MW00357134

BEGINNING
MAC OS® X SNOW LEOPARD™ PROGRAMMING

BEGINNING

Mac OS® X Snow Leopard™ Programming

Michael Trent and Drew McCormack

WILEY

Wiley Publishing, Inc.

Beginning Mac OS® X Snow Leopard™ Programming

Published by
Wiley Publishing, Inc.
10475 Crosspoint Boulevard
Indianapolis, IN 46256
www.wiley.com

ISBN: 978-0-470-57752-3

Manufactured in the United States of America

10 9 8 7 6 5 4 3 2 1

For general information on our other products and services please contact our Customer Care Department within the United States at (877) 762-2974, outside the United States at (317) 572-3993 or fax (317) 572-4002.

Wiley also publishes its books in a variety of electronic formats. Some content that appears in print may not be available in electronic books.

Library of Congress Control Number: 2009940871

For Angela, Katie, and Sophie

—MT

For Jennifer, Gileesa, and Rylan

—DMc

CREDITS

ABOUT THE AUTHORS

 MICHAEL TRENT has been programming in Objective-C since 1997 and programming Macs since well before that. He is a professional computer programmer and engineering manager, a technical reviewer for numerous books and magazine articles, and an occasional dabbler in Mac OS X open source projects. Currently, he is using Objective-C and Apple Computer's Cocoa frameworks to build professional and consumer applications for Mac OS X. Michael holds a Bachelor of Science degree in Computer Science and a Bachelor of Arts degree in Music from Beloit College in Beloit, Wisconsin. He lives in Pittsburgh, Pennsylvania, with his family.

 DREW McCORMACK has a Ph.D. in Chemical Physics and has worked much of his career as a computational scientist. Recently, he founded The Mental Faculty (www.mentalfaculty.com), an independent company developing applications for the Mac and iPhone in the fields of science and education. (The Mental Faculty's flagship product is the flashcard study application Mental Case, which can be found at www.macflashcards.com.) Drew is a board member and regular contributor to the MacResearch web site (www.macresearch.org), and is a lead on the Core Plot project (www.code.google.com/p/core-plot), an undertaking with the aim to develop a complete open source graphing framework for Cocoa.

ACKNOWLEDGMENTS

I WOULD LIKE TO THANK STEVE KOCHAN for his early help with this project. Thanks also to Brett Halle, Pete Steinauer, Yaniv Gur, and many others for their encouragement. Most of all, I would like to thank my wife, Angela, and my daughters, Katie and Sophie, for putting up with all the late nights.

—MICHAEL TRENT

I WISH TO THANK MY WIFE, Jennifer, and children, Gileesa and Rylan, for suffering first hand all of my wacky schemes. Thanks also to my brother — and mentor — Cody McCormack.

—DREW McCORMACK

CONTENTS

INTRODUCTION

MAC OS X REPRESENTS A UNION OF many different operating system technologies. At its core you will find Unix, an operating system once reserved for high-end servers and workstations, now found on common desktop systems. With Unix comes a whole history of tools, computer languages, and runtime environments. At a higher level, you will find Cocoa, derived from the application toolkits found on NeXTSTEP and OpenStep — a result of Apple's merger with NeXT in 1997. In Mac OS X you will also find Carbon, a library made from elements of the original Macintosh operating system. The original Mac OS API remains for older projects, although Apple is de-emphasizing its role in Mac OS X. Other technologies have found their way into Mac OS X through the open source community, and Apple is hard at work developing new technologies unique to Mac OS X.

Although the operating system is composed of all these separate pieces, Mac OS X still looks and feels like a single piece of software. The Macintosh's legendary user interface still shines brightly today, providing a consistent look and feel for the applications on your system. When you sit down to use your computer, it just works for you. And aside from a few cosmetic differences — say using a command-line interface or a graphical interface — rarely are you aware of the differences between all these operating system technologies.

Under the covers, there are fundamental differences between these operating system technologies. For example, Carbon still provides its own special memory data types, and Cocoa requires its own object-oriented runtime. But there are no firm boundaries between these technologies; Cocoa can call Carbon API and vice versa. And though these technologies have their own history, strengths, and weaknesses, they are all still part of the same Mac OS X operating system.

With the release of Mac OS X Snow Leopard, Apple has spent two years fine-tuning these pieces. Instead of focusing on a number of new features, Apple has been working on what it has: making things faster, using fewer resources, and smoothing out the edges. As a result, Snow Leopard feels as though it is one operating system — the whole greater than the sum of its parts.

WHO THIS BOOK IS FOR

This book is for anyone who wants to get started writing programs that run on Mac OS X. Every Mac OS X system comes with everything you need: a complete set of development tools and resources. But finding the place to start can be challenging. This book provides a great starting point for programming on Mac OS X and shows you how to find more information on your own.

This book will appeal most to the hobbyist programmer who already has some exposure to a programming language. Experience with C or Objective-C, although helpful, is not required. You can learn the basics of these languages, as well as concepts such as object-oriented programming (OOP), as you go.

If you are an experienced programmer familiar with one aspect of Mac OS X programming (such as shell scripting or Carbon), you can use this book to explore other aspects of Mac OS X programming. In addition, you learn how to incorporate these new techniques into your existing programming style.

HOW THIS BOOK IS STRUCTURED

This book takes a hands-on approach to learning the material, using the Wrox "Try It Out" format. After you learn about a particular element, you are presented with step-by-step instructions that walk you through using that element. You are encouraged to follow along on your own system by typing the examples, running them, and if necessary debugging them when they don't work quite right. A detailed explanation of the example follows the step-by-step instructions under a "How It Works" heading.

Some examples take the form of small standalone projects, designed to illustrate one particular concept or technique. When appropriate, examples build on material presented in earlier chapters or examples, providing an opportunity to see the new material in a non-trivial context. Many of the examples focused on Mac OS X application development build on an application called Slide Master, a functional image/slideshow browser that you build piece by piece. Whenever possible, larger tasks have been broken down into smaller examples to make them easier to digest.

Each chapter includes a few exercises at the end, again illustrating the lessons presented earlier. You can work through these examples on your own, at your own pace. Complete answers to each exercise are provided in the appendix, so you can check your work or get a hint if you get stuck. Keep in mind that in programming there's usually more than one way to do something; our solution isn't necessarily the only correct one.

Chapters are collected into three broad categories or parts: Mac OS X Developer Resources, Application Programming, and Script Programming. This keeps related material together and helps with the flow of information from topic to topic. You are encouraged to cover the material in order so that you don't miss anything. If you want to skip ahead for a specific topic, make a point of coming back to the earlier material at a later time.

Here's a brief summary of what you'll find in each chapter:

In Chapter 1, "The Mac OS X Environment," you learn about Mac OS X's system architecture. You also get a little hands-on experience using Mac OS X's built-in command-line interface.

In Chapter 2, "Developer Tools," you find out about the resources that come with your copy of Mac OS X. You also learn how to find current versions of these resources on the Internet.

In Chapter 3, "Xcode," you explore the application used to build Mac OS X programs. A few simple examples introduce you to writing source code, building a finished product, and debugging programs one line of code at a time.

Chapter 4, "Interface Builder," walks you through the process of designing a graphic user interface on Mac OS X. Examples in this chapter illustrate useful techniques for building an interface that conforms to Apple's guidelines.

In Chapter 5, "The Application," you pick apart the individual elements that make up an application on Mac OS X. You learn how application resources are stored and how applications work in multiple languages.

Chapter 6, "The C Language," offers a brief introduction to the C programming language. If you are new to C, you will want to read this chapter before continuing on to Chapters 7, 8, 9, or 10. In addition to learning how to write programs in C, you learn how non-trivial C programs are divided among several source files.

Chapter 7, "The Objective-C Language," builds on Chapter 6 to teach you about Objective-C, the object-oriented language used by the Cocoa application frameworks.

In Chapter 8, "Introduction to Cocoa," you discover how to write your own Cocoa applications, from designing a user interface to writing the final code. The Cocoa application frameworks do a lot of work for you, freeing you up to concentrate on the unique aspects of your own application.

Chapter 9, "Document-Based Cocoa Applications," explores how to use Cocoa to build a program that works with documents of user data.

Chapter 10, "Core Data-Based Cocoa Applications" describes how to use Core Data to store collections of Objective-C objects. It also focuses on using Cocoa Bindings for passing data between Core Data and document UI.

In Chapter 11, "Overview of Scripting Languages," you examine scripting languages available on the Mac OS X system. Many of these languages extend Mac OS X's command-line interface in one way or another. You get a sense of what sets each language apart and what tasks each language is best suited to perform.

Chapter 12, "The Bash Shell," covers Mac OS X's default command-line interpreter in detail. You learn how to write shell scripts that interact with command-line tools installed on your system.

In Chapter 13, "AppleScript and AppleScriptObjC," you learn about Apple's high-level application scripting language, AppleScript. AppleScript enables you to communicate with and automate tasks in Mac OS X applications.

Chapter 14, "JavaScript, Dashboard, and Dashcode," focuses on the JavaScript language, a scripting language used to make Dashboard widgets and modern web applications. You will use the Dashcode developer tool to write and debug JavaScript programs.

Appendix A, "Exercise Answers," provides the solutions to the exercises that appear at the end of each chapter throughout this book. Also be sure to check out Appendix B, "Developer Resources," which offers valuable information that you may find helpful as you develop applications.

WHAT YOU NEED TO USE THIS BOOK

As we mentioned earlier, your Mac OS X installation already has everything you need to get started. You will also need an Internet connection to access Apple Computer's developer web site. We used the Safari web browser to access these pages, but other web browsers (Internet Explorer, Firefox, and so on) should work fine.

Examples and figures in this book were made using Mac OS X v10.6 Snow Leopard and Xcode 3. Although many code examples will still work on earlier versions of Mac OS X, a few have been updated using features new to Snow Leopard. Apple periodically makes new versions of Xcode available for download. Earlier versions of Xcode can be obtained at no charge from Apple's web site. You can find more information on Apple's developer web site, Apple Developer Connection, in Chapter 2.

CONVENTIONS

To help you get the most from the text and keep track of what's happening, we've used a number of conventions throughout this book.

TRY IT OUT

The *Try It Out* is an exercise you should work through, following the text in the book.

1. It usually consists of a set of steps.

2. Each step has a number.

3. Follow the steps through with your copy of the database.

How It Works

After each *Try It Out*, the code you've typed will be explained in detail.

 WARNING *Boxes such as this one hold important, not-to-be-forgotten information that is directly relevant to the surrounding text.*

 NOTE *Tips, hints, tricks, and asides to the current discussion are offset and placed in italics similar to this.*

The following are styles used in the text:

We *highlight* important words in italics when they are introduced.

We show keyboard strokes like this: Ctrl-A.

We show file and folder names, URLs, and code within the text in a special monofont typeface, like this: `persistence.properties`.

SOURCE CODE

As you work through the examples in this book, you may choose either to type in all the code manually or to use the source code files that accompany the book. All of the source code used in this book is available for download at http://www.wrox.com. Once at the site, simply locate the book's title (either by using the Search box or by using one of the title lists) and click the Download Code link on the book's detail page to obtain all the source code for the book.

 NOTE *Because many books have similar titles, you may find it easiest to search by ISBN; this book's ISBN is 978-0-470-57752-3.*

Once you download the code, just decompress it with your favorite compression tool. Alternately, you can go to the main Wrox code download page at http://www.wrox.com/dynamic/books/download.aspx to see the code available for this book and all other Wrox books.

ERRATA

We make every effort to ensure that there are no errors in the text or in the code. However, no one is perfect, and mistakes do occur. If you find an error in one of our books, like a spelling mistake or faulty piece of code, we would be very grateful for your feedback. By sending in errata you may save another reader hours of frustration and at the same time you will be helping us provide even higher-quality information.

To find the errata page for this book, go to http://www.wrox.com and locate the title using the Search box or one of the title lists. Then, on the book details page, click the book errata link. On this page you can view all errata that has been submitted for this book and posted by Wrox editors. A complete book list including links to each book's errata is also available at www.wrox.com/misc-pages/booklist.shtml.

If you don't spot "your" error on the book errata page, go to www.wrox.com/contact/techsupport.shtml and complete the form there to send us the error you have found. We'll check the information and, if appropriate, post a message to the book's errata page and fix the problem in subsequent editions of the book.

P2P.WROX.COM

For author and peer discussion, join the P2P forums at p2p.wrox.com. The forums are a Web-based system for you to post messages relating to Wrox books and related technologies and interact with other readers and technology users. The forums offer a subscription feature that e-mails you topics of your choosing when new posts are made to the forums. Wrox authors, editors, other industry experts, and your fellow readers are present on these forums.

At `http://p2p.wrox.com` you will find a number of different forums that will help you not only as you read this book, but also as you develop your own applications. To join the forums, just follow these steps:

1. Go to `p2p.wrox.com` and click the Register link.

2. Read the terms of use and click Agree.

3. Complete the required information to join, as well as any optional information you wish to provide, and click Submit.

4. You will receive an e-mail with information describing how to verify your account and complete the joining process.

 NOTE *You can read messages in the forums without joining P2P but in order to post your own messages, you must join.*

Once you join, you can post new messages and respond to messages other users post. You can read messages at any time on the Web. If you would like to have new messages from a particular forum e-mailed to you, click the "Subscribe to this Forum" icon by the forum name in the forum listing.

For more information about how to use the Wrox P2P, be sure to read the P2P FAQs for answers to questions about how the forum software works, as well as many common questions specific to P2P and Wrox books. To read the FAQs, click the FAQ link on any P2P page.

PART I
Mac OS X Developer Resources

The Mac OS X Environment

➤ How the Mac OS X operating system is structured, including what the major areas of the system are and how they work together

➤ How to use Mac OS X's command-line interface

➤ How applications take advantage of the operating system services on Mac OS X

➤ How Apple encourages a common look and feel for Mac OS X applications

Welcome to the wonderful world of Mac OS X, the next-generation operating system from Apple Computer!

The Mac OS X operating system powers modern Macintosh computers. After many long years and a few scrapped attempts to modernize the older Mac OS operating system, Apple released Mac OS X in April 2001. Since then, Apple has released a steady stream of upgrades and system updates. This book was written around Mac OS X v10.6 Snow Leopard, the latest version.

To write software for Mac OS X, you need to know your way around the system. By now you may already be familiar with Mac OS X's applications and user interface style. Those things all rest on top of a number of subsystems and services that make up the Mac OS X operating system.

INTRODUCING THE MAC OS X

What comes to mind when you think of Mac OS X? Is it the applications you use? Perhaps you recall Mac OS X's distinctive user interface? Or maybe you think of Mac OS X's stability? In truth, Mac OS X embodies all these things.

The Mac OS X operating system is often described as a collection of layers, as seen in Figure 1-1.

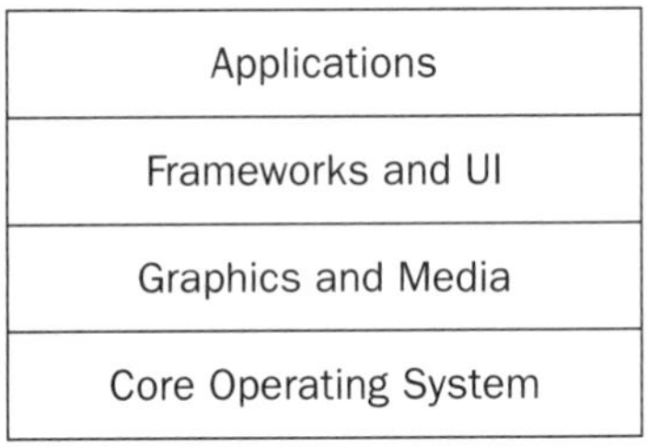

You are probably already familiar with the topmost layer: the applications that run on Mac OS X (such as Mail, iTunes, Safari, and so on). These applications are all written against a collection of application *frameworks*. These frameworks are special libraries that provide the code and all the other resources (icons, translated strings, and so on) to perform common tasks. For example, the Cocoa framework contains a number of resources necessary to make a Cocoa application.

Applications
Frameworks and UI
Graphics and Media
Core Operating System

FIGURE 1-1

All Mac OS X applications use graphics to some extent, ranging from simply presenting its user interface to processing graphical data such as QuickTime movies. The system provides several specialized libraries for working with graphics and graphics files.

These layers rest on the broad shoulders of the core operating system, which at the lowest level is responsible for making your Macintosh run. For example, the core OS handles reading from and writing to your hard drive and random access memory (RAM), it manages your network connections, it powers down the computer when it falls to "sleep," and so on. In fact, any program that talks to your hardware in any way ultimately goes through the core OS.

Throughout this book you examine Mac OS X in detail through Slide Master, an application that builds and displays photo slideshows. You will build Slide Master bit-by-bit as you learn more about how the elements of Mac OS X come together. The Slide Master application and its source code can be downloaded from Wiley's web site; so you can check your work against our complete solution as you go.

This is a good time to take a quick tour of Slide Master. You can download Slide Master from Wiley's web site, make a slideshow, and view your handiwork. In doing so, you touch on all the major areas of the Mac OS X operating system.

TRY IT OUT Slide Master

1. Download the files for this chapter from www.wrox.com. Refer to the Introduction for instructions on finding the files you need from the Wrox web site. You can search for the book by its ISBN number: 978-0-470-57752-3. You are looking for a file named MacOSXProg Chapter01.zip.

2. Uncompress the MacOSXProg Chapter01.zip archive using your favorite decompression tool. (Mac OS X supports uncompressing .zip files directly in the Finder.) Inside you will find the Slide Master application, a folder of pictures called Images, and a folder of source code.

3. Run the Slide Master application by double-clicking it in Finder. The application opens an untitled document window.

4. Add the pictures in the Images folder to Slide Master by choosing Slide Show ➪ Add Slide. You can select all the files at once from the open panel. The images appear in a drawer to the side of the document window and the main window displays the selected image, as shown in Figure 1-2. You can use the arrow keys to change the selection.

FIGURE 1-2

5. Export a slideshow as a QuickTime movie by choosing File ➪ Export. Slide Master writes out a QuickTime movie and opens it with QuickTime Player.

6. Save your document by choosing File ➪ Save.

How It Works

Slide Master is a document-based application, which means that it provides a user interface for individual documents. In this case, documents are collections of slides that you can sift through and export as QuickTime movies. Slide Master documents can be opened, saved, and closed using the File menu. Other document-based applications also support printing, although Slide Master does not.

Much of the functionality you see here comes from Slide Master's application framework: Cocoa. The Cocoa application framework provides the implementation for the things you see on the screen: windows, pictures, menus, buttons, and so on. Cocoa also provides support for managing the document: reading and writing document files, closing the document when its window is closed, and routing menu commands to the selected document. Finally, Cocoa provides tools for storing application data, including working with user preferences and storing lists of items in memory.

Of course Slide Master uses QuickTime to generate movie files. You are probably already familiar with QuickTime, both through QuickTime Player and through web browsers that support the display of QuickTime movies. But QuickTime also makes most, if not all, of its functionality available to applications through its framework interface.

When you save a Slide Master document, the document file contains a list of image files that are part of your slideshow, not the actual images themselves. As a result, these documents can be relatively small. Behind the scenes, Slide Master uses aliases to track these image files so that they can be found if the files are moved around on your disk. These aliases are the same aliases you can create in the Finder, although they are embedded in your document rather than saved separately to disk.

You learn more about Cocoa, QuickTime, and other technologies later in this chapter, and as you proceed through this book.

THE CORE OPERATING SYSTEM

The heart of Mac OS X is based on the Unix operating system. Unix was developed by AT&T in the early 1970s. In those days, computers were large and expensive, and Unix was intended as a way to share computing resources between multiple users at once. It was likely that an organization at that time could afford only one computer for all its members, and Unix provided a way for people to use that computer simultaneously without getting in each other's way.

Over the years, Unix development has split off into many distinct "flavors" of Unix, all headed up by different groups of people, all with somewhat different goals. BSD and Linux are two such examples. Each version of Unix shares some portion of the original vision and typically implements a common set of libraries and commands.

Unix is regarded as a robust operating system whose scalability and innate networking capability make it ideal for use as a server. In fact, most of the modern-day Internet is powered by Unix servers of one version or another. It turns out that these features are also desirable in modern desktop operating systems. So it is no surprise that when Apple was seeking to modernize the original Macintosh operating system, it turned to Unix.

Mac OS X's core operating system is a Unix flavor called *Darwin*. As with most Unix flavors, Darwin's source code is freely available, allowing interested parties to see exactly how the core operating system works. Apple maintains several resources for programmers interested in Darwin, including a way for people-at-large to contribute changes and bug fixes back to Apple.

Although Mac OS X tries to hide Darwin from the average user, there are some places where the Unix command line pokes through. The most obvious example is the Terminal application, found in `/Application/Utilities`. You can use Terminal to work directly with Darwin's command-line tools. A more subtle example includes the way you describe file locations on Mac OS X: by using a *file path*. A file path is a string of text that describes a file's location.

The original Mac OS operating system abhorred file paths and tried its best to avoid them; but even so, it devised a convention for describing a path to a file. Mac OS file paths are composed of a disk volume name followed by several folder names and possibly a file, all separated by colons, as in `Macintosh HD:Applications:Utilities:Terminal.app`.

PROGRAM, PROCESS, APPLICATION — WHAT'S THE DIFFERENCE?

Much of the time you can use the terms *program* and *process* interchangeably to refer to something that's *executable*. But these terms do have distinct definitions. The word *program* refers to a file on disk containing a series of computer instructions. When this file is executed (or run, launched, and so on), the computer starts processing the instructions in the file. *Process* describes the act of executing the file. To borrow an example from the kitchen, it may help to think of a program as a recipe for baking a cake, and the process as the act of baking that cake.

Ultimately, an *application* is just a program. On Mac OS X, however, programs can take many forms: simple tools typed in a command-line interface, a program you can double-click in the Finder, a plug-in file loaded by other programs, and so on. To avoid some confusion, we use the term *application* in this book to refer specifically to programs that appear in the Finder; we use the term *program* when no distinction is necessary.

Although there are places where this old convention still exists, Mac OS X mostly uses Unix's method of describing file paths: a series of directories from the *root* directory all separated by slashes, as in `/Applications/Utilities/Terminal.app`. The root directory contains all the files and directories on a Mac OS X system and is referred to simply as `/`. The path `/Applications` refers to a file or directory named `Applications` in the root directory. A path that begins with the root slash is called an *absolute* (or *full*) *path* because it describes a precise file location. If the root slash is not included, the path is called a *relative path* because it is relative to your current location.

NOTE *If you look in* `/Applications/Utilities` *in the Finder, you might notice that there is no* `Terminal.app`; *instead there's just a program called Terminal. By default, Finder and other applications hide file extensions such as .app and .txt from you. So the application at* `/Applications/Utilities/Terminal.app` *appears simply as Terminal. The Core OS makes no attempt to hide extensions from you; if you browse the file system using Mac OS X's command-line interface, you can see all these extensions. You learn more about Mac OS X's command-line interface later in this chapter.*

Darwin is composed of several parts, including a kernel, a system library, and numerous commands, as illustrated in Figure 1-3.

The Kernel

The heart of a Unix operating system is its *kernel*. The kernel is the program that loads when the computer is first turned on and is responsible for managing all the hardware resources available to the computer. The kernel is also responsible for running the other programs on the system, scheduling process execution so that they can share the central processing unit (CPU) and other resources, and preventing one process from seeing what another process is doing. These last two responsibilities are more commonly known as *preemptive multitasking* and *protected memory*, respectively.

Applications	Command-line Tools
Frameworks and UI	
Graphics and Media	
Core Operating System	
System Library	
Kernel	

FIGURE 1-3

Because Unix prevents programs from accessing the computer hardware or other programs directly, it protects against the most common forms of system crashes. If a process misbehaves in one way or another, the system simply terminates the process and continues on its way. In other words, the misbehaving process crashes. In some operating systems, a misbehaving process can stomp all over other applications, or even break the operating system itself, before the system is able to terminate the process. As a result, poorly written programs can cause the entire computer to freeze or crash. Not so on Unix; because a process cannot modify other processes, including the kernel, there is virtually no risk of a bad process bringing down the entire operating system.

Although the kernel is responsible for accessing hardware, much of the knowledge of specific hardware details is delegated to *device drivers*. Device drivers are small programs that are loaded directly into the kernel. Whereas the kernel might know how to talk to hard disks, a specific device driver generally knows how to talk to specific makes and models of hard disks. This provides a way for third parties to add support for new devices without having to build it into Apple's kernel. Mac OS X includes default drivers for talking to a wide variety of devices, so much of the time you won't need to install separate drivers when you install new third-party hardware.

The System Library

The kernel is responsible for critical functions such as memory management and device access, so programs must ask the kernel to perform work on its behalf. Programs communicate with the kernel through an application program interface (API) provided by a special library. This library defines some common data structures for describing system operations, provides functions to request these operations, and handles shuttling data back and forth between the kernel and other programs. This library is simply called the *system library*.

As you might imagine, every program on Mac OS X links against this library, either directly or indirectly. Without it, a program would be unable to allocate memory, access the file system, and perform other simple tasks.

> **WHAT IS AN API?**
>
> All libraries and frameworks provide a collection of functions and data structures that programs can use to perform a task. For example, the system library provides functions for reading from files, and QuickTime provides functions for playing back QuickTime movies. These functions and data structures are collectively known as the library's *application program interface*, or API.

The system library takes the form of a dynamic library installed as `/usr/lib/libSystem.B.dylib`. Mac OS X also includes a framework called `System.framework` in `/System/Library/Frameworks` that refers to this library. The files that define the Darwin interface live in the `/usr/include` directory. By the way, neither of these directories is visible from Finder; Mac OS X actively hides much of the complexity of Darwin from the average Mac user.

Unix Commands

Unix users interact with their systems using command-line tools. These tools typically perform very specialized functions, such as listing files in a directory or displaying files on-screen. The advantage of supplying many specialized tools lies in the way commands can be combined to form more sophisticated commands. For example, a command that lists the contents of a directory can be combined with a program that lists text in "pages" for easy reading.

As you have learned, you use the Terminal application to gain access to Darwin's command-line tools.

The following Try It Out looks at Darwin's command-line interface. You start by browsing files using the command line, looking up command information in Darwin's online help system, and running a command that displays its own arguments.

TRY IT OUT   **Experiencing Darwin's Command-Line Interface**

1.   In the Finder, go to Applications ➪ Utilities and launch the Terminal application. You will see a few status lines of text ending in a command-line prompt (your lines may look slightly different from what is shown here):

```
Last login: Sat May 15 23:28:46 on ttys000
Macintosh:~ sample $
```

2.   When you're using Terminal, there are commands that let you navigate the file system. The Terminal application always keeps track of where you are, maintaining the notion of your *current directory*. You can display the contents of the current directory using the ls (list) command that follows. As a matter of fact, the Terminal window is currently "in" your home directory. Your results may vary from what's printed here, but they will match what you see in the Finder when you browse your home directory. (Throughout this book, any text you are asked to type on the command line is indicated in **bold**.)

```
Macintosh:~ sample $ ls
Desktop         Downloads       Movies          Pictures        Sites
Documents       Library         Music           Public
```

3.   You can display more information about the files in your home directory by passing additional arguments, called *flags*, into ls. By using ls –l, you can build what is often called a *long list*. Again, your results may differ from what is printed here:

```
Macintosh:~ sample$ ls -l
total 0
drwx------+  4 sample  staff   136 Jul 16 01:49 Desktop
drwx------+ 10 sample  staff   340 Jul 22 00:10 Documents
drwx------+  6 sample  staff   204 Jul 21 10:22 Downloads
drwx------+ 31 sample  staff  1054 Jul 16 00:05 Library
drwx------+  3 sample  staff   102 Jul 15 09:19 Movies
drwx------+  4 sample  staff   136 Jul 18 23:34 Music
drwx------+  4 sample  staff   136 Jul 15 09:19 Pictures
drwxr-xr-x+  5 sample  staff   170 Jul 15 09:19 Public
drwxr-xr-x+  5 sample  staff   170 Jul 15 09:19 Sites
```

4.   You can view the contents of a specific directory by specifying its name as the argument to ls. Note that this argument can co-exist with other flags you might want to use:

```
Macintosh:~ sample$ ls -l Library
total 0
drwx------+ 11 sample  staff   374 Jul 18 23:37 Application Support
drwx------+  2 sample  staff    68 Jul 15 09:19 Assistants
drwx------+  5 sample  staff   170 Jul 15 09:19 Audio
drwx------   4 sample  staff   136 Jul 22 00:12 Autosave Information
drwx------  23 sample  staff   782 Jul 20 23:39 Caches
drwxr-xr-x   6 sample  staff   204 Jul 15 15:44 Calendars
drwx------+  2 sample  staff    68 Jul 15 09:19 ColorPickers
drwx------+  3 sample  staff   102 Jul 15 09:19 Compositions
drwxr-xr-x   3 sample  staff   102 Jul 21 10:35 Cookies
drwx------+  3 sample  staff   102 Jul 15 09:19 Favorites
```

```
drwx------+  9 sample  staff   306 Jul 18 23:37 FontCollections
drwx------+  2 sample  staff    68 Jul 15 09:19 Fonts
drwxr-xr-x   2 sample  staff    68 Jul 16 00:05 Fonts Disabled
drwx------+  3 sample  staff   102 Jul 15 09:19 Input Methods
drwx------+  2 sample  staff    68 Jul 15 09:19 Internet Plug-Ins
drwx------+  2 sample  staff    68 Jul 15 09:19 Keyboard Layouts
drwxr-xr-x   4 sample  staff   136 Jul 18 23:35 Keychains
drwx------   3 sample  staff   102 Jul 15 12:29 Logs
. . .
```

5. Two new questions immediately come to mind: exactly what is `ls -l` telling you, and what other flags can you pass into `ls`? The answer to both of these questions resides in Darwin's online help system, which is better known as the Unix Manual. You can consult the manual by using the `man` command and including the name of another command as the argument:

```
Macintosh:~ sample$ man ls
LS(1)                    BSD General Commands Manual                    LS(1)
NAME
     ls - list directory contents
SYNOPSIS
     ls [-ABCFGHLPRTWZabcdfghiklmnopqrstuwx1] [file ...]
DESCRIPTION
     For each operand that names a file of a type other than directory, ls
     displays its name as well as any requested, associated information.  For
     each operand that names a file of type directory, ls displays the names
     of files contained within that directory, as well as any requested, asso-
     ciated information.
     If no operands are given, the contents of the current directory are dis-
     played.  If more than one operand is given, non-directory operands are
     displayed first; directory and non-directory operands are sorted sepa-
     rately and in lexicographical order.
     The following options are available:
     -A      List all entries except for . and ...  Always set for the super-
:
```

6. The arguments you are allowed to pass to a Unix command depend entirely on the command. As you have seen, the `ls` command accepts filenames, and the `man` command accepts the names of other Unix commands. The `echo` command accepts arbitrary arguments and simply repeats them on the screen. It turns out that this command is especially useful when writing shell scripts, as you see in Chapter 11.

```
Macintosh:~ sample$ echo hello, my name is sample
hello, my name is sample
```

How It Works

In spite of appearances, Terminal doesn't understand any of the commands you just entered. In fact, Terminal's only job is to read input from your keyboard and display text coming from a special program called a *shell*. Terminal starts your shell for you when its window appears. The shell is a special program that provides a command-line prompt, parses instructions into command names and lists of arguments, runs the requested commands, and passes back the resulting text.

When the shell has decided which command to launch, the shell starts that command and passes the remaining flags and arguments into the command for further evaluation. That's why ls, man, and echo all interpret their arguments in different ways. Flags are also interpreted by individual commands, so it's not uncommon to use a particular flag in more than one Unix command, although the flag might have different meanings.

One thing to watch out for: Unix shells historically are *case-sensitive*, meaning that the command LS is not the same as ls, the directory library is not the same as the directory Library, and so on. Mac OS X's default file system, HFS+, is case-insensitive, and much of the time the shell can figure out what you mean. But if you had some trouble with the commands in the preceding Try It Out, make sure you entered the text exactly as it appears here.

You have only just scratched the surface of what the shell can do. You will continue to learn more about the shell as you continue through the book.

GRAPHICS AND MEDIA LAYERS

Much of the user experience on Mac OS X is built around graphics. All the elements you see on the screen — windows, menus, buttons, and text — are graphics. It comes as no surprise that Mac OS X has several subsystems dedicated to graphics, as shown in Figure 1-4.

Mac OS X provides a rich graphics library for doing two-dimensional drawings, called Quartz 2D. The Quartz 2D library is specific to Mac OS X, although it uses industry-standard graphic formats, such as PDF. Mac OS X also includes OpenGL for those interested in three-dimensional drawings. Although popularized by cross-platform video games, Mac OS X itself uses OpenGL for certain operations. Finally, QuickTime is built into Mac OS X, providing support for what Apple occasionally calls four-dimensional drawing. QuickTime is also available for Microsoft Windows operating systems, and for older versions of Mac OS. All these programming libraries rely on the Quartz Compositor for actually drawing their content.

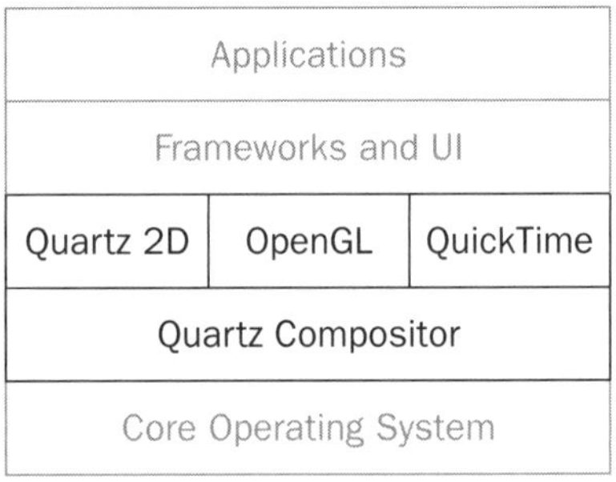

| Applications |
| Frameworks and UI |

| Quartz 2D | OpenGL | QuickTime |

| Quartz Compositor |
| Core Operating System |

FIGURE 1-4

The following sections look at these subsystems in more detail.

The Quartz Compositor

The Quartz Compositor is a private system service that oversees all graphics operations on Mac OS X. Apple does not provide a means for developers to interact with the Quartz Compositor directly, so we won't look at it in detail here. The Quartz Compositor plays such an important role in Mac OS X's graphic strategy, however, that it pays to understand what it does.

Among its many duties, the Quartz Compositor handles these tasks:

> **Manages all the windows on your screen** — Although the actual look of the window may come from an application or an application framework such as Cocoa or Carbon, the Quartz Compositor provides most of the window's guts: where the window sits on the screen, how the window casts its drop shadow, and so on.

> **Ensures that graphics are drawn appropriately, regardless of which library or libraries an application may be using** — In fact, an application may use commands from Quartz 2D, OpenGL, and QuickTime when drawing a given window. The Quartz Compositor ensures that the drawing reaches the screen correctly.

> **Collects user events from the core operating system and dispatches them to the Application Frameworks layer** — User events such as keystrokes and mouse movements are collected from drivers in the core operating system and sent to the Quartz Compositor. Some of these events are passed along where they may be interpreted by the application. The Quartz Compositor will also send its own special events to the application for responding to special conditions, such as when the user brings the application to the foreground or when a window needs to be updated.

The Quartz Compositor was designed with modern best practices for graphics in mind. For example, the drawing coordinate space uses floating-point values, allowing for sub-pixel precision and image smoothing. Compositing operations can take advantage of available hardware. Transparency is supported natively and naturally in all drawing operations.

Apple has been able to capitalize on this architecture to provide a number of exciting features, such as Quartz Extreme and Exposé. Quartz Extreme allows graphic operations to take full advantage of the graphics processing unit (GPU) found on modern video cards to provide hardware-accelerated drawing. This has two benefits. The GPU is specially optimized for common drawing operations, so drawing is much faster than when using the computer's CPU. Second, by offloading drawing onto the GPU in the video card, Quartz Extreme frees up the CPU for other tasks. Although in the past, developers needed to use OpenGL to do hardware-accelerated drawing, Quartz Extreme provides this support to Quartz 2D as well, and ultimately to QuickTime. Exposé allows the user to quickly view all windows at once. It is a very handy way to find a specific window that might be buried underneath a number of other windows, as shown in Figure 1-5.

The Quartz Compositor is one of the most fundamental parts of Mac OS X. Although you will not be working with it directly in this book, you will feel its influence in almost everything you do.

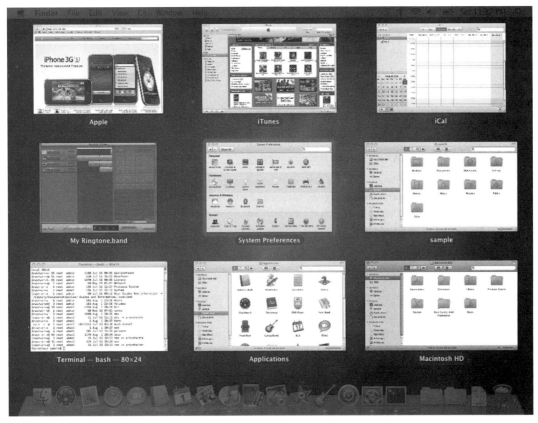

FIGURE 1-5

WHAT ARE PDF FILES?

PDF stands for Portable Document Format. The PDF standard was invented by Adobe as a means for describing documents that can be displayed or printed virtually anywhere. The file specification itself is *open*, meaning the public-at-large can view the format and write their own tools for reading and generating PDF documents. Adobe continues to own and develop the standard.

Mac OS X reads and writes PDF documents as its preferred native image file format. You can save any document in PDF format simply by "printing" it and clicking Save as PDF in Mac OS X's print panel. PDF files can be displayed in Mac OS X's Preview application.

Quartz 2D

The Quartz 2D graphics library is Mac OS X's native graphics library. It is responsible for all the two-dimensional drawing performed by Mac OS X. As you might imagine, Quartz 2D provides an interface for drawing two-dimensional shapes, such as lines and rectangles, and compositing images. It is also capable of drawing sophisticated curves, arbitrary shapes expressed as paths or vectors, and color gradients. Quartz 2D also includes support for generating and displaying PDF files.

The Quartz 2D programming interface is provided by CoreGraphics, which is part of the ApplicationServices framework: `/System/Library/Frameworks/ApplicationServices.framework`. The Quartz 2D API is very powerful and is best approached by an experienced programmer. In this book, you focus more on the drawing API in the Application Frameworks layer, which is a little easier to use.

OpenGL

OpenGL is a powerful, cross-platform graphics library for doing 2D and 3D graphics. Although OpenGL is owned by SGI, the OpenGL specification is governed by an independent consortium called the OpenGL Architecture Review Board — ARB for short. As a voting member of the ARB, Apple contributes to the OpenGL community as a whole, in addition to improving the state of OpenGL on Mac OS X.

One of OpenGL's most compelling features is its tight integration with video card technology. Many OpenGL commands, such as image and shape drawing, blending, and texture-mapping, can be performed directly by the video card's GPU. Recall that the GPU is optimized to perform these operations very quickly, and after graphic operations have been unloaded onto the video card, the CPU is free to perform other computational functions. The net result of this tight integration is very fast drawing.

Performance combined with its cross-platform nature makes OpenGL uniquely suited for certain kinds of situations, including scientific research, professional video editing, and games. If you have played a 3D video game on Mac OS X, you've seen OpenGL in action. For that matter, if you have used one of Mac OS X's built-in screen saver modules, you've seen OpenGL.

OpenGL's programming interface is spread across two frameworks: core OpenGL functionality lives in the OpenGL framework (`/System/Library/Frameworks/OpenGL.framework`), and a basic cross-platform Application Framework called GLUT resides at `/System/Library/Frameworks /GLUT .framework`. As with Quartz 2D, the OpenGL API is fairly advanced and better suited for more experienced programmers.

QuickTime

Apple Computer invented QuickTime back in 1991 as a way to describe, author, and play back video on Macintosh computers running System 6 and System 7. Since then, QuickTime has exploded into a cross-platform library encompassing a variety of multimedia file formats and algorithms. QuickTime provides tools for working with digital video, panoramic images, digital sound, MIDI, and more. It has spawned entire genres of software, including CD-ROM adventure games, digital audio/video editing suites, and desktop video conferencing.

Mac OS X increased Apple's commitment to QuickTime by building it directly into the operating system. Though versions of QuickTime shipped with Mac OS releases since the earliest days of QuickTime, Mac OS X actually relies on QuickTime in ways earlier OS versions did not. For example, Finder uses QuickTime to allow you to preview video and audio files directly in the Finder when using column view. Mac OS X's Internet connectivity apps, including iChat and Safari, make substantial use of QuickTime.

Mac OS X Snow Leopard introduces QuickTime X, integrating QuickTime more tightly into the Mac OS X architecture than before. Although QuickTime has taken advantage of available video hardware resources for years, QuickTime X has been redesigned around the multiple CPUs and powerful programmable GPUs found in current Macintosh computers. QuickTime X also reintroduces some simple editing features into QuickTime Player, so you can make and edit videos without additional software.

The QuickTime X API is supplied by the QTKit framework: `/System/Library/Frameworks/ QTKit.framework`. The QuickTime programming interface has undergone nearly 20 years of evolution, and many of its concepts are quite advanced.

Core Animation

Animations can make tasks more appealing or more understandable. When you activate Exposé, all your windows reorganize on your screen with a sweeping animation. When you minimize a document, it flows into the Dock. When using Cover Flow in the Finder or in iTunes, files flip smoothly to and fro.

Mac OS X v10.5 Leopard introduced a new technology called Core Animation to manage common animations. Core Animation takes flat, two-dimensional images called "layers" and basically pushes them around. Layers are drawn using the GPU, freeing up the CPU to manage the actual business of animation. You can use Core Animation to animate a number of individual parameters, such as the layer's position, its angle of rotation (in three-dimensional space), its size, how transparent it is, and so on.

The Core Animation API is part of the QuartzCore framework: `/System/Library/Frameworks/ QuartzCore.framework`.

APPLICATION FRAMEWORKS AND UI

All applications rely on common interface elements to communicate with the user. By packaging these elements in a library, an operating system can make sure all applications look and behave the same way. And the more functionality the operating system provides "for free," the less work application developers need to do themselves.

Toward that end, Mac OS X provides a number of application frameworks, as shown in Figure 1-6, upon which programmers can build their applications: Cocoa, Carbon, and the Java JDK. These frameworks, described in more detail in the following sections, all provide the basic concepts essential for application design: how events are processed by the application, how window contents are organized and drawn, how controls are presented to the user, and so on.

It is important that all applications present their user interface (UI) in a consistent manner, regardless of which application framework the program uses. In other words, all windows, menus, buttons, text fields, and so on should look and behave the same way on Mac OS X. These UI elements together on Mac OS X form a distinctive user experience that Apple calls the Aqua user interface. Consistency among apps is so important that Apple has published guidelines enumerating the proper way to use Aqua user interface elements; these guidelines are called the Apple Human Interface Guidelines.

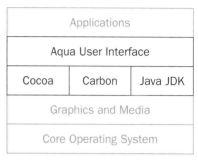

FIGURE 1-6

Each of these application frameworks is appropriate in different situations. In addition, these application frameworks are not mutually exclusive. An application may draw on features from all three frameworks.

Cocoa

The Cocoa application framework provides programmers with a means of building feature-rich Mac OS X applications quickly. The roots of Cocoa lie in NeXTSTEP, the operating system that powered NeXT computers in the early 1990s. When Apple announced Mac OS X in 1998, the API was re-christened Cocoa, and introduced alongside Carbon as Mac OS X's application development strategy.

Cocoa is an object-oriented API written in Objective-C, an object-oriented language descended from ANSI C and Smalltalk. Programmers work with Cocoa by creating objects and hooking them together in various ways. Objects provide a convenient way for programmers to extend basic application functionality without having to design the entire application from the ground up. Put another way, Cocoa allows you to focus on writing the code that makes your application unique, rather than forcing you to write the code that all applications must share.

The Cocoa API is divided between two frameworks:

➤   **The AppKit framework** (/System/Library/Frameworks/AppKit.framework): Provides high-level objects and services for writing applications, including Aqua UI elements.

➤   **The Foundation framework** (/System/Library/Frameworks/Foundation.framework): Provides objects and services useful for all programs, such as collection data types, Unicode string support, and so on.

These features are divided into two separate frameworks so programs can use Foundation's utility classes without having to bring in a full graphical user interface (GUI). For example, a command-line tool written in Objective-C might simply use Foundation.

Carbon

What we know as Carbon today started out as the programmatic interface to the original Macintosh operating system. Although sufficient for writing Macintosh applications, the API had some problems that made transitioning to a new core operating system impossible. In 1998,

Apple set out to revise the traditional Mac OS API and eliminate these problems, which would give existing Macintosh developers an easy path for migrating their code to Mac OS X. This revised API was called Carbon.

It used to be the case that you needed to work with Carbon to do a number of useful things in Mac OS X. For example, programmers interested in working with aliases, customized menus, or QuickTime all needed to use Carbon, even if they were writing a Cocoa application. Many of these things are no longer true in Mac OS X Snow Leopard. Cocoa programmers can now access things either through Cocoa or through specialized frameworks, such as QTKit.

If you are interested in porting a traditional Mac OS application to Mac OS X, Carbon is a good place to start. However, Apple has begun encouraging programmers to move away from Carbon altogether. Many Carbon technologies simply don't play well with modern hardware such as accelerated GPUs or modern software such as Core Animation. Apple has chosen to stop investing in Carbon to spend time on newer, more interesting technology.

The Carbon API is built around a collection of C interfaces, spread across several frameworks, including the Carbon framework (`/System/Library/Frameworks/Carbon.framework`), the Core Services framework (`/System/Library/Frameworks/CoreServices.framework`), and the ApplicationServices framework (`/System/Library/Frameworks/ApplicationServices.framework`). The Carbon framework includes a number of interfaces for working with high-level concepts, such as UI elements, online help, and speech recognition. CoreServices provides interfaces for working with lower-level Carbon data structures and services. ApplicationServices fits somewhere between the other two, building on CoreServices to provide important infrastructure supporting the high-level interfaces in the Carbon framework, such as Apple events, font and type services, and speech synthesis.

Java JDK

Mac OS X comes with built-in support for Java applications. Java is an object-oriented programming language created by Sun Microsystems for developing solid applications that can deploy on a wide variety of machines. Java itself is best thought of as three separate technologies: an object-oriented programming language, a collection of application frameworks, and a runtime environment, as described in the following list:

> **Java the programming language** — Designed to make writing programs as safe as possible. Toward that end, Java shields the programmer from certain concepts that often are a source of trouble. For example, because programmers often make mistakes when accessing memory directly, Java doesn't allow programmers to access memory in that way.

> **Java the application framework** — Provides a number of ways to develop applications using the Java programming language. Java and Cocoa are similar in many ways; for example, many of the objects and concepts in Cocoa also appear in Java.

> **Java the virtual machine** — Provides the runtime environment, called a virtual machine, in which all Java programs live. This virtual machine protects Java programs from subtle differences one encounters when trying to deploy programs on a variety of systems. For

example, different systems may have widely divergent hardware characteristics, supply different kinds of operating system services, and so on. Java Virtual Machine levels the playing field for all Java apps, so that Java programmers do not need to worry about these issues themselves.

Java's greatest strength is that it enables you to easily write applications that are deployable on a wide variety of computers and devices. In this respect, Java has no equal. On the other hand, for the purposes of writing a Mac OS X–specific application, the Java application frameworks have some serious drawbacks. Because Java must deploy on several different computers, Java's approach to application design tends to focus on commonly available technologies and concepts. It is difficult to gain access to features unique to Mac OS X, such as the power of CoreGraphics, through Java's application frameworks, because those features are not available on all Java systems. Because this book focuses on technologies specific to Mac OS X, we will not examine Java in further detail.

APPLE HUMAN INTERFACE GUIDELINES

All Mac OS X programs share a specific look and feel that makes them instantly recognizable as Mac OS X programs. This creates the illusion that all the applications on your system were designed to work together — even though your applications may have been designed by different people, all with different interests. After you learn how to use one application, you have a pretty good idea of how to use all applications.

Apple provides a document, called the Apple Human Interface Guidelines, which spells out how Mac OS X applications should look and behave. Applications written against one of Mac OS X's application frameworks start with a bit of an advantage: all the UI elements provided by these frameworks meet the specifications in the Apple Human Interface Guidelines. All the controls in Figure 1-7 are drawn using the Cocoa application framework; notice that they all look like Mac OS X controls.

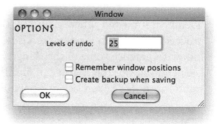

FIGURE 1-7

Unfortunately, simply using the right controls isn't enough to make an Aqua-compliant interface. A large part of UI design is in collecting and organizing controls so they make sense. The Apple Human Interface Guidelines provide metrics for how far apart related controls and groups of controls should be and where certain kinds of controls should go. The Aqua guidelines specify specific fonts and font sizes for UI elements. It also specifies when certain features are appropriate, such as default buttons, hierarchical menu items, and so on. Figure 1-8 illustrates the same controls from Figure 1-7, laid out in compliance with the Apple Human Interface Guidelines — note that it looks much cleaner.

The information in the Apple Human Interface Guidelines is quite extensive. It covers all the user interface elements available within Mac OS X, such as windows, menus, controls, separators, text labels, and icons. All Mac OS X programmers should be familiar with the Apple Human Interface Guidelines to know what correct Aqua user interfaces are supposed to look like, and how they're supposed to behave.

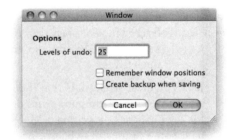

FIGURE 1-8

SUMMARY

You have seen how the major elements of Mac OS X come together on your computer. The applications you use every day are but one element. These applications are built on application frameworks, system services, and ultimately Mac OS X's core operating system; all these pieces contribute to your application experience. The high-level picture might look similar to Figure 1-9.

In the next chapter, you learn about the developer resources bundled with Mac OS X. These include tools used during the development process, as well as online documentation and other resources. Before proceeding, you can use the exercises that follow to practice some of the things you learned in this chapter. You can find the solutions to these exercises in Appendix A.

Applications			Command-line Tools
Aqua User Interface			
Cocoa	Carbon	Java JDK	
Quartz 2D	OpenGL	QuickTime	
Quartz Compositor			
System Library			
Kernel			

FIGURE 1-9

EXERCISES

1. The `apropos` command returns a list of manual pages that match one or more keywords. Try entering the following commands into Terminal:

    a. apropos copy

    b. apropos copy file

    c. apropos "copy file"

    Which of these commands provides the best result?

2. You have seen how you can use `man` to read the online help for a specific command. Type `man man` into Terminal and read about what `man` is capable of. For example, what does `man -k "copy file"` do?

▶ WHAT YOU LEARNED IN THIS CHAPTER

Kernel	the heart of the Core OS, responsible for talking to hardware and running programs
System Library	API for "talking to" the Core OS
Quartz Compositor	the process responsible for all application drawing and event handling
Quartz 2D	API for drawing rich 2D graphics
OpenGL	an open, standard API for drawing hardware accelerated 2D and 3D graphics
QuickTime	a framework for reading and creating multimedia files
CoreAnimation	a framework for animating user interfaces and other application content
Cocoa	a collection of frameworks used for writing Mac OS X applications using the Objective-C programming language
Carbon	a collection of frameworks used for older Mac OS and Mac OS X applications

Developer Tools

WHAT YOU WILL LEARN IN THIS CHAPTER:

➤ How to install the developer tools that came with your copy of Mac OS X

➤ Where to find the tools and documentation you just installed

➤ How to use the Apple Developer Connection web site

Since the earliest releases of Mac OS X, a complete set of developer tools has come bundled with the operating system. These tools range from text editors and compilers to debuggers and performance analyzers. Mac OS X even comes with a large collection of developer documentation and examples to help explain how these developer tools and development libraries should be used. Those interested in programming on Mac OS X have everything they need to get started.

Apple Computer also has a large developer support web site called Apple Developer Connection or ADC, found at `http://developer.apple.com/`. Here Apple posts the most updated versions of its developer tools, documentation, and examples. This site also provides resources for small businesses interested in developing and distributing a product to the Macintosh community. If you are an ADC member, you can even file bug reports on Apple's software to help resolve issues you may discover on your own.

INSTALLING THE DEVELOPER SOFTWARE

As we have said, Apple bundles development tools along with the Mac OS X operating system. However, these tools are often an optional part of the installation process, and all the necessary components might not yet be installed on your system. If your copy of Mac OS X came pre-installed on a new Macintosh, these tools may be installed already. Otherwise, you need to install the necessary pieces from your Mac OS X CDs.

In Mac OS X Snow Leopard, the developer tools live in a package called `Xcode`. You can find this package on your install DVD. The Installer will ask you to customize the Xcode installation, and you can just accept the default options. If you're not sure, go ahead and install everything.

DEVELOPER APPLICATIONS

The Mac OS X developer package includes several applications for your use during the development process. You can find most of these applications in the `/Developer/Applications` folder. Some of these tools are essential, such as those used for editing source code and building programs. Other tools are more specialized, such as the performance analysis tools and graphics utilities. In the sections that follow, you learn about many of these tools and how you can put them to use.

Build Tools

Of the programs installed in `/Developer/Applications`, two stand out as being indispensable in the development process: Xcode and Interface Builder. Together they include all the functionality required to design, build, and debug programs on Mac OS X.

Xcode is the centerpiece of the Mac OS X development environment. It includes tools for writing, building, and debugging programs, all in a single application. Xcode also provides easy access to much of the developer documentation on your system. Xcode scales easily from building command-line tools and applications, to building libraries and plug-ins. You learn much more about Xcode in Chapter 3.

Interface Builder builds Carbon and Cocoa user interfaces for use in Xcode projects. You build interfaces by arranging windows, controls, and other elements graphically with your mouse. You learn much more about Interface Builder in Chapter 4.

Both Xcode and Interface Builder are up to the challenge of building whatever program you might need. In fact, Apple uses these same tools to build most of the applications and frameworks that make up Mac OS X. And by making Xcode and Interface Builder available with Mac OS X, Apple is giving you a great head start on building your software.

Performance Tools

Once you have dealt with the petty matters of writing some software and working out the bugs, your thoughts may turn to the question of performance. When you run your program, you may see the spinning wait cursor (or the *rainbow wheel* or *spinning pizza of death*, whatever you call it). This cursor means your program has stopped processing user events and has become temporarily unresponsive. This unresponsiveness can be caused by many factors that normally boil down to two root causes: excess computation and memory management problems. In other words, *time* vs. *space*.

Mac OS X includes Instruments, an application you can use to diagnose most of your performance problems. It helps you find common memory problems, troublesome file usage, and computation bottlenecks. You learn more about Instruments in a little bit. Instruments resides in `/Developer/Applications` along with Xcode and Interface Builder.

Mac OS X includes several additional utilities for examining where you spend your time and how you allocate your memory. These tools all live in `/Developer/Applications/Performance Tools`. Many of these tools match functionality available in Instruments. One tool that stands apart from the others is Shark, a sampling tool that finds performance bottlenecks and suggests ways you can eliminate them.

ON PROGRAMS, STACKS, AND BACKTRACES

Programs are made up of a series of machine instructions gathered into functions or routines. These functions normally call other functions to do work. Your program can't exit a given function until all that function's sub-functions have completed. You might think of these functions as a stack of plates at a cafeteria. When your program enters a function, push a plate on the stack; when the function completes, pop the plate off the stack. The topmost plate represents your program's current function.

This metaphor for describing how functions work is so natural, we refer to a program's list of running functions as its *stack*, *frame stack,* or *call stack*. The individual function calls are sometimes called *frames*.

Debugging tools often show you where you are in your program by displaying the entire stack. Traditionally, you start with the current frame and work all the way back to the very first function. This list is called a *backtrace* because you *trace back* from the current frame.

All these utilities work by analyzing your program's state as it runs. These kinds of tools are generally known as *profilers*. Profilers normally require you to build your program in a special way so that the utility can carefully watch your program's execution. Mac OS X's utilities require no such preprocessing and can be run on any application, whether you wrote it or not. They work by periodically (several times a second) peeking at your program's stack and aggregating the results.

Instruments

Instruments analyzes your programs for different kinds of performance problems. Most of the actual work of analyzing your program is done by smaller tools called *instruments*, from which the utility gets its name. Instruments provides a common user interface (UI) for configuring and running these smaller instruments.

These instruments are organized in a timeline similar to GarageBand. Start by dragging instruments into the timeline from a Library, or by opening a preconfigured template. You can watch performance statistics change in real-time as your program runs. When you see something interesting, you can go back and look at it by scrubbing the playhead back in time.

The following table lists some of the instrument tools available to Instruments. These tools are covered in more depth in the next several sections.

TOOL	DESCRIPTION
Leaks	Watches how your program allocates memory and looks for leaks; best used in conjunction with the ObjectAlloc instrument
ObjectAlloc	Watches how your program manages reference-counted objects and detects autorelease problems
Spin Monitor	Automatically samples programs when they display the wait cursor
Thread States	Watches how your program creates and uses threads
Time Profiler	Shows how your program's call stack changes over time
User Interface	Records user events, allowing you to replay them later

ObjectAlloc and Leaks

ObjectAlloc keeps track of when your application allocates and frees memory. It records the position in your program's call stack where each allocation occurs, allowing you to find places where you're using a lot of memory. ObjectAlloc is specifically useful for tracking reference-counted memory objects such as Objective-C objects and CoreFoundation data structures.

Reference counting is a memory management technique where you keep track of the number of things referring to a piece of memory. If someone is interested in the memory, they *retain* it, or increase the memory's reference count by one. When they are done with the memory, they *release* it, or decrease the reference count by one. When an object's reference count goes to 0, its memory is freed. Foundation introduces an interesting concept called *autoreleasing*. Autoreleasing is a way of marking an Objective-C object to be released later. It's useful for hanging onto an object temporarily without worrying about precisely when it is released.

Leaks watches memory, looking for places where your program lost its reference to a memory allocation without freeing it. We call this situation a *leak*. If you aren't quite sure what memory allocation means or what a leak is, don't worry; you learn more about this in Chapter 6.

Figure 2-1 shows ObjectAlloc and Leaks in action.

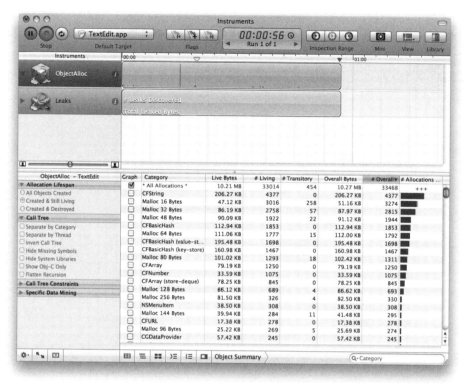

FIGURE 2-1

Time Profiler and Spin Monitor

Time Profiler shows you how a program's call stack changes over time. Simply start your program while using the Time Profiler instrument. When you finish recording, you can analyze the results to find out where your program spent most of its time during the recording period.

Time Profiler works by pausing your program several times a second and recording your program's call stack at that point in time. It then trends the data in several ways, including measuring the frequency of each specific frame in the call stack, and tracking the size of the call-stack changes. For example, if a specific function call appears in half your program's call stacks, Time Profiler calls that out.

By default, Time Profiler shows you the most common stacks where your program was sampled, sorted by frequency. This is useful when you're looking at very computation-intensive programs, because this view shows you which functions you need to make faster. This view is called an *inverted call tree*. Sometimes your performance problem is deeper in your backtrace, and you need to see how your program spent its time in your code. In this situation, you can display the normal call tree, and then drill down into the stack trace, layer by layer. Each step of the way, you can see how much time your program spent at that stack frame. Figure 2-2 shows Time Profiler's normal call tree view.

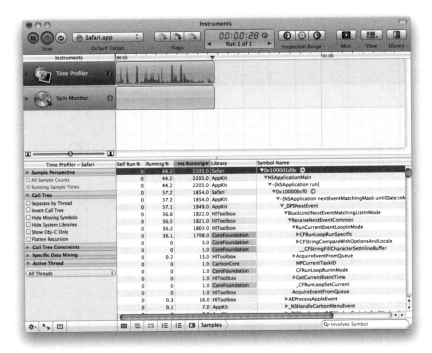

FIGURE 2-2

Imagine that your program has become unresponsive. It no longer responds to user events, and Mac OS X automatically shows the spinning wait cursor. You want to sample your program to find out what is chewing up its time, but you don't want to have to search through a lot of instrument data to find the trouble spots.

Spin Monitor helps you deal with these situations by automatically sampling applications that go into the busy state (display the spinning wait cursor). Just start the Spin Monitor instrument and wait for your app to go off and start spinning. When that happens, Spin Monitor generates a sample report similar to the one produced by Time Profiler. Because Spin Control works passively, you can just start it and leave it running as you go about your business.

Thread States

Every process on Mac OS X uses one or more *threads* to process machine instructions. A thread basically represents the capability to do work on the system at any given time. In the same way in which Mac OS X's preemptive multitasking kernel can run two processes at the same time, a process with two threads can do two activities at the same time.

Programmers often turn to threads to improve program performance. For example, on Macintosh systems with more than one CPU, a programmer can use threads to perform work on both CPUs at once. Also, a program such as the Finder might perform a long file-copy operation in a background thread while responding to user events in the main thread.

But writing multi-threaded programs can be challenging, because programmers must deal with the fact that a program is performing two or more things at once. You can get into trouble if two threads start competing for the same resource. For example, if you have two programs trying to write to the same file at the same time, the file contents might get mixed up. Similarly, multiple threads trying to write to the same data structures might instead scramble their program's memory. Creating additional worker threads comes at some cost, so you can actually hinder performance if you get carried away with threads.

Thread States shows you the state of your program's threads. Each thread is plotted in a bar graph in the timeline clip, allowing you to see when it's busy and when it's idle, as shown in Figure 2-3.

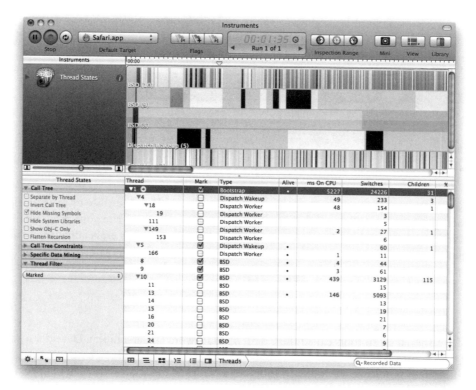

FIGURE 2-3

User Interface

The User Interface instrument records the keyboard and mouse events coming into your application. Each event is displayed in the results window along with a thumbnail image summarizing the event, as shown in Figure 2-4.

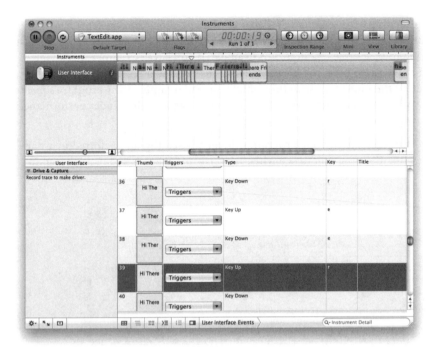

FIGURE 2-4

Using the User Interface instrument couldn't be simpler. Simply add User Interface to your timeline, run your program, use it normally, and then stop recording. Next time you run your program, Instruments will play your keyboard and mouse events back for you. This is especially useful when used in conjunction with other instruments; you can automatically replay the same set of steps while watching your performance. As you fix problems in your application, you can rerun your test scenarios and verify that performance has improved.

Shark

Apple provides a special set of tools called the Common Hardware Understanding Development Tools, or CHUD Tools for short. These tools work very closely with your Mac's hardware to diagnose performance problems. The CHUD Tools come with the other Mac OS X developer tools. You'll find the CHUD tools in a folder at `/Developer/Applications/Performance Tools/CHUD`.

Of all the CHUD Tools from Apple, the most popular is Shark, as shown in Figure 2-5. Although it's part of the CHUD toolset, you will find Shark in `/Developer/Applications/Performance Tools`, not in the CHUD folder.

Shark is similar to the Time Profiler instrument in that it records programs' call stacks over a period of time and trends the results. Shark differs from Time Profiler in that it samples your entire system, not just a single application. Shark takes your call-stack data one step further by showing your frame's assembly code, and even the source code, if available. So when Shark indicates that you're spending a suspicious amount of time in a particular function, you can actually view the source code for that function right there. And if that isn't enough, Shark even suggests specific ways in which you can improve your function's performance. The only catch is that some of Shark's advice is appropriate only for advanced programmers.

You can find a complete user guide under Shark's Help menu. Shark also comes with PowerPC, Intel, and ARM assembly command reference guides to help you understand Shark's assembly code view.

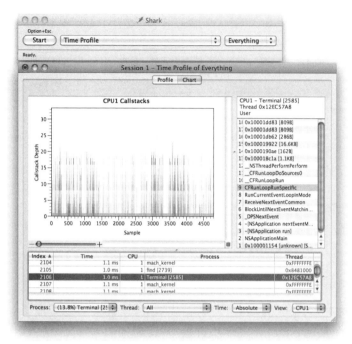

FIGURE 2-5

Other Utilities

Mac OS X's developer tools include other utilities that can make your life easier. Though these utilities are not as indispensable as Xcode, Interface Builder, or Instruments, it's worth spending some time getting to know them. A number of the more interesting utilities appear in the following table and are described in more depth in the next sections. All these tools live at /Developer/ Applications/Utilities, except where otherwise noted.

TOOL	DESCRIPTION
FileMerge	Compares two files or directory trees, and merges the differences
Icon Composer	Builds icon files (.icns) used for your application
PackageMaker	Builds Installer packages
Pixie	Magnifies portions of your screen to look for minute drawing problems
Property List Editor	Edits property list files
Script Editor	Writes and tests AppleScript programs

FileMerge

FileMerge lets you compare two text files side by side and see how they differ. As you scroll through the files, FileMerge highlights places where text has been added, removed, or moved within the files. You can also use FileMerge to compare entire directories of files, as shown in Figure 2-6.

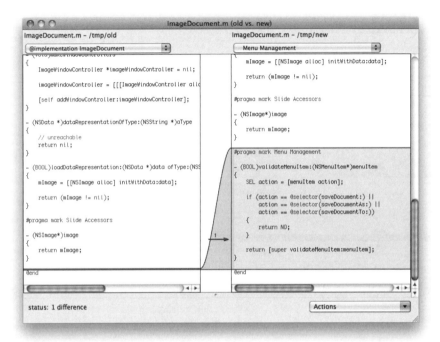

FIGURE 2-6

FileMerge gets its name from its ability to merge changes between two files into a third file. You simply scroll through both files and, for each change, pick which one you want to keep. You can then save a new version of the file that contains all the common text with the changes you specified. This is very useful when you're looking at two versions of the same Xcode project. You can use FileMerge to see where the two projects differ, and select which changes you want to keep on a change-by-change basis.

Icon Composer

Icon Composer, shown in Figure 2-7, is a small utility for making Mac OS X icon (.icns) files. Despite its name, you cannot draw icons in Icon Composer; you need to draw your icons in some other program and save various sizes of the icons as separate files. You can then drag your files into Icon Composer and save the result as a .icns file. You learn more about using .icns files in Chapter 5.

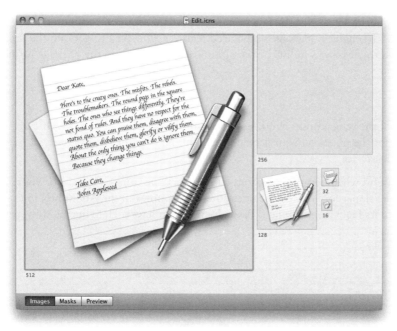

FIGURE 2-7

PackageMaker

PackageMaker builds packages for use in Installer, Mac OS X's built-in software installer. After you've written your own programs, you might want to distribute them as packages to help simplify the installation process for your users. You simply point PackageMaker at a directory of files, fill out the form shown in Figure 2-8, and create your package.

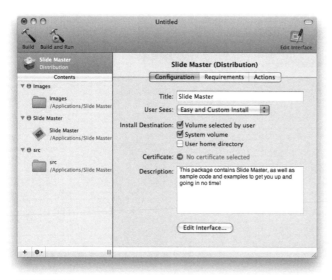

FIGURE 2-8

Packages can actually support a lot of custom functionality, more than can be configured using PackageMaker's interface. To enable a package's advanced features, you need to get into the details of the package format. PackageMaker's online help contains detailed notes on the package format, along with a few examples.

Pixie

Pixie magnifies the area of the screen under your mouse cursor, as shown in Figure 2-9. It can also display color values for the pixels on your screen. You can find Pixie in `/Developer/ Applications/Graphics Tools`.

These features are very useful when designing custom UI elements and other graphics for your programs. Unlike other developer tools, Pixie includes some usage notes in the About box in the Pixie menu, rather than in its Help menu. In fact, Pixie doesn't even have a Help menu. However, the program is easy to master.

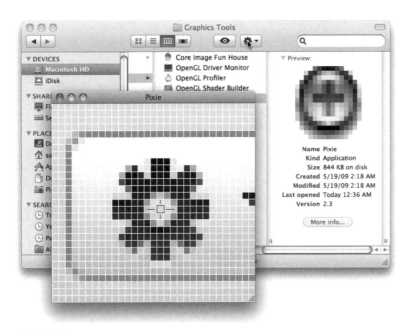

FIGURE 2-9

Property List Editor

Property List Editor is, as its name implies, a program that edits *property lists*. Property lists are text or binary files that store structured data. Property List Editor displays property lists in an outline view so that you can easily navigate them, as shown in Figure 2-10.

Property lists are commonly used for such things as application preferences, configuration files, and even some document formats. You learn more about property lists and see some examples of how they are used in Chapter 5.

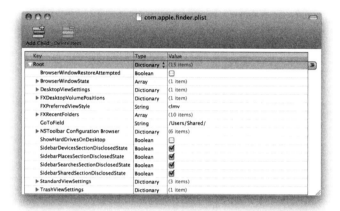

FIGURE 2-10

Script Editor

Script Editor is an application for writing and running AppleScripts. Strictly speaking, Script Editor isn't a developer tool; it's a standard part of Mac OS X. You can find Script Editor in `/Applications/AppleScript`.

Script Editor is a specialized tool for working with AppleScripts. It validates your AppleScript syntax as you write and use colors and text styles to highlight various parts of your script. You can also run AppleScripts from Script Editor and display the results in the main editor window, as shown in Figure 2-11. After you've written an AppleScript, you can save it as a self-contained application for future use; this lets you distribute AppleScripts without sharing your script's code with others. These applications are really just simple AppleScripts, not full-featured applications such as TextEdit or Finder.

You learn more about AppleScript in Chapter 13.

FIGURE 2-11

Command-Line Tools

As you learned in Chapter 1, Unix development is traditionally done through command-line tools. Although Mac OS X includes applications for designing, building, and debugging programs on Mac OS X, the developer packages include several powerful command-line tools as well. In fact, many of the applications you've read about in this chapter have command-line equivalents.

Some of the more interesting command-line utilities appear in the following table and are described in more detail in the next sections. You access these tools through the Terminal application.

TOOL	DESCRIPTION
cc/gcc	Compiles C and other programming languages
diff	Compares two files or directory trees
gdb	Debugs programs written in C and other programming languages
sample	Shows how your program's call stack changes over time
sh/bash/tcsh	Interprets Unix commands and runs shell scripts
top	Tracks performance statistics for the entire system

cc/gcc

Since the very beginning, Unix operating systems have come with a built-in C compiler: cc. In the old days, this compiler was necessary to install software: you would download a program's source code and compile it specifically for your system.

Sometime later, the Free Software Foundation created and distributed a free, multi-language compiler called gcc. The organization's goal was to ensure computer users would always have access to a royalty-free compiler they could use without cost. Today, gcc has essentially replaced cc on most modern Unix systems, and Mac OS X is no exception. Even if you type cc instead of gcc, you get the gcc compiler.

Of course, Mac OS X's primary tool for building programs is Xcode, as you see in Chapter 3. In reality, Xcode uses the gcc compiler for building your C, C++, and Objective-C code. But you can still drive the gcc compiler yourself from the command-line. This is especially useful for compiling software intended for other Unix systems on Mac OS X.

diff

diff is a command-line tool for examining two text files and showing how they differ, much like FileMerge. The method for comparing two files is fairly straightforward. The following example shows a method that has been added to a new version of the ImageDocument.m file. diff supports many options for customizing its output, and you can learn a lot more about this utility from its manual (man) page.

```
Macintosh:~ sample$ diff old/ImageDocument.m new/ImageDocument.m
60a61,71
> - (BOOL)validateMenuItem:(NSMenuItem*)menuItem
> {
>     SEL action = [menuItem action];
>
>     if (action == @selector(saveDocument:)) {
>         return NO
>     }
>
>     return YES;
> }
>
Macintosh:~ sample$
```

gdb

gdb is a source-level debugger distributed by the Free Software Foundation. You can use it to step through your program's call stack as it's running, examine your program's variables and the contents of its memory, and so on. If your program crashes while you're debugging it, gdb shows you precisely where it crashed. As with the Unix shell, you interact with gdb by issuing command-line instructions, as shown in the following example:

```
Macintosh:~ sample$ gdb Slide\ Master.app/Contents/MacOS/Slide\ Master
GNU gdb 5.3-20030128 (Apple version gdb-309) (Thu Dec  4 15:41:30 GMT 2003)
Copyright 2003 Free Software Foundation, Inc.
...
Reading symbols for shared libraries .... done
(gdb) break main
```

```
Breakpoint 1 at 0xedf68: file /Projects/Slide Master/main.m, line 13.
(gdb) run
Starting program: Slide Master.app/Contents/MacOS/Slide Master
Breakpoint 1, main (argc=1, argv=0xbfffffe9c) at /Projects/Slide Master/main.m:13
13          return NSApplicationMain(argc, argv);
(gdb)
```

You've learned that the primary tool for debugging programs on Mac OS X is Xcode. But just as Xcode uses the gcc tool to compile your program's source code, Xcode actually uses gdb to help you debug your program. Xcode provides a nice graphical interface on top of gdb that is easy to learn and is well-suited for most debugging tasks. Once in a while, programmers drop down to gdb's command line to access the debugger's more advanced features. You can learn more about Xcode in Chapter 3; if you're interested in learning more about gdb, you can bring up an extensive command reference by typing help at the (gdb) prompt.

sample

sample is a command-line tool that generates reports for Instruments' Time Profile instrument. It's fairly simple to use; you just enter the name or *process identifier* of the program you want to sample and the number of seconds you want to record, as shown in the following code example. A process identifier is a unique number that identifies the process on your system. You can find a process's identifier using command-line tools such as ps or top, or using the Activity Monitor application.

```
Macintosh:/tmp sample$ sample Finder 2
Sampling process 256 each 10 msecs 200 times
Sample analysis of process 256 written to file /tmp/Finder_256.sample.txt
Macintosh:~ sample$
```

Output is saved to a file in the /tmp/ directory by default. Although not as user-friendly as Instruments, you may find yourself using sample quite a bit, especially if you spend a lot of time in Terminal. It's often faster to type sample Finder 2 than to go and find Instruments, launch it, attach to the Finder, and so on. You can also open sample reports in Instruments by choosing File ➪ Import Data. You can learn more about the options you can pass to sample from its man page.

sh/bash/tcsh

In Chapter 1, you learned how to run command-line functions from Terminal. Again, the Terminal itself knows nothing about how to interpret your commands. Instead, it delegates all that responsibility to the Unix shell.

The original Unix shell is called sh (for *shell*) and supports a fairly simple command language. Every sh command begins with a program name. This program is responsible for parsing the other arguments in the sh command and doing the requested work. The sh command language also includes support for redirecting a program's input and output to files. For example, you can capture all the output from a command by redirecting its output to a file. Realizing the utility of sh's command language, its authors devised a means of processing commands from a file rather than from user input. These files are called *shell scripts*, because they are *scripts* of *shell* commands.

But sh is not without limitations, and many people have sought to build a better shell to replace sh. Individual shells come into, and subsequently out of, favor all the time. Two modern sh replacements include bash (the "Bourne Again Shell," a reference to one of the original sh authors) and `tcsh`, both of which come with Mac OS X. `bash` is a modern replacement derived (if only in spirit) from the original `sh` command syntax. It is quite common on Linux and other Unix systems and is the default shell for Mac OS X. `tcsh` is a modern replacement for an older shell, `csh`, which featured a number of improvements over the original `sh` command: a history and command aliases.

You can find shells installed with other fundamental command-line utilities in `/bin`. You can run a shell simply by typing its name in the command line; the `exit` command quits out of the shell. You can change your default shell with the `chsh` command, as shown in the following code. The change takes effect when you open a new Terminal window.

```
Macintosh:~ sample$ chsh -s /bin/tcsh
chsh: netinfo domain "." updated
Macintosh:~ sample$
```

You learn more about the shell and shell scripting in Chapter 12. You can also learn a lot about how individual shells work, including their command syntax and other features, by reading their man pages.

top

`top` displays system performance statistics such as CPU load, memory usage, and processor time consumed per process in your Terminal window. Unlike the other performance tools you've learned about so far, `top` updates itself automatically and displays its results live. It is the command-line equivalent of the Activity Monitor utility found in `/Applications/Utilities`.

Although it's really more of a system maintenance command than a developer tool, `top` is useful as a developer tool. Because `top` displays its results live, you can use it to watch how your program's CPU load and memory requirements change while you are using your program. For example, you should make sure your program is using 0 percent of the CPU when you aren't actively using the program; using CPU unnecessarily will affect the battery life on portable machines. Also make sure your program is using a minimum of other system resources: threads, memory, and so on. You can learn a lot more about how to use `top` from its man page.

DEVELOPER DOCUMENTATION AND EXAMPLES

Mac OS X includes a lot of documentation for people interested in writing Mac OS X programs. You have already seen some examples of this documentation, such as the online help that comes with most of the system's developer tools. Documentation also exists for frameworks such as Carbon and Cocoa; this includes API reference, conceptual or high-level documentation, and even examples that illustrate how these frameworks should be used.

Much of Mac OS X's developer documentation resides in the Apple Developer Connection Reference Library. You can download, search, and read the Reference Library directly within Xcode, so it is in easy reach while you are working on your programs. The Reference Library can also be found on the Apple Developer Connection web site. You will learn more about the Apple Developer Connection later in this chapter.

Xcode's Developer Documentation window lets you access the Reference Library. You can open the Developer Documentation window, shown in Figure 2-12, from Xcode's Help menu. Type a word or phrase into the Search field to search through the documentation on your system. Xcode will look through class and function references, overview documentation, and source code examples. You will learn more about Xcode in the next chapter.

FIGURE 2-12

Earlier, you learned how to use Mac OS X's man page system to get help for command-line tools. Although man pages aren't strictly intended as developer documentation, they do contain a lot of information specifically for developers. For example, most of Mac OS X's Darwin API reference is published through man pages rather than HTML or PDF documents. The same is true of some third-party libraries and languages, such as OpenGL, Tcl, and Perl.

Conceptual Documentation

When you're learning how to use a particular library or framework on Mac OS X, one of the first places you should turn to is the framework's conceptual documentation. The conceptual documentation is designed to teach you the fundamentals of using that framework, such as describing basic data structures and concepts and how the different parts of the framework interact with each other and with other frameworks. The conceptual documentation also contains tutorials that illustrate how the pieces come together and give you a chance to practice what you've learned.

The best place to find this conceptual documentation is in the Apple Developer Connection Reference Library. You can find the library's main index by opening Xcode's Developer Documentation window and choosing Mac OS X 10.6 Core Library from the Home toolbar item. The library contains thousands of documents organized by resource type, topic, and framework. You can also search for documents by title if you are looking for something specific. Figure 2-13 shows the Core Reference Library's top-level page.

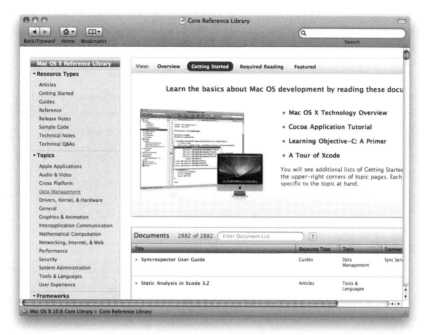

FIGURE 2-13

The Resource Types section groups documents by how they're written or by audience. For example, the Resource Types section collects all the Getting Started documents into one place. The following table describes the library resource categories.

RESOURCE TYPE	DESCRIPTION
Articles	Documents meant to quickly illustrate a single topic, such as using a development tool or working with specific technologies.
Getting Started	Short pages that link articles, guides, and reference documentation for a specific topic.
Guides	Conceptual documentation about a framework or technology, including detailed discussions, tutorials, and small examples.
Reference	Thorough documentation describing classes, functions, tools, and file formats at a low level. You will read more about this documentation later.
Release Notes	Lists of changes and additions to libraries and tools.
Sample Code	Xcode projects, AppleScripts, and other source files that illustrate how to use libraries or other technologies.
Technical Notes	Similar to Articles, Technical Notes are short documents describing a specific technical topic, such as debugging certain kinds of problems or explaining common programming techniques.
Technical Q&As	Short technical notes written in a question-and-answer format.

The documents shown in the following table and explained in more detail in the following sections describe important Mac OS X concepts that aren't specific to individual technologies. You have already learned about some of them in Chapter 1, but they bear repeating. You can find these documents in the Mac OS X section of the documentation index, except where otherwise noted.

DOCUMENT	DESCRIPTION
Apple Human Interface Guidelines	Describes the elements of the Aqua user interface
Mac OS X Technology Overview	Describes Mac OS X's system architecture
A Tour of Xcode	Gives a brief overview of Xcode and links to more-detailed references

Apple Human Interface Guidelines

You already learned about the role of the Apple Human Interface Guidelines in Chapter 1. To recap, the Apple Human Interface Guidelines describe how Aqua UI elements should look and behave, how they should interact with each other, when to develop your own custom controls, and how to make them "fit in" with the rest of Aqua. In other words, they define the rules that all Mac OS X applications are supposed to follow. You can find this document in the Mac OS X section of the documentation index.

Mac OS X Technology Overview

The Mac OS X Technology Overview describes how the various pieces of Mac OS X come together into a complete system. It includes an overview of information you can't find easily in other places, including the following:

➤ Mac OS X's directory layout

➤ File system issues specific to Mac OS X

➤ How bundles, applications, and frameworks are packaged

➤ Strategies for internationalizing Mac OS X software

Although the Technology Overview goes into a reasonable amount of detail on these topics, it stops short of providing an API reference for working with the technologies themselves. So, for example, you should turn to the System Overview to learn what a bundle is, what features they offer, and conceptually how bundles are used. After you understand all this, you can turn to Carbon- or Cocoa-specific documentation to learn about the particular API available for working with bundles directly.

The Technology Overview is available in the Mac OS X section of the documentation index.

A Tour of Xcode

The Xcode application is a complex tool. Although it's easy to get started using Xcode to write Mac OS X programs, there are many advanced features lurking beneath its surface. In Mac OS X Snow Leopard, Apple divided Xcode's User Guide into a series of detailed documents. A Tour of Xcode collects these user guides into a list called Recommended Reading for Xcode Developers, which is located in the Tools section of the documentation index.

API Reference

After you understand the fundamental concepts behind a particular framework and work through a tutorial or two, you will want to roll up your sleeves and start writing some code. Before too long, you will have questions about how the framework's API handles a certain problem, or if it provides a particular feature. To find the answers, you can turn to the framework's API reference.

As with conceptual documentation, the best place to find an API reference is in the ADC Reference Library index. You will find API references listed under the Reference resource type or in one of the libraries listed in the Frameworks section.

Most frameworks have a Framework Reference document that links to additional pages of class and function documentation. For example, you will find an index of AppKit classes, protocols, and other API references on the Application Kit Framework Reference page in the AppKit section. The exact content of an API reference file depends on the technology. Figure 2-14 shows the Application Kit Framework Reference for Objective-C. The top-level page links to additional pages for individual Objective-C classes and other information. Class pages contain documentation for each of the class's methods.

Figure 2-15 shows one such method entry. The page defines the method signature and then describes the function's inputs and outputs, expected behavior, and anything else you need to know to use the function.

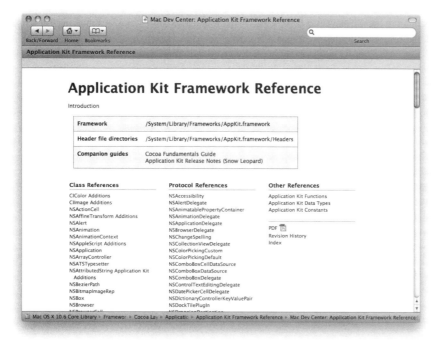

FIGURE 2-14

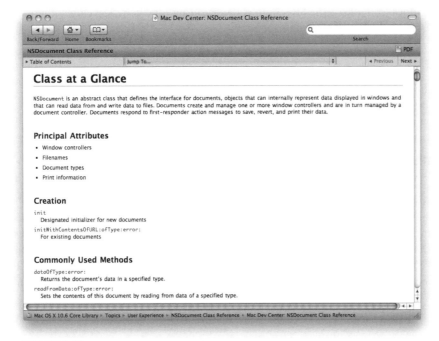

FIGURE 2-15

This API reference is arguably the most important piece of Mac OS X's developer documentation. You use it to discover what a framework is capable of and to learn how to write code that uses that framework's specific features. Without the API reference, you could still learn a lot about a framework's API definition from its header files, but you'd have to guess at what the interface does and how it's used. Feel free to bookmark the reference pages you visit often so that you can return to them quickly.

Examples

You will find many examples in the ADC Reference Library. These examples range from small snippets of code that illustrate specific points to full-blown applications. Again, you can browse for these examples in Xcode's Developer Documentation window under the Reference Library's Sample Code section.

You will also find a few examples in /Developer/Examples. These examples are editable by any user with administrative privileges. If you created your user account when you installed Mac OS X, or when you turned on your new computer for the first time, you have an administrator account. That means you can open and build these projects right where they are. However, it's still a good idea to always make copies of these examples before you build them; that way, if you accidentally edit or change something, you can always go back to the original.

You will find the complete source code to TextEdit and Sketch here in /Developer/Examples. You may already be familiar with TextEdit, the text editor that lives in /Applications. The TextEdit source code shows you how to build a complete Cocoa application, including working with documents, basic scriptability, and printing. TextEdit is quite old for a Cocoa app, and it doesn't use some of the newer additions to Cocoa, such as Cocoa's document abstraction. Sketch is a drawing application written in Cocoa that's a little more current than the TextEdit example.

Man Pages

In Chapter 1, you learned about the Unix *manual* and how you can use the man command to view information about Mac OS X's command-line programs. Even the command-line tools installed by the developer packages have man pages. But the manual contains information beyond command-line reference.

Most of the Darwin programmer documentation lives in the manual system. This includes API references for the C functions in the system libraries. It also contains API references for other libraries and languages that are part of Darwin, including entries for Perl, Tcl, and OpenSSL. In addition, you can find notes on file formats, directory layouts, and other conceptual documentation in the manual.

Man pages are gathered into different sections, with each section indexed by numbers. Historically, these sections have special meaning, as shown in the following table.

SECTION	DESCRIPTION
1	Commands
2	System Calls
3	Library Functions
4	Devices and Device Drivers
5	File Formats
6	Games
7	Miscellaneous
8	System Maintenance

Although most of the man pages available on Mac OS X still follow this old format, there are some things to consider. Information about command-line utilities tend to live in sections 1 and 8. Similarly, the C API reference for Darwin is spread between sections 2 and 3, but the difference between these sections is somewhat obscure. Although section 4 includes a few man pages related to devices and device drivers, you won't find information about Mac OS X's driver layer, IOKit, in the man system. Instead, you can find IOKit information in the ADC Reference Library, along with other Mac OS X–specific technologies.

Other projects have expanded the original section list to meet their own needs. For example, Perl documentation lives in section *3pm*, which is sort of a part of section 3. You really don't need to worry about these new sections (or sections in general) except when you have trouble pulling up certain man pages.

When you ask for a man page, the man command searches its sections for a matching page and returns the first one it finds. So if pages in two or more sections share the same name, man displays only one of those files. In these cases, you have to ask for the proper section number in addition to the page name. For example, man 2 open asks the system for the open man page in the System Calls section, not the page in the Commands section. You can use the apropos and man -k commands you learned about in Chapter 1 to print page names and section numbers that match specific keywords, as shown here:

```
Macintosh:~ sample$ man -k "copy file"
CpMac(1)                    - copy files preserving metadata and forks
File::Copy(3pm)             - Copy files or filehandles
cp(1)                       - copy files
cpio(1)                     - copy file archives in and out
ditto(8)                    - copy files and directories to a destination directory
```

Also, if you know that a page appears in more than one section, but you're not sure which, you can use man -a to print all the pages that match a specific name. For example, man -a open displays all the open man pages, one after another.

Mac OS X's man pages live in the /usr/share/man directory. This directory is part of the underlying Darwin system and isn't visible from Finder by default. You can either use Terminal or choose Finder's Go ➪ Go to Folder command to examine this directory. Here you'll find the individual sections broken out for you, each one containing the individual man files. Most of these files appear in an old Unix text markup language called troff that you won't be able to read in normal text editors, web browsers, or word processors. If you're wondering why these files are in usr/share/man, you can find the answer in the hier man page.

APPLE DEVELOPER CONNECTION

Mac OS X is constantly evolving, and the same is true of its developer information. Apple is constantly revising its tools, documentation, and examples to reflect the changes in Mac OS X and the needs of its developers. You can tap into this information from the Apple Developer Connection (ADC) web site: http://developer.apple.com/. Figure 2-16 shows the Apple Developer Connection home page at the time this book was written. As with all things on the Internet, it may change by the time you read this. Some of the information is available to the public-at-large, and those pages can be viewed using any web browser. Other content is available with an Apple Developer Connection account. You can sign up for an Online Membership to the ADC program for free, which gives you access to most, if not all, of the material on the ADC web site. You can learn more about the ADC membership levels at http://developer.apple.com/products/membership.html.

FIGURE 2-16

The Apple Developer Connection is split into two main areas: the Macintosh Developer Program and the iPhone Developer Program. It turns out iPhone and Mac programmers use most of the same tools, libraries, and techniques, so there is some overlap in developer content. But there are some unique differences between these two areas, and Apple tracks access to these areas separately. If you want to develop Macintosh applications, make sure you sign up for a Mac Developer Program account.

When you're online, you will find a treasure trove of information, ranging from software downloads to video tutorials. For example, you can find information about licensing the QuickTime or FireWire logo for use in your Mac OS X product. Or you might find information about debugging Mac OS X's kernel. Some highlights of the ADC web site follow.

Documentation

The ADC web site contains the most recent versions of Mac OS X's developer documentation, and many links into this documentation appear on the ADC home page. You can also find the ADC Reference Library at the following URL: http://developer.apple.com/referencelibrary/. This page, shown in Figure 2-17, should look familiar to you — it's an Internet version of the developer documentation index you saw in Xcode.

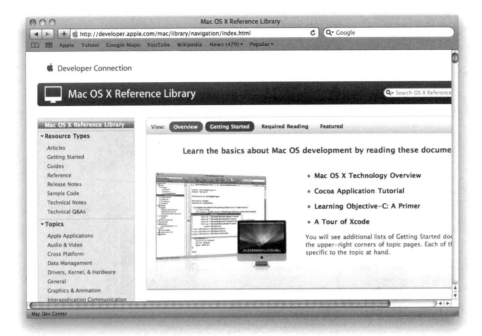

FIGURE 2-17

In fact, the similarities between the ADC web site and the documentation in Xcode are not coincidental. The documentation installed by Xcode is a snapshot of the ADC web site, ensuring that you have complete and reasonably recent information even if you aren't connected to the Internet. And if you are connected, your local files contain links to resources on the ADC web site, creating a seamless bridge between both sets of documentation.

All the documentation in the ADC Reference Library is available without an ADC membership. You should be able to access this information quickly and easily using your favorite web browser.

Examples

The ADC web site also includes developer examples to help you learn more about how Mac OS X's technologies work. They are cross-referenced throughout the ADC web site, so there are many ways to discover these examples. The most direct way is to follow the link from the Apple Developer Connection home page to the Sample Code area at `http://developer.apple.com/samplecode/`. Figure 2-18 shows the content of the Sample Code page. Again, this content mirrors what's available to you locally, although the samples on the ADC web site may be more current than what you'll find on your computer.

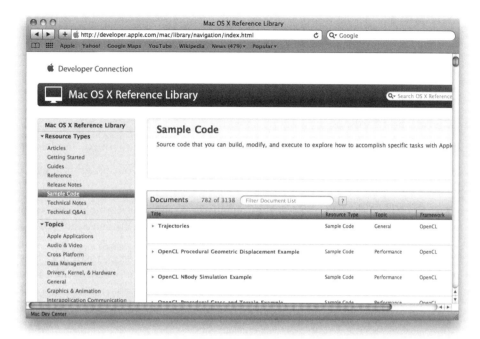

FIGURE 2-18

All the examples in the ADC Source Code library are available at no cost and do not require an ADC membership.

Mailing Lists

Apple maintains a number of mailing lists about specific developer topics. These mailing lists are available at http://lists.apple.com/. Here you can discuss various topics with other interested users and developers. Apple also provides archives of older messages, so you can easily check if a question has already appeared on a mailing list. All of Apple's mailing lists are publicly available. You only need an email address to subscribe to a mailing list. You can browse old mailing list archives using your favorite web browser.

Developer Tools

Apple also provides tool updates on the Apple Developer Connect web site. Unlike the Reference Library and Sample Code areas, the tool downloads are available only to ADC members. However, these tools are available with the free Online Membership plan.

When you log into the ADC account with your membership, you'll see a special members-only section cordoned off from the rest of the ADC site. Here you have access to a Download Software menu where you'll find updates to developer tools such as Xcode and Web Objects, Software Development Kits (SDKs) for other technologies, and other downloads.

Developer Support

Another benefit of having an Apple Developer Connection account is access to a number of developer support services. All these services are available from the ADC home page. These services include the following:

➤ The ability to report bugs against Apple software using Bug Reporter

➤ Discounts on Apple hardware

➤ Use of Apple's compatibility labs by appointment only in Cupertino, Tokyo, and Beijing

➤ Access to Developer Technical Support, which can help you with your programming problems and questions, one support incident at a time

The level of service available to you depends on your membership plan. For example, Bug Reporter and mailing lists are available to all ADC members. All member levels can purchase support incidents for access to Developer Technical Support; paying membership levels get a few starting support incidents with their memberships. Hardware discounts and access to compatibility labs are available for paying memberships only. You can find a complete breakdown of the services available at each membership level at `http://developer.apple.com/products/membership.html`.

SUMMARY

Apple provides a number of developer tools and information to help you write programs on Mac OS X. Much of this information is available in Xcode for quick access. Recent information is available at the Apple Developer Connection web site at `http://developer.apple.com/`.

In this chapter, you learned

➤ How to install the developer tools that came with your copy of Mac OS X

➤ Where to find the tools and documentation you just installed

➤ How to use the Apple Developer Connection web site

In the next chapter, you learn about the Xcode application, which provides the tools you need to develop Mac OS X programs. Before proceeding, however, try the exercises that follow to test your understanding of the material covered in this chapter. You can find the solutions to these exercises in Appendix A.

EXERCISES

1. Use the Time Profiler instrument to watch the Stickies program launch. Let the program sit idle for a few seconds before stopping the sample process. Where did Stickies spend most of its time? If you need some help using the Instruments application, check the documentation under the Help menu.

2. Which man sections contain a page named `intro` on your system? Use a single `man` command to read them all. Feel free to consult `man`'s man page for help at any time.

WHAT YOU LEARNED IN THIS CHAPTER

Xcode	Mac OS X's development environment for writing Mac OS X applications
Interface Builder	a tool for building graphical user interfaces
Instruments	a tool for analyzing program computation and memory performance
Shark	a tool that analyzes the performance of a program or the operating system and suggests specific improvements
Backtrace	a list of stacks in the order they were called, helpful in describing what part of a program is currently running
`diff`	a command-line tool that shows the differences between two text files
`gcc`	the command-line C, C++, and Objective-C compiler used by Xcode
`gdb`	a command-line, source-level debugger used by Xcode

3

Xcode

WHAT YOU WILL LEARN IN THIS CHAPTER:

➤ How to create new projects in Xcode

➤ How to organize files in an Xcode project

➤ How Xcode can help you write and format your code

➤ How to build and run your application, and examine your project in Xcode's built-in debugger

➤ How to access online documentation through Xcode

When programming for Mac OS X, you spend most of your time in Xcode. Xcode is an Integrated Development Environment, or IDE, meaning that Xcode provides all the tools you need to write, build, and debug Mac OS X programs in a single application.

Xcode's text editing tools are specifically designed for writing computer programs. Source code is typically displayed in a small monospaced font so that programmers can tell at a glance if their code is formatted properly. In addition, source code can be color-coded so that specific parts of the program stand out. For example, comments that aren't compiled into your program may appear in a different color from the rest of the code.

Xcode also provides tools for building your source code within easy reach. You can easily change your build settings to adapt to different situations, such as testing or deploying your program. If for some reason your code will not compile, Xcode displays the list of errors encountered in the build process and allows you to fix your mistakes.

After your code has compiled into the final application, you can launch the program directly from Xcode. If the program doesn't work right, or if it crashes, you can diagnose the problem using Xcode's built-in debugger. The debugger allows you to walk through your program line by line and examine the state of your program's variables as it runs.

During the development process, you may find yourself checking and double-checking the developer documentation on your system. Xcode provides a full-featured documentation browser within easy reach, so you don't need to fumble with a web browser or PDF viewer to review the API. A number of shortcuts make looking up specific functions, methods, and data types very easy.

STARTING A NEW PROJECT

Every application starts out as a blank page — basically a lump of clay. You are responsible for shaping that page or figurative lump into the application you see in your mind's eye. This really is a creative process very similar to writing, painting, or sculpting, except that your medium is source code.

Xcode gives you a head start with a new project by supplying you with templates that include some of the basic files, code, and other resources you need to get started. All these resources are bundled together into an Xcode *project*, which provides a way for you to organize all the files for your program in a single place.

TRY IT OUT   **Creating a Default Project**

1.   Launch `/Developer/Applications/Xcode.app`. A welcome screen will appear, as shown in Figure 3-1. Options for getting started with Xcode appear along the left, and eventually a list of recently opened projects will appear along the right.

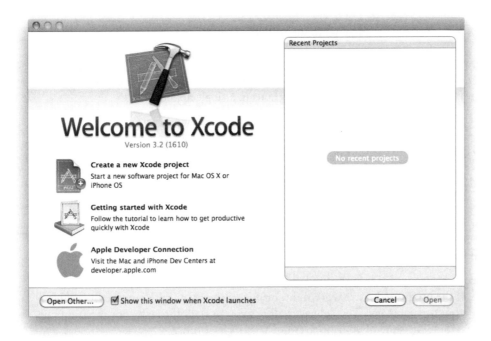

FIGURE 3-1

2. Choose the Create A New Xcode Project option. A New Project window appears, such as the one in Figure 3-2.

FIGURE 3-2

3. Select the Command Line Tool project type from the Application list and click the Choose button. A standard save panel will appear, giving you a chance to name your project and choose the directory it will live in.

4. Name your project Hello, pick a directory in which to save your new project (use your Documents directory if you aren't sure), and click Save. At this point, you see Xcode's project interface, as shown in Figure 3-3. The project window contains a toolbar, a Groups & Files list on the left side, a wider file list in the upper-right corner, and a file editor in the lower-right corner. The file list on the right contains three entries: a Hello application, a Hello.1 file, and a main.c file. The file editor simply says No Editor.

FIGURE 3-3

5. Double-click `main.c`, and the file appears in a new window. Notice that `main.c` already contains the following code. Keep this code for now:

```
#include <stdio.h>

int main (int argc, const char * argv[]) {
    // insert code here...
    printf("Hello, World!\n");
    return 0;
}
```

code snippet MacOSXProg ch03/Hello/main.c

6. Click the Build and Run button in `main.c`'s window. Xcode flashes some status information at the bottom of `main.c`'s window, ending with the message: `Debugging of "Hello" ended normally`.

7. Choose Run ⇨ Console. A new window appears and displays the following message (your results may not match exactly):

```
[Session started at 2009-08-03 23:16:36 -0400.]
GNU gdb 6.3.50-20050815 (Apple version gdb-1339) (Sat May 23 05:39:07 UTC 2009)
Copyright 2004 Free Software Foundation, Inc.
GDB is free software, covered by the GNU General Public License, and you are
```

Available for
download on
Wrox.com

```
welcome to change it and/or distribute copies of it under certain conditions.
Type "show copying" to see the conditions.
There is absolutely no warranty for GDB.  Type "show warranty" for details.
This GDB was configured as "x86_64-apple-darwin".tty /dev/ttys002
Loading program into debugger…
Program loaded.
run
[Switching to process 3480]
Running…
Hello, World!

Debugger stopped.
Program exited with status value:0.
```

How It Works

When you create a new project, Xcode also creates simple source files for you. The content of the source files depends on the kind of project you created, but typically the source files represent a general placeholder so that you can get the ball rolling. Because you are creating a simple command-line tool, Xcode creates a very basic C program shell. Normally you replace the placeholder code with something more original.

NOTE *When describing computer programs written in languages that require compilation, we refer to the text file containing human-readable instructions as source code. Source files typically use special file extensions that identify the language the source code is written in. For example, the* .c *extension designates code written in C, Objective-C programs end in* .m, *and C++ files generally use* .cpp. *Some source files are meant to share common data structures and interfaces among several other files. Those files are called header files, or simply headers. C, Objective-C, and C++ use the* .h *file extension to designate header files.*

After the program was built, you asked Xcode to run the program for you. This particular workflow, first built and then run, is so common that Xcode provides a single command to perform both functions: Build and Run.

Xcode ran the program and displayed the results in the Run Log window. When the program finished, Xcode printed the following:

```
Program exited with status value:0.
```

This means that the program ran to completion without errors. All Mac OS X programs return a numeric error code when they finish: By convention, 0 means the program ran correctly and any other value means something went wrong. Notice that your program explicitly returned its error code just before it ended:

```
return 0;
```

WORKING WITH FILES

As with the Finder, Xcode allows you to specify how your project files are organized. Unlike the Finder, your changes don't necessarily reflect how the files are stored on disk. Just as it does when creating a project, Xcode automates some of the busywork of creating new source files.

TRY IT OUT   Using Xcode's Groups and Files Viewer

1. Create a new Command Line Tool project and name it `Hello2`.

2. Close the Hello2 project group; then Option-click the disclosure triangle to open it again. The project group and all its subgroups will expand, as shown in Figure 3-4. Notice that the Products file `Hello2` is drawn in red; that's because the `Hello2` program doesn't exist yet.

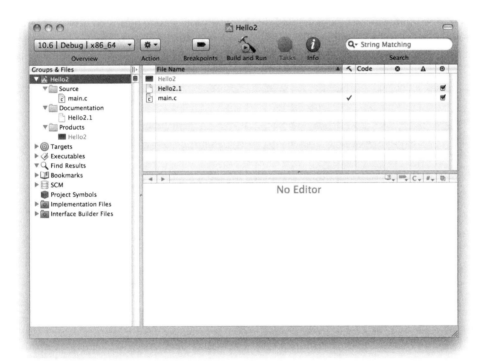

FIGURE 3-4

3. Click each of the groups below the Hello2 project group: Source, Documentation, and Products. Notice the contents of the file list changes to match the contents of your selection. When the Hello2 project group is selected, all the files in `Hello2` appear in the list; when Source is selected, only `main.c` appears in the list.

4. If necessary, click once on Source to select it, and then click it again after a short pause. Make sure you click to the right of the disclosure triangle. You can now rename the Source group to My Source Files.

5. Select and then click main.c and rename your source file to Hello2.c.

6. Click Hello2.1 and drag it into your My Source Files group.

7. Select the Documentation group and press the Delete key. The group is removed from your project.

8. Select Hello2.1 again and choose Project ➪ Group. A new group appears containing the Hello2.1 file, and the group is ready to be renamed. Name this new group Man Pages.

9. Drag the new Man Pages group to the same level as the My Source Files and Products groups. If you have trouble, drag down and to the left toward the Products group's disclosure triangle; make sure the circle at the end of the drag indicator is to the left of the Products group folder icon. Figure 3-5 shows what your project should look like now.

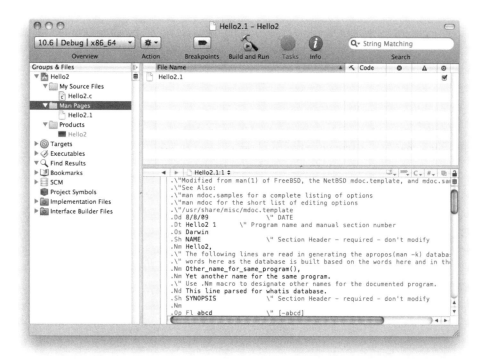

FIGURE 3-5

10. Select your My Source Files group and choose File ➪ New File. A New File assistant appears, resembling Figure 3-6, and allows you to select the kind of file you want to create.

FIGURE 3-6

11. Choose C and C++ from the Mac OS X list, select C File, and click the Next button. The assistant changes, giving you a chance to name your file, as shown in Figure 3-7.

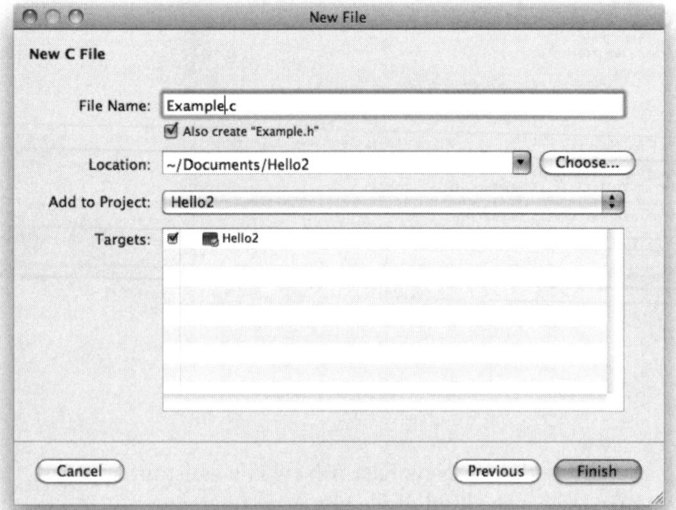

FIGURE 3-7

12. Name the file `Example.c`.

13. Make sure the Also Create "Example.h" checkbox is checked, as shown in Figure 3-7. Ignore the others settings for now.

14. Click Finish. Two files, `Example.c` and `Example.h`, will appear in the My Source Files group, and `Example.h` is visible in the project's file editor. Your project should now resemble Figure 3-8.

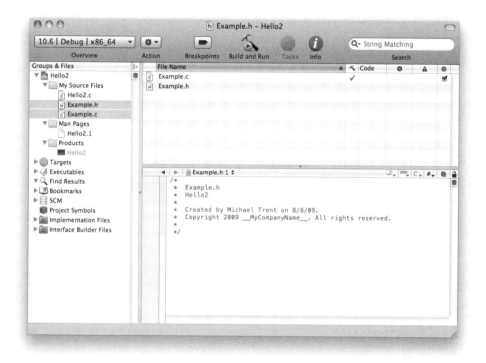

FIGURE 3-8

15. Select the group named Implementation Files. The list of files changes to include only your `.c` files.

16. Select the group named Project Symbols. The file list changes to a list of symbols, including the symbol name, the kind of symbol it is, and the file where the symbol can be found, as shown in Figure 3-9.

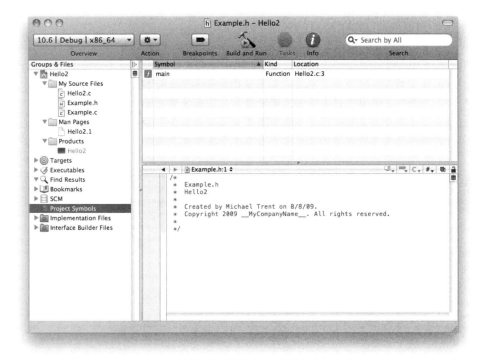

FIGURE 3-9

17. Select the entry for the main symbol. Hello2.c appears in the file editor with the first line of the main function selected. Double-click the entry for the main symbol, and Hello2.c will appear in a new window.

How It Works

The Groups & Files list uses the Option key to open all the subgroups within a parent group. There often are many ways to perform a given task in Xcode, such as selecting a command in the main menu bar or in a contextual menu, or clicking, command-clicking, or Option-clicking text. Your toolbar might also include an Action pop-up menu that provides quick access to some of the commands you'll find in the contextual menu.

When you rename files, Xcode actually changes the name of the file on disk. In this example, the file main.c changed to Hello2.c when the file was renamed. This is often very helpful, because Xcode tends to lose track of source files if you rename them in the Finder or in Terminal. If Xcode cannot find a file, it will draw its name in red.

Xcode uses groups to organize your code. Although groups resemble folders similar to what you might see in the Finder, they don't necessarily map to real folders. Groups are just containers in which you can organize your files. You can create them, rename them, remove them, and copy files in and out of them, however you like, without affecting how your source files are stored on disk.

Your project has some built-in groups for organizing information you might want within easy reach. For example, you can pull up a list of recent find results in the Find Results group, get a quick list of all your build problems in the Errors and Warnings group, or see all the symbols defined within your project from the Project Symbols group.

 NOTE *The term "symbol" refers to the names of elements within a source file or program, including function names, variable names, class names, data type names, structure definitions, and so on. For example, all C programs define a function symbol named "main" representing the start of the program.*

Xcode also provides something called *smart groups*. Smart groups filter your source file based on a set of rules. For example, the Implementation Files group is a smart group that displays all files that end with .c or .m file extensions. Smart group rules are specified using *regular expressions*, which is a small but sophisticated language for recognizing patterns within strings. You can select a smart group and choose File ➪ Get Info to see what patterns the group is filtering on.

When you created a new source file, Xcode helped out by automatically supplying a new header file with the same name. Xcode also added a little bit of code to get you started. These templates vary by the kind of file you are creating, so it's a good idea to start with a file template that most closely resembles what you need.

WRITING YOUR CODE

Most of your time in Xcode will be spent reading and writing the source files that make up your program. Xcode's source code editor has a number of features to make this time as productive as possible. Some of these features are passive, such as drawing different parts of your source code in different colors or styles. This helps you quickly recognize elements of your program at a glance. Other features are active, such as providing commands for quickly formatting large areas of code.

In the following example, you write a small C program called Calculator that lets you add and subtract numbers. The program consists of two functions: the main function, which interacts with the user via Mac OS X's command-line interface, and a calculate function that does some arithmetic. The calculate function takes two numbers and an operator and returns the result of applying the operator to the numbers. If you aren't familiar with the C programming language, don't worry too much about what the code is doing; this is really just a chance to get used to Xcode's text editor. Alternatively, you can skip ahead to Chapter 6, where you learn about writing programs in C.

TRY IT OUT   **Working in the Code Editor**

1.   Choose Xcode ➪ Preferences. Xcode's Preferences window appears.

2.   If necessary, select the General preference pane.

3.   If necessary, check the Open Counterparts In Same Editor button.

4.   Select the Text Editing preference pane.

5.   Check the Show Line Numbers button. The Show Gutter button should already be checked; if not, you should check Show Gutter as well.

6.   Select the Indentation preference pane and uncheck Syntax-Aware Indenting.

7.   Click OK. Xcode's Preferences window closes.

8.   Create a new Command Line Tool project and name it Calculator.

9.   Select the Source group and create a new C file named Calculate.c in your project. Make sure you create the accompanying header file Calculate.h. Both files will be added to your Source group, and Calculate.h will appear in your project window's file editor, as shown in Figure 3-10. Notice the file editor has a small button bar just above the text editing area. In particular, this small button bar contains grayed-out left and right arrows, a pop-up menu with Calculate.h already selected, and a few other tools.

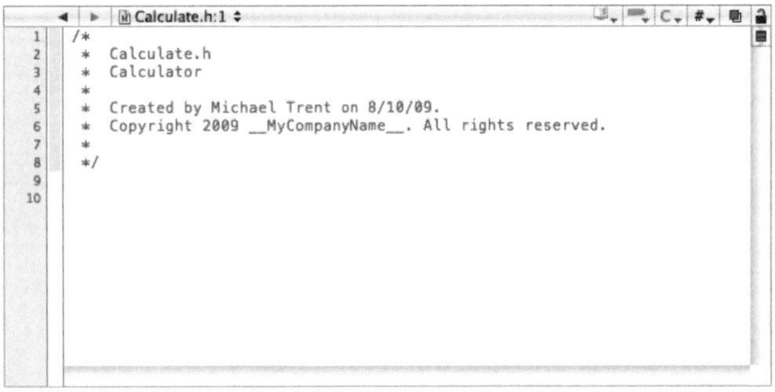

FIGURE 3-10

10. Add the following line of code to `Calculate.h`:

```
int calculate(int a, int b, char operator);
```

code snippet MacOSXProg ch03/Calculator/Calculate.h

11. Choose View ⇨ Switch to Header/Source File. The source editor window switches to display the contents of `Calculate.c`. Notice that the left arrow is no longer grayed out and the pop-up menu now says `Calculate.c`.

12. Click the left arrow. This moves you back to the last file you were working with: `Calculate.h`. The back button disables itself while the right forward button is enabled.

13. Save your changes to `Calculate.h` now.

14. Click the pop-up menu to view its contents. You will see entries for `Calculate.h` and `Calculate.c` as well as items that clear the file history and control its size.

15. Select `Calculate.c` from the file history pop-up menu. Once again, the contents of the source editor change to reflect `Calculate.c`.

16. Add the following code to the end of the file, typed exactly as shown here. As you enter the code, notice that Xcode draws different parts of your program in different colors. The added color is called *syntax coloring* and helps you spot keywords, strings, and so on in your code.

Available for download on Wrox.com

```
#include <stdio.h>
#include <stdlib.h>

int calculate(int a, int b, char operator)
{
int result

switch (operator) {
case '+':
result = a + b;
break;
case '-'
result = a - b;
break;
default:
printf("unknown operator: %c\n", operator)
exit(1);
}

return result;
}
```

code snippet MacOSXProg ch03/Calculator/Calculate.c

17. Select all the text within the `calculate` function. That corresponds to lines 17–31 in Figure 3-11.

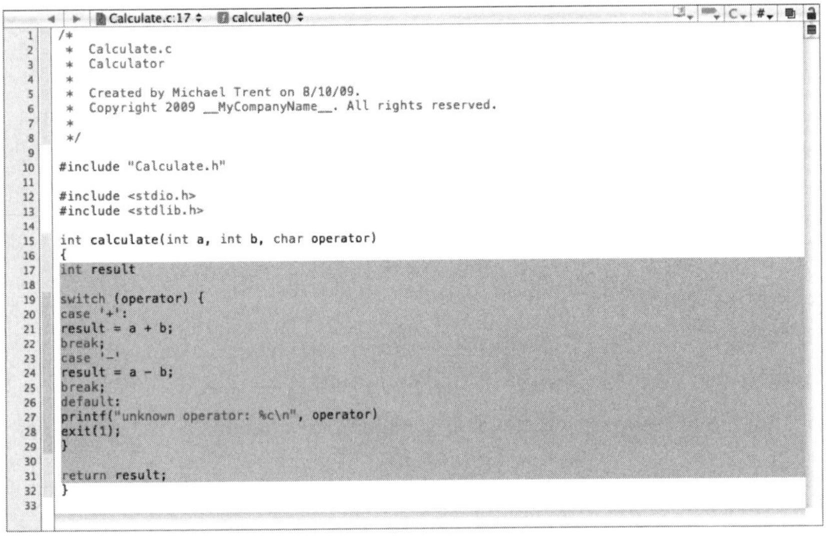

FIGURE 3-11

18. Choose Edit ➪ Format ➪ Shift Right. The selection indents four spaces to the right.

19. Select the three lines of code that comprise the first `case` statement. That corresponds to lines 20–22 in Figure 3-11.

20. Press Command-] to invoke the Shift Right command. The selection indents four more spaces to the right.

21. Change the selection to the last two lines in that same `case` statement, lines 21 and 22 in Figure 3-11, and indent the text four more spaces to the right.

22. Repeat steps 19–21 until the `switch` statement is indented as shown here:

```
switch (operator) {
    case '+':
        result = a + b;
        break;
    case '-'
        result = a - b;
        break;
    default:
        printf("unknown operator: %c\n", operator)
        exit(1);
}
```

23. Make sure your text insertion point is in the `calculate` function; if not, click line 19 to set the selection. By now you may have noticed there is a second pop-up menu in the small button bar, next to the file history pop-up menu. The menu currently says `calculate()`.

24. Move the text insertion point cursor to the very top of the file. Use the mouse if you like, or press Command-up arrow on your keyboard. The second pop-up menu changes to <No selected symbol>.

25. Click this second pop-up to reveal its menu. You will see a small menu with a single item: `calculate()`. This menu is showing you all the symbols in your file.

26. Select the `calculate()` item. The selection changes to highlight the `calculate` function's name and arguments.

27. Save your changes to `Calculate.c`.

28. Select `main.c` from your project's file list on the right side of the project window. If you have trouble finding `main.c`, look in your project's Source group in the Groups & Files list.

29. Replace the contents of `main.c` with the following code. Use your Tab key to indent text as you type. Similar to the Shift Right command, the Tab key will insert four spaces into your file; unlike the Shift Right command, the spaces are added at the insertion point, not at the beginning of the line. If you get into trouble, you can fix your indenting with the Shift Left and Shift Right menu commands.

```c
#include <stdio.h>
#include <stdlib.h>

#include "Calculate.h"

int main (int argc, const char * argv[])
{
    int a, b, count, answer;
    char op;

    // print the prompt
    printf("Enter an expression: ");

    // get the expression
    count = scanf("%d %c %d", &a, &op, &b);
    if (count != 3) {
        printf("bad expression\n");
        return 1
    }

    // perform the computation
    answer = calculate(a, b, op);

    // print the answer
    printf("%d %c %d = %d\n", a, op, b, answer);

    return 0;
}
```

code snippet MacOSXProg ch03/Calculator/main.c

30. Save your changes to `main.c`.

31. Command–double-click the word `calculate` in your `main` function. The `Calculate.c` file appears in the same file editor, with the `calculate` function name selected.

How It Works

You started by turning on line numbers in Xcode's *gutter*. The gutter is the region just to the left of the source editor's text area. The line numbers are a handy way to keep track of precisely where you are in a source file. You also configured Xcode to use the same source editor for viewing your source and header files. This is a handy feature for easily switching between a header and its implementation, or when using Command–double-click to jump to code in another file.

Xcode retains a history of files you have viewed in a given source editor. You can easily flip through these files using the source editor's small button bar, called a *navigation bar*. The navigation bar includes forward and back buttons as you might find in a web browser. It also includes a history pop-up from which you can select any of the files in your file history, regardless of how far forward or back they are. The history pop-up uses darkened file icons to remind you about unsaved files.

The navigation bar also includes a pop-up button of symbols defined in your source files. In this example, each of your files contained only one symbol, a function; normally source files contain many symbols. The symbol pop-up menu is a helpful way to search for a specific symbol. You can jump directly to the place where a symbol is defined by Command–double-clicking the symbol name as it appears in your source file. This is helpful if you can't remember exactly where a symbol is defined, saving you the step of searching for it.

As you noticed earlier, Xcode drew different parts of your program in different colors. This helps you distinguish between various parts of your program at a glance. For example, comments might be drawn in green, reserved language keywords might be drawn in purple, strings might be drawn in red, and so on. You probably also noticed Xcode drew your text in a monospaced font. Because all characters have the same width — even spaces — it's easy to align your text vertically.

If, for whatever reason, you do not like the default colors or font settings, you can easily change them in Xcode's Fonts & Colors preferences panel. For each part of your program (strings, comments, and so on), you can specify the specific color, font, size, and style (such as bold or italic) to use. For example, you could display your source code in a nice fixed-width font, but display your comments in a hot pink symbol font if you thought that might help.

Although C, Objective-C, and C++ languages do not require you to indent your code, code written in these languages is indented by default. Although specific styles of indenting exist, there can be a wide variation between individual programmers. You will probably end up using Shift Left and Shift Right a lot.

You might be wondering why you turned off Syntax-Aware Indenting, and if that can help you indent the code in your source files. If so, you're right! Let's take a second look at indenting.

A Second Look at Indenting

In the previous example, you learned two different ways of indenting your code: using the Tab key to insert four spaces at the text insertion point, and using the Shift Left and Shift Right menu commands to quickly remove or insert four spaces at the beginning of a line. Xcode provides a third way of indenting your code: indenting automatically.

TRY IT OUT Indenting Automatically

1. In Xcode, open your Calculator project from the previous Try It Out.

2. Open the `Calculate.c` file in a source editor.

3. Select all the text and press Command-[(Shift Left) repeatedly until all the code is mashed against the left side of the window.

4. Without changing the selection, choose Edit ➪ Format ➪ Re-Indent. Xcode indents all your code for you.

5. Save your changes to `Calculate.c` and close the window.

6. Open Xcode's Preferences panel.

7. Select the Indentation toolbar item.

8. Turn on Syntax-Aware Indenting and leave the other settings alone. Your settings should match those in Figure 3-12.

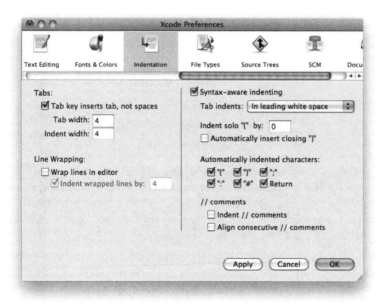

FIGURE 3-12

9. Click OK to save your preference changes.

10. Open `main.c` and delete all the text in the file.

11. Re-enter the code from the previous example. The code is reprinted here for your convenience. This time, do not do any formatting yourself; do not press the Tab key or add extra spaces, and do not use the Shift Left or Shift Right menu commands.

```c
#include <stdio.h>
#include <stdlib.h>
#include "Calculate.h"
int main (int argc, const char * argv[])
{
    int a, b, count, answer;
    char op;
    // print the prompt
    printf("Enter an expression: ");

    // get the expression
    count = scanf("%d %c %d", &a, &op, &b);
    if (count != 3) {
        printf("bad expression\n");
        return 1
    }

    // perform the computation
    answer = calculate(a, b, op);

    // print the answer
    printf("%d %c %d = %d\n", a, op, b, answer);

    return 0;
}
```

code snippet MacOSXProg ch03/Calculator/main.c

12. Save your changes to `main.c`.

How It Works

Xcode's Re-Indent command looks at the selection and neighboring code and tries its best to indent the selection appropriately. You can find the Re-Indent command in the source editor's contextual menu as well as on the Format menu. Unfortunately, the menu item doesn't have a macro assigned by default. If you find yourself using Re-Indent often, you might consider adding your own macro. You can use Xcode's Key Bindings preferences panel to customize Xcode's menu macros.

By turning on Syntax-Aware Indenting, Xcode automatically formats your code as you type. You don't need to use the Tab key or the Shift Left and Shift Right menu commands to line up your code. Both auto-indenting and the Re-Indent command use the same formatting algorithms, so the features play well together. Because you won't need to stop and format your code manually, auto-indenting can save you a lot of time.

However, neither indenting method is perfect. Under some rare circumstances, the Re-Indent command might misinterpret how you want your code to be formatted. Or maybe you don't agree with the style in which Xcode indents your text. Perhaps you just find auto-indenting distracting. If any of these are true, you can simply fall back to the Tab key and Shift Left and Shift Right menu items to manually format your code.

BUILDING AND RUNNING

After you have written a reasonable amount of code, the urge to build your project may strike. Building your project is the first step toward validating that you have entered your code correctly. Of course, compiling does not guarantee your program actually works! Remember: computers only understand what you said, not what you meant. After you build your project, however, you can run your program and make sure it does what you want.

In the next Try It Out example, you actually build the `Calculator` project you saw earlier. Along the way, you correct a few build errors introduced during the editing process. Finally, you verify that `Calculator` works correctly by running the program and testing its results.

TRY IT OUT   **Building Your Calculator Project**

1. In Xcode, open the `Calculator` project you created and saved earlier.

2. Click the Build and Run button. If you entered the code exactly as it was provided earlier, the project will fail to compile. The project window's status area notes that the build failed, and you may see some error messages in your file editor.

3. Choose Build ➪ Build Results. A window resembling Figure 3-13 appears and lists the build errors along with a toolbar, a file editor, and a few other controls. This window is called the Build Results window.

4. Select the first error in the list. The `main.c` source file will appear in the file editor. A line of code is selected near where the error occurred, also shown in Figure 3-13. Line 18 is missing a semicolon.

5. Add a semicolon to line 18:

```
return 1;
```

6. Save `main.c`.

FIGURE 3-13

7. Try rebuilding `Calculator`. The build will fail again, and the Build Results window will update to show errors in `Calculate.c`.

8. Select the first error for `Calculate.c`. Again, the contents of `Calculate.c` appear in the file editor. This time, line 17 is missing a semicolon.

9. Add a semicolon to line 17:

```
int result;
```

10. Select the fourth error in the list. Line 24 becomes selected. The `case` statement on line 23 should end with a colon.

11. Add a colon at the end of line 23:

```
        case '-':
```

12. Select the last error in the list. Notice that line 27 is also missing a semicolon.

13. Add a semicolon to line 27:

```
            printf("unknown operator: %c\n", operator);
```

14. Save `Calculate.c`.

15. Rebuild `Calculator` again using the Build button on the Build Results window. This time, the compile should succeed. If it doesn't, go back and review your changes.

16. Choose Run ⇨ Run. The Build Results and project windows' status bar will say `GDB: Running`. So far, so good.

17. Choose Run ⇨ Console. The Debugger Console window will appear, as shown in Figure 3-14. The console is asking you to enter an expression.

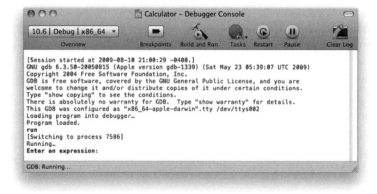

FIGURE 3-14

18. Enter **44 + 7**, and press Return. The Run Log displays the results of your program. It looks as though it's working correctly.

```
Enter an expression: 44 + 7
44 + 7 = 51

Debugger stopped.
Program exited with status value:0.
```

19. Run `Calculator` again by clicking the Build and Run button on the Debugger Console window.

20. Enter **44 - 7** and press Return. The Run Log will display the following results. Again, so far so good.

```
Enter an expression: 44 - 7
44 - 7 = 37

Debugger stopped.
Program exited with status value:0.
```

21. Run `Calculator` again, and enter **6 * 9**. This time `Calculator` prints an error message and quits early. Although it's unfortunate that `Calculator` doesn't know how to multiply, that doesn't qualify as a bug in your program. You simply haven't taught it how to multiply yet.

```
Enter an expression: 6 * 9
unknown operator: *
Debugger stopped.
Program exited with status value:0.
```

22. Run `Calculator` again, and enter **two plus two**. `Calculator` prints a new error message and quits. Again, this is the expected result.

```
Enter an expression: two plus two
bad expression
Debugger stopped.
Program exited with status value:1.
```

23. Close the Debugger Console window.

24. Return to the Build Results window and choose Build ⇨ Clean. Click the Clean All button. A warning appears, as shown in Figure 3-15, advising that you are about to delete your compiled program.

25. Click the Clean button. Xcode does a little work, and your Build Results window notes that the command succeeded.

26. In the Build Results window's Overview pop-up menu, change the Active Configuration from Debug to Release.

27. Click the Build button. The build should again succeed.

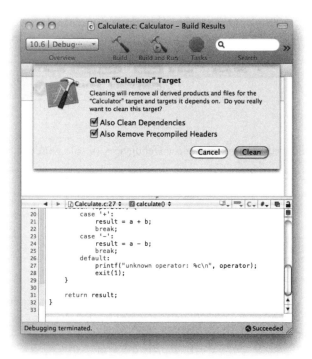

FIGURE 3-15

How It Works

When you ask Xcode to build your project, Xcode actually does a number of smaller tasks for you and presents the results all at once. The first thing Xcode does is convert all your source code to machine-friendly instructions using a tool called a *compiler*. The compiler's main job is to take your instructions written in a programming language such as C or Objective-C and convert them to instructions under-standable by your computer's CPU. These instructions are called *object code*. Object code is typically stored in special files, called *object files*; these files are transitional in nature and their existence is handled entirely by Xcode.

The second thing Xcode does while building your project is combine all your object files to form an executable binary file. This process is called *linking*, and it is performed using a special tool called, you guessed it, a *linker*. A linked file is self-contained and can easily be copied and used on other computers, assuming those computers are running the same operating system and are in the same processor family.

Either of these processes may encounter problems such as syntax errors, missing files, and the like. Xcode reports these errors in the Errors and Warnings group and in the Build Results window. You must address these errors before you can link and run your program. The `Calculator` code contained a few minor syntax errors to help you practice fixing these problems.

Notice that Xcode actually reported more problems in your program than you fixed. A single error in a source file may actually result in several problems within the C compiler. So the fact that adding a semicolon to one line of code in `main.c` fixed all the compile errors there is not all that surprising. This is true of Objective-C and C++ as well.

When working on fairly small projects, you might think that Xcode will simply build all the files in your project. In reality, Xcode builds all the files in the current *target*. A target collects all the files, resources, and settings required to build a specific program. An Xcode project can contain several targets. For example, a project that builds an application, a framework, and a plug-in would be composed of three different targets. Although the target abstraction is a powerful feature for people working on larger or more complicated projects, this book focuses on examples with only one target.

Xcode's Build Styles allows you to generate your object code differently depending on what you intend to do with your program. A specific build style contains options for the compiler, linker, and other build tools that control the way your project builds. For example, the Debug build style tells the compiler to generate debugging symbols along with your code, and might tell the linker not to fully link your program. The Release build style doesn't generate debugging symbols, but it does enable optimizations and instructs the linker to fully link your program so you can give it to other people.

Xcode also has a command for cleaning your build results: Clean. The Clean command removes the build results associated with the current target. Build results include temporary files such as your project's object files and some other information cached by Xcode; it also includes your compiled program. You typically use this command to make sure your next project build starts from a clean state and won't get any leftover state from a previous build. You might also clean your project before giving the source code to someone else because build results can add several megabytes to your source directory.

FINDING PROBLEMS WITH THE STATIC ANALYZER

In the last section, you saw how the compiler reports problems found while building your project. Xcode presented those errors and warnings inline in your source file, and also in the Build Results window. But you didn't really know if your program worked properly until you ran it and put it through its paces. Wouldn't it be nice if Xcode could find logic errors in your program for you, and report them as build errors?

Xcode can find logic problems in your program and report them to you before you run your program, using a new Snow Leopard feature called the Static Analyzer. The Static Analyzer traces through your program, watches how you use each variable, and looks for problems. It can find problems that are sometimes tricky to find through traditional testing and debugging, although it unfortunately doesn't replace those activities.

In the next Try It Out, you will run the Static Analyzer on your `Calculator` example. First though, you'll need to give the Static Analyzer something to find. If you aren't comfortable enough with programming to follow along with this section, feel free to skip ahead to Chapter 6 to learn about the C programming language. Then come back and give the Static Analyzer a second try, it will be here waiting for you.

TRY IT OUT   Using the Static Analyzer

1.   In Xcode, open the `Calculator` project you created and saved earlier.

2.   Build your project and verify that Xcode finds no build errors or warnings. If you do see problems, look over the previous example carefully.

3.   Choose Build ➪ Build & Analyze. Again, Xcode should find no errors or warnings.

4.   Open `main.c` and change lines 21–25 to match the following code:

```
// perform the computation
answer = calculate(a, b, op);
int aa;

// print the answer
printf("%d %c %d = %d\n", a, op, b, aa);
```

5.   Save `main.c`.

6.   Build the project again using Build ➪ Build. Observe that the program still compiles error-free.

7.   Choose Build ➪ Build & Analyze again and open the Build Results window. This time, Xcode found some problems, shown in Figure 3-16.

FIGURE 3-16

8. In the Build Results window, select the first error in the list: `Value stored to 'answer' is never read`. Xcode will scroll to that warning in your `main.c` source file. Xcode is telling you that you never actually use the result of the `calculate` function, even though you went to the trouble of storing that result in `answer`.

9. Select the second error in the list: `Pass-by-value argument in function call is undefined`. This warning may not make sense to you at first glance.

10. Click the triangle next to this error, or press the right arrow on your keyboard. Xcode shows you two new details about this error.

11. Select the first detail: `1. Variable 'aa' declared without an initial value`. The Build Results window selects the code where `aa` is declared and then draws a number of blue arrows, shown in Figure 3-17. These arrows show the path through your code that the Static Analyzer took when it found this problem.

FIGURE 3-17

12. Select the second detail: `2. Pass-by-value argument in function call is undefined`. An arrow appears between where the variable `aa` was defined without an initial value and where you read the value of `aa`. Now the problem is clear. The solution is to remove the bad `aa` variable and print the value of `answer` before the function ends.

13. Return your code back to the way it was at the beginning of this example, as shown here:

```
// perform the computation
answer = calculate(a, b, op);

// print the answer
printf("%d %c %d = %d\n", a, op, b, answer);
```

14. Save your changes to `main.c`.

How It Works

The Build & Analyze command found some problems that the simple Build command missed. When you build, Xcode will only show you errors from the compiler and the linker that interfere with the process of putting your program together. In this case, the problem in `Calculator` was syntactically correct. Because Build & Analyze first builds your project, you might want to get into the habit of using Build & Analyze instead of Build.

When the Static Analyzer examines your program, it starts by looking at every possible path through code. `Calculator`'s `main` function has two code paths: one where you enter the `if` statement and return early, and one where you don't enter the `if` statement and you return at the end. The Static Analyzer checked both paths looking for problems with how you used your variables.

Two classes of problems the Static Analyzer is concerned with are situations when you read from a variable before it is initialized, or when you write to a variable without reading it later. In the first case, your program will get back some random result, often causing problems with unpredictable symptoms. In the second case, only writing to a variable more often than not is a problem — maybe you are ignoring an error result that you really should check, or maybe you simply forgot to use the information you asked for.

Xcode's Static Analyzer currently works with the C and Objective-C programming languages. At the time of this writing, the Static Analyzer did not support C++ or non-C based languages.

USING THE DEBUGGER

Sometimes your program won't work properly, and even after you spend hours staring at your source code, it isn't obvious what has gone wrong. For times such as these, Xcode has a built-in debugger. The debugger allows you to step through your code as the program is running and watch the state of your variables change.

TRY IT OUT Debugging Changes to Calculator

1. In Xcode, open your `Calculator` project that you saved earlier.

2. Make sure the Project file's Overview pop-up says the Active Configuration is Debug. Change it if necessary.

3. If you changed your project's Active Configuration, clean your build results using the Build ⇨ Clean menu item.

4. Open `Calculate.c`.

5. Make a copy of the second `case` statement at lines 23–25, and paste them back at line 26. The calculate function should look similar to the following code:

Available for
download on
Wrox.com

```c
int calculate(int a, int b, char operator)
{
    int result;

    switch (operator) {
        case '+':
            result = a + b;
            break;
        case '-':
            result = a - b;
            break;
        case '-':
            result = a - b;
            break;
        default:
            printf("unknown operator: %c\n", operator);
            exit(1);
    }

    return result;
}
```

code snippet MacOSXProg ch03/Calculator3/Calculate.c

6. Change `case '-':` at line 26 to **`case '*':`**.

7. Save `Calculate.c`.

8. Build and run your project.

9. Open the Debugger Console with the Run ⇨ Console menu item and enter **4 ★ 5**. `Calculator` prints the following result. Obviously, something is wrong.

```
Enter an expression: 4 * 5
4 * 5 = -1
Debugger stopped.
Program exited with status value:0.
```

10. Open `main.c` in your project window's file editor.

11. Click in the gutter on the left side of the window at line 6, where the `main` function is defined. A blue marker appears there, as shown in Figure 3-18. Notice also the Build and Run toolbar item has changed to Build and Debug.

FIGURE 3-18

12. Choose Build ⇨ Build and Debug – Breakpoints On or press the Build and Debug item in the project window toolbar. Your program starts and then stops at the first line of code in your `main` function, as shown in Figure 3-19. The current line of code is highlighted in blue and marked with a red arrow. Notice also that a new toolbar has appeared above the file editor's navigation bar. These are mini debugger controls.

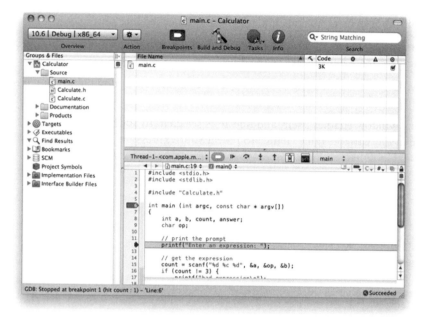

FIGURE 3-19

13. Choose Run ➪ Debugger. The Debugger window appears as shown in Figure 3-20. The Debugger window has a toolbar with a number of debugger commands, a list showing your program's stack, a second list showing the current stack's variables, and a file editor.

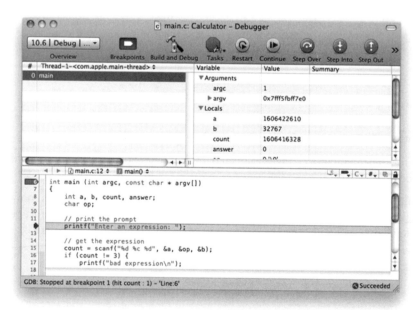

FIGURE 3-20

14. Click the debugger toolbar's Step Over button. The selection advances to line 15.

15. Click the Step Over button again. The selection disappears, and the debugger's toolbar changes so that only the Pause and Terminate buttons are enabled.

16. Return to the Debugger Console menu, using Run ➪ Console if necessary. You will find your program is running, waiting for you to enter an expression.

17. Enter **4 * 5**. The Debug window enables itself, and line 16 is selected. In addition, the entries for a, b, count, and op in the Variable table change to reflect your expression. Figure 3-21 shows what the debugger should look like.

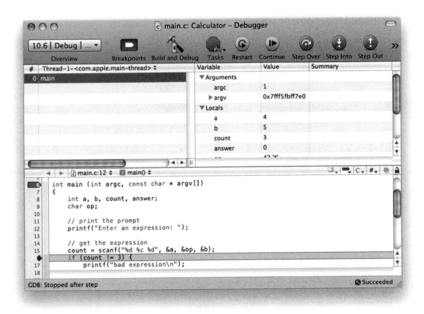

FIGURE 3-21

18. Click the Step Over button. The selection advances to line 22.

19. Click the Step Into button. The debugger changes to display the contents of the Calculate.c file, where line 19 is selected. The calculate symbol appears in the stack list, just above main.

20. Click the Step Over button. The selection advances to line 27, as shown in Figure 3-22. And now the problem becomes clear. You changed the calculate function to include a new * operator, but you didn't change the logic that computes the answer to multiply your numbers. It looks like b, which is currently 5, will be subtracted from a, which is currently 4, to yield –1.

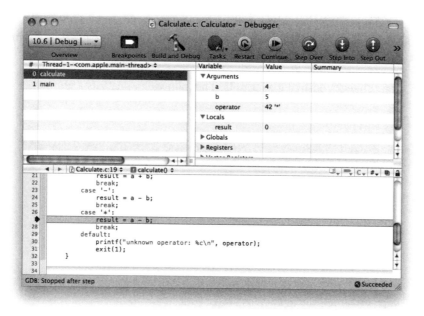

FIGURE 3-22

21. Click the Step Over button. Sure enough, the Variable table shows `result` changing to –1.

22. Click the Tasks button, which currently looks like a stop sign, to quit the program.

23. Without leaving the debugger, correct `Calculate.c` by changing the operator at line 27 from – to *.

24. Save your changes to `Calculate.c`.

25. Choose Build ⇨ Build and Run – Breakpoints Off. Xcode compiles your project. Assuming that you didn't make any mistakes, your program will continue without stopping at the breakpoint in `main`.

26. Enter **4 * 5** in the Debugger Console window. `Calculator` prints the following result. It looks like you've fixed the problem.

```
Enter an expression: 4 * 5
4 * 5 = 20
Debugger stopped.
Program exited with status value:0.
```

How It Works

You started by changing your build style to Debug and cleaning any previous build results. Before you try to debug a program, make sure you are working with a Debug build. Otherwise, the debugger will not work properly, and you'll see strange results.

Xcode's debugger has the power to pause your program, control when the program's instructions are fed to the processor, and examine or change the contents of the program's memory. A paused program is actually in a state of suspended animation: a process exists, but machine instructions are not being processed. The debugger can also execute your program a few instructions at a time. This allows you to watch how your program's state changes bit-by-bit as it runs. The following table lists a number of common debugging commands.

COMMAND	DESCRIPTION
Restart	Terminates the current debug session and starts a new one from the beginning. This is useful if you find you've missed the point where a bug occurred.
Pause	Suspends your program, allowing you to see which lines of code are currently being executed as well as your program's variables.
Continue	Resumes execution of a suspended program.
Step Over	Advances the program to the next line of code. If the current line of code is a function call, Step Over simply allows it to run normally as if it were a single instruction. In other words, this command steps over the function.
Step Into	Advances the program to the next line of code. If the current line of code is a function call, Step Into descends into the function call. In other words, this command steps into the function.
Step Out	Advances the program until the current function ends.
Step Into Instruction	Similar to Step Into except that this command runs your program one machine instruction at a time. Note that a single line of source code may be expanded into several machine instructions.

The marker that appeared when you clicked on the source editor's gutter is called a *breakpoint*. Breakpoints instruct the debugger to pause (break*)* your program when you reach that spot (point*)* in the file. If you don't set a breakpoint, the debugger simply runs your program until you click the Pause button, your program completes normally, or your program crashes.

You may have noticed that although you set a breakpoint on line 6, the debugger actually stopped on line 12. Xcode allows you to set breakpoints on arbitrary lines in your source file, even places where there isn't any code. In those cases, Xcode's debugger stops at the first opportunity after the breakpoint.

The debugger displays the state of your program's variables in the Variable table. Each variable is displayed along with its value. If a variable changes as you step through your code, Xcode draws the variable in red. The Variable table isn't for display only; you can actually change a variable's value simply by double-clicking the Value cell and entering a new value.

The debugger also displays your current stack history in the list in the Debugger window's upper-left corner. In other words, this list shows your program's *stack*. Each entry in the stack represents a function call or *stack frame*. The topmost entry represents the function your program is currently "in"; that function was called by the second entry in the list, which was called by the third entry, and so on. You can click a stack frame to see your program's state at that function. The stack is extremely useful for figuring out how your program ended up in the current function.

There often isn't enough room in the debugger to display your program's output, so Xcode provides a separate window, called the Debugger Console window, for that purpose. The Debugger Console can also read input from the keyboard.

Xcode's Debugger window includes a source editor, so you can easily keep track of where you are in your program. This source editor works the same as the other source editors you have seen: you can edit code, you can use source editor's history to switch between files, and so on. This is really useful when you find a simple bug in your program: just correct the code in the debugger, rebuild, and try again.

ONLINE DOCUMENTATION

As you may remember from Chapter 2, Xcode provides a ton of documentation within easy reach. This includes API documentation for various system frameworks, conceptual documentation that illustrates how various services should be used, and Darwin's man page system. In the following Try It Out example, you learn how to use the documentation tools in Xcode to access the online Cocoa documentation. The techniques illustrated here apply to other online documentation, such as Carbon, QuickTime, and so on.

TRY IT OUT   Searching the Online Documentation

1.   Create a new Command Line Tool project, but this time change the project type from C to Foundation. You'll find the type in a pop-up menu that appears after you select the Command Line Tool option but before you click Choose, shown in Figure 3-23.

FIGURE 3-23

2. Name your project **Greetings**.

3. Open `Greetings.m` in your project window's file editor, and replace its contents with the following code:

```
#import <Foundation/Foundation.h>

int main (int argc, const char *argv[])
{
    NSAutoreleasePool *pool = [[NSAutoreleasePool alloc] init];

    NSString *user = NSFullUserName;
    NSString *time = nil; // get the current time ...

    printf("Hello %s,\n", [user UTF8String]);
    printf("It is now %s.\n", [time UTF8String]);

    [pool drain];
    return 0;
}
```

Available for download on Wrox.com

code snippet MacOSXProg ch03/Greetings/Greetings.m

Notice you haven't actually initialized the `time` variable to something useful. You need to find some kind of function or method call that returns the current time.

4. Choose Help ➪ Developer Documentation. A window titled Xcode Quick Start appears, as shown in Figure 3-24. The window resembles a simple web browser, with Forward, Back, Home, and Bookmark buttons and a Search field.

FIGURE 3-24

5. Choose Mac OS X Snow Leopard Core Library from the Home pop-up button. You will see the ADC Reference Library documentation for Snow Leopard. This is the same documentation you saw in Chapter 2.

6. Choose Cocoa from the list of topics, choose Frameworks from the first row of options, and choose Foundation Framework Reference (HTML) from the list of Cocoa frameworks.

7. Select `NSDate` from the list of Foundation classes. The Developer Documentation window displays information about `NSDate`. Notice a simplified navigation bar has appeared at the top of the scroll view, with Table of Contents, Jump To, Previous, and Next buttons.

8. Click the Jump To pop-up in the navigation bar. You will see an entry in this menu for each section in the document, beginning with high-level concepts and ending with method documentation for `NSDate`.

9. Select `descriptionWithCalendarFormat:timeZone:locale:` from the symbol pop-up. The Developer Documentation window jumps to the entry describing `descriptionWithCalendarFormat:timeZone:locale:`, as shown in Figure 3-25.

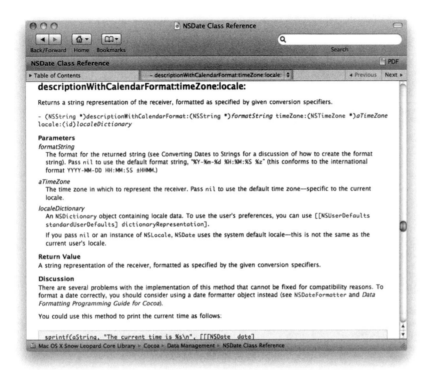

FIGURE 3-25

This method returns the current time with a particular formatting. The example provided in the documentation looks like what you are searching for.

10. Close the Developer Documentation window and return to `Greetings.m` in your project window.

11. Change line 8 to match the following code and save the file:

```
NSString *time = [[NSDate date] descriptionWithCalendarFormat:@"%H:%M:%S %Z"
                                                     timeZone:nil
                                                       locale:nil];
```

12. Build and run the project. You will see a compile warning appear on line 7, the same line will be selected with a grey highlight, and the window's status bar will read `GDB: Program received signal: "EXEC_BAD_ACCESS"`. Looks like the program crashed on launch.

13. Open the Debugger window by selecting Run ⇨ Debugger. The debugger appears, displaying the precise place where the program crashed, as noted in Figure 3-26. The assembly code displayed in the debugger may not be that helpful to you, but don't panic.

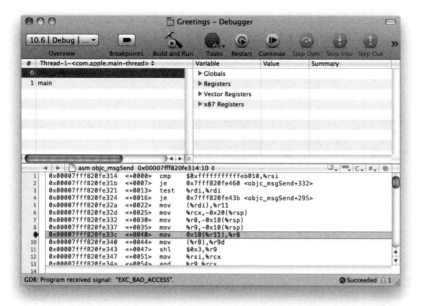

FIGURE 3-26

14. Click the entry for main in the stack list. The debugger updates to match the contents of Figure 3-27. It looks like the program has crashed trying to print the full username. It looks as though the compile warning comes from line 7, where the full username is stored in the user variable. That's no coincidence.

FIGURE 3-27

15. Stop debugging the program by clicking the Tasks button.

16. Option–double-click NSFullUserName. A small window will appear containing documentation for NSFullUserName, as shown in Figure 3-28. This small window is called the Quick Help window. It turns out that the NSFullUserName symbol is a function call, not a constant.

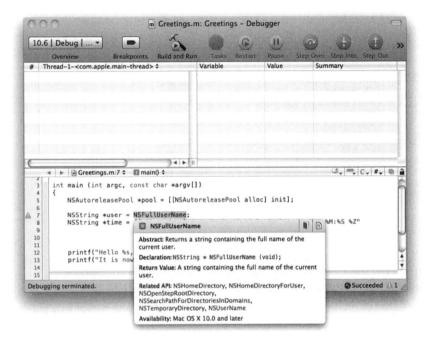

FIGURE 3-28

17. Return to main.m and change line 7 to match this code:

```
NSString *user = NSFullUserName();
```

18. Build and run the project, and then check the output in the Debugger Console. Your results should be similar to the following:

```
Hello Your Name,
It is now 01:31:39 US/Pacific.
Debugger stopped.
Program exited with status value:0.
```

19. Open Xcode's Developer Documentation window again.

20. Enter NSString in the search field at the top of the window. A list of symbols and documents will appear on the left side of the window, resembling Figure 3-29. Notice that the Symbol table automatically updates itself as you type. Eventually an entry for the NSString Objective-C class should percolate near the top of the list. If not, you may need to reveal more search results before you find it.

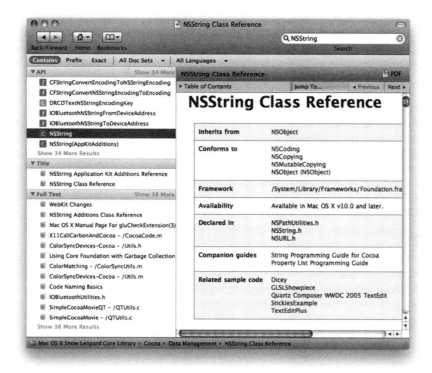

FIGURE 3-29

21. Select the NSString class from the API list. The Developer Documentation window displays documentation for the NSString class.

22. Select UTF8String from the Jump To pop-up menu (it's toward the very bottom of the menu). It looks as though UTF8String returns a const char * type, which should be exactly what printf expects.

23. Return to Greetings.m and Option–double-click printf. An entry for printf appears in the Quick Help window. This confirms that printf takes a const char * type, but it doesn't go into much detail.

24. Return to the Developer Documentation window and type **printf** into the Search field. A large number of results will appear in the API and file lists.

25. Change the search options from Contains to Exact in the small toolbar just above the API list. Now only one entry for printf will appear in the API list.

26. If necessary, select printf from the API list. The printf man page will appear in the Developer Documentation window.

How It Works

The code in this example looks a little different from the earlier examples because it is Objective-C. Don't worry about following along with the specifics of what this program is doing; you learn more about Objective-C in Chapter 6.

In this example, you ran your program without first starting the debugger or setting a breakpoint. In Snow Leopard, Xcode always runs the debugger to help you debug unexpected crashes such as this one. Recall that the debugger executes your program until it hits a breakpoint, the program terminates normally, you click the Pause button, or the program crashes. When you opened the Debugger window, your program's debugging information was right there waiting for you.

The Developer Documentation window displays information about many of the high-level frameworks on the system. You can navigate the documentation in the following two main ways:

➤ Browse through the documentation as you might browse through a web site, clicking through a series of hyperlinked entries. This is a great approach if you aren't quite sure what you are looking for.

➤ Search for documentation on specific symbols, such as classes, functions, and so on, by typing the symbol name into the Search field. This is a great approach if you are looking for more information on a specific thing.

You can also bring up a Quick Help window by holding down the Option key while double-clicking on symbols in your source files. The Quick Help window displays brief summary information about a symbol. For example, Option–double-clicking NSDate displays a short abstract for Cocoa's NSDate class. Do not confuse this with Command–double-clicking symbols: Command–double-clicking NSDate shows you NSDate's definition in the NSDate.h header file.

In many cases, Darwin man pages will display in the Developer Documentation window. Recall from Chapter 2 that manual pages are organized into separate sections. If necessary, you can specify the section name along with the page, such as 1 printf for the printf command-line tool and 3 printf for the printf C function. In cases where it's hard to search for a specific page, you may have better results using the Help ➪ Open Man Page menu item, or by just using Terminal.

SUMMARY

The Mac OS X development workflow is built around the Xcode IDE. You used Xcode to write and build a number of small projects. Xcode's source editor gave you a hand by providing several tools for arranging and navigating your source code. The integrated build system and run log turned your code into a useful program. And when things didn't go right, the debugger allowed you to see what was really going on in your program. Xcode even threw in a documentation browser for good measure.

The Developer Documentation window also includes a Tools group where you can find documentation for most of the developer tools in Mac OS X, including Xcode. This chapter presents enough information to help you get started with Xcode. You can learn a lot more about Xcode by reading its online manual.

In the next chapter, you learn how to use Interface Builder, a tool for building graphical user interfaces. Before proceeding, however, try the exercises that follow to test your understanding of the material covered in this chapter. You can find the solutions to these exercises in Appendix A.

EXERCISES

1. Use Xcode to look up the man page for the functions in the following table:

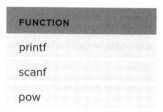

FUNCTION
printf
scanf
pow

2. The `Calculator` program can only perform integer math. Extend `Calculator` to do double-precision floating-point computations. These double-precision values will use the `double` data type, rather than the `int` data type. For example, you need to change the `calculate` function to accept and return `doubles` instead of `ints`. Feel free to skip ahead to Chapter 6 if you want to learn more about these data types. But this is mostly an opportunity to practice using Xcode to build and run a program.

    The "3 printf" and "3 scanf" man pages tell you how to read and write double-precision numbers to standard I/O. Make sure the decimal point is printed only when necessary:

    ```
    Enter an expression: 1 + 2
          1 + 2 = 3
    Enter an expression: 1 + 2.1
          1 + 2.1 = 3.1
    ```

3. Common mathematical functions and operators appear in the following table. Extend your `Calculator` changes in Exercise 2 to incorporate these new operators:

NAME	KEY	FUNCTION/OPERATOR	EXAMPLE
Divide	"/"	/	x = y / z;
Integer Divide	"\"	/	x = (int)y / (int)z;
Modulo	"%"	%	x = (int)y % (int)z;
Power	"^"	pow()	x = pow(y, z);

    You need to add the following line of code near the top of `Calculate.c`, along with the other `include` statements:

    ```
    #include <math.h>
    ```

▶ **WHAT YOU LEARNED IN THIS CHAPTER**

Project	an Xcode file representing your entire program
Source Files	text files containing your program's source code
Templates	sample project and source files with existing content
Symbols	names of variables, functions, classes, etc. used by your project
Targets	an Xcode feature that represents project output: an application, a command-line tool, a framework, etc.
Navigation Bar	editor controls that help you navigate within and between source files
Syntax Aware Editing	automatic source code formatting
Static Analyzer	a tool that finds many programming errors at build time
Debugger	a tool that lets you watch your program's state change as you run it
Breakpoint	a place in source code that tells the debugger to pause your program

4

Interface Builder

WHAT YOU WILL LEARN IN THIS CHAPTER:

➤ How to build menus and controls

➤ How to make windows resizable

➤ How to use Interface Builder's Inspector to configure individual interface elements

➤ How to test your interface directly in Interface Builder

Interface Builder, as its name implies, is a tool for building graphical user interfaces (GUIs). You design interfaces by dragging windows, controls, and other elements into your interface and arranging them with your mouse. People often refer to this kind of tool as a *WYSIWYG* editor because What You See Is What You Get. Because you're already familiar with these techniques (moving files, sorting your e-mail, and so on), it's easy to get started designing user interfaces (UIs) in Interface Builder.

All your interface information is stored in a *nib* file. Nib files can describe an entire interface, or they can describe only a subset of an interface, such as a menu bar or window. As such, nib files are used by plug-ins (such as System Preferences panes) as well as applications.

After your interface has been built, you can test the interface and make sure everything has been laid out correctly. In this chapter, you learn the fundamentals of using Interface Builder — you learn more about Cocoa-specific features in Chapters 8, 9, and 10.

STARTING A NEW INTERFACE

As with Xcode, Interface Builder has templates that help you get started with a new nib file. These templates are grouped by application framework, so you can quickly zero in on the kind of interface you need.

TRY IT OUT Creating a New Interface

1. Launch /Developer/Applications/Interface Builder. You should see a Choose A Template window resembling Figure 4-1, along with two other windows which you will learn about in a moment.

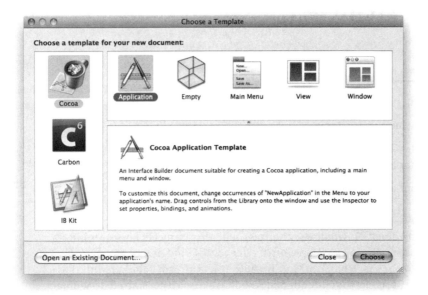

FIGURE 4-1

2. Select Application from the list of Cocoa projects and press the Choose button. The Template window has been replaced by three new windows. Figure 4-2 shows all five windows currently on your screen. The Untitled window represents your nib file and contains a menu bar and a window. The contents of the menu bar and window are displayed in detail in their own windows. The Library window contains UI elements that you can use when building your interface. The fifth window is the Inspector window. Its title and contents depend on the selected panel and the current selection.

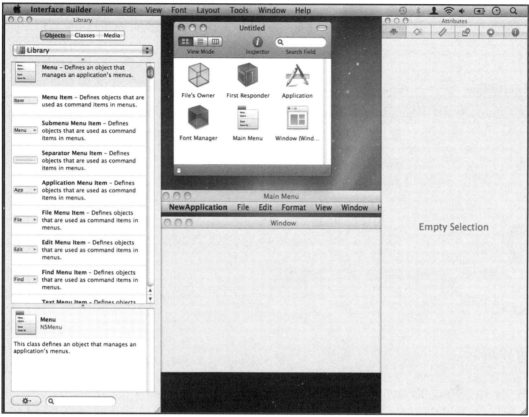

FIGURE 4-2

3. Close the window representing your interface's main window. This window is simply named Window and has no content.

4. Double-click the Window (Window) icon in your nib file. The window representing the main window reappears. Also notice that the Inspector displays some settings for your window, shown in Figure 4-3.

5. Click once on the Window (Window) icon's label and wait a moment. The label changes to an editable text field, allowing you to rename the window icon in your nib file. Change its name to **My Window**. Notice that the title of the window you opened in the previous step doesn't change.

6. Click the Main Menu icon in your nib file. The contents of the Inspector window change to reflect the settings of your main menu. This behavior is common among all inspector windows; Inspector contents change along with the current selection.

FIGURE 4-3

7. Choose File ⇨ Simulate Interface. Interface Builder opens your interface in a program called Cocoa Simulator. The Cocoa Simulator displays your menu bar and window, as shown in Figure 4-4.

8. Quit Cocoa Simulator, and you are returned to Interface Builder.

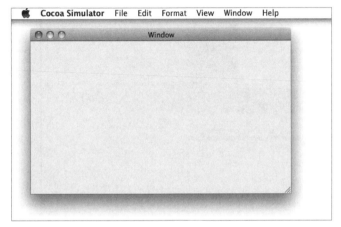

FIGURE 4-4

How It Works

When you create a new nib file in Interface Builder, it offers to initialize the file from one of a series of templates. Interface Builder needs to know if the interface is going to be used with Carbon or Cocoa. Even if you want to start from a blank slate, you need to specify the empty template appropriate for your application framework.

Your nib file appears in a small window, which provides a place to store menu bars, windows, and other UI elements. Interface Builder refers to the elements in your interface as *objects*. An object is essentially a specific item of a particular type. If your nib file contains two windows, you will find two window objects in your nib file. In this example, you created a nib file with main menu and window instances. Object icons in your nib can be renamed. The name is merely a label for your benefit — it has no effect on the final user interface.

Some object contents are displayed graphically within Interface Builder using additional windows. For example, your application's main menu was represented within a window. And representing an application's main window as a window seems natural enough.

Interface Builder provides two powerful tools in the form of utility panels: the Inspector and the Library. The Inspector displays information about the current selection. You use the Inspector to customize the instances in your nib file. The Library contains different kinds of interface elements. The specific contents of the Library depend on the kind of interface being edited (Carbon or Cocoa) and sometimes on what developer tools you have installed. Normally, you use the Library window by dragging interface elements into your nib file or its helper windows.

After your interface has been designed, you can quickly check your work with the Simulate Interface command. Simulate Interface runs your interface in a special test mode, giving you the opportunity to try out the controls, check that your window's keyboard focus moves properly when you press the Tab key, verify that windows look good when they are resized, and similar tasks. You quit the simulation by pressing Command-Q or by selecting Quit from your interface's menu bar.

It is interesting to note at this point that Interface Builder did not generate any source code to test your interface. The behavior of your interface is controlled entirely by the Cocoa and Carbon frameworks. All the information necessary to rebuild your interface is stored in your nib file and is interpreted by the Cocoa and Carbon frameworks at runtime. You learn more about how Cocoa uses nib files in Chapter 8.

BUILDING MENUS

Every Mac OS X program has a main menu bar — that familiar sight at the top of your computer's screen. Although every application adds its own menus and menu items, there is a fair amount of similarity between each program. For example, most programs have File, Edit, Window, and Help menus. The guidelines for how menus should look and behave can be found in the Apple Human Interface Guidelines, which you learned about in Chapter 2.

In this Try It Out example, you create a menu bar for a Cocoa application. Interface Builder provides some nice graphical tools for building menus, and it also sets up many of the common menus for you.

TRY IT OUT   Building Cocoa Menus

1. In Interface Builder, create a new Cocoa Main Menu project. Note that you can open the Choose A Template window with File ⇨ New, if necessary. Your nib window and a window representing the Main Menu appear.

2. Click once on the File menu in your menu bar window. The File menu drops down, as shown in Figure 4-5. Notice that a bunch of items have already been filled in for you. The Inspector now shows settings for the File menu.

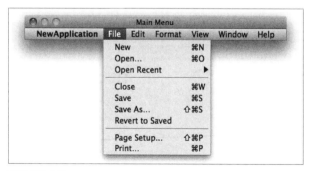

FIGURE 4-5

3. Click once on the New item in your nib's File menu. You have now selected the New item. Notice the Inspector has changed again, this time showing settings for the menu item.

4. Double-click the NewApplication menu on the left side of your interface's menu bar. You can rename the menu to something more appropriate.

5. Name the menu `Cocoa Example` and press Return.

6. Click Cocoa Example to reveal its menu. Note that this time the menu has a number of items, including a Preferences menu item. Figure 4-6 shows what the Cocoa Example menu should look like.

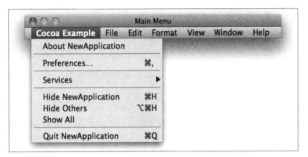

FIGURE 4-6

7. Rename the About NewApplication item to `About Cocoa Example`. While you're here, also rename the Hide NewApplication and Quit NewApplication items to `Hide Cocoa Example` and `Quit Cocoa Example`.

8. Remove the Format menu by selecting it in your menu bar and pressing Command–Delete.

9. In the Library window, select Submenu Menu Item. If you have trouble finding it, try searching for it by typing `Submenu` into the Search field at the bottom of the Library window. When selected, the Library window should resemble Figure 4-7.

10. Drag the Submenu Menu Item from the Library into your interface's menu bar and drop it between the View and Window menus. A new Menu menu appears, as shown in Figure 4-8. You can re-order the menu items by dragging them with the mouse, if necessary.

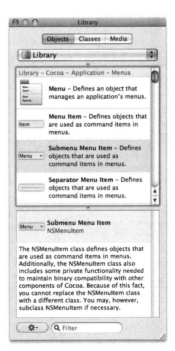

FIGURE 4-7

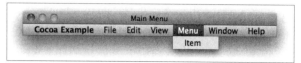

FIGURE 4-8

11. Rename Menu to **Extras**.

12. Select Item from the Extras menu.

13. Rename the item to **Empty The Trash**. Notice the item's name in the Inspector window also changed to Empty The Trash.

14. Click the gray box next named Key Equiv. in the Inspector window. The gray box will be lit with a curious highlight. You can now define a keyboard shortcut for this menu item.

15. Hold down the Command and Shift keys and press E. The contents of the gray box are replaced by symbols representing Command-Shift–E, shown in Figure 4-9.

16. Duplicate the Empty The Trash menu item with Edit ➪ Duplicate.

17. Change the new item's name to **Shred The Trash**.

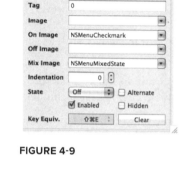

FIGURE 4-9

18. Double-click the Command-Shift–E symbols in your menu item. A box appears around the key equivalent, indicating that you can change it, as shown in Figure 4-10.

19. Change Shred The Trash's key equivalent to Command-Option-Shift-E.

FIGURE 4-10

20. In the Inspector, check the Alternate checkbox for the Shred The Trash menu item.

21. Choose File ➪ Simulate Interface. Your menu bar appears in the Cocoa Simulator.

22. Check the Cocoa Example menu to make sure your changes took effect.

23. Click once on the Extras menu to reveal the menu. Notice that there is only a single menu item: Empty The Trash.

24. Hold down the Option key. The Extras menu item changes to Shred The Trash.

How It Works

Every application in Mac OS X has a main menu bar. This menu bar is composed of several menus, which are in turn composed of menu items. Interface Builder normally creates a main menu bar for you. You can add menus and menu items to your nib by dragging these items in from Interface Builder's Library window.

Interface Builder's Library contains the following objects that you will find useful when building menus:

Empty menus and menu items, such as Menu Item and Submenu Menu Item — You can drag the Submenu Menu Item into the main menu bar to create new menus, or you can drag it into other menus to create submenus.

Pre-built menus such as Application, File, Text, and Format — Some of these items are automatically included in the main menu bar, and some can be added manually for enabling certain kinds of operations. For example, if you're working on a text-editing application, you might want to add Text and Font menus to your menu bar.

A Separator Menu Item — Menu separators help group menu items into collections of related items. They aren't selectable; they simply separate other menu items.

An entire menu bar — As with the Submenu Menu Item, the Menu object represents an individual menu. However, this menu can't be dragged into the menu bar or other menus; it can only be dragged into your nib window. This is useful for defining menus that don't live in your main menu bar, such as contextual menus or Dock menus.

After you've arranged your menus the way you want them, you can edit the individual menu items. You can do simple tasks such as naming the item and setting its key equivalent from the menu itself by double-clicking the menu item. More complicated changes require Interface Builder's Inspector.

Note that the Cocoa Simulator's application menu did not change to Cocoa Example, even though you renamed the application menu in the nib file. The system does not actually use the application menu item's name at runtime. Instead, it uses the application's display name, which is stored in the application's bundle. You learn more about the application bundle in Chapter 5.

Mac OS X lets you create alternate or dynamic menu items that change when specific modifier keys (usually Option) are pressed. Alternate items allow applications to provide more menu options without cluttering the menu with lots of items. In this example, you created a menu item Empty The Trash that changes to Shred The Trash when you hold down the Option key. The Finder's File menu is an example of alternate menus in action. If you tap the Option key while holding down the File menu, you see a number of menu items change. For example, File ⇨ Close Window changes to File ⇨ Close All. Note that alternate menu items must share the same menu key character but use different modifier keys to work properly.

When you tested your interface, the new menu items were disabled. Cocoa automatically handles enabled and disabled states for its menu items. In general, if a menu item is hooked up to something, Cocoa enables the item; otherwise the item is disabled. You haven't learned how to hook up menu items yet, so these items are disabled. You learn about hooking up menu items in Chapter 8.

BUILDING WINDOWS

Applications use windows in many different ways. Document windows, such as those used by word processors or image viewers, tend to be large, resizable windows that contain only a few UI elements. Utility windows and inspectors tend to have a lot of controls packed into a small area.

Dialog boxes, alerts, and sheets are often the simplest windows, containing only enough items to ask a simple question and collect an answer from the user.

Interface Builder's drag-and-drop interface should be well suited for building windows. Theoretically, all you need to do is drag some controls into your window and you're good to go. In practice, you also need to make sure the controls are arranged properly in the window, accounting for both your application's needs and the spacing rules set forth in the Apple Human Interface Guidelines. Fortunately for you, Interface Builder includes some useful tricks that make this easy.

In the following Try It Out, you build a window to be used as a *modal* dialog box or a sheet. A modal window locks out portions of your application's interface until you close that window. Modal dialog boxes block the entire application, whereas sheets block access only to the window in which they appear. The window contains a number of controls arranged in a specific layout. The window also includes OK and Cancel buttons that allow the user to dismiss the window. As is often the case with small dialog boxes and sheets, this window will not be resizable.

This example is the basis for the first exercise at the end of this chapter. If you want to try your hand at that exercise, be sure to save your work.

TRY IT OUT   Building a Dialog Window

1. In Interface Builder, create a new Cocoa Empty project. Your nib window appears. Unlike the earlier examples, no other windows are associated with your interface yet.

2. Select Library ⟹ Cocoa ⟹ Application ⟹ Windows from the Library window's topmost pop-up menu. The Library will display only Window items in its object list, and should resemble Figure 4-11.

3. Drag the Window item from the Library into your nib file. An icon named Window (Window) appears in your nib, and the Inspector shows the window's settings.

4. Uncheck the Close, Minimize, and Resize buttons. The Inspector should resemble Figure 4-12.

5. Double-click the Window (Window) icon. A blank window representing your window appears. Soon you will add controls to this new blank window.

6. Select Library ⟹ Cocoa ⟹ Views & Cells ⟹ Inputs & Values from the Library window's object pop-up menu. The Library displays items for displaying static and editable text, as well as other controls.

FIGURE 4-11

7. Drag a Label item out of the Library and into the center of your blank window. This creates a new label in your window.

8. Double-click the label to change its text. Replace Label with **First Name:**. Press Return or click once outside the label to end the text entry process.

9. Click the label to select it. Control points appear around the text. Note that the label is just large enough to fit its text.

10. Drag the label toward the upper-left corner of the window. As you approach the corner, blue guides appear about 20 pixels from the left and top of the window. Figure 4-13 shows these guides in action. These guides help suggest a place for your label that is consistent with the Apple Human Interface Guidelines.

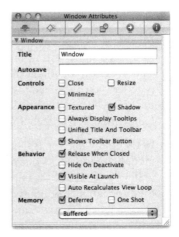

FIGURE 4-12

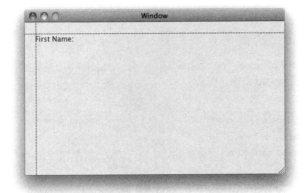

FIGURE 4-13

11. Be sure the label is selected. The Inspector displays information about this label.

12. Change the label's text to be right-aligned by clicking the fourth control in the list of Alignment buttons. Figure 4-14 shows the Inspector with right alignment selected.

13. Drag a Text Field object out of the Library and into your window.

FIGURE 4-14

14. Move the text field so that it sits to the right of the First Name: label. Guides appear, suggesting the proper distance between the text field and its label, as shown in Figure 4-15. A guide also aligns the label and text field's baselines.

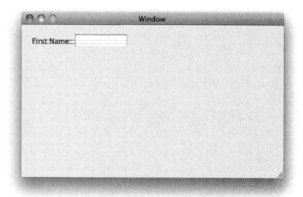

FIGURE 4-15

15. Be sure the text field is selected and choose the Size palette from the Inspector's top button bar. The Size palette is represented by a small yellow ruler. The Inspector displays size and layout information for your text field, as shown in Figure 4-16.

16. Change the text field's frame width to 200 pixels. The text field immediately changes to reflect this new size.

17. Use the mouse to select both items and choose Edit ⇨ Duplicate. New items appear on top of the originals, offset a few pixels down and to the right.

18. Drag the new items directly below the originals. The left edges should line up. As you move down, Interface Builder may suggest two positions next to each other: one when the text fields are 6 pixels away and one when the text field is 8 pixels away. Choose the greater of these two gaps.

19. Rename the new label from First Name: to **Last Name:**.

20. Duplicate the first two items again, and position the new items directly below the First Name: and Last Name: fields.

21. Rename the new label **Email:**. Figure 4-17 shows the window's layout so far. Notice that the controls are aligned to the top and left of the window, but there is a lot of unused space below and to the right.

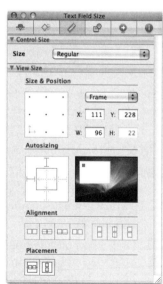

FIGURE 4-16

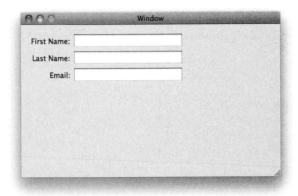

FIGURE 4-17

22. Make the window narrower by clicking in the window's resize control and dragging it to the left. As before, Interface Builder uses guides to suggest a reasonable distance between the window's right edge and your controls. Don't worry about keeping your window's height exactly the same; you can tighten up the window's lower edge after you've finished adding items to the window.

23. Select Library ➪ Cocoa ➪ Views & Cells ➪ Buttons from the Library window's object pop-up menu. A variety of buttons appear in the Library.

24. Drag the Push button from the Library into your window.

25. Move the button to the right side of the window below the Email: text field. Guides appear, suggesting a position about 20 pixels away from the window's right edge and 8 pixels away from the text field.

26. Press the down arrow button four times. Your button should now be about 12 pixels away from the editable Email: text field. Don't worry about making it precisely right — you'll learn how to double-check the distance between controls later.

27. Select the Attributes section from the Inspector's top button bar. It's the first icon in the bar.

28. Use the Inspector to change the button's title to **OK**. Notice Interface Builder automatically set the key equivalent for your button: the Inspector's Key Equiv. field displays a symbol for the Return key. The button will draw with a dark highlight, indicating Return can be used to choose this button.

29. Drag a new push button from the Library into your window. Position this button to the left of your OK button. Again, Interface Builder's guides will suggest a reasonable place for this button: about 12 pixels to the left of the OK button.

30. Use the Inspector to name this button `Cancel`. Notice Interface Builder set the button's key equivalent to the Escape key.

31. Now you can finish resizing the window so that it fits all its controls snugly. The guides suggest the proper 20-pixel buffer between the controls and the window's edges. Figure 4-18 illustrates your final window.

32. Choose File ➪ Simulate Interface. Your window appears on-screen, giving you a chance to test your controls.

33. Press Command-Q to end the test.

FIGURE 4-18

How It Works

Perhaps you are wondering why your new Empty nib file started out with some objects already in it. Cocoa nibs have three special objects in them at all times: File's Owner, First Responder, and Application. These special objects are defined by Cocoa, and they're used to bind controls to the application code. They cannot be removed or renamed. You can simply ignore these items for now.

You build window interfaces much as you would build menu interfaces: by dragging interface elements from the Library window into your interface. When building windows, Interface Builder uses guides to automatically suggest layouts consistent with the Apple Human Interface Guidelines. These guides appear when you move and resize interface elements.

Even though you removed your window's close, resize, and minimize controls, you were still able to resize, close, and minimize that window when designing your interface. The window that Interface Builder uses to represent the interface you're editing can always be resized, closed, and minimized. Think of this representation as Interface Builder's *window editor*, not actually your window. After you test the interface, you will find that your window really isn't resizable.

The Library window contains dozens of interface elements in its list, and sometimes it can be a bit overwhelming. You can filter the items in the Library in two ways: using the filter pop-up menu at the top of the window and using the Filter Search field at the bottom of the window. Using the filter pop-up is a great way to browse for items relevant to your task at hand, whether it is building a menu bar or laying out a window.

When laying out the first text field, you used the Inspector to set its size to a specific value. You also used the Inspector to edit button and label attributes. These values were located in different views of the Inspector, and each view was accessible through the Inspector's button bar. Interface Builder buries a lot of interesting, framework-specific functionality in these Inspector views. You learn more about some of these views in Chapter 8, but you might take some time to explore them on your own.

Interface Builder resized your text label to exactly fit its contents. When manually resizing text labels, Interface Builder will snap to the natural border of your text for you, but you have the power to make the label as large or as small as you want.

Interface Builder also set your button key equivalents for you, keying off of the button names. The Inspector interface for setting a button key equivalent is the same as that for menu items. Even when Interface Builder automatically chooses a key equivalent, you get to have the last word.

MAKING WINDOWS RESIZABLE

When designing windows, you need to consider what will happen when the user tries to resize them. For some windows, such as simple sheets and dialog boxes, you may choose to prohibit resizing. But most user-friendly interfaces allow the user to resize windows as they see fit.

An interface element normally responds in two possible ways when a window is resized. The element may remain stationary, fixed in an area of the screen, or the element may change size along with the window. Some elements may do both: remain fixed vertically and resize themselves horizontally. Interface Builder provides tools for defining what happens to its contents when a window is resized.

In the following Try It Out, you build a simple, resizable Cocoa window. Figure 4-19 shows the window in two sizes. Don't worry too much about what this interface is supposed to represent; it's really just an opportunity to practice item layout.

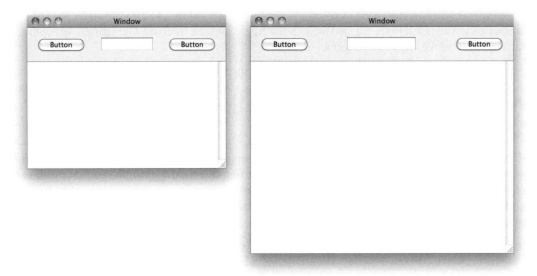

FIGURE 4-19

Building a Resizable Cocoa Window

1. In Interface Builder, create a new Cocoa Window project. Your nib appears along with an empty window.

2. Select the empty window and verify in the Inspector that the Minimize, Close, and Resize buttons are all checked.

3. Drag a Push button from the Library and place it in the upper-left corner of your window. Use the guides to place the button a comfortable distance of 20 pixels from the window edges.

4. Drag a second button from the Library and place it in the upper-right corner of your window.

5. Drag a Text Field from the Library and place it between the two buttons. Use the guides to make sure that the text field lines up vertically with the buttons. Don't worry about centering the text field right now.

6. Make sure the text field is selected. If not, select it using the mouse.

7. Hold down the Option key and move the mouse over the window. Special red guides appear to measure out the distance from the text field's boundaries to those of the window. Figure 4-20 shows these guides in action. The specific horizontal distances may differ from those shown here.

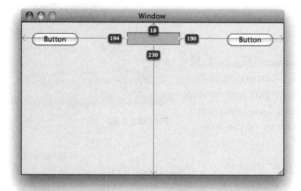

FIGURE 4-20

8. While still holding down the Option key, tap the left or right arrow key on the keyboard. This nudges the text field by a single pixel. Continue nudging the text field until it is centered in the window.

9. Drag a multi-line Text View object from the Library into your window. Position it so that it fills the window's remaining space, as shown in Figure 4-21. If you have trouble finding the Text View object, try typing **Text Field** in the Library's Filter Search field.

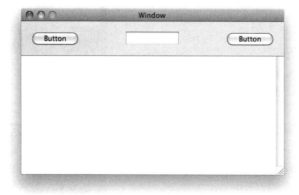

FIGURE 4-21

10. Choose File ➪ Simulate Interface to check your work. Your window is displayed in test mode.

11. Grab the window by its resize control and resize the window in a bunch of different directions. Start using small, circular motions and move toward progressively larger movements. You'll find some of the controls are pinned to the lower-left corner of the window, while others are pinned to the upper-left corner. If you make the window very small, the buttons are covered by the text field. If you make the window very large, the items sit still as the window grows underneath them.

12. Press Command-Q to quit the simulator.

13. Select the button in your window's upper-left corner.

14. Press Command-3 to select the Inspector's Size view. Figure 4-22 shows the layout values, along with an unusual Autosizing control. The Autosizing control is composed of red struts and springs (arrows) arranged around a light-gray rectangle. This control tells you this button is anchored to the upper-left corner of the window and isn't resizable.

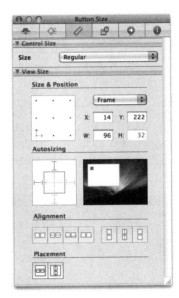

FIGURE 4-22

15. Click the button in the upper-right corner of your window.

16. In the Autosizing control, click the left strut to deselect it, and click the right strut to select it. If you click on the wrong thing, just click it again to toggle it back to its previous state. The Autosizing control should now resemble Figure 4-23. This button is now anchored to the upper-right corner of the window.

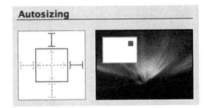

FIGURE 4-23

17. Select the text field at the top of the window.

18. Deselect the Autosizing control's left strut.

19. Click the horizontal spring running through the gray box. Remember the springs resemble straight red arrows. The Autosizing control should now resemble Figure 4-24.

20. Select the text view at the bottom of your window.

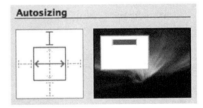

FIGURE 4-24

21. Select both of the Autosizing control's springs within the gray box. The control should look similar to the one in Figure 4-25.

22. Choose File ➪ Simulate Interface to check your work. Your window appears in test mode.

23. Resize the window in a bunch of different directions. At first it looks as though the interface is resizing correctly. The buttons stay in their corners, the text field expands and

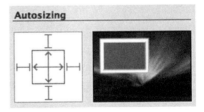

FIGURE 4-25

contracts horizontally, and the text view fills the remaining available space. But if you make the window too small, the text field goes away; when that happens, making the window large again leaves the text field in an unusual state. The solution to this problem is to set a minimum size for the window.

24. Quit test mode using Command-Q. Interface Builder's UI returns to normal.

25. Click your window's title bar to select it. Alternatively, you can select the Window (Window) icon in your nib file. Figure 4-26 shows the Inspector's Size controls for your window. Some of the values may not match exactly.

26. Select the Minimum Size checkbox. The Width and Height controls will become active.

27. Click the Use Current button underneath the Minimum Size Width and Height fields. The Width and Height fields will update to match the dimensions of your window.

28. Choose File ⇨ Simulate Interface to check your work.

29. Resize the window in a bunch of different directions. The window elements will resize correctly. The window won't shrink beyond the dimensions specified in step 27.

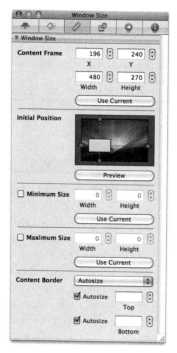

FIGURE 4-26

How It Works

Initially your window's controls seemed pinned to the upper-left or lower-left corner of the window. In Cocoa programming, graphics coordinates are normally relative to a window's lower-left corner. So without any additional resizing information, a control is pinned to the lower-left corner by default. Interface Builder helps you out a little by anchoring controls near the top edge of their window to that top edge.

You used a special Autosizing control for configuring how Cocoa interface elements resize. This Autosizing control consists of red struts (lines), red springs (arrows), and a light-gray rectangle. The light gray rectangle represents the interface element, or control, you are editing, and the red struts and springs describe how your interface element responds when its parent window changes. You enable or disable these struts and springs by clicking them with your mouse.

The four struts outside the light-gray rectangle represent the distance between your control and the window's border. An enabled strut means that the control's position doesn't change along that edge. This has the effect of anchoring the control in a specific location. If a strut is disabled, the distance between the interface element's edge and the window's edge may change when the window is resized. Here your upper-left button had struts on the top and left side, locking the button against the upper-left corner of the window. The two springs within the light-gray rectangle represent the size of your interface element. Enabled springs mean the size can change, and disabled springs mean the size remains constant. You enabled the text field's horizontal spring, and left the vertical spring disabled. This allowed the text field's width to change with the window while keeping the height constant.

WHY SPRINGS?

You're probably wondering why these simple red arrows are called springs instead of, well, arrows. The reason is historical. Interface Builder's Autosizing control used to use straight lines called struts and springy lines called springs. A strut inside or outside the gray box meant "this dimension doesn't change," and a spring inside or outside the gray box meant "this dimension can change." This system confused many people who were new to Cocoa, and so it looks as though Apple decided to make things clearer by redesigning the Autosizing control. Interface Builder's documentation still refers to flexible space within the gray box as springs, even though they look similar to arrows.

Sometimes you can get into trouble when a window gets too small. This often happens when you have one or more controls that change size along with the window. The solution to this problem is to set your window's minimum size. Normally your layout in Interface Builder already is the minimum size; it's easier to design a small interface and allow it to grow bigger than the other way around.

The resizing rules for controls and windows often aren't obvious at a glance, and manually checking each control's Autosizing values can be tedious. The Simulate Interface command again proves its value by providing a quick and easy way to test your resize logic from Interface Builder. It also encourages experimentation; if you're not sure what a specific set of Autosizing values will do, just test it out.

SUMMARY

Interface Builder is a powerful tool that's essential for designing UIs on Mac OS X. It allows you to design, build, and test UIs using simple editing concepts, such as drag and drop. Interface Builder also lets you fine-tune your interfaces using its Inspector.

In the next chapter, you learn about the structure of a Mac OS X application. Before proceeding, however, try the exercises that follow to test your understanding of the material covered in this chapter. You can find the solutions to these exercises in Appendix A.

EXERCISES

1. Modify the example dialog you built in the Try It Out "Building a Dialog Window" to make it resizable. All the controls should be pinned to the upper-left corner of the window. Allow the text fields to expand when the window is resized.

2. Carbon and Cocoa both support a tab control that lets you display several sets of controls in the same area. Unlike the examples you've seen so far, you can actually put controls inside a tab control: simply switch to the tab you want and drag buttons, text fields, and the like into that tab.

   Build the interface shown in Figure 4-27 using a Cocoa Window nib file. This window need not be resizable.

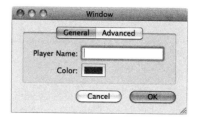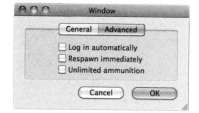

FIGURE 4-27

▶ WHAT YOU LEARNED IN THIS CHAPTER

Nib File	a file containing application UI elements
Library Panel	a window containing UI elements and other helpful objects
Attributes Inspector	an inspector panel for setting object options
Size Inspector	an inspector panel for setting object size, and for configuring how objects resize when their window or parent object resizes
Cocoa Simulator	a utility for quickly testing a UI
Guides	lines that suggest where UI objects should go
Struts	a resizing tool showing how an object anchors itself to its window or parent object
Springs	a resizing tool showing how an object stretches when its window or parent object resizes

PART II
Application Programming

5

The Application

WHAT YOU WILL LEARN IN THIS CHAPTER:

➤ How applications and other bundles are structured

➤ What kind of files you find in a bundle

➤ How application preferences are stored

Mac OS X applications seem simple enough. They appear with friendly icons that bounce in the Dock when you launch them, display a window or two, and then you're on your way. If you want, you can move the application out of the system-wide /Applications directory and into a folder of your choosing. You can even drag some applications into Mail or iChat to send a copy to your friends!

But in reality, Mac OS X applications are sophisticated things. They are composed of executable code, a user interface (UI), and other resources. An application can even include files that translate the UI into other languages. When packaged correctly, an application looks and feels as if it really were a single file. This packaging scheme is called a *bundle*, or sometimes *wrapper* or *package*.

Bundles organize executable code and other resources by storing files in a special directory tree. The bundle format can store resources for specific languages and countries (called *localizations*) as well as resources that are language-independent. Bundles can also store executable code for various platforms, allowing the system to pick a specific version of a program based on the system on which it's running. The Finder, Dock, and other Mac OS X programs treat bundles as if they are single files, giving you the flexibility of a directory tree with the convenience of a file.

Although applications themselves are self-contained, they do store some data in other places on your computer. These data normally represent things such as your application preferences — the directory that opens by default when you bring up an Open panel — the contents of an Open Recent menu, and the like. All these settings are stored in one of a few common locations using a common file format.

BASIC BUNDLE STRUCTURE

Mac OS X uses bundles for a number of file formats, including applications, frameworks, plug-ins, and certain kinds of documents. You are already familiar with applications and frameworks. Plug-ins are bundles that can be loaded into applications or frameworks at runtime. For example, graphics programs commonly use plug-ins to import functionality into the application. Also, the QuickTime framework can load new codecs, importers, and other things with plug-ins. Some applications use bundles to store document data. For example, Xcode project files are bundles. Not all documents are bundles, however.

Bundles offer a number of different features depending on the specific kind of bundle format in use. No one format takes advantage of all bundle features. The following table outlines the features supported for each bundle format.

	APPLICATIONS	FRAMEWORKS	PLUG-INS	DOCUMENTS
Opaque Directory	✓		✓	✓
Versioned Bundles		✓		
The `Info.plist` File	✓	✓	✓	
Executable Code	✓	✓	✓	
Global Resources	✓	✓	✓	✓
Localized Resources	✓	✓	✓	

Opaque Directory

Various parts of the operating system, including the Finder, Dock, and Open/Save panels can treat a bundle directory as if it really is a single file. This prevents people from casually viewing a bundle's contents and making changes to its files and directories. Because users can't see inside these bundles, we refer to them as *opaque directories*.

Opaque directories are common for applications, plug-ins, and document bundle types. When users open one of these bundles in the Finder, they expect an application to launch (either the selected application or an application that works with the selected plug-in or document). As a result, these bundles are opaque. Framework bundles are not opaque because you need to look inside a framework to see its header files, documentation, and other browsable resources.

The system keeps track of opaque bundle directories in a number of ways. The first way is simply by checking the file extension. All application bundles (directories that end in .app) are made opaque automatically. The second way is by setting a piece of file metadata called a *bundle bit*. If a directory's bundle bit is set, the system knows it should treat the bundle as a file, and not as a directory. Thirdly, an application can register a file extension for bundled document types with the system; when the system encounters a directory with that extension, it knows it needs to be treated as a file. This is normally also how document icons are associated with files on Mac OS X.

Versioned Bundles

Frameworks on Mac OS X actually use an older bundle format than other bundle types. This type supports a built-in bundle versioning scheme where all the bundle's files are separated into special subdirectories within the bundle. This allows several versions of a framework to safely live within a single framework bundle.

At the top level of the bundle, you will find a Versions directory that stores all the version-specific subdirectories. Normally, frameworks are versioned by a single English letter, starting with *A*. However, frameworks can also use more meaningful version numbers.

Along with the Versions directory, you will find *symbolic links* pointing to specific files and directories in the current version. This helps people find and work with the current bundle version without having to know which version they are actually using. When a program is first built, it normally uses the current version of the bundle. However, the program keeps track of the version it used at build time. If a new version of the framework is added in the future, the application continues to look for the version it built against. The application runs only if that older framework version is still installed.

NOTE *A symbolic link, or symlink, is a special Unix file that refers to another file or directory. When you open a symlink, Mac OS X opens the symlinks target file or directory instead. You normally create symlinks using the ln command in Terminal.*

Because symlinks are part of the Unix system, they use paths to refer to these target files. There is no guarantee that a symlink points to a valid target file. For example, the target may have been deleted, or someone might have moved or renamed it.

Symlinks resemble alias files created by Mac OS X's Finder. The major difference between symlinks and aliases is that aliases use a method other than a file path to refer to their targeted files. As a result, aliases continue to point to their target files even if the target is moved or renamed. On the other hand, alias files do not work with traditional Unix commands, which expect full paths.

Here is an example of a versioned bundle:

```
FunFramework.framework
FunFramework.framework/FunFramework
FunFramework.framework/Resources
FunFramework.framework/Versions
FunFramework.framework/Versions/A
FunFramework.framework/Versions/A/FunFramework
FunFramework.framework/Versions/A/Resources
FunFramework.framework/Versions/A/Resources/English.lproj
FunFramework.framework/Versions/A/Resources/English.lproj/InfoPlist.strings
FunFramework.framework/Versions/A/Resources/Info.plist
FunFramework.framework/Versions/Current
```

More modern bundles do not support versioning. Instead of gathering their files up into a versions directory, they push their bundle contents into a `Contents` directory at the top level, as shown in the following code:

```
FunBundle.bundle
FunBundle.bundle/Contents
FunBundle.bundle/Contents/Info.plist
FunBundle.bundle/Contents/MacOS
FunBundle.bundle/Contents/MacOS/FunBundle
FunBundle.bundle/Contents/Resources
FunBundle.bundle/Contents/Resources/English.lproj
FunBundle.bundle/Contents/Resources/English.lproj/InfoPlist.strings
```

The Info.plist File

Most bundles contain a special file called an `Info.plist`, which contains special information about the bundle: its name, a human-readable copyright string, an identifier meant to uniquely represent the bundle, and other settings. The `Info.plist` file is commonly used by application, framework, and plug-in bundles to provide specific information about their features to the system. You will find `Info.plist` at the top level of the bundle's content directory.

The `Info.plist` is a *property list*. Property lists are special files that can hold an arbitrary hierarchy of data on Mac OS X. Data can be referenced either by name (known as a *key*) or with a numeric index, depending on how the data is organized. Data in the `Info.plist` file is most often looked up by key. The following table provides keys commonly found in the `Info.plist` file, along with an explanation of their use.

INFO.PLIST KEY	USAGE
CFBundleDocumentTypes	A list of document types supported by an application. Each entry in this list includes the document's type, file extension, OS type, and a reference to its icon, and other settings.
CFBundleExecutable	The filename of the executable found within the bundle; common to application and plug-in bundles.

INFO.PLIST KEY	USAGE
CFBundleGetInfoString	Text displayed by the Finder when the user brings up the Info window for this bundle.
CFBundleIconFile	The filename of this bundle's icon. This key is used only for application bundles.
CFBundleIdentifier	A string representing a unique identifier for this bundle. These strings are normally expressed in a format beginning with a company's reversed domain name followed by the program name; for example, com.apple.mail or com.wrox.Slide Master.
CFBundleName	The name of the bundle. This key can be localized, so it takes precedence over the bundle's filename when determining what name to display to the user.
CFBundlePackageType	A four-character code representing the bundle's Type code. It is normally APPL for applications and FMWK for frameworks. Plug-in bundles might use a variety of type codes.
CFBundleSignature	A four-character code representing this bundle's Creator code used to identify this bundle. It is typically used by Mac OS X when deciding which application should open a document by default.
CFBundleVersion	The version string for this version; for example, "1.0.3" or "4.1b3fc2".
NSMainNibFile	For Cocoa applications, the name of the nib file containing the main menu.
NSPrincipalClass	The name of an Objective-C class designated as the principal class for a Cocoa application or plug-in bundle. In the case of Cocoa applications, this must either be NSApplication or an NSApplication subclass.

The keys shown in the preceding table represent only the most common Info.plist keys used by the system. Other keys do exist but are appropriate only for certain situations, such as for applications that run without appearing in the Dock. You can also define your own data keys if you want.

Bundles with an Info.plist file often also contain one or more InfoPlist.strings files. These files contain localized copies of human-readable values in the Info.plist. For example, the CFBundleGetInfoString key represents text displayed when the user examines the bundle in the Finder, and normally is translated along with other strings in the bundle. However, other values, such as CFBundleIdentifier, are not meant to be localized. You learn more about localization in the section "Localized Resources" later in this chapter.

You can find more information about `Info.plist` keys in Mac OS X's conceptual documentation for Runtime Configuration Guidelines: Snow Leopard Core Library ➪ Mac OS X ➪ Runtime Configuration Guidelines.

Executable Code

Bundles can contain executable code, as is the case for application, framework, and plug-in bundles. Executable files live in a special directory named after the system for which the code is intended. Mac OS X defines two such directories: `MacOS` for native Mac OS X programs and `MacOSClassic` for programs that must run natively on Mac OS 9 or earlier. This mechanism allows one bundle to contain code that runs natively on Mac OS X and earlier systems.

Modern Macintosh computers use Intel processors — the same processors used by Windows PCs. Older Macintosh systems used PowerPC (PPC) processors. It's worth mentioning that a single native Mac OS X executable in this `MacOS` directory can potentially run on either Intel or PPC systems. Apple calls programs built to run on both kinds of Mac systems *universal binaries*. This architectural variance was built into the binary file format, not into the bundle format, as was the case of classic Mac OS support.

As of Snow Leopard, Apple has dropped support for PPC Macintoshes, so the era of the universal binary may be drawing to a close. Apple dropped support for the Classic Mac OS runtime environment in Mac OS X much earlier — around the time of the Intel transition. But the flexibility is there in case you ever need it.

Global Resources

All bundles support *global resources*, which are files required by the bundle regardless of what platform or localization the bundle is running under. For example, global resources might include file icons, images, sounds, and other resources that don't need to be translated. Global resources live in a `Resources` directory inside the bundle's `Content` directory.

The system provides functions for searching a bundle's contents for its resources. These functions will always find global resources before returning other kinds of resources, so don't think of global resources as a "default" resources available when all else fails. Global resources are meant to be truly localization independent.

Localized Resources

In contrast to global resources, *localized resources* are meant to contain resources that are appropriate only for a specific language or locale. For example, localized resources might include UI (`.nib`) files, Unicode strings (`.strings`) files, and other resources that may need to be translated into other languages.

Localized resources live in *Language Project* directories, commonly known as *lprojs* (named for their .lproj file extension), which live in the bundle's Resources directory. Language project directories gather up resources for a specific language or locale into a single directory named after that language or locale. For example, files appropriate for English speakers will be grouped together into an English.lproj directory.

Again, the system provides functions for searching bundles for localized resources, assuming a global version of the resource does not exist. The system searches for localizations according to the user's settings in the International System Preferences pane. By separating code and global resources from resources that need to be localized, it's easy to see how Mac OS X makes it easy to support single applications that can seamlessly run in many languages.

Although technically any bundle can hold localized resources, document bundles normally are not localized.

EXAMINING APPLICATION BUNDLES

Although the Finder goes out of its way to display bundles as files, it does provide some tools for peeking into package contents. You can open the bundle directly and examine the entire application bundle.

Unix commands make no attempt to disguise the true nature of application bundles — the very concept of bundles is alien to a Unix system. Terminal is another good way to reveal the contents of an application.

In the Try It Out example that follows, you use both the Finder and Terminal to examine the contents of the Mail Application's bundle.

TRY IT OUT   Examining the Mail Application

1. In the Finder, select /Applications/Mail.

2. Control-click the Mail application's icon. A contextual menu appears.

3. Select the Show Package Contents menu item. A new Finder window appears and contains a folder named Contents.

4. Select the Contents folder.

5. If necessary, change the window to Column mode by choosing View ➪ As Columns. The Finder window displays a number of files and folders, as shown in Figure 5-1.

6. Select the MacOS directory. Inside you will see a single file named Mail.

7. Select that Mail file. The Finder claims Mail is a Unix executable file.

FIGURE 5-1

8. Scroll the Finder window to the left if necessary and select `Contents/Resources`. This directory is full of all kinds of files: AppleScript files, image files saved in TIFF format, `lproj` directories, and so on. Figure 5-2 shows a few of those files.

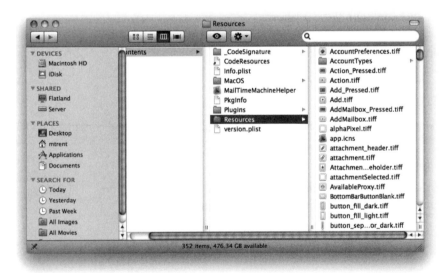

FIGURE 5-2

9. Scroll down until you see an `lproj` directory and select it. Figure 5-3 shows the Finder window with `da.lproj` selected. The `lproj` directory contains a number of other files, primarily Interface Builder and Strings files.

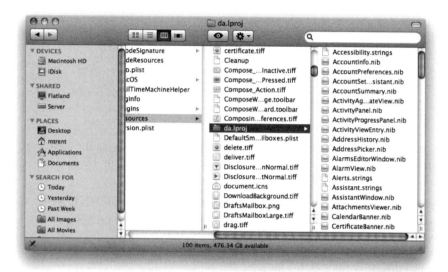

FIGURE 5-3

10. Close this window.

11. Launch `/Applications/Utilities/Terminal`.

12. Change the current directory to `/Applications` using the `cd` command as follows:

```
Macintosh:~ sample$ cd /Applications
Macintosh:Applications sample$
```

13. Type **find Mail.app**. Pages of information will scroll by. You can use Terminal's scrollbar to go back and see the whole list. Here is a portion of the results:

```
Macintosh:/Applications sample$ find Mail.app
Mail.app
Mail.app/Contents
Mail.app/Contents/_CodeSignature
Mail.app/Contents/_CodeSignature/CodeResources
Mail.app/Contents/CodeResources
Mail.app/Contents/Info.plist
Mail.app/Contents/MacOS
Mail.app/Contents/MacOS/Mail
Mail.app/Contents/MailTimeMachineHelper.app
```

```
Mail.app/Contents/MailTimeMachineHelper.app/Contents
Mail.app/Contents/MailTimeMachineHelper.app/Contents/_CodeSignature
Mail.app/Contents/MailTimeMachineHelper.app/Contents/_CodeSignature/CodeResources
Mail.app/Contents/MailTimeMachineHelper.app/Contents/CodeResources
Mail.app/Contents/MailTimeMachineHelper.app/Contents/Info.plist
Mail.app/Contents/MailTimeMachineHelper.app/Contents/MacOS
Mail.app/Contents/MailTimeMachineHelper.app/Contents/MacOS/MailTimeMachineHelper
Mail.app/Contents/MailTimeMachineHelper.app/Contents/PkgInfo
Mail.app/Contents/MailTimeMachineHelper.app/Contents/Resources
[ . . . ]
```

14. Quit Terminal.

How It Works

When you run an application, the Finder looks inside the application's bundle and selects the appropriate executable for your system. In the preceding case of Mail, there was only one executable file: `Mail.app/Contents/MacOS/Mail`. That executable file is the "real" Mail program.

Also, when you run an application, the system decides which language to use. This choice is driven by your settings in the Language & Text System Preferences pane and by the `lproj`s available in your application. The system goes through each language in the Language & Text preference pane's list in order until it finds an `lproj` for that language; the system picks the first `lproj` it finds. The application then uses the files in that `lproj` directory for its UI. This selection process is all automatic; the application programmer only needs to make sure localized resources are available for a given language. In the case of Mail, the system looks for localized resources in `Mail.app/Contents/Resources/English.lproj` when running in English. The system pulls resources from only one localization; it does not mix and match resources from multiple localizations.

The other files that make up the Mail application live in the global resources directory, `Mail.app/Contents/Resources`. The files stored in this directory do not contain language-specific information. In this example, the global resource directory contains a lot of TIFF images (`.tiff`), icon files (`.icns`), and so on. Normally, image files display the same image regardless of language, so they are commonly treated as global resources.

The Finder provides a contextual menu command for opening up a bundle and seeing its contents. This is useful for all kinds of bundles that masquerade as files, not just applications.

The Unix `find` command walks down a directory tree and performs a variety of operations on the files and directories it finds. In this example, you told `find` to walk through the entire `Mail.app` directory tree and print the path to each file or directory therein. People new to Unix commands are often confused by `find` because its name suggests it scrounges through directories looking for specific files ("find me this file!"). Although `find` can do that, it is capable of a whole lot more; you may discover that even the basic way you used `find` in this example is extremely useful. When you have some time, read through `find`'s man page entry to learn what it is capable of.

BUILDING AN APPLICATION BUNDLE

Bundles are basically directories, and building a bundle could be as simple as just creating a folder in the Finder. However, much of the bundle's power is wrapped up in its specific directory tree and `Info.plist` file. Xcode manages most of the complexity of building bundles for you as part of your project build process.

In the following Try It Out, you explore this capability in Xcode by building the project and application bundle for the Slide Master application. If you haven't already done so, you will want to download the Slide Master source from `www.wrox.com`. You can use our copy of Slide Master to copy from if you get into trouble. You can also pull icons and other resources out from our copy.

TRY IT OUT Building the Slide Master Bundle

1. In Xcode, create a new Cocoa document-based Application project named **Slide Master**. Make sure the Create Document-Based Application is checked before you click the Choose button, as shown in Figure 5-4.

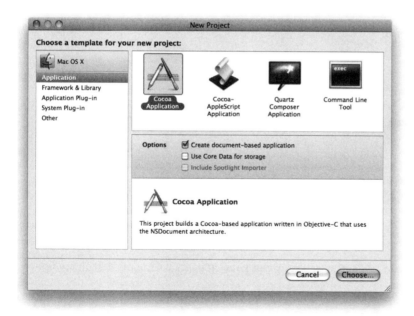

FIGURE 5-4

2. Build and run the new project. After a few moments of building, your new Slide Master application appears. Right now the application just displays a window saying `Your document contents here`. Slide Master appears in the Dock using a generic app icon, as shown in Figure 5-5.

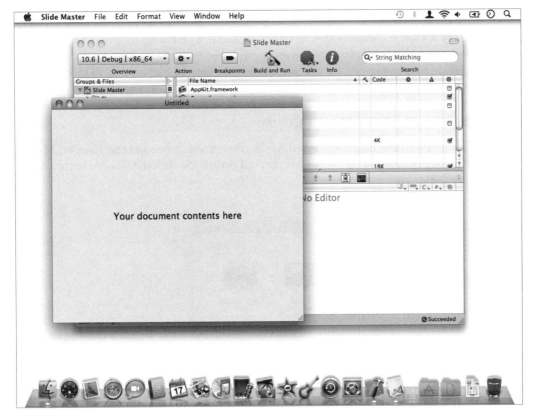

FIGURE 5-5

3. Choose Slide Master ➪ About Slide Master. An About panel appears with some default credits and the generic app icon.

4. Quit Slide Master.

5. In Terminal, type **cd** but don't press return. Make sure you leave a space after the **cd** command.

6. In the Finder, locate your new Slide Master program. If you're not sure where it might be, search for **Slide Master.app** in your Xcode project window, select it from the list, and choose Reveal In Finder from the Action menu in Xcode's toolbar.

7. Drag the Slide Master icon from Finder into your Terminal window. The path to the application appears on your Terminal command line, resembling Figure 5-6. Your results will differ depending on where your Slide Master project lives. Normally you will find your built programs in a new directory called `build` inside your project directory.

FIGURE 5-6

8. Press Return to change the current directory to that of your application bundle.

9. Enter **find .** to list the entire contents of your bundle. The list should resemble the following:

```
.
./Contents
./Contents/Info.plist
./Contents/MacOS
./Contents/MacOS/Slide Master
./Contents/PkgInfo
./Contents/Resources
./Contents/Resources/English.lproj
./Contents/Resources/English.lproj/Credits.rtf
./Contents/Resources/English.lproj/InfoPlist.strings
./Contents/Resources/English.lproj/MainMenu.nib
./Contents/Resources/English.lproj/MyDocument.nib
```

10. Switch back to Xcode and select Slide Master in the Groups & Files list. The file list changes to display the source files and other resources that make up your project.

11. Open `Credits.rtf`. This is where the credits you saw in step 3 came from. Go ahead and make the credits more meaningful to you. Then save and close the file.

12. Choose Project ⇨ Add To Project. A sheet appears where you can choose files to add.

13. Navigate to the Slide Master project you downloaded from www.wrox.com and select `appl.icns`. If you haven't downloaded the project yet, you can borrow TextEdit's icon from here: `/Developer/Examples/AppKit/TextEdit/Edit.icns`. When you select the file, the sheet shown in Figure 5-7 appears.

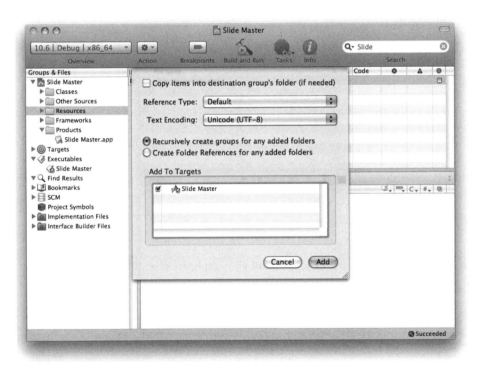

FIGURE 5-7

14. Check the Copy Items Into Destination Group's folder checkbox and click the Add button to dismiss the sheet. The file will appear in your Groups & Files list.

15. If necessary, rename the icon file to **appl.icns**.

16. Choose Project ⇨ Add To Project again and then add slim.icns to your project. Again, borrow from TextEdit if you don't have the Slide Master example project handy. Make sure you copy the file into your project.

17. Drag your icon files into the Resources group. Your project should resemble the one shown in Figure 5-8.

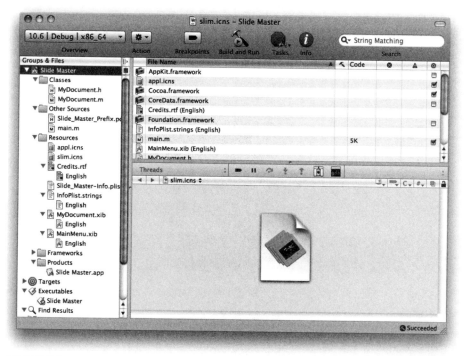

FIGURE 5-8

18. Open the Targets group in the Groups & Files list.

19. Select the item representing your Slide Master application.

20. Get information for this target by choosing File ⇨ Get Info. A Target Info window appears, displaying settings for your target.

21. Select the Build tab in the Target Info window. The window displays lists of build options, as shown in Figure 5-9. Note `Product Name` is set to `Slide Master` and `Wrapper Extension` is set to `app`.

FIGURE 5-9

22. Select the Properties tab in the Target Info window. You will now see an area where you can enter information about your application, as shown in Figure 5-10.

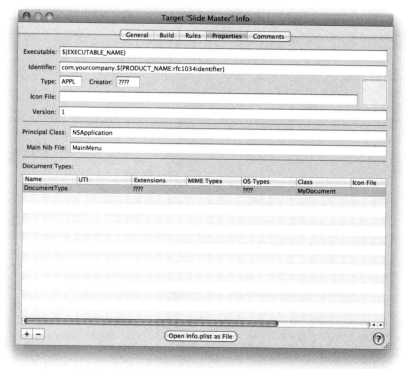

FIGURE 5-10

23. Change Identifier to **com.wrox.Slide Master**.

24. Change Icon File to **appl.icns**.

25. Change Creator to **slid**.

26. Change the Version to **1.0**. Your Target Info window should now resemble the one shown in Figure 5-11.

27. Close the Target Info window.

28. Build and run the new project. After building, Slide Master should launch and your icon should appear in the Dock.

29. Choose Slide Master ⇨ About Slide Master. The About panel now uses your application icon and your updated credits text.

30. Choose File ⇨ Open. An Open panel appears, allowing you to browse for files. However, all the files will be grayed out and unselectable.

31. Cancel out of the Open panel and quit Slide Master.

FIGURE 5-11

32. Re-open the Target Info window by double-clicking the Slide Master target; if necessary, select the Properties tab. Notice a table named Document Types at the bottom of the window. The table has one entry, for a document named `DocumentType`.

33. Change the entry for `DocumentType` to match the information in Figure 5-12.

FIGURE 5-12

34. Build and run the new project. After building, Slide Master should launch.

35. Choose File ⇨ Open. An Open panel should now allow you to select files ending with a `.slim` extension. If you don't happen to have any `.slim` files, save some slideshows from the version of Slide Master you downloaded off the Web. If you haven't downloaded Slide Master yet, just use TextEdit to create a text file with a `.slim` extension.

36. Open a slideshow file. Again, your placeholder window appears.

37. Quit Slide Master.

38. Find and open the `Slide_Master-Info.plist` file in Xcode's Groups & Files list. If you have trouble, select the Slide Master project group and enter **Info** in the toolbar's Search field. When you open the file, a Property List editor appears, displaying the contents of your file; it should resemble the one shown in Figure 5-13. You will see that the results in this file match the values you entered into your target's Info panel shown in Figure 5-12.

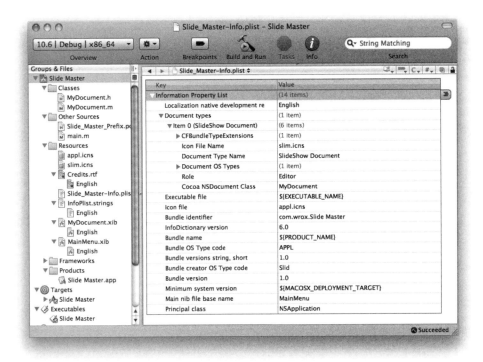

FIGURE 5-13

How It Works

Slide Master works with slideshow documents (`.slim` files), so the Cocoa Document-Based Application template is the logical choice for your project. This project template is set up to emit a complete Cocoa application at build time. When you built the project, Xcode laid out Slide Master's bundle directory structure and copied default resources into it. The result is a normal application, although it doesn't do much yet.

Much of your program's bundle is derived from its project files. For example, your application's credits file and icon are stored in files embedded in the application bundle. In fact, your entire UI is copied into the application bundle. The bundle also includes information about what document types your program will recognize, and what icon to use for those types. This document-binding information is stored in the bundle's `Info.plist` file. Xcode stores your `Info.plist` as `Slide_Master-Info.plist` in your project, and it renames it to `Info.plist` during the build process.

If necessary, you can change key details of your bundle from the Build tab in Xcode's Target Info window. For example, you can customize your bundle's extension or rename your `Info.plist` file to something else. Normally, you don't need this kind of control for applications and frameworks, but plug-in bundles often use custom file extensions.

Xcode provides several ways to modify your `Info.plist` file. One way is to use the Properties tab in Xcode's Target Info window, which is convenient for projects that do not require anything special of their `Info.plist` file. Alternatively, you can simply open your project's `Info.plist` file in a source editor and view its contents as a property list. This is useful for those projects that require custom settings in their `Info.plist` file. Remember that the `Info.plist` file can contain any number of data keys, not just those shown here.

Navigating through deep directory trees can be a tedious task in Terminal, for novice and expert users alike. Terminal and the Unix shell include a number of shortcuts that make this chore easier. One such shortcut is the capability to drag files and folders into Terminal instead of typing their entire path. This allows those comfortable with the Finder to save a bit of typing.

The Slide Master icons have unusual names: `appl.icns`, `slim.icns`, and so on. These files have been named after the OS type that those icons represent. For example, `appl` represents the application and `slim` represents slideshow documents. This is not a requirement by Xcode or the system; it is merely a way to remember what each icon is for. You can name icons whatever you like, provided you enter the proper filename in your program's `Info.plist`.

APPLICATION PREFERENCES

Most programs provide a preferences panel that allows users to customize the application to fit their needs. By convention, applications are supposed to store their preferences in a specific place with a specific file format. The system also provides tools that encourage developers to enforce these conventions.

TRY IT OUT   **Examining Preference Files**

1. Launch `/Applications/TextEdit`. TextEdit displays a new, untitled text document.

2. Choose TextEdit ➪ Preferences. A Preferences window appears, as shown in Figure 5-14.

3. Click the Restore All Defaults button. This returns TextEdit's preferences to what they were when Mac OS X was first installed. If you have already customized TextEdit's preferences, you might write down your settings so that you can restore them later.

4. Close the Preferences window.

5. Enter some text in the text document. Anything will do; you just need enough text for TextEdit to note that the document needs to be saved.

6. Save the document to the Desktop. Name it **Document**.

7. Quit TextEdit.

8. In the Finder go to the `Library/Preferences` directory in your home directory. You will see a number of files and folders. The majority of files are property lists, or `.plist` files.

9. Open the `com.apple.TextEdit.plist` file. The file should open in a program called Property List Editor, as shown in Figure 5-15.

10. If necessary, Option-click the disclosure triangle next to the Root entry. The outline expands to show the entire contents of the `.plist` file.

11. Quit Property List Editor.

12. Launch `/Applications/Utilities/Terminal`, or switch to it if it is already running.

13. Enter **defaults read com.apple.TextEdit**. Terminal displays some data in an ordered fashion, as illustrated in the following code (your results may not match this exactly):

FIGURE 5-14

```
[Zazredia:~] mtrent% defaults read com.apple.TextEdit
{
    NSNavBrowserPreferedColumnContentWidth = 186;
    NSNavLastRootDirectory = "~/Desktop";
    NSNavPanelExpandedSizeForSaveMode = "{537, 422}";
    NSNavPanelExpandedStateForSaveMode = 1;
}
```

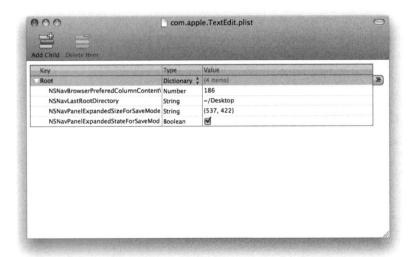

FIGURE 5-15

14. Launch TextEdit again and open the Preferences window.

15. Uncheck the Delete Backup File checkbox found on the Open And Save tab and close the Preferences window.

16. Quit TextEdit.

17. In Terminal, enter **defaults read com.apple.TextEdit** again. The output of the `defaults` command will change to resemble the following:

```
[Macintosh:~] sample% defaults read com.apple.TextEdit
{
    DeleteBackup = 0;
    NSNavBrowserPreferedColumnContentWidth = 186;
    NSNavLastRootDirectory = "~/Desktop";
    NSNavPanelExpandedSizeForSaveMode = "{537, 422}";
    NSNavPanelExpandedStateForSaveMode = 1;
}
```

18. Enter **defaults write com.apple.TextEdit DeleteBackup 1**. Terminal should accept this command without comment.

19. Again enter **defaults read com.apple.TextEdit**. The results should resemble the following:

```
[Macintosh:~] sample% defaults write com.apple.TextEdit DeleteBackup 1
[Macintosh:~] sample% defaults read com.apple.TextEdit
{
    DeleteBackup = 1;
[ ... ]
```

20. Launch TextEdit and open the Preferences window. The Delete Backup File checkbox is selected again.

21. Quit TextEdit.

22. In Terminal, enter **defaults read com.apple.screensaver**. An error message appears, claiming that the `com.apple.screensaver` domain doesn't exist.

23. Enter **defaults -currentHost read com.apple.screensaver**. Some Screen Saver settings should appear. If they don't, change your Screen Saver settings in System Preferences and try again.

24. Enter **ls ~/Library/Preferences/ByHost**. You will see a number of files, including one beginning with `com.apple.screensaver` as shown here:

```
[Zazredia:~] mtrent% defaults -currentHost read com.apple.screensaver
{
    CleanExit = YES;
    PrefsVersion = 100;
    moduleDict =     {
        moduleName = Arabesque;
```

```
            path = "/System/Library/Screen Savers/Arabesque.qtz";
            type = 1;
        };
    }
    [ ... ]
```

How It Works

Most applications store preferences of some kind. Normally, preferences are edited in an application's Preferences pane. Other settings might be set more transparently, such as an application that remembers its window positions. Mac OS X will even save some settings on an application's behalf, such as open panel settings.

Normally, your application preferences are stored in your `Library/Preferences` directory. By designating a place for preferences to be stored, the system makes it easy for you to manage your own preference files (for example, by removing old preferences if necessary) and discourages applications from writing preferences in other, less appropriate, places.

Actually, Mac OS X defines a number of places in which programs can store preference files. Consider that a Mac OS X system might have multiple user accounts. Because preferences are generally user-specific, each user has his or her own collection of preferences. However, some preferences may be appropriate for all users on the system. Also consider that in larger networked environments, home directories might live on a file server, and the user might share the same home directory among several computers. Some preferences may be appropriate only for a specific system, whereas other preferences might be shared among all systems. The following table outlines the various `Preferences` directories on a Mac OS X system.

DIRECTORY	PURPOSE
`~/Library/Preferences`	Normally, user preferences are saved into their `Library/Preferences` directory. In large networked environments, these settings are appropriate for all machines that the user might log into. This is the most common location for preferences on a Mac OS X system.
`~/Library/Preferences/ByHost`	User preferences specific to a particular machine are stored in a `ByHost` subdirectory of the user's `Preferences` directory. For example, screen savers tend to make assumptions based on a computer's display hardware, and thus save machine-specific preferences. Normally, these machine-specific preference files are tagged with the computer's primary Ethernet address as a simple means of uniquely identifying individual computers.

DIRECTORY	PURPOSE
`/Library/Preferences`	Preferences specific to all users on a given system are saved in the system-wide `/Library/Preferences` directory. For example, preferences related to starting up your computer or for running Software Update are stored here. But in general, such settings are rare.
`/Network/Library/Preferences`	In large networked environments, preferences intended for all users on all machines can be written to a special file server directory found at `/Network/Library/Preferences`. These settings, too, are rare.

In addition to providing common places for saving preference files, Mac OS X provides a common file format for saving preference data: the property list. As you saw in the `Info.plist`, property lists can hold a wide variety of structured data. This makes property lists ideal for storing application preferences as well.

Preferences are meant to be created lazily. Application installers shouldn't install preference files along with other file data; instead, application preferences should be created by the application when the user actually sets a preference. In addition, the application doesn't need to write out every preference value when it saves a file; it can write out only values that differ from the default settings. You saw this when looking at TextEdit's preferences: the `DeleteBackup` key was absent when it had nothing meaningful to store. Of course, you were able to manually set `DeleteBackup` to its default value, but you could also have simply removed the `DeleteBackup` key entirely.

Applications that use Mac OS X's built-in preferences system benefit from a number of features. One of these benefits is a convenient API for working with preferences files. In the case of Cocoa applications, the system takes care of reading and writing your preferences automatically; the application only needs to work with the preference values themselves. You learn more about these APIs in Chapter 8.

Another benefit of using Mac OS X's built-in preferences system is that a number of tools exist for working with preference files. These tools include the Property List Editor application and the `defaults` command-line tool you saw in this example. Property List Editor is a normal document-based application that works with property list files in general. The `defaults` tool is specifically designed to work with preference files. When using `defaults`, you reference settings by their preference domain rather than by filename. An application's preference domain is normally the same as its `CFBundleIdentifier`. You can use the `-currentHost` flag to easily distinguish between normal and machine-specific preferences. You can learn more about the `defaults` command by reading its man page.

You may have noticed that the `defaults` command displays preference information in an unusual format. Normally, property list files are a binary container format. The `defaults` command appears to display the same data, but in a format using square and curly brackets to designate groups of values. It turns out that this is actually an obsolete version of the property list file, used in systems prior to Mac OS X. In earlier Mac OS X versions, Apple used a more modern XML format for property lists, but as of Snow Leopard, it looks as if the binary format has completely replaced the XML format.

Both Property List Editor and `defaults` allow you to change the content of your preference files. This comes with a quick word of caution. Although the property list format is common to most preference files, the semantic meaning of the content of the property list is specific to the application that wrote the file. Editing an application's preference file by hand may cause that application to misbehave or crash if you make an inappropriate change. If you get into trouble with a corrupt or damaged preference file, just delete it; the application creates a new one.

Not all applications follow these conventions. Some applications write their own preference file format to the `Library/Preferences` directory; some store their files in other places entirely. This can actually cause problems for certain kinds of Macintosh environments. For example, many administration tools make use of the standard preference locations and file formats to allow system administrators to easily configure entire rooms of Macintosh computers at once. Applications that do not save preferences in standard locations using the standard format will not play well with these tools.

SUMMARY

In this chapter, you learned that

➤   Mac OS X uses bundles to wrap a collection of files into self-contained directories that appear as files in Finder and other programs.

➤   Bundles store resources, including those intended for specific localizations.

➤   The system provides standard locations and file formats for storing preference files, and tools for viewing and editing them.

In the next chapter, you learn about the C programming language. C is commonly used in writing Unix programs, and it also forms the base of the Objective-C programming language used by Cocoa. Before proceeding, however, try the exercises that follow to test your understanding of the material covered in this chapter. You can find the solutions to these exercises in Appendix A.

EXERCISES

1.   You have seen how an application's bundle structure defines various properties for an application. Use the techniques for examining bundles you learned in this chapter to answer the following questions.

   a.   How many document types does the TextEdit application support?

   b.   What is the Preview application's bundle signature?

   c.   What is Terminal's bundle identifier?

d. Some document types actually are bundles rather than solitary files. Examine an Xcode project (bundles with an `.xcodeproj` extension). What kind of files might you find in an Xcode project?

e. What is the current bundle version of the AppKit framework?

2. The `defaults` command provides a convenient way for working with application preferences from Terminal. You can read and write preference values without having to manually find and edit the preference file. Use the `defaults` command to perform the following tasks; if necessary, check the `defaults` man page for help.

a. List all your machine-independent preference domains.

b. List all your machine-specific preference domains.

c. Display your Terminal preferences.

d. Create a new preference file called `MyExamplePref` with a single key `Autosave` set to `1`.

e. Add key `colors` to your `MyExamplePref` preferences with an array of values: `red, orange, yellow`.

f. Delete the Autosave key from your `MyExamplePref` preferences.

▶ **WHAT YOU LEARNED IN THIS CHAPTER**

Bundle	a directory structure containing multiple files, usually masquerading as a single file
Info.plist	a file found in most bundles containing common metadata such as the bundle's name and copyright string
Global Resources	files that are appropriate for all languages and locales, usually stored at the top level of a bundle
Localized Resources	files appropriate only for a specific language or locale, usually stored in an lproj directory within a bundle
Property List	files of type plist that can hold an arbitrary hierarchy of data on Mac OS X
User Preferences	property list files of application settings that are specific to a user
Host-Specific Preferences	property list files of application settings that are specific to a single computer
defaults	a command-line utility for reading and editing preference files

The C Language

WHAT YOU WILL LEARN IN THIS CHAPTER:

➤ How to write programs in the C programming language

➤ How to write C programs using the structured programming style used in the Mac OS X C frameworks, including Core Foundation, Quartz 2D, Core Audio, and OpenGL

C is probably the most successful programming language that there has ever been. Whether you realize it or not, most of the software you use daily has something to thank C for. Operating systems, such as Mac OS X, are invariably written in C, and most applications make use of one or more frameworks that are entirely written in C. Popular languages, such as Java, also take much of their syntax from C. Let's face it, apart from the fact that it is still very much in use today, C is the Latin of computer languages.

C also forms the basis of Objective-C , which is a more modern variant used for most new application development on Mac OS X. Objective-C is the core language for the Cocoa frameworks, which you learn about in Chapter 8.

Half the battle of learning to program new applications on Mac OS X is learning to program in Objective-C, which you learn about in Chapter 7. And more than half that battle is learning C. Objective-C is a superset of C, meaning it has everything that C has and a bit more. If you already know C, you are well on your way to mastering Objective-C and Cocoa development (which you learn about in Chapter 8).

In this chapter, you learn the basics of C, which will serve you well whether or not you continue to develop for Mac OS X. By the end, you should be able to read existing C code without too much trouble, and you will have the prerequisites to write programs in Objective-C.

A LITTLE HISTORY

C is the mother of many popular languages, including Objective-C, Java, and C++. Even scripting languages such as Perl owe much to this venerable old workhorse. C began its journey to greatness at Bell Labs in 1969, where Ken Thompson and Dennis Ritchie created it. It was used to write the first Unix operating system, from which Mac OS X ultimately descends. Other operating systems, such as Windows and Mac OS, also owe a lot to C.

In 1989, the American National Standards Institute (ANSI) published the first official standard for C. C was already very popular by this time, but standardization is always an important point in the history of a programming language. Before this, a watershed book by Brian Kernighan and Dennis Ritchie, *C Programming Language* (Prentice Hall, 1978), had become the de facto standard for C. In 1999, the International Standards Organization (ISO) published an update to the 1989 standard, known to developers as C99.

These days, C is used as a modern assembler. C was one of the first high-level languages, but relative to more modern programming languages such as Objective-C and Java, it is actually quite low-level. For programmers, it has transplanted much of the functionality of assembler and is often only used when performance is critical.

NOTE Assembler *is a very low-level language that is normally used only by computers as an intermediate step to producing object code, which can be run by the computer's CPU. In the early days of computers — and sometimes still today — a programmer often had to write assembler code for high performance because hand-written assembler code could sometimes yield more efficient code than a compiler produces.*

GETTING STARTED

Every C program begins execution in the main function. It is the first piece of code that is run, and it's responsible for ensuring that other parts of your code are executed appropriately. Sometimes a main function can be a few lines, as is often the case in software written with the Cocoa frameworks (which you learn about in Chapter 8). At other times it may constitute the whole program. Here is a simple example to get started:

```
#include <stdio.h>

int main (int argc, const char * argv[]) {
    printf("Why me? Why C?");
    return 0;
}
```

The first line in this snippet is called a *preprocessor directive.*

```
#include <stdio.h>
```

The preprocessor, which is explained in more detail later in this chapter, is a program that passes over the source code, modifying it, before the compiler is called to turn the program into binary *machine code* that the computer can run. This particular line tells the preprocessor to replace the directive with all the text from the file stdio.h. The file stdio.h is part of the standard C library, and the preprocessor automatically knows where to find it. This type of file is known as a *header file*, and it contains definitions that can be used in C programs. Header files are an important part of C, and you generally need to write many of them to define the functions and data structures in your programs.

The `main` function itself begins on the next line:

```
int main (int argc, const char * argv[]) {
```

The word `int` at the beginning of the line is known as the *return type*. It is the type of number that the `main` function returns to the environment in which it was started. For a `main` function, the return type is a whole number or *integer*, which is written as `int` in C. Returning a value of 0 from the `main` function indicates that the run was successful, and any non-zero value indicates an error occurred.

 NOTE *Returning 0 to indicate success may seem odd if you have worked with other programming languages. This oddity also carries over into Unix, which is based on C; Unix commands also return 0 to indicate success, with a non-zero value returned if an error arises.*

The `main` function is listed next to `int`, followed by a block of code in parentheses. This block of code is known as the *parameter list*. The `main` function can be passed a number of character strings by the environment that runs it. For example, if a program is started on the command line, a number of filenames or options that control the program's behavior could be passed to the `main` function. The parameter list contains *parameters*, in this case `argc` and `argv`. Parameters in turn are *variables*, which are entities in which you can store values. In this case, `argc` has the type `int`, which means it is an integer. Its value is the number of strings being passed to the `main` function. `argv` holds the character strings themselves. The type of `argv` is quite involved, so we leave that discussion for the later section "Characters and Strings."

The *body* of the `main` function is included between braces (that is, `{ . . . }`), and looks like this:

```
printf("Why me? Why C?");
return 0;
```

The first of these two lines is a *function call*. A *function* is a separate unit of code that you can jump to in order to carry out some task, before returning to the original point in the code. A function has a number of parameters, executes a block of source code, and returns a value. The function in this case is called `printf`, and its definition is in the header file `stdio.h` included earlier. This is a popular C function that prints a character string to the program's output. In this case, the text `Why me? Why C?` should appear in the output of the program when it is run.

The final line of the `main` function just returns the integer number 0. As explained earlier, this indicates to the environment running the program that it succeeded. The `return` statement is used to return values and exit the `main` function immediately.

Note that each line of code in the example `main` function ends in a semicolon. C does not assume a line has ended until it sees a semicolon, whether a return has been inserted or not. So this code is equivalent to the `return` statement previously used:

```
return
    0;
```

C makes no distinction between the two. Note that unlike some other languages, you do not need any character to indicate that a line continues. C takes the opposite approach — you need a character to indicate a line has ended.

In the next Try It Out, you compile your first C program with Xcode and run it. The program in question is an old favorite: Hello World. Xcode inserts a Hello World program whenever it creates a new C project.

TRYITOUT   Compiling and Running a C Program with Xcode

1. Create a new Command Line Tool project with Xcode. You can find Command Line Tool in the New Project panel under Application. Call the project **MyFirstMain.**

2. In the Groups & Files view on the left, open the Source group and click `main.c` so you can view its source in the editor.

3. You should already see the following code, which is inserted by Xcode:

Available for
download on
Wrox.com

```c
#include <stdio.h>

int main (int argc, const char * argv[]) {
    // insert code here . . .
    printf("Hello, World!\n");
    return 0;
}
```

code snippet MacOSXProg ch06/MyFirstMain/main.c

4. Compile and run this program by clicking the Build and Go toolbar item.

5. Bring up the Debugger Console (shown in Figure 6-1) by choosing Console from the Run menu.

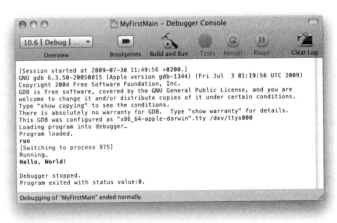

FIGURE 6-1

How It Works

This is an example of the infamous Hello World program that is the bane of every beginning programmer, whatever the language they are learning. It simply prints out "Hello, World!" when it is run, as you will have seen in the Debugger Console and can also see in Figure 6-1.

 NOTE *Apple, with its uncanny knack for fine details, has apparently spent more effort on punctuation than most in its Hello World program.*

The details of this example are very similar to the `main` function discussed earlier. This `main` function also uses the definitions provided in the header file `stdio.h`, and in particular, the function `printf`. The `main` function generated by Xcode includes a comment line, not present in the earlier example. The comment line looks like this:

```
// insert code here . . .
```

A *comment* is a message to the programmer, which is ignored by the compiler. The double forward slashes tell the compiler to ignore any text that appears up to the end of the line (that is, the next return character). The comment is telling you that the code given is disposable, and can be replaced by your own, which hopefully does something more useful than printing out "Hello, World!"

Apart from the text destined for display, the `printf` statement includes two extra characters that you may have found perplexing: `\n`. These two characters together in a C string indicate that a new line character should be inserted. C does not insert new line characters automatically after printing a string; you have control over where and when new lines appear in the output.

VARIABLES AND DATA TYPES

The `main` functions in the previous sections demonstrate that even the simplest of C programs include operations on data, even if it is just writing it to the program output. Any non-trivial program needs to represent different types of data, and reference it in a way that a programmer can understand. C has many built-in data types, including integer, decimal, and character types. To store and reference data, C has *variables*, which are labels applied to pieces of data.

You should already recognize the fundamental integer type of C: `int`. It appeared in the previous sections as the type of the variable: `argc`. An `int` is a whole number that can be positive, negative, or `0`. There are also other variations on the integer, including integers that cannot take negative values (`unsigned int`), integers that take up less space but have a more restricted range of values (`short int`), and integers that take up more space but can take a wider range of values (`long int`). The following table provides the most important integer types in C.

INTEGER TYPE	MINIMUM VALUE	MAXIMUM VALUE	SIZE IN BYTES
int	-2147483648	2147483647	4
short int	-32768	32767	2
long int	-2147483648	2147483647	4
unsigned int	0	4294967295	4

There are other variations on these types, but these are by far the most important and the ones you will encounter the most.

Now that you know what integer types are available, it would be nice to know how to use them. You can create integer *literals* in your code, which are values inserted directly, but you can also create integer *variables*, which can be used to store integers and change value while the program is running. Here is a piece of code to demonstrate some of the things you can do with integers:

```c
#include <stdio.h>

int main( int argc, const char * argv[]) {
    int var1;
    int var2, var3 = 5;
    var1 = 10;

    var2 = var1 * var3;
    printf("var2 is %d\n", var2);   // Should be 50

    unsigned int var4 = 4294967295;
    printf("var4 is %u\n", var4);   // Should be 4294967295

    var4 = var4 + 1;
    printf("var4 is %u\n", var4);   // Should be 0

    return 0;
}
```

code snippet MacOSXProg ch06/IntegerOperations/main.c

There is quite a lot happening in this code, so we will take it one step at a time, beginning with the variables at the start of the main function.

```c
int var1;
int var2, var3 = 5;
var1 = 10;
```

The first two lines are *declarations*: they declare the type of variable. In this case, the variables var1, var2, and var3 are all of the int type. var3 is not only declared, it is also initialized to the value 5, and so 5 is put in the memory associated with var3 when it is created. You can also see from the declaration of var2 and var3 that multiple variables of the same type can be declared on the same line if commas separate them.

WARNING *You may be wondering if the variable names chosen have any significance. The answer is no. They can be just about anything you like, with a few limitations: variable names can contain only alphanumeric characters and the underscore character, and variable names cannot begin with a number. Other than that, you are free to choose any variable names you like, but try to make them understandable so that others reading your code can follow it easily.*

The next two lines perform an arithmetic operation on the variables, and print the value of var2.

```
var2 = var1 * var3;
printf("var2 is %d\n", var2);  // Should be 50
```

var2 is first set to the value of var1 multiplied by var3, and then the printf function — which you were introduced to previously — prints the value of var2 to the program's output. The expected value is 50, or 10 by 5, as indicated in the comment.

 NOTE *Don't concern yourself with the form of the string passed to the* printf *function — the details are discussed later in this chapter in the section "Input/Output."*

The next lines introduce an unsigned integer variable and demonstrate what can happen if you are not wary of the range limitations in the preceding table:

```
unsigned int var4 = 4294967295;
printf("var4 is %u\n", var4);  // Should be 4294967295

var4 = var4 + 1;
printf("var4 is %u\n", var4);  // Should be 0
```

The variable var4 is declared and set to a very particular number. If you look to the preceding table, you will see that this is the maximum value in a range of unsigned integers. The next line prints var4, and the value should be as expected. However, var4 is then incremented by one, which takes it outside the range of allowed values for unsigned int. What happens? The program continues without error, but var4 *wraps* around to the lower limit of its range, namely 0. This behavior can be expected with all of C's numerical types, and you should be on your guard not to introduce hard-to-find bugs in this way.

 NOTE *The variable* var4 *was declared in the middle of the* main *function, not at the beginning. Some programming languages, including C originally, require that all declarations reside at the beginning of the function in which they appear. This has recently changed in the case of C so that you are allowed to declare variables anywhere in the code.*

You can't get far with integers alone, so C has a variety of decimal number types. These are referred to as *floating-point numbers* in C, because the decimal point is able to "float" to any position in the number. The following table shows the most important floating-point numbers you will encounter in C programs.

FLOATING-POINT TYPE	SMALLEST VALUE	LARGEST VALUE	SIZE IN BYTES
float	1.175494e-38	3.402823e+38	4
double	2.225074e-308	1.797693e+308	8

In this case, the largest negative number has not been presented, because it has the same magnitude as the largest value, but the smallest non-zero number has been given instead. Infinitely many decimal numbers exist, even between two values such as `0.0` and `1.175494e-38`, which are very close together. A computer can't represent any decimal number, so it uses the closest number it can find whenever a floating-point number arises that it can't represent exactly.

NOTE *If you already have experience with other programming languages, you may be wondering when we are going to discuss Boolean types. A Boolean value is one that can be true or false. Actually, C didn't originally have a Boolean type. Instead,* `0` *was treated as false, and any other number as true. This is still the common approach in C programs, though C99 did introduce a Boolean type to the language:* `bool`.

OPERATORS

In the previous examples, you saw some simple operators in use, adding and multiplying numbers and variables. C has a variety of different operators, some that you need to use nearly every time you sit down to program, and others that you rarely see. The following table shows some of the most important arithmetic and logical operators in C.

OPERATOR	SYMBOL	DESCRIPTION	EXAMPLE
Addition	+	Adds two numbers	5.46 + 7.2
Subtraction	–	Subtracts the second number from the first number	8 – 6
Multiplication	*	Multiplies two numbers	7 * 19.5
Division	/	Divides the first number by the second number	10 / 2
Modulus	%	Finds the remainder after integer division	11 % 2
Logical OR	||	True if one or both expressions are true	1 || 0
Logical AND	&&	Only true if both expressions are true	1 && 1
Not	!	True if the expression is false, and vice versa	!0

OPERATOR	SYMBOL	DESCRIPTION	EXAMPLE
Increment	++	Increases the integer variable by one	++i
Decrement	––	Decreases the integer variable by one	––i
Addition Assignment	+=	Adds the LHS to the RHS and assigns a value to the LHS	i += j
Subtraction Assignment	–=	Subtracts the LHS from the RHS and assigns a value to the LHS	i –= j
Assignment	=	Assigns a variable on the LHS to the RHS	i = 5
Equality	==	Tests if two values are equal	1 == 1
Inequality	!=	Tests if two values are not equal	1 != 1
Greater Than	>	Tests if the first value is greater than the second value	10 > 5
Less Than	<	Tests if the first value is less than the second value	10 < 5
Greater or Equal	>=	Tests if the first value is greater than or equal to the second value	10 >= 5
Less or Equal	<=	Tests if the first value is less than or equal to the second value	15 <= 19

LHS = Left-Hand Side
RHS = Right-Hand Side

The table begins with the usual suspects of arithmetic operators. These behave pretty much as you would expect. The only one to be wary of is the division operator. If you divide an integer number by another integer number, the result is always an integer, whether the numbers divide exactly or not. For example, in the following expression, the variable var ends up taking the value 2, not 2.2:

```
int var = 11 / 5;
```

Even in the following case, the variable will be 2.0, rather than 2.2:

```
float var = 11 / 5;
```

Integer division can lead to some very interesting bugs if you are not careful. A general rule of thumb for avoiding integer division is to make sure that when you want the correct floating-point number to come out of a division of two numbers, one of them has to be a floating-point number. Here are some ways you can ensure that:

```
float var1 = 11 / 5;      // No good! We want var1 to be 2.2, not 2.0
float var2 = 11.0 / 5;    // Fine. Now var2 is 2.2

float var3 = 11;
float var4 = var3 / 5;    // Again fine. var3 is a float, so float division is used.
```

If you are now cursing C for having ever been invented, note that sometimes you may actually want the result of an integer division. And furthermore, you may want the remainder left after the division. You can use the modulus operator in such instances, as shown in the following example:

```
int anInt = 5;
int divInt = anInt / 2;   // divInt will become 2
int modInt = anInt % 2;   // modInt will become 1
```

In this example, integer division is used to get the whole number of times that 2 goes into `anInt`, and the modulus gets the leftover. You could use the `modInt` value to test whether `anInt` is odd or even, for example.

Logical operators appear next in the table. These are most commonly used in tests. For example, in the following code, a number is tested to see if it is outside a given range:

```
if ( x < 0 || x > 5 ) printf("x is outside the range 0 to 5 inclusive.");
if ( x < 0 && x > 5 ) printf("Wrong! x can't be in two places at once.");
if ( x < 0 && !(x < -5) ) printf("x is -5, -4, -3, -2, or -1");
if ( x < 0 && x >= -5 ) printf("x is -5, -4, -3, -2, or -1 (again)");
```

The `if` statement, which tests an expression and carries out the corresponding action in the case of a true (non-zero) result, has been introduced here. The `if` statement is discussed in detail later in this chapter, but here it shows typical uses of logical operators. Each test compares the integer variable x with integer constants, such as 0 and 5, to see if the variable is in a given range. The first test, for example, checks whether x is less than 0 or greater than 5. If it is, a message is printed to indicate that x falls outside the range 0 to 5, inclusive.

The third `if` statement demonstrates the NOT operator. The test is whether x is less than 0 and not less than –5. In other words, this tests if x is greater than or equal to –5, and less than 0, as indicated by the next test. Note the brackets used with the NOT operator: these ensure that the expression x < -5 is evaluated before the NOT operator is applied. If you don't do this, you could get some unexpected results. For example, if x is equal to 6, then x < -5 should be false, so !(x < -5) will be true. But !x < -5 will be false! That's because the NOT operator has *precedence* over the less-than operator, so the expression will be evaluated similar to this: !x is evaluated first, and has the value 0 (false), because x is 6, which corresponds to true. So now the comparison is 0 < -5, which is false.

> **NOTE** *You need to be careful to consider operator precedence in your expressions, and use parentheses to enforce your will whenever in doubt. Precedence of operators is discussed later in this section.*

C has various operators for changing the value of a variable. The increment operator ++ is used to increase an integer by 1. The decrement operator – reduces an integer by 1. Any of the basic arithmetic operators can also be combined with an equals sign to produce an operator that first evaluates the right-hand side (RHS) of the expression, performs an operation between the left and right sides, and lastly, assigns the result to the variable on the left. Here are some examples of these types of operators:

```
int i = 5;
i++;        // i is now 6
i--;        // i is 5 again
i += 1;     // i is now 6
i *= 2;     // i is now 12, i.e., 6 * 2

int j = 2;
i -= j + 1;  // i is 9
```

The last two statements demonstrate clearly how these operators work. In the last expression, i is set as the value of itself minus the RHS. The following would be exactly equivalent:

```
i = i - (j + 1);
```

This is actually a good way to remember how these operators work. Simply imagine an expression using the assignment operator, =, in which the LHS also appears at the beginning of the RHS.

The remaining operators are fairly self-explanatory. There are the usual comparison operators, such as greater than, less than, greater than or equal, and less than or equal. The equality operator is ==, which you should be careful not to confuse with the assignment operator =. The following is a common bug made by beginning C programmers:

```
int a = 1, b = 2;
if ( a = b ) printf("a was equal to b");
```

If you think this code will not print anything, think again. The expression a = b sets a to the value of b, which is 2. The if statement tests the value of a after the assignment, which is non-zero, so the result of the test is considered to be true, and the printf statement is performed, printing the text.

One thing you may be wondering about is the order in which operators are evaluated in C, or the *operator precedence*. The following table gives the operators in order of precedence. Operators appearing in a given row have the same precedence, with the level of precedence decreasing down the table. Expressions are evaluated in order from the operator of highest precedence to that of lowest precedence. To override operator precedence, you can always turn to parentheses, the contents of which are evaluated before any operators.

OPERATOR PRECEDENCE
! ++ --
* / %
+ -
< <= >= >
== !=
&&
||
= += -=

Now that you know about simple data types and operators, it's time to move on to more advanced data types. In the next section, you learn about arrays and closely related types known as *pointers*, which enable you to store multiple data values in a single variable.

ARRAYS AND POINTERS

Integers and floating-point variables are useful to be sure, but what do you do if you need to represent lots of numbers of the same type? Coming up with unique variable names for each one could be quite tiresome. Take the following code, for example:

```
int var0 = 1;
int var1 = 5;
int var2 = 3;
int var3 = 2;
. . .
int var9 = 7;
```

If you had to make up variable names to represent a thousand values similar to this, you would soon lose any interest you might have had in writing C programs.

Luckily, C provides *array variables*, which are variables containing many values of the same data type. If you consider the preceding code, you will notice that each variable name starts with var and has a number appended to make it unique. Arrays work the same way, except the number, or *index*, is not part of the variable's name. Here is an example similar to the preceding code, but using an array instead of multiple, simple variables:

```
int var[10];
var[0] = 1;
var[1] = 5;
var[2] = 3;
var[3] = 2;
. . .
var[9] = 7;
```

The array variable var contains 10 integers. You can see that from the way it has been declared: the number 10 in square brackets is the size of the array. The indexes are used to access the *elements* of the array range between 0 and 9, and appear in the square brackets directly after the variable name. Array indexes in C always begin at 0; this differs from some other programming languages that begin counting at 1.

 NOTE *If the preceding examples have you wondering what the advantage of using arrays is over lots of different variables, you will have to wait until we get to the section on loops to find out. The advantage may not be evident looking at the examples so far, where each array element has been assigned on a separate line of code, but it will become clearer when you have a means of moving through the elements of an array without explicitly referring to each one individually.*

If you don't explicitly set the value of an array element, its value is undefined. It could have any value, and you shouldn't try to access its value until you have *initialized* it. There is a shorthand way of initializing an array that can save you typing in the same variable name over and over. When you declare the array, you can set its contents as this:

```
int var[10] = {1,5,3,2,2,3,4,5,6,7};
```

The numbers in the braces on the right are used to initialize the contents of the array var. Actually, the size of the array is even optional in this case, because the compiler can see how long the array should be from the number of entries used to initialize the array, so the following is also legal:

```
int var[] = {1,5,3,2,2,3,4,5,6,7};
```

You still need to include the square brackets to indicate that the variable is an array, but you do not need to enter the size of the array explicitly.

An array is stored as a block of *contiguous* memory, meaning there are no gaps in the data. The computer stores the numbers together, with var[1] just before var[2], which is just before var[3], and so forth. The C compiler calculates where a particular array element is by calculating how far it is *offset* from the beginning of the array. So the array is stored as the memory address of var[0], and whenever another element of the array is accessed, the compiler simply calculates how far it is from var[0], giving its address in memory. For example, var[2] is two steps from var[0], so it must be stored two memory addresses after the address of var[0].

In C, a variable that holds a memory address is known as a *pointer*. You can create pointers explicitly in your programs, and retrieve the pointer of any variable. You can also perform *pointer arithmetic*, calculating new pointers from existing ones. Here is some code to demonstrate basic properties of pointers:

```
int *p;
int a = 5;
p = &a;
printf("%d\n", *p);  // This should print 5

*p = 2;
printf("%d\n", a);   // This should print 2
```

A pointer is declared whenever an asterisk appears before the variable's name. In the preceding code, int *p; declares a pointer variable called p. This pointer points to the address in memory of an int. The value of p was not initialized, so you don't know what it is pointing to in the beginning, and you shouldn't use it until it has been assigned.

After declaring and initializing an int variable called a, the next line assigns the pointer to the address of a, similar to this:

```
p = &a;
```

The operator & is called the *address-of operator*. It gives the memory address of the variable it precedes, in this case a. This address has been assigned to the pointer p, so p points to a.

The value pointed to by p is printed next.

```
printf("%d\n", *p);
```

It is important to recognize the distinction between the pointer's value, which is an address in memory, and the value it points to, which is an int in this case. To access the pointer's value, you simply use the pointer variable, such as when the pointer was assigned to the address of a. When you want to access the value pointed to by the pointer, you need to *dereference* it by inserting an asterisk immediately in front of the pointer variable. This asterisk tells the compiler to use the value that the pointer points to, rather than the memory address stored in the pointer. Because p points to a's address, the value of a is printed, namely 5.

 WARNING *When you are first learning C, it is easy to confuse dereferencing a pointer with declaring a pointer because both use the asterisk character in the same way. You should try to make this distinction in your head early on: inserting an asterisk when declaring a variable indicates that the variable is a pointer to the type, and inserting an asterisk in other parts of the code indicates that the value pointed to by the pointer will be used, not the memory address stored in the pointer.*

Pointer dereferencing is demonstrated further on the next line of code:

```
*p = 2;
```

In this case, the value pointed to by p is set to 2. Because p points to the same memory as a, this will also change the value of a. When a is printed on the last line, the output should show 2 instead of the initial value of 5.

 NOTE *How big is a pointer variable? The answer depends on the type of computer and operating system you are using, and even the compiler settings that were used to compile an application. In early versions of Mac OS X, the size of a pointer was 32 bits, or 4 bytes. You may have heard the term 32-bit operating system; this refers to the size of the pointers used to store memory addresses. Mac OS X Snow Leopard has support for both 32-bit and 64-bit pointers, which makes it possible for an application to address much more memory. Snow Leopard is a 64-bit operating system.*

Pointers and arrays are closely related in C, as you may have gathered from the preceding discussion. An array is represented internally as a pointer to some memory, and in C programming, it is quite common to use the two interchangeably, as the following example shows:

```
int a[3];
*a = 2;       // Sets a[0]
*(a+1) = 5;   // Sets a[1]
*(a+2) = 10;  // Sets a[2]

int *p;
p = &a[1];
printf("%d\n", *p);     // Should print a[1], which is 5
printf("%d\n", *(p-1)); // Should print a[1-1], which is a[0], which is 2
```

An array a has been declared, but its contents have been set as if a were a pointer. That's because in C, an array and a pointer are equivalent. Take the first assignment:

```
*a = 2;
```

This sets the value pointed to by an int pointer to 2. The variable a points to the first element of the array — the element at index 0 — so setting *a sets the first element of a.

The next two lines are a little more involved:

```
*(a+1) = 5;   // Sets a[1]
*(a+2) = 10;  // Sets a[2]
```

You can do arithmetic with pointers, just as you can with integers. When you add an integer to a pointer, the result is a new pointer offset from the original by the amount added. Adding 1 to an int pointer results in the memory address of the next int in memory. Adding 2 results in a memory address that is 2 integers further in memory. In the example, *(a+1) is equivalent to a[0+1], which is a[1], so the value of a[1] is set to 5. The same logic can be applied to the line for *(a+2).

The last block of code in the example introduces a new pointer, p, which is set to the address of array element a[1], like this:

```
p = &a[1];
```

The right-hand side of this expression uses the address-of operator, &. It takes the address of the array element a[1], which means p is assigned the address of a[1]. You could also write the equivalent expression, like this:

```
p = a+1;
```

Hopefully the examples of pointer arithmetic have taught you enough to realize that these two expressions achieve the same end result.

The last two lines of the example print the value pointed to by p, and the int in the memory address preceding p. The latter is given by the expression *(p-1). This pointer arithmetic demonstrates that you aren't restricted to merely adding offsets to pointers, but you can also subtract them. You can even use operators such as ++ and – with pointers, as well as += and -=.

In the following Try It Out, you write a program to test your knowledge of pointer arithmetic. The program asks you questions about pointers used to access data stored in an array, and you enter the answers in the console. When you are finished, a score is printed to tell you how many you got right.

TRY IT OUT **Working with Pointers**

1. Create a new Command Line Tool project with Xcode and name it **Pointy**.

2. Open the `main` function in the editor by opening the Source group in the Groups & Files view and clicking the `main.c` file.

3. Replace the default code provided by Xcode with the following in `main.c`:

```c
#include <stdio.h>

/* Pointy is a program to test your pointer arithmetic.
   The user is asked to answer questions about the value pointed
   to by an integer pointer. */
int main (int argc, const char * argv[]) {

    printf("Pointy: A program to test your pointer arithmetic\n");

    int intArray[] = {10,20,30,40,50};
    printf("The variable intArray holds these values: %d %d %d %d %d\n",
        intArray[0], intArray[1], intArray[2], intArray[3], intArray[4] );

    int answer;
    int score = 0;

    // Question 1
    int *p;
    p = intArray + 3;
    printf("p is set to 'intArray + 3'. What is the value of *p? ");
    scanf("%d", &answer);
    if ( answer == *p ) {
        ++score;
        printf("Very good!\n");
    }
    else {
        printf("No, the answer is %d\n", *p);
    }

    // Question 2
    ++p;
    printf("After applying ++p, what is the value of *p? ");
    scanf("%d", &answer);
    if ( answer == *p ) {
        ++score;
        printf("Very good!\n");
    }
    else {
        printf("No, the answer is %d\n", *p);
    }

    // Question 3
    p = &intArray[4] - 1;
    printf("p is set to &intArray[4] - 1; What is the value of *p? ");
    scanf("%d", &answer);
```

```
if ( answer == *p ) {
    ++score;
    printf("Very good!\n");
}
else {
    printf("No, the answer is %d\n", *p);
}

printf("You got %d out of 3.\n", score);

return 0;
}
```

code snippet MacOSXProg ch06/Pointy/main.c

4. Build and run the program by clicking the Build and Go toolbar item.

5. Open the Debugger Console by choosing Console from the Run menu. You should see some introductory text and a question. Type the answer to the question, and the questions that follow, into the Debugger Console. Be sure to enter only integer values in response to the questions, or the program may behave unexpectedly.

6. You should be told after each question whether you have the answer correct, and at the end you will be told your score. Keep rerunning the program by clicking the Restart toolbar button in the Debugger Console window until you get all questions correct.

How It Works

The code for this example may seem complex at first, but it is very repetitive. It begins by initializing some data, and then asks three questions. The source code for each question is virtually identical, so only the code used to ask the first question is discussed.

 NOTE *Duplicating code that is the same or almost the same throughout your program is a bad idea, because when you need to change something, you need to track down all the different pieces of copied code and change those as well. This is a big waste of time and effort, and can introduce bugs. A better way is to write the code once in a function, and call the function at each point that you need to execute the code. Functions are discussed in more detail later in this chapter.*

Before the `main` function even starts, there is some introductory text in the form of a comment for the programmer. You have already seen single-line comments, which begin with a `//` and continue to the end of the line, but in this case the multiple-line variety is used. Multiple-line comments can be one or more lines, begin with the symbols `/*`, and end with `*/`. Anything in between is completely ignored by the compiler.

After printing an introductory message, the `main` function begins like this:

```
int intArray[] = {10,20,30,40,50};
printf("The variable intArray holds these values: %d %d %d %d %d\n",
    intArray[0], intArray[1], intArray[2], intArray[3], intArray[4] );

int answer;
int score = 0;
```

This initializes the variable `intArray` to be an array of integers, with five entries. The `printf` statement writes the values in the array to output, so that the user can see what is in the array and is able to answer the questions. Two other variables are also declared, `answer` and `score`. The `score` variable, which will be used to count how many questions are answered correctly, is initialized to 0. The `answer` variable is used to store the answers typed in by the user.

The code for the first question looks like this:

```
// Question 1
int *p;
p = intArray + 3;
printf("p is set to 'intArray + 3'. What is the value of *p? ");
scanf("%d", &answer);
if ( answer == *p ) {
    ++score;
    printf("Very good!\n");
}
else {
    printf("No, the answer is %d\n", *p);
}
```

A new pointer variable `p` is declared and set to be `intArray+3`. A `printf` statement then prompts the user to enter the answer to a question about `*p`, the value pointed to by `p`.

A second function, `scanf`, is used to read what the user types. `scanf` is also from the header file `stdio.h`, and reads anything entered on *standard input*, which in this case is what the user types on the keyboard. Do not concern yourself too much with the call to `scanf`; it simply expects to read an integer from input, and puts the value of the integer read into the `int` variable `answer`. You will learn more about `scanf` in the section "Input/Output" later in this chapter.

Another new construction is introduced on the next lines: the `if/else` statement. You have already seen `if` statements, and this is simply a variation on the theme. If the value in parentheses evaluates to a non-zero number, it is considered true, and the code in the braces following the `if` is evaluated. If the expression in the parentheses is 0, it is considered false, and the code in the braces after the `else` statement is evaluated instead. The `if/else` construction is described in detail later in this chapter.

In the preceding example, the value entered by the user, which is stored in the variable `answer`, is compared for equality with the value pointed to by `p`. If it is the same, the user was right, so the `score` variable is incremented and a congratulatory message is printed. If the user was wrong, the correct answer is printed, and the `score` variable is left unchanged.

After all questions have been answered, the program writes the user's score and stops.

CONDITIONAL BRANCHING

In the previous section, you became acquainted with *conditional branching*, whether you realized it or not. Branching occurs in a program when execution can jump to different parts of the code depending on the situation. The term *branching* refers to the way that program execution can follow different paths, like a monkey climbing a tree or someone rowing up a river. In the case of the `if/else` construction, the program chooses between jumping to the block of code just after the `if` statement or to the block of code after the `else` statement. The path followed depends on whether the condition in parentheses is true or false. This explains the "conditional" in "conditional branching": the branch followed depends on whether a condition is true or false.

Consider the following `if/else` construct:

```
if ( everestIsHigh ) {
    printf("Everest is apparently a high mountain");
}
else {
    printf("Which world do you call home?");
}
```

This is the same form of `if/else` used in the previous example. If the value in parentheses, `everestIsHigh`, evaluates to a non-zero value, the code in the `if` block will be evaluated; otherwise, the code in the `else` block is evaluated. Each code block is enclosed in braces, and may consist of zero or more statements. The placement of the braces is entirely at your discretion, because C ignores extra whitespace, including new lines. The following rewrite of the example is also perfectly legal, but not advisable:

```
if ( everestIsHigh ) { printf("Everest is apparently a high mountain"); } else
{
    printf("Which world do you originate from?"); }
```

Common conventions for brace placement include putting the opening brace at the end of a line and the end brace alone on a line, as in the first example in the preceding text, and putting each brace on a separate line, such as this:

```
if ( everestIsHigh )
{
    printf("Everest is apparently a high mountain");
}
else
{
    printf("Which world do you originate from?");
}
```

You may also see this variation:

```
if ( everestIsHigh )
    {
    printf("Everest is apparently a high mountain");
    }
else
    {
    printf("Which world do you originate from?");
    }
```

The point is that all these variations are legal in C. It is up to you to choose a style that makes your code legible for yourself and other programmers who may need to read your code.

If you have only a single statement in a code block, it is even possible to leave out the braces altogether, as in the following example:

```
if ( everestIsHigh )
    printf("Everest is apparently a high mountain");
else
    printf("Which world do you originate from?");
```

In practice, this can be a risky exercise, because if you ever need to add an extra statement to one or other of the code blocks, chances are you will forget to add the braces. Take a look at this code, for example:

```
if ( everestIsHigh )
    printf("Everest is apparently a high mountain");
else
    printf("Which world do you originate from?");
    ++i;
```

This code is equivalent to the following:

```
if ( everestIsHigh ) {
    printf("Everest is apparently a high mountain");
}
else {
    printf("Which world do you originate from?");
}
++i;
```

However, it is not equivalent to the following code, as you may have thought:

```
int everestIsHigh = 1;
if ( everestIsHigh ) {
    printf("Everest is apparently a high mountain");
}
else {
    printf("Which world do you originate from?");
    ++i;
}
```

It is reasonable, however, to leave out the braces when you use a solitary `if`, without an `else` branch, as shown in the following example:

```
if ( everestIsHigh ) ++highMountainCount;
```

You have already seen this form of `if` in many of the examples. It is fairly safe to use, because you are unlikely to accidentally forget to add braces when you add a new statement to the `if` block.

Often, you don't have only two different branches to choose from, but instead you have a whole range of choices. You can use `if/else if/else` constructions in such cases, as shown here:

```
float mountainHeight = 6000.0; // Height in feet

if ( mountainHeight > 15000.0 ) {
    printf("A monster!");
}
else if ( mountainHeight > 10000.0 ) {
    printf("I've seen bigger.");
}
else if ( mountainHeight > 5000.0 ) {
    printf("You call that a mountain!");
}
else {
    printf("Mountain? Or molehill?");
}
```

The `if/else if/else` construct is basically a number of `if` statements chained together, with an optional `else` at the end. The code following the first condition that evaluates to true is used, and all other code is skipped. In the example, the `mountainHeight` variable is tested to see if it is greater than `15000.0` feet. If so, `A monster!` is printed, and execution continues after the last `else` branch — all other branches are ignored. If the first test fails, the condition of the first `else if` is tested. If that is true, `I've seen bigger.` is printed and execution jumps to after the `else`, and so on. If none of the `else if` conditions evaluate to true, the code in the `else` block is performed.

C includes another conditional branching construction for choosing between discrete integer values: `switch/case`. The `if/else if/else` construction is general, and can be used whenever you have multiple branches. The `switch/case` construction is less general, but a bit more compact, and can help improve the legibility of your programs. Here is an example of `switch/case`:

```
int age = 3;
switch (age) {
    case 0:
        printf("Newborn\n");
        break;
    case 1:
        printf("Baby\n");
        break;
    case 2:
    case 3:
        printf("Toddler\n");
        break;
    case 4:
```

```
            printf("Pre-schooler\n");
            break;
        case 5:
            printf("School Kid\n");
            break;
        default:
            printf("That ain't no kid!\n");
    }
```

switch is used to branch based on the value of an integer variable. In the preceding example, the age of a child is represented as an integer. The switch statement tests the value of age against each case in order. The case statement includes a single integer value, followed by a colon. If the integer in the case equals the value of the variable in the switch, the code under the case is executed.

Despite what you might expect, after a case has been matched, all the code below that case is executed until a break statement is encountered, even if some or all of the code appears under a different case. The switch/case construction is different from if/else if/else in this sense, because after an if or else if block has been evaluated, execution automatically jumps to the end. With switch/case, you are responsible for making sure that the program jumps to the end when it should. You do this with the break keyword.

In the preceding example, case 2: appears immediately in front of case 3:, and includes no code of its own. If the child is two years old, execution continues from the case 2: branch to the case 3: branch, where Toddler\n gets printed. Only after the break statement does execution jump to the end of the switch. The other cases each have a single call to printf, followed by a break. The optional default block is equivalent to else: it gets executed if no other case matches.

The last conditional branching construction discussed here is actually an operator: a *ternary* operator. It is ternary because it has three parts. You can use the ternary operator as a shorthand way of choosing one value or another based on the value of a condition. Here it is in action:

```
// Ice cream id's
const int CHOCOLATE = 0;
const int STRAWBERRY = 1;

// People id's
const int MOM = 0;
const int DAD = 1;

// Set person
int person = DAD;

// Dad's favorite is Chocolate
int favorite;
favorite = ( person == DAD ? CHOCOLATE : STRAWBERRY );
```

The ternary operator appears at the end of this example:

```
person == DAD ? CHOCOLATE : STRAWBERRY
```

The ternary operator consists of a condition — in this case, the comparison between the variable person and the constant DAD — followed by a question mark, and then two expressions separated by a colon. The ternary operator is used here to set the value of the variable favorite, according to the value of person. If person is equal to DAD, favorite is set to the value of CHOCOLATE; otherwise, it is set to STRAWBERRY.

> **NOTE** *It is a good idea to enclose the ternary operator in parentheses when it is used in expressions like the previous one, because they help avoid surprises that can arise due to operator precedence.*

The ternary operator's condition appears before the question mark. If the condition evaluates to a non-zero value, it is considered true, and the value of the expression before the colon is evaluated and returned. If the condition evaluates to 0 (that is, false), the value of the expression after the colon is used.

To clarify matters, the statement containing the ternary operator in the preceding code is equivalent to the following more-verbose if/else construct:

```
if ( person == DAD ) {
    favorite = CHOCOLATE;
}
else {
    favorite = STRAWBERRY;
}
```

The ternary operator can be useful for writing more-compact code, when there are only two branches and branching is being used to set a variable or to evaluate part of a larger expression, as in the following:

```
const int FEET = 0;
const int INCHES = 1;
float height = 6.0;
int units = FEET;
float heightInInches = ( units == FEET ? 12 : 1 ) * height;
```

In this example, the ternary operator has been embedded in a larger expression, rather than being used to set a variable directly. The value of the variable units is compared with the value of the variable FEET. If the value of units is in feet, the ternary operator evaluates to 12; otherwise, it is 1. The operator thus chooses the conversion factor for multiplying by height. If the units are already inches, the conversion factor is 1, but if the height variable is in feet, it is multiplied by 12 to convert the value into inches.

You may have noticed the keyword const used in the preceding examples. It is not strictly necessary, but it can help prevent bugs. const tells the compiler that the value of a variable may not change after it has been initialized. If you try to change the value of a const, you will get an error from the compiler.

NOTE *Constant variables are often given names that are all capitalized. This is a convention to make code more readable, but it is not a requirement of the C language itself.*

LOOPS

If there is one thing that computers are good at, it is repetitive tasks. C has various constructs for repeating a block of code, which is known as *looping*. Looping is also a form of branching because at the end of a loop, execution can either continue or return to the beginning of the loop.

The simplest form of loop in C is the `while` loop. `while` keeps looping until a condition is no longer true. The condition is tested whenever execution returns to the beginning of the loop after each *iteration*. A `while` loop takes this form:

```
while ( condition ) {
    . . .
}
```

The order of events in a `while` loop goes as follows: When the `while` is encountered, the condition in parentheses is tested. If it is true, the block of code between the braces after `while` is executed, and execution jumps from the closing brace back to the `while` statement, where the condition is tested again. This continues until the condition evaluates to 0 (false), at which point execution jumps immediately after the last brace and continues.

Here is a concrete example of a `while` loop:

```
int i = 0;
while ( i < 2 ) {
    printf("%d\n", i);
    ++i;
}
```

The execution of this example code proceeds as follows:

1. When the `while` is first encountered, i is equal to 0, which is less than 2, so execution jumps to the code in the braces.

2. The `printf` statement is executed, printing 0 to standard output.

3. i is then incremented to 1.

4. At the closing brace, execution jumps back to `while`, and again performs the test. Because i is 1, and this is still less than 2, the code in the braces is executed again.

5. After execution has jumped back to `while` again, i is equal to 2. Because 2 is not less than 2, the condition is not met, so the program jumps to the last brace, and continues with the rest of the program. The code between the braces is not performed in this case.

A disadvantage of `while` loops is that if you are not careful, you can end up in an *infinite loop*. This arises when the condition in the `while` statement never evaluates to false, and no other provision for escaping the loop is made. Here is the simplest infinite loop we can think of:

```
while (1) {
}
```

If you run this code, and wait for it to end, you could be waiting a while (pardon the pun). Because 1 never equates to 0, the loop will never finish — it will be infinite.

 NOTE *This concept is so important to computing that Apple named its campus driveway after it. The street address of the Apple campus is 1 Infinite Loop.*

Nevertheless, you will occasionally see a `while` loop with its condition equal to 1. Does that mean such loops will never end? Not necessarily, because you can *break out* of a loop in other ways. The C command `break`, which you encountered in the context of `switch`/`case` statements, can also be used to escape a `while` loop, like this:

```
int i = 0;
while (1) {
    if ( i >= 5 ) break;
    printf("%d\n", i);
    ++i;
}
```

This code is actually equivalent to the first `while` loop example given previously. It will loop until i is greater than or equal to 5, at which point the `if` condition will evaluate to true, and the `break` will be performed. Execution then jumps immediately to the closing brace, and continues.

Another common loop in C programming is the `for loop`. In theory, you can do everything a `for` loop can do with a `while` loop, but the `for` loop is often easier to read and understand. The structure of a `for` loop is a little more complex, but after you get used to it, it is straightforward enough. It takes the following form:

```
for ( initialization; condition; update ) {
    . . .
}
```

As you can see, the `for` loop has parentheses just as the `while` loop does, but it expects more than just a single condition. Three entries are required, separated by semicolons. The first is an initialization statement, which is performed only once at the beginning. The second is a condition that determines whether the loop should continue or not, just like the while loop has. The last are statements that are executed at the beginning of each new iteration, which are usually used to update indexing variables.

A for loop typically looks something like this:

```
int i;
for ( i = 0; i < 2; i++ ) {
    printf("%d\n", i);
}
```

This code performs the same operations as the first example of while shown previously. The program flow goes like this:

1. When the for loop is first encountered, the initialization block is executed, setting i to 0.

2. The condition is then checked, and because i is less than 2, the code in the braces is executed.

3. The printf statement prints the value of i, which is 0, to standard output.

4. Control jumps from the closing brace back to the for statement. The update statement is executed first, incrementing i to 1.

5. Next the condition is tested. Because i is still less than 2, the code in braces is executed again, and 1 is printed.

6. When the for statement is encountered for the third time, the update operation increments i to 2. Then the condition is checked, but this time it is false, so control jumps immediately to the closing brace without performing the printf, and continues with the rest of the program.

for loops are most commonly used to perform operations on arrays. Here is an example of adding the elements of two arrays, and storing the result in a third:

```
int array1[] = {1,2,3,4,5};
int array2[] = {2,3,4,5,6};
int array3[5];

int i;
for ( i = 0; i < 5; ++i ) {
    array3[i] = array1[i] + array2[i];
}

for ( i = 0; i < 5; ++i ) printf("%d ", array3[i]);
printf("\n");
```

Arrays array1 and array2 are initialized to each hold five elements. The array array3 is given a size, but its elements are not initialized. The for loop loops over i values from 0 to 4 inclusive, executing the summation in braces, which sets the elements of array3 to the sum of the corresponding elements of array1 and array2. The last for loop prints the values of array3 one after the other, separated by a space. The last printf adds a new line character to the end.

NOTE The for *loop responsible for printing* array3 *does not include any braces. Braces are not necessary in this case because there is only one statement to be performed. This is a general aspect of C that you have already encountered for* if *statements.*

You should take careful notice of the form of the for loops used in the preceding code, because it is very common. Whenever you need to iterate over the elements of an array, you generally use a for statement with the following three characteristics:

➤ The index variable is initialized to 0, corresponding to the first element in the array.

➤ The condition expression requires that the index variable be less than the array length.

➤ The index is incremented after each iteration.

This structure is summarized by the following form:

```
int i;
for ( i = 0; i < array_length; ++i ) {
 . . .
}
```

If you stick to this formula for iterating array elements, you should rarely go astray.

 WARNING for *loops often lead to what are called off-by-one or fence-post bugs, particularly for beginner programmers. An off-by-one bug arises when the loop iterates one too many or too few times, either not treating all the array elements, or treating too many and going outside the bounds of the array. (The latter can lead to program crashes known as segmentation faults, because the segment of memory assigned to the array was exceeded.)*

The best way to avoid these types of bugs is to develop a convention that works, and always use that convention. The for *loop convention shown is a good example. If you always use* i < array_length, *for example, instead of sometimes using* i <= array_length - 1, *you are much less likely to make a mistake.*

In the following Try It Out, a program is developed that uses loops to perform a simple statistical analysis of some data stored in an array.

TRY IT OUT Statistical Analysis of Array Data

1. Create a new Command Line Tool project with Xcode and call it **Statistics.**

2. Open the file main.c in the editor by clicking it in the Groups & Files view. You can find it in the Source group.

3. Replace the default code inserted by Xcode with the following:

Available for
download on
Wrox.com

```c
#include <stdio.h>
#include <stdlib.h>

int main (int argc, const char * argv[]) {
    const int DATA_SIZE = 1000;
    float heightData[DATA_SIZE];

    // Initialize data randomly.
    int i;
    for ( i = 0; i < DATA_SIZE; ++i ) {
        float randNum = (float)rand() / RAND_MAX;   // From 0.0 to 1.0
        heightData[i] = 150.0 + ( randNum * 70.0 ); // 150.0 to 220.0 centimeters
    }

    // Calculate statistics
    float maxHeight = 0.0, minHeight = 1000.0;
    float sum = 0.0, average;
    for ( i = 0; i < DATA_SIZE; ++i ) {
        sum += heightData[i];
        if ( heightData[i] > maxHeight ) maxHeight = heightData[i];
        if ( heightData[i] < minHeight ) minHeight = heightData[i];
    }
    average = sum / DATA_SIZE;

    // Print results
    printf("Average Height (cm): %f\nMaximum Height (cm): %f\n"
            "Minimum Height (cm): %f\n",
        average, maxHeight, minHeight);
    return 0;
}
```

code snippet MacOSXProg ch06/Statistics/main.c

4. Click the Build and Go toolbar item to compile and run the program.

5. Open the Debugger Console by choosing Console from the Run menu, and verify that it contains results similar to, although not exactly the same as, what's shown in Figure 6-2.

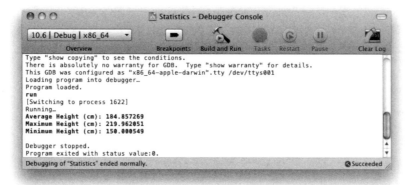

FIGURE 6-2

How It Works

This program calculates a number of statistics for a data array of the heights of 1,000 people, given in centimeters. Rather than use real data, the data is generated randomly within a realistic range of values. The statistics calculated are the average or mean, the maximum height, and the minimum height. You will need to use the techniques in this example many times in your C programming. For example, calculating the maximum or minimum value in an array is a very common programming task.

The declaration of the array holding the data makes use of a constant integer called DATA_SIZE.

```
const int DATA_SIZE = 1000;
float heightData[DATA_SIZE];
```

Using a constant like this is good practice. If instead of using a constant, you just typed 1000 anywhere in your program that the array size was needed, you would soon discover that changing the amount of data can be very inconvenient. You have to find every point in the code where you typed 1000, and change it to the new size. If you use a constant variable, as in the example, you have to change only the value of the constant whenever you want to change the size of your array. The rest of the program is automatically updated, because there is no reference to 1000, only to the constant variable.

The code to randomly initialize the height data looks like this:

```
// Initialize data randomly.
int i;
for ( i = 0; i < DATA_SIZE; ++i ) {
    float randNum = (float)rand() / RAND_MAX;  // From 0.0 to 1.0
    heightData[i] = 150.0 + ( randNum * 70.0 ); // 150.0 to 220.0 centimeters
}
```

This loops over the elements in the array. For each element, a random number between 0.0 and 1.0 is generated and put in the variable randNum. randNum is used to generate a value for the height between 150.0 and 220.0 centimeters, which is inserted in the heightData array.

NOTE *The function* `rand` *returns an* `int` *between 0 and the constant* `RAND_MAX`. *The declarations of both rand and* `RAND_MAX` *come from the* `stdlib.h` *file that has been included at the beginning of the program.*

To generate a random float between 0.0 and 1.0, the `int` returned by `rand` is first converted to a `float`, similar to this:

```
(float)rand()
```

This is called a *cast*. You force the compiler to convert the `int` from `rand` into a `float`. Putting a data type in parentheses, as this does, tells the compiler you want to cast the number or variable that follows to a different type.

The random `float` is divided by the `int` `RAND_MAX`, so the result is a `float` between 0.0 and 1.0. The floating-point number `randNum` is then used to generate a height between 150.0 and 220.0. You can verify for yourself that the code given achieves this result, if `randNum` is between 0.0 and 1.0.

The statistics are calculated in the second loop, as shown here:

```
// Calculate statistics
float maxHeight = 0.0, minHeight = 1000.0;
float sum = 0.0, average;
for ( i = 0; i < DATA_SIZE; ++i ) {
    sum += heightData[i];
    if ( heightData[i] > maxHeight ) maxHeight = heightData[i];
    if ( heightData[i] < minHeight ) minHeight = heightData[i];
}
average = sum / DATA_SIZE;
```

To calculate the average, the sum of all heights is first calculated and then divided by the total number of people. The variable `sum` is used to accumulate the sum of heights. It is first initialized to 0.0, and has `heightData[i]` added to each iteration of the loop. The variable `average` is set to `sum` divided by `DATA_SIZE` after the loop.

To calculate the maximum height, the variable `maxHeight` is used. It is first initialized to a very small height value, namely 0.0. In each iteration of the loop, `heightData[i]` is compared with the current value of `maxHeight`. If it is larger, `maxHeight` is set to `heightData[i]`, which is the new maximum height. If not, no action is taken. When the loop completes, `maxHeight` will hold the largest value in the array.

Evaluating the minimum height is similar, except the variable used to accumulate it, `minHeight`, is initialized to a very large value. Whenever `heightData[i]` is smaller than `minHeight`, `minHeight` is updated.

The last lines of the `main` function simply print out the values of `average`, `minHeight`, and `maxHeight`.

FUNCTIONS AND BLOCKS

Many of the examples you have seen thus far have included the `printf` statement, but what is `printf` exactly? `printf` is a *function* in the C standard library that prints a string to standard output. A function is a block of code that can be executed from any other point in your program. When you execute a function, you are said to be *calling* it. When you call a function, your program performs the code in the *function body*, before returning to the point of the call.

 WARNING *The standard library is a collection of functions and constants provided with every C compiler. It includes functions for reading and writing files, and manipulating strings, among other things. C programmers need to use the standard library in virtually every piece of code they write.*

Here is a simple example of a function, with calling code:

```c
#include <stdio.h>

int AddFunc(int a, int b) {
    return a + b;
}

int main( const int argc, const char *argv[] ) {
    printf("%d\n", AddFunc(1,2) );
    return 0;
}
```

This defines a function called `AddFunc`, which adds two `int`s together. The function has two *parameters*, which are called `a` and `b`. Parameters are variables that are initialized with values passed to the function when it is called. The values passed are called *arguments*, and in the preceding example, the arguments to `AddFunc` are 1 and 2, the numbers appearing in parentheses after `AddFunc` in the `printf` statement.

When the function `AddFunc` is called from inside the `printf` statement, it initializes the variables `a` and `b` to the values of the arguments passed, which in this case are 1 and 2. It then returns the value of `a + b`, which is 3, to the calling code. The *return value* is then used at the point in the code that the call was instigated, so in this case, the value 3 would be printed by `printf`.

Functions are not required to take any arguments, nor are they required to return anything. You can use the keyword `void` when there is nothing to return and/or to be passed in via the parameter list, like this:

```c
void DoNothingFunc( void ) {
}
```

You must use `void` when there is no return value, but the `void` in the parameter list is optional, so you could rewrite `DoNothingFunc` like this:

```
void DoNothingFunc() {
}
```

When a function is called, it must already be declared. You could try to keep all your functions in order, so each has been declared before any other function needs to call it, but this is a hassle, and, in certain cases, impossible. Instead, C allows you to declare a function without writing its body (or *implementation*). These function declarations are known as *signatures*.

It is possible in C for two functions to call one another, and even that a function call itself. (The latter is known as *recursion*.) In the case of two functions calling one another, it is not possible to declare each function before each call without using function signatures.

Here is an example in which two functions call one another, with both functions' signatures declared in the beginning:

```
#include <stdio.h>

// Function signatures
unsigned int calcSum(unsigned int n, unsigned int sum);
unsigned int addToSum(unsigned int n, unsigned int sum);

/* Adds the numbers from n to 10 to sum,
   and returns the result. */
unsigned int calcSum(unsigned int n, unsigned int sum) {
    if ( n > 10 )
        return sum;
    else
        return addToSum(n, sum);
}

// Used by calcSum
unsigned int addToSum(unsigned int n, unsigned int sum) {
    return calcSum(n+1, n+sum);
}

// Main function
int main() {
    printf( "%d\n", calcSum(1, 0) );
    return 0;
}
```

The mechanics of this example are quite involved, but the important thing for you to realize is that `calcSum` calls `addToSum`, even though `calcSum`'s implementation appears first. This is possible because `addToSum` has already been declared before the definition of `calcSum`, by means of a function signature at the beginning. The signature is nothing more or less than the interface that appears at the beginning of a function, which defines the function's name, parameter list, and return value.

Without going into too much detail, the example demonstrates a rather obscure way of adding the numbers from 1 to 10. calcSum is called first from main with the value 1 for the parameter n, and 0 for sum. Because n is not greater than 10, calcSum calls addToSum, passing 1 and 0 as arguments. addToSum calls back to calcSum, but passes the value of n+1 and n+sum as arguments. Back in calcSum, the new value of n is 2, and sum is 1. Because n is still not greater than 10, addToSum is again called, this time with 2 and 1 as arguments. This merry-go-round continues until n is greater than 10, at which point calcSum returns sum, which is the sum of numbers to that point.

This is a rather complex piece of recursion, and you should not worry yourself too much with it. It is only important that you understand that a function can call another function before it is defined, as long as its signature has been declared.

There is one more aspect of C functions that you should grasp before moving on, and it has to do with the arguments passed. C follows a convention known as *pass-by-value*. What this means in practice is that any argument passed to a function is copied before it is used in the function, and any changes you make to the corresponding parameter have no effect on the argument. Here is an example to demonstrate this important point:

```
void func(int param) {
    param = 5;
}

int main() {
    int a = 2;
    func(a);
    printf("%d\n", a);
    return 0;
}
```

The million-dollar question is: What will be printed? You may say 5, because when you call func, it sets param to 5, but alas you would be wrong. Because C uses pass-by-value, the argument a passed in main to func is copied, so that when the parameter param is modified in func, the original argument does not change. After returning to the main function, the variable a is still 2, and this is what gets printed.

But what if you want to change a variable passed to a function? How can you do it? The simple answer is that you must pass a pointer to the variable, rather than the variable itself. Here is the preceding example rewritten so that a really does get modified by func before returning to main:

```
void func(int *param) {
    *param = 5;
}

int main() {
    int a = 2;
    func(&a);
    printf("%d\n", a);
    return 0;
}
```

If you run this version of the program, 5 will be printed for the value of a. Notice that func now expects a pointer to an int. It sets the value pointed to by the pointer param to 5 by using the dereferencing operator *. The call to func uses the address-of operator & to pass a pointer to a, rather than a itself. When func sets the value pointed to by param to 5, it is actually setting a to 5, because param is a copy of the memory address of a.

When you pass a pointer to a function, the function receives a copy of the pointer, just as with any other type, but the data pointed to by the pointer is not copied. This means that you can allow a function to change a variable passed to it by passing the pointer to the variable, rather than the variable itself. The pointer will be copied, but the function will still be able to access the data pointed to by dereferencing the pointer copy.

The only exception to the pass-by-value rule is arrays. The contents of an array that gets passed to a function are not copied; instead, the array is passed as a pointer to its first element. This pointer is copied, but the array data is not. If the function makes changes to the data in the array, the array data will reflect these changes after the function returns.

Mac OS X v10.6 saw the introduction of a new construct to the C language: *blocks*. You can think of blocks as being inline, anonymous functions. Blocks have a parameter list and return value, just as functions do, but have no name.

The following example demonstrates some of the differences between functions and blocks:

```c
#include <stdio.h>

typedef float (^OperationBlock)(float val);

float Operate( OperationBlock block, float value ) {
    return block(value);
}

int main (int argc, const char *argv[]) {
    int maxIndex = 2;
    float f = 10.0;
    f = Operate(
        ^(float v){
            int j;
            for ( j = 0; j < maxIndex; ++j ) {
                v += j;
            }
            return v;
        }, f);
    printf("%f\n", f);    // Prints out 11.0

    return 0;
}
```

The block itself is the following piece of code:

```c
^(float v){
    int j;
    for ( j = 0; j < maxIndex; ++j ) {
```

```
        v += j;
    }
    return v;
}
```

It looks similar to a function definition, but has a caret (^) in place of a name. In this case, there is also no return type; the return type is optional for blocks, as long as the compiler can figure out what type it should be. A `float` variable is returned, so the compiler knows the return type must be `float`.

In the previous example, the block is passed as an argument to the function `Operate`. Blocks can be passed between program elements, and even stored in variables or arrays. The `Operate` function calls the block returning the result, like this:

```
float Operate( OperationBlock block, float value ) {
    return block(value);
}
```

The block parameter in the `Operate` function has the type `OperationBlock`, which is defined by a `typedef` as follows:

```
typedef float (^OperationBlock)(float val);
```

This rather convoluted form of type definition declares `OperationBlock` as a block type that returns a `float`, and takes a single `float` as an argument. Using `typedef`s such as this to declare block signatures can make the rest of your code considerably more readable.

There is one more aspect of blocks that distinguishes them from ordinary functions: a block can access variables defined in the scope in which it was defined. You can see this in the previous example. The variable `maxIndex` is used inside the block, even though it originates outside the block and is not passed through the argument list. This ability of blocks to "carry around" extra data means they can be used in ways that standard functions aren't.

 NOTE *Blocks are a new and advanced construct in Mac OS X, and can't be covered in depth here. However, they do play a very important role in Grand Central Dispatch, a technology introduced in Mac OS X v10.6, to help developers take full advantage of multi-core systems. If your code is performance-intensive, you should take a closer look at blocks.*

CHARACTERS AND STRINGS

Since beginning your sojourn into C, you have made use of many strings. Each `main` function gets passed an array of strings, for example, and every `printf` call has at least one string. Discussion of strings was put off until now because they are a bit more difficult to use than other basic data types such as `int` and `float`.

As you will undoubtedly have guessed, you can create a literal string by simply putting it between double quotation marks. But how do you declare a string variable? This is trickier, because a string variable is actually an array of characters, which have the type char in C.

char variables have a size of 1 byte. They can represent ASCII characters, which include letters and numbers, as well as punctuation. A literal char is a single character between single quotation marks. Here is an example of creating a char variable, and setting it to the letter A:

```
char cVar = 'A';
```

A char can also change its value, just as an int or float. You could change the value of cVar later in the program to b, like this:

```
cVar = 'b';
```

As with any variable, if you don't want the value of a character variable to change, you can make it constant, as shown in this example:

```
const char constCharVar = 'c';
```

Because an array is equivalent to a pointer to the first element of the array, and strings are just arrays of chars, strings are usually given the type char*. Here is an example of initializing a string:

```
char *myString = "Hello, World!";
```

This string can be printed like this:

```
printf("%s", myString);
```

To declare a string without initializing it to a literal value, you simply follow the same steps that you would take to declare an array. For example:

```
char anotherString[100]; // This string has room for 100 chars
```

But how do you set the characters in this array when the array has been declared? The first approach is to use the usual means of setting the elements in an array, such as this:

```
anotherString[0] = "H";
anotherString[1] = "e";
anotherString[2] = "l";
anotherString[3] = "l";
anotherString[4] = "o";
anotherString[5] = "\0";
```

Printing anotherString will result in Hello appearing in the output. Take careful note of the last character entered into the string, "\0". This is known as the *terminating null character*. Because C stores arrays as a simple pointer to the first element, it doesn't actually know how long they are after they are declared. Strings inherit this problem from arrays, so to tell the compiler where the string ends, you have to insert the terminating null character. The terminating null character has the special form of a backslash followed by a zero.

NOTE *You may have noticed that there was no terminating null character used in the previous literal strings. Literal strings have a terminating null character added automatically. The only thing you have to remember is to make enough space in your strings to accommodate this extra character. For example, if your literal string has 10 characters, and you want to copy its contents into a string variable, your variable needs to be at least 11 characters long to contain the 10 characters of the literal string and the terminating null character.*

Setting the characters in a string one-by-one, as in the preceding example, may only be convenient for certain applications. It wasn't very convenient in this particular case, for example. It would be better if you could just copy the contents of a literal string directly into the string variable. C doesn't provide direct language support for such an operation. The following, for example, will *not* copy the contents of a literal into a string variable, despite what you might expect:

```
char stringVar[10];
stringVar = "Hello";
```

What this code does is take the pointer corresponding to `stringVar`, and assign it to the address of the first `char` in the literal `"Hello"`. This is probably not what you want.

Even though there is no built-in language support for copying string contents, C provides functions to do so in its standard library. You need to include the file `string.h` to use these functions. Here is an example of copying a string with a function from `string.h`:

```
#include <string.h>
. . .
char stringVar[10];
strcpy(stringVar, "Hello");
```

`strcpy` copies the contents of the second string into the first, including the terminating null character. If there is no terminating null character in the second string, your program will likely crash when it is run. In this example, there is a terminating null, because a literal string always has a hidden terminating null character.

NOTE *C is reasonably compact when compared to other languages. A lot of functionality is provided in the standard library, rather than via the language itself. Where other languages provide built-in string manipulation operations, C provides most of this through functions in the standard library. Even* printf, *which is used to print to output, is simply a function in the standard library.*

Another function from `string.h` is `strncpy`, which can be used to copy one string into another, up to a maximum number of characters. It can be a bit safer to use than `strcpy`, because it will not go on forever, looking for a terminating null character. Here is the preceding example, using `strncpy` instead of `strcpy`:

```
#include <string.h>
. . .
char stringVar[10];
strncpy(stringVar, "Hello", 10);
```

In this instance, a maximum length of 10 has been used, because you know that `stringVar` cannot accommodate more than 10 characters.

There are many other functions in the standard library for working with strings. The following table gives some of the more useful functions declared in the file `string.h`.

FUNCTION	SIGNATURE	DESCRIPTION
strcat	`char *strcat(char *first, const char *second)`	Appends or concatenates the second string to the end of the first; returns the modified first string.
strncat	`char *strncat(char *first, const char *second, int n)`	Appends or concatenates the second string to the end of the first, taking at most n characters; returns the modified first string.
strcmp	`int strcmp(const char *first, const char *second)`	Compares the two strings. A return value less than 0 means that the first string precedes the second alphabetically; a value of 0 means the two strings are equal; and a positive value means the first string comes after the second.
strncmp	`int strncmp(const char *first, const char*second, int n)`	Compares the two strings as in `strcmp`, but only up to a maximum of n characters.
strstr	`char *strstr(const char *first, const char *second)`	Searches for the second string in the first string. If it is found, a pointer to the first character of the located string is returned. If it is not found, NULL is returned.
strlen	`int strlen(const char *first)`	Returns the length of the string passed.

WARNING *The table of functions for manipulating strings is fairly straightforward, but the keyword* NULL *may have you worried. If so, worry not.* NULL *is actually just another way of saying 0, and is used to indicate that a pointer is not pointing to any useful address. In the table, it can be returned from* strstr *whenever the second string is not found in the first string. You can compare the pointer returned with* NULL *to see if the string was found.*

Returning NULL *for a pointer in C is a very common way of saying that something didn't go as planned. Perhaps an error occurred, or something was not found, as is the case for* strstr. *Passing* NULL *as the value of a pointer to a function is a common way of telling the function that the corresponding argument is not needed for this call.*

You've probably noticed that in many examples, though not all, the main function has two parameters, with a signature like this:

```
int main( const int argc, const char* argv[] );
```

None of the examples up to this point in the chapter have actually made use of these parameters, so what are they? These parameters allow arguments to be passed to a program when it is run. The number of arguments passed is `argc`, or the *argument count*. The values of the arguments passed in are stored in `argv`, the *argument values*. `argc` is a simple integer, but the declaration of `argv` is more involved. `argv` is an array of pointers to `char`. A pointer to `char` is a string, so `argv` is actually an array of strings. Each entry in the array is a different argument for the `main` function.

You can access these arguments like this:

```
int main( const int argc, const char* argv[] ) {
    printf("arg0 is %s", argv[0]);
    printf("arg1 is %s", argv[1]);
    return 0;
}
```

The first entry in the array, `argv[0]`, is reserved for the name of the program. The other entries, up to index `argc-1`, are the arguments for the program. How these arguments are passed to the program depends on the manner in which the program is run.

NOTE *The* %s *in* printf *is a formatting directive, which is used to print string variables. This is covered in the next section, along with other aspects of formatting.*

Sometimes you will see a main function declared like this:

```
int main( const int argc, const char** argv );
```

In this case, the second parameter is given as a *pointer to a pointer*. Because an array is equivalent to a pointer in C, this declaration is equivalent to the preceding one.

INPUT/OUTPUT

Programs aren't very useful unless you can get data into and out of them. This aspect of computing is known as *input/output* or I/O. You have already seen many examples of I/O earlier in this chapter. Every time a program contains printf or scanf, it is performing I/O, either printing data to output or reading it from input. It is also common to read from or write to files. This section covers basic aspects of I/O in C programming.

As you are now well aware, printf can be used to print strings to standard output. Variables and other values can be embedded in the string via format characters, which are preceded by a %. The following table provides the most important format characters.

FORMAT CHARACTERS	TYPES
%d, %i	int, short, long
%u	unsigned int
%f, %e, %g	float, double
%c	char
%s	char* (string)
%p	pointer

The format characters appear in the string passed to printf. Expressions for the values corresponding to the format characters appear after the string, separated by commas. Here is an example of printing a complex string containing several values:

```
int i = 5;
float f = 100.6;
char *str = "This is the winter of our discontent";

printf("Shakespeare said: \"%s\". \n\tThis, while he ate %d eggs, "
       "each weighing %f grams.\n", str, i+10, f);
```

If you can't fit a string on one line, you can either leave it as a single line and let it wrap around in your editor, or you can break it in two, as in this example. Two neighboring string literals are concatenated to form a single string, which is passed to printf.

The use of quotations inside a string is made possible by *escaping* the special meaning of the quotation marks. You do this by adding a backslash character before each quotation mark. This principle applies to all characters with special meaning. Another example is the % symbol, which generally implies a format character. If you want to print the backslash character itself, you need to use two backslashes together.

Non-formatting characters with a special meaning are preceded by a backslash. For example, \n represents a new line character, and \t is the tab character. If you want to print \n or \t rather than a new line or tab, you can again use the double-backslash trick, entering \\n or \\t in your string.

You are not restricted to simple variables and literals in calls to printf. As you can see from the example, any expression is allowed. In this case, i+10 has been passed. Of course, this applies to functions in general, not just printf.

 NOTE *If you take the time to type in the preceding example and run it, don't be too surprised if the weight of each egg in the example is not printed as 100.6 grams, but something such as 100.599998 grams. This has to do with the way the computer stores floating-point numbers. It cannot internally represent all floating-point numbers, so it represents only some, and chooses the closest internal representation it can find for any given value. In this case, 100.599998 is the closest float to 100.6 that the computer can represent.*

When you want to read something in from standard input, you use scanf, which reads a string with a particular format, in the same way that printf writes one. The same format characters that apply to printf also apply to scanf. Here is an example of using scanf to read two floating-point numbers, and one integer, from standard input (the user's keyboard):

```
#include <stdio.h>

int main() {
    float f1, f2;
    int i;
    printf("Enter two floats and an int: ");
    scanf("%f%f%d", &f1, &f2, &i);
    printf("You typed: %f, %f, and %d.\n", f1, f2, i);
    return 0;
}
```

The program is simple enough: It requests that the user type in two floats, followed by an int, using the printf function. scanf is then used to read the numbers. The format characters in the string passed as the first argument to scanf indicate what value types can be expected. After the format string, a list of pointers to variables is passed. (You can tell that pointers are being passed because each variable is preceded by an &, the dereferencing operator.) These variables contain the values read after the call. Finally, another printf statement writes the data back out again.

Note that scanf takes pointers to variables as arguments, and not the variables themselves, as is the case for printf. This is because scanf must change the variables' values inside the function. As you learned earlier in this chapter, because C uses pass-by-value, the only way to change the value of a variable passed to a function is to pass the address of the variable to be modified, rather than its value.

> **NOTE** *If you try this out, you will find that* scanf *is fairly tolerant of your input, although results may be meaningless if you don't type in what is requested. For example, if you enter an* int *instead of a* float, *it works fine, because an integer number can be easily converted to a floating-point number. But try entering a* float *in place of the requested* int, *and you may get surprising results, depending on the form of the* float *that you enter. For example, entering* **4.5** *will return* 4, *which is not so surprising, but entering* .3 *returns* 6, *which is a little more difficult to fathom!*

Unlike printf, scanf ignores whitespace in the format string, so the following statement is equivalent to the original:

```
scanf("%f %f %d", &f1, &f2, &i);
```

Two functions that are not directly related to I/O, but are closely related to scanf and printf, are sscanf and sprintf. These functions behave very similarly to scanf and printf, except that they read and write to and from strings, respectively, rather than input and output. Here is a simple example of using sscanf and sprintf:

```
char str[34];
sprintf( str, "Have a nice birthday on the %dth.", 20 );
printf("%s\n", str);

int i;
float f;
char s[20];
char *readStr = "20 1.4 hey there";
sscanf( readStr, "%d%f%s", &i, &f, s );
printf("%d:%f:%s\n", i, f, s);
```

If you compile and run this in a main function, you will see output something like this:

```
Have a nice birthday on the 20th.
20:1.400000:hey
```

sprintf includes the same parameters as printf, except it takes an extra one at the beginning of the parameter list, which is the string it is to write to. In this case, the variable str is passed, which is 34 characters long. If you count how many letters there are in the output string, you should come to 33. So an extra char has been included in the variable str. This is by design: if you recall, a string should include a terminating null character, and that occupies the extra place. In general, you should make your strings at least one larger than the maximum expected number of meaningful characters that they need to contain.

sscanf has the same parameters as scanf, but it too has an extra string at the beginning of the parameter list. It reads out of this string, according to the format passed as the second argument. In this case, it reads the int 20, the float 1.4, and the string hey. You will notice that it stopped reading the string at the first whitespace rather than continuing on to read in there. The sscanf and scanf functions assume that whitespace delineates the end of an entry.

Variations of scanf and printf also exist for reading and writing to files: fscanf and fprintf. Not surprisingly, these functions take the same arguments as scanf and printf, with the addition of an extra FILE pointer passed first. The following example opens two files, reading from one, and writing to the other, using fscanf and fprintf, respectively:

```c
#include <stdio.h>

int main() {
    FILE *inpFile, *outFile;

    // Open files
    inpFile = fopen("/var/tmp/temp.inp", "r");
    outFile = fopen("/var/tmp/temp.out", "w");

    // Read from inpFile
    float f1, f2, f3;
    fscanf( inpFile, "%f%f%f", &f1, &f2, &f3 );

    // Write to outFile
    fprintf( outFile, "The three floats were: %f, %f, and %f.", f1, f2, f3 );

    // Close files
    fclose(inpFile);
    fclose(outFile);

    return 0;
}
```

This program begins by declaring two pointers to variables of the type FILE. The FILE type is not as simple as a float or int. It is a struct, which you will learn about later in the chapter. In the meantime, you can use FILE pointers without actually understanding what they contain or how they work.

In this case, the function fopen is used to open two files, and the FILE pointers are assigned to the return values. fopen takes two parameters: a string with the path to the file and a string indicating the operations permitted on the file.

The second parameter tells fopen whether the file is for reading, writing, or some combination. The following table shows strings that can be passed as the second argument to fopen.

STRING	FILE OPERATION
r	Read only
w	Write only
a	Append to the end of an existing file
r+	Read and write an existing file
w+	Read and write a new file
a+	Read and write an existing file, beginning at the end

In the example, "r" is passed for the input file, indicating it will be read, and "w" is passed for the output file, indicating it will only be written to.

 NOTE *The paths chosen for the files were both in the directory* /var/tmp. *This is a good directory to practice with reading and writing files because everything there is treated as temporary and disposable, and it is less likely that you will accidentally overwrite or change an important file.*

fscanf and fprintf work as expected, taking the respective file pointers as the first argument. After reading data from inpFile, and writing the same data to outFile, both files are closed using the function fclose. After fclose, the FILE pointers are no longer valid, and should not be used.

Many other functions are defined in the standard library for reading and writing standard input and output, and files. The following table lists some of the more important functions, for use in your programs.

FUNCTION	SIGNATURE	DESCRIPTION
gets	`char *gets(char *line);`	Reads a string from standard input up to a new line character, and copies the string into the `line` variable. It also returns the pointer to the `line` string. If the end of file is encountered before a line is read, the `line` variable is not set, and `NULL` is returned.
fgets	`char *fgets(char *line, int n, FILE *file);`	Same as `gets`, except that it reads from the file associated with the file pointer file. A maximum of n-1 characters can be read. If a new line is encountered, or the maximum number of characters is reached, the line is returned, including the new line and a terminating null character.
getchar	`char getchar();`	Reads a single character from standard input.
fgetc	`char fgetc(FILE *file);`	Reads a single character from the file passed. If the end of the file is encountered, the special value `EOF` is returned.

In the following Try It Out, you write a program called *Grepper*, which is a simplified version of the Unix command `grep`. Grepper goes through a file one line at a time, searching for a string passed to it when run. If it finds the string in a line, the whole line is printed. In this way, you can see whether a file contains a particular word, for example, and the lines on which the word appears.

TRY IT OUT Searching a File

1. Create a new Command Line Tool project in Xcode and call it **Grepper**.

2. Open the source file `main.c` and replace the content with the following code:

Available for download on Wrox.com

```c
#include <stdio.h>
#include <string.h>

// Global constants
const int MAX_STRING_LENGTH = 256;

// Main function
int main (int argc, const char * argv[]) {
    // Make sure there are two arguments given, the filename
```

```
// and the search string
if ( argc != 3 ) return 1; // Indicate error

// Get input file paths from standard input
const char *inpPath = argv[1];

// Get string to search for
const char *searchString = argv[2];

// Open files
FILE *inpFile;
inpFile = fopen(inpPath, "r");

// Loop over lines in the input file, until there
// are none left
char line[MAX_STRING_LENGTH];
while ( fgets(line, MAX_STRING_LENGTH-1, inpFile) ) {
    if ( strstr(line, searchString) ) {
        printf("In file %s:\t%s", inpPath, line);
    }
}

// Close files
fclose(inpFile);
return 0;
}
```

code snippet MacOSXProg ch06/Grepper/main.c

3. Build the program by choosing Build from the Build menu.

4. Select the Grepper executable in the Executables group of the Groups & Files view.

5. Choose File ⇨ Get Info or use the key combination Command-I.

6. Open the Arguments tab in the Grepper Info window, and click the + button to add a new argument. Enter a path to any text file that you would like to search for a string. (This could even be the `main.c` program in the Grepper project itself.)

7. Add a second argument, and enter the string you would like to search in the file. The Grepper Info window should now look similar to Figure 6-3.

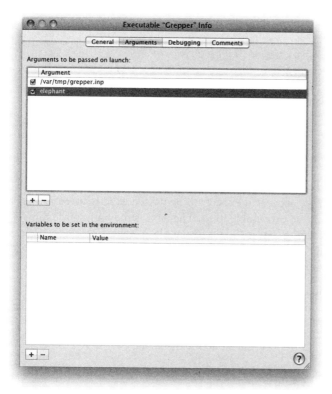

FIGURE 6-3

8. Now run the program by choosing Run from the Run menu, and bring up the Debugger Console to check the results (Run ⇨ Console). You should see each of the lines from the input file that contains the search string.

How It Works

Grepper utilizes many of the skills that you have learned up to this point in the chapter, from string handling to I/O, and conditional branching to loops. After the `#include` statements, a variable is declared outside the `main` function. This variable has *global scope*, which means it can be accessed from anywhere in the program, not just inside a particular function, for example. In this case, it could also have been placed inside the `main` function, but there will be other cases, where the variable needs to be accessed outside of `main` as well, and making it global is one way to facilitate this.

In general, global variables should be avoided, because they can make a program more difficult to understand. You can't see the variable being passed through to a function via the parameter list, so it can make it difficult to follow the flow of data in a program. One case where global data is acceptable is for constant variables that need to be accessed at many points throughout a program. The previous example, `MAX_STRING_LENGTH`, is just such a case, because it stipulates the size of string variables used throughout Grepper.

WARNING *The* scope *in global scope* refers to where a particular variable can be accessed, and how long it remains in existence. Variables with global scope are visible everywhere in a program, and exist for the runtime of the program, but for most variables, this isn't the case. Variables declared inside functions are created when the function begins, and destroyed when it ends. These variables are called local variables *because they exist only locally to the function. In fact, variables declared in any code block — a section of code enclosed in braces — exist only while that block is executing.*

The `main` function first checks that `argc` is 3, because it expects to be passed exactly three values in `argv`. The first, as always, is the name of the executable itself. The next is the path to the file that should be scanned, and the last is the string that is sought in the file. You entered these input parameters in the Inspector window of the Grepper executable just before you ran it. Xcode passes these parameters to Grepper when it starts.

If there are three arguments, the next action taken is to assign the last two arguments to variables, one for the input file path (`inpPath`), and one for the string (`searchString`). The `inpPath` variable is then used with `fopen` to open the input file for reading.

The program then begins to loop over lines, checking each one for the string.

```
char line[MAX_STRING_LENGTH];
while ( fgets(line, MAX_STRING_LENGTH-1, inpFile) ) {
    if ( strstr(line, searchString) ) {
        printf("In file %s:\t%s", inpPath, line);
    }
}
```

Just before the loop, a string variable is created to store each line of the file. It is given the length defined earlier at global scope. This should be adequate as long as your file does not have any very long lines. *Very long* in this case is greater than 255 characters because `MAX_STRING_LENGTH` is `256` and you should always save one character for the terminating.

The `while` loop condition needs some explaining. It is a call to a function that you haven't seen before: `fgets`. `fgets` is declared in the file `string.h`, which is included at the beginning of the program. The `fgets` function reads a line of text from the file passed as the third argument, up to a maximum length given by the second argument. So it keeps reading until it either encounters a new line character (`\n`) or reaches the maximum line length. In either case, it sets the value of the string passed as the first argument to the line read, and returns the same string variable via its return parameter. If the end of the file is reached before anything is read, it returns `NULL`.

You may be wondering why both the first parameter value and the return value are set to the line string. One reason is that you can easily test if anything was read, and thus whether you should keep reading. That is precisely how it has been used here: the `while` loop will continue until a zero value is returned by `fgets`. `NULL` is a zero value, so it will keep reading lines until the end of the file is encountered.

The `if` construct in the loop uses the function `strstr`, which was introduced in the previous section "Characters and Strings." This function searches the string passed as the first argument for the string passed second. If it finds the second string in the first, a pointer to the location of the second string is returned. If it is not found, `NULL` is returned. The `if` tests whether the return is non-zero, so any line for which `NULL` is returned by `strstr` is ignored, and any line containing the search string is printed.

The last lines of `main` simply close the input file and return `0`, indicating success.

NOTE *Grepper assumes that no line will exceed 255 characters, plus one terminating null character. If a line is longer than this, Grepper will not operate correctly. This type of situation is referred to as buffer overflow, and is a common source of security breaches. For example, an unscrupulous hacker could use buffer overflow to cause a program like FTP to crash, and run more malicious programs in its place. If your programs are potential security risks, you should take extra care to put checks into your code that ensure buffer overflow can't happen.*

DATA STRUCTURES

Up to this point in the chapter, you have dealt with only simple data types such as `int`, `float`, and `char`. C was one of the first languages to facilitate *structured programming*, part of which entails creating more complex data relationships than you have seen so far. C provides a number of constructions to group data, and this section introduces you to them.

Sometimes it is necessary to represent variables that can take only a few discrete values. For example, a variable representing the type of a pet could be represented by an integer restricted to a small range of values. Such a variable is referred to as an *enumerated type*. C provides the `enum` data type to represent enumerated types. Consider this example:

```c
typedef enum { DOG, CAT, BIRD } Pet;

Pet myPet = CAT;

switch (myPet) {
    case DOG:
        printf("I have a dog!\n");
        break;
    case CAT:
        printf("I have a cat!\n");
        break;
    case BIRD:
        printf("I have a bird!\n");
```

```
        break;
    default:
        printf("I have an undefined beast\n");
}
```

The keyword `typedef` is used in conjunction with the keyword `enum` to define a new type called `Pet`. This type can take three meaningful values: `DOG`, `CAT`, and `BIRD`. A variable called `myPet` is then declared to be of the type `Pet`, and is initialized to `CAT`. A `switch` statement checks the type of `myPet`, printing a message depending on its value.

C simply represents enumerated types as integers, so they can be used anywhere an `int` can be used. For example, you can subscript an array with an `enum` like this:

```
int averagePetLifetime[3];

averagePetLifetime[DOG] = 20;
averagePetLifetime[CAT] = 15;
averagePetLifetime[BIRD] = 5;
```

Unless indicated otherwise, the first entry in an `enum` gets the value 0; the second, 1; the third, 2; and so forth. You can override this behavior by explicitly indicating the integers corresponding to the entries, like this:

```
typedef enum { DOG = 1, CAT = 2, BIRD = 3} Pet;
```

Whenever no integer is explicitly assigned to one of the values, it is given the value of the previous value incremented by 1. So this example could also be written as follows:

```
typedef enum { DOG = 1, CAT, BIRD} Pet;
```

In theory, you can do without `enum`s in your programming, but your code becomes considerably easier to read if you use them, because the values assigned have a clear meaning. Assigning a variable to `DOG` is much easier to understand than assigning it to 1, where 1 only implies a dog.

Another data structure available in C is `struct`. A `struct` allows you to group variables. Here is a `struct` you might use to represent a person:

```
typedef enum { BLUE, GREEN, BROWN } EyeColor;

struct Person {
    char *firstName, *secondName;
    char *address;
    float height;
    float weight;
    EyeColor eyeColor;
};
```

The `struct` can include variables of any type, including other `struct`s. To use a `struct`, you need to make a variable, or *instance*, such as this:

```
struct Person me;
```

You can then access the variables inside the `struct` using the `.` operator. To set them, you can do this:

```
me.firstName = "Bob";
me.secondName = "Bobbs";
me.address = "1 Holy Smoke Crescent, Who Knows Where, USA";
me.height = 180.0;
me.weight = 90.0;
me.eyeColor = BLUE;
```

To use the variables, you can do this:

```
float weightInPounds = me.weight * KILOS_TO_POUNDS;
```

In other words, the members of a `struct` are just like ordinary variables in every way, except that you have to reference them by giving the name of the `struct` variable, followed by a point, and then the name of the member.

Most programmers find typing in `struct Person me;` annoying after a while, so they use the same trick you saw for `enum`s; namely, they define the `struct` as a new type. The following code shows you how:

```
typedef struct Person_ {
    char *firstName, *secondName;
    char *address;
    float height;
    float weight;
    EyeColor eyeColor;
} Person;

Person me;
me.height = 180.0;
```

As you can see, this saves you from having to type `struct` in front of every variable you declare. If you look carefully, you will see two names ascribed to the `struct`: `Person_` and `Person`. `Person` is actually not the name of a `struct`, but a type, which in this case happens to be a `struct` called `Person_`. The name of the `struct`, `Person_`, may be omitted, in which case you have an *anonymous struct*. However, it is good practice to name a `struct`, even if you don't have any immediate reason to. That's because you sometimes need to make reference to the `struct` inside its own definition as shown here:

```
typedef struct ListNode_ {
    float value;
    struct ListNode_ *nextNode;
} ListNode;
```

It is perfectly legal in C to include pointer variables to the `struct` you are declaring inside the declaration itself. If you used an anonymous `struct`, this would not be possible, because you can't refer to the `struct`'s type, and the type name `ListNode` is yet to be declared.

This example also demonstrates that, just as with any other type of variable, you can declare a variable that is a pointer to a struct. When you want to access a member of such a variable, it looks like this:

```
(*me).address = "55 Melancholy Road, Loserville";
```

You first have to dereference the pointer to the struct, and then apply the . operator to get the address. This is not very pretty, so C provides the following equivalent notation:

```
me->address = "55 Melancholy Road, Loserville";
```

The hyphen followed by a greater-than symbol is a shorthand way of accessing the members of a pointer to a struct.

MEMORY MANAGEMENT

Up to this point, all the variables you have created have been stored in a part of memory known as the *stack*. The stack is a contiguous block of memory, meaning that it forms one continuous segment unbroken by gaps. Whenever a function is entered, the local variables declared there are pushed onto the end of the stack. When the function returns, the variables are popped off the stack again, effectively destroying them.

Stack variables can't be used for every situation, so C also gives you access to another part of memory for storing variables called the *heap* or *free store*. When you put a variable "on the heap," you are responsible for managing its memory yourself. In other words, you have to request that the memory be assigned to the variable, and you are also responsible for freeing the memory when you are finished with it. If you don't do this, you can end up with a *memory leak*, where the amount of memory used by your program rises over time, perhaps even causing your computer to slow or crash.

Variables that have their values stored on the heap are always pointers. They point to the location in memory where the data is stored. Here is an example of creating and freeing a heap variable:

```c
#include <stdlib.h>
#include <stdio.h>

int main() {
    float *heapVar;
    heapVar = malloc( sizeof(float) );

    *heapVar = 4.0;
    printf( "%f\n", *heapVar );

    free(heapVar);

    return 0;
}
```

The variable heapVar is declared as a pointer, and then assigned to the return value of the function malloc, which is declared in stdlib.h. The name malloc stands for *memory allocation* — it takes a single argument, which is an integer indicating how many bytes of memory are required to hold the variable. You could enter 4 here, because you know that a float has 4 bytes, but this would be a mistake: If float were to be redefined on the Mac to have more than 4 bytes, or, if you port your program to a platform where float has 8 bytes, your code will no longer run.

Instead of *hard coding* the size of float, you can use the function sizeof to find out how many bytes are in a float. The sizeof function will work with any data type, including pointers, though you should be careful not to confuse the size of the pointer itself with the size of what it is pointing to. In this example the return value of sizeof(float) is passed to malloc, which allocates the requested 4 bytes, and returns a pointer to the memory.

 WARNING malloc *returns a special kind of pointer called a* void pointer. *A void pointer is a general pointer to memory, with no associated data type. You can declare a void pointer variable with the type* void*.

Rather than having to provide a different version of malloc *for each pointer type, the designers of C elected to have a single function that returns a void pointer. A void pointer can be cast to any other type of pointer implicitly by the compiler, so they effectively killed all birds with one stone.*

After assigning the target of the heapVar pointer, the memory is destroyed or freed. free is a bit easier to use than malloc because you don't have to pass a size. You simply pass the pointer, and the memory it points to on the heap will be freed for use at a later time.

malloc and free will work with any C data type, as long as you remember that you need to use it with pointer variables. Here is an example of creating a *linked list* of floating-point values:

```
#include <stdlib.h>
#include <stdio.h>

int main() {

    typedef struct ListNode_ {
        float data;
        struct ListNode_ *nextNode;
    } ListNode;

    typedef struct List_ {
        ListNode *firstNode;
    } List;

    // Create a list on the stack, and add a node to it
    List list;
    list.firstNode = malloc(sizeof(ListNode));
    list.firstNode->data = 2.0;
```

```
        list.firstNode->nextNode = NULL; // NULL indicates there are no more nodes

        // Add a new node in front of the other one
        ListNode *newNode = malloc(sizeof(ListNode));
        newNode->data = 3.0;
        newNode->nextNode = list.firstNode;
        list.firstNode = newNode;

        // Print out the values in the list
        ListNode *currentNode = list.firstNode;
        while ( currentNode ) {
            printf("Node value: %f\n", currentNode->data);
            currentNode = currentNode->nextNode;
        }

        // Free the memory of all nodes
        currentNode = list.firstNode;
        while ( currentNode ) {
            ListNode *next = currentNode->nextNode;
            free(currentNode);
            currentNode = next;
        }

        return 0;
    }
```

 NOTE *A linked list is a data container, which has similarities to C's arrays. The primary difference is that they can grow and shrink to fit the amount of data they need to store. C does not have any built-in linked list type, but you can certainly create linked lists in C using* structs, *as shown in the example. A more advanced implementation would provide functions for adding data to the list, and removing it again.*

A linked list is made up of zero or more nodes. Each node holds a piece of data, in this case a `float`. The nodes are linked in the sense that the first node in the list has a pointer to the second, which has a pointer to the third, and so forth. The last node points to NULL, indicating that the list is finished.

Nodes are represented by the type `ListNode`, which is a `struct` that contains a single `float`, and a pointer to the next node in the list.

```
    typedef struct ListNode_ {
        float data;
        struct ListNode_ *nextNode;
    } ListNode;
```

Note that the `struct`, `ListNode_`, is referenced inside the `struct` itself to define a pointer to the next node.

The `List` type is a `struct` that holds a single pointer to the first node in the list.

```
typedef struct List_ {
    ListNode *firstNode;
} List;
```

The `List` is declared and initialized as follows:

```
// Create a list on the stack, and add a node to it
List list;
list.firstNode = malloc(sizeof(ListNode));
list.firstNode->data = 2.0;
list.firstNode->nextNode = NULL; // NULL indicates there are no more nodes
```

The `firstNode` member of the `struct` variable `list` is assigned to the pointer returned from `malloc`. When the memory for the node has been allocated, the data can be set, in this case to `2.0`. The `nextNode` pointer in the `ListNode struct` is assigned to `NULL`, to reflect the fact that this is the last node in the list at this point. The next portion of code inserts a second node at the beginning of the list. This is slightly more complex, because the newly inserted node must point to the first node created as shown here:

```
// Add a new node in front of the other one
ListNode *newNode = malloc(sizeof(ListNode));
newNode->data = 3.0;
newNode->nextNode = list.firstNode;
list.firstNode = newNode;
```

The primary difference is that the `nextNode` pointer in `newNode` is set to the `firstNode` pointer of `list`. The `firstNode` variable is then updated to point to `newNode`, making it the first node in the list. It is important that these operations are carried out in this order. If instead `list.firstNode` was assigned to `newNode`, there would be no way of assigning `newNode->nextNode` to the original node in the list.

The next section of code prints the values of the list. This demonstrates how you can traverse a list with a loop:

```
// Print out the values in the list
ListNode *currentNode = list.firstNode;
while ( currentNode ) {
    printf("Node value: %f\n", currentNode->data);
    currentNode = currentNode->nextNode;
}
```

The `currentNode` variable is initialized to the first node. A `while` loop is used to move through the list, until `currentNode` is `NULL`, which indicates that the end of the list has been reached. The data stored in the current node is printed each time around the loop, and `currentNode` is updated to point to the following node.

The final `while` loop is similar, although not exactly the same. Its purpose is freeing the memory that was allocated for the nodes earlier in the program.

```
// Free the memory of all nodes
currentNode = list.firstNode;
while ( currentNode ) {
    ListNode *next = currentNode->nextNode;
    free(currentNode);
    currentNode = next;
}
```

The current node is again initialized to the first node, and the while loop continues until currentNode is NULL. The difference lies in an extra pointer declared inside the body of the loop: next. This is used to temporarily store the address of the next node in the list. The reason this is necessary is that the current node is being freed, and the nextNode pointer will be freed with it. Without the temporary pointer, you would not know the memory address of the next node in the list, and therefore could not free the nodes in the rest of the list.

THE PREPROCESSOR

This section covers a topic that isn't really part of the C language at all: the *C preprocessor*. A preprocessor is a program that goes through a piece of code before it is passed to the compiler, and modifies it. The C preprocessor is heavily used by C programmers, and is also used when programming in derived variants of C such as C++ and Objective-C.

 NOTE *On Mac OS X, the standard C compiler is* gcc, *which is part of the GNU Compiler Collection (GCC). To confuse matters, the preprocessor is part of* gcc, *so you may not even realize that you are using it. Usually it automatically runs before the compiler. If you want to use the* gcc *preprocessor without compiling afterward, you can pass the* -E -P *options.*

The C preprocessor is used for a range of tasks, most of which ensure that compilation can proceed without a hitch. Here are some ways in which the C preprocessor is used:

➤   To incorporate the source code of one file in another file.

➤   To include different code based on a condition, such as whether you are debugging.

➤   To replace a macro label wherever it is found with a piece of code. For example, it can be used to replace PI with a number such as 3.1415972.

In this section, you learn how you can achieve these goals with the C preprocessor.

When you communicate with the preprocessor in your source code, you give it *directives*. These are commands to do something, and they are all preceded by a # symbol. The first directive, and probably the most widely used, is #include. Its purpose is to tell the preprocessor to include the text of another file in the current file, at the position of the #include. Here is an example:

```
My birthday is on
#include "Birthday"
at
#include "Venue"
```

When the preprocessor sees the #include lines in a source file, it will look for the files Birthday and Venue. If the preprocessor finds the values, it will insert the text contained in these files into the source file, replacing the #include directives. The preprocessed file might end up looking something like this:

```
My birthday is on
March the 21st
at
Under the C
```

All this happens before the compiler itself is called, so the compiler will never see the #include, only the text from Birthday and Venue.

You will undoubtedly have noticed that the preceding example is not C. What this demonstrates is that the C preprocessor is not part of the C language, and doesn't care what contents are in the file that it is processing. In fact, the C preprocessor is often used with other languages, such as Fortran, which doesn't have a preprocessor of its own.

The #include directive is very important in C programming. Nearly every source file will have one or more includes, just as in the example. These includes are used to import declarations of functions and data structures needed to compile the source code. Without the #include directive, the programmer would have to duplicate these declarations in each source file that required them.

The #include directive can also be used to include declarations from a library or framework. In this case, triangular parentheses are used instead of quotes:

```
#include <math.h>
```

This directive includes the file math.h from the C standard library, which defines a number of mathematical functions and constants.

The C preprocessor also allows you to define *macros*. A macro is basically a label for a piece of text that will be inserted whenever the macro is found in the file. Here is a simple example:

```
#define MY_AGE 21
```

This defines the macro MY_AGE to be 21. Note that MY_AGE is not the number 21, but a string with the value 21. Macros are just strings of characters to the preprocessor. You could instead write the following, and the preprocessor would not complain:

```
#define MY_AGE twenty something
```

This directive would replace any instances of MY_AGE in the file with the text twenty something. Whether that makes sense will depend on what you are using the macro for. In any case, the preprocessor itself will not complain, but the compiler may not like what it finds in the preprocessed file.

 NOTE *Although the preprocessor will generally treat macro definitions with numbers as strings of characters, it is capable of simple arithmetic operations, and in such cases, a number string can be handled as an integer. This is explained further a little later.*

Using a macro is very easy — you simply insert the macro's label in your file wherever you like. Here is a simple example:

```
Since turning MY_AGE a few months ago, I have had an overwhelming desire to
learn C. Perhaps mid-life is finally upon me!
```

The preprocessor replaces MY_AGE with the string 21, giving the following preprocessed source:

```
Since turning 21 a few months ago, I have had an overwhelming desire to
learn C. Perhaps mid-life is finally upon me!
```

The only restriction on where you can place a macro is that it should not appear in a string, between quotations. If it does, the preprocessor will treat the macro label as a literal string, and not replace it. For example, the following will remain unchanged by the preprocessor, because MY_AGE appears in quotations:

```
Since turning "MY_AGE" a few months ago, I have had an overwhelming desire to
learn C. Perhaps mid-life is finally upon me!
```

Interestingly, you can also define macros that define nothing at all. This is useful for conditional branching. Yes, even the preprocessor is capable of checking for conditions, and taking different actions accordingly. The following defines a condition for the preprocessor:

```
#define USE_SMALL_BUFFER
```

After the preprocessor sees this line, it will consider USE_SMALL_BUFFER as defined, even though it has not been assigned a value.

NOTE By now you will probably have realized that macros are usually named in uppercase letters, with underscores separating words. This is a convention only to help distinguish them from standard variables. The preprocessor does not require you to use the convention, but it is good to do so. Otherwise, other programmers may have trouble understanding your code.

The preprocessor can check conditions with the `#ifdef` and `#ifndef` directives like this:

```
#ifdef USE_SMALL_BUFFER
const int bufferSize = 1024;
#else
const int bufferSize = 2048;
#endif
```

An equivalent way of writing this code is as follows:

```
#ifndef USE_SMALL_BUFFER
const int bufferSize = 2048;
#else
const int bufferSize = 1024;
#endif
```

In both these cases, the `#else` block is optional. The `#ifdef` directive checks if a macro has been defined earlier. If it has been, the text up until the next directive is included. If the macro has not been defined, the text following it is not included, but any text after the `#else` directive — if it exists — will be included. The `#ifndef` directive is exactly the opposite of `#ifdef` — its text is included if a macro is *not* defined.

`#ifdef` is actually a shorthand way of writing `#if defined`. There is also an `#elif` directive, which stands for `else if`. This allows you to include many different branches, each one with a different block of text. The first matching block is included. For example:

```
#if defined USE_SMALL_BUFFER
const int bufferSize = 1024;
#elif defined USE_MEDIUM_BUFFER
const int bufferSize = 2048;
#else
const int bufferSize = 4096;
#endif
```

The preprocessor first checks if `USE_SMALL_BUFFER` is defined. If it is, the line setting `bufferSize` to `1024` is included. If `USE_SMALL_BUFFER` is not defined, the `#elif` condition is tested; if `USE_MEDIUM_BUFFER` is defined, the line setting `bufferSize` to `2048` is included. Finally, if neither of the conditions is met, the line in the `#else` block is included, setting the `bufferSize` variable to `4096`.

Simple arithmetic is also allowed in macro definitions. Take this reworking of the preceding example:

```
#define BUFFER_BLOCK_SIZE 1024

#if defined USE_SMALL_BUFFER
    #define BUFFER_SIZE BUFFER_BLOCK_SIZE
#elif defined USE_MEDIUM_BUFFER
    #define BUFFER_SIZE BUFFER_BLOCK_SIZE * 2
#else
    #define BUFFER_SIZE BUFFER_BLOCK_SIZE * 4
#endif

const int bufferSize = BUFFER_SIZE;
```

Here you can see that it is possible to use a previously defined macro in the definition of a new one. The macro BUFFER_BLOCK_SIZE is used to define the macro BUFFER_SIZE, and simple arithmetic is used in the last two definitions.

The arithmetic allowed in conditionals like these is not very advanced, but it's adequate for most purposes. You can use simple integer arithmetic, such as adding or subtracting, but arithmetic with decimal numbers is not possible. You can compare integers and strings, testing for equality, or for one value being greater or less than another. Here is an example demonstrating some of the arithmetic operators available:

```
#define MY_AGE 21
#define MIDDLE_AGE 40
#define OLD_AGE 60

#if MY_AGE >= OLD_AGE * MIDDLE_AGE
printf("Humans do not live that long.\n");
#elif MY_AGE > \
        OLD_AGE + MIDDLE_AGE
printf("Should you be using a computer at your age?\n");
#elif MY_AGE >= OLD_AGE
printf("Better sit down.\n";
#elif MY_AGE == MIDDLE_AGE
printf("Life is just beginning.\n");
#elif MY_AGE > MIDDLE_AGE
printf("Better slow down.\n");
#else
printf("A spring chicken, eh?\n");
#endif
```

 NOTE *This example is intended to demonstrate the use of arithmetic operators with the preprocessor and is not intended to reflect the authors' personal definitions of middle and/or old age, or the activities appropriate for a person of a given age.*

Jokes aside, the preceding code includes the operators *, +, >, >=, and ==. You should also have noticed this strange-looking construction:

```
#elif MY_AGE > \
      OLD_AGE + MIDDLE_AGE
```

Apart from the strange logic used, the backslash is new. A backslash at the end of a preprocessor line is a *line continuation symbol*. It indicates to the preprocessor that the next line belongs with the current one, and should be treated as a single logical expression. The preceding is equivalent to the following:

```
#elif MY_AGE > OLD_AGE + MIDDLE_AGE
```

The preprocessor requires that a line be explicitly continued. This is opposite from the C language itself, which requires explicit termination of a line.

Macros are not just restricted to simple string substitution. They can actually take arguments, assuming a role more like that of functions. Here is an example of a macro that calculates the maximum of two different numbers:

```
#define MAX(a, b) ( a > b ? a : b )
```

Consider this code:

```
float f = MAX(1.0, 10.0);
```

It will look like this after the preprocessor is finished with it:

```
float f = (1.0 > 10.0 ? 1.0 : 10.0 );
```

Note that the preprocessor doesn't actually evaluate the macro. It simply performs a textual substitution of the arguments passed to it, and then inserts the result directly in the code.

Macros with arguments can be particularly useful when you have some code that can be applied for many different types. Instead of writing a different function for each of the possible types, each with a slightly different parameter list, you could write one macro. MAX is actually a good example of this principle, because it works regardless of the type of number you feed to it.

```
float f = MAX(1.0, 10.0);
int i = MAX(5, 2);
```

As you can see, the same macro, MAX, is used with both floating-point numbers and integers in this example. You could not do this with a function: you would need to have one function to find the maximum of two floats (MaxFloats), and one to find the maximum of two ints (MaxInts).

The examples you have seen up to this point in the chapter have all been concentrated in a single file, with the code executed directly in the main function. Of course, this is practical only for the simplest of programs. Usually, many different files are used, and then code organization becomes an issue. The next section deals with how you should organize your C programs.

ORGANIZING PROGRAMS

As explained in Chapter 3, C programs typically comprise many source files with the extension
.c. These files contain the definitions of the functions and variables that make up the program.
Each source file is usually accompanied by a *header file*, which has the extension .h. A header file
declares the parts of the source file that should be visible to the rest of the program, which may
include macros, global variables, data types, and function signatures. Any .c file can utilize the
declarations in a header file by including it with the #include preprocessor directive.

Take the following example: you have a function called DoSomething, and a struct called Monkey,
and you want to put them into a separate file from the main function. You could write a header file,
Monkey.h, which contains declarations and definitions, such as this:

```
#ifndef MONKEY_H
#define MONKEY_H

typedef struct {
    char *name;
} Monkey;

void DoSomething(Monkey *monkey);

#endif
```

The first thing you will notice is that there are some preprocessor directives that don't have anything
to do with the code itself. These directives are called *guards*. Definitions such as the struct
Monkey can only be defined once, or the compiler will report an error. To avoid this, the guard is
introduced, to ensure that the definitions in the header file get imported only once, no matter how
many times #include "Monkey.h" appears.

The first line of the guard checks if the macro MONKEY_H is defined. If not, the preprocessor includes
the definitions and declarations, and also defines MONKEY_H. The next time the header is included,
MONKEY_H is defined, and the code is excluded. In this way, the declarations and definitions in
Monkey.h are included only once per compilation.

The main.c file can use the definitions and declarations in Monkey.h by including it, like this:

```
#include <stdio.h>
#include "Monkey.h"

int main() {
    return 0;
}
```

The `struct Monkey` and the function `DoSomething` are now accessible inside the `main` function, as shown in the following:

```
#include <stdio.h>
#include "Monkey.h"

int main() {
    Monkey monkey;
    monkey.name = "Bonzo";
    DoSomething(&monkey);
    return 0;
}
```

The last piece of the puzzle is the `Monkey.c` file, which must provide a definition of `DoSomething`. Here is one possibility:

```
#include "Monkey.h"

void DoSomething(Monkey *monkey) {
    printf("%s stands on his head.\n", monkey->name);
}
```

Because the `Monkey.c` file also needs the definitions and declarations in `Monkey.c`, it also includes the header file `Monkey.h`. The `Monkey.c` file includes a definition of the function `DoSomething`, which simply prints a sentence using the name of the `Monkey` passed to it.

The `struct Monkey` does not get defined in `Monkey.c` because it was already defined in `Monkey.h`. `Monkey` must be defined in `Monkey.h`; otherwise, the compiler doesn't know what member variables it includes and cannot compile files such as `main.c` that access the variables of `Monkey`. This is not the case for the function `DoSomething`, because the compiler needs to know only the signature of a function to compile the call in `main.c`. The implementation of `DoSomething` is not needed, so it is defined in `DoSomething.c`.

> **NOTE** *In general, you need to give the compiler enough details in a header file that it can compile any file using the header, but no more than that. Every time you make a change to a header file, any file that includes that header must be recompiled when you click Build. If your program becomes large, you will want to put the bare minimum in header files, so that you don't spend your time waiting for unnecessarily long builds for every small change you make.*

To finish your exploration of C in the following sections, you are going to write a program that spans multiple files and uses many of the aspects of C you have read about in this chapter. The program itself is a simple address book, which allows you to add addresses, retrieve them, and save them to disk.

TRY IT OUT   Getting Started with MyAddressBook

1. Create a new Command Line Tool project in Xcode and call it **MyAddressBook.**

2. Create a new C file called `Person.c` in the Source group. To do this, select the Source group in the Groups & Files view on the left, and then choose File ➪ New File. Under the file group C and C++, choose C File, and click the Next button. Enter the name and make sure that the Also Create "Person.h" checkbox is selected, as shown in Figure 6-4. When you are ready, click the Finish button, and Xcode creates two files: `Person.c` and `Person.h`.

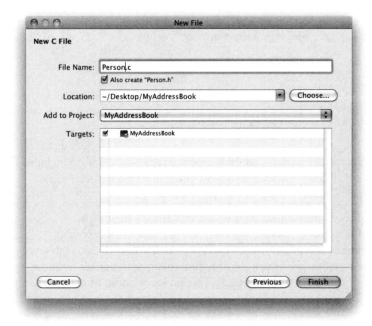

FIGURE 6-4

3. Replace the contents of the `Person.h` and `Person.c` files, as well as `main.c`, with the code given in the following listing:

PERSON.H

```
#ifndef PERSON_H
#define PERSON_H

typedef struct {
    char *name;
    char *address;
} Person;

Person* AllocPerson();
```

```
void InitPerson( Person *person, char *name, char *address );
void DeallocPerson( Person *person );

#endif
```

code snippet MacOSXProg ch06/MyAddressBook 1/Person.h

PERSON.C

```
#include "Person.h"
#include <stdio.h>
#include <stdlib.h>
#include <string.h>

Person* AllocPerson() {
    return malloc( sizeof(Person) );
}

void InitPerson( Person *person, char *name, char *address ) {
    int nameLength = strlen(name) + 1;
    person->name = malloc( sizeof(char) * nameLength );
    strcpy( person->name, name );

    int addressLength = strlen(address) + 1;
    person->address = malloc( sizeof(char) * addressLength );
    strcpy( person->address, address );
}

void DeallocPerson( Person *person ) {
    free( person->name );
    free( person->address );
    free( person );
}
```

code snippet MacOSXProg ch06/MyAddressBook 1/Person.c

MAIN.C

```
#include <stdio.h>
#include "Person.h"

int main () {
    Person *person = AllocPerson();
    InitPerson(person, "Joe Citizen", "1 Hopalong Avenue, MediumRare, USA");
    printf("Name: %s\nAddress: %s\n", person->name, person->address);
    DeallocPerson(person);
    return 0;
}
```

code snippet MacOSXProg ch06/MyAddressBook 1/main.c

4. Compile and run the program by clicking the Build and Go toolbar item, and view the output in the Debugger Console.

How It Works

The MyAddressBook program is considerably more complex than anything you have seen to this point. It makes use of all the aspects of C that you have already encountered, and uses them in a particular style of *structured programming* that is very common in C programming.

 NOTE *The style of programming demonstrated in this example is used, for example, in the Mac OS X frameworks Core Foundation and Quartz 2D. Even if you don't end up programming in C, at some point you will inevitably need to use one of these frameworks, or one of the other C frameworks in Mac OS X. When that time comes, the information you have garnered from this example will serve you very well.*

In structured programming, data is arranged into `struct`s, and functions are written to operate on the data in each `struct`. Together, the `struct` and functions that operate on it are referred to as an *Abstract Data Type (ADT)*, because they represent an abstraction of something, such as a person or an automobile. This style of programming lays the foundations for object-oriented programming (OOP), which you learn about in Chapter 7.

You should generally begin to study a program that you are not familiar with by considering the *interfaces* it declares. These are the entities in a program that are visible to other parts of the program, and are given in the header files. From the header files, you can learn how a program is structured and get a general idea of how it works, without knowing the finer details of how things are implemented.

You can find the interface of the `Person` ADT in `Person.h`. The `Person` ADT stores two strings: one to contain the name of the person, and another to contain the address. The only functions declared are for *constructing* and *destructing* the `Person` instance. Functions that allocate memory, initialize the ADT, and deallocate memory are common to all ADTs.

Every ADT provides methods for construction and destruction. Construction is the process of allocating memory for an ADT and initializing its data. Usually `malloc` is used to allocate memory. Destruction is freeing the memory associated with an ADT, usually with the `free` function, as well as any other resources it might be using, such as files.

The `Alloc . . .` functions allocate memory in which to store the ADT. Mostly, the implementation of an `Alloc . . .` function simply calls `malloc` and returns the pointer to the new memory. This is the case for `AllocPerson`.

The `Init . . .` functions allocate and initialize any variables in the ADT. The `Dealloc . . .` method frees the data structures, as well as the ADT variable itself. As you can see in the preceding code, `DeallocPerson` frees the memory associated with the `name` and `address` variables, and then frees the `Person struct` itself.

The `main` function is some simple test code to create a new `Person`, print its data, and deallocate it again. Writing test code in this manner as you go can be very useful, rather than leaving your testing until the end when the whole program is written. Testing late in the game can make finding bugs much more difficult than if you test small chunks of the program at a time.

The `main` function demonstrates the pattern used for constructing and destructing ADT variables when using structured programming. Memory for the variable is first allocated by calling an `Alloc . . .` function, rather than using `malloc` directly.

```
Person *person = AllocPerson();
```

The pointer returned is assigned to the pointer variable used to represent the instance. Note that this variable is always a pointer. After the allocation of memory, an `Init . . .` function is called.

```
InitPerson(person, "Joe Citizen", "1 Hopalong Avenue, MediumRare, USA");
```

This allocates memory for any variables in the type and initializes them. When it is no longer needed, the variable is deallocated.

```
DeallocPerson(person);
```

This pattern of allocation, initialization, and deallocation is an important aspect of structured programming and OOP, which are introduced in Chapter 7.

Having written the `Person` ADT, you write the `AddressBook` ADT in the following Try It Out, which stores multiple `Person` instances and can be used to save them to a file.

TRY IT OUT   Writing the AddressBook ADT

1. Open the MyAddressBook project in Xcode, and using the approach described in the preceding Try It Out for creating files for the `Person` ADT, add files called `AddressBook.c` and `AddressBook.h`.

2. Insert the following code in the new files, and replace the existing `main` function as well:

ADDRESSBOOK.H

```
#ifndef ADDRESSBOOK_H
#define ADDRESSBOOK_H

#include "Person.h"
#include <stdio.h>

typedef struct {
    Person *persons[]; // An array of pointers to Person
```

```
    int numPersons;
    int maxNumPersons;
} AddressBook;

AddressBook* CreateAddressBook( const char *pathToAddressBookFile );

AddressBook* AllocAddressBook();
void InitAddressBook( AddressBook *addressBook, const int maxNumPersons );
void InitAddressBookWithFile( AddressBook *addressBook, FILE *file);
void DeallocAddressBook( AddressBook *addressBook );

AddressBook* AddPerson( AddressBook *addressBook, Person *person );

Person* FindPerson( AddressBook *addressBook, char *name );

void SaveToFile( AddressBook *addressBook, FILE *file);

#endif
```

code snippet MacOSXProg ch06/MyAddressBook 2/AddressBook.h

ADDRESSBOOK.C

Available for download on Wrox.com

```
#include "AddressBook.h"
#include <stdio.h>
#include <stdlib.h>
#include <string.h>

void ReadLine( FILE *file, char *line, const int maxLength ) {
    fgets(line, maxLength-1, file);
        // This reads up to new line, and includes new line
    int l = strlen(line);
    line[l-1] = '\0';
        // Replace the new line character with a null terminating char
}

// Create an address book. If the address book file exists, create the book
// from the file. Otherwise, create an empty address book.
AddressBook* CreateAddressBook( const char *pathToAddressBookFile ) {
    AddressBook *addressBook = AllocAddressBook();
    FILE *file;
    file = fopen( pathToAddressBookFile, "r" );
    if ( NULL == file ) {
        // Create new address book
        InitAddressBook( addressBook, 1000 );
    }
    else {
        // Read address book from file
        InitAddressBookWithFile( addressBook, file );
        fclose(file);
    }
    return addressBook;
}

AddressBook* AllocAddressBook() {
```

```
        return malloc( sizeof(AddressBook) );
    }

    void InitAddressBook( AddressBook *addressBook, const int maxNumPersons ) {
        addressBook->persons = malloc( sizeof(Person*) * maxNumPersons );
        addressBook->maxNumPersons = maxNumPersons;
        addressBook->numPersons = 0;
    }

    void InitAddressBookWithFile( AddressBook *addressBook, FILE *file ) {
        int numPersons, maxNumPersons;
        fscanf(file, "%d", &numPersons);
        fscanf(file, "%d", &maxNumPersons);
        fgetc(file); // Remove the new line character

        // Call the other initializer first.
        InitAddressBook( addressBook, maxNumPersons );

        int i;
        for ( i = 0; i < numPersons; ++i ) {
            int nameLength, addressLength;

            // Read person's name
            char name[256];
            ReadLine( file, name, 255 );

            // Read person's address
            char address[256];
            ReadLine( file, address, 255 );

            // Create new person
            Person *p = AllocPerson();
            InitPerson( p, name, address );

            // Add person to address book
            AddPerson( addressBook, p );
        }
    }

    void DeallocAddressBook( AddressBook *addressBook ) {
        // Dealloc all Persons first
        int i;
        for ( i = 0; i < addressBook->numPersons; ++i )
            DeallocPerson(addressBook->persons[i]);

        // Now free persons array
        free(addressBook->persons);

        // Free address book
        free(addressBook);
    }

    // Adding a person passes ownership of the person to the AddressBook.
    // The return value is the address book if the person was added successfully,
    // NULL otherwise.
```

```c
AddressBook* AddPerson( AddressBook *addressBook, Person *person ) {
    int n = addressBook->numPersons;

    // Check that the persons array is big enough. Otherwise indicate error.
    if ( ++n > addressBook->maxNumPersons ) return NULL;

    // Array is big enough, so add the new person.
    addressBook->numPersons = n;
    addressBook->persons[n-1] = person;

    return addressBook;
}

// Find a person in the address book according to their name. If the person
// with the name is not found, NULL is returned.
Person* FindPerson( AddressBook *addressBook, char *name ) {
    int i;
    for ( i = 0; i < addressBook->numPersons; ++i ) {
        Person *person = addressBook->persons[i];
        if ( strcmp( person->name, name ) == 0 ) return person;
    }
    return NULL;
}

void SaveToFile( AddressBook *addressBook, FILE *file) {
    fprintf(file, "%d\n", addressBook->numPersons);
    fprintf(file, "%d\n", addressBook->maxNumPersons);

    int i;
    for ( i = 0; i < addressBook->numPersons; ++i ) {
        Person *p = addressBook->persons[i];
        fprintf(file, "%s\n", p->name);
        fprintf(file, "%s\n", p->address);
    }
}
```

code snippet MacOSXProg ch06/MyAddressBook 2/AddressBook.c

MAIN.C

```c
#include <stdio.h>
#include "Person.h"
#include "AddressBook.h"

int main () {
    AddressBook *addressBook = AllocAddressBook();
    InitAddressBook(addressBook, 1000);

    // Add a person to the address book
    Person *person = AllocPerson();
    InitPerson(person, "Joe Citizen", "1 Hopalong Avenue, MediumRare, USA");
    AddPerson(addressBook, person);

    // Add another
    person = AllocPerson();
    InitPerson(person, "Jill Citizen", "2 Hopalong Avenue, MediumRare, USA");
```

```
    AddPerson(addressBook, person);

    // Search for person in the address book
    person = FindPerson(addressBook, "Joe Citizen");
    printf("Found person\nName: %s\nAddress: %s\n", person->name,
        person->address);

    DeallocAddressBook(addressBook);
    return 0;
}
```

code snippet MacOSXProg ch06/MyAddressBook 2/main.c

3. Compile and run the program by clicking the Build and Go toolbar item, and bring up the Debugger Console.

How It Works

The `AddressBook` ADT is declared in the header file `AddressBook.h`. The data of `AddressBook` is declared in the following `struct`:

```
typedef struct {
    Person *persons[]; // An array of pointers to Person
    int numPersons;
    int maxNumPersons;
} AddressBook;
```

The `numPersons` variable is used to store the number of entries currently in the address book, and `maxNumPersons` stores the upper limit on the number allowed. The entries themselves are stored in the variable `persons`, which is an array of `Person` pointers.

The functions declared for `AddressBook` are the following:

```
AddressBook* CreateAddressBook( const char *pathToAddressBookFile );

AddressBook* AllocAddressBook();
void InitAddressBook( AddressBook *addressBook, const int maxNumPersons );
void InitAddressBookWithFile( AddressBook *addressBook, FILE *file);
void DeallocAddressBook( AddressBook *addressBook );

AddressBook* AddPerson( AddressBook *addressBook, Person *person );

Person* FindPerson( AddressBook *addressBook, char *name );

void SaveToFile( AddressBook *addressBook, FILE *file);
```

The `AllocAddressBook` function is provided for allocating memory for an `AddressBook`. Two different functions are provided for initializing an `AddressBook` after it has been allocated: `InitAddressBook` and `InitAddressBookWithFile`. The function `CreateAddressBook` allocates and initializes an `AddressBook` in one call, and `DeallocAddressBook` is responsible for deallocating the memory associated with an `AddressBook`, and all its member variables.

The other functions declared in the AddressBook.h file are AddPerson, for adding a new Person; FindPerson, for finding an existing Person; and SaveToFile, for saving the whole AddressBook to a file. This file can be read later to initialize a new AddressBook with the same information as the one saved, using the function InitAddressBookWithFile.

The InitAddressBook function in AddressBook.c looks like this:

```
void InitAddressBook( AddressBook *addressBook, const int maxNumPersons ) {
    addressBook->persons = malloc( sizeof(Person*) * maxNumPersons );
    addressBook->maxNumPersons = maxNumPersons;
    addressBook->numPersons = 0;
}
```

This function allocates an array of pointers to Persons and sets addressBook->persons with it. The other initializer function, InitAddressBookWithFile, calls InitAddressBook to do the initial memory allocation before adding addresses from the file.

```
void InitAddressBookWithFile( AddressBook *addressBook, FILE *file ) {
    int numPersons, maxNumPersons;
    fscanf(file, "%d", &numPersons);
    fscanf(file, "%d", &maxNumPersons);
    fgetc(file); // Remove the new line character

    // Call the other initializer first.
    InitAddressBook( addressBook, maxNumPersons );

    int i;
    for ( i = 0; i < numPersons; ++i ) {
        int nameLength, addressLength;

        // Read person's name
        char name[256];
        ReadLine( file, name, 255 );

        // Read person's address
        char address[256];
        ReadLine( file, address, 255 );

        // Create new person
        Person *p = AllocPerson();
        InitPerson( p, name, address );

        // Add person to address book
        AddPerson( addressBook, p );
    }
}
```

The loop reads one person's information at a time from the file. The number of Persons in the file is read first, along with the maximum number of Persons allowed in the address book. After the call to InitAddressBook, the loop reads one name and address at a time, allocates and initializes a new Person with the information, and adds it to the AddressBook with the AddPerson function.

The order in which the data is read from the file in InitAddressBookWithFile has to be exactly the same as the order in which it was written. The function SaveToFile is used for writing the AddressBook to a file as follows:

```
void SaveToFile( AddressBook *addressBook, FILE *file) {
    fprintf(file, "%d\n", addressBook->numPersons);
    fprintf(file, "%d\n", addressBook->maxNumPersons);

    int i;
    for ( i = 0; i < addressBook->numPersons; ++i ) {
        Person *p = addressBook->persons[i];
        fprintf(file, "%s\n", p->name);
        fprintf(file, "%s\n", p->address);
    }
}
```

As you can see, it first prints the number of Persons, and the maximum number allowed. This is exactly the same order that InitAddressBookWithFile read them in. The loop prints the name and address of each person in turn, in the same order in which they are read.

 WARNING *The capability to store information even after a program stops running is known as* persistence. *This can entail storing data on file, but it could also involve more advanced means such as using a database. Being able to save your ADTs to some form of storage, and retrieve them again, is very useful, and many ADTs will define functions for performing these actions.*

The function CreateAddressBook can be used to allocate and initialize a new AddressBook in a single function call. The function first checks to see if there is already an AddressBook stored on file. If so, it initializes the new AddressBook with the information stored using the function InitAddressBookWithFile, like this:

```
AddressBook* CreateAddressBook( const char *pathToAddressBookFile ) {
    AddressBook *addressBook = AllocAddressBook();
    FILE *file;
    file = fopen( pathToAddressBookFile, "r" );
    if ( NULL == file ) {
        // Create new address book
        InitAddressBook( addressBook, 1000 );
    }
    else {
        // Read address book from file
        InitAddressBookWithFile( addressBook, file );
        fclose(file);
    }
    return addressBook;
}
```

To check if the file exists, an attempt is made to open it with `fopen`. If a `NULL` pointer is returned, the file does not exist. If there is no file, an empty `AddressBook` is initialized with the function `InitAddressBook`.

The `AddPerson` function in `AddressBook.c` adds a `Person` pointer to the end of the `persons` array as shown here:

```
AddressBook* AddPerson( AddressBook *addressBook, Person *person ) {
    int n = addressBook->numPersons;

    // Check that the persons array is big enough. Otherwise indicate error.
    if ( ++n > addressBook->maxNumPersons ) return NULL;

    // Array is big enough, so add the new person.
    addressBook->numPersons = n;
    addressBook->persons[n-1] = person;

    return addressBook;
}
```

Care is taken to check that there is room for adding the new `Person`, by comparing the new value of `addressBook->numPersons` with the maximum allowed value `addressBook->maxNumPersons`. The latter is used to allocate the `persons` array in `InitAddressBook`; ignoring the maximum would cause data to be written outside the array, and either corrupt other data or crash the program.

 NOTE *The use of the increment operator ++ preceding the variable* n, *as in* ++n, *causes* n *to be incremented before its value is returned. This is different from* n++, *which returns the value of* n *before it has been incremented. You need to be careful not to confuse the two operators, because they can lead to very different outcomes.*

To find a person in the `AddressBook`, the `FindPerson` function simply loops over all the `Persons` in the `persons` array, and checks if a match is found for the name passed.

```
Person* FindPerson( AddressBook *addressBook, char *name ) {
    int i;
    for ( i = 0; i < addressBook->numPersons; ++i ) {
        Person *person = addressBook->persons[i];
        if ( strcmp( person->name, name ) == 0 ) return person;
    }
    return NULL;
}
```

The `strcmp` function compares the name passed with the name of a `Person` in the `persons` array. If they match — if 0 is returned — the `Person` is returned from `FindPerson`. If no `Person` matches, `NULL` is returned.

The last function you should consider is the `DeallocAddressBook` function, because it demonstrates the sort of actions you must take to clean up when you destruct an ADT variable.

```
void DeallocAddressBook( AddressBook *addressBook ) {
    // Dealloc all Persons first
    int i;
    for ( i = 0; i < addressBook->numPersons; ++i )
        DeallocPerson(addressBook->persons[i]);

    // Now free persons array
    free(addressBook->persons);

    // Free address book
    free(addressBook);
}
```

You can see that a call is made to every `Person` in the `persons` array. This brings up the issue of *ownership*, because by deleting a `Person`, the `AddressBook` is assuming that no other part of the program needs to use it anymore. The `AddressBook` is considered to own any `Person` passed to the `AddPerson` function, and is thus responsible for deleting it when the time comes.

 NOTE *An important part of memory management when programming with this structured form of C is to decide who owns each variable, and is thus responsible for deleting it. Not making a clear decision about this could lead to memory leaks, or variables being deallocated when they are still needed.*

The `DeallocAddressBook` function continues by freeing the `persons` array. Note that this happens after all the `Persons` contained in the array have been deallocated. If you freed the array first, you would not have any way to access its contents. The final act of `DeallocAddressBook` is to deallocate the `AddressBook` itself.

The `main` function is again used for testing purposes as follows:

```
int main () {
    AddressBook *addressBook = AllocAddressBook();
    InitAddressBook(addressBook, 1000);

    // Add a person to the address book
    Person *person = AllocPerson();
    InitPerson(person, "Joe Citizen", "1 Hopalong Avenue, MediumRare, USA");
    AddPerson(addressBook, person);

    // Add another
    person = AllocPerson();
    InitPerson(person, "Jill Citizen", "2 Hopalong Avenue, MediumRare, USA");
    AddPerson(addressBook, person);

    // Search for person in the address book
```

```
        person = FindPerson(addressBook, "Joe Citizen");
        printf("Found person\nName: %s\nAddress: %s\n", person->name, person->address);

        DeallocAddressBook(addressBook);
        return 0;
    }
```

This creates an `AddressBook` instance, adds two `Person` instances to it with the `AddPerson` function, searches for one of the `Persons` with the `FindPerson` function, and prints details of the `Person` found.

With basic data storage, ADTs are now defined for MyAddressBook. The next Try It Out moves on to deal with an ADT called `Controller`, which interacts with the user of the program and modifies the `AddressBook` instance according to requests from the user.

TRY IT OUT Finishing MyAddressBook

1. Using the approach described earlier for creating files for the `Person` and `AddressBook` ADTs, add files called `Controller.c` and `Controller.h` to the MyAddressBook project.

2. Insert the following code into the new files and replace the existing `main` function:

CONTROLLER.H

Available for
download on
Wrox.com

```
#ifndef CONTROLLER_H
#define CONTROLLER_H

#include <stdio.h>
#include "Person.h"
#include "AddressBook.h"

typedef struct {
    AddressBook *addressBook;
    char *pathToAddressBookFile;
} Controller;

Controller* AllocController();
void InitController(Controller *controller);
void DeallocController(Controller *controller);

void PrintIntroductoryMessage(Controller *controller);
void PrintUserOptions(Controller *controller);

int ProcessUserChoice(Controller *controller, char c);
void ProcessNewPersonRequest(Controller *controller);
void ProcessFindPersonRequest(Controller *controller);
void ProcessSaveRequest(Controller *controller);

#endif
```

code snippet MacOSXProg ch06/MyAddressBook 3/Controller.h

CONTROLLER.C

```c
#include "Controller.h"
#include <stdio.h>
#include <stdlib.h>
#include <string.h>
#include "Person.h"
#include "AddressBook.h"

Controller* AllocController() {
    return malloc( sizeof(Controller) );
}

void InitController(Controller *controller) {
    controller->pathToAddressBookFile = "/var/tmp/addressbook.txt";
    controller->addressBook =
        CreateAddressBook(controller->pathToAddressBookFile);
}

void DeallocController(Controller *controller) {
    DeallocAddressBook( controller->addressBook );
    free(controller);
}

void PrintIntroductoryMessage(Controller *controller) {
    printf("Welcome to MyAddressBook\n");
    printf("With this program, you can add addresses, retrieve them,\n"
 "and store them on file.\n");
}

void PrintUserOptions(Controller *controller) {
    printf("\nYou can either\n"
            "a) Add an address\n"
            "f) Find an address, or\n"
            "s) Save your addresses\n"
            "q) Save and Quit\n");
    printf("Please enter your choice (a, f, s, or q): ");
}

// Return value is 1 if the program should stop running, and 0
// if it should continue.
int ProcessUserChoice(Controller *controller, char choice) {
    int shouldStop = 0;
    switch (choice) {
        case 'a':
            ProcessNewPersonRequest(controller);
            break;
        case 'f':
            ProcessFindPersonRequest(controller);
            break;
        case 's':
            ProcessSaveRequest(controller);
            break;
```

```
            case 'q':
                ProcessSaveRequest(controller);
                shouldStop = 1;
                break;
            default:
                printf("You entered an invalid choice. Try again.\n");
        }
        return shouldStop;
    }

    void ProcessNewPersonRequest(Controller *controller) {
        char name[256];
        printf("You chose to add an address.\n");
        printf("Please enter the name of the person to add: ");
        gets(name);
        char address[256];
        printf("Please enter the address of the person on one line: ");
        gets(address);
        Person *p = AllocPerson();
        InitPerson( p, name, address );

        if ( ! AddPerson( controller->addressBook, p ) )
            printf("An error occurred while trying to add the new address.\n");
    }

    void ProcessFindPersonRequest(Controller *controller) {
        char name[256];
        printf("You chose to find an address.\n");
        printf("Please enter the name of the person to find: ");
        gets(name);

        // Print details of person if found. Otherwise tell the user that
        // the person could not be found.
        Person *p = FindPerson( controller->addressBook, name );
        if ( p )
            printf("The address of %s is\n%s\n", p->name, p->address );
        else
            printf("The address of %s could not be found.\n", name );
    }

    void ProcessSaveRequest(Controller *controller) {
        FILE *file = fopen(controller->pathToAddressBookFile, "w");
        SaveToFile(controller->addressBook, file);
        fclose(file);
    }
```

code snippet MacOSXProg ch06/MyAddressBook 3/Controller.c

MAIN.C

Available for
download on
Wrox.com

```
#include <stdio.h>
#include <string.h>
#include "Person.h"
#include "AddressBook.h"
#include "Controller.h"
```

```
int main () {
    Controller *controller = AllocController();
    InitController(controller);

    PrintIntroductoryMessage(controller);

    // Main run loop
    int exitMainLoop = 0;
    while ( !exitMainLoop ) {
        PrintUserOptions(controller);
        char line[256];
        gets( line );
        if ( strlen(line) > 1 ) {
            printf("You entered too many characters. Try again.\n");
        }
        else {
            exitMainLoop = ProcessUserChoice( controller, line[0] );
        }
    }

    DeallocController(controller);

    return 0;
}
```

code snippet MacOSXProg ch06/MyAddressBook 3/main.c

3. Compile and run the program by clicking the Build and Go toolbar item, and bring up the Debugger Console.

4. Follow the instructions printed by the program in the Debugger Console window. Add a few names and addresses. Search for one of the names you have entered, and also search for a name that you haven't added, just to see what happens. Try entering an invalid option to see how the program reacts.

5. When you have finished playing with MyAddressBook, choose the Save and Quit option. Now rerun the program, and search for one of the names you entered before you quit. The program should find and print the address, even though it was added in a different session.

How It Works

As you now know, the MyAddressBook program has three ADTs: `Person`, `AddressBook`, and `Controller`. A `Person` is a type that stores information about an entry in the address book — in particular, the name and address. The `AddressBook` type contains many instances of the type `Person`, which represents all the entries in the address book. The last ADT, `Controller`, is a type that interacts with the user and updates the data objects as required.

WARNING *This design is known as* Model-View-Controller (MVC), *and is very important in Cocoa programming, which you learn about in Chapter 8. Put simply, the data objects, such as* Person *and* AddressBook, *make up the Model. The View is the interface with the user, in this case a console with keyboard input. (In Cocoa programming, the View is usually the Aqua graphical user interface.) The Controller is the intermediary between the View and the Model, and is in charge of keeping the two synchronized with one another.*

The `Controller` has the usual functions for constructing and destructing the ADT, but it also includes functions that print information for the user and process user input.

```
typedef struct {
    AddressBook *addressBook;
    char *pathToAddressBookFile;
} Controller;

Controller* AllocController();
void InitController(Controller *controller);
void DeallocController(Controller *controller);

void PrintIntroductoryMessage(Controller *controller);
void PrintUserOptions(Controller *controller);

int ProcessUserChoice(Controller *controller, char c);
void ProcessNewPersonRequest(Controller *controller);
void ProcessFindPersonRequest(Controller *controller);
void ProcessSaveRequest(Controller *controller);
```

The `Controller struct` holds the `AddressBook` used in the program, in the variable `addressBook`. It also contains a path to the file where the address book can be saved.

The `Process . . .` functions handle different user requests. `ProcessNewPersonRequest` is for adding a new entry to the address book, and `ProcessFindPersonRequest` is for finding a person in the address book. Saving the address book to a file is handled by `ProcessSaveRequest`. The `ProcessUserChoice` function takes a `char` entered by the user, and chooses the appropriate `Process . . .` method to call for that choice. If the user presses a, for example, the `ProcessUserChoice` function ends up calling `ProcessNewPersonRequest`.

The `Controller.c` file contains most of the code for interacting with the user. When the user makes a choice, the `main` function calls the function `ProcessUserChoice` as follows:

```
int ProcessUserChoice(Controller *controller, char choice) {
    int shouldStop = 0;
    switch (choice) {
        case 'a':
            ProcessNewPersonRequest(controller);
            break;
```

```
        case 'f':
            ProcessFindPersonRequest(controller);
            break;
        case 's':
            ProcessSaveRequest(controller);
            break;
        case 'q':
            ProcessSaveRequest(controller);
            shouldStop = 1;
            break;
        default:
            printf("You entered an invalid choice. Try again.\n");
    }
    return shouldStop;
}
```

As you can see, this is really just a big `switch`. A processing method is chosen based on the letter entered by the user. When the user chooses q, the address book is saved by `ProcessSaveRequest`, and the flag `shouldStop` is set to 1. This causes the `main` function to exit.

When the user chooses to add a new address, the `ProcessNewPersonRequest` is called. It asks the user for the name and address of the new entry, creates a new `Person`, and adds it to the `AddressBook` as shown here:

```
void ProcessNewPersonRequest(Controller *controller) {
    char name[256];
    printf("You chose to add an address.\n");
    printf("Please enter the name of the person to add: ");
    gets(name);
    char address[256];
    printf("Please enter the address of the person on one line: ");
    gets(address);
    Person *p = AllocPerson();
    InitPerson( p, name, address );

    if ( ! AddPerson( controller->addressBook, p ) )
        printf("An error occurred while trying to add the new address.\n");
}
```

The address book is stored in the variable `controller->addressBook`, and gets created in the `InitController` function. Note that the return value of `AddPerson` is checked to see if it is `NULL`, because a `NULL` return value is used to indicate that an error has occurred, such as when the array of `Persons` is too small to hold the new entry.

The `ProcessFindPersonRequest` is very straightforward: it simply calls the `AddressBook`'s `FindPerson` function and returns the result.

ProcessSaveRequest first opens a file for writing, and then asks the AddressBook to save its contents on the file using the SaveToFile function, and finally closes the file again.

```c
void ProcessSaveRequest(Controller *controller) {
    FILE *file = fopen(controller->pathToAddressBookFile, "w");
    SaveToFile(controller->addressBook, file);
    fclose(file);
}
```

The path to where the AddressBook will be stored is fixed in this example — it's initialized in InitController to /var/tmp/addressbook.txt. In a more advanced program, the user would be able to set this path.

The Controller creates a new AddressBook by calling the function CreateAddressBook from AddressBook.c. As you saw earlier, this function first checks to see if there is already an AddressBook stored on file. If so, it initializes the new AddressBook with the information stored using the function InitAddressBookWithFile. If not, it creates a new empty AddressBook.

The main function is relatively simple. It creates a Controller, asks it to print an introductory message for the user, and then loops until the Controller indicates that it should stop.

```c
int main () {
    Controller *controller = AllocController();
    InitController(controller);

    PrintIntroductoryMessage(controller);

    // Main run loop
    int exitMainLoop = 0;
    while ( !exitMainLoop ) {
        PrintUserOptions(controller);
        char line[256];
        gets( line );
        if ( strlen(line) > 1 ) {
            printf("You entered too many characters. Try again.\n");
        }
        else {
            exitMainLoop = ProcessUserChoice( controller, line[0] );
        }
    }

    DeallocController(controller);

    return 0;
}
```

Each iteration of the loop prints a request for the user to choose an operation. The function PrintUserOptions is used for this purpose. The main function then uses the gets function to read the whole line of input typed by the user. If this line is longer than one character, an error message is printed. If exactly one character was entered (excluding the new line character), the character is passed to the `Controller` function `ProcessUserChoice`, which takes the appropriate action. `ProcessUserChoice` returns a non-zero value when the program should stop. After the loop exits, the `DeallocController` method frees the memory of the `Controller` and the `AddressBook` that it contains.

This concludes your exploration of the C programming language. C is useful in itself, but it becomes really useful as the basis for other languages, such as Objective-C, which you learn about in the next chapter. Ninety percent of Objective-C is just plain C, so having completed this chapter, you are well on your way to understanding Objective-C and learning to program with the Cocoa frameworks (which you learn about in Chapter 8).

SUMMARY

This chapter has been a crash course in one of the most important languages on Mac OS X. Along the way you have learned

➤   That C is the Latin of programming languages, underpinning operating systems such as Mac OS X and fathering modern languages such as Objective-C, Java, and C++.

➤   About various aspects of C, such as variables, pointers, functions, conditional branching, memory management, and looping.

➤   About structured programming in C, where data structures are coupled with functions to form abstract data types (ADTs). This style of programming is used in fundamental Mac OS X frameworks such as Core Foundation, Quartz 2D, and Core Audio. It is also the basis of object-oriented programming (OOP).

In the next chapter, you learn about Objective-C, which together with the Cocoa frameworks (Chapter 8) form the basis of most new application developments in Mac OS X. Before proceeding, however, try the exercises that follow to test your understanding of the material covered in this chapter. You can find the solutions to these exercises in Appendix A.

EXERCISES

1.   Modify the Grepper C program so that it can search in multiple files for a string. Assume that the filenames are given as the first arguments to the `main` function, and that the search string is given last. Test it by adding more than one file to the arguments of the Grepper executable in Xcode. Also modify the program so that line numbers are printed after the filename in the program output.

2.   Change MyAddressBook so the user can request that an entry be removed from the address book.

▶ WHAT YOU LEARNED IN THIS CHAPTER

C	the Latin of programming languages, forming the basis of most modern operating systems
Function	a block of source code that can be executed via a call from other parts of the program
Variable	a labeled piece of data
Operator	modifies or operates upon data
Array	a collection of data elements identifiable by index
Pointer	an address in memory
Branching	taking a different path through the code based on run-time conditions
Loop	a construct for the repetitive execution of a block of code
Block	an anonymous, inline function
String	textual data consisting of one or more characters
I/O	stands for input/output, the process of reading and writing data to and from disk
struct	a data structure that can hold multiple different variables of different types
Abstract Data Type (ADT)	an entity with data and functionality
Structured Programming	an approach to organizing programs using ADTs
Preprocessor	a program that can be used to modify source code before the compiler attempts to compile it

7

The Objective-C Language

WHAT YOU WILL LEARN IN THIS CHAPTER:

➤ What OOP is, and its most important characteristics

➤ The extensions to C defined by the Objective-C 2.0 language, including object-oriented programming

➤ How to write object-oriented programs in Objective-C, using the Foundation framework from Cocoa

Objective-C is an *object-oriented programming* (*OOP*) language that forms the basis of most software development on Mac OS X. It is a superset of the C programming language, which means that you can use C code directly in an Objective-C program. In fact, much of an Objective-C program is simply C. What's left is a small number of extensions to facilitate OOP, which can potentially make your life a lot easier as a programmer.

The philosophy of Objective-C is a minimalist one. The object-oriented (OO) features of Objective-C were designed as a compact and easy-to-understand extension to C. This is in contrast to C++, for example, which is also a superset of C, but which includes many different extensions to standard C, and is relatively difficult to learn. Anyone that understands C++, or any other OO language for that matter, can learn Objective-C in a few hours. For those with no understanding of OOP, Objective-C is one of the better languages with which to learn it, because of its simplicity.

Just because Objective-C is easy to learn and simple to use does not mean it gives away anything to other languages when it comes to expressiveness. In many ways, Objective-C is more powerful than other languages, by way of its dynamism, as you will learn as you proceed through this chapter. Cocoa developers, extolling the virtues of the Objective-C/Cocoa combination, often claim that they are much more productive than they ever were with any other combination of language and framework. After you have completed this chapter as well as Chapters 8 through 10, which cover the Cocoa frameworks, you can be the judge.

OBJECT-ORIENTED PROGRAMMING

Before you begin to learn Objective-C, you need to know a little bit about what it was designed to achieve. OOP has really caught on during the last 20 years or so, but it is now the de facto standard for all programming languages. Nearly all development these days takes place in the OO style — even in non-OO languages such as C!

So what is OOP? The main distinction between programming in an OO language such as Objective-C and programming in a procedural language such as C is that data and the functions that operate on that data are grouped into entities called *objects*. An object has both data and behavior: the data are the variables belonging to the object, and the behavior is defined by the object's functions.

An object is actually a variable or *instance* of a particular *class*. A class defines what data and functions a particular type of object has. For example, a class called Person could declare that Person objects have a name and address, and that they have functions to create a new Person, delete an existing Person, and perform operations such as changing a Person's address.

 NOTE *If you worked through the chapter on C programming, you should realize by now that OOP has many similarities with the structured programming example you encountered in the simple address book program MyAddressBook. Indeed, structured programming with Abstract Data Types (ADTs) was a forerunner of OOP, and is still used today to achieve some of the benefits of OOP in programming languages that do not support object orientation, such as C.*

The variables in an object are called *instance variables* or *attributes*. They are very similar to the variables in a C struct. The functions associated with an object are called *methods*, and are similar, though not the same, as functions in C.

An important aspect of OOP is being able to hide the data in an object from other parts of the program. This is known as *encapsulation*, because the object encapsulates its own data, and can choose what to make accessible to the rest of the program and how it will do so. Encapsulation is important, because it reduces the dependencies between different parts of a program. If you know that a certain variable can be accessed only from within a certain class, you have much less to think about when searching and changing code that uses that variable.

A second aspect of OOP is the capability to directly reuse the instance variables and member functions of one class inside another class. This is known as *inheritance*, and classes related in this way often mimic the relationships found in the real world. For example, a dentist is a type of person. You could say that a dentist *inherits* the characteristics of a person, as well as possessing some unique attributes that a general person does not exhibit. If you were modeling this in an OO program, you may create a Dentist class, which inherits all the data (that is, attributes) and behavior (that is, member functions) of a class Person. Thus, Dentist is said to be a subclass of Person.

The last major aspect of OOP languages not possessed by procedural languages is *polymorphism*. The word may be terrifying, but the meaning is less so: polymorphism is the capability of something to behave differently depending on the circumstances. In the context of OOP, it refers to the ability of a single *method invocation* — the OO equivalent of a function call — to execute different code depending on an object's class.

To make the discussion more concrete, take a real-world example: a `Man` is a type of `Person`, and a `Woman` is a type of `Person`. Each could be considered subclasses of `Person`. Assume that a `Person` has a life expectancy, which depends on its specific type — its subclass. A `Man`, for example, may have a life expectancy of only 70 years, while a `Woman` may expect to live for 77 years. If you have an object of the class `Person`, you will get a different answer to the question "What is your life expectancy?" depending on the specific subclass of `Person` you are talking to. In programming terms, the same method invocation — `lifeExpectancy`, for example — executes either code in the class `Man` or some code in the class `Woman`, depending on the type of `Person` used to invoke the method.

If this all seems a bit abstract, don't worry; it will become clearer when you see how these concepts are put into practice. At this point, it is only necessary that you get a vague feeling for what OOP is, and some of its more important attributes.

CLASSES AND OBJECTS

Objective-C takes the concepts presented in the previous section, and makes minimal extensions to C to implement them. Classes in Objective-C are comprised of two basic code structures: the *interface block* and the *implementation block*.

The interface block defines the interface of a class, which includes its instance variables and methods. The interface is usually found in a header file, because it should be accessible to the rest of the program. Here is an interface block for a class similar to the `Person` type defined in the MyAddressBook program from Chapter 6:

```
@interface Person : NSObject
{
    NSString *name;
    NSString *address;
}

-(id)initWithName:(NSString *)name andAddress:(NSString *)address;
-(void)dealloc;
-(NSString *)name;
-(NSString *)address;

@end
```

The interface block begins with the keyword `@interface`, and ends with `@end`. After the `@interface` keyword, the name of the class is given, followed by a colon and the name of the *superclass*. The superclass of `Person` is `NSObject`, just as `Person` is a subclass of `NSObject`.

`Person` inherits all the data and methods of the class `NSObject`. `NSObject` is an important Cocoa class from which nearly all classes ultimately descend. You learn more about this class as you go.

After the superclass, a block in braces declares the data belonging to the class. This part of the class interface is similar in many ways to a C `struct`, and the preceding code bears a close resemblance to the `struct Person` used in the MyAddressBook program in Chapter 6. The main difference is that C strings are represented by the simple type `char*`, but in Objective-C/Cocoa programming, variables of the class `NSString*` are usually used instead.

The `NS` that appears at the beginning of every Cocoa class name is a prefix used to avoid naming conflicts. An application or framework will often use a unique prefix for class names, so that the chance of two different classes having the same name is minimized.

 NOTE *The choice of* NS *may seem obscure, until you realize that Cocoa descends from a technology called OPENSTEP, which was jointly created by NeXT Computers and Sun Microsystems. Apple acquired the technology in 1996 and renamed it Cocoa. There is some controversy as to what* NS *actually stands for: some claim it is short for NeXTSTEP, the forerunner of OPENSTEP, while others believe it is an abbreviation of NeXT and Sun.*

After the instance variables, the method declarations appear. An Objective-C method signature looks considerably different from a C function, though there are many similarities, too. As with a C function, a method has a name, but this name is partitioned into sections, one for each parameter that the method declares. You learn more about how Objective-C methods are declared in the next section. For now, you simply need to recognize that the preceding example declares four different methods, one on each line.

The implementation block of the `Person` class could take the following form:

```
@implementation Person

-(id)initWithName:(NSString *)name andAddress:(NSString *)address {
...
}

-(void)dealloc {
...
}

-(NSString *)name {
...
}

-(NSString *)address {
...
}

@end
```

The implementation usually appears in a file with the extension .m, and the same base name as the header file in which the interface block appeared. In this case, the Person interface would probably be in the file Person.h, and the implementation in Person.m.

The implementation block is similar to the interface block, but has no data section. It contains the definitions of the methods declared in the interface block, between @implementation and @end keywords. The name of the class is given directly after the @implementation keyword, just as it was for the interface block.

In Objective-C, it is perfectly legal, and indeed common, to have multiple interface blocks, and multiple implementations per class. They don't even have to be in the same files. The extra blocks define *categories*, and the code in them has all the same privileges as the main interface and implementation blocks. The only difference is that a category cannot define any new data: the interface block cannot declare instance variables, only methods.

Here is the interface block of a category for the Person class:

```
@interface Person ( MeasurementsCategory )
-(float)heightInMeters;
-(float)weightInKilos;
@end
```

The implementation would look like this:

```
@implementation Person ( MeasurementsCategory )

-(float)heightInMeters {
...
}

-(float)weightInKilos {
...
}

@end
```

As you can see, a category has an additional label, given in parentheses after the class name in both the interface and implementation blocks. This label must be unique on a per-class basis, but can otherwise be any legal identifier. Note that the category implementation doesn't have to be in a separate implementation block, but can also be placed in an existing one.

In the Person example, a category called MeasurementsCategory has been defined. The interface block declares two methods: heightInMeters and weightInKilos. Note that there is no data block, because that is not allowed in a category.

The methods declared in MeasurementsCategory are treated exactly the same as methods declared in the main interface block. Everything you learn in the following sections about methods and how they work applies equally well to category methods as methods declared in the main interface block.

Objective-C places no special restrictions on the kind of methods defined in a category. For example, you can replace an existing method in a category. This allows you to change the behavior of a class without writing a subclass. You should be wary, however, that you cannot easily call the original method from inside your category method when you do this.

Finally, Objective-C 2.0 introduced a new type of category, the *class extension*. Class extensions are unnamed, anonymous categories that extend the main interface block. Class extensions are often used to declare methods in the .m file that are intended to be private to the class. The methods declared in a class extension should be defined in the main class implementation block. Here is an example of a class extension to the `Person` class that declares a single method (`calculateHeight`):

```
@interface Person ()
-(void)calculateHeight;
@end

@implementation Person

-(void)calculateHeight {
    ...
}

...

@end
```

 NOTE *Objective-C 2.0 is a revision to the language introduced by Apple in Mac OS X 10.5. It includes a number of improvements to the original Objective-C language, including class extensions, properties, and fast enumeration. You will learn about these new features later in this chapter.*

METHODS

Now you take a closer look at how methods are defined and called, or *invoked*, to be more consistent with the OO terminology.

Consider the first method of the previous `Person` class:

```
-(id)initWithName:(NSString *)name andAddress:(NSString *)address;
```

The method's name is broken into two segments: `initWithName:` and `andAddress:`. The full name of this method is `initWithName:andAddress:`, which is quite a mouthful, but has the advantage of reading as a sentence. After each section of the name, there is a colon, which is actually considered part of the name itself, and then a parameter. The type of the parameter is given in parentheses, followed by the parameter name.

It is also legal to have parameters with only a colon, and no preceding label, such as this:

```
-(void)methodWith3Parameters:(NSString *)param1 :(float)param2 :(int)param3;
```

The method name in this case is `methodWith3Parameters:::` — the colons are significant.

The parameter types in a method declaration are also optional, but if you exclude them, the parameter is assumed to be an object. A generic object has the type id in Objective-C, as shown in the following method declaration:

```
-(void)doSomethingWithObject:(id)object1 andObject:(id)object2;
```

Here is an equivalent declaration:

```
-(void)doSomethingWithObject:object1 andObject:object2;
```

By now, you know that Objective-C methods also have return values, just as C functions do. In the first example in this section, the return value was of the type id, a generic object. In the subsequent examples, there is no return value, so the return type was given as void, just as in C.

The hyphen that you see preceding every method signature is not just for decoration; it indicates an *instance method*. An instance method is one that belongs to an object or instance of the class. Instance methods have an extra hidden argument passed to them when they are invoked: the object that the method belongs to. This object can be accessed inside an instance method using the variable self. For example, it is not uncommon to see methods similar to the following in Objective-C classes:

```
-(void)run {
    [self takeYourMark];
    [self go];
}
```

Here the method run invokes two other methods, takeYourMark and go, both of which belong to the same class. It uses the self variable to refer to the object for which the other methods are invoked.

Another type of method is also found in Objective-C: the *class method*. Class methods are preceded by a + symbol rather than a hyphen. Class methods are shared by all objects of a particular class, and do not get passed an object hidden in the self variable; instead, the class itself is passed in via the self variable. Here is how you declare a class method for the Person class:

```
+(int)totalNumberOfPersons;
```

This method describes a property of the class Person, and not of an individual Person object, so it is appropriate to make it a class method.

Because a class method is invoked on the class itself, rather than on a particular instance of the class, you cannot access the instance variables inside a class method. Instance variables belong to instances (objects) of the class, not the class itself.

The only aspect of methods not yet considered is how you can actually invoke them. The syntax for invoking an Objective-C method is quite different from calling a C function. Here is an example of invoking one of the instance methods introduced earlier:

```
[obj doSomethingWithObject:arg1 andObject:arg2];
```

The whole invocation appears between square brackets. The object to which the method belongs — in this case, the object `obj` — comes first, followed by the segmented method name. After each colon in the name, an argument is given. In this case, the argument variables are called `arg1` and `arg2`.

Method invocations can be embedded in one another. Consider the following variation on the preceding example:

```
[[otherObj getObject] doSomethingWithObject:arg1 andObject:[anotherObj getArg]];
```

The original method invocation now has two additional invocations embedded within it. Each invocation is enclosed in square brackets. The first invokes the `getObject` method of the object `otherObj`. The return value of `getObject` becomes the object for which `doSomethingWithObject:andObject:` is invoked. The other embedded method is `getArg`, which is invoked for the object `anotherObj`, with the return value becoming the second argument to `doSomethingWithObject:andObject:`.

You may find the syntax used to invoke methods in Objective-C unusual at first, particularly if you are used to other calling conventions, but you soon get used to it, and when you do, you may even find it preferable to other styles. To better grasp how the Objective-C syntax works, here is the previous method as it might be written in Java or another C-like OO language:

```
otherObj.getObject().doSomething(arg1, anotherObj.getArg());
```

The Java way is a little shorter, but it's not as explicit about what arguments are being passed to `doSomething`. The Objective-C approach has the advantage of being more *self-documenting*, at the expense of being more verbose. Both approaches work well in practice, and which of the two is best is really a question of personal preference.

Class methods are invoked the same way as instance methods, but they must be invoked on a class. You can give the class explicitly, as in this example:

```
[Person totalNumberOfPersons];
```

Alternatively, you can give the class via the `class` method of an object, similar to this:

```
[[person class] totalNumberOfPersons];
```

The variable `person` is assumed here to be an instance of the class `Person`. The method `class` returns the class of any object.

> **NOTE** *Class methods in Objective-C are a bit different from the analogous methods found in Java or C++. In Objective-C, class methods behave just as instance methods do. For example, they can be inherited and overridden, concepts that you learn more about later in this chapter. In other languages, class methods — which are often called* static *methods — are similar to C functions and do not exhibit the OO characteristics of instance methods.*

In the following Try It Out example, you rewrite the Grepper program from Chapter 6 in Objective-C. This will give you an idea of what Objective-C looks like, and the way objects and classes are used.

TRY IT OUT Rewriting Grepper in Objective-C

1. Create a new project in Xcode. In the New Project panel, choose the project type Command Line Tool in the group Application. From the Type pop-up button, choose Foundation. Name the project **Grepper in Objective-C**.

2. Find the file Grepper in Objective C.m in the Source group of the Groups & Files list on the left. Select it so that its source code appears in the editor.

3. Replace the code in the open file, which was generated by Xcode, with the following:

Available for
download on
Wrox.com

```
#import <Foundation/Foundation.h>

int main (int argc, const char * argv[]) {
    NSAutoreleasePool * pool = [[NSAutoreleasePool alloc] init];

    @try {
        // Make sure there are two arguments given, the filename
        // and the search string
        if ( argc != 3 ) {
            NSException *exception =
                [NSException exceptionWithName:@"GrepperException"
                    reason:@"Wrong number of arguments passed to main."
                    userInfo:nil];
            @throw exception;
        }

        // Get input file path from standard input
        NSString *inpPathString =
            [NSString stringWithCString:argv[1] encoding:NSUTF8StringEncoding];

        // Get string to search for
        NSString *searchString =
            [NSString stringWithCString:argv[2] encoding:NSUTF8StringEncoding];

        // Read file into string
        NSError *error = nil;
        NSStringEncoding fileEncoding;
        NSString *fileString =
            [NSString stringWithContentsOfFile:inpPathString
                usedEncoding:&fileEncoding
                error:&error];

        // Split file string into lines
        NSArray *lines = [fileString componentsSeparatedByString:@"\n"];

        // Loop over lines, printing any that contain the search string
        NSFileHandle *so = [NSFileHandle fileHandleWithStandardOutput];
        for ( NSString *line in lines ) {
            // Find range of search string
```

```
        NSRange searchStringRange = [line rangeOfString:searchString];

        // If string was found, write it to standard output
        // Also add a new line character
        if ( searchStringRange.location != NSNotFound ) {
            NSString *s =
            [NSString stringWithFormat:@"In file %@:\t%@\n",
             inpPathString, line];
            [so writeData:[s dataUsingEncoding:NSUTF8StringEncoding]];
        }
    }
}
@catch (NSException *e) {
    NSLog(@"The following error occurred: %@", [e reason]);
}

[pool release];
return 0;
}
```

code snippet MacOSXProg ch07/ Grepper in Objective C /Grepper in Objective C.m

4. Choose Build from the Build menu to compile the program.

5. Open the Executables group in Groups & Files, click the Grepper in Objective C executable, and choose Get Info from the File menu. Select the Arguments tab, and add two arguments to the first table, by twice clicking the + button under the table. The first argument should be a path to a text file in which you would like to search. (It could even be the source code for this example.) The second argument should be the string that will be sought in the file. Close the Get Info panel.

6. Click the Build and Go toolbar item to run the program, and bring up the Console by choosing Console in the Run menu. You should be able to see the lines from the file you entered that contain the search string.

How It Works

This example, though short, is dense with Cocoa classes, so you are not expected to grasp it all at once. However, you should try to get a feel for Objective-C code, and how closely intertwined Objective-C is with Cocoa. Cocoa is to Objective-C what the Standard Library is to C.

At the top of the file, there is a preprocessor directive that is not recognized by the standard C preprocessor: #import. An #import statement is similar to #include, but it imports a file's content only once. Any further imports are ignored. In other words, it fulfills the same role as the #ifdef guards discussed in Chapter 6, but in a much easier and concise manner.

The #import statement imports the Foundation framework, which is part of Cocoa. It provides the functionality of Cocoa that is not related to the graphical user interface (GUI); that's why you can use it in a command-line tool such as Grepper, which has no GUI.

The main function begins by creating an object of the type NSAutoreleasePool. This has to do with memory management, and you should ignore it for the time being; it is discussed in depth later.

The main body of the code appears in a block between the Objective-C keywords `@try` and `@catch`. These are used for exception handling. Exception handling is about treating exceptional occurrences and errors. Objective-C provides facilities for exception handling that allow you to jump from anywhere in the `@try` block to the `@catch` block whenever an exception arises. An example of this appears at the top of the `@try` block as shown here:

```
if ( argc != 3 ) {
    NSException *exception =
        [NSException exceptionWithName:@"GrepperException"
            reason:@"Wrong number of arguments passed to main."
            userInfo:nil];
    @throw exception;
}
```

This is the same as the test performed in the original Grepper program to ensure there are exactly two arguments passed when the program is started. In the original program, if the condition was not met, the program simply returned a non-zero value. In this case, an exception is thrown: an object of the class `NSException` is created, and the keyword `@throw` is used to jump to the `@catch` block.

In the `@catch` block, the exception is caught, and the reason for the exception, which was included in the `NSException` when it was created, is output to the program log, using the function `NSLog` as follows:

```
@catch (NSException *e) {
    NSLog(@"The following error occurred: %@", [e reason]);
}
```

`NSLog` is virtually the same in its workings as `printf`, but it expects to be passed an `NSString` as the first argument, not a `char*`. A literal `NSString` is created using double quotes, preceded by an `@` symbol. Note also the formatting character `%@`, which is used when an object is to be printed — in this case, it's the reason for the exception, which is an `NSString`. When this formatting character is encountered, the `description` method of the object is called to get an `NSString` representing its value.

After the argument count test, several `NSstrings` are created as shown here:

```
// Get input file path from standard input
NSString *inpPathString =
    [NSString stringWithCString:argv[1] encoding:NSUTF8StringEncoding];

// Get string to search for
NSString *searchString =
    [NSString stringWithCString:argv[2] encoding:NSUTF8StringEncoding];

// Read file into string
NSError *error = nil;
NSStringEncoding fileEncoding;
NSString *fileString =
    [NSString stringWithContentsOfFile:inpPathString
        usedEncoding:&fileEncoding
        error:&error];

// Split file string into lines
NSArray *lines = [fileString componentsSeparatedByString:@"\n"];
```

Various methods are used to create the strings, including `stringWithCString:encoding:` to create strings from the `char*` string parameters of the `main` function, and `stringWithContentsOfFile:usedEncoding: error:`, which reads the file at the path passed and places its contents in an `NSString` object.

To make processing the file string easier, it is split into an array of lines. A Cocoa array class, `NSArray`, is used to contain the lines. Other than `NSString`, `NSArray` is probably the most widely used Cocoa class there is. It is similar to an array in C, in that you can store and retrieve objects by index, but it is also more powerful. You learn more about it in Chapter 8, which covers the Cocoa frameworks.

The last part of the `@try` block loops through the lines in the `NSArray`, and searches each one for the search string passed to the main function like this:

```
// Loop over lines, printing any that contain the search string
NSFileHandle *so = [NSFileHandle fileHandleWithStandardOutput];
for ( NSString *line in lines ) {
    // Find range of search string
    NSRange searchStringRange = [line rangeOfString:searchString];

    // If string was found, write it to standard output
    // Also add a new line character
    if ( searchStringRange.location != NSNotFound ) {
        NSString *s =
            [NSString stringWithFormat:@"In file %@:\t%@\n",
                inpPathString, line];
        [so writeData:[s dataUsingEncoding:NSUTF8StringEncoding]];
    }
}
```

A special `for` loop called a *fast enumeration* is used to iterate over the different lines in the array. Fast enumeration was introduced in Objective-C 2.0, and it is designed specifically for looping quickly over elements in Cocoa container classes such as `NSArray`.

To use fast enumeration, you declare the looping variable inside the `for` loop parentheses, and follow it by the keyword `in` and the container object (such as `NSArray`).

The `NSString` method `rangeOfString:` is used to search each line for the string stored in the variable `searchString`. This method returns an `NSRange`, which is a standard C `struct`, *not* an Objective-C class. As a result, you can treat `searchStringRange` as a stack variable, rather than a pointer to a heap object. Objective-C requires all objects be allocated from the application heap, and must always be represented as pointers. You learn more about how to create an Objective-C object later in this chapter.

`rangeOfString:` returns an `NSRange` with its location variable set to the constant `NSNotFound` if the string is not found. The `if` statement checks `searchStringRange` for the string, and writes the line to standard output when it is found. Standard output is represented by the variable `so`, which is a variable of the class `NSFileHandle`. `NSFileHandle` is the Objective-C class equivalent of C's `FILE` type.

DATA HIDING

An important aspect of OOP is encapsulation of data. Encapsulation requires that a language include facilities for *data hiding* so that the programmer can control access to data from outside a class. Objective-C provides three keywords for this purpose: `@public`, `@protected`, and `@private`.

These keywords can be inserted into the data section of a class's interface block and applies to any data that follows, up to the end of the block or the next keyword.

For example, imagine that you want to restrict access to the name attribute of the Person class, but wish to make the address attribute directly accessible to the rest of the program. You could declare the class like this:

```
@interface Person : NSObject
{
    @public
    NSString *address;

    @private
    NSString *name;
}

...

@end
```

The @public keyword makes an instance variable globally accessible. Any part of your program can directly retrieve the value of a public variable or modify its value. The @private keyword indicates that data may be accessed only from within the specific class in which it appears — in this case, Person. @protected gives access to the data from within the class in which it appears, but also from *descendents* of that class — subclasses of the class, subclasses of subclasses of the class, and so forth. If no keyword is given, instance variables are assumed to have protected accessibility.

In general, you should make as much data in your classes protected or private as possible. Public data is frowned upon in OOP, because any change in the way the data is represented in the class can potentially require global changes to your program. For example, imagine that instead of using an NSString to store the address in Person, you decide you want to use another class. Because your program has direct access to the address variable, you have to track down every point in the program where the address is accessed and update the code. This is not only a time-consuming operation, but it can also be error-prone, leading to bugs in your program.

So how should you access instance variables from outside the class itself? You can define methods explicitly for the purpose of getting and setting each instance variable that needs to be accessed from outside the class. Such methods are called *accessor methods* or *accessors*. Here is how you could declare the Person class with accessor methods, thus giving the rest of your program controlled access to the data it contains:

```
@interface Person : NSObject
{
    @private
    NSString *address;
    NSString *name;
}

-(NSString *)name;                       // Getter method for name
-(void)setName:(NSString *)newName;      // Setter method for name
```

```
-(NSString *)address;                      // Getter method for address
-(void)setAddress:(NSString *)newAddress;  // Setter method for address

...

@end
```

Accessors generally come in pairs, with a setter and a getter for each instance variable, but occasionally you may want to allow only data to be read, in which case, you would supply only a getter. The getter simply returns the value of the instance variable, and the setter takes the new value of the variable as an argument and sets the variable to that value.

Apart from restricting access to data, accessors also play a crucial role in memory management in Objective-C. They are thus even more important in Objective-C than in other languages, such as Java. A bit later, you learn how to write accessor methods, but for now it is enough to understand their purpose and importance.

 NOTE *Objective-C 2.0 introduced a shorthand way of generating accessor methods known as* declared properties. *Properties are equivalent to handwritten accessors, but are more concise and less cumbersome. Properties are covered later in this chapter.*

SUBCLASSING

Each class in Objective-C can have a *superclass* from which it inherits data and methods. Only *single inheritance* is allowed, meaning that each class may only have a maximum of one superclass.

Languages such as C++ allow multiple inheritance, where each class may have many superclasses. Other languages, such as Java, do not. Multiple inheritance is a hotly debated issue among OO programmers: it seems a powerful feature, but you also have to be careful how you use it, or it can lead to serious design issues and make a program difficult to understand.

NAMING CONVENTIONS

The naming convention used in the example is that the getter shares the name of the instance variable, and the setter name begins with set, and ends with the variable name in mixed-case format.

Naming of accessors in Objective-C/Cocoa programming is not simply a question of whatever takes your fancy. You should stick to the convention used here, because the Cocoa frameworks include various technologies, such as Bindings, that work only if your code adheres to the convention. Adopting a different naming scheme will effectively prevent you from using important features of Cocoa in your programs. You learn more about Bindings in Chapters 8 through 10.

NOTE *Languages such as Objective-C and Java have opted for single inheritance, but add a second mechanism to mimic one of the better aspects of multiple inheritance: the ability to have two classes not in the same inheritance tree share some interface. Objective-C provides* protocols *for this purpose, which are covered later in this chapter.*

When you are programming with Cocoa in Objective-C, all your objects will have a superclass. Most classes in a Cocoa program descend from the class NSObject, which contains much of the basic functionality in Cocoa, including memory management.

Recall from the discussion earlier in this chapter that a subclass inherits all the data and methods of its superclass. The following class inherits all the methods in SuperClass:

```
@interface SubClass : SuperClass
{
    @private
    int subClassInt;
}

-(id)init;
-(void)dealloc;

-(void)subClassMethod;

@end
```

If the SuperClass interface looks like this:

```
@interface SuperClass : SuperDuperClass
{
    @private
    int superClassInt;
}

-(id)init;
-(void)dealloc;

-(void)superClassMethod;

@end
```

SubClass will include the integer instance variable superClassInt and the method superClassMethod, as if SubClass had declared them itself. (Note that the SubClass has no direct access to superClassInt, because it is private to SuperClass, but the data for superClassInt is included in SubClass.)

The SuperClass also inherits from SuperDuperClass, so all the instance variables and methods in SuperDuperClass are also included in SubClass, as though it had declared them itself. SubClass is said to be a *descendent* of SuperDuperClass, and includes its methods and data via inheritance from SuperClass. SuperDuperClass is an *ancestor* of SubClass.

The following code makes use of SubClass, demonstrating that methods inherited from the superclass can be invoked for the subclass:

```
SubClass *subClassObj = [[SubClass alloc] init];
[subClassObj superClassMethod];
[subClassObj release];
```

The method alloc is inherited from NSObject and allocates memory for the SubClass object. init initializes it and returns a pointer, which is stored in the variable subClassObj. The method superClassMethod, which is defined in SuperClass, is then invoked on the SubClass object as though it were defined in that class. Finally, the method release from NSObject is invoked to indicate that the object is no longer needed.

> **NOTE** alloc *and* release *form an integral part of memory management in Cocoa and are covered in detail later in this chapter.*

You may have noticed that SubClass has declared two methods that are also declared by SuperClass: init and dealloc. A subclass is allowed to redefine any of the methods it inherits from its superclass and, implicitly, from any of its ancestors. This is called *overriding*. The subclass can even invoke the superclass method from inside the overriding method. This is a way of extending the functionality of a method in a subclass.

> **NOTE** *A subclass can override superclass methods, but it cannot override superclass instance variables. Two different instance variables cannot have the same name, even if one is in the superclass and the other in a subclass.*

Take this typical implementation of dealloc, which is a method inherited from NSObject and is used to deallocate an object when it is no longer needed:

```
-(void)dealloc {
    [instanceVar release];
    [super dealloc];
}
```

This method first invokes the `release` method of the instance variable `instanceVar`, and then invokes the `dealloc` method of the superclass. Methods in the superclass can be called using the variable `super`. Effectively, the `dealloc` method in the superclass has been extended in the subclass to include the line that invokes `release`.

The keyword `super` is used to access the contents of the superclass. In this case, the `dealloc` method of the superclass is invoked at the end of the `dealloc` method of the subclass. This *chaining* of method invocations is very common in OOP.

 NOTE *Languages such as Java and C++ allow not only for method overriding, but also method* overloading. *Overloading is giving the same name to two different methods in a class. The methods are distinguished by their parameters, so it must be clear from the arguments passed in the calling code which of the overloaded methods is intended. Objective-C does not have method overloading, but it is not really needed, because the sectioned naming scheme means that you rarely want two methods with the same name. For example, imagine that you have a method called* execute *in Java or C++, which is overloaded to take either an argument of type* ClassA *or an argument of type* ClassB. *In Objective-C, the argument types are usually incorporated into the method name, so you would probably name the two methods something like* executeWithClassA: *and* executeWithClassB:. *This approach has the added advantage of making your code more readable.*

An object of a given class can always be used where an object of an ancestor class is expected. This is an example of polymorphism, and an extremely important concept in OOP. Because a descendent class contains all the methods and data of its ancestors, objects of the descendent class can do everything defined by the ancestor classes (and more), and may thus be used wherever an object of the ancestor class is expected.

The easiest way to understand this is to consider an example. In the Foundation framework of Cocoa, the `NSString` class is used to represent string objects that are immutable, meaning they cannot change after they have been created. There is also a subclass of `NSString` called `NSMutableString`. `NSMutableString` inherits all the data and methods of `NSString`, of course, and introduces a number of new methods that allow its contents to be modified. Because `NSMutableString` is a subclass of `NSString`, it can be used wherever an `NSString` is expected. Take this function, for example:

```
NSString* PrintAndReturnString(NSString *string) {
    NSLog(string);
    return string;
}
```

Looking at this function, you may be led to think that `PrintAndReturnString` can be used only with objects of the class `NSString`. This is not true. It can be used with objects of any class descending from `NSString`, including `NSMutableString`. So the following calling code is perfectly legal:

```
NSString *str = PrintAndReturnString(@"Some NSString");
NSMutableString *mstr = [NSMutableString stringWithString:@"Some NSMutableString"];
mstr = (NSMutableString *)PrintAndReturnString(mstr);
```

On the first line, a literal `NSString` is passed to the `PrintAndReturnString` function, and the return value is assigned to the variable `str`. On the last two lines, an `NSMutableString` instance is created with the `stringWithString:` method, and this too is passed to `PrintAndReturnString`. In both calls to `PrintAndReturnString`, the object passed will be printed by the `NSLog` function, which is similar to C's `printf` function.

You may have noticed that assigning the return value to `mstr` on the last line required a cast to `NSMutableString*`. Wasn't it stated that you could use an `NSMutableString` wherever an `NSString` is expected? That's right, but we didn't say you could use an `NSString` wherever an `NSMutableString` is expected. The assignment of the return value of `PrintAndReturnString` to `mstr` attempts to assign an `NSString*` to an `NSMutableString*` variable. Although you know that the string returned from `PrintAndReturnString` is actually an `NSMutableString`, not just an `NSString`, the compiler does not know and must assume an `NSString` is being returned. To compile this code, you need to cast the `NSString` returned to an `NSMutableString`. This is called *downcasting*, because you are casting down the inheritance hierarchy from an ancestor class to one of its descendents.

Being able to substitute objects of a descendent class wherever an object of an ancestor class is expected is the primary source of polymorphism in OO programs. Because you can use different descendent classes in the same code, such as in `PrintAndReturnString`, that code can be made to behave differently depending on the class of object used — it can behave polymorphically. Polymorphism is difficult to grasp at first, but it's an essential aspect of OOP.

MESSAGING

Now that you know about inheritance in Objective-C, you are ready to consider method invocation, or *messaging*. It is called messaging because it is similar to sending a message to an object, asking it to do something. Messaging has similarities to function calling, but it is important to realize that it is a higher-level operation: a single message will often entail several behind-the-scenes function calls.

When you send a message, such as the following, a chain of events is set in motion:

```
[obj doSomething];
```

The function `objc_msgSend` is called, with the object and an identifier for the message `doSomething` passed as arguments. `objc_msgSend` is a function in the *Objective-C runtime*, which is a library of functions and data structures in every Objective-C program.

objc_msgSend performs a search for a function matching the arguments passed to it. It first looks in the class of obj to see if a doSomething method has been defined there. If not, it moves to the superclass to see if doSomething appears there. It then moves to the superclass of the superclass, and so forth, until a doSomething method is found. When doSomething is located, the corresponding function is called. If it is not found in any of the ancestors of the class of obj, an error occurs.

As you can see from this example, messaging is a high-level operation, often leading to several function calls. It is also very powerful, because a programmer can influence the messaging procedure in various ways. For example, it is possible to intercept any message that does not appear in the inheritance tree, and *forward* it to another object. This can be used to mimic multiple inheritance, or to easily implement a so-called *proxy* class, which passes most of its messages on to another class or program, perhaps via a network.

Each method has a unique identifier in the Objective-C runtime, called a *selector*. A selector has the C type SEL. You can get the selector of a method by using the @selector keyword, as in this example:

```
[obj performSelector:@selector(doSomething) withObject:nil];
```

The performSelector:withObject: method can be found in NSObject. It takes a selector and an object as arguments, and invokes the method passing the object as the sole argument. If the object has the value nil, which is the Objective-C equivalent of NULL for object values, no argument is passed. The preceding line of code is thus equivalent to the following:

```
[obj doSomething];
```

Selectors can be very powerful, because they allow you to store method names in variables and pass them around as arguments to functions or methods of other objects. It is possible, for example, to read a string from file, convert it to a selector using the Cocoa function NSSelectorFromString, and invoke the corresponding method of an object. This sort of flexibility is considerably more difficult to achieve in most other programming languages.

PROTOCOLS AND INFORMAL PROTOCOLS

Objective-C is a language with single inheritance, meaning that each class can have, at most, one superclass. But there is a mechanism for defining shared behavior between classes that are not related by inheritance: *protocols*. Protocols can be used to define a set of methods that a class must implement. It is a bit like a class without any data, consisting of an interface declaring the methods that are implemented, and nothing more. There is no limit to the number of protocols a class can conform to, and there is no limit to the number of classes that can conform to a single protocol. With protocols, you can get some of the advantages of multiple inheritance, without the drawbacks.

DYNAMIC VERSUS STATIC TYPING

Programming languages generally fall into two basic categories: *statically typed* and *dynamically typed*. Statically typed languages such as C++ and Java require that the type of an object be explicitly known when the program is compiled, so that the compiler can check if it has been used in a valid way. This means that a programmer is often forced to explicitly cast object types to compile, making code more verbose and difficult to read. It also makes sending an arbitrary message to an object more involved or, worse still, impossible. In C++, for example, it is not possible to send arbitrary messages to objects without manually building the capability into your program.

Objective-C is a dynamically typed language, meaning that it does not require that an object type be given explicitly for the compiler to check. Instead, the type is effectively checked at *runtime*, because whenever an object is used inappropriately — by sending it an invalid message, for example — an error will occur. By postponing *type checking* until runtime, Objective-C can avoid the casting required in statically typed languages, making the code easier to read. It also makes it more flexible, because you can easily invoke arbitrary methods on objects, without having to indicate what object classes are involved in the transaction.

Static typing has the advantage that it can catch certain programmer errors a bit faster than dynamic typing, because you don't have to run the program first. For this reason, Objective-C offers static typing extensions. In theory, you could give all object variables in your programs the type id, but it is generally better to include an explicit type where that is known. Objective-C allows you to do this, and you are warned by the compiler if it detects that you are using an object in an invalid way. No error will arise though — only a warning — and your program will still compile. In contrast to statically typed languages, object types in Objective-C are used only to alert the programmer to potential problems, and are not needed to compile the code.

Here is an example of a protocol declaration:

```
@protocol Execution
-(void)execute;
-(void)stopExecution;
@end
```

This looks like an interface block without the data section, and with the @interface keyword replaced by @protocol. A protocol has no implementation block — it only defines interface. It is up to a class conforming to the protocol to provide the implementation. Here is the interface of a class called Task that conforms to the Execution protocol:

```
@interface Task : NSObject <Execution>
{
}
@end
```

Protocols that a class conforms to are added after the superclass in triangular brackets. If there are multiple protocols, they are separated by commas. It is not necessary to re-declare the protocol methods in the conforming class's interface block, though you can if you want.

`Task` must implement the methods in the `Execution` protocol, and could look similar to this:

```
@implementation Task

-(void)execute {
...
}

-(void)stopExecution {
...
}

@end
```

The implementation block makes no reference to the protocol, but it must provide implementations for the methods declared in the protocol.

The advantage of protocols is that completely unrelated classes can conform to the same protocol, and thus be used in similar contexts. Imagine that in addition to `Task`, you have a second class that conforms to `Execution` called `Television`. There would seem to be no relation between `Task` and `Television`, but they both conform to `Execution`, so you could write a function similar to the following that would work with an object of either type:

```
void StartAndStop( id <Execution> executableObj ) {
    [executableObj execute];
    [executableObj stopExecution];
}
```

The parameter of this function has the type `id <Execution>`. The class is given first, which in this case is the generic `id` type. Any protocols that the object must conform to, such as `Execution`, are given next in triangular brackets. Because both `Task` and `Television` conform to `Execution` — they are both *executable* — an object of either type can be passed to the `StartAndStop` function. `StartAndStop` uses only the methods from the `Execution` protocol, and both `Task` and `Television` are required to define these methods.

You could call the `StartAndStop` function with any object conforming to the `Execution` protocol, as in this example:

```
Task *task = [[Task alloc] init];
StartAndStop(task);

Television *tele = [[Television alloc] init];
StartAndStop(tele);
```

The `Execution` protocol requires that all of its methods be implemented by each conforming class. Sometimes this is what you want, and sometimes it isn't.

When you have a situation where you want to give classes the option of leaving some methods out, you can use a protocol with optional methods. By including the keyword `@optional` in a protocol, you can indicate that certain methods do not have to be defined in the classes that conform to the protocol.

 NOTE *Before Objective-C 2.0 arrived, protocols could not include optional methods. To get around this, developers used categories of the* `NSObject` *class to declare informal protocols. The net effect was the same: classes could choose whether or not to implement the methods in the informal protocol. These days, you can better use protocols with optional methods than informal protocols, because the latter is not a language construct and has no compiler support.*

A common use for protocols with optional methods is *delegation*. A *delegate* is an object that is sent messages by another object when certain events occur. Here is how you declare such a protocol for the `Task` class:

```
@protocol TaskDelegate

@optional

-(BOOL)taskExecutionShouldBegin:(Task *)task;
-(void)taskExecutionDidBegin:(Task *)task;

-(BOOL)taskExecutionShouldStop:(Task *)task;
-(void)taskExecutionDidStop:(Task *)task;

@end
```

And here is how you write a class that conforms to the `TaskDelegate` protocol, and can thereby act as the delegate of a `Task`:

```
@interface TaskObserver <TaskDelegate>
{
}
@end

@implementation TaskObserver

-(BOOL)taskExecutionShouldBegin:(Task *)task {
    ...
    return YES;
}

-(void)taskExecutionDidStop:(Task *)task {
    ...
}

@end
```

The class `TaskObserver` implements two of the methods of the `TaskDelegate` protocol. The method `taskExecutionShouldBegin:` is sent by a `Task` object to its delegate whenever the `execute` method is called, and execution is about to begin. The `Task` object passes itself as the only argument so that the delegate knows which `Task` object is sending the message. The use of the word SHOULD in the title is a convention that indicates that the delegate determines whether or not the action may proceed. By returning a `true` value, the execution continues; a `false` value would prevent execution from proceeding.

> **NOTE** In the Cocoa frameworks, BOOL is defined to represent the type of Boolean values, because originally C had no such built-in type. (C99 includes a built-in Boolean type.) In practice, BOOL is simply a C type. BOOL can take the value YES, which is defined as a non-zero value, or NO, which is zero.

The other method defined in `TaskObserver`, `taskExecutionDidStop:`, is sent when the `stopExecution` method of `Task` is invoked, after execution has ended. Note that `TaskObserver` did not provide implementations for `taskExecutionDidBegin:` or `taskExecutionShouldStop:`. This is the primary advantage of optional methods in a protocol — a class can choose which of the methods it will implement.

> **NOTE** The opposite of the `@optional` keyword in protocol definitions is `@required`. You can use this to indicate that certain methods must be provided by conforming classes. But because `@required` is the default, you usually don't write it explicitly.

One question remains: How does `Task` call its delegate? First, a class with a delegate usually supplies the accessor methods `setDelegate:` and `delegate`, or the equivalent property. A `TaskObserver` object could become a `Task` delegate with code similar to the following:

```
Task *task = [[Task alloc] init];
TaskObserver *observer = [[TaskObserver alloc] init];
[task setDelegate:observer];
```

`Task` then includes code similar to the following at any point that it needs to message its delegate:

```
id del = [self delegate];
if ( [del respondsToSelector:@selector(taskExecutionShouldBegin:)] )
    [del taskExecutionShouldBegin:self];
```

This code first gets the delegate and stores it in the local variable `del`, which is of the generic class type `id`. The `if` condition sends a message to the delegate, asking whether it implements the method `taskExecutionShouldBegin:`. The `NSObject` method `respondsToSelector:` is used for this purpose. If the delegate implements the method, then the message `taskExecutionShouldBegin:` is sent with `self` — the `Task` instance — as the argument. If `del` is not set, or it doesn't implement the `taskExecutionShouldBegin:` method, no action is taken.

The preceding example dealt with optional methods in protocols as they are used to implement a delegation relationship, which is a common application, but by no means the only one. Other applications also exist, and many involve mixing required and optional methods in the same protocol.

NAMING CONVENTIONS

At several points in this chapter, you encountered Objective-C conventions. Conventions are not built into the language proper, but nonetheless pervade Objective-C/Cocoa programming. Understanding these conventions can be just as important as grasping the formal aspects of the language.

Objective-C has many conventions, and some of them apply to naming. You may think that you can name functions, variables, and classes in any way you like, within the rules laid down by the Objective-C grammar. That is true, but if you do not stick to the naming conventions of Objective-C/Cocoa, your programs will be at a disadvantage, and not have access to certain functionality.

You have probably already worked out most of the naming conventions, simply by reading the example code. Classes should be in *mixed-case* format, with all words beginning with a capital letter. Following this rule, you might have a class named `ClassWithALongName`. Variables should also be in mixed-case format, with all words except the first beginning with a capital letter. For example, you might have a variable named `variableWithALongName`. So you might have a class called `ClassWithALongName`, and a variable called `variableWithALongName`.

Accessor methods, which were introduced earlier, should also follow a convention: Setters should begin with `set` and be followed by the corresponding variable in mixed-case form, such as `setVariableWithALongName:`. Getters should have the same name as the variable they are accessing, such as `variableWithALongName`.

Why is all this so important? Cocoa assumes that you will follow these conventions, and builds that assumption into certain important technologies. One of these is *Key-Value Coding (KVC)*, which is used to implement *Bindings*, which you learn about in Chapters 8 through 10. KVC allows you to get and set instance variables using strings, or *keys*, rather than calling an accessor directly. For example, to get the value of an instance variable called `date`, you could do the following:

```
NSDate *d = [obj valueForKey:@"date"];
```

Note that there is no call to the accessor `date`. Instead, the method `valueForKey:` searches the methods defined in the class of `obj`, looking for an accessor called `date`. If it finds one, it calls it and returns the result. If not, it looks to see if there is an instance variable called `date`. If there is, it returns that directly.

You can also set `date` using KVC as follows:

```
NSDate *d = [NSDate date];
[obj setValue:d forKey:@"date"];
```

In this case, the `setValue:forKey:` method looks for an accessor called `setDate:`. If it finds such an accessor, it is called with `d` as an argument. If `setDate:` does not exist in the class, `setValue:forKey:` checks for an instance variable called `date`. If such a variable is found, it is set to `d` directly.

KVC is an important part of Cocoa programming, which facilitates many of its cooler features. Interface Builder, for example, would not be nearly as powerful without KVC, and Bindings would probably not have materialized at all without KVC. These technologies rely on the ability to get and set object properties with keys, and for this to work, you need to follow the conventions laid down, or they will not work with your classes.

CREATING AND DESTROYING OBJECTS

An important part of any OOP language is being able to create and destroy objects. In Objective-C, creation or *instantiation* of objects occurs in two stages: *allocation* and *initialization*. The NSObject method `alloc` takes care of allocating the memory needed to store the instance variables of an object. You should practically never need to override `alloc` to implement your own memory allocation scheme.

Initialization occurs in a method called an *initializer*. An initializer is a just a method like any other, and could be given any name; however, Cocoa convention says that it should begin with `init`. Initializers are responsible for allocating and initializing any instance variables, as well as ensuring that an initializer in the superclass is called. Here is an example of an initializer:

```
-(id)init {
    if ( self = [super init] ) {
        [self setCount:0];
        [self setGreeting:@"Hello"];
    }
    return self;
}
```

The `if` statement may seem a bit strange. It first assigns the `self` variable to the return value of the `init` method in the superclass. In Objective-C, it is acceptable for an initializer to replace an object with a different instance and return that, so assigning `self` to the return value of `super`'s `init` is good practice, even though `self` generally will not change.

The return value of an assignment is simply the value of the left-hand side (LHS) after the assignment — in this case, the value of `self`. Another Cocoa convention says that if there is an error in an initializer, that initializer should return `nil`. The `if` statement checks whether `self` is `nil`. (Non-nil values are the same as non-zero values in an `if` statement, and thus considered true.) If it is a non-nil value, the instance variables are initialized, which, in the preceding example, involves invoking two setter methods.

An initializer must return the object it has initialized. In the example, `self` is returned, which is the case for most of the initializers you will encounter. Returning the initialized object makes it easier to embed initializer invocations in longer expressions, such as this:

```
Cat *cat = [[[Cat alloc] initWithName:@"Bob"] autorelease];
```

You learn about the `autorelease` method in the next section, but what this example demonstrates is the way in which initializers are often used in Objective-C code.

A class can have many initializers, but it only has one *designated initializer*. The designated initializer is yet another Objective-C convention. Usually, the designated initializer is the most general initializer in a class, the one that gives you the most control over the contents of an object. For example, take this class representing cats:

```
@interface Cat : NSObject
{
    NSString *name;
    unsigned age;
}

-(id)init;
-(id)initWithName:(NSString *)newName;
-(id)initWithName:(NSString *)newName andAge:(unsigned)newAge; // Designated

-(void)setName:(NSString *)newName;
-(NSString *)newName;

-(void)setAge:(unsigned)newAge;
-(unsigned)newAge;

@end
```

The three initializers belonging to the class `Cat` would probably be chained together in the implementation block, in this manner:

```
@implementation Cat

-(id)init {
    return [self initWithName:@"No Name"];
}

-(id)initWithName:(NSString *)newName {
    return [self initWithName:newName andAge:0];
}
```

```
-(id)initWithName:(NSString *)newName andAge:(unsigned)newAge {
    if ( self = [super init] ) {
        [self setName:newName];
        [self setAge:newAge];
    }
    return self;
}

...

@end
```

The designated initializer is the most general one: `initWithName:andAge:`. It allows you the most control over the contents of a `Cat` object. Other initializers do no initializing of their own, but instead invoke their sibling initializers to do the work for them. These invocations all end up back at the designated initializer, which actually takes the steps of invoking the superclass initializer, setting the instance variables, and returning the initialized object.

Because designated initializers are a convention, they have no language support. Therefore, it is important that you document in your code which of the initializers in a class is the designated initializer. The reason this is important is that subclasses should nearly always call the designated initializer of their superclass. This prevents strange things from happening during the initialization process.

 NOTE NSObject *is the root of the whole Cocoa class hierarchy, and many of your classes will inherit directly from this class. The only initializer that* NSObject *has is* init, *which is the designated initializer by default. Whenever you subclass* NSObject *directly, you need to invoke the* init *method of the* super *variable.*

When you no longer need an object, you have to be able to delete it. In Cocoa, object deletion takes place in the `dealloc` method. You should never call the `dealloc` method directly though. Instead, you call either the `release` or `autorelease` method when you don't need an object anymore. These methods, which are defined in `NSObject`, are covered in detail in the next section. They simply indicate that an object is no longer needed by a particular part of the program. When all parts of the program using the object have released it, the `dealloc` method is called behind-the-scenes to delete it.

 NOTE *The* release, autorelease, *and* dealloc *methods are only used in code that performs memory management manually (as discussed in the next section). If you are using automatic garbage collection for memory management, you do not call these methods, and the* dealloc *method is not used.*

Here is the `dealloc` method for the `Cat` class:

```
-(void)dealloc {
    [name release];
    [super dealloc];
}
```

A `release` message is sent to the `name` string to indicate that it is not needed anymore by the `Cat` object. If it is still being used by other parts of the program, it will not be deleted. When it is not needed anywhere in the program, the string's `dealloc` method gets invoked.

Although you should never invoke the `dealloc` method of an object directly from outside a class, it is acceptable — indeed necessary — to invoke it from within the `dealloc` method of a subclass, as in the preceding example. Like an initializer, the `dealloc` method should always invoke the `dealloc` method of its superclass, usually after it has released the class's instance variables. If you don't do this, a memory leak will arise.

> **NOTE** *If you are using garbage collection, you do not need to write a* `dealloc` *method or manually manage your memory. If you need to clean up some resources when an object is deleted, you can implement the* `finalize` *method.* `finalize` *gets called when an object is deleted by the garbage collector.*

In addition to object initialization, Objective-C also provides a means of initializing data used class-wide. The `initialize` class method is called once before a class is used for the first time. You can set up any data structures needed by the class in this method. Here is an example of setting user preference defaults in an `initialize` method, which is a common use of the method:

```
+(void)initialize {
    NSUserDefaults *defs = [NSUserDefaults standardUserDefaults];
    [defs registerDefaults:
        [NSDictionary dictionaryWithObject:@"/var/tmp" forKey:@"TempDir"]];
}
```

The class `NSUserDefaults` is used to store preferences for a program. The `standardUserDefaults` method returns a shared object that is used throughout the program. The `registerDefaults:` method sets default values, which are used when a particular preference has not been set explicitly somewhere else in the program or found in the user's preferences file.

An `NSDictionary` is passed to the `registerDefaults:` method. An `NSDictionary` is a container class similar to an `NSArray`; but rather than using indexes to access stored data, `NSDictionary` uses *keys*. The data in an `NSDictionary` is unordered, so using an index to reference it makes no sense; instead, you supply a key, which is a label that uniquely identifies a particular data value. Usually, `NSString`s are used as keys, although this is not a requirement. The data value can be any object that you want to store in the dictionary. The NSDictionary used in the preceding code is created with only a single entry, which has the NSString key @"TempDir" and the NSString value @"/var/tmp".

MEMORY MANAGEMENT

There are two types of memory management that can be used in an Objective-C/Cocoa program: the traditional manual scheme, which is based on *reference counting*, and an automated scheme introduced in Mac OS X 10.5 that uses *garbage collection*.

 NOTE *The default when you create a new Xcode project is the reference counting scheme. You can turn on garbage collection in the Build settings of the project root, or for each separate target. Just change the Objective-C Garbage Collection setting to Required.*

If you are using garbage collection, you don't generally need to worry about memory management. The runtime environment ensures that as long as an object is still needed, it will remain in existence. When it is no longer needed, the finalize method gets invoked — if there is one — and the object is deleted.

In the rest of this chapter, and throughout this book, we work with the manual reference counting scheme. This scheme is still in widespread use, and requires more explanation than the garbage collection scheme. You can generally convert a piece of reference counted code into garbage collected code simply by removing calls to methods such as retain, release, and autorelease, and by removing the dealloc method of any classes.

 NOTE *A secondary benefit of using reference counting is that your code can be reused on the iPhone. At the time of this writing, garbage collection was not available on the iPhone, though it is likely to be supported at some point in future.*

The reference counting scheme works as follows: The NSObject class contains an integer instance variable that keeps track of how many entities in the program are using a given object. When the integer, which is known as the *retain count*, drops to 0, the object is not needed anymore, and the dealloc method is called to delete it.

When you initialize an object, it is given a retain count of 1. If you take no further action, the object will remain in existence for the lifetime of the program. You indicate that an object is not needed by sending it a release message, which reduces the retain count by 1. If the retain count drops to 0, the object gets deallocated.

You can also explicitly indicate that an object should remain in existence by sending it a `retain` message, which increases the retain count by 1. `retain` is used when part of your code needs to ensure that an object instantiated elsewhere remains in existence.

 NOTE *In the same way that objects have a retain count of 1 when they are first initialized, they also have a retain count of 1 when they are copied using the* `NSObject` *method* `copy`, *or a similar method such as* `copyWithZone:` *or* `mutableCopy`. *Any copy method produces an object with a retain count of* 1.

In some cases, you can't release an object, even if you do not need it anymore. One such case is when the object must be returned from a method or function. If you invoke `release`, the object may get deallocated, and then the return value would be undefined. For these cases, Cocoa provides the `autorelease` method. `autorelease` has the same effect as `release` in that it decreases the retain count by 1, but this action is delayed to a later time. After you invoke `autorelease`, you can keep using the object without fear that it will be deallocated. At a later time, the retain count of the object will be automatically decreased by 1, and if the retain count drops to `0`, the object will be deleted.

The workings of `autorelease` may seem mysterious, but there is really nothing sinister about it. When you invoke the `autorelease` method of an object, the object is passed to another object of the class `NSAutoreleasePool`. The autorelease pool stores a list of objects that need to be released at a later time. When the autorelease pool is released, it sends a release message to each of the objects on its list.

Usually `NSAutoreleasePool` operates behind the scenes in a Cocoa application, and you don't need to worry about the details of how it works and when it is released. In some situations, such as when you write a program without a graphical interface, you need to instantiate and release your own `NSAutoreleasePool`.

At this point, you may think that memory management in Cocoa is a complex exercise, but nothing could be further from the truth. With the following simple guidelines it becomes a breeze:

➤ Any program unit (for example, a class or a function) that initializes, retains, or copies an object is also responsible for releasing that object.

➤ Any invocation of an initializer, `retain`, or `copy` method should be balanced by a `release` or `autorelease` invocation.

➤ When an object is no longer needed by a program unit, but must be passed or returned to another program unit, `autorelease` should be used rather than `release`.

The next Try It Out contains an example that creates and releases many objects using the techniques described in this section.

TRY IT OUT Memory Management with Cats

1. Create a new Foundation Command Line Tool project in Xcode. Select Command Line Tool in the Application group of the New Project pane, and then choose Foundation from the Type pop-up button. Name the project **Memories of Cats**.

2. Select the Memories of Cats.m file in the Groups & Files view in the group Source. In the editor, replace the default code with the following:

```objc
#import <Foundation/Foundation.h>

@interface Cat : NSObject <NSCopying>
{
}

-(id)copyWithZone:(NSZone *)zone;

+(id)createCat;

@end

@implementation Cat

-(id)copyWithZone:(NSZone *)zone {
    return [[Cat alloc] init];
}

+(id)createCat {
    Cat *cat = [[Cat alloc] init];
    return [cat autorelease];
}

@end

int main() {
    NSAutoreleasePool *pool = [[NSAutoreleasePool alloc] init];

    Cat *cat1 = [[[Cat alloc] init] autorelease];
    Cat *cat2 = [Cat createCat];
    Cat *cat3 = [[Cat alloc] init];
    NSLog(@"Retain count of cat1 is: %i", [cat1 retainCount]); // Prints 1
    NSLog(@"Retain count of cat2 is: %i", [cat2 retainCount]); // Prints 1
    NSLog(@"Retain count of cat3 is: %i", [cat3 retainCount]); // Prints 1

    Cat *cat4 = [cat3 copy];
    NSLog(@"Retain count of cat3 is: %i", [cat3 retainCount]); // Prints 1
    NSLog(@"Retain count of cat4 is: %i", [cat4 retainCount]); // Prints 1

    [cat3 release];    // Deallocates cat3
    [cat4 retain];
    NSLog(@"Retain count of cat4 is: %i", [cat4 retainCount]); // Prints 2

    [cat4 release];
    NSLog(@"Retain count of cat4 is: %i", [cat4 retainCount]); // Prints 1
```

```
[cat4 release];    // Deallocates cat4
[pool release];    // Deallocates cat1 and cat2

return 0;}
```

code snippet MacOSXProg ch07/Memories of Cats/Memories of Cats.m

3.   Click the Build and Run toolbar item to compile and run the program, and choose Console from the Run menu.

4.   Read the output in the Console, and try to understand what each of the memory management method invocations in the example are doing to the retain count of each of the Cat objects.

How It Works

This code is not intended to represent typical Cocoa code, and you should not write your programs to look this way. The point of the exercise is simply to get acquainted with the various memory management methods and monitor their effect on the retain count of objects.

A very sparse Cat class is declared and defined first. It contains no instance variables and only two methods. The copyWithZone: method is required to allow Cat objects to be copied. It is declared in the NSCopying protocol and used by the NSObject method copy. An NSZone is an object that describes a section of memory, but it can be ignored here. The copyWithZone: method returns an exact copy of the messaged object. Because Cat has no instance variables, it is only necessary to initialize and return a new Cat.

The content of the main function is sandwiched between the instantiation and destruction of an NSAutoreleasePool. This keeps track of the autoreleased objects, and sends them a release message when the autorelease pool is deallocated.

The variable cat1 is initialized first, to a Cat object that is autoreleased. This Cat is automatically deallocated by the NSAutoreleasePool at the end of the function.

cat2 is initialized with a Cat returned by the class method createCat. createCat initializes a Cat and autoreleases it before it is returned, so the net effect is the same as for cat1 — the Cat returned is deallocated when the NSAutoreleasePool is deallocated.

 NOTE *The class method* createCat *falls into the category of convenience initializer. Many classes provide methods that initialize and return an autoreleased object, because it is easier for the user of the class than calling* alloc, init . . ., *and* autorelease. *By way of example,* NSString *has many such methods:* stringWithFormat:, stringWithString:, stringWithContentsOfFile:, *and so on. The list is almost endless! All these methods return an autoreleased object, so you don't need to release the objects in your code.*

cat3 is set to a Cat that is initialized by init, but not autoreleased. An NSLog call prints out the retain count, which should be 1, because a newly initialized object should have a retain count of 1. The retainCount method of NSObject returns the retain count of an object. A bit further on, cat3 gets copied, which does not affect its retain count, and then it gets released. At this point, the retain count drops to 0, so the Cat is deallocated immediately, with its dealloc method called.

cat4 is initialized to be a copy of cat3. As you can see by the code for the copyWithZone: method of the Cat class, the object returned has a retain count of 1, just as if it were newly initialized. This is a Cocoa convention — copied objects are returned with a retain count of 1. Two NSLog calls follow, which should verify that cat4 has a retain count of 1, and that cat3 is unaffected by the copy operation.

cat4 is then subject to a retain invocation, which increments its retain count to 2. This is again verified in a call to NSLog. A release follows, which decrements the retain count to 1, before cat4 finally meets its end at the hands of yet another release. Don't worry, cat4's passing is quick and humane, with immediate deallocation, rather than the prolonged agony of the NSAutoreleasePool.

ACCESSOR METHODS AND PROPERTIES

You already met accessor method interfaces earlier in this chapter, but you are about to find out how you can implement them. Accessor methods are even more important in Objective-C than they are in other languages, such as Java, because they are used for systematic memory management. If you follow this system, you will rarely have any problem with memory leaks or disappearing objects in your code. If you don't, you may end up in an Objective-C–grade horror movie.

 NOTE *Actually, the reference to a horror movie is appropriate, because Cocoa provides a class called* NSZombie *for tracking down memory management problems in which objects are released too many times, or they're sent messages after they have been deallocated.* NSZombie *is a class that comes into play when you set the environment variable* NSZombieEnabled *to* YES *before running your program. With the environment variable set, whenever an object is deallocated, its class is effectively changed to* NSZombie. *If a message is sent to the object after it has been deallocated, it will go to* NSZombie, *which will throw an exception that tells you the details of the mismanaged object.*

There are actually several ways to write accessor methods. Each approach works, and it is up to you to choose the one that you are most comfortable with. To demonstrate some of the ways to write accessors, consider the following class interface:

```
@interface WeatherConditions
{
    float temperature;
    NSDate *date;
    WeatherStation *weatherStation;
}

-(float)temperature;
-(void)setTemperature:(float)newTemp;
```

```
-(NSDate *)date;
-(void)setDate:(NSDate *)newDate;

-(WeatherStation *)weatherStation;
-(void)setWeatherStation:(WeatherStation *)newStation;

@end
```

The question is, how do you implement the accessor methods in the `WeatherConditions` class?

The `float` variable `temperature` is an easy case, because it is a simple type, not an object. It does not need to be allocated or deallocated, so it can simply be returned from the getter, and set directly in the setter like this:

```
-(float)temperature {
    return temperature;
}

-(void)setTemperature:(float)newTemp {
    temperature = newTemp;
}
```

The `NSDate` variable `date` is a bit more difficult. It is a Cocoa class that represents a time or date. A getter accessor is easy enough to write, because it can simply return the `date` instance variable, but the setter is more involved. Here is one approach:

```
-(NSDate *)date {
    return date;
}

-(void)setDate:(NSDate *)newDate {
    if ( newDate != date ) {
        [date release];
        date = [newDate retain];
    }
}
```

The `setDate:` method includes an `if` statement to check whether the new date and the existing stored date are the same. If they are, the setter does nothing; if they differ, it replaces the old date with the new one. To do this, it first releases the old date, and then retains the new date, assigning it to the `date` instance variable. The `retain` indicates that the `newDate` object is needed by the `WeatherConditions` object, and ensures it will not be deallocated. Releasing the old date indicates that it is no longer needed by `WeatherConditions` and may be deallocated if it is not needed elsewhere.

Why so much trouble just to set `date`? Why not simply release the old date and assign the new one while retaining it, as shown in the following:

```
-(void)setDate:(NSDate *)newDate {
    [date release];
    date = [newDate retain];
}
```

The problem with this is that it doesn't account for instances when `newDate` and `date` are the same object. If they are, the object will be released by the first line of the setter and may be deallocated before the second line is executed. This is why it is necessary to check whether the two are the same before carrying out the exchange. Other ways of getting around the pathological case where the new object is the same as the old one also exist. By way of example, here is one of them:

```
-(void)setDate:(NSDate *)newDate {
    [date autorelease];
    date = [newDate retain];
}
```

This does not suffer the fate of the previous version, because the autoreleased object is guaranteed to exist at least for the life of the method. The only disadvantage of this approach is that if there happen to be a lot of calls to `setDate:`, an unnecessarily high number of `NSDate` objects may end up hanging around waiting to be released by the `NSAutoreleasePool`. In most cases, this doesn't happen, but you should keep it in mind.

The previous setters use the `retain` method to ensure that the new `NSDate` is not deallocated. This implies that the `NSDate` object may be shared with other parts of the program and will not be exclusive to the `WeatherConditions` object. It is often better to copy small objects as follows, rather than retain them:

```
-(void)setDate:(NSDate *)newDate {
    if ( newDate != date ) {
        [date release];
        date = [newDate copy];
    }
}
```

Here, the `WeatherConditions` object creates its own copy of the `NSDate`, so it doesn't need to worry about another section of the code modifying the `NSDate` later. For small objects, such as `NSDate` and `NSString`, it is a good idea to use `copy` rather than `retain`, just to be sure that your class's encapsulation is not violated.

There is one last link in the memory management chain: the `dealloc` method. `dealloc` must release any instance variables that a class has retained, copied, or initialized. This is what `dealloc` would look like for the `WeatherConditions` class:

```
-(void)dealloc {
    [weatherStation release];
    [date release];
    [super dealloc];
}
```

Objective-C 2.0 introduced a shorthand way of generating accessor methods known as *properties*. These can save you a lot of typing, and yet work in much the same way as handwritten accessor methods.

There are two parts to creating a property: declaring it in the interface block of the class, and directing the compiler to generate it in the class implementation. Here is how you declare the `WeatherConditions` class using properties instead of accessor methods:

```
@interface WeatherConditions
{
    float temperature;
    NSDate *date;
    WeatherStation *weatherStation;
}

@property float temperature;
@property (copy) NSDate *date;
@property (retain) WeatherStation *weatherStation;

@end
```

A property declaration begins with the keyword `@property`, followed by an optional set of *property declaration attributes*, and ending with the type and name of the property, which is usually the same as the instance variable.

The property declaration attributes allow you to indicate to the compiler what sort of accessors you would like it to generate. When no declaration attributes are supplied, the compiler generates accessors that simply assign variables, doing no special memory management. This is the case for the `temperature` property, and because the `float` type is not an object, it works fine in this case. You can also explicitly include the declaration attribute `assign` if you choose.

When working with objects, you have to be careful to indicate how they should be treated when a property is set. In the previous example, the declaration attribute `copy` has been included for the `date` property, which will cause the compiler to generate an accessor that copies the new object, rather than retaining it. However, when setting the `weatherStation` property, a `retain` is used, rather than a `copy`.

 NOTE *This example covers the most important property declaration attributes, but there are others. For example, you can use* `getter` *and* `setter` *to explicitly set the name of the generated accessors, if you do not want to use the standard names (such as* `getter=longDate`*). The* `readonly` *attribute is a common attribute, and indicates to the compiler that only a getter is needed — no setter should be generated. Lastly, the attribute* `nonatomic` *can make the accessors run faster by excluding code designed primarily for use in multithreaded programs.*

There are a number of choices for implementing properties. You can write accessors yourself if you need to customize them. You can use the `@synthesize` keyword in the `@implementation` block of the class to have the compiler generate any accessors that you haven't included yourself. Or you can use the `@dynamic` keyword to tell the compiler that you are not supplying any accessors in the class implementation, but that the accessors will be available at runtime. The latter is useful if you are using the Core Data framework, which automatically generates accessor methods for you at runtime. (Core Data is covered in Chapter 10.)

By far the most common of these is `@synthesize`. Here is how you would use `@synthesize` with the `WeatherConditions` class:

```
@implementation WeatherConditions

@synthesize temperature, date, weatherStation;

-(void)dealloc {
    self.date = nil;
    self.weatherStation = nil;
    [super dealloc];
}

@end
```

The first thing you will notice is that the class is considerably reduced in size because all those accessor methods can be thrown out, and are replaced by a single `@synthesize` statement. You can have one or more `@synthesize` statements; in this case, all properties have been combined into one.

It is also possible to have a property take a name that is different from the corresponding instance variable. You do this by assigning the property name to the instance variable name, in this way:

```
@synthesize temperature = temp;
```

In this example, the instance variable would be called `temp`, and the property would be `temperature`.

The previous class implementation includes a `dealloc` method. It is important to remember that properties do not imply automatic memory management — they are just a shorthand way of writing accessor methods. You still have to release your objects in the `dealloc` method.

In this particular `dealloc` method, the properties are assigned to `nil`, which has the net effect that they are released. Note that a different syntax has been used to refer to the properties: the so-called *dot notation*. Rather than using the standard square braces like this:

```
[self setWeatherStation:nil];
```

Objective-C 2.0 allows you to use dot notation like this:

```
self.weatherStation = nil;
```

You can use the same dot notation to invoke the getter method. For example:

```
self.weatherStation = other.weatherStation;
```

The property `weatherStation` of the object `other` is being accessed here using dot notation. The getter — or synthesized getter — of the object is invoked to retrieve the property value.

> **NOTE** *The dot notation feels very familiar to developers coming from other programming languages, but it caused quite a controversy when it was introduced with Objective-C 2.0. Many felt it was just a marketing trick to attract developers from other platforms. To this day, there are respected developers who refuse to use the dot notation, and instead opt to access properties using the traditional square brace syntax.*

In the following Try It Out, you rewrite the MyAddressBook program in Objective-C. This brings together all the aspects of Objective-C that you have learned here, and contrasts the style of Objective-C programming directly with programming in the C language.

TRY IT OUT   Beginning MyAddressBook in Objective-C

1. Create a new project in Xcode. In the New Project panel, choose Command Line Tool in the Application group, and make sure that Foundation is selected in the Type pop-up button. Name the project **MyAddressBook in Objective C.**

2. Create the files `Person.h` and `Person.m` in the Source group of the Groups & Files view. To do this, select the Source group and then choose File ➪ New File. In the New File sheet, choose Objective-C Class in the Cocoa Class group. Name the file `Person.m` and ensure that the Also Create "Person.h" checkbox is checked.

3. Create files called `IOUtility.h` and `IOUtility.m` in the same way you created `Person.h` and `Person.m` in step 2.

4. Replace the default code in each of these files, as well as the default code in the file `MyAddressBook in Objective C.m`, with the following source code:

PERSON.H

```
#import <Foundation/Foundation.h>

@interface Person : NSObject {
    @private
    NSString *name;
    NSString *address;
}

@property (readonly) NSString *name;
@property (copy) NSString *address;

-(id)initWithName:(NSString *)aName andAddress:(NSString *)anAddress;
-(id)initWithName:(NSString *)aName;

@end
```

code snippet MacOSXProg ch07/ MyAddressBook in Objective C 1/Person.h

PERSON.M

```objc
#import "Person.h"

@implementation Person

@synthesize name, address;

// Designated
-(id)initWithName:(NSString *)aName andAddress:(NSString *)anAddress {
    if ( self = [super init] ) {
        name = [aName copy];
        self.address = anAddress;
    }
    return self;
}

-(id)initWithName:(NSString *)aName {
    return [self initWithName:aName andAddress:@"Address Unknown"];
}

-(void)dealloc {
    [name release];
    [address release];
    [super dealloc];
}

-(NSString *)description {
    return [NSString stringWithFormat:@"Name: %@\nAddress: %@", name, address];
}

@end
```

code snippet MacOSXProg ch07/ MyAddressBook in Objective C 1/Person.m

IOUTILITY.H

```objc
#import <Foundation/Foundation.h>

void WriteToStandardOutput(NSString *string);
NSString* ReadFromStandardInput();
```

code snippet MacOSXProg ch07/ MyAddressBook in Objective C 1/ IOUtility.h

IOUTILITY.M

```objc
#import "IOUtility.h"

void WriteToStandardOutput(NSString *string) {
    NSFileHandle *so = [NSFileHandle fileHandleWithStandardOutput];
    [so writeData:[string dataUsingEncoding:NSUTF8StringEncoding]];
}

// Reads input line, and removes new line character
NSString* ReadFromStandardInput() {
    NSFileHandle *si = [NSFileHandle fileHandleWithStandardInput];
```

```
    NSData *data = [si availableData];
    NSString *string = [[[NSString alloc] initWithData:data
        encoding:NSUTF8StringEncoding] autorelease];
    NSCharacterSet *set =
        [NSCharacterSet characterSetWithCharactersInString:@"\n"];
    return [string stringByTrimmingCharactersInSet:set];
}
```

code snippet MacOSXProg ch07/ MyAddressBook in Objective C 1/ IOUtility.m

MYADDRESSBOOK IN OBJECTIVE C.M

Available for download on Wrox.com

```
#import <Foundation/Foundation.h>
#import "Person.h"
#import "IOUtility.h"

int main (int argc, const char * argv[]) {
    NSAutoreleasePool *pool = [[NSAutoreleasePool alloc] init];

    Person *person = [[[Person alloc] initWithName:@"Joe Citizen"
        andAddress:@"1 Hopalong Avenue, MediumRare, USA"] autorelease];
    WriteToStandardOutput([person description]);

    [pool release];
    return 0;
}
```

code snippet MacOSXProg ch07/ MyAddressBook in Objective C 1/MyAddressBook in Objective C.m

5. Build and run the program by clicking the Build and Run toolbar item. Examine the output by choosing Console in the Run menu.

How It Works

The `Person` class is a *model* class, which is a class that is used to store data. It is quite similar to the abstract data type (ADT) of the same name used in the C version of the program. It contains two instance variables, both of which are `NSString`s checkbox used to store the name and address of an entry in the address book. (The C version contained two `char*` strings.)

The `Person` class demonstrates the use of initializer chaining, with a designated initializer. It also has properties declared for the `name` and `address` instance variables. Note that the `name` property is read-only, so it has no generated setter. This is a design decision: for the purposes of this address book program, it was decided that a person could not change their name, although changing their address should be allowed. Making `name` read-only prevents a `Person` object from changing the name. The name variable of `Person` is said to be *immutable*.

The `Person` class also contains the method `description`. This method is actually inherited from the `NSObject` class, and has been overridden. It can be used to provide a user-readable description of an object in the form of an `NSString`. Anytime you use the `stringWithFormat:` method to create a new `NSString` and include the formatting character `%@`, which is the placeholder for an object, the `description` method of the object is called and returns an `NSString` that describes the object.

The `description` method of `Person` is used in other parts of the program to write out the details of the `Person` for the user.

The `WriteToStandardOutput` function uses the class `NSFileHandle` to write to the standard output stream as follows:

```
void WriteToStandardOutput(NSString *string) {
    NSFileHandle *so = [NSFileHandle fileHandleWithStandardOutput];
    [so writeData:[string dataUsingEncoding:NSUTF8StringEncoding]];
}
```

The class method `fileHandleWithStandardOutput` returns an `NSFileHandle` that corresponds to standard output. Writing to this file handle with the method `writeData:` causes the data to appear in standard output. The string passed to the `WriteToStandardOutput` method is converted into data in the UTF-8 format, which is the format used by the console. The `NSString` method `dataUsingEncoding:` returns an autoreleased `NSData` object, which is a Cocoa class that wraps around raw bytes of data. The constant `NSUTF8StringEncoding` is used to indicate that the data format should be UTF-8.

The `ReadFromStandardInput` function reads a line from the console, and returns it as an autoreleased `NSString` like this:

```
NSString* ReadFromStandardInput() {
    NSFileHandle *si = [NSFileHandle fileHandleWithStandardInput];
    NSData *data = [si availableData];
    NSString *string = [[[NSString alloc] initWithData:data
        encoding:NSUTF8StringEncoding] autorelease];
    NSCharacterSet *set =
        [NSCharacterSet characterSetWithCharactersInString:@"\n"];
    return [string stringByTrimmingCharactersInSet:set];
}
```

An `NSFileHandle` for standard input is retrieved with the method `fileHandleWithStandardInput`, and the line of data is read in with `availableData`. The `NSData` object returned is converted to an `NSString` using the initializer `initWithData:encoding:`. The string created is autoreleased. A new string is created with the new line character removed from the end using the `NSString` method `stringByTrimmingCharactersInSet:`. An `NSCharacterSet` is simply a set of characters; the one used here contains only the new line character, so the `stringByTrimmingCharactersInSet:` method trims any new line characters from either end of the string before returning the result.

The `main` function in this example is used for testing purposes. An `NSAutoreleasePool` is initialized at the beginning and released at the end. In between, a `Person` object is created, and the function `WriteToStandardOutput` is used to write the `NSString` returned by the `Person`'s `description` method to standard output.

In the next Try It Out, you write the `AddressBook` class, which stores the `Person` objects containing the addresses in the address book.

TRY IT OUT   Writing the AddressBook Class

1. Open the MyAddressBook in Objective C project, and create the files `AddressBook.h` and `AddressBook.m` in the Source group of the Groups & Files view. Choose the file type Objective-C Class in the Cocoa Class group of the New File sheet.

2. Replace the default code in each of these files, as well as the contents of `MyAddressBook in Objective C.m`, with the following source code:

ADDRESSBOOK.H

Available for
download on
Wrox.com

```
#import <Foundation/Foundation.h>

@class Person;

extern NSString *AddressBookFilePath;

@interface AddressBook : NSObject {
    @private
    NSMutableDictionary *personForNameDict;
}

+(id)sharedAddressBook;

-(id)initWithFile:(NSString *)path;

-(void)writeToFile:(NSString *)path;
+(void)writeSharedAddressBookToFile;

-(void)addPerson:(Person *)newPerson;
-(Person *)personForName:(NSString *)name;

@end
```

code snippet MacOSXProg ch07/ MyAddressBook in Objective C 2/ AddressBook.h

ADDRESSBOOK.M

Available for
download on
Wrox.com

```
#import "AddressBook.h"
#import "Person.h"

// Path to address book file
NSString *AddressBookFilePath = @"/var/tmp/addressbookobjc";

@implementation AddressBook

+(id)sharedAddressBook {
    static AddressBook *sharedAddressBook = nil;
    if ( ! sharedAddressBook ) {
        // Load from file if the file exists
        NSFileManager *fm = [NSFileManager defaultManager];
        if ( [fm fileExistsAtPath:AddressBookFilePath] ) {
            sharedAddressBook =
                [[AddressBook alloc] initWithFile:AddressBookFilePath];
        }
```

```
        else {
            // Create a new AddressBook
            sharedAddressBook = [[AddressBook alloc] init];
        }
    }
    return sharedAddressBook;
}

-(id)init {
    if ( self = [super init] ) {
        personForNameDict = [[NSMutableDictionary alloc] init];
    }
    return self;
}

-(void)dealloc {
    [personForNameDict release];
    [super dealloc];
}

-(id)initWithFile:(NSString *)path {
    if ( self = [super init] ) {
        personForNameDict = [[NSMutableDictionary alloc] init];
        NSString *string = [NSString stringWithContentsOfFile:path
            usedEncoding:nil error:nil];
        NSScanner *scanner = [NSScanner scannerWithString:string];
        NSString *name, *address;
        while ( ![scanner isAtEnd] ) {
            [scanner scanUpToString:@"\n" intoString:&name];
            [scanner scanString:@"\n" intoString:NULL]; // Remove end of line
            [scanner scanUpToString:@"\n" intoString:&address];
            [scanner scanString:@"\n" intoString:NULL]; // Remove end of line
            Person *person = [[Person alloc] initWithName:name
                andAddress:address];
            [self addPerson:person];
            [person release];
        }
    }
    return self;
}

-(void)writeToFile:(NSString *)path {
    NSMutableString *string = [NSMutableString string];
    for ( Person *person in [personForNameDict allValues] ) {
        [string appendString:person.name];
        [string appendString:@"\n"];
        [string appendString:person.address];
        [string appendString:@"\n"];
    }
    [string writeToFile:path atomically:YES
        encoding:NSUTF8StringEncoding error:nil];
}
```

```objc
+(void)writeSharedAddressBookToFile {
    [[AddressBook sharedAddressBook] writeToFile:AddressBookFilePath];
}

-(void)addPerson:(Person *)newPerson {
    [personForNameDict setObject:newPerson forKey:newPerson.name];
}

-(Person *)personForName:(NSString *)name {
    return [personForNameDict objectForKey:name];
}

@end
```

code snippet MacOSXProg ch07/ MyAddressBook in Objective C 2/ AddressBook.m

MYADDRESSBOOK IN OBJECTIVE C.M

```objc
#import <Foundation/Foundation.h>
#import "IOUtility.h"
#import "Person.h"
#import "AddressBook.h"

int main (int argc, const char * argv[]) {
    NSAutoreleasePool *pool = [[NSAutoreleasePool alloc] init];

    AddressBook *addressBook = [[[AddressBook alloc] init] autorelease];

    // Add a person to the address book
    Person *person = [[[Person alloc] initWithName:@"Joe Citizen"
        andAddress:@"1 Hopalong Avenue, MediumRare, USA"] autorelease];
    [addressBook addPerson:person];

    // Add another
    person = [[[Person alloc] initWithName:@"Jill Citizen"
        andAddress:@"2 Hopalong Avenue, MediumRare, USA"] autorelease];
    [addressBook addPerson:person];

    // Search for person in the address book
    person = [addressBook personForName:@"Joe Citizen"];
    WriteToStandardOutput(@"Found person");
    WriteToStandardOutput([person description]);

    [pool release];
    return 0;
}
```

code snippet MacOSXProg ch07/ MyAddressBook in Objective C 2/MyAddressBook in Objective C.m

3. Build and run the program by clicking the Build and Run toolbar item. Examine the output by choosing Console from the Run menu.

How It Works

The AddressBook class stores Person objects in a Foundation container class called NSMutableDictionary. An NSMutableDictionary stores key-value pairs, such as an NSDictionary; in fact, it is a subclass of NSDictionary. The difference is that an NSMutableDictionary is mutable and can be modified after creation. You can add or remove key-value pairs to an existing NSMutableDictionary.

AddressBook has the following two methods for adding and finding Person objects:

```
-(void)addPerson:(Person *)newPerson {
    [personForNameDict setObject:newPerson forKey:[newPerson name]];
}

-(Person *)personForName:(NSString *)name {
    return [personForNameDict objectForKey:name];
}
```

The addPerson: method sets an object in the personForNameDict instance variable, with the Person's name as the key. The setObject:forKey: method of NSMutableDictionary serves this purpose. Note that no attempt is made to check whether a Person with that name is already in the NSMutableDictionary, so the newPerson instance will replace any instance with the same name that already exists. A dictionary can have only one value per key.

The personForName: method can be used to retrieve a Person from the AddressBook. The objectForKey: method of NSDictionary is used, which returns the object corresponding to the key passed, or nil if no object with that key exists in the dictionary.

The init and dealloc methods of AddressBook are responsible for initializing and releasing personForNameDict.

```
-(id)init {
    if ( self = [super init] ) {
        personForNameDict = [[NSMutableDictionary alloc] init];
    }
    return self;
}

-(void)dealloc {
    [personForNameDict release];
    [super dealloc];
}
```

However, you don't generally need to call init directly, because AddressBook is a singleton class, which means usually there is only one instance of AddressBook used in the whole program. The method sharedAddressBook is used to access this instance. Rather than creating a new AddressBook, sharedAddressBook is called and takes care of initializing the AddressBook object as follows:

```
+(id)sharedAddressBook {
    static AddressBook *sharedAddressBook = nil;
    if ( ! sharedAddressBook ) {
        // Load from file if the file exists
```

```
        NSFileManager *fm = [NSFileManager defaultManager];
        if ( [fm fileExistsAtPath:AddressBookFilePath] ) {
            sharedAddressBook =
                [[AddressBook alloc] initWithFile:AddressBookFilePath];
        }
        else {
            // Create a new AddressBook
            sharedAddressBook = [[AddressBook alloc] init];
        }
    }
    return sharedAddressBook;
}
```

A `static` variable called `sharedAddressBook` is declared and initialized to `nil`. Being declared `static` means that it will not disappear when the method returns, but will remain for the life of the program. The `if` statement checks if the variable is `nil`; if not, it simply returns the `AddressBook` to the calling code. If the variable is `nil`, a new `AddressBook` must be created.

> **NOTE** *Singletons are quite common in Cocoa, and indeed most OO frameworks. For certain classes, it does not make sense to create multiple instances, and in these cases, a singleton object is shared instead. One example of this is the `NSFileManager` class, which is used to interact with the file system. The method `defaultManager` is used to retrieve the shared instance.*

The new `AddressBook` can either be retrieved from a file, which involves invoking the initializer `initWithFile:`, or created empty with the `init` initializer. The Foundation class `NSFileManager`, which is used to perform operations that are typically handled by the Finder (for example, moving and removing files or creating directories), is used to check for the existence of the `AddressBook` file. The `fileExistsAtPath:` method returns `YES` if the file exists at the path passed, or `NO` otherwise. According to the return value of this method, the `sharedAddressBook` method chooses between the `initWithFile:` and `init:` methods to initialize the new `AddressBook` instance.

Reading and writing to and from a file is achieved using the two methods `initWithFile:` and `writeToFile:`. (The convenience class method `writeSharedAddressBookToFile:` is also provided to write the shared address book to file; this simply invokes `writeToFile:`.) The `writeToFile:` method writes the name and address of each entry in the `personForNameDict` dictionary to a file as follows:

```
-(void)writeToFile:(NSString *)path {
    NSMutableString *string = [NSMutableString string];
    for ( Person *person in [personForNameDict allValues] ) {
        [string appendString:person.name];
        [string appendString:@"\n"];
        [string appendString:person.address];
        [string appendString:@"\n"];
    }
    [string writeToFile:path atomically:YES
        encoding:NSUTF8StringEncoding error:nil];
}
```

Fast enumeration is used to move through the values of the NSMutableDictionary. Each Person's name is appended to an NSMutableString, followed by the address. (NSMutableString is a subclass of NSString. The value of an NSMutableString can change after it is created, unlike instances of NSString.) After each string is appended, a new line character is appended, so that when the data is read back in, the end of each string can be located.

 NOTE *You may see a pattern emerge in the naming of certain Cocoa classes.* NSString, *which is immutable, has a subclass called* NSMutableString, *which is mutable.* NSDictionary, *which is immutable, has a subclass called* NSMutableDictionary, *which is mutable. In fact, many of the most important Cocoa Foundation classes have mutable and immutable variants.*

The mutable classes have all the methods of the corresponding immutable classes, as well as extra methods for changing the object's attributes. For this reason, the mutable class is always a subclass of the immutable one.

The initWithFile: method reads the data back in and adds it to the personForNameDict, like this:

```
-(id)initWithFile:(NSString *)path {
    if ( self = [super init] ) {
        personForNameDict = [[NSMutableDictionary alloc] init];
        NSString *string = [NSString stringWithContentsOfFile:path];
        NSScanner *scanner = [NSScanner scannerWithString:string];
        NSString *name, *address;
        while ( ![scanner isAtEnd] ) {
            [scanner scanUpToString:@"\n" intoString:&name];
            [scanner scanString:@"\n" intoString:NULL]; // Remove end of line
            [scanner scanUpToString:@"\n" intoString:&address];
            [scanner scanString:@"\n" intoString:NULL]; // Remove end of line
            Person *person = [[Person alloc] initWithName:name andAddress:address];
            [self addPerson:person];
            [person release];
        }
    }
    return self;
}
```

The method begins by initializing the personForNameDict. After reading the contents of the file with the NSString method stringWithContentsOfFile:, an NSScanner is used to extract the names and addresses. NSScanner is a class that can scan through strings, looking for strings and numbers.

The while loop keeps iterating until the end of file is reached, which is signaled by the NSScanner method isAtEnd returning YES. Each iteration of the loop scans in the name and address strings with the method scanUpToString:intoString: and discards the end of line character with the scanString:intoString: method. Passing NULL as the second argument to this method causes the string to be scanned, but ignored.

At the completion of each loop iteration, a new `Person` is created with the name and address read, and added to the `AddressBook` with the `addPerson` method.

The `main` function is again used for testing purposes. It creates an `AddressBook` object, adds two `Person` objects to it, searches for a `Person` with `personForName:`, and writes the details to standard output.

In the next Try It Out, you write the `Controller` class, which is used to interact with the user. You also introduce a class that represents different operations the user can perform. This section provides a good demonstration of inheritance and polymorphism in OOP.

TRY IT OUT   Writing the Controller and Command Classes

1. Open the MyAddressBook in Objective C project, and create the files `Controller.h` and `Controller.m` in the Source group of the Groups & Files view. Choose the file type Objective-C Class in the Cocoa Class group of the New File panel.

2. Similarly, create files called `Commands.h` and `Commands.m` in the Source group.

3. Replace the content of each of these files, as well as the content of `MyAddressBook in Objective C.m`, with the following source code:

CONTROLLER.H

```
#import <Foundation/Foundation.h>

@class AddressBook;

@interface Controller : NSObject {
}

-(void)printIntroductoryMessage;
-(BOOL)processUserRequest;
-(void)printUserOptions;
-(BOOL)processUserChoice:(NSString *)choice;

@end
```

code snippet MacOSXProg ch07/ MyAddressBook in Objective C 3/Controller.h

CONTROLLER.M

```
#import "Controller.h"
#import "Commands.h"
#import "IOUtility.h"

static NSDictionary *commandClassForChoiceDict;

@interface Controller ()

-(NSDictionary *)requestCommandInfoFromUser:(Class)commandClass;
```

```objectivec
@end

@implementation Controller

+(void)initialize {
    NSMutableDictionary *dict = [NSMutableDictionary dictionary];
    for ( Class c in [Command commandClasses] ) {
        [dict setObject:c forKey:[c commandIdentifier]];
    }
    commandClassForChoiceDict = [dict retain];
}

-(void)printIntroductoryMessage {
    NSString *message =
        @"Welcome to MyAddressBook\n"
        @"With this program, you can add addresses, retrieve them,\n"
        @"and store them on file.\n";
    WriteToStandardOutput(message);
}

-(BOOL)processUserRequest {
    // Offer user options
    [self printUserOptions];
    WriteToStandardOutput(@"Please enter a choice: ");

    // Read choice, and get first character
    NSString *choice = ReadFromStandardInput();
    if ( choice.length == 0 ) return NO;
    choice = [choice substringToIndex:1];

    // Process choice
    return [self processUserChoice:choice];
}

-(void)printUserOptions {
    NSArray *commandClasses = [Command commandClasses];
    NSMutableString *str =
      [NSMutableString stringWithString:@"The options are\n"];
    for ( Class c in commandClasses ) {
        [str appendString:c.commandIdentifier];
        [str appendString:@":\t"];
        [str appendString:c.commandDescription];
        [str appendString:@"\n"];
    }
    WriteToStandardOutput(str);
}

-(BOOL)processUserChoice:(NSString *)choice {
    BOOL shouldStop = NO;
    NSString *outputString;
    Class commClass = [commandClassForChoiceDict objectForKey:choice];
    if ( Nil == commClass ) {
        outputString = @"Invalid choice.\n";
```

```
    }
    else {
        NSDictionary *infoDict = [self requestCommandInfoFromUser:commClass];
        AddressBook *ab = [AddressBook sharedAddressBook];
        Command *comm = [[[commClass alloc] initWithAddressBook:ab] autorelease];
        outputString = [comm executeWithInfoDictionary:infoDict];
        if ( nil == outputString ) {
            shouldStop = YES;
        }
        else {
            // Append new line
            outputString = [outputString stringByAppendingString:@"\n"];
        }
    }
    if ( nil != outputString ) WriteToStandardOutput(outputString);
    return shouldStop;
}

-(NSDictionary *)requestCommandInfoFromUser:(Class)commandClass {
    NSMutableDictionary *infoDict = [NSMutableDictionary dictionary];
    NSArray *reqInfo = [commandClass requiredInfoIdentifiers];
    if ( [reqInfo count] > 0 ) {
        WriteToStandardOutput(@"Please enter the following information:\n");

        // Request each piece of info, and enter in a dictionary.
        for ( id req in reqInfo ) {
            WriteToStandardOutput([NSString stringWithFormat:@"%@: ", req]);
            NSString *info = ReadFromStandardInput();
            [infoDict setObject:info forKey:req];
        }

    }
    return infoDict;
}

@end
```

code snippet MacOSXProg ch07/ MyAddressBook in Objective C 3/Controller.m

COMMANDS.H

```
#import <Foundation/Foundation.h>
#import "AddressBook.h"
#import "Person.h"

@interface Command : NSObject
{
    @private
    AddressBook *addressBook;
}

+(NSArray *)commandClasses;

-(id)initWithAddressBook:(AddressBook *)ab;
```

```
-(AddressBook *)addressBook;

@end

@interface Command (AbstractMethods)

+(NSString *)commandIdentifier;
+(NSString *)commandDescription;
+(NSArray *)requiredInfoIdentifiers;  // Info needed from the user
-(NSString *)executeWithInfoDictionary:(NSDictionary *)infoDict;

@end

@interface QuitCommand : Command
{
}
@end
```

code snippet MacOSXProg ch07/ MyAddressBook in Objective C 3/Commands.h

COMMANDS.M

```
#import "Commands.h"

static NSArray *commandClasses;

@implementation Command

+(void)initialize {
    commandClasses = [[NSArray arrayWithObjects:
      [QuitCommand class],
        nil] retain];
}

+(NSArray *)commandClasses {
    return commandClasses;
}

-(id)initWithAddressBook:(AddressBook *)ab {
    if ( self = [super init] ) {
        addressBook = [ab retain];
    }
    return self;
}

-(void)dealloc {
    [addressBook release];
    [super dealloc];
}

-(AddressBook *)addressBook {
    return addressBook;
}
```

```
@end

@implementation QuitCommand

+(NSString *)commandIdentifier {
    return @"q";
}

+(NSString *)commandDescription {
    return @"Save and quit";
}

+(NSArray *)requiredInfoIdentifiers {
    return [NSArray array];
}

-(NSString *)executeWithInfoDictionary:(NSDictionary *)infoDict {
    [AddressBook writeSharedAddressBookToFile];
    return nil;
}

@end
```

code snippet MacOSXProg ch07/ MyAddressBook in Objective C 3/Commands.m

MYADDRESSBOOK IN OBJECTIVE C.M

```
#import <Foundation/Foundation.h>
#import "IOUtility.h"
#import "Controller.h"

int main (int argc, const char * argv[]) {
    NSAutoreleasePool *outerPool = [[NSAutoreleasePool alloc] init];

    // Print introduction
    Controller *controller = [[[Controller alloc] init] autorelease];
    [controller printIntroductoryMessage];

    // Run loop
    BOOL exitRunLoop = NO;
    while ( !exitRunLoop ) {
        NSAutoreleasePool * pool = [[NSAutoreleasePool alloc] init];
        exitRunLoop = [controller processUserRequest];
        [pool release];
    }

    [outerPool release];
    return 0;
}
```

code snippet MacOSXProg ch07/ MyAddressBook in Objective C 3/MyAddressBook in Objective C.m

4. Compile and run the program by clicking the Build and Run toolbar item, and open the console by choosing Console from the Run menu.

5. Follow the instructions in the console. Quit the program by typing **q** at the prompt.

6. Rerun the program by selecting Run from the Run menu. Try entering invalid responses to see how the program reacts.

How It Works

This version of MyAddressBook is perhaps overkill for the simple problem it solves, but the intention is to expose you to as many of the principal Foundation classes of Cocoa as possible, as well as the OO features of Objective-C. You could easily produce a program that mimics the source code of the C version of MyAddressBook more closely, but it would not demonstrate the OO features of Objective-C very well. Instead, the design of MyAddressBook has been changed somewhat to make full use of OO features such as inheritance and polymorphism.

The Controller class performs a similar role to the Controller ADT in the C version of MyAddressBook. It acts as the interface between the model classes, which store the data, and the user interface, which in this case is simply a console. It has methods for printing introductory messages, printing the options available to the user, and processing the user's choices. Most of these methods use the functions WriteToStandardOutput and ReadFromStandardInput, which were defined in the files IOUtility.h and IOUtility.m.

The printUserOptions method of the Controller class is responsible for printing the various commands a user can choose from.

```
-(void)printUserOptions {
    NSArray *commandClasses = [Command commandClasses];
    NSMutableString *str =
        [NSMutableString stringWithString:@"The options are\n"];
    for ( Class c in commandClasses ) {
        [str appendString:[c commandIdentifier]];
        [str appendString:@":\t"];
        [str appendString:[c commandDescription]];
        [str appendString:@"\n"];
    }
    WriteToStandardOutput(str);
}
```

What you will notice about this code is that there is no explicit mention of any of the options. There is no reference to adding a new person, saving the address book, or any other operation that the user can request. The C version of the program included a large switch statement that would call different processing functions based on the character entered by the user. Here, the OO features of Objective-C have been used to create a more flexible design.

The way it works is this: each option is represented by a subclass of the class Command. The Command class is called an *abstract class*, because you never actually create an instance of Command, only its subclasses. However, you do use the interface of Command, as you can see from the printUserOptions method.

`printUserOptions` begins by calling the `Command` class method `commandClasses`. This returns an `NSArray` containing all the subclasses of `Command`, which represent the different options available to the user. The built-in Objective-C keyword `Class` is used to represent the generic type of a class, in the same way that `id` is the generic type of an object.

The `printUserOptions` method then initializes an `NSMutableString`. A fast enumeration `for` loop iterates over the `Command` subclasses and calls the class methods `commandIdentifier` and `commandDescription`. The return values of these methods are `NSStrings`, which are appended to the `NSMutableString`. The strings returned represent the character option that the user can enter to select the command and a description of what the command does, respectively. When all subclasses of `Command` have been queried, the `NSMutableString str` is written to standard output.

The `printUserOptions` method is a good example of OOP and polymorphism. The methods `commandIdentifier` and `commandDescription` are declared in the interface of `Command`, but the `Command` class does not provide the implementation. Instead, the subclasses of `Command` implement the methods. When an invocation of `commandIdentifier` is made in the `for` loop, it ends up invoking the `commandIdentifier` method of a subclass of `Command`, not the `Command` class implementation.

To understand the design of the `Command` class hierarchy somewhat better, consider the `Command` class itself. Its interface can be found in `Commands.h`, as shown here:

```
@interface Command : NSObject
{
    @private
    AddressBook *addressBook;
}

+(NSArray *)commandClasses;

-(id)initWithAddressBook:(AddressBook *)ab;

-(AddressBook *)addressBook;

@end

@interface Command (AbstractMethods)

+(NSString *)commandIdentifier;
+(NSString *)commandDescription;
+(NSArray *)requiredInfoIdentifiers;  // Info needed from the user
-(NSString *)executeWithInfoDictionary:(NSDictionary *)infoDict;

@end
```

The initializer takes an `AddressBook` object, which is needed by many of the `Command` subclasses. The `AddressBook` itself is stored in the `Command` class, and accessed from the subclasses using the `addressBook` accessor method. It also includes the `commandClasses` method that you have already seen, and the `commandIdentifier` and `commandDescription` class methods.

The *abstract methods* in the `Command` class — those without an implementation — are declared in a category. If you declare them in the main interface block of the class, the compiler issues a warning that it cannot find the methods' implementations. Using a category avoids the warning, as well as making it clear to other programmers that the methods are abstract, and therefore need to be overridden.

The `commandClasses` method returns an `NSArray` that is also called `commandClasses`, which gets initialized in the `initialize` class method as follows:

```
+(void)initialize {
    commandClasses = [[NSArray arrayWithObjects:
        [QuitCommand class],
        nil] retain];
}

+(NSArray *)commandClasses {
    return commandClasses;
}
```

At this point, only one command exists, `QuitCommand`, which saves the address book and quits the program. The `commandClasses` variable is declared at the top of the file like this:

```
static NSArray *commandClasses;
```

You have already seen the keyword `static` several times. It ensures that the variable remains in existence for the lifetime of the program.

The `initialize` method uses the `NSObject` method `class` to retrieve the `Class` type of each subclass of `Command`, and inserts them into a new `NSArray` with the method `arrayWithObjects:`. You will probably use this convenience constructor of `NSArray` often. It takes a comma-separated series of objects, and must be terminated by a `nil` argument.

Two other methods are included in the `Command` class interface. The first is `requiredInfoIdentifiers`, which returns an `NSArray` of `NSStrings`. Many of the `Command` subclasses need extra information to process a user request. For example, to add a new address to the address book, a person's name and address are needed. This method returns the strings used to identify the information that must be entered by the user.

The `Controller` class uses the returned array in the `requestCommandInfoFromUser:` method to get the information from the user, and puts the results in a mutable dictionary.

```
-(NSDictionary *)requestCommandInfoFromUser:(Class)commandClass {
    NSMutableDictionary *infoDict = [NSMutableDictionary dictionary];
    NSArray *reqInfo = [commandClass requiredInfoIdentifiers];
    if ( [reqInfo count] > 0 ) {
        WriteToStandardOutput(@"Please enter the following information:\n");

        // Request each piece of info, and enter in a dictionary.
        for ( id req in reqInfo ) {
            WriteToStandardOutput([NSString stringWithFormat:@"%@: ", req]);
            NSString *info = ReadFromStandardInput();
            [infoDict setObject:info forKey:req];
        }

    }
    return infoDict;
}
```

This method basically consists of a `for` loop that prints out a request for each piece of information required by the `Command`, and stores the user response in an `NSMutableDictionary` with the request string as key.

The last method of the `Command` class is `executeWithInfoDictionary:`. This method gets passed in the dictionary of user responses created in `requestCommandInfoFromUser:` and executes the `Command`. The parameter `infoDict` holds the information requested from the user. If the `Command` has output, it can be returned as an `NSString`.

The only part of the puzzle not yet addressed is how the `Controller` actually creates a `Command` and executes it. That takes place in the `processUserChoice:` method as shown here:

```
-(BOOL)processUserChoice:(NSString *)choice {
    BOOL shouldStop = NO;
    NSString *outputString;
    Class commClass = [commandClassForChoiceDict objectForKey:choice];
    if ( Nil == commClass ) {
        outputString = @"Invalid choice.\n";
    }
    else {
        NSDictionary *infoDict = [self requestCommandInfoFromUser:commClass];
        AddressBook *ab = [AddressBook sharedAddressBook];
        Command *comm = [[[commClass alloc] initWithAddressBook:ab] autorelease];
        outputString = [comm executeWithInfoDictionary:infoDict];
        if ( nil == outputString ) {
            shouldStop = YES;
        }
        else { // Append new line
            outputString = [outputString stringByAppendingString:@"\n"];
        }
    }
    if ( nil != outputString ) WriteToStandardOutput(outputString);
    return shouldStop;
}
```

This method starts by attempting to retrieve a `Class` from the `NSDictionary` `commandClassForChoiceDict`, which is the `static` variable created in the `initialize` method. This dictionary maps the option characters that a user enters to the classes that represent the command in the program. The return value of `objectForKey:` is assigned to the variable `commClass`, which is then compared to `Nil`. `Nil` is an Objective-C keyword that is the zero-value of a `Class` variable, in the same way that `nil` is the zero-value of the `id` type.

If a `Command` class is found that corresponds to the `choice` string, it is used with the methods described earlier. First, the `Controller` method `requestCommandInfoFromUser:` is invoked to create the `NSDictionary` `infoDict`, which contains information for the `Command`. Then an object of the class `commClass` is created and assigned to the `Command` variable `comm`. `comm` is executed, with `infoDict` passed as argument, and the returned string is stored in `outputString`. If `outputString` is not `nil`, it is printed, and the method returns.

The advantage of the OO design used here is that the `Controller` class is quite generic. It makes no reference to the various commands available to the user — this functionality has been split off into the `Command` class hierarchy. To add a new command (that adds a person to the address book, for example), you only have to write a new subclass of `Command`, and add the new class to the array returned by the `commandClasses` method of the `Command` class. The `Controller` class remains unaltered.

The `main` function creates the `Controller` object, and includes a run loop that repeatedly calls the `Controller` to process the next user request.

```
NSAutoreleasePool *outerPool = [[NSAutoreleasePool alloc] init];

// Print introduction
Controller *controller = [[[Controller alloc] init] autorelease];
[controller printIntroductoryMessage];

// Run loop
BOOL exitRunLoop = NO;
while ( !exitRunLoop ) {
    NSAutoreleasePool * pool = [[NSAutoreleasePool alloc] init];
    exitRunLoop = [controller processUserRequest];
    [pool release];
}

[outerPool release];
```

This code includes two `NSAutoreleasePool` instances. One is created to encompass the whole body of the `main` function. This one should exist in any Foundation Tool that you write, because otherwise you might end up with a memory leak. For example, the `controller` instance is autoreleased, and the `outerPool` is responsible for releasing it at the end of the `main` function.

The second autorelease pool is inside the `run` loop. This one is not strictly necessary, but has been added to prevent memory usage from increasing too much. If this pool did not exist, every autoreleased object created inside the loop would remain in existence until the whole program finished. This is wasteful of memory, so a second autorelease pool is created that releases autoreleased objects once per iteration of the `run` loop. This code also demonstrates that it is perfectly acceptable to use multiple `NSAutoreleasePool` objects. When an object's `autorelease` method is invoked, the object is added to the last pool created.

 NOTE *The* `main` *function used in this example contains a* `while` *loop referred to as a run loop. You usually don't need to create a loop such as this in Cocoa programming, because it is created for you. An object of the class* `NSRunLoop` *is used for this purpose.*

In the following Try It Out, you add the `Command` subclasses that enable you to create and store addresses.

TRY IT OUT   **Adding Command Subclasses**

1.   Open the MyAddressBook in Objective C project and add the following source code to the bottom of the `Commands.h` and `Commands.m` files:

COMMANDS.H

```objc
@interface NewPersonCommand : Command
{
}
@end

@interface FindPersonCommand : Command
{
}
@end

@interface SaveAddressBookCommand : Command
{
}
@end
```

code snippet MacOSXProg ch07/ MyAddressBook in Objective C 4/Commands.h

COMMANDS.M

```objc
@implementation NewPersonCommand

+(NSString *)commandIdentifier {
    return @"n";
}

+(NSString *)commandDescription {
    return @"Add a new address";
}

+(NSArray *)requiredInfoIdentifiers {
    return [NSArray arrayWithObjects:@"Name of person", @"Address", nil];
}

-(NSString *)executeWithInfoDictionary:(NSDictionary *)infoDict {
    NSString *name = [infoDict objectForKey:@"Name of person"];
    NSString *address = [infoDict objectForKey:@"Address"];
    Person *p = [[[Person alloc] initWithName:name andAddress:address]
        autorelease];
    [[self addressBook] addPerson:p];
    return [NSString stringWithFormat:
        @"Address for %@ was added to the address book.", name];
}

@end

@implementation FindPersonCommand
```

```
+(NSString *)commandIdentifier {
    return @"f";
}

+(NSString *)commandDescription {
    return @"Find an address";
}

+(NSArray *)requiredInfoIdentifiers {
    return [NSArray arrayWithObject:@"Name of person"];
}

-(NSString *)executeWithInfoDictionary:(NSDictionary *)infoDict {
    NSString *name = [infoDict objectForKey:@"Name of person"];
    Person *p = [[self addressBook] personForName:name];
    return ( p == nil ? @"Address not found" : [p description] );
}

@end

@implementation SaveAddressBookCommand

+(NSString *)commandIdentifier {
    return @"s";
}

+(NSString *)commandDescription {
    return @"Save address book";
}

+(NSArray *)requiredInfoIdentifiers {
    return [NSArray array];
}

-(NSString *)executeWithInfoDictionary:(NSDictionary *)infoDict {
    [AddressBook writeSharedAddressBookToFile];
    return @"Address book saved";
}

@end
```

code snippet MacOSXProg ch07/ MyAddressBook in Objective C 4/Commands.m

2. Modify the `initialize` method of the `Command` class in `Commands.m` as follows:

```
+(void)initialize {
    commandClasses = [[NSArray arrayWithObjects:
        [NewPersonCommand class],
        [FindPersonCommand class],
        [SaveAddressBookCommand class],
        [QuitCommand class],
        nil] retain];
}
```

3. Compile and run the program by clicking the Build and Run toolbar item.

4. Open the console by choosing Console from the Run menu. Enter a few names and addresses, and then try to retrieve them again with a find request. Try saving the address book and then quit.

5. Rerun the program by selecting Run from the Run menu. Try to find one of the addresses you entered before quitting in step 4.

How It Works

To improve your understanding of how the `Command` subclasses work, consider the `NewPersonCommand` class, which is used to add a new entry to the address book. For this, a person's name and address are needed. The `NewPersonCommand` class returns strings from the `requiredInfoIdentifiers` method, which are used to request that the user enter a name and address.

```
+(NSArray *)requiredInfoIdentifiers {
    return [NSArray arrayWithObjects:@"Name of person", @"Address", nil];
}
```

The `executeWithInfoDictionary:` method of `NewPersonCommand` creates the new `Person` and adds it to the `AddressBook` as follows:

```
-(NSString *)executeWithInfoDictionary:(NSDictionary *)infoDict {
    NSString *name = [infoDict objectForKey:@"Name of person"];
    NSString *address = [infoDict objectForKey:@"Address"];
    Person *p = [[[Person alloc] initWithName:name
        andAddress:address] autorelease];
    [[self addressBook] addPerson:p];
    return [NSString stringWithFormat:
        @"Address for %@ was added to the address book.", name];
}
```

The user-supplied information is passed to the method by the `Controller` via the `infoDict` `NSDictionary`. The identifiers returned from `requiredInfoIdentifier` are used as the keys to extract the information. A string is returned from the method that indicates that a new entry has successfully been added to the address book.

The other subclasses of `Command` that were introduced have a similar structure to `NewPersonCommand`. It is left to you to investigate them further on your own.

SUMMARY

This chapter introduced you to one of the most important languages on Mac OS X for application development. You learned

➤ What object-oriented programming (OOP) entails, including the important concepts of encapsulation, inheritance, and polymorphism

➤ That Objective-C is a superset of C that introduces powerful OOP capabilities with minimal extensions

➤ Aspects of Objective-C such as classes, protocols, categories, methods, properties, data hiding, messaging, and memory management

➤ How to write a Foundation Tool in Objective-C that makes use of fundamental Cocoa classes from the Foundation framework, leveraging the OO capabilities of Objective-C

In the next chapter, you learn about the Cocoa frameworks, which form the basis of most new application development on Mac OS X and are tightly coupled with Objective-C. Before proceeding, however, try the exercises that follow to test your understanding of the material covered in this chapter. You can find the solutions to these exercises in Appendix A.

EXERCISES

1. In this exercise, you practice working with some of the most important Cocoa Foundation classes. You need to use these classes every time you write a Cocoa program, so it is essential that you get used to them.

Create a new Foundation Tool project called Discus, and in the `Discus.m` file, add code to store information about a few CDs, DVDs, and Blu-ray discs in your collection. Store details of each disc in an `NSDictionary` and use an `NSArray` to hold all the dictionaries. The details you might consider storing could include the type of media (CD, DVD, or Blu-ray); the title; where in your house it is located; and the artist or director. After the data has been stored in the array, retrieve a few pieces of information and print them to the console using the `NSLog` function.

Finally, look up `NSArray` in the Xcode documentation and read about the methods `writeToFile:`, `atomically:`, and `initWithContentsOfFile:`. Use these methods to save the data for your disc collection to a file on your desktop; then read it back. Write the whole `NSArray` to the console using `NSLog` to verify that it was read correctly. Also examine the contents of the file on your desktop in a text editor such as TextEdit.

2. Update the Objective-C version of MyAddressBook so that it allows the user to remove an entry from the address book. Compare the changes you make in the Objective-C version to those you made in Exercise 2 of Chapter 6.

▶ WHAT YOU LEARNED IN THIS CHAPTER

OOP	object-oriented programming, a popular programming paradigm based on combining data and behavior in objects
Objective-C	the C-based OOP language used to develop applications for Mac OS X
Class	an OO entity used to declare the data and functionality of a particular type of object
Object/Instance	an entity with data (instance variables) and behavior (methods)
Method	a function belonging to a particular object or class
Messaging	the high-order mechanism of invoking methods in Objective-C
Encapsulation	the ability of an object to protect its data from being accessed from outside its class
Inheritance	an OO relationship between two classes in which one — the *subclass* — incorporates the data and methods of the other — the *superclass*
Polymorphism	the ability of an entity to behave in different ways depending on the runtime conditions
Reference Counting	a manual memory management scheme used in Objective-C which requires the developer to maintain a count of all references to an object
Garage Collection	a fully automated memory management scheme, whereby objects are automatically deleted when they are no longer in use
Interface	an Objective-C block that declares the variables and methods in a class
Implementation	an Objective-C block that includes the bodies of the methods in a class
Accessor Methods	methods that allow indirect access to the data in an object from outside the class
Properties	an Objective-C 2.0 feature that provides a shorthand way to generate accessor methods
Foundation	a framework used in every Cocoa program which provides fundamental classes for memory management, storing and representing data, and interacting with the operating system

Introduction to Cocoa

WHAT YOU WILL LEARN IN THIS CHAPTER:

➤ How to use outlets and actions to connect Cocoa application interfaces to your custom code

➤ How to use Cocoa Bindings as an alternative to outlets and actions

➤ How Apple uses the Model/View/Controller design pattern to build reusable, extendable classes

People use the word "Cocoa" in different ways to describe different things. For example, Cocoa can refer to the Objective-C programming language and dynamic runtime. In Chapter 7, you learned how to write simple programs in Objective-C. Some of that material, such as object reference counting, is specific to Cocoa.

Cocoa also applies to the Objective-C frameworks and libraries commonly used by Cocoa applications. Two principal frameworks among these include AppKit and Foundation. A few other frameworks seem to be a part of the Cocoa family in one way or another, including the PreferencePanes and WebKit frameworks.

The Foundation framework contains Objective-C objects, protocols, and functions that are useful to Mac OS X programs in general, regardless of whether they are meant to be user-friendly applications or low-level system utilities. For example, things such as collection classes, file I/O, and memory utilities are defined in Foundation. Also, some functionality commonly thought of as high-level application functionality lives in Foundation because it doesn't involve any user interface (UI). The management of both undo and user preferences are part of Foundation.

The AppKit framework builds upon Foundation to implement classes essential for high-level applications, often limiting itself to graphic elements displayed on-screen. For example, windows, buttons, and menus are all AppKit features. Also, some specialized objects live in AppKit, even though they don't themselves define UI directly, such as objects responsible for doing font and text layout.

As a topic, Cocoa is huge. The API reference alone would make a hefty book if it was printed. Fortunately, Cocoa's API reference is installed on your hard drive, where you can search through it at your leisure. This chapter builds upon your experience from Chapter 7 about writing Objective-C programs, and shows you how to write simple Cocoa applications. You use the techniques you learn here in Chapters 9 and 10 to build a more complete application.

CONNECTING COCOA INTERFACES

In earlier chapters, you learned how to use Xcode to create a Cocoa application shell and use Interface Builder to design its UI. Those examples stopped short of actually connecting the interface to code. In fact, Cocoa provides two different complimentary ways of hooking up UIs.

Older Cocoa applications and programs with fairly specialized needs may choose to work with the UI directly. In these cases, you are responsible for keeping the controls synchronized with the state of their application. In other words, you must initialize your controls with your application data, and you must grab a new value from the controls when they change. This technique is direct and easy to grasp, but it can be hard to work with to create large UIs.

In Mac OS X v10.3 Panther, Apple introduced Cocoa Bindings, a new way of connecting Cocoa controls to custom Objective-C objects. Cocoa Bindings let you hook your application's controls to specific pieces of data. When your data changes, Cocoa Bindings updates the control. When the control changes, Cocoa Bindings updates your data. Cocoa Bindings helps alleviate some of the tedium of connecting larger interfaces by hand, but some specialized interfaces may be difficult to convert entirely to Cocoa Bindings.

Modern Cocoa applications use both techniques in their UIs. Fields that naturally reflect application data, such as text fields and sliders, may be connected using Cocoa Bindings. Other controls, such as push buttons and controls with customized drag-and-drop behavior, may continue to bind manually.

Connecting Interfaces Manually with Outlets and Actions

Before getting started with connecting Cocoa interfaces, you need to understand a few simple concepts: *instances*, *actions*, and *outlets*. Everything you worked with in Interface Builder so far is an *instance*: menus, menu items, controls, windows, and so on. Not only are these conceptually instances of each control, but they are also literally instances of Objective-C classes. That is to say, each element in your interface is one or more Objective-C objects. Recall from Chapter 7 that Objective-C objects are composed of instance variables and methods that operate on those variables.

An Interface Builder *action* is a specific kind of Objective-C method that is sent whenever a control is triggered. All actions have the same basic method signature: a void method that accepts a single argument.

```
- (IBAction)textFieldChanged:(id)sender;
```

Here, IBAction is really the same as void; it's just a marker to remind you that this method is known to Interface Builder as an action. The sender parameter is normally a pointer to the control that triggered the action. For example, when you click the button, it sends its action message to a target object. You set both the target object and the action in Interface Builder.

Similarly, an *outlet* is an instance variable that points to another object known to Interface Builder. Objects often contain references to other objects to facilitate communication between these objects. In the case of the button mentioned earlier, the button needs to know about its target. Often these references are handled automatically, but sometimes you need to explicitly tell one object about another object in Interface Builder. Outlets serve that purpose.

Most of the controls in the Interface Builder's Library window have specific outlets and actions predefined. This gives you a good base to start from when hooking your controls up to something. Normally, you will define your own classes within Interface Builder, define outlets and actions, and instantiate those classes. Then you can connect the interface to your own classes and customize its behavior with code.

In the following examples, you build a simple program called Email Formatter, which takes some text data and reformats it in a particular way. The UI shown in Figure 8-1 should look familiar to you; it's similar to the "Building a Dialog Window" example in Chapter 4.

Interface Builder is easy to use, if not exactly intuitive, to create simple interfaces. But the process of binding objects to controls can be repetitive and difficult in larger interfaces. Interface Builder includes several time-saving shortcuts to help streamline this process, and you learn many of these shortcuts along the way.

FIGURE 8-1

After you've built the interface, you perform the following four basic steps to get the application working:

1. First you set the key view loop so that the interface focus changes correctly when the user taps the Tab key. You didn't see this in Chapter 4 because it requires working with outlets, but it's good practice to do this before you jump in and create your own objects.

2. You declare a new Objective-C class inside Interface Builder that will manage your interface. This includes defining the class's outlets and actions.

3. You then instantiate the class within your nib file and connect it to your controls.

4. Finally, you complete your object's definition by writing some code in Xcode.

The following Try It Out walks you through building a simple interface.

Building the Email Formatter Interface

1. In Xcode, create a new Cocoa Application project named **Email Formatter**. Make sure all the options are unchecked — you just want a simple Cocoa application.

2. Double-click the `MainMenu.xib` nib file. It opens in Interface Builder.

3. In Interface Builder, lay out the interface shown in Figure 8-2. If you need a refresher on arranging controls in Interface Builder, feel free to flip back to Chapter 4 and read the "Building Windows" section again. Don't forget to make these items resizable.

4. Click twice on the Text View in your interface window. The first time you click, Interface Builder selects the containing scroll view. On the second click, Text View is selected.

FIGURE 8-2

5. Change the Text View Attributes settings to match those shown in Figure 8-3. Note that Text View is not editable, and doesn't support rich text, undo, or the Font Panel.

6. Click the window background to select it, or select Window (Email Formatter) in your MainMenu window. Make sure your interface window is visible at launch time, as shown in Figure 8-4. Normally this setting is on by default.

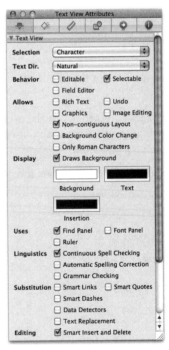

FIGURE 8-3

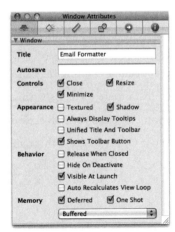

FIGURE 8-4

How It Works

There isn't much new here, because you got a lot of practice building UIs in Chapter 4. However, there are some important things to note. One is the horizontal separator shown in Figure 8-2. This control can be found in the Library under the name Horizontal Line and is actually an instance of the NSBox object. As you might expect, NSBox is used to collect items into a box, but Interface Builder includes special one-dimensional NSBox instances for drawing horizontal and vertical lines in nib files.

Simple Cocoa Application projects normally have only one window that contains most, if not all, of the application's UI. These windows normally are visible at launch time, and Interface Builder provides a helpful checkbox for displaying the window automatically. This setting isn't appropriate when you have more than one window, such as in a document-based application; in those cases, you tend to make windows visible programmatically. You learn more about working with documents in Chapter 9.

NSTextView instances are very customizable, allowing you to adjust each one to your specific needs. In this case, you just need a read-only view to display some string results. The text view should be selectable so you can copy text out of it and paste it into other applications. You can enable a bunch of other features in Interface Builder, including support for multiple fonts, undo/redo support, and automatic spell checking.

In the next Try It Out example, you define your window's key view loop so that you can use the Tab key to switch between controls in the window.

TRY IT OUT   Setting the Key View Loop

1. In Interface Builder, arrange your MainMenu nib file, your window editor, and the Inspector window so that you can easily see all three windows at the same time. Make sure the window editor is the frontmost window.

2. Hold down the Control key, click the editable text field next to the First Name label, and drag out without letting go of the mouse button. A line appears, joining the text field to the mouse cursor as shown in Figure 8-5.

3. Move the mouse over the editable Last Name text field and let go of the mouse button. A black overlay window appears, listing a bunch of options as shown in Figure 8-6. This overlay acts as a contextual menu. You can scroll up and down the list by moving your mouse over the up and down arrows. Note that the list contains Outlets and Received Actions sections, each one with a number of individual choices.

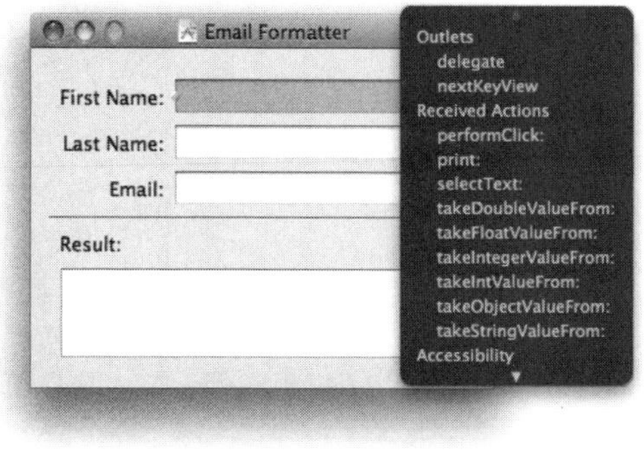

FIGURE 8-5

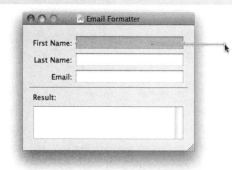

FIGURE 8-6

4. Scroll up in the list until the Outlets section is visible. The Outlets section has two items: `delegate` and `nextKeyView`.

5. Select the `nextKeyView` outlet. The overlay disappears and a line connecting both text fields flashes a few times.

6. Follow steps 2 through 5 again to connect the remaining objects to each other. Start by Control-dragging from the editable Last Name text field to the Email text field, and end by connecting the Result text view back to the First Name field.

7. Select your interface window, and then switch to the Inspector's Connections panel. A list of connections appears, as shown in Figure 8-7. As with the overlay list from Figure 8-6, the Connections list has sections for Outlets and Received Actions. Each item in the Connections list has a small circle along the right side of the Inspector.

8. Click in the circle next to `initialFirstResponder` and, while holding down the mouse, drag to the First Name editable text field. A line connecting the `initialFirstResponder` outlet to the text field appears, as shown in Figure 8-8. This line is the same one you saw in step 2. Let go of the mouse to complete the connection.

9. Test the interface and verify that the key view loop is correct by tabbing through the items. The key focus, normally indicated by a blue focus ring, should visit each control in turn. Note that the text view doesn't get a focus ring. If the text view just swallows the Tab key (inserts a tab as text), that means you haven't marked the control as non-editable yet. To do so, select the text view and uncheck the Editable box in the Inspector window's attributes view.

FIGURE 8-7

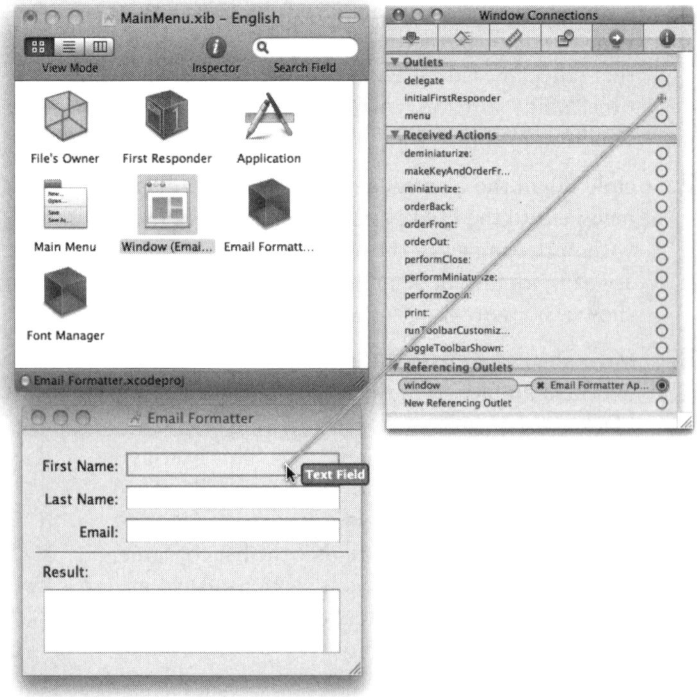

FIGURE 8-8

How It Works

You can set outlets either by Control-dragging from one instance to another, or by dragging from the Connections Inspector to a target instance. Control-dragging between instances is often convenient when you want to make a connection between two objects quickly. The Connections Inspector is often convenient when you want to make a number of connections from the same object. If you Control-click an object without dragging, Interface Builder will create a floating standalone connections window, which is handy if you don't want to use the Inspector.

When Control-dragging to set an outlet, you must remember to start the drag from the object whose outlet you want to set. That is, if you want to set a window's `initialFirstResponder` outlet to a text field, you must start the drag from the window and end at the text field. You cannot set the window's outlets when starting the drag from another object. This is a little more intuitive when you're dragging from the Connections Inspector, because you are clearly changing the outlet for the selected object.

When you're connecting the text controls to each other, you have to manually scroll up to reveal the Outlets section each time. This is because Interface Builder assumes you want to set actions when making a connection between two controls. Note that only controls and menu items have actions; when you start a drag from windows and other objects, Interface Builder reveals the Outlets section for you.

 NOTE *Mac OS X interfaces are meant to be navigable from the keyboard. At a minimum, this means you can switch between text controls using the Tab key. However, you can turn on full keyboard access from the Keyboard system preference pane, which allows you to tab between all kinds of controls.*

In Cocoa, controls are responsible for handling their own keyboard and mouse events. The selected control gets the first opportunity to handle incoming events. This control is called the *first responder*. Normally, the control just handles the event itself. For example, a text field updates itself when you type text. If the control doesn't know how to interpret an event, it can pass the event to something else. You learn more about the first responder and event handling in Chapter 9.

When you press the Tab key, the selected control will attempt to change the focus to the next control in the window. For this to work properly, you usually supply the next control through the selected control's `nextKeyView` outlet. Remember, outlets are really special instance variables. When the first responding control receives the tab event, it will look at its `nextKeyView` instance variable and make the object it finds there the new first responder.

By default, the Cocoa system will attempt to figure out what the next control should be based on the location of other controls in the window, but it's good practice to set the key view loop directly. AppKit decides if it should use the default behavior or trust the settings in the controls by checking the window's `initialFirstResponder` outlet. `initialFirstResponder` points to the control that should be active when the window first appears on-screen. If you want to define your own key view loop in Interface Builder, you must remember to set the window's `initialFirstResponder`.

In the next Try It Out example, you make a new Objective-C class that manages your interface. This includes defining the class's outlets and actions.

TRY IT OUT **Declaring a Custom Controller**

1. In Xcode, create a new Objective-C class file named **EmailController.m.** Make sure you create the corresponding EmailController.h header file.

2. Replace the contents of EmailController.h with the following code:

```objc
#import <Cocoa/Cocoa.h>

@interface EmailController : NSObject
{
    IBOutlet NSTextField *emailField;
    IBOutlet NSTextField *firstNameField;
    IBOutlet NSTextField *lastNameField;
    IBOutlet NSTextView *resultTextView;
}

- (IBAction)textFieldChanged:(id)sender;

@end
```

code snippet MacOSXProg ch08/Email Formatter/EmailController.h

3. Save your changes to EmailController.h.

4. In Interface Builder, find an Object item in the Library and drag it to your MainMenu.xib nib file window. A new blue cube will appear in your window, as shown in Figure 8-9.

5. Select the new Object and switch to the Identity Inspector. The Identity Inspector has a field where you can enter a custom class name for this object and some other controls, resembling Figure 8-10.

FIGURE 8-9

FIGURE 8-10

6. Change the object's class from the default `NSObject` to `EmailController`. As you start typing, Interface Builder will automatically suggest class names found within your Xcode project.

7. Switch to the Connections Inspector. The list of Outlets and Received Actions contains the new instance variables and methods you added to your `EmailController.h` file, as shown in Figure 8-11.

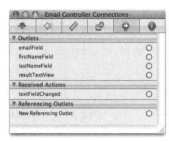

How It Works

FIGURE 8-11

Information about common Cocoa controls, including their outlets and actions, is built directly into Interface Builder. This information allows you to hook Cocoa controls to each other. You used these built-in settings to set your application's key loop in this example.

You can use Xcode to define new classes in Interface Builder. Simply create a new Objective-C class and add outlets and actions to your class's interface. Interface Builder will read the changes to your Xcode project and update itself automatically. If you have trouble getting Interface Builder to recognize your classes, try dragging your header file into your nib window, or select File ➪ Read Class Files.

Earlier in this chapter, you learned that outlets are really instance variables and actions are really methods. You also learned `IBOutlet` and `IBAction` are simply markers that help remind you about which of your instance variables are outlets and which of your methods are actions. Interface Builder also uses these markers when reading your header files. Without them, Interface Builder won't find any of your outlets or actions.

After you've declared your class, you can instantiate it in your nib file by dragging in a generic object and setting its class. This allows you to connect your object to other user interface elements in your nib file, as you see shortly. Note that you really are creating an instance of your object in your nib file; when the nib file loads, a new instance of your object will be created and initialized with the settings in the nib file. Your nib assumes ownership of this object, so you don't need to worry about retaining or releasing it yourself.

In the next Try It Out, you create an instance of your Objective-C controller class and connect it to your UI. You will try out two ways of connecting objects to each other: Control-dragging between nib file instances and connecting objects to a standalone Connections list.

TRY IT OUT Connecting Controls to Your Controller

1. Control-click the Email Controller instance in `MainMenu.xib`. The standalone Connections list appears, showing you the outlets and actions that Email Controller supports. It should look exactly as shown in Figure 8-12.

2. Connect the `emailField`, `firstNameField`, `lastNameField`, and `resultTextView` outlets to the corresponding controls in your interface window by dragging from the Connections list.

FIGURE 8-12

3.   Control-drag from the First Name editable text field to the Email Controller instance in your nib window. A small list appears, showing you an outlet named `delegate` and an action named `textFieldChanged:`.

4.   Choose the `textFieldChanged:` action. The small list disappears.

5.   Drag from the `textFieldChanged:` circle in the standalone Connections list to the Last Name editable text field. This time, the Connections list changes indicating that there are multiple connections for this received action. Your Connections list should resemble Figure 8-13.

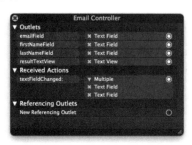

6.   Drag from the `textFieldChanged:` circle in the Connections list to the Email editable text field to complete the interface.

7.   Save your nib file.

FIGURE 8-13

How It Works

You saw how to connect outlets in the previous example, and for the most part, there were no surprises. This was a good opportunity to practice using the standalone Connections list to quickly set up a number of connections to a single object.

You also learned how to set actions. For the most part, setting actions is similar to setting outlets, except you start the Control-drag operation from the control. This whole issue of Control-dragging can be a bit confusing for people new to Cocoa, because it's not always obvious where you should start dragging from. There is a simple rule to keep this straight: always start the Control-drag from the element you are modifying. The following table lists a few examples that illustrate this point.

WHAT YOU WANT	WHAT YOU DO
Set a window's `initialFirstResponder` from the window to the text field.	The window is being modified, so Control-drag to a text field.
Set a text field's `nextKeyView` to a button.	The text field is being modified, so Control-drag from the text field to the button.
Connect a button to an object's `clickedOK:` action.	The button is being modified, so Control-drag from the button to the object.

Working with the Connections list, be it the standalone HUD-style window or the Connections Inspector, tends to be a lot more intuitive. Because the actions in the list represent the received action, you are actually modifying the destination of the drag, not the source. When you make a connection from `textFieldChanged:` to a text field, you are actually changing the text field. But the language in the list flips this around so you can configure outlets and actions with the same gesture.

In the next Try It Out example, you write the code for your `EmailController` class. Then you are able to build and run the Email Formatter program.

TRY IT OUT Writing Your Controller

1. Open `EmailController.m` in Xcode. The class implementation is currently empty, as shown here:

```
#import "EmailController.h"

@implementation EmailController

@end
```

2. Add the following `textFieldChanged:` method to the class:

Available for
download on
Wrox.com

```
- (IBAction)textFieldChanged:(id)sender
{
    NSString *string = [NSString stringWithFormat:@"%@ %@ <%@>",
        [firstNameField stringValue],
        [lastNameField stringValue],
        [emailField stringValue]];

    [resultTextView setString:string];
}
```

code snippet MacOSXProg ch08/Email Formatter/EmailController.m

3. Save your changes to `EmailController.m`.

4. Build and run your project. Xcode compiles your code, builds your application wrapper, and runs your program.

5. Insert values in the text fields. As you do so, the Result view displays the information formatted as a verbose e-mail address. You can select the text in the Result field and copy and paste or drag and drop the full address into an e-mail program such as Mail.

How It Works

Interface Builder knows a lot about your `EmailController` object, including the names and types of `EmailController`'s outlets and the name of its action. This information was required for hooking your interface's controls up to a custom object.

But Interface Builder doesn't know anything about your implementation code. You need to supply that yourself in Xcode. In this example, all you need to do is supply some code for the `textFieldChanged:` method. Interface Builder didn't try to generate this code for you. For that matter, Interface Builder didn't generate any code at all for the other objects in your nib file.

This is a pretty big deal, especially if you've used WYSIWYG development environments that automatically generate the entire code for all your interface elements. Those systems actually write large pieces of your source code for you as you change your interface layout. Although those tools spare you the time and trouble to write that code, it can be difficult to find where you should insert your own changes. If you make a mistake, you run the risk of losing your custom code the next time you make a trivial change to your interface. When using Cocoa, you write only the code that's unique to your application; all the default control behaviors are provided directly by the Cocoa frameworks.

The `textFieldChanged:` method does three things. First, it gets the content of the text fields using its `-stringValue` methods. The `NSTextField` objects inherit `-stringValue` from their superclass, `NSControl`. The `NSControl` class is the common ancestor for all controls that trigger actions when they change.

Second, the `textFieldChanged:` method builds a new `NSString` object that joins the other strings together using `+stringWithFormat:`. You may remember `NSString`'s `stringWithFormat:` and `NSLog` from Chapter 7. This string holds the newly formatted e-mail address.

Third, it assigns the resulting string to the `resultTextView` using its `-setString:` method. Again, `resultTextView` is an instance of `NSTextView`, which in spite of appearances, isn't really an `NSControl` subclass such as `NSTextField`. As a result, it doesn't use the same methods for getting and setting data.

In Chapter 7, you also learned a little about how `NSAutoreleasePool` objects work; every example you saw created and released its own autorelease pool instance. You may be wondering why this example has no autorelease pool. It turns out it does, but AppKit is managing it for you. Every event is processed in its own autorelease pool, meaning all the temporary objects created during event handling are released before processing the next event. That also means you can't hang onto these autoreleased objects in an instance variable (or a global variable) without retaining them first. Note that that's exactly what the `NSTextView` will do when you call `setString:`. As a general rule in Cocoa programs, you don't need to worry about autoreleased objects as long as you never hang onto them between events.

After you've completed the `textFieldChanged:` method, you can build and run your application. When your application's nib file loads, Cocoa creates and initializes your `EmailController` object. And when you change the text fields, `textFieldChanged:` is called to rebuild the Result text view. If you want, you can set a breakpoint in `textFieldChanged:`, run your application in Xcode's debugger, and watch as the Result text view is rebuilt. Note that copy and paste, select all, drag and drop, and other features work without you doing anything special on your end. You are beginning to reap the benefits of Cocoa.

Working with Cocoa Bindings

You now have a pretty good idea of the work involved in connecting a Cocoa UI. Most of the hard work is done in Interface Builder: you design your user interface, then you declare your classes, and then you do a lot of dragging to connect the interface to your custom classes. When that's done, all you have to do is fill in the remaining source code, and you're good to go.

Although this isn't a big deal for the Email Formatter example, there's a lot of busy work involved in building a large UI. Consider an Inspector window with dozens or hundreds of controls. Each control needs its own outlet, you have to remember to initialize the controls to useful values, and you have to remember to update the controls if somehow your data changes behind the scenes. You also need to track when each control changes, either by using separate actions or by funneling groups of controls into a single action. Even the Email Formatter application, which has only three editable controls, captures edits in a single action method. AppKit provides a number of little tricks, such as control tags, to help facilitate this kind of control management. But there's another way to hook up Cocoa UIs that avoids much of this busywork.

Apple introduced *Cocoa Bindings*, a new way of connecting Cocoa controls to your custom Objective-C objects, to deal with some of these scalability issues. Instead of connecting a control to outlet instance variables and action methods, Cocoa Bindings lets you connect a control directly to an object's value. When the control changes, Cocoa Bindings updates the value for you. What's more, when the value changes, Cocoa Bindings automatically updates the control for you as well. There's a lot going on behind the scenes to make this work; but you really don't need to worry about how it works to get started with Cocoa Bindings.

In the following Try It Out, you build a version of Email Formatter that uses Cocoa Bindings to manage its UI. After you build your UI, the following three steps remain to complete the application:

1. You create an NSObjectController instance and connect it to a custom data object. This is the Cocoa Bindings equivalent of the EmailController class from the first Email Formatter example.

2. You connect your controls to the NSObjectController.

3. You finish the implementation of your custom class in Xcode.

TRY IT OUT   Building the Email Formatter 2 Interface

1. In Xcode, create a new Cocoa Application project named **Email Formatter 2.**

2. Double-click the MainMenu nib file. It opens in Interface Builder.

3. In Interface Builder, select the Window (Email Formatter 2) instance and press the Delete key to remove it from your nib file.

4. Now open the MainMenu nib file from your first Email Formatter program. You should be able to find it in Interface Builder's File ⇨ Open Recent menu. If not, you can find it in your Email Formatter Xcode project.

5. Copy the Window instance from the first Email Formatter nib file by clicking the Window (Email Formatter) icon and choosing Edit ⇨ Copy.

6. Close the original Email Formatter nib file.

7. Paste the Window into your new nib file by choosing Edit ⇨ Paste.

How It Works

Copying the Window instance from your first Email Formatter project to your second saved you a bit of time. For the most part, the entire Window instance structure was preserved, including the controls and their key view loop. However, all your controls' actions were cleared. This is just as well, as you won't be setting actions in this example.

In the next Try It Out, you declare an EmailAddress class to store the data displayed by your interface and create an NSObjectController instance to manage the relationship between your controls and the EmailAddress class.

TRY IT OUT   Creating an NSObjectController

1. In Xcode, create a new Objective-C class file named `EmailAddress.m`. Make sure you create the corresponding `EmailAddress.h` header file. Don't worry about editing these files for now.

2. In Interface Builder, find the Object item in the Library and drag it to your `MainMenu.xib` nib file. A new blue cube appears in your window.

3. Change your new object to a subclass of `EmailAddress` using the Identity Inspector. Interface Builder should auto-complete to the name EmailAddress, indicating Interface Builder already knows about the class you defined in step 1.

4. Find the Object Controller item in the Library and drag it to your nib file. The Object Controller looks similar to a cube in a green bubble. Your nib file should resemble Figure 8-14.

FIGURE 8-14

5. Set the Object Controller's `content` outlet to your Email Address instance by Control-dragging from the Object Controller icon to the Email Address icon, or by using the Connections Inspector.

6. In the Attributes Inspector, change the Object Controller's Class Name from `NSMutableDictionary` to **EmailAddress.**

7. Save your work.

How It Works

Cocoa Bindings uses `NSController` subclasses to marshal data between your custom objects and your controls. Currently, there are many such `NSController` subclasses, including `NSObjectController`, `NSUserDefaultsController`, and `NSArrayController`. `NSArrayController` is useful for working with arrays of custom objects, such as when you're working with lists of information. `NSUserDefaultsController` is a special kind of `NSObjectController` that reads and writes values to your preference file automatically.

You added an `NSObjectController` object to your interface because your data object is a simple `NSObject` subclass. The `NSObjectController` is used for managing single objects. By default, `NSObjectController` assumes you are working with `NSMutableDictionary` instances. When using `NSObjectController` with your own classes, you must manually set the class name.

You still created a custom object in Interface Builder, `EmailAddress`, even though you're working with Cocoa Bindings. This custom object won't talk to your controls directly; as a result, you don't need to create any outlets or actions. Your `NSObjectController` instance handles that for you. Instead, `EmailAddress` will basically store the values that appear in your controls. Because `NSObjectController` needs this information, you connect your `EmailAddress` instance to the `NSObjectController`'s outlet.

In the next example, you connect the controls to your new `NSObjectController` instance.

TRY IT OUT Connecting Controls to NSObjectController

1. Select the editable First Name text field in your Window editor.

2. Choose the Bindings panel in the Inspector window. The Bindings Inspector appears, as shown in Figure 8-15.

3. Click the Value disclosure triangle under the Value section to reveal the group of controls shown in Figure 8-16. Note that Object Controller already appears in the Bind To pop-up menu.

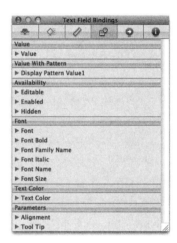

FIGURE 8-15

FIGURE 8-16

4. Enter **firstName** in the Model Key Path text field and press Return. Note that the Bind To checkbox automatically enables itself, and the group of disabled controls under the Model Key Path value is enabled.

5. Follow the preceding steps to set the Last Name text field's Model Key Path to **lastName** and the Email text field's Model Key Path to **email**.

6. Click once on the Result text view. Note that the Bindings view changes to include only Availability and Parameters sections. Also note that the Inspector window's title reads Scroll View Bindings.

7. Double-click the Result text view. The Inspector window's title is now Text View Bindings, and the Bindings view includes a Value section. If you have trouble selecting the text view inside the scroll view, try clicking toward the top of the control where the first line of text would be if the text view had something in it.

8. If necessary, click the Value disclosure triangle under the Value section to reveal the group of controls. These controls resemble the ones you saw in Figure 8-16.

9. Enter `formattedEmail` in the Model Key Path text field and press Return. Again note that the disabled group of controls under Model Key Path is enabled.

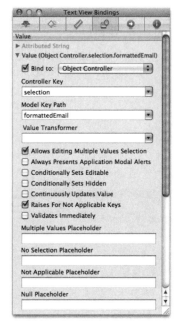

FIGURE 8-17

10. Turn off the Conditionally Sets Editable checkbox. The Bindings settings should match those shown in Figure 8-17.

How It Works

You use the Bindings Inspector to associate a UI element with a particular piece of data. First, you use the Bind To pop-up menu to specify the `NSController` subclass you want to bind to. In this example, Interface Builder automatically selected `NSObjectController`, because it was the only one available in your nib file.

Then you specify a *controller key,* which helps provide some context when talking to your controller. In this example, and for all `NSObjectController` bindings, this value will always be `selection`. Other kinds of controllers, such as `NSArrayController`, can use the Controller Key Value to specify more specifically which object or objects you want to bind.

Finally, you specify a *model key path* that identifies the data you are looking for. In this example, the model key path values are simply names of values in your `EmailAddress` object, although you haven't defined those values yet. In more sophisticated examples, the model key path might include a list of objects to traverse to find the data.

There are two subtle gotchas regarding your `NSTextView`. When you built your interface the first time (in the Email Formatter example), you turned off the ability to use multiple fonts. This allows you to treat the content of the text view as a simple string, just as in the preceding text fields. You see why this is important in the next section. If that option was enabled, Cocoa Bindings would expect you to work with `NSData` objects that contain *rich text* data, such as those found in RTF files. In that case, the Bindings Inspector would show the "data" or Attributed String section instead of the Value section seen earlier in Figure 8-17. If you find yourself in this situation, just turn off the data binding, turn off the text view's Use Multiple Fonts checkbox, and enable the value binding.

The second `NSTextView` gotcha involves editability. Again, when you create the interface, you turn off the `NSTextView`'s Editable flag. If you use Cocoa Bindings, the Editable flag is ignored by default; instead, editability can be controlled through the bindings themselves. That is, you can configure controls to be editable only when another condition is true; for example, you can enable one checkbox automatically when the checkbox above it is enabled. Because you want your text view to always be read-only, you have to turn off the Bindings view's Conditionally Sets Editable setting.

In the next example, you write the code for your `EmailAddress` model object. Then you can build and run Email Formatter 2.

TRY IT OUT **Writing Your EmailAddress Class**

1. Open `EmailAddress.h` in Xcode. The class interface is currently empty, as shown here:

```
@interface EmailAddress : NSObject
{

}

@end
```

2. Change the declaration of `EmailAddress` to include the following instance variables:

```
@interface EmailAddress : NSObject
{
    NSString *firstName;
    NSString *lastName;
    NSString *email;
}
@end
```

code snippet MacOSXProg ch08/Email Formatter 2/EmailAddress.h

3. Save your changes to `EmailAddress.h`.

4. Switch to `EmailAddress.m`.

5. Add the following methods to the `EmailAddress` object:

```
@implementation EmailAddress

+ (NSSet *)keyPathsForValuesAffectingValueForKey:(NSString *)key
{
    NSSet *keyPaths = [super keyPathsForValuesAffectingValueForKey:key];

    if ([key isEqualToString:@"formattedEmail"]) {
      NSSet *dependentKeys = [NSSet setWithObjects:@"firstName",
                                                   @"lastName",
                                                   @"email",
                                                   nil];

      keyPaths = [keyPaths setByAddingObjectsFromSet:dependentKeys];
    }

    return keyPaths;
}

- (NSString *)formattedEmail
{
    if (firstName && lastName && email) {
        return [NSString stringWithFormat:@"%@ %@ <%@>", firstName, lastName,
```

```
    email];
    }

    return nil;
}

@end
```

code snippet MacOSXProg ch08/Email Formatter 2/EmailAddress.m

6. Save your changes to `EmailAddress.m`.

7. Build and run your project. Xcode compiles your code, builds your application wrapper, and runs your program.

How It Works

There are two things happening in your `EmailAddress` class. First, **EmailAddress** is receiving values for the First Name, Last Name, and Email text fields. Second, `EmailAddress` is providing the formatted e-mail address upon request. That's the same two things as in the `EmailController` class from your first Email Formatter example, but here you're working with Cocoa Bindings instead of outlets and actions.

Cocoa Bindings uses strings to represent model key paths. You have already learned that these model key paths identify pieces of data in your object. When the time comes to actually get the data from your object, Cocoa Bindings looks for model key paths either in instance variables or accessor methods. Three of your key paths — `firstName`, `lastName`, and `email` — were defined as instance variables in your `EmailAddress` object. Because all three of these values need to be available to `EmailAddress` at any given time (to build the resulting, formatted e-mail address), instance variables are a convenient choice of implementation. All you have to do is make sure the instance variables' names match the key paths in the nib file, and Cocoa Bindings manages the rest for you.

You may also remember accessor methods (methods used to get and set instance variable values) from Chapter 7. Your fourth key path, `formattedEmail`, was implemented as an accessor method. Doing this gave your `EmailAddress` object the opportunity to construct the `formattedEmail` value upon demand. If it were instead implemented as an instance variable, you would need to find some other way of rebuilding the value when one of the text fields changed.

Note in both cases that the specific data types for `EmailAddress`'s values were specified by the instance variable and accessor definitions themselves. You did not need to specify the exact type in your nib file. The Cocoa Bindings system recognizes many different data types. In this example, you worked entirely with `NSString` instances; you could just have easily worked with simple scalar types such as `int`, `float`, or `BOOL`. Other kinds of controls are better suited for working with other kinds of data types. For example, an `NSImageView` might work with `NSImage` instances directly; `NSTextViews` that display rich-text work with `NSData` objects and `NSAttributedStrings`.

The mechanism for accessing your objects' values by a key path is called *Key Value Coding*, and is one of the technologies Cocoa Bindings is based on. You have already seen Key Value Coding in action when accessing the values in your `EmailAddress` object. Key Value Coding also defines how the value for each key is found, how to handle requests for keys that aren't available, navigating through multiple objects to find specific data, and other advanced topics.

However, Key Value Coding doesn't explain why your application knew to request the `formattedEmail` value when your text fields changed. You used a special class method named `+keyPathsForValuesAffectingValueForKey:` to tell Cocoa Bindings that `formattedEmail` depends on the values of your other keys. This method is built into `NSObject` and is part of a mechanism called *Key Value Observing*.

Key Value Observing is another core technology behind Cocoa Bindings. It refers to the ability of Cocoa Bindings to watch your objects, note when they change, and communicate that change to others. This is often used to keep controls synchronized with their bound values. For example, when an object's value is changed through an accessor method, Key Value Observing will make sure the controls that refer to this value are updated automatically. This automatic update works only for changes made through accessor methods or Key Value Coding, not for direct assignment to instance variables. In this example, when your `NSObjectController` changed the value of `EmailAddress`'s `firstName`, `lastName`, and `email` values through Key Value Coding, Key Value Observing told the `NSObjectController` that the `formattedEmail` value also needed to be updated. Then the `NSObjectController` used Key Value Coding again to read the new value of `formattedEmail`.

This example has only just scratched the surface of Cocoa Bindings, Key Value Coding, and Key Value Observing. You see a few more examples of bindings throughout this chapter. If you want to learn more about bindings, including how bindings work and what they can do, you should check the Xcode's Documentation window. You can start by reading the conceptual documentation for Cocoa Bindings, available either through the Cocoa conceptual documentation list or through the `NSController` reference documentation.

The Model/View/Controller Design Pattern

You may have noticed the term "controller" appearing in both of the previous examples. In the first Email Formatter application, the word appears in the name of your custom Objective-C object, `EmailController`. In the second application, you learned that Cocoa Bindings is built around a series of classes derived from `NSController`. And there are some similarities about how these controllers were used; in both cases, your user interface was bound directly to your controller objects. This was not a coincidence.

Most Cocoa objects follow a programming convention known as the Model/View/Controller design pattern. Model/View/Controller, which is abbreviated MVC, refers to a particular way of organizing objects to encourage code reuse. Objects are separated into one of three categories, from which the MVC design pattern derives its name: model objects, views, and controllers.

A *model* encapsulates a particular set of data or an algorithm. Models are normally limited in scope, and do not imply how the data is meant to be displayed. One example of a model object you've seen so far is `NSString`. An `NSString` object represents a Unicode character string; it supplies storage for the string data and methods for accessing and manipulating that data. At the same time, `NSString` doesn't provide any support for drawing strings in UIs. By keeping model objects focused on the data they represent, they are easily usable in any situation that calls for that kind of data.

Objects responsible for presenting information to the user are called *views*. Concrete examples of views abound in Cocoa; for example, windows, buttons, menus, and text fields are all views. Many AppKit classes even use the term in their class names, such as NSTextView and NSImageView. View objects aren't directly concerned with the details of how data is stored, or what the data might represent. This allows views to be easily reused whenever you need that kind of UI element.

Controllers fill the gap between the general-purpose model and view objects. Mechanically, this means a controller pulls data out of the model and hands it to the view for display, and when the view changes (the user changed the value of a control), the controller pulls the new data out of the view and records it in the model. This also means the controller provides the context in which the model and view objects are used. For example, although an NSString is just a collection of Unicode characters, and an NSTextField knows how to draw an NSString in an editable control, the EmailController object knows that a particular string containing an e-mail address should go into the Email NSTextField control. Because controllers are specific to a particular UI, they normally aren't reusable in the same way that model and view objects are. Cocoa Bindings try to solve this reusability problem by providing a standard mechanism for shuttling values between your model objects and your views.

The MVC design pattern is an abstract notion, and you can implement its concepts in different ways. For example, a controller object might also double as a model in a simple example where you aren't interested in reusing the model elsewhere. This was the case in your first Email Formatter application: the EmailController object was responsible for reacting to UI changes as well as performing your model-specific behavior (converting the inputs into a formatted e-mail address). Conversely, Email Formatter 2's EmailAddress object was strictly a model object.

SUMMARY

Cocoa provides the building blocks for Mac OS X applications. These building blocks take the form of Objective-C classes found in AppKit, Foundation, and other frameworks. You work with these building blocks in both Interface Builder and Xcode.

Since the beginning, Cocoa has constantly evolved to make it easier for programmers to create their applications. You can see this evolution even in the simplest Cocoa examples. Hooking up UIs to code in Cocoa with outlets and actions is easy, and is a huge improvement over other libraries where you have to memorize large numbers or generate massive quantities of code. Hooking up UIs with Cocoa Bindings is even easier than that.

Cocoa owes a lot of its configurability to its object-oriented design, as well as to the Objective-C language. Design patterns such as Model/View/Controller encourage programmers (even Apple's Cocoa programmers) to organize their code so it is easy to extend and reuse. Principles of these design patterns are built deeply into Cocoa's DNA. The Objective-C runtime provides the power under the hood of technologies such as Cocoa Bindings.

In this chapter you learned

> ➤ How to bind your application's UI to your custom code using outlets and actions. Outlets and actions provide a way for you to manually connect objects together in Interface Builder.

➤ How to bind your application to your custom code using Cocoa Bindings. When you use Cocoa Bindings, you no longer need to create outlets and actions that exist only to marshal data into and out of your user interface.

➤ About the Model/View/Controller design pattern and how it can encourage code reuse.

In the next chapter, you learn about document-based Cocoa applications, including how to create a document-based UI, how to wire the UI up to document data, and how events are routed to these documents. Before proceeding, however, try the exercises that follow to test your understanding of the material covered in this chapter. You can find the solutions to these exercises in Appendix A.

EXERCISES

1. Create a color calculator application that takes a Red, Green, and Blue value between 0 and 1 and displays the corresponding color in an `NSColorWell` control.

2. Extend the color calculator program to display new Red, Green, and Blue values when the user changes the `NSColorWell`, in addition to the existing behavior. You can get the red, green, and blue color components from an `NSColor` object, although when, you're working with arbitrary colors, you should convert them to an RGB color space first. See the `NSColor` documentation for more information.

▶ **WHAT YOU LEARNED IN THIS CHAPTER**

Instance	an Objective-C object visible in Interface Builder files
Outlet	a reference to an instance that can be set within Interface Builder, often marked with an `IBOutlet` keyword
Action	an Objective-C method that can be triggered from Cocoa controls, often marked with an `IBAction` keyword
Cocoa Bindings	a mechanism for associating a control in a window with data in an object
Key Value Coding	Cocoa Bindings technology responsible for looking up and setting data by name or path
Key Value Observing	Cocoa Bindings technology responsible for detecting and responding to changes in model data
NSController	a Cocoa class used for managing Cocoa Binding relationships between controls and one or more model objects
Controller Key	the name of the controller method used to fetch model objects, set in Interface Builder when using Cocoa Bindings
Model Key Path	the name of a property used to get and set data from a model object, set in Interface Builder when using Cocoa Bindings
Model	in the Model/View/Controller design pattern, an object that encapsulates data or an algorithm
View	in the Model/View/Controller design pattern, an object that presents information to the user
Controller	in the Model/View/Controller design pattern, an object that manages the communication between model and view objects

Document-Based Cocoa Applications

WHAT YOU WILL LEARN IN THIS CHAPTER:

➤ How to use an NSDocument subclass to store your document data

➤ How to use an NSWindowController subclass to organize and display your document interface

➤ How to bind menu items to your documents using Interface Builder

Macintosh applications have presented user data as documents since the very beginning. A document is a convenient way to organize a user interface: a document can be displayed in its own window. A document is also a convenient way to organize file data: a document is its own self-contained file or bundle.

In Mac OS X, document-based apps can take many forms. The archetypical document-based application is TextEdit. You can open text files in TextEdit and display the content of those files in their own window. You can edit the content of a file directly in its window, and when you are done you can save and close the document. From there it's an easy jump to viewing Pages or Preview files as documents. If you're willing to relax the way you treat the user interface and how data is stored, you can view Mail, iChat, and Safari as document-based applications. E-mail messages are self-contained and Mail displays these messages either as their own windows, or in a one-window mail viewer. And sending a new mail message is a lot like saving and closing a text document.

So far you have seen how to use Cocoa to build small, single-window applications. And using those techniques, you can even build applications that use more than one window. But you need to learn some new techniques to build good document-based applications that follow Apple's Human Interface Guidelines.

In this chapter you learn:

➤ To use an NSDocument subclass to store your document data

➤ To use an NSWindowController subclass to organize and display your document interface

➤ How to bind menu items to your documents using Interface Builder

WORKING WITH DOCUMENTS

The AppKit framework includes classes to help manage documents of information in a Cocoa program. When you use these classes, AppKit handles your documents' files and windows for you. You need to focus on your documents' data and how to connect it to your user interface.

AppKit's document support can be used in two different ways, depending on how sophisticated your interface is or what kind of hurry you are in. In both cases you begin by creating your own custom subclass of NSDocument. The NSDocument class provides basic behavior for a document, including reading from and writing to files, tracking open windows, managing document changes, undo, printing, and so on.

Your NSDocument subclass can manage its own windows directly. It contains model code for storing document data in memory and working with files, as well as controller information such as populating the user interface and updating the model when the interface changes (and vice versa).

Having NSDocument manage its own windows has a few advantages for people new to Cocoa programming. Primarily it simplifies your application code by keeping all your document knowledge in one class. It's easy to work with document-based applications using this method. Also, for very small projects with only a few objects, it may not make sense to burden the application with a more sophisticated design. On the other hand, more complicated classes may suffer from mingling interface controller code with the document model code.

AppKit provides an NSWindowController class that you can use to separate document model logic from its interface control. NSWindowController manages the life cycle of a window, including loading the window from a nib file, managing how the window appears on-screen, and tearing everything down when the window is closed. In addition to providing general window behavior, a custom NSWindowController subclass can also manage a window's contents: the window controller can initialize its controls from your document's state, and update that state when the controls change.

Because NSDocument can handle window management itself, use of custom NSWindowControllers in a document-based application is largely optional. There are benefits to separating out document model logic from interface controller code. For example, you may want to create instances of your documents where you don't load a user interface, such as in a background-only daemon or when handling AppleScript commands. Also, you need to use NSWindowController subclasses if your application needs to display more than one window per document, such as in a CAD program or a video-editing application. NSDocument can only handle one window per document by default.

Creating a New Document

In the following Try It Out sections, you build a simple image viewer application that uses a custom NSWindowController class along with a custom NSDocument class. Rather than building a small standalone example, you build this functionality directly into the Slide Master project you started in Chapter 5. This gives Slide Master the capability of viewing slides in individual windows, outside the context of a slideshow, as shown in Figure 9-1. Images appear in their own window; if the window isn't large enough to display the entire image, scrollbars appear.

You add this functionality to Slide Master in three steps:

1. First you build Slide Master's image window. This window contains an NSImageView object that can display image data; the image view resides within an NSScrollView object that knows how to scroll views too large to fit in a specific area.

2. Next you define your custom NSWindowController subclass and set it as the nib file's owner. This allows you to connect the interface to your custom controller class. You also write the code that initializes your window content from document data.

3. You create your custom NSDocument subclass in Xcode. This class is responsible for reading image data from disk and creating your window controller instances.

FIGURE 9-1

TRY IT OUT   Configuring a Scrollable Image View

1. In Xcode, open the Slide Master project you created in Chapter 5. If you haven't built this project yet for some reason, flip back to Chapter 5 and follow the example in the "Building an Application Bundle" section.

2. Control-click the `MyDocument.xib` interface file and choose the Reveal In Finder option from the contextual menu. The Finder will activate and display the `MyDocument` file.

3. Make a copy of the `MyDocument` interface file named `ImageDocument`.

4. In Xcode, add `ImageDocument` to the Slide Master project. If you like, drag `ImageDocument` to the Resources group in your project's Groups & Files list. You can also use Project ➪ Add To Project to choose the file.

5. Double-click the `ImageDocument.xib` interface file. It will open in Interface Builder.

6. In Interface Builder, select the "Your document contents here" text label and press Delete to remove it from your window.

7. Find an Image Well item in the Library and drag it to your window. This object represents an instance of the `NSImageView` control used to draw images. Don't bother resizing the control; you manage the size of this image view programmatically in your window controller class a little later.

8. In the Attributes Inspector, set the Scaling to None and set the Border to None. The Attributes Inspector should resemble Figure 9-2. Note that when you turn the border off, the image view is no longer obviously visible in the window editor. Only its bounding box selection handles indicate the image view's location.

9. Select Layout ➪ Embed Objects In ➪ Scroll View. The image view is replaced by a scroll view containing that image view.

10. Resize the scroll view so that it fills the entire screen. Double-check Size & Position in the Size Inspector — if Interface Builder positions the scroll view at –1, –1 changes X and Y to 0, 0. Also make sure the scroll view will grow and shrink as the window is resized.

11. Disable the scroll view's border and turn on Automatically Hide Scrollers. Also set the scroll view's background color to white. The Attributes Inspector will resemble the one in Figure 9-3.

12. Double-click within the scroll view area; this selects the image view again. You may need to click in the lower-left corner of the scroll view to hit the image view.

13. Verify that the image view will not grow or shrink when the window is resized using the Size inspector.

FIGURE 9-2

FIGURE 9-3

How It Works

The NSImageView class is a simple control that draws images. It's useful in cases such as this where you need to draw an image in a window. NSImageView objects can also be editable, meaning you can change the image by dragging in a new image file from the Finder. These kinds of image views are often called *image wells*, so called because editable image views often appear inset in the window.

Rather than exposing scrollbars as individual controls in Interface Builder, Cocoa provides a new view class that manages the entire scrollable area: NSScrollView. An NSScrollView instance does all the work required for checking its size against the size of its content and configuring the scrollbars accordingly. You can even tell NSScrollView to hide scrollbars when they aren't necessary.

You normally create NSScrollView instances using Interface Builder's "Embed Objects In" menu item. This menu item takes the current selection and wraps it in a container view, such as NSScrollView or NSBox. You can drag an NSScrollView into your window from the Library if you need to set this manually, but the Embed Objects In menu tends to be more convenient.

You can access an NSScrollView's content simply by double-clicking in its content area. You will notice the selection rectangle change slightly to reflect the scroll view's contents. Also, the Inspector window will change to reflect the new selection. Selecting the scroll view again can be difficult, especially if the scroll view fills the entire window; one way is to double-click the window instance in the Instances tab. This will select the window and clear the selection. You can then click normally to select the scroll view. When you built your interface, you didn't resize the NSImageView control, and you made sure that the control doesn't change size along with the window. This may seem odd when compared with the other examples you've seen so far. You didn't change the control's size because Slide Master controls its area programmatically: when you open a large image, Slide Master resizes the NSImageView to fit the image. If you changed the size of the control, that's okay; it will have no bearing on the finished product. You made sure the NSImageView doesn't resize with the window because its viewable area is being managed by an NSScrollView. When the window changes size, your NSScrollView changes with it, allowing you to see more of the picture. But the picture itself, including its size, remains constant — even when the window is resized.

In the following Try It Out, you declare a custom NSWindowController subclass and designate it the owner of your nib file. This is a prerequisite step for hooking your document's user interface up to your code. You then complete the window controller implementation.

TRY IT OUT   Setting the Nib File's Owner

1. In Xcode, create a new NSWindowController subclass named ImageWindowController.m. Remember to change the Subclass Of pop-up menu from NSObject to NSWindowController before clicking Next. Also remember to create the ImageWindowController.h header file.

2. Replace the content of ImageWindowController.h with the following code:

Available for download on Wrox.com

```
#import <Cocoa/Cocoa.h>

@interface ImageWindowController : NSWindowController
{
    IBOutlet NSImageView *mImageView;
}

- (void)resizeWindowToFitImage;

@end
```

code snippet MacOSXProg ch09/Slide Master 1/ImageWindowController.h

3. Save your changes to ImageWindowController.h.

4. In Interface Builder, double-click the File's Owner object in your ImageDocument interface. Interface Builder will select the File's Owner object and open the Identity Inspector.

5. Change Class from MyDocument to ImageWindowController.

6. Switch to the Connections Inspector. You should see two Outlets, as in Figure 9-4: a new mImageView outlet and a Window outlet. The Window outlet will already be connected to your window.

7. Connect the mImageView outlet to the image view in your scroll view. Again, you may need to aim toward the lower-left corner of your scroll view to find the image view.

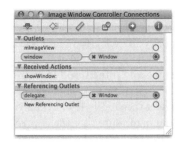

8. Save your changes to ImageDocument.xib.

FIGURE 9-4

9. In Xcode, replace the content of `ImageWindowController.m` with the following code:

```objc
#import "ImageWindowController.h"
#import "ImageDocument.h"

@implementation ImageWindowController

- (void)windowDidLoad
{
    [super windowDidLoad];

    // get the image from the document
    NSImage *image = [[self document] image];

    // set the image
    [mImageView setImage:image];
    [mImageView setFrameSize:image.size];

    // resize the window to fit the new image
    [self resizeWindowToFitImage];
}

- (void)resizeWindowToFitImage
{
    NSWindow *window = self.window;
    NSRect frame = window.frame;
    NSPoint topLeftPoint;

    // get the window's top left point
    topLeftPoint.x = frame.origin.x;
    topLeftPoint.y = frame.origin.y + frame.size.height;

    // size the window to fit our image size exactly
    frame = [window contentRectForFrameRect:frame];
    frame.size = [[[self document] image] size];
    frame = [window frameRectForContentRect:frame];

    // re-adjust the frame origin
    frame.origin.x = topLeftPoint.x;
    frame.origin.y = topLeftPoint.y - frame.size.height;

    // set the new frame
    [window setFrame:frame display:window.isVisible];
}

@end
```

code snippet MacOSXProg ch09/Slide Master 1/ImageWindowController.m

10. Save your changes to `ImageWindowController.m`.

How It Works

In Cocoa applications, interface files are opened on behalf of a particular object, which is known as the interface file's *owner*. You can think of the interface file's owner as the object that actually loaded the nib file. In this case, the interface is owned by your ImageWindowController class. This makes sense, because the ImageWindowController manages the window and image well. Your MainMenu interface is owned by the NSApplication class, because NSApplication is responsible for finding and loading the interface file with the menu bar.

An interface file can reference its owner using the built-in File's Owner instance. Unlike other controller instances you've seen in Interface Builder so far, the File's Owner exists before the interface is loaded. For example, the EmailController object you created in Chapter 8 was created by the interface. You use the Identity Inspector to change the class of a selected object. The Class field auto-completes to classes Interface Builder knows about. The field and its neighboring pull-down menu attempt to display only class names that are appropriate for your selection. In this case, the File's Owner can be any kind of NSObject subclass, so the Class pull-down list displays a lot of choices. After you define your ImageWindowController class in Xcode, you are able to make it the File's Owner's class in Interface Builder. You can also use this technique to create and use a custom class for other instances. For example, you can create a custom subclass of NSButton and configure a button instance to use your class; in that case, the Custom Class list would only display NSButton and your custom subclass.

The code for ImageWindowController follows the same Outlets and Actions technique you learned about in Chapter 8. The code uses the mImageView outlet to push an image into the window. If your image view is an editable image, your code would most likely read changes from the mImageView outlet. You could just as easily use Cocoa Bindings for managing the image view.

Note that the mImageView instance variable has a special prefix: m. When working with larger classes it's often helpful to prefix your instance variables in some way so you can easily distinguish them from other kinds of variables. The practice of using m as a prefix is common among many Objective-C programmers. Apple reserves the underscore prefix (as in _window) for Cocoa's instance variables, so you should avoid using that prefix in your own classes.

NSWindowController calls its windowDidLoad method after its window has been loaded and before it appears on-screen. You can use this method to configure your window interface the first time. Because Slide Master's image window isn't editable, this is the only time the interface needs to be initialized. Editable interfaces need to reload their controls whenever the underlying document has changed. When using Cocoa Bindings this is usually automatic, but when using Outlets and Actions you need to handle this yourself.

Slide Master automatically resizes its image windows to match the dimensions of the image data. All the logic for doing this is contained in ImageWindowController's resizeWindowToFitImage method. ImageWindowController calls this method when initializing its controls from the document.

In Cocoa, screen area is measured in rectangles. Cocoa rectangles are themselves described as having an origin point, and a size. The Foundation framework provides data types for all three of these values: NSRect, NSPoint, and NSSize. These types are C-style structures, not real Objective-C objects. They are defined as follows:

```
typedef struct _NSPoint {
    float x;
    float y;
} NSPoint;
```

```
typedef struct _NSSize {
    float width;
    float height;
} NSSize;
typedef struct _NSRect {
    NSPoint origin;
    NSSize size;
} NSRect;
```

You can work these data types either by setting their values directly, or by using constructor functions such as NSMakeRect or NSMakePoint.

Normally when changing the size of a window, you work with *frame rects*, or rectangles, which describe the area of the entire window including its title bar. Because you want your window to enclose an existing image, you need to specify the window's *content rect*, or the rectangle describing only the window's content. NSWindow provides methods for converting between frame and content rect coordinates:

```
- (NSRect)contentRectForFrameRect:(NSRect)frameRect;
- (NSRect)frameRectForContentRect:(NSRect)contentRect;
```

When drawing in Cocoa, the coordinate plane's origin is the lower-left corner of the drawable area. For example, when drawing in a custom view, the origin is the lower-left corner of that view, and when positioning windows on-screen, the origin is the lower-left corner of the screen. This complicates window positioning because conceptually we think of a window's upper-left corner as being the window's origin. ImageWindowController adjusts for that difference when programmatically resizing windows. In the next Try It Out, you create ImageDocument, an NSDocument subclass, to manage Slide Master's image windows. You also modify your project so Slide Master recognizes image files as valid documents. You are then able to build and run Slide Master.

TRY IT OUT   Writing a Custom NSDocument Subclass

1.   In Xcode, create a new Cocoa Objective-C subclass of NSDocument named ImageDocument.m. Also remember to create the ImageWindowController.h header file.

2.   Open ImageDocument.h and replace its content with the following code:

```
#import <Cocoa/Cocoa.h>

@interface ImageDocument : NSDocument
{
    NSImage *mImage;
}

@property (nonatomic, readonly) NSImage *image;

@end
```

code snippet MacOSXProg ch09/Slide Master 1/ImageDocument.h

3. Open `ImageDocument.m`. Xcode has added a lot of starter code to this file for you, including some usage notes. This provides a good place to start when hooking up your document functionality.

4. Replace the `ImageDocument.m` content with the following code:

```
#import "ImageDocument.h"
#import "ImageWindowController.h"

@implementation ImageDocument

#pragma mark Document Initialization

- (id)init
{
    self = [super init];
    if (self) {

        // Add your subclass-specific initialization here.
        // If an error occurs here, send a [self release] message and return nil.

    }
    return self;
}

- (void)dealloc
{
    [mImage release];

    [super dealloc];
}

- (void)makeWindowControllers
{
    ImageWindowController *imageWindowController = nil;

    imageWindowController = [[[ImageWindowController alloc] initWithWindowNibName:
        @"ImageDocument"] autorelease];

    [self addWindowController:imageWindowController];
}

- (NSData *)dataOfType:(NSString *)typeName error:(NSError **)outError
{
    // unreachable
    return nil;
}
```

```
- (BOOL)readFromData:(NSData *)data ofType:(NSString *)typeName error:(NSError **)
    outError
{
    mImage = [[NSImage alloc] initWithData:data];

    return (mImage != nil);
}

#pragma mark Slide Accessors

@synthesize image = mImage;


#pragma mark Menu Management

- (BOOL)validateMenuItem:(NSMenuItem*)menuItem
{
    SEL action = menuItem.action;

    if (action == @selector(saveDocument:) ||
        action == @selector(saveDocumentAs:) ||
        action == @selector(saveDocumentTo:))
    {
        return NO;
    }
    return [super validateMenuItem:menuItem];
}

@end
```

---

code snippet MacOSXProg ch09/Slide Master 1/ImageDocument.m

Everything here should be recognizable as Objective-C code, except perhaps for the `#pragma mark` commands. These are just markers for your use, like comments. You'll learn about them in a moment.

5. Save the `ImageDocument` files.

6. In Xcode's project window, select the Slide Master target and choose File ➪ Get Info. The Target Info window appears.

7. Select the Properties tab and add a new document type called Image Document. The Image Document type resembles the SlideShow Document type you added back in Chapter 5, with a few differences. Set the document Class to `ImageDocument`, set Extensions to `tif tiff jpg gif pdf` (do not include a dot; separate the extensions with a space), and set the Role to Editor, as shown in Figure 9-5. You don't need an icon for this document type. Also, make sure the new Image Document type appears after the SlideShow Document type in the list; that way, Slide Master continues to create untitled SlideShow Documents when you select File ➪ New.

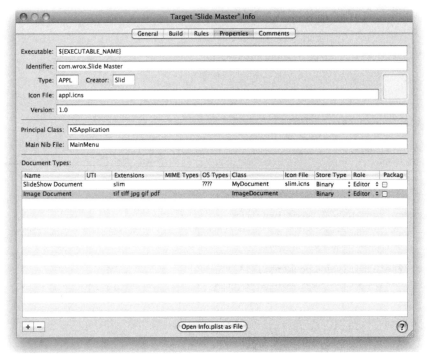

FIGURE 9-5

8. Build and run Slide Master. The Slide Master application opens various image files and displays them in a simple window, much as the Preview application does. As you resize the window, scrollbars appear. However, when the window is larger than the image data, the image always draws in the lower-left corner rather than in the center of the window. If you are unable to open image files, check your Slide Master target Properties settings from the previous example; make sure that the document Class (`ImageDocument`) and Extensions (`tif tiff jpg gif pdf`) settings are correct. If necessary, refer to Figure 9-5.

9. Select the File menu and look at its menu items. Slide Master only views images, it doesn't edit them; the various Save operations are disabled.

How It Works

Your `NSDocument` subclass needs to provide two pieces of information to Cocoa: how its windows should be loaded, and how its data should be read from and written to disk. Simple applications that use an `NSDocument` subclass as an interface controller as well as a document model can implement the `windowNibName` method:

```
- (NSString *)windowNibName;
```

The `windowNibName` method associates an interface file directly with that class. In other words, the document object is the File's Owner for that interface file.

Document classes that delegate window management to NSWindowController objects should use the makeWindowControllers method instead of windowNibName. ImageDocument uses makeWindowControllers to initialize its window controllers. Window controllers normally manage windows found in a nib file, and in these cases you simply need to pass the nib file's name to initWithWindowNibName:. When created, you can add the window controller to your document by calling addWindowController:. Note that this is the last time Slide Master's ImageDocument class deals with the image window interface; the rest is handled by ImageWindowController.

NSDocument defines several methods for reading and writing file data, the most common of which are dataOfType:error: and readFromData:ofType:error: as shown here:

```
- (NSData *)dataOfType:(NSString *)typeName error:(NSError **)outError
- (BOOL)readFromData:(NSData *)data ofType:(NSString *)typeName error:(NSError **)
  outError
```

The NSData objects refer to the data being written to or read from the file. NSData is a class that stores an arbitrary array of binary or text data. The typeName variable stores the name of the document type describing the data. Document-based applications can use the same document class to work with different kinds of documents; the document class can differentiate between the document types using this value. Recall from Chapter 5 that this information lives in the application's Info.plist file, and you set it in Xcode's Target editor. Slide Master currently handles two kinds of documents: Image Documents and Slide Show Documents. Because each document type uses its own custom NSDocument subclass, you don't need to worry about the type value here. Finally, your document can return error information to AppKit by assigning NSError objects to the outError variable. It is optional, but it's a good idea to provide error information if you have it.

You may have noticed the outError variable has a type of NSError ** instead of simply NSError *. That's because outError is a pointer to the address of an NSError object. Recall from Chapter 6 that C (and Objective-C) follows the *pass-by-value* convention. You learned that when you call functions and methods, arguments are copied so that the function or method can't change them. You also learned that when passing pointers or C arrays as arguments, you can change the data to which the pointer is pointing and the contents of the C arrays. This is a handy way for C functions and Objective-C methods to return an arbitrary number of results. In the case of dataOfType:error:, AppKit passed you the address of an NSError object and invited you to change it if necessary.

AppKit uses an object called NSImage to store and work with image data. For example, NSImageView uses NSImage objects in much the same way NSTextView uses NSString objects. NSImage objects can be created from a variety of different sources, such as a path to a file or raw image data encoded in an NSData object. Your ImageDocument simply creates an NSImage object by passing the file data from readFromData:ofType:error: to NSImage's initWithData: method. Note that ImageDocument holds a reference count on this image until the document is deallocated. Slide Master's ImageDocument class cannot save image data back out again. It is meant to be used as an image viewer only. As a result, its dataRepresentationOfType: method returns nil instead of actually doing anything. It turns out this code path is unreachable, meaning it will never be called, because ImageDocument disables the Save and Save As menu items in its validateMenuItem: method.

AppKit calls validateMenuItem: just before displaying menus. Each object that is a target of a menu command receives one validateMenuItem: call for each item to which it responds. This provides an opportunity for target objects to modify menu and menu item states prior to display, typically to enable or disable menu items. If `–validateMenuItem:` returns YES, the item will be enabled; otherwise the menu will be grayed out.

Your `validateMenuItem:` method distinguishes between menu items by checking their actions directly. Each action is an Objective-C method selector, or SEL data type. You can refer to selectors as SEL variables by wrapping them with the `@selector()` directive. For example, this:

```
@selector(saveAs:)
```

refers to your `ImageDocument`'s saveAs: method. `ImageDocument` simply checks for the save methods defined by the `NSDocument` superclass and returns NO when found. Otherwise `ImageDocument` passes the message back to its superclasses.

You added a few `#pragma mark` directives to your `ImageDocument` class. These directives have nothing to do with how your class is compiled; they merely insert comments into Xcode's function pop-up menu in the navigation bar. You can even insert separator items into the function pop-up menu with the following code:

```
#pragma mark -
```

As you start adding more and more functions to a source file, the function pop-up becomes hard to navigate. You can use the `#pragma mark` directives to identify groups of related symbols, and add some structure to the function pop-up.

At this point you have a complete document-based application. You can open image documents by selecting image files from the Open menu item. You can also open images by dragging them onto your application's icon in Finder or in the Dock. After you've opened a few files you can retrieve them again quickly with the File ⇨ Open Recent menu item. You can minimize and zoom your window, and if you Command-click the name in your window's title bar, you'll see a pop-up menu showing exactly where that file lives on your disk.

What? You don't remember writing code that does all that? That's because you didn't. Cocoa handles all these things for you. All you have to do is tell Cocoa what kind of files you are interested in, write the code that reads those files from disk (in this case, one entire line's worth), and hook up a user interface. Although the user interface was the lion's share of the code, it really wasn't all that much work.

There is one problem with Slide Master's image document window: if you make the window larger than the image, the picture won't be centered in the window. The `NSScrollView` class draws its content in its origin, which you've just learned is the scroll view's lower-left corner. Although this is reasonable behavior for something such as a text view, image viewers look better when they center their content.

One fix for this problem is to change the nib file to resize the `NSImageView` instance along with the scroll view and window. You also need to resize the image view in the nib file to match the size of its scroll view. Then the image draws in the center of the window when the window is larger than the image. `NSImageView` provides this behavior by default. But now you'll have another problem: if the window is smaller than the image, scrollbars will not appear. `NSScrollView` compares the size of its content view to its own size to configure the scrollbars; if both views are the same size, no scrollbars will appear. If you don't make the image view exactly match the scroll view size in the nib file, you will see even more unpredictable behavior within Slide Master.

To solve this problem cleanly, you need to change the way your NSImageView resizes. When the window is larger than the image, the NSImageView should grow along with the window. This allows you to take advantage of NSImageView's ability to center images in a large area. When the window is smaller than the image, the NSImageView should remain the same size as the image. Then NSScrollView will display scrollbars allowing you to reveal the portions of the images not currently on-screen. Because NSImageView doesn't have this functionality already, you need to create your own image view class that resizes the way you want. The easiest way to do that is by subclassing NSImageView. You learn how to do this in the next section.

SUBCLASSING CONTROLS IN INTERFACE BUILDER

Occasionally you need to create your own custom controls to provide the right user experience within your application. Although you can create new controls from scratch by creating a custom NSControl subclass, you can often start from an existing control and just add your custom behavior. After all, if you need a special control that acts like a slider, you could save a lot of time and trouble by re-using the implementation in the NSSlider class.

This practice of starting from an existing control applies to Interface Builder as well. After you have decided to subclass a control from an existing class, drag the existing class into your interface from the Library and then change its Class in the Identity Inspector. You have already seen examples of both these techniques: you have dragged many controls out of the Library, and you have changed the class of a nib's File's Owner instance. You simply need to apply these techniques to other controls to modify their behavior through subclassing.

In the following Try It Out, you create a custom image view class that provides some custom resize logic for that view. This image view is meant to resize itself freely when its window changes size, as long as the image view is never smaller than its contents. This custom class simply inherits the rest of its behavior from the existing NSImageView class.

TRY IT OUT   Creating a Custom NSImageView Subclass

1.   In Xcode, create a new Objective-C object subclassed from NSObject named SlideImageView.m. Remember to create the corresponding header file.

2.   In SlideImageView.h, change the superclass for SlideImageView from NSObject to NSImageView:

```
@interface SlideImageView : NSImageView
{
}
@end
```

code snippet MacOSXProg ch09/Slide Master 2/SlideImageView.h

3. Replace the content of `SlideImageView.m` with the following code:

```
#import "SlideImageView.h"

@implementation SlideImageView

- (void)setFrameSize:(NSSize)viewSize
{
    NSScrollView *scrollView = self.enclosingScrollView;

    // if the image view is installed in a scroll view, make sure we preserve
    // the original file dimensions, so scrolling works correctly.
    if (scrollView) {
        NSSize imageSize = self.image.size;
        NSSize scrollSize = scrollView.documentVisibleRect.size;

        // first, disregard the area used by scroll bars (if any)
        viewSize.width = MIN(viewSize.width, scrollSize.width);
        viewSize.height = MIN(viewSize.height, scrollSize.height);

        // second, make sure the view is at least as big as the image itself
        viewSize.width = MAX(viewSize.width, imageSize.width);
        viewSize.height = MAX(viewSize.height, imageSize.height);
    }

    // set the adjusted frame size
    [super setFrameSize:viewSize];
}

@end
```

code snippet MacOSXProg ch09/Slide Master 2/SlideImageView.m

4. Replace `ImageWindowController`'s `windowDidLoad` method with the following code:

```
- (void)windowDidLoad
{
    [super windowDidLoad];

    // set the image
    [mImageView setImage:[[self document] image]];

    // resize the window to fit the new image
    [self resizeWindowToFitImage];
}
```

code snippet MacOSXProg ch09/Slide Master 2/ImageWindowController.m

5. Save your changes to source files.

6. Open the `ImageDocument` interface file in Interface Builder.

7. Double-click the `NSScrollView` in your document window to select its `NSImageView`. Again, you may need to click in the lower-left corner of the scroll view to hit the image view.

8. In the Size Inspector, manually resize the image view to match the area of your scroll view. The image view should be 507 pixels wide and 413 pixels high. If you have trouble resizing the view, try setting its origin to 0,0 using the Size Inspector. Also make sure the image view grows and shrinks when its parent scroll view and window are resized. The Size Inspector should resemble Figure 9-6.

9. Change the image view's class from `NSImageView` to `SlideImageView` using the Class Inspector.

10. Save the `ImageDocument` interface file.

11. Build and run Slide Master. Now when you resize image documents, the image will remain centered when the window is large, and scrollbars will appear when the window is small.

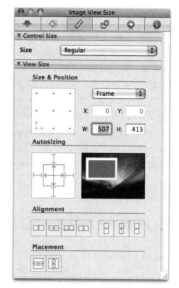

FIGURE 9-6

How It Works

When you use a custom class for an object instantiated in the interface, Cocoa creates an object of that class at runtime. This works much the same way as `NSObject` subclasses that reside in a nib's Instances tab. In both cases the objects are created and owned by the nib file.

Interface Builder keeps track of an object's original class even after you change the object's class. It uses this information to determine what kind of control to draw in the nib file and what information should be displayed in the Inspector. Though you changed your `NSImageView` instance to a `SlideImageView`, Interface Builder still treats it as an `NSImageView` instance; you could set its attributes or reset its class if you like. On the other hand, if you created your `SlideImageView` subclass from a simple `NSView` instance, Interface Builder would not recognize the `SlideImageView` as an `NSImageView` subclass. Note that the `NSView` instance in the Library is labeled "Custom View," because normally you designate these objects as a custom class.

When you first configured the image view, you were careful to make sure it didn't resize with the window or scroll view. Instead, you set the image size programmatically when the image document was opened. But now you've carefully positioned the image view and made it resizable. That's because your `SlideImageView` subclass now expects the image view's frame to change when the window is resized. In fact, `SlideImageView` customizes this resize process.

Your `SlideImageView` extends the `NSImageView` class by providing a new `setFrameSize:` method. The `setFrameSize:` method is actually defined by the `NSView` superclass, and is used to change a view's size. This method is called whenever the image document's window is resized, because the `SlideImageView` instance is still set to resize itself in the nib file. Before passing the resize request back to the superclass,

`SlideImageView` makes sure the new frame size is at least as large as its image. That's simply a matter of checking the image size against the image's visible area, and using the larger of the two.

Because the image document uses an `NSScrollView` to manage the image's scrollbars, `SlideImageView` can ask the `NSScrollView` for its visible area. The `NSScrollView` class has a `documentVisibleRect` method that returns the visible area as an `NSRect`; this rectangle doesn't include the scroll view's scrollbars. You are familiar with using outlets to create relationships between two objects, and in this case you could have created an outlet in `SlideImageView` for storing a reference to the `NSScrollView` instance. However, the `NSView` class provides a convenient method called `enclosingScrollView` that returns the `NSScrollView` for any given view; if a view isn't in a scroll view, `enclosingScrollView` returns `nil`. This provides an easy alternative to using an outlet for this purpose.

CONNECTING MENUS

In Cocoa, menu items behave a lot like controls. For example, menu items can send an action to a target object. Unlike controls, which normally talk to specific controller objects, menu commands are usually handled by an application's current selection. For example, the Copy command copies the content of the selected control, regardless of which control or which window is selected. In either case you connect menus using the same kinds of techniques you've seen earlier in this chapter.

In the following Try It Out, you add some basic zoom commands to Slide Master's View menu. The new menu items are handled by the image document. You configure the menus in two steps:

➤ First, you design the menus in Interface Builder, and connect them to custom actions in the nib file's First Responder instance.

➤ Then, you implement the menu actions in the `ImageDocument` class.

TRY IT OUT   **Connecting Menus to the First Responder**

1. In Xcode, double-click the `MainMenu.xib` nib file. The nib file opens in Interface Builder.

2. In Interface Builder, double-click the First Responder object in the nib file window. Interface Builder selects the First Responder and switches to the Attributes Inspector. The Inspector displays a number of action methods, as shown in Figure 9-7.

3. Use the + button to add the following new actions to the First Responder.

ACTION
`zoomActualSize:`
`zoomIn:`
`zoomOut:`

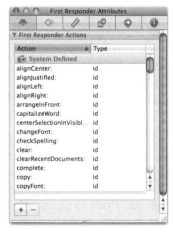

FIGURE 9-7

When you're done, the Inspector should resemble Figure 9-8.

4. Remove the Format menu from the main menu by selecting it and pressing Delete twice. The first Delete will remove the Format menu's items, and the second Delete will remove the Format menu itself from the menu bar.

5. Add Actual Size, Zoom In, Zoom Out, and a separator item to the View menu. Assign 0, +, and – key equivalents to these items. Flip back to Chapter 4 if you need a refresher on building menus with Interface Builder. Your finished View menu should look similar to the one in Figure 9-9.

6. Control-drag from the Actual Size menu to the First Responder object in your nib file window. A list of First Responder actions appears, shown in Figure 9-10. Notice that your mouse is already positioned next to the action named `zoomActualSize:`.

FIGURE 9-8

7. Select `zoomActualSize:` from the list. The Actual Size menu item is now connected to the `zoomActualSize:` action.

8. Repeat steps 6 and 7 to connect the Zoom In menu item to `zoomIn:` and the Zoom Out menu item to `zoomOut:`.

9. Save the `MainMenu` nib file.

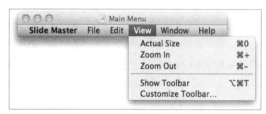

FIGURE 9-9

How It Works

Connecting menu items works just like connecting controls. Control-drag from the menu item to the target object and select one of the target's actions. Remember you can also drag from the Connection Inspector's Sent Actions item to the First Responder, if you don't like Control-dragging. Although you didn't do so in this example, you can also assign menus and menu items to other objects' outlets.

The View menu items are meant for the currently active slideshow document. Because you don't know which instance that might be at runtime, or if there even is an active document, you need a placeholder to reflect that information in your nib file. Your nib file's First

FIGURE 9-10

Responder instance is exactly that placeholder. Recall from the Email Formatter examples that you manually set your window's `initialFirstResponder` to a specific item, and that the first responder changed as you tabbed from item to item. First Responder is AppKit shorthand for the currently active control.

Messages sent to the nib file's First Responder instance may not necessarily be handled by the first responder. They may instead be handled by one of a number of objects involved in handling events in your application. These objects collectively make up your *responder chain*, or the specific list of objects that might respond to a given event. If a particular instance doesn't respond to an event, it passes the event to the next element in the responder chain; this process continues until either the event is handled, or until the entire chain is searched. The following table shows basically how the responder chain interprets events.

RESPONDER	DESCRIPTION
The key window's first responder	The key window is the window receiving keyboard events. This is often the same as the main window. However, windows derived from the `NSPanel` object may become key without being the main window. Inspector windows such as Interface Builder's Inspector are often derived from `NSPanel`. The first responder by definition gets the first chance to respond to an event.
The key window	If the first responder will not handle this event, the key window has an opportunity to do so.
The main window's first responder	The main window is the currently active `NSWindow` class. Again, its first responder gets the first chance to respond to an event.
The main window	As with the key window, the main window has the opportunity to handle events ignored by its contents.
The application	If the key and main windows or their content don't handle an event, the `NSApplication` instance itself gets one last chance to handle it.

Other instances might be involved in the responder chain as well. The window and application instances might have *delegate* objects associated with them. Delegate objects are other objects, often simply `NSObject` subclasses, which can respond to messages in lieu of a particular object. If a window or application doesn't handle an event, the delegate will get a chance to handle it before the event is passed up the chain.

When writing a document-based application, Cocoa will insert your window controller and document instances into the responder chain. Window controllers are inserted between their window and that window's delegate. Documents are inserted right before the application. The `NSDocumentController` class, an AppKit-supplied controller that manages creating and opening documents, is inserted at the end of the chain. The following table illustrates the responder chain for Slide Master when an image document is active. Because the key window is the same as the main window, the responder chain doesn't call them out separately.

RESPONDER	DESCRIPTION
The window's first responder	This is the NSScrollView instance in your image window.
The window's view hierarchy	Each superview between the scroll view and the window gets an opportunity to handle the actions. Currently, this is the window's content view.
The document window	Again, the window has a chance to respond.
The window's window controller	This is your ImageWindowController class.
The window's delegate	In Slide Master, the image window's delegate is the ImageWindowController. But it could theoretically be another object.
The document	This is your ImageDocument.
The application	Again, the application has a chance to respond.
The application's delegate	Slide Master does not currently have an application delegate. You will create one later.
The document controller	The NSDocumentController object responsible for creating and opening documents is the last stop in the chain.

Both window controller and document objects appear in the responder chain. Which class should you use when hooking up your menu items? The choice is yours. A good rule of thumb is to hook into the window controller if the menu item needs to cooperate with other controls (such as Copy/Paste) and hook into the document if the command depends only on document state.

In the following Try It Out, you receive the new zoom actions in the ImageWindowController, implement the zoom logic, and then test your changes.

TRY IT OUT   Receiving Menu Commands in a Document

1. In Xcode, open the ImageWindowController.m file.

2. Add the following code at the end of the class:

```
#pragma mark Zoom Menu Items

- (void)zoomActualSize:(id)sender
{
    NSScrollView *scrollView = mImageView.enclosingScrollView;

    if (scrollView)
```

```
        {
            NSClipView *clipView = scrollView.contentView;

            // compute normal clip bounds from the frame
            NSRect bounds = clipView.frame;
            bounds.origin = NSZeroPoint;

            // reset the clip view bounds
            [clipView setBounds:bounds];

            // manually update the scrollbars.
            [scrollView tile];
        }
    }

- (void)zoomIn:(id)sender
{
    NSScrollView *scrollView = mImageView.enclosingScrollView;

    if (scrollView) {
        NSClipView *clipView = scrollView.contentView;

        NSRect visible = scrollView.documentVisibleRect;
        NSRect bounds = clipView.bounds;

        // magnify the visible area by shrinking the clip view bounds.
        bounds.size.width *= 0.5f;
        bounds.size.height *= 0.5f;

        // adjust the bounds origin so the image remains centered while zooming.
        bounds.origin.x = NSMidX(visible) - bounds.size.width * 0.5f;
        bounds.origin.y = NSMidY(visible) - bounds.size.height * 0.5f;

        [clipView setBounds:bounds];

        // manually update the scrollbars.
        [scrollView tile];
    }
}

- (void)zoomOut:(id)sender
{
    NSScrollView *scrollView = mImageView.enclosingScrollView;

    if (scrollView) {
        NSClipView *clipView = scrollView.contentView;

        NSRect visible = scrollView.documentVisibleRect;
        NSRect bounds = clipView.bounds;
        NSRect frame = clipView.frame;

        // reverse the zoom in effect by increasing the clip view bounds.
        bounds.size.width *= 2.0f;
        bounds.size.height *= 2.0f;
```

```
                // constrain the zoom out to fit the actual size.
                bounds.size.width = MIN(bounds.size.width, frame.size.width);
                bounds.size.height = MIN(bounds.size.height, frame.size.height);

                // adjust the bounds origin so the image remains centered while zooming.
                bounds.origin.x = NSMidX(visible) - bounds.size.width * 0.5f;
                bounds.origin.y = NSMidY(visible) - bounds.size.height * 0.5f;

                [clipView setBounds:bounds];

                // manually update the scrollbars.
                [scrollView tile];
        }
}
```

code snippet MacOSXProg ch09/Slide Master 3/ImageWindowController.m

3. Save your changes to `ImageWindowController.m`.

4. Build and run Slide Master. When a SlideShow Document is active (currently still displaying the "Your document contents here" placeholder) the items in the View menu are disabled. When you open an image file, the Actual Size, Zoom In, and Zoom Out menu items are enabled.

5. Verify that you can zoom into an image multiple times. While zoomed in, scrollbars work normally. You can return the image to normal by zooming out a number of times or with the Actual Size menu command.

How It Works

Recall that both the image document and window controller are in the responder chain. When the SlideShow window was frontmost, neither the active window controller nor the document implemented the new zoom commands. As a result, Cocoa automatically disabled the zoom menu items. After you opened an image and made its window frontmost, the `ImageWindowController` became part of the responder chain and Cocoa activated the zoom menu items.

It turns out responding to the menu items was relatively easy. All you had to do was define action methods in your window controller and Cocoa did the rest for you. On the other hand, the zooming logic is fairly complicated. It turns out `NSImageView` doesn't support rotating or scaling images, or other advanced-image manipulations. Programmers who need that kind of functionality are best off using `IKImageView`, which is part of ImageKit in the Quartz framework.

To understand what the zoom logic is doing here, you need to understand two things: how view frames and view bounds interact with each other, and how `NSScrollView` uses this interaction to implement scrolling.

Every `NSView` has a frame rect. The frame rect describes the position and size of the view as expressed in terms of its parent. When you set an object's position and size using Interface Builder's Size Inspector, you are modifying the object's view frame. Similarly, the code you wrote to resize image views worked with frames.

Every NSView also has a bounds rect. The bounds rect describes the position and size of the view relative to *itself*. Normally a view's bounds rect is the same size as its frame rect, and the bounds origin is 0, 0. Changing the bounds rect origin has the effect of shifting how the view's contents get drawn without changing the position of the view in its window (that would be the frame, remember?). Changing the bounds rect size has the effect of scaling the view's contents. For example, when you have a view whose frame is 100 points wide and whose bounds are 50 points wide, you're saying "draw only 50 points but stretch it out to fill all 100 points."

Modifying view bounds really isn't that common, and there tend to be other ways of shifting or scaling content. For example, IKImageView handles scale, rotation, and translation transformations directly instead of relying on bounds rect changes. That said, NSScrollView relies on these bounds transformations to implement scrolling.

The scroll view works with two other views: the document view and the content view. The document view is the view you want to scroll through, and you must provide this view to the scroll view. In the case of Slide Master's image document, the document view is the SlideImageView object. The content view is a utility view representing the portion of the document view you can actually see. Content views are all instances of NSClipView, and are created by the scroll view automatically. The content view has the same size as its parent scroll view (without the scrollbars) and its position doesn't change. In other words, its frame is fixed to the scroll view.

When you scroll around, the scroll view asks its content view to draw a different part of the document view. It does this by changing the content view's bounds origin. Recall that changing the bounds rect's origin has the effect of shifting the views contents, or in other words, scrolling them.

As you have seen, this process is entirely automatic. You can implement scrolling without really knowing how the mechanism works, and you don't need to write code that deals with the content view at all. Apple's documentation for NSScrollView and NSClipView emphasizes this point. Most of the time you shouldn't reach into the scroll view and modify its NSClipView instance; you should instead message the scroll view directly.

If you did that, you took advantage of the NSClipView's relationship to the scroll view and your image to implement a simple image zoom. Instead of changing the bounds rect's origin you changed the bounds rect's size, which as you recall will scale to the NSClipView's contents. As the bounds rect gets smaller, the image gets larger and vice versa. The zoom methods also adjust the bounds origin to keep the viewable area centered while zooming. The magnification can be removed by resetting the bounds rect's size to that of the frame rect. One problem here is that the scroll view won't update its scrollbars when you modify the clip view's bounds directly. So you need to ask the scroll view to update using the tile method.

SUMMARY

The Cocoa frameworks go beyond a simple toolkit for windows, menus, and buttons. They also provide a lot of common application behavior. By giving you such things as an Open Recent window and a pop-up menu embedded in your window title bar for free, they encourage you, and everyone else, to use them. As a result, nearly every Cocoa application has these features, and Mac OS X feels all the more consistent and unified.

AppKit's document-based application architecture is built around three classes: NSDocument, NSWindowController, and NSDocumentController. You easily built a document-based application using only two of those classes; you didn't see NSDocumentController at all. For simple applications such as this, you could even forego NSWindowController, although there are advantages to keeping your code structured in model, view, and controller classes.

In this chapter you learned:

> ➤ How to use NSDocument to read files from disk and how to manage a user interface with NSWindowController. Wiring up the user interface in Interface Builder was just as easy as in last chapter's examples. You connected your interface to your nib's File Owner instead of directly creating a controller object in the nib file.

> ➤ How to extend existing Cocoa objects through subclassing. Interface Builder even works with your custom subclasses, providing a convenient way to extend existing controls such as NSImageView and NSButton.

> ➤ How to use the responder chain and the first responder to route menu commands to the active document. To deliver the message to the current document, you need to connect the menu items to the nib's First Responder item.

> ➤ How to use NSScrollView to create a scrollable interface. You even learned a little bit about how NSView's frame and bounds rectangles control drawing, and how NSScrollView works under the covers.

In the next chapter, you will learn about using Core Data to make a custom document file. You will learn how CoreData also manages Undo and Redo for you. Finally you will work with other Cocoa classes to finish the Slide Master application. Before proceeding, however, try the exercises that follow to test your understanding of the material covered in this chapter. You can find the solutions to these exercises in Appendix A.

1. Create a document-based application that reads and writes text files. You can use the following:

```
- (id)initWithData:(NSData *)data encoding:(NSStringEncoding)encoding
```

to read file data into an `NSString`, and you can use

```
- (NSData *)dataUsingEncoding:(NSStringEncoding)encoding
```

to write strings into a text file. In both cases, pass `NSMacOSRomanStringEncoding` in as the encoding. The user interface should feature one large `NSTextView` for viewing and editing this text data. Consider a way to get the text data out of the text view when it's time to save the document.

2. Extend your application in the last example to use the following methods for reading and writing strings to a document:

```
- (id)initWithContentsOfURL:(NSURL *)url usedEncoding:(NSStringEncoding *)enc
      error:(NSError **)error
- (BOOL)writeToURL:(NSURL *)url atomically:(BOOL)useAuxiliaryFile encoding:
      (NSStringEncoding)enc error:(NSError **)error
```

Here's another hint: you need to find alternatives to `dataOfType:error:` and `readFromData:ofType:error:` that deal with URLs instead of `NSData` objects. Check in Cocoa's online developer documentation for `NSDocument`: Help ➪ Documentation.

▶ WHAT YOU LEARNED IN THIS CHAPTER

NSDocument	A model object encapsulating a document, commonly backed by a file
NSWindowController	A controller object that manages a document window and its controls
makeWindowControllers	NSDocument method responsible for creating one or more window controllers for a document
windowDidLoad	NSWindowController method commonly used to initialize window controls and other states
drawRect	NSView method used to draw a view or control on screen
frame	A rectangle describing a view's size and position in its parent window or superview
bounds	A rectangle describing a view's size and position relative to its contents
First Responder	An object, usually a control in a window, that gets the first chance to handle user actions
Responder Chain	An ordered list of responders managed by AppKit that may respond to user actions

10

Core Data-Based Cocoa Applications

WHAT YOU WILL LEARN IN THIS CHAPTER:

➤ How to design a document data model in an object graph

➤ How to observe, change, and sort Core Data objects using Cocoa Bindings

➤ How to create your own Core Data objects and insert them into a managed object context

➤ How to manually set and get values from Core Data objects

➤ How Core Data and Cocoa Bindings interact with other Cocoa archiving technologies

In the last chapter you learned a few things about document-based applications. In the examples and exercises you dealt with simple documents, text files and images, and how to focus on user interface and dataflow issues. Applications often want to store their own data, in a format specific to that application. What do you do if a file format doesn't exist that Cocoa knows about? You make one.

There are many ways to deal with your own document format. And Cocoa itself has made many attempts at solving this problem over the years. The property list format you saw in Chapter 5 is one example. Many Cocoa programs use property lists to store their own document data, because they are easily understood, many tools exist for working with them, and with a little effort they can store any kind of Objective-C object. Recently, Core Data has emerged as a preferred way of solving this problem among many Cocoa programmers.

Core Data provides a way to store collections of Objective-C objects in a database. When talking about a document-based application, you can think of these Core Data databases simply as files — especially with Core Data handles, with all the particulars of pushing objects into, and out of, the database. There are other benefits to using Core Data, as you will soon see.

Apple describes Core Data as an advanced programming topic. Core Data assumes you understand Objective-C programming, are comfortable with Cocoa Bindings, and that you organize your objects according to the Model/View/Controller design pattern. On the other hand, Apple encourages Core Data use in document-based applications. Core Data is also the preferred method for storing application data in iPhone applications, even very simple ones. You are ready to dig into Core Data because you've already learned about Objective-C, bindings, and Model/View/Controller during the past few chapters.

ARCHIVING OBJECTIVE-C OBJECTS

Even when using Core Data it helps to understand how Objective-C objects are converted into a format that can be saved to disk or written over a network. This process is often called *archiving*, *flattening*, or *serializing*. Regardless of the term you use, the idea is the same: convert an Objective-C object into a single piece of data.

The Foundation framework provides several ways of retrieving data from files on disk. The right approach for you depends on the nature of your application and your data. Some of these methods are listed here:

➤ **Programs that need low-level access to files can use the** NSFileHandle **class to open files and read data.** NSFileHandle provides basic support for opening a file and reading a number of bytes from the file; you can pass the resulting data to NSString or NSNumber initialization methods to interpret the data as usable values. The NSStream subclasses, NSInputStream and NSOutputStream, provide low-level support for data that might reside in a number of different places, including in the file system, in memory, on the network, and so on.

➤ **Common Foundation objects know how to write themselves to disk automatically.** For example, you can read and write an NSString using the initWithContentsOfFile: encoding:error and writeToFile:atomically:encoding:error methods. Other objects that can read and write themselves to disk include NSData, NSArray, and NSDictionary. Note you can use only the NSArray and NSDictionary classes to write out objects that can be found in property lists: NSData, NSDate, NSNumber, NSString, and other NSArray and NSDictionary objects. In fact, the NSDictionary and NSArray classes' writeToFile: options:error: method is normally how you write property lists.

➤ **You can encode one or more Objective-C objects into a single NSData item, and then write that NSData item to disk using its** writeToFile:atomically: **method.** This works well for programs that keep their state in Objective-C model objects. Foundation provides classes that manage this encoding process: NSArchiver and NSKeyedArchiver. Foundation also provides a protocol, NSCoding, which other objects can conform to. This allows you to pass your own objects to Foundation's archiving classes. Many Cocoa objects can be encoded by default, including all the property list classes previously mentioned. Serialized data is stored in a binary format, unlike property lists, which are text.

You can use any of these techniques in your `NSDocument` subclass's file handling code. Xcode's template for new `NSDocument` subclasses is slightly biased toward the approach of encoding objects into an `NSData` object. This technique is fairly practical for Cocoa applications, where document state is normally stored in one or more model objects.

When using Core Data, sometimes you fall back on these techniques to store existing Objective-C objects that are not directly managed by Core Data. One common example is the `NSColor` object. Colors are not directly managed by Core Data, nor can they be directly inserted into a property list. To save a color object you either need to archive it with `NSKeyedArchiver` or you need to pull the low-level data out of the object and manage the archiving process yourself. Core Data gives you a chance to transform objects similar to this into a format that can be managed, so don't entirely forget these old ways.

MODELING OBJECTS WITH CORE DATA

One major difference between Core Data and other archiving approaches is that Core Data requires you to describe the objects you are archiving in advance. With the approaches you've read, objects are archived as they are — the archiving system has no special knowledge of these objects. Having this information up front allows Core Data to automatically manage your objects, both in memory and in storage. It also allows Core Data to manage the relationship between objects.

Core Data refers to a collection of related objects as an *object graph*. Figure 10-1 shows an example object graph. Each node in the object graph is called an *entity*. You can think of entities as classes in an Object-Oriented programming language such as Objective-C. As with a class, each entity defines a number of traits or *properties*. Entities may be children of other entities similar to how classes inherit from a superclass. Objects can also store data as *attributes*. Similar to instance variables, attributes represent specific pieces of information.

Entities in the graph are connected to one another through *relationships*. Relationships may be one-way in cases where an entity points to another object, or they may be bi-directional where entities refer to each other. A relationship that connects to a single object is called a *to-one* relationship. Relationships where an object refers to many other objects in a list are called *to-many* relationships.

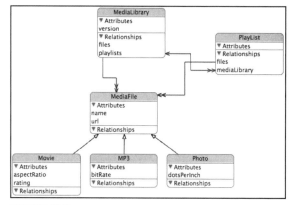

FIGURE 10-1

The similarity to object classes is no accident. The object-graph is a way of modeling object-oriented programs: identifying the classes and describing the relationships between them. Object graphs, such as the one in Figure 10-1, are often drawn using specific symbols and patterns collectively known as Unified Modeling Language (UML). You can easily imagine how an object graph such as this might be used to create a collection of Objective-C classes.

In practice, Core Data doesn't need to construct custom Objective-C classes for you, though it will if you ask. Normally Core Data uses the NSManagedObject class for object graph model objects. The specific details of an object's relationships and attributes are stored in its NSManagedObject instance. Given a managed object, you can ask for its attributes and relationships through Cocoa Binding properties. This creates the illusion that a managed object is actually a custom Objective-C class of a particular type, even when you haven't written any custom code.

You supply object graph information to Core Data in a special data model file that is part of your Xcode project. The data model file uses the .xcdatamodel file extension. Xcode has a special editor for viewing and changing these files, shown in Figure 10-2. Think of this file as part of your program's source code — you need to edit this file to tell Core Data how your program's model objects look. In return, Core Data manages all these objects for you.

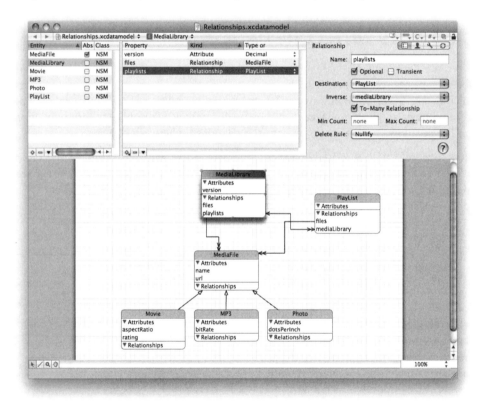

FIGURE 10-2

In the following Try It Out you will add a data model file to the Slide Master project and use it to model the slideshow document. This example focuses on your document's model structure. You will hook the data model up to the user interface later.

TRY IT OUT   Building a Core Data Object Graph

1. In Xcode, add a group to the Groups & Files list. Name it Models.

2. Create a new file in the Models group. Use the data model template for this file, shown in Figure 10-3. Name the file SlideShowDocument.xcdatamodel.

FIGURE 10-3

3. A file chooser panel will appear resembling Figure 10-4. If you already had model objects in your project, Xcode would use them to build part of your object graph.

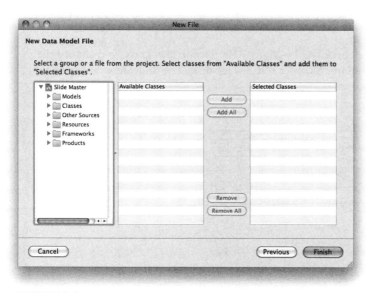

FIGURE 10-4

4. Click Finish. A new empty `SlideShowDocument.xcdatamodel` file has been added to your project and is selected. Xcode's editor has changed from the usual text view to a special data modeling tool you saw in Figure 10-2.

5. In the Entity table, click the + button twice. Two entities will appear in the table: Entity and Entity1. Also, small boxes will appear in the data model's diagram view.

6. Double-click the first entity in the Entity table, and rename it SlideShow. The corresponding box in the diagram view also changes to SlideShow.

7. While SlideShow is still selected in the Entity table, click the + button on the Property table. A pull-down menu will appear, shown in Figure 10-5.

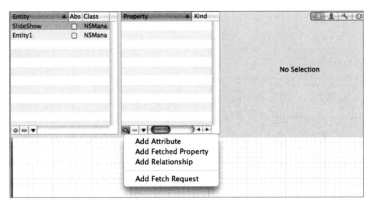

FIGURE 10-5

8. Select Add Relationship from the menu. A property named newRelationship will appear both in the table and in SlideShow's diagram. Also, a settings panel will appear to the right of the Property table.

9. Rename newRelationship to slides, check the To-Many Relationship checkbox, and change the Delete Rule to Cascade. You can ignore the other settings for now. The SlideShow Entity should now look like Figure 10-6.

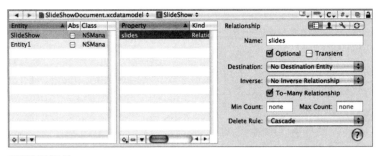

FIGURE 10-6

10. In the Entity table, rename Entity1 to Slide.

11. In the Property table, create a new Attribute named `image`. Change its Type from Undefined to Transformable, as shown in Figure 10-7.

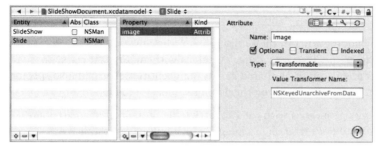

FIGURE 10-7

12. Create a new Slide Relationship named `slideShow`. Set the Destination to SlideShow and set Inverse to slides. Now is a good time to rearrange the boxes in the diagram view so you can see them better.

13. Save `SlideShowDocument.xcdatamodel`. Your file should resemble Figure 10-8.

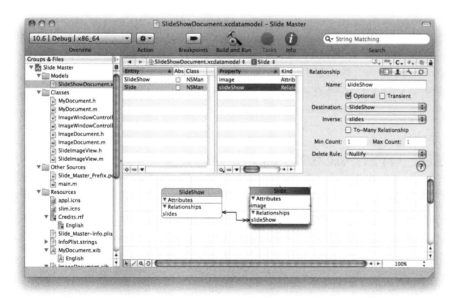

FIGURE 10-8

How It Works

Xcode supplies templates and tools for working with data model files. These data model files become part of your program, similar to your source code, nib files, and other resources. You created your data model from a data model file template. If instead you had checked both the Create Document-based

Application and Use Core Data For Storage options when you created the Slide Master project, Xcode would have created this file for you.

One benefit of having data model support built into Xcode is tighter integration with other files in your project. When you create a new data model file from scratch, Xcode offers to read classes from existing files and preload them into your object graph. You can ask Xcode to generate Objective-C classes from the Entities in your data model file.

You add Entities to the data model by adding rows to the Entity table. Although you created concrete entities, you can use the Entity table to create *abstract entities*. Much as with an abstract class, an abstract entity defines properties that are meant to be shared across many entities. You can also specify the base class for your entity. Currently you are relying on the default value, NSManagedObject.

After you have an entity, you can edit its properties with the Property table. You created an attribute property named image. This attribute will hold your slide's image, which will be an instance of AppKit's NSImage class. As with variables, attributes have a data type. Core Data knows how to work with a variety of scalar data types including numbers, strings, and dates. You made image a transformable type, which means image refers to some kind of Objective-C object that can be converted to an NSData object using a value transformer. It turns out NSImage responds to the <NSCoding> protocol, which means you can use NSKeyedArchiver to transform your image data. The NSKeyedArchiver happens to be Core Data's default value transformer, so you don't need to specify a custom Value Transformer Name.

You also created a relationship property called SlideShow, which points from each Slide to the SlideShow that contains it. By designating SlideShow's slides attribute as the Inverse relationship, you created a two-way connection between Slide and SlideShow. Yes, you could have done that by switching back to SlideShow, selecting slides, and specifying a new Destination, but the Inverse control saves you those extra steps. Recall that SlideShow's slides property is a To-Many relationship. That means SlideShow can refer to many slides, but each slide can be a member of only one SlideShow.

CONNECTING USER INTERFACE TO CORE DATA

In most of the earlier examples you explicitly wrote Objective-C objects that provided your program logic. And most of the time you manually connected these custom objects to your user interface through Outlets and Actions. This worked just fine, but all the customization means there's a certain amount of work you must do before you get to the interesting bit of your program: you have to create files, type in the class interface, type in the class implementation, drag lines one by one in Interface Builder, and so on. All this work amounts to a tax you must pay each time you try to do something. It's not clear who benefits from this tax, but it's definitely not you.

Core Data tries to bypass a lot of this busywork by doing it all for you. All you have to do is tell it what kind of "classes" you want, and what "variables" they each have. When told, Core Data manages the details of creating the class, creating the variables, wiring up the accessors, saving them to disk at the right times, and so on.

This sounds familiar to other Cocoa technologies you've worked with: Cocoa Bindings and Properties. You learned about Properties in Chapter 7, where you used them to synthesize accessors for Objective-C instance variables. You declared what kind of variable accessors you wanted (such as "readonly" or "readwrite, retain") and the Objective-C runtime provided those accessors for you. You saw Cocoa Bindings in Chapter 8, when you built the Email Formatter 2 application. You told Cocoa what values you were interested in, and Cocoa told you when those values changed.

You see the pattern here. These are all *data driven* systems. You tell them what you want in advance, and they behave as if you did all the manual work of building those systems. As a result, Core Data, Cocoa Bindings, and Properties mesh really well together.

The examples in this chapter use Cocoa Bindings to hook the Core Data document to its user interface. It should be said there is no requirement that you use Cocoa Bindings or Properties when using Core Data. This means you always have an out: if something isn't working for you, or if you can't get Cocoa Bindings to do what you want, you can always fall back to doing it the long way (it's just more work, and sometimes it gets messy).

In the following Try It Out sections you build Slide Master's SlideShow UI and bind it to the document data. Then you test your work. This takes place in three steps:

1. You do some housekeeping in the Slide Master project: replacing `MyDocument` with a `SlideShowDocument` class, and building the `SlideShowWindowController` to manage your UI.

2. You build the user interface and use Cocoa Bindings to hook the controls up to object controllers.

3. Finally, you add a SlideShow Entity to your `SlideShowDocument`.

At that point your UI will be fully bound and you run and test your program.

TRY IT OUT   Replacing the MyDocument Class

1. In Xcode, remove the `MyDocument.h` and `MyDocument.m` files.

2. Create new `SlideShowDocument.h` and `SlideShowDocument.m` from the Cocoa Objective-C Class template. Be sure to subclass from `NSDocument` before naming the files.

3. Create new Cocoa Objective-C `NSWindowController` subclass files named `SlideShowWindowController.h` and `SlideShowWindowController.m`.

4. Open `SlideShowDocument.h` and replace its contents with the following code:

```
#import <Cocoa/Cocoa.h>

@interface SlideShowDocument : NSPersistentDocument
{
}
@end
```

code snippet MacOSXProg ch10/Slide Master 1/SlideShowDocument.h

5. Open `SlideShowDocument.m` and replace its contents with the following code. Note that the default `windowNibName` method was replaced by a `makeWindowControllers` method. You don't need special code to read and write the document.

```
#import "SlideShowDocument.h"
#import "SlideShowWindowController.h"

@implementation SlideShowDocument

#pragma mark Document Initialization

- (void)makeWindowControllers
{
    SlideShowWindowController *slideShowWindowController = nil;

    slideShowWindowController = [[[SlideShowWindowController alloc]
        initWithWindowNibName:@"SlideShowDocument"] autorelease];

    [self addWindowController:slideShowWindowController];
}

@end
```

code snippet MacOSXProg ch10/Slide Master 1/SlideShowDocument.m

6. Rename the `MyDocument` nib file to `SlideShowDocument.xib`. (Recall from Chapter 3 that you can rename files by clicking their names in the Groups & Files list.)

7. Open the `SlideShowDocument` nib file in Interface Builder.

8. In the nib file's Classes tab, create a new `NSWindowController` subclass called `SlideShowWindowController`.

9. Set the File's Owner class to the new `SlideShowWindowController` class.

10. Make sure that the File's Owner's `window` outlet is connected to the document window instance. If not, make the connection.

11. Save the `SlideShowDocument` nib file.

12. In Xcode's project window, select the Slide Master target and choose Project ➪ Get Info. The Target Info window appears.

13. Select the Properties tab and change the class for the SlideShow Document from `MyDocument` to `SlideShowDocument`.

14. Build and Run Slide Master. The default "Your document contents here" window should still appear on launch and when you choose File ➪ New.

How It Works

Xcode always uses a `MyDocument` class for new document-based projects. The class name appears in source files, in the `MyDocument` nib file, and in the `Info.plist`. If you want your class names to be more relevant to your project, you need to change all these different areas. It's often easier to simply replace the source files with new ones than to rename them and change all the references to `MyDocument` within the source code. That leaves you with the task of updating the nib file and `Info.plist` by hand.

`SlideShowDocument` subclasses from `NSPersistentDocument`, which is the base class for all Core Data-based documents. `NSPersistentDocument` handles all the Core Data-specific parts of the document system and integrates them with `NSDocument`. For example, `NSPersistentDocument` manages Core Data's storage, and handles all the details of initializing the storage when the document is opened and writing the storage when the document is saved. You will learn more about Core Data's storage in the next two sections.

Now that your document classes are in order, you can build the interface.

TRY IT OUT   Binding User Interface to Core Data

1. Open the `SlideShowDocument.xib` nib file.

2. Drag an Object Controller from the Library into your nib file's object window, and rename it SlideShow Controller.

3. In the Attributes Inspector, change the object controller's Mode to Entity, set the Entity Name to SlideShow, enable Prepares Content, and make sure Editable is enabled. The Inspector will resemble Figure 10-9.

4. In the Bindings Inspector bind the Content Object to the File's Owner and change the Model Key Path to `document.slideShow`.

5. Bind the Managed Object Context to the File's Owner and change the Model Key Path to `document.managedObjectContext`. The Bindings Inspector will now look like Figure 10-10.

6. Drag an Array Controller from the Library into your nib file's object window and rename it Slides controller.

7. In the Attributes Inspector change the object controller's Mode to Entity, set the Entity Name to Slide, enable Prepares Content, and make sure Editable is enabled. Leave the other settings alone. The Object Controller portion of the Inspector will again resemble Figure 10-9.

FIGURE 10-9

8. In the Bindings Inspector, bind the Content Set to SlideShow Controller, and change the Model Key Path to `slides`.

9. Just as with step 5, bind the Managed Object Context to the File's Owner, and change the Model Key Path to `document.managedObjectContext`.

10. Remove the "Your document contents here" placeholder from your document's window.

11. Drag a Table View from the Library into your window. Don't worry about resizing the table view, or placing it anywhere.

12. Click once on the table view to select its enclosing scroll view.

13. In the scroll view's Size Inspector change the view so that it resizes horizontally and vertically and is anchored to the window's sides.

14. Select the table view by clicking again on the scroll view. The Inspector's title bar will change from Scroll View Size to Table View Size.

15. Change the Row Height to 34. Leave the other settings alone.

16. In the Table View Attributes Inspector, change the table's attributes to match those in Figure 10-11. Note there is only one column, and columns can be resized but not reordered. The table view allows multiple selections, but doesn't allow empty selections. Finally, rows draw with alternating background colors.

17. Drag an Image Cell from your Library into your table column. The table's placeholder contents will change to show a little image icon.

18. With the table selected, click once in your table column area to select the table column. If you deselected the entire table view, you can select the table column by double-clicking it quickly. The Inspector's title will change to Table Column Attributes.

FIGURE 10-10

19. Set the table column's title to Image. Turn off User Resizable and Editable.

20. In the Table Column Bindings Inspector bind Value to Slides Controller and change the Model Key Path to `image`. The Bindings Inspector will look like Figure 10-12.

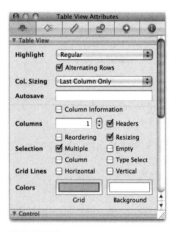

FIGURE 10-11

FIGURE 10-12

21. Drag a Gradient Button from your Library into your window. Position it against the bottom edge of the table at the left corner.

22. Change the button's title to +, resize the button to 26 pixels wide, and anchor the button to the lower-left corner of the window.

23. Copy the button, name the copy -, and position it just to the right of the table view.

24. Control-drag from the + button to the Slides array controller and connect to the add: action.

25. Connect the – button to the Slides array controller's remove: action.

26. Select the table view and both buttons together and choose Layout ➪ Embed Objects In ➪ Custom View. Your window will now resemble Figure 10-13.

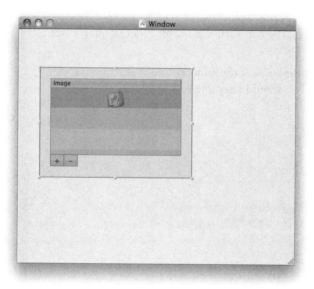

FIGURE 10-13

27. Use the resize handles on the custom view to fit it snugly to your table view and buttons. You don't want any extra space around the edges of the table.

28. In the Custom View Size Inspector, change the view so that it resizes horizontally and vertically and is anchored to the window's sides.

29. Drag an image view from your Library into your window. Place it to the right of the table view group. You don't need to be exact so long as it's near the table's right side, and you don't need to resize the image view.

30. In the Image View Attributes Inspector, change the Scaling to Proportionally Down, set the Border to None, and check the Editable checkbox.

31. In the Size Inspector, make sure the image view shrinks and grows properly when its window is resized. Also anchor the edges to the sides of the window.

32. In the Bindings Inspector bind Value to Slides Controller and change the Model Key Path to `image`. The Bindings Inspector will look like Figure 10-12, except the Controller Key should still say `selection`.

33. In the Image View Identity Inspector, change the view's Class to `SlideImageView`. We want this image view to behave the same as in our image documents.

34. Select both the table view group and the image view together and choose Layout ➪ Embed Objects In ➪ Split View. Both controls are now enclosed in a split view, with the table on the left and the image on the right.

35. Resize the split view so it fills the entire window. You may have trouble moving and resizing the split view if it isn't selected first. You can select the split view by clicking its split divider. The split view will resize by growing the table view. You can shrink the table to a reasonable size by dragging the split divider to the left.

36. In the Size Inspector, anchor the split view to the sides of the window and make sure the view resizes horizontally and vertically. Your window should resemble Figure 10-14.

FIGURE 10-14

How It Works

Here you built on your experiences in Chapters 8 and 9 to build a more sophisticated user interface. You have seen most of these tasks before: adding controls to a window, moving and resizing them, embedding them into scroll views, making action connections from buttons, and even using Cocoa Bindings. Let's look at some of the new things you saw in this example.

First you created an object controller that represents the main SlideShow model object. In the Email Formatter 2 program from Chapter 8 your object controller was bound to an object that was instantiated by the nib file. In Slide Master you bound the object controller to the document's slideshow by way of the File's Owner: the `SlideShowWindowController`. The window controller has a `document` accessor for returning its NSDocument subclass. You used that accessor when you set the Model Key Path to `document.slideShow`. You haven't written a `slideShow` accessor for your document yet, but you will very soon.

When you are using Cocoa Bindings with Core Data, your object controllers need to know about the storage system Core Data is managing. That's the role of the Managed Object Context setting. Cocoa's `NSManagedObjectContext` acts as a container for `NSManagedObject` objects, and every managed object will live in one (and only one) managed object context. The managed object context is the piece of Core Data code responsible for reading and writing these objects to a file, managing undo and redo, and the like. Every Core Data-based document has a `NSManagedObjectContext` provided by the `NSPersistentDocument` base class. You bound the object controllers to the document's managed object context with the `document.managedObjectContext` Model Key Path. Again, you found the document by going through the window controller's `document` accessor.

An array controller is a kind of object controller that deals with lists of objects. The `NSArrayController` class manages all the low-level details of working with an array: getting an item at a specific index, adding an item, removing an item, moving an item in the list, and so on. `NSArrayController` also manages a selection, which is very useful for table views and other controls that manage more than one object. You can also filter the contents of a `NSArrayController` to display only a subset of the array. Because your SlideShow Entity refers to a list of Slide Entities, you need to use an array controller to manage that list.

When binding controls to an array controller you need to be aware of which item in the array the control needs. For example, table views often display all the objects in the array in a particular arrangement, with each row in the table representing an object in the array. The table view takes care of indexing each item into the array for you, so long as you tell it which array controller to use. When binding table columns to an array controller, you usually want to bind the column's value to the array controller's `arrangedObjects`, and then ask those objects for the model data you want. Set the table column's Controller Key to `arrangedObjects`. The Model Key Path set to `image` is similar to saying the following in Objective-C property dot notation:

```
value = arrayController.arrangedObjects.image;
```

If you try entering `arrangedObjects.image` into Interface Builder as the Model Key Path or the Controller Key, Interface Builder will break the message up and store `arrangedObjects` as the Controller Key and `image` as the Model Key Path.

On the other hand, image views often want to display a specific image from your model, or only the selected image from an array controller. When binding image views to an array controller, you often want to set the Controller Key to `selection`. The image view will ask the array controller for the list of selected objects, and ask those objects for their data.

Now that the controls are bound to an array controller you need some way to add objects to the array controller. Ideally Slide Master would do this in code using some user-friendly UI, such as drag-and-drop or a menu command. But it's easy to create simple add and remove buttons and connect them to the array controller's add: and remove: actions.

In this example, you configured the table column to display images. Changing the column's data type involved dragging a cell from the Library to the table column. In Cocoa, cells are subclasses of NSCell that do most of the real work for a control object, such as drawing a button or a text field. By breaking this behavior out of the NSControl object, the behavior of these controls can be reused elsewhere. For example, an NSImageView is a control that holds an NSImageCell. NSTableView controls can display images using the same NSImageCell class. By default, table columns display and edit text with NSTextFieldCell.

Image views and image view cells can be bound to model objects in one of three ways: as an NSImage Value, as an NSString Value Path pointing to a file, and as an NSURL Valueurl pointing to a file. The Value Path and Valueurl bindings are read-only: they can only be used when displaying images. The Value binding can be used for reading and writing to the model. Remember that image views are controls; you can change their values by dragging an image onto them from the Finder. Slide Master uses the Value binding to respond to the control change instead of dragging an action connection in Interface Builder. Because the Value binding expects NSImage objects, you bound it to your model's image attribute.

You grouped the table view with its add and remove buttons into a custom view so that they would move and resize together as a unit. When the custom view resizes, its contents also resize, following the same rules as if they were in a window by themselves. This step is important because you need to hand the table view and its buttons to a split view.

The NSSplitView class separates two or more views with a movable divider. The split view handles all the work of resizing the objects when the divider moves, and for the most part the usual resizing rules apply here. The only problem here is that NSSplitView can only manage one view per split area. If you simply select the table view, the add button, the remove button, and the image view and grouped them into a split view, the new split view would have four views in it, one for each view. By grouping the table and its buttons into a single unit, the split view saw those controls as a single view and shared the same split area.

Now your user interface has been built and bound to your document. You'd be ready to go right now except that the SlideShowDocument has no accessor for the slideShow property. Now when you run Slide Master, you should see an error message in Xcode's debugging console telling you that Cocoa can't find a property for slideShow:

```
GNU gdb 6.3.50-20050815 (Apple version gdb-1344) (Fri Jul  3 01:19:56 UTC 2009)
Copyright 2004 Free Software Foundation, Inc.
GDB is free software, covered by the GNU General Public License, and you are

welcome to change it and/or distribute copies of it under certain conditions.
Type "show copying" to see the conditions.
There is absolutely no warranty for GDB.  Type "show warranty" for details.
This GDB was configured as "x86_64-apple-darwin".tty /dev/ttys002
Loading program into debugger…
Program loaded.
run
[Switching to process 6928]
Running…
2009-09-26 11:49:19.763 Slide Master[6928:a0b] [<SlideShowDocument 0x100449cd0>
    valueForUndefinedKey:]: this class is not key value coding-compliant for the
```

```
    key slideShow.
2009-09-26 11:49:19.770 Slide Master[6928:a0b] [<SlideShowDocument 0x100473c50>
    valueForUndefinedKey:]: this class is not key value coding-compliant for the
    key slideShow.
```

The slideShow property isn't just an instance variable, it is the root object of your document model. It needs to be an object in your document's Managed Object Context. Unfortunately, Core Data doesn't create this object for you. In the next Try It Out, you will create your document's root SlideShow object.

TRY IT OUT   Creating a Root Document Object

1. In Xcode, open SlideShowDocument.h and change the SlideShowDocument interface to the following code:

Available for
download on
Wrox.com

```
@interface SlideShowDocument : NSPersistentDocument
{
        NSManagedObject* mSlideShow;
}

@property (nonatomic, readonly) NSManagedObject* slideShow;

@end
```

code snippet MacOSXProg ch10/Slide Master 2/SlideShowDocument.h

2. Switch to SlideShowDocument.m and replace the entire SlideShowDocument implementation with the following code:

Available for
download on
Wrox.com

```
@implementation SlideShowDocument

#pragma mark Document Initialization

- (id)initWithType:(NSString *)typeName error:(NSError **)outError
{
    self = [super initWithType:typeName error:outError];

    if (self) {
        // create a new SlideShow entity object and insert it into the managed
        // object context. store it in mSlideShow so the UI code can find it.
        NSManagedObjectContext *context = self.managedObjectContext;

        mSlideShow = [[NSEntityDescription
            insertNewObjectForEntityForName:@"SlideShow"
                    inManagedObjectContext:context] retain];
    }

    return self;
}

- (BOOL)configurePersistentStoreCoordinatorForURL:(NSURL *)url
```

```objc
ofType:(NSString *)fileType modelConfiguration:(NSString *)configuration
storeOptions:(NSDictionary *)storeOptions error:(NSError **)error;
{
    BOOL result = [super configurePersistentStoreCoordinatorForURL:url
                                                ofType:fileType
                                     modelConfiguration:configuration
                                           storeOptions:storeOptions
                                                  error:error];

    if (result) {
        // our document is now open and the managed object context is ready.
        // retrieve the SlideShow entity object from the managed object context
        // and store it mSlideShow.
        NSManagedObjectContext *context = self.managedObjectContext;

        // get the entity description for SlideShow
        NSEntityDescription *entity = [NSEntityDescription
            entityForName:@"SlideShow" inManagedObjectContext:context];

        // build a fetch request that looks for this entity
        NSFetchRequest *fetchRequest = [[[NSFetchRequest alloc] init]
            autorelease];
        [fetchRequest setEntity:entity];

        // fetch
        NSError *fetchError = nil;
        NSArray *fetchResults;
        fetchResults = [context executeFetchRequest:fetchRequest
                                    error:&fetchError];

        // we expect to find only one slide show object. more than one or less
        // than one is an error.
        if ([fetchResults count] == 1) {
            [mSlideShow release];
            mSlideShow = [[fetchResults objectAtIndex:0] retain];
        } else {
            if (fetchError != nil) {
                [self presentError:fetchError];
            }

            result = NO;
        }
    }

    return result;
}

- (void)makeWindowControllers
{
    SlideShowWindowController *slideShowWindowController = nil;

    slideShowWindowController = [[[SlideShowWindowController alloc]
        initWithWindowNibName:@"SlideShowDocument"] autorelease];
```

```
        [self addWindowController:slideShowWindowController];
}

#pragma mark Properties

@synthesize slideShow = mSlideShow;

@end
```

---

code snippet MacOSXProg ch10/Slide Master 2/SlideShowDocument.m

3. While you're in Xcode, open `SlideImageView.m` and add the following method to the `SlideImageView` implementation:

```
- (void)drawRect:(NSRect)rect
{
    [[NSColor whiteColor] set];
    NSRectFill(rect);

    [super drawRect:rect];
}
```

4. Build and run Slide Master. If you see errors while building, go back and make sure the code changes are correct. Because Slide Master's SlideShow window doesn't appear on launch, you need to review the nib file for errors. If all is well, Slide Master's SlideShow document will appear, as shown in Figure 10-15.

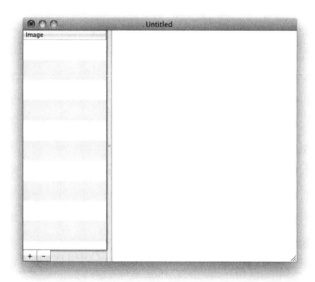

FIGURE 10-15

5. Press the + button. The first row in the Image table will turn dark, indicating there's now an item in the table, and that item is selected.

6. Drag an image into the window. The image will appear both in the large image area and also in the table.

7. Repeat steps 5 and 6 a number of times until you have added two or three images to your document. Your document should resemble Figure 10-16.

FIGURE 10-16

8. Select Edit ➪ Undo. The most recent image will disappear, leaving the current row empty.

9. Select Edit ➪ Undo again. The empty row will disappear.

10. Select Edit ➪ Redo twice. The new row and image will return.

11. Select File ➪ Save and save your document.

12. Close your document.

13. Reopen the document using the File ➪ Open Recent menu.

14. Find your document in the Finder and select File ➪ Get Info. Your file size will likely be in megabytes, depending on the pictures you add.

How It Works

Slide Master's slideshow document contains one SlideShow Entity. From the point of view of the data model, the SlideShow Entity represents the document's data model. When working with Core Data documents you need to take some manual steps to create and find the root object when the document is initialized.

When a document is first created, you need to create a default instance of your root object and register it with Core Data's managed object context. The NSDocument class provides a method named `initWithType:error:` which gets called only for new untitled documents. This method is the ideal place to create your root slideshow object.

Creating a managed object in a managed object context is ordinarily a two-step process: first to get the entity description for that object, and then to create the new managed object with that description. The entity description, represented by `NSEntityDescription`, is essentially the box you created in Xcode's data model editor describing all the properties for an entity. `NSEntityDescription` provides a convenient class method for creating a `NSManagedObject` from an entity name and a `NSManagedObjectContext`.

When opening an existing document, you need to retrieve the root object after the document object is initialized and after the file contents have been loaded. `NSPersistentDocument` uses a method named `configurePersistentStoreCoordinatorForURL:ofType:modelConfiguration:storeOptions:error:` to open the connection to a document's file. You can override this method and retrieve the root object after calling `super`.

You retrieve objects from the manage object context through fetch requests, represented by the `NSFetchRequest` class. A fetch request contains all the information about the object or objects you are looking for, including an `NSEntityDescription` and other optional search terms. When the fetch request is executed, the managed object context searches through its contents looking for objects that match your request. The fetch results are returned in an array, as fetch requests may return any number of objects.

While you were in your program's code, you made a small change to the `SlideImageView` so that it draws a white background behind its image. `SlideImageView` overrides the `NSImageView`'s `drawRect:` method and changes the way the object is drawn. By overriding an existing `drawRect:` classes method, you can control whether the changes draw in front or behind the existing drawing.

After all that work, Slide Master is ready to go. As promised, Cocoa Bindings did all the work of loading your controls and updating the model, Core Data managed all the reading and writing of your document files, and you received undo and redo for free. Success!

But there are problems:

➤ Although it was easy to create small add and remove buttons to manage the contents of your table view, they aren't very convenient to use. Adding more than one slide can be a real chore.

➤ You may have noticed when undoing and redoing slide changes that the list of images in the table view suddenly reordered itself. This illustrates a weakness of Core Data: To-Many relationships are unordered sets, not ordered arrays. As such, Core Data makes no guarantees about the order the results will appear in.

➤ SlideShow document files can be quite big. That's because the slideshow embeds the entire image into the document.

All these problems have solutions. In fact, they each have many solutions. You will explore these solutions in the following sections.

SELECTING FILES WITH OPEN PANELS

As you know, AppKit's NSDocument class handles your application's File ⇨ Open menu command for you. It reads the list of supported file extensions and file types out of your application's Info. plist file, and displays files of that type in an open panel. When you select one of those files, AppKit instantiates the document class appropriate for the selected file and passes the file contents to the document.

Sometimes you need to drive the open panel yourself. You might be working on an application that doesn't have documents, or your document may itself refer to one or more files. In either case, working with the open panel is fairly easy.

The NSOpenPanel class defined by AppKit provides all the functionality necessary to run an open panel modally, either as a sheet or as a separate dialog window. NSOpenPanel is itself based on the NSSavePanel class, used for driving a corresponding save file window. Although NSSavePanel provides some of the basic implementation, NSOpenPanel extends this to include filtering for specific files and file types, returning multiple files, selecting directories as well as files, and other features.

In the following Try It Out, you use an open panel to add image files to a slideshow document.

TRY IT OUT   Running an Open Panel

1.   Open MainMenu.xib in Interface Builder.

2.   Add the following actions to the First Responder. If necessary, refer back to Connecting Menus in Chapter 9:

ACTION
addSlidesWithOpenPanel:
removeSlides:

3.   Drag a Submenu Menu Item from the Library to the menu bar, and drop it between the View and Window menus. Name the menu Slide Show.

4.   Add the following items to the Slide Show menu and connect them to the corresponding First Responder action:

COMMAND	FIRST RESPONDER ACTION
Add Slides ...	addSlidesWithOpenPanel:
Remove Slides	removeSlides:

5.   Save your changes.

6.   In Xcode, open SlideShowWindowController.h, add the mSlidesController instance variable shown next, and save the file:

```
@interface SlideShowWindowController : NSWindowController
{
    IBOutlet NSArrayController *mSlidesController;
```

```
}

@end
```

code snippet MacOSXProg ch10/Slide Master 3/SlideShowWindowController.h

7. Open `SlideShowDocument.xib` in Interface Builder.

8. Connect the First Responder's `mSlidesController` outlet to the Slides Controller array controller, and save the file.

9. In Xcode, open `SlideShowWindowController.m` and replace its contents with the following code:

```objc
#import "SlideShowWindowController.h"
#import "SlideShowDocument.h"

@interface SlideShowWindowController ()
- (void)openPanelDidEnd:(NSOpenPanel *)openPanel returnCode:(int)returnCode
    contextInfo:(void *)contextInfo;
@end


@implementation SlideShowWindowController

#pragma mark Open Panel UI

- (void)addSlidesWithOpenPanel:(id)sender
{
    NSOpenPanel *openPanel = [NSOpenPanel openPanel];
    SEL selector = @selector(openPanelDidEnd:returnCode:contextInfo:);
    NSArray *types = nil;

    // get the list of image types
    types = [NSImage imageFileTypes];

    // configure the open panel
    [openPanel setAllowsMultipleSelection:YES];
    [openPanel setCanChooseDirectories:NO];
    [openPanel setCanChooseFiles:YES];
    [openPanel setResolvesAliases:YES];

    // run the open panel as a sheet
    [openPanel beginSheetForDirectory:nil
                                 file:nil
                                types:types
                        modalForWindow:self.window
                         modalDelegate:self
                        didEndSelector:selector
                           contextInfo:nil];
}

- (void)openPanelDidEnd:(NSOpenPanel *)openPanel returnCode:(int)returnCode
    contextInfo:(void *)contextInfo
{
    if (returnCode == NSOKButton) {
```

```
        [self.document addSlidesAtURLs:openPanel.URLs];
    }
}

- (void)removeSlides:(id)sender
{
    [mSlidesController remove:sender];
}

@end
```

---

code snippet MacOSXProg ch10/Slide Master 3/SlideShowWindowController.m

10. Open `SlideShowDocument.h` and add the following method to the `SlideShowDocument` interface:

```
- (void)addSlidesAtURLs:(NSArray*)urls;
```

11. Switch to `SlideShowDocument.m` and add the following code to the bottom of the `SlideShowDocument` implementation:

```
#pragma mark Adding Slides

- (void)addSlidesAtURLs:(NSArray*)urls
{
    // get the managed object context
    NSManagedObjectContext *context = self.managedObjectContext;

    // get a mutable set of slides
    NSMutableSet *slides = [[mSlideShow valueForKey:@"slides"] mutableCopy];

    // for each url...
    for (NSURL *url in urls) {
        // ... open an image
        NSImage *image = [[[NSImage alloc] initWithContentsOfURL:url]
            autorelease];

        // ... create a slide for the image and add it to the slides set
        if (image) {
            NSManagedObject *slide = [NSEntityDescription
                insertNewObjectForEntityForName:@"Slide"
                        inManagedObjectContext:context];

            [slide setValue:image forKey:@"image"];

            [slides addObject:slide];
        }
    }

    // write the slides set back into the slide show
    [mSlideShow setValue:slides forKey:@"slides"];
}
```

---

code snippet MacOSXProg ch10/Slide Master 3/SlideShowDocument.m

12. Save your changes to the `SlideShowWindowController` and `SlideShowDocument` files.

13. Build and run the Slide Master project.

14. Choose Slide Show ➪ Add Slides. The open panel appears as a sheet on the Slide Show window. You can select one or more image files from this panel. When you press OK, the new images are added to the document.

15. Select one or more images in the table view and choose Slide Show ➪ Remove Slides. The selected images are removed from the document.

How It Works

You began by declaring a method called `openPanelDidEnd:returnCode:contextInfo:` in a class extension. This method is a private utility, intended to be used only from within the `SlideShowWindowController` class. Objective-C doesn't have a concept of private methods; that is, methods that can be called only from within their own class. You can discourage other objects from using a method by omitting it from your class's header file. You can then define the methods in your implementation file using an Objective-C category or class extension. You learned about categories in Chapter 7.

You work with `NSOpenPanel` by getting a pointer to the shared open panel instance:

```
NSOpenPanel *openPanel = [NSOpenPanel openPanel];
```

After you have the shared instance you can configure the open panel to match your specific situation. For example, when adding slides with the Slide Show ➪ Add Slides command, Slide Master configures the open panel to allow a selection of multiple files. Slide Master resolves alias files, such as those created by the Finder.

The open panel can be run either as a sheet or a dialog. Dialogs are processed *synchronously*. In other words, code that opens a dialog waits until the dialog is closed before continuing on its way. As a result, programming a dialog is easy; you simply call a method that invokes one (such as `NSOpenPanel`'s `runModalForTypes:` or `runModalForDirectory:file:types:`) to show and run the open panel, and check the return code to find out if the user confirmed or canceled the operation. Sheets are handled *asynchronously*, meaning code that starts a sheet operation will return right away, before the sheet has closed. This allows a sheet to lock out user events for the parent window, but allows other windows in your application to keep working. This also complicates the task of finding out how and when the sheet was dismissed.

`SlideShowWindowController` runs the `NSOpenPanel` as a sheet by invoking its `beginSheetForDirectory: file:types:modalForWindow:modalDelegate:didEndSelector:contextInfo:` method. This method is easy to understand if you pick it apart section by section.

The first two parts of the method signature, `beginSheetForDirectory:` and `file:`, allow you to specify the directory or file that is selected by default in the open panel. `SlideShowWindowController` passes `nil` to get the default behavior. The third part, represented by the `type:` segment, allows you to specify an array of file extensions and HFS types appropriate for this file. HFS types are four character codes specific to the HFS filesystem that identify the type of a file. Although Mac OS X applications tend to prefer file extensions, older documents may use HFS types instead of file extensions. `SlideShowWindowController` passes in the list of extensions and types that `NSImage` knows, provided by the call to NSImage's imageFileTypes method. modalForWindow: takes the NSWindow instance to which the open panel will be anchored. SlideShowWindowController uses its own window instance. The last three arguments refer to a callback method that will be called when the NSOpenPanel is dismissed.

The first of these arguments, the modalDelegate: segment, refers to the object that will be notified when the sheet closes. This is normally the same object that requested the sheet in the first place, which in this example is the SlideShowWindowController object. The didEndSelector: argument specifies the modal delegate's callback method that will fire when the sheet is dismissed. The method is specified by a SEL data type, which you can get using the @selector() function. According to the documentation from NSOpenPanel, these callbacks must match the following method signature (which matches the method you declared earlier):

```
- (void)openPanelDidEnd:(NSOpenPanel *)sheet returnCode:(int)returnCode
    contextInfo:(void *)contextInfo
```

That means the names in the method may be different as long as the number and types of arguments do not change. Finally, the contextInfo: segment designates a pointer that will be passed into the "did end selector" when the sheet ends. This provides an alternative way to pass information between the code that starts the sheet and the code that closes the sheet, which is especially helpful if this code is in different objects. If you aren't interested in this information, you can set it to nil.

Finally, your openPanelDidEnd:returnCode:contextInfo: method will take the result from the open panel and pass it to the SlideShowDocument's addSlidesAtURLs: method. All it needs from the open panel is the list of file paths, which it gets using NSOpenPanel's URLs method.

The code that creates new slides and adds them to the managed object context is very similar to the code you wrote earlier to create a new document root object. First you get the set of existing slides from the mSlideShow root object. After creating a new instance of the Slide Entity in the document's managed object context you set its image and add it to the set of slides. Finally you push the new slide set into the mSlideShow root object. Now you can quickly add images to the slideshow document without going through the + button. While you are in the neighborhood, you hook up a removeSlides: command, which calls the same remove: method as the – button.

At this point, you could edit your SlideShowDocument.xib nib file and remove the + and – buttons. On the other hand, they don't seem to be hurting anything. The choice is yours.

CREATING NEW DOCUMENTS

So far Cocoa has handled document management for you. But there are times when it would be nice to create new documents yourself. Consider an import command that creates a new document from a collection of existing files.

Consider also Xcode's project window and source code windows. It is easy to imagine that Xcode's project window is a document. You can also view and edit source files using Xcode even if you don't have a project window open, so these standalone source code windows are probably also documents. When you double-click a source file in an Xcode project, you're creating a new source file document. It doesn't really matter that you didn't use the File ➪ Open command or double-click the file in the Finder.

In the next Try It Out you will write a File ➪ Import command that asks the user for one or more files and then stores them in a new, untitled document.

TRY IT OUT Creating a New Document

1. In Xcode, create files for a new Objective-C NSObject subclass called ApplicationDelegate.

2. Open MainMenu.xib in Interface Builder.

3. Drag an object from the Library to your nib objects window. Set the object's class to ApplicationDelegate.

4. Connect the File Owner's delegate outlet to the ApplicationDelegate object.

5. Add a newSlideShowWithOpenPanel: action to the First Responder.

6. Open the File menu in the menu bar and a separator item and an Import item below the Revert to Saved menu item. Your finished File menu should resemble the one in Figure 10-17.

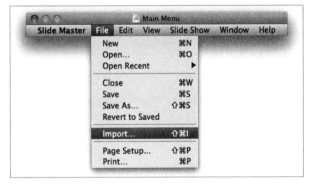

FIGURE 10-17

7. Connect the Import menu item to the First Responder's newSlideShowWithOpenPanel: action.

8. Save MainMenu.xib.

9. Open SlideShowDocument.h and add the following method to the SlideShowDocument interface:

```
+ (SlideShowDocument *)newFromFolderWithOpenPanel;
```

10. Switch to SlideShowDocument.m and add the following class extension above the SlideShowDocument implementation block:

```
@interface SlideShowDocument ()
- (void)importFolderAtURL:(NSURL*)dirURL;
@end
```

11. Add the `newFromFolderWithOpenPanel` class method at the top of the `Document Initialization` section:

```
#pragma mark Document Initialization
+ (SlideShowDocument *)newFromFolderWithOpenPanel
{
    SlideShowDocument *document = nil;
    NSOpenPanel *openPanel = [NSOpenPanel openPanel];
    int returnCode;

    // configure the open panel
    [openPanel setAllowsMultipleSelection:NO];
    [openPanel setCanChooseDirectories:YES];
    [openPanel setCanChooseFiles:NO];
    [openPanel setResolvesAliases:YES];

    // run the panel
    returnCode = [openPanel runModalForDirectory:nil
                                            file:nil
                                           types:nil];

    // if the user selected a directory, import the images found there.
    // if the user canceled, return nil and trust the autorelease pool
    // to release the document.
    if (returnCode == NSOKButton) {
        NSError *error;

        document = [[[SlideShowDocument alloc] initWithType:@"SlideShow Document"
            error:&error] autorelease];
        [document importFolderAtURL:openPanel.URL];
    }

    return document;
}
```

code snippet MacOSXProg ch10/Slide Master 4/SlideShowDocument.m

12. Add the following method at the end of the `Adding Slides` section:

```
- (void)importFolderAtURL:(NSURL*)dirURL
{
    NSFileManager *fileManager = [NSFileManager defaultManager];
    NSMutableArray *urls = [NSMutableArray array];
    NSDirectoryEnumerator *enumerator = [fileManager enumeratorAtURL:dirURL
                                    includingPropertiesForKeys:[NSArray array]
                                                       options:0
                                                  errorHandler:nil];
    for (NSURL *url in enumerator)
```

```
    {
        [urls addObject:url];
    }

    [self addSlidesAtURLs:urls];
}
```

13. Open `ApplicationDelegate.m` and replace its contents with the following code:

```
#import "ApplicationDelegate.h"
#import "SlideShowDocument.h"

@implementation ApplicationDelegate

- (void)newSlideShowWithOpenPanel:(id)sender
{
    SlideShowDocument *slideDoc = [SlideShowDocument newFromFolderWithOpenPanel];

    if (slideDoc) {
        NSDocumentController *documentController = [NSDocumentController
            sharedDocumentController];

        [slideDoc makeWindowControllers];
        [slideDoc showWindows];

        [documentController addDocument:slideDoc];
    }
}

@end
```

14. Save your changes to the `SlideShowDocument` and `ApplicationDelegate` files.

15. Build and run your application. When you choose the File ⇨ Import command, you can choose a directory instead of individual images. When you select a directory, a new slideshow document window appears complete with your selected images.

How It Works

You began by adding a new `newFromFolderWithOpenPanel` class method to `SlideShowDocument`. This class method provides a way for Slide Master to create a new slideshow document pre-initialized with the contents of a directory chosen by the user. Because this is a class method, the method can be called without first instantiating `SlideShowDocument`. This is useful because this method is itself responsible for creating a `SlideShowDocument` instance.

Although the `newFromFolderWithOpenPanel` class method also drives the `NSOpenPanel`, its needs are very different from the `addSlidesWithOpenPanel:` method. Because the slideshow document has just been created and its window isn't yet on-screen, you can't run the open panel as a sheet. Instead, `newFromFolderWithOpenPanel` runs the open panel as a modal dialog using the `runModalForDirectory:file:types:` method. Because `newFromFolderWithOpenPanel` doesn't need to customize the dialog, it passes `nil` in as all the arguments to `runModalForDirectory:file:types:`. When you click the OK button, the `newFromFolderWithOpenPanel` will make a call to `importFolderAtPath:`.

The `importFolderAtPath:` method enumerates the contents of the specified directory and passes its files to the existing `addSlidesAtURLs:` method. `SlideShowDocument` uses Foundation's `NSFileManager` object to get information about the file system. One of the features `NSFileManager` supplies is the ability to create an `NSDirectoryEnumerator` object for finding the contents of a directory. `NSDirectoryEnumerator` works just like the more general `NSEnumerator` class, except `NSDirectoryEnumerator` is designed to specifically return file URLs and other file system characteristics.

Your `ApplicatonDelegate`'s `newSlideShowWithOpenPanel:` method completes the menu action. First it acquires a new, pre-initialized `SlideShowDocument` instance using the `newSlideShowWithOpenPanel` class method. It then displays the document interface and adds it to the application's document list. The document list is maintained by a class called `NSDocumentController`. You rarely need to access this class directly in a document-based application; normally it works behind the scenes managing your documents for you. Because Slide Master has a customized way of creating new documents, it must talk to the document controller directly.

Remember the `newSlideShowWithOpenPanel:` is implemented in the `ApplicationDelegate` class so that the File ⇨ Import menu command is always enabled. If you implemented `newSlideShowWithOpenPanel:` in `SlideShowDocument` or `SlideShowWindowController` you would only be able to use File ⇨ Import if a document was already open.

SORTING RESULTS

Core Data represents To-Many relationships as an unordered set. Any time you ask for a collection of objects from a To-Many relationship they will come back in random order. This works well for cases where model objects don't have any explicit order, such as songs in an iTunes library. But it causes trouble in cases where you need to store an ordered list in your model. You've seen this problem first-hand when the table view suddenly rearranges itself during undo, redo, and the Add Slides menu item.

Modeling ordered relationships in a relational database is a tricky problem. It's difficult partly because there are many ways to interpret the problem, but also because there are many ways to go about modeling an ordered relationship. If you have a small dataset, tracking the order inside your child objects will constantly page all your objects in from disk when you rearrange the list. If you have a large dataset, tracking the order in a separate entity will be at the expense of keeping this entity synchronized with your To-Many relationship. Either way, you need to model the ordered relationship yourself.

Cocoa Bindings supports sorting array or set contents based on some criteria. For many ordered relationships, you can substitute sorting for modeling a real ordered To-Many relationship. For example, you could return all text strings in alphabetical order. Or you could return all song files sorted by artist and album name.

In the next Try It Out you will sort your Slide Entities by creation date. This will fix the random reordering problems you see during undo and redo.

TRY IT OUT   **Sorting Core Data Results**

1.   In Xcode, open `SlideShowDocument.xcdatamodel`. The slideshow object graph will appear in the data model editor.

2.   Select the Slide Entity and add a new attribute named `creationDate`. Set its Type to Date.

3.   Save `SlideShowDocument.xcdatamodel`.

4.   With `SlideShowDocument.xcdatamodel` still selected, choose the File ➪ New File menu item. In the New File template browser you will see a new Cocoa Class template named Managed Object Class. This option is only visible if a data model file is selected in your project.

5.   Select the Managed Object Class template and click Next. A panel appears asking for details about your project.

6.   Click Next. The panel changes again, this time to a list of entities in the selected data model file.

7.   Check the Slide Entity, make sure Generate Accessors and Generate Obj-C 2.0 Properties are checked, and click Finish. New files `Slide.m` and `Slide.h` are added to your project.

8.   Open `Slide.m` and add the following code to the Slide implementation:

```
- (void)awakeFromInsert
{
    [super awakeFromInsert];

    self.creationDate = [NSDate date];
}
```

code snippet MacOSXProg ch10/Slide Master 5/Slide.m

9.   Open `SlideShowWindowController.m` and add the following code to the top of the `SlideShowWindowController` implementation:

```
#pragma mark Window Initialization

- (void)windowDidLoad
{
    [super windowDidLoad];

    NSSortDescriptor *descriptor = [NSSortDescriptor sortDescriptorWithKey:
        @"creationDate" ascending:YES];
    NSArray *descriptors = [NSArray arrayWithObject:descriptor];

    [mSlidesController setSortDescriptors:descriptors];
}
```

code snippet MacOSXProg ch10/Slide Master 5/SlideShowWindowController.m

10. Save your changes to `Slide.m` and `SlideShowWindowController.m`.

11. Build and run Slide Master. Test adding images using the Add Slides menu and test removing them with Undo. The contents of the table view will remain sorted in the order they were originally added to the document.

How It Works

The idea is simple: keep track of the date and time when a Slide object was created, and display the list of slides in creation order. This approach will work well in Slide Master so long as there is no way to rearrange the image list.

Adding a `creationDate` attribute to the Slide Entity is easy; you just edit the data model file. Setting the `creationDate` attribute when the object is created requires writing some code. It turns out all managed objects receive a call to `awakeFromInsert` when they are created and added to a managed object context. The `awakeFromInsert` method will be called exactly once in an object's lifetime. That makes it an ideal place to initialize `creationDate`. Foundation provides the `NSDate` class for working with moments in time, and `[NSDate date]` is a quick way to get a date object representing the current date and time.

Array controllers can have optional sort rules applied to them. Each rule is represented by an `NSSortDescriptor` class. You can create a sort descriptor for each model key you want to sort on and group them together into an array. Here you built a sort descriptor for the `creationDate` property.

Sort rules are often configured dynamically using some kind of filtering UI. In those situations you can bind your array controller's sort descriptor array to your data model using Cocoa Bindings. In the case of Slide Master's image table, the sort rules will not change, so you can set these rules once. `NSWindowController` classes receive `windowDidLoad` messages when their nib files are loaded from disk and connected to the File's Owner. This is also the earliest time you can access your window controller's outlets. It is the ideal spot to initialize outlets and other window controller settings that depend on the nib file.

USING TRANSIENT OBJECTS

Currently, the Slide Master document stores images directly in its document as data. Core Data transforms the image data into live `NSImage` objects when Slide Master requests a slide from the managed object context. For each slide, the same `NSImage` instance is shared between the table view and the main image view. Having only one instance of the image in memory can be handy when working with very large images.

Although it's nice that slideshow files are self-contained, large images result in large document sizes. The image data may be stored in a large uncompressed format instead of what might be a smaller JPEG file. If the document referred to its images by URL or file path, the file format would shrink considerably.

You can bind image views and cells to URLs instead of `NSImage` objects, but then you'd have two new problems. First the URL image view binding is read-only. Also it's likely the main image and table views would create their own in-memory copy of each image.

You can use transient Core Data attributes to solve these problems. A transient attribute is one that doesn't get saved to the persistent object store. They're meant to hold a temporary state that can easily be derived from other attributes. Even though they aren't saved they are still tracked by Core Data, and you can get them and set them like other attributes. If you store a transient NSImage object in the Slide Entity, you can still share that image between the main image view and the table view while writing URLs to your file.

In the next Try It Out you change Slide Master to store images by URL, and you use a transient attribute to cache the in-memory image in each Slide Entity.

TRY IT OUT   Storing Images by URL

1. In Xcode, open SlideShowDocument.xcdatamodel.

2. Select the Slide Entity and add a new attribute named imageURL. Set its Type to Transformable.

3. Select the Slide Entity's image attribute and select the Transient checkbox.

4. Save SlideShowDocument.xcdatamodel.

5. Open Slide.h and add a property declaration for imageURL, shown here:

Available for download on Wrox.com

```
@property (nonatomic, retain) id image;
@property (nonatomic, retain) id imageURL;
@property (nonatomic, retain) NSDate * creationDate;
@property (nonatomic, retain) NSManagedObject * slideShow;
```

code snippet MacOSXProg ch10/Slide Master 6/Slide.h

6. Switch to Slide.m and replace the implementation with the following code:

Available for download on Wrox.com

```
@implementation Slide

@dynamic image;
@dynamic imageURL;
@dynamic creationDate;
@dynamic slideShow;

- (void)awakeFromInsert
{
    [super awakeFromInsert];

    self.creationDate = [NSDate date];
}

- (void)awakeFromFetch
{
    [super awakeFromFetch];

    NSImage *image = [[[NSImage alloc] initWithContentsOfURL:self.imageURL]
        autorelease];
```

```
        [self setPrimitiveValue:image forKey:@"image"];
    }

    @end
```

code snippet MacOSXProg ch10/Slide Master 6/Slide.m

7.   Open SlideImageView.h and add the instance variable and property shown here:

```
@interface SlideImageView : NSImageView
{
    NSString *mURLKeyPath;
}

@property (nonatomic, retain) NSString *URLKeyPath;

@end
```

code snippet MacOSXProg ch10/Slide Master 6/SlideImageView.h

8.   Switch to SlideImageView.m and add the following code to the class implementation:

```
- (void)dealloc
{
    [mURLKeyPath release];

    [super dealloc];
}

@synthesize URLKeyPath = mURLKeyPath;

- (void)concludeDragOperation:(id < NSDraggingInfo >)sender
{
    // get the drag pasteboard
    NSPasteboard *pasteboard = [sender draggingPasteboard];

    // make sure the pasteboard contains something NSURL recognizes
    NSArray *types = [NSURL readableTypesForPasteboard:pasteboard];
    if (types.count > 0) {
        // get the URL
        NSURL *fileURL = [NSURL URLFromPasteboard:pasteboard];

        // get the "value" binding settings
        NSDictionary *binding = [self infoForBinding:@"value"];
        if (binding) {
            id observed = [binding objectForKey:NSObservedObjectKey];
            id path = [binding objectForKey:NSObservedKeyPathKey];

            // push the image into the model
            NSImage *image = [[[NSImage alloc] initWithContentsOfURL:fileURL]
                autorelease];
            [observed setValue:image forKeyPath:path];

            // push the URL into the model
```

```
                    [observed setValue:fileURL forKeyPath:mURLKeyPath];
                } else {
                    // this isn't what we expected, let super handle it
                    [super concludeDragOperation:sender];
                }
            }
        }
    }
```

code snippet MacOSXProg ch10/Slide Master 6/SlideImageView.m

9. Open `SlideShowWindowController.h` and add a `mSlideImageView` outlet shown here:

```
@interface SlideShowWindowController : NSWindowController
{
    IBOutlet NSArrayController *mSlidesController;
    IBOutlet SlideImageView    *mSlideImageView;
}
```

code snippet MacOSXProg ch10/Slide Master 6/SlideShowWindowController.h

10. Switch to `SlideShowWindowController.m` and initialize the `mSlideImageView` instance variable in `windowDidLoad`:

```
- (void)windowDidLoad
{
    [super windowDidLoad];

    NSSortDescriptor *descriptor = [NSSortDescriptor sortDescriptorWithKey:
        @"creationDate" ascending:YES];
    NSArray *descriptors = [NSArray arrayWithObject:descriptor];

    [mSlidesController setSortDescriptors:descriptors];

    mSlideImageView.URLKeyPath = @"selection.imageURL";
}
```

code snippet MacOSXProg ch10/Slide Master 6/SlideShowWindowController.m

11. Save your code changes.

12. Open `SlideShowDocument.xib` in Interface Builder.

13. Connect the File's Owner's `mSlideImageView` outlet to the main image view, and save your changes.

14. Build and run Slide Master. An untitled slideshow document will appear as usual.

15. Add slides to the document using Slide Show ➪ Add Slides. Replace a few slides by selecting an image in the list and dragging a new file into the image view. Both the image view and the list will update.

16. Save your file, close its window, and examine it in the Finder. The file should now only be a few kilobytes in size, rather than a few megabytes.

17. Reopen your file in Slide Master. All the images will display.

How It Works

The slideshow document user interface is still bound to the Slide Entity's `image` property. This means the user interface continues to ask for `NSImage` objects from Core Data. By making `image` a transient property you told Core Data to stop archiving this value in your document. You are now responsible for setting the `image` by hand.

When a new Slide Entity is created it won't have an `image`, but if that Slide Entity is being created from a file, it will have an `imageURL`. You used the `awakeFromFetch` method to initialize `image` at that time. This `awakeFromFetch` method is explicitly for initializing transient variables in this way. When setting the `image`, you used the `NSManagedObject`'s `setPrimitiveValue:forKey:` method to avoid triggering unnecessary changes.

When you drag a file into the main image view, your custom `SlideImageView` object will push both the `image` and the `imageURL` values into the Slide. Because the image view's writable `value` binding is already set, it makes sense to reuse it here. It might be better to add some code to `Slide.m` to reload `image` when `imageURL` changes instead. You could have hardcoded the URL binding information in your `SlideImageView` class, but storing the information in an instance variable and initializing the object in the `SlideShowWindowController` makes the object a little more reusable. Remember, you are sharing this class with the image document.

APPLICATION PREFERENCES

Cocoa doesn't provide any special support for application preference windows, other than reserving a menu item for Preferences in new application nib files. You can simply apply the techniques and shortcuts you learned in earlier examples to build a window with controls, record the values when they change, and tell other parts of the application that they need to respond to that change. Cocoa Bindings do a very good job of managing this kind of problem.

In this example, you add a simple preference window to Slide Master, shown here in Figure 10-18. This window runs as a modal dialog just to keep things simple. You will use Cocoa Bindings to manage the values of the controls in your window, and observe the changes as they happen.

FIGURE 10-18

You complete the following Try It Out in two steps:

➤ First, you build the new user interface, including binding these controls with Cocoa Bindings.

➤ Then, you complete the custom code required to run the window modally and interpret the values.

TRY IT OUT   Creating a Preference Window Interface

1. Open Slide Master's `MainMenu` nib file in Interface Builder.

2. Add an `orderFrontPreferencePanel:` action to the First Responder.

3. Connect your menu bar's Slide Master ⇨ Preferences menu item to the First Responder's `orderFrontPreferencePanel:` action.

4. Save the `MainMenu` nib file.

5. Create a new empty Cocoa nib file. A new nib window appears, containing only the File's Owner, First Responder, and Application instances.

6. Build the window interface shown in Figure 10-19. The rectangular control is called a *color well*. You can find it in the Library under the name `NSColorWell`.

7. Select the OK push button and set its tag to 1 using the Attributes Inspector.

8. In the color well's Bindings settings, bind Value to the Shared User Defaults Controller and change the Model Key Path to `backgroundColor`. Also select `NSKeyedUnarchiveWithData` from the Value Transformer combo box. The Bindings settings should now look similar to Figure 10-20. Also note that a Shared Defaults controller instance has appeared in the nib's Instances tab.

FIGURE 10-19

9. Save your nib file with the name `PreferencesWindow`, and save it to your Slide Master project's `English.lproj` directory. Interface Builder asks if you want to add the nib file to your Slide Master project. Click the Add button to add the `PreferencesWindow.xib` nib file to Slide Master.

10. In Xcode, create files for an `NSWindowController` subclass named `PreferencesWindowController`.

11. Open `PreferencesWindowController.h` and replace its contents with the following code:

FIGURE 10-20

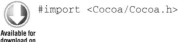

```
#import <Cocoa/Cocoa.h>

@interface PreferencesWindowController : NSWindowController
{
}

- (IBAction)handleOKCancel:(id)sender;

@end
```

code snippet MacOSXProg ch10/Slide Master 7/PreferencesWindowController.h

12. Back in Interface Builder, change File Owner's Class to `PreferencesWindowController` in the Identity Inspector.

13. Connect the OK and Cancel buttons to the File's Owner's `handleOKCancel:` action. If you have trouble seeing the `handleOKCancel:` action in Interface Builder, try manually reloading your nib's class files using File ➪ Reload All Class Files.

14. Connect the File's Owner's `window` instance variable to your preference window.

15. Save your nib file again.

How It Works

Cocoa Bindings provides an `NSController` subclass, called `NSUserDefaultsController`, for working with preferences. You can bind controls to this controller simply by choosing the Shared User Defaults option from the Bind To pop-up menu. Interface Builder will create the defaults controller instance for you.

Recall from Chapter 5 that user defaults are stored as property list values: `NSString`, `NSDate`, `NSData`, `NSNumber`, and so on. Color values are defined by `NSColor` objects, which cannot be written to property lists or used directly with Cocoa Bindings. To deal with this problem, Cocoa Bindings lets you supply a value transformer used when moving values into and out of controls. You are already familiar with transforming model objects into data objects using value transformers, because Core Data has a similar restriction.

Your `PreferencesWindowController` subclass is primarily concerned with opening and closing the window, and running the window in a modal event loop. Because your preference controls are bound through Cocoa Bindings, you don't need to create outlets or actions to track them. `PreferencesWindowController` provides a `handleOKCancel:` method for responding to the OK and Cancel buttons. This method distinguishes between the OK and Cancel buttons by checking the sender's tag value. The OK button's tag was set to 1, which is the same value defined by the `NSOKButton` constant you saw when working with the Open panel.

In the next Try It Out example, you write the code that loads and drives the preferences window.

Running the Modal Preferences Window

1. In Xcode, open `PreferencesWindowController.h` and add the `sharedInstance` and `runModal` methods shown here:

```
@interface PreferencesWindowController : NSWindowController
{
}

- (IBAction)handleOKCancel:(id)sender;

+ (PreferencesWindowController*)sharedInstance;
- (void)runModal;

@end
```

code snippet MacOSXProg ch10/Slide Master 7/PreferencesWindowController.h

2. Switch to `PreferencesWindowController.m` and replace its contents as follows:

```
#import "PreferencesWindowController.h"

@implementation PreferencesWindowController

+ (PreferencesWindowController*)sharedInstance
{
    static PreferencesWindowController *sharedInstance = nil;

    if (sharedInstance == nil) {
        sharedInstance = [[PreferencesWindowController alloc]
            initWithWindowNibName:@"PreferencesWindow"];
    }

    return sharedInstance;
}

- (void)runModal
{
    NSUserDefaultsController *defaultsController = [NSUserDefaultsController
        sharedUserDefaultsController];

    // do not apply changes immediately; instead wait for the OK button.
    [defaultsController setAppliesImmediately:NO];

    // run the modal window
    int code = [NSApp runModalForWindow:[self window]];

    if (code == NSOKButton) {
        // save the defaults changes
        [defaultsController save:nil];
    } else {
        // discard the defaults changes
        [defaultsController revert:nil];
    }

    [self close];
}

- (IBAction)handleOKCancel:(id)sender
{
    // stop the modal loop and return the button's tag as the stop code
    [NSApp stopModalWithCode:[sender tag]];
}

@end
```

code snippet MacOSXProg ch10/Slide Master 7/PreferencesWindowController.m

3. Open `ApplicationDelegate.m` and add the following `#import` directive near the top of the file:

```
#import "PreferencesWindowController.h"
```

4. Add the following methods to the `ApplicationDelegate` implementation:

```
- (void)applicationWillFinishLaunching:(NSNotification *)notification
{
    NSColor *color = [NSColor whiteColor];
    NSData *colorData = [NSKeyedArchiver archivedDataWithRootObject:color];
    NSDictionary *defaults = [NSDictionary dictionaryWithObjectsAndKeys:
        colorData,  @"backgroundColor",
        nil];

    [[NSUserDefaults standardUserDefaults] registerDefaults:defaults];
}

- (void)orderFrontPreferencePanel:(id)sender
{
    [[PreferencesWindowController sharedInstance] runModal];
}
```

code snippet MacOSXProg ch10/Slide Master 7/ApplicationDelegate.m

5. Open `SlideImageView.h` and add an `mBackgroundColor` instance variable and a `setBack-groundColor:` method. The following code shows the entire `SlideImageView` interface:

```
@interface SlideImageView : NSImageView
{
    NSString *mURLKeyPath;
    NSColor *mBackgroundColor;
}

@property (nonatomic, retain) NSString *URLKeyPath;
@property (nonatomic, retain) NSColor *backgroundColor;

@end
```

code snippet MacOSXProg ch10/Slide Master 7/SlideImageView.h

6. Switch to `SlideImageView.m` and add mBackgroundColor to your `dealloc` method:

```
- (void)dealloc
{
    [mURLKeyPath release];
    [mBackgroundColor release];

    [super dealloc];
}
```

code snippet MacOSXProg ch10/Slide Master 7/SlideImageView.m

7. Add a `@synthesize` statement for your new property, define a setter method that calls `setNeedsDisplay`, and use the property in `SlideImageView`'s `drawRect:` method:

```objectivec
@synthesize backgroundColor = mBackgroundColor;

- (void)setBackgroundColor:(NSColor *)color
{
    if (mBackgroundColor != color) {
        [mBackgroundColor release];
        mBackgroundColor = [color retain];

        [self setNeedsDisplay];
    }
}

- (void)drawRect:(NSRect)rect
{
    NSColor* backgroundColor = self.backgroundColor;
    if (backgroundColor) {
        [backgroundColor set];
        NSRectFill(rect);
    }

    [super drawRect:rect];
}
```

code snippet MacOSXProg ch10/Slide Master 7/SlideImageView.m

8. Open `SlideShowWindowController.m`, add the following `initWithWindowNibName:` and `dealloc` methods, and redefine the `windowDidLoad` method:

```objectivec
- (id)initWithWindowNibName:(NSString *)windowNibName
{
    self = [super initWithWindowNibName:windowNibName];
    if (self) {
        NSUserDefaults *userDefaults = [NSUserDefaults standardUserDefaults];

        // watch for backgroundColor changes
        [userDefaults addObserver:self
                    forKeyPath:@"backgroundColor"
                        options:NSKeyValueObservingOptionNew
                        context:NULL];
    }

    return self;
}

- (void)dealloc
{
    NSUserDefaults *userDefaults = [NSUserDefaults standardUserDefaults];

    // remove backgroundColor observer
    [userDefaults removeObserver:self forKeyPath:@"backgroundColor"];

    [super dealloc];
}
```

```
- (void)windowDidLoad
{
    [super windowDidLoad];

    NSSortDescriptor *descriptor = [NSSortDescriptor sortDescriptorWithKey:
        @"creationDate" ascending:YES];
    NSArray *descriptors = [NSArray arrayWithObject:descriptor];

    [mSlidesController setSortDescriptors:descriptors];

    mSlideImageView.URLKeyPath = @"selection.imageURL";

    // set the initial background color
    NSUserDefaults *userDefaults = [NSUserDefaults standardUserDefaults];
    NSData *data = [userDefaults objectForKey:@"backgroundColor"];
    NSColor *color = [NSKeyedUnarchiver unarchiveObjectWithData:data];
    mSlideImageView.backgroundColor = color;
}
```

code snippet MacOSXProg ch10/Slide Master 7/SlideShowWindowController.m

9. Add the following method to the end of the `SlideShowWindowController` implementation:

Available for
download on
Wrox.com

```
#pragma mark Observing

- (void)observeValueForKeyPath:(NSString *)keyPath ofObject:(id)object change:
        (NSDictionary *)change context:(void *)context
{
    NSData *data = [change objectForKey:NSKeyValueChangeNewKey];
    NSColor *color = [NSKeyedUnarchiver unarchiveObjectWithData:data];

    [mSlideImageView setBackgroundColor:color];
}
```

code snippet MacOSXProg ch10/Slide Master 7/SlideShowWindowController.m

10. Save your changes to Slide Manager's source files.

11. Build and run Slide Master. You can bring up the preference panel by choosing Slide Master ⇨ Preferences. When you change the color and click the OK button, all the open slideshow documents update themselves.

How It Works

`PreferencesWindowController` manages Slide Manager's preference panel. This class is a *singleton* class, meaning there is always one instance of this class available at any time. The `Preferences WindowController` class guarantees this through its `sharedInstance` factory method. The first time `sharedInstance` is called it will allocate and initialize the window controller; subsequent calls to `PreferencesWindowController` will simply return this first instance. `ApplicationDelegate` should not release the instance returned by `sharedInstance` because it didn't explicitly allocate or copy the object itself.

The shared `PreferencesWindowController` instance runs its window as a modal dialog box by sending a `runModalForWindow:` message to an object named `NSApp`. `NSApp` is the shared instance of the `NSApplication` singleton class; `NSApp` is initialized by AppKit automatically when your program starts. You use the `NSApp` object to access certain kinds of AppKit features that are provided through the `NSApplication` interface. Running modal dialog and sheets are examples of `NSApplication` features. You can read the documentation for `NSApplication` to get a complete list of features available through the `NSApp` object.

`NSApplication`'s `runModalForWindow:` method will make the supplied window visible, and run that window in its own modal session. This means only that window will receive user events; other actions, such as clicking on other windows, are not permitted. The `runModalForWindow:` method will not return until something causes the modal session to stop. In this example, your OK and Cancel button handler, `handleOKCancel:`, ends the modal session by calling `NSApp`'s `stopModalWithCode:` method. You can also end a modal session by calling `NSApp`'s `stopModal` method.

The value passed into `stopModalWithCode:` will be returned by `runModalForWindow:`, providing a simple way to pass state from your OK and Cancel button handlers back to the code that started the modal session. `PreferencesWindowController` uses the predefined `NSOKButton` and `NSCancelButton` constants for this purpose, but you can use whatever values you want. You have the choice of completing the requested task either in your OK button action method, or later after `runModalForWindow:` concludes. Pick whichever technique works best for you.

Your `ApplicationDelegate` object does two more things now: it registers a set of initial user defaults when Slide Master launches, and it runs the `PreferencesWindowController` dialog box when the Preferences menu item is selected. The `NSApplication` class defines two dozen or so messages it might send to its delegate object, one of which is `applicationWillFinishLaunching:`. The `ApplicationDelegate` object will receive this message early in the application's launch cycle, making it a reasonably good place to initialize your application state.

The Cocoa class for working with user preferences is `NSUserDefaults`. You acquire the instance of this singleton class using its `standardUserDefaults` class method. You can access individual default values using methods similar to `NSMutableDictionary`: `objectForKey:`, `setObject:forKey:`, and so on; you have already learned how to access these values using Cocoa Bindings. You can register a set of initial default values that `NSUserDefaults` will use when a value can't be found in the preferences file. For example, if Slide Master's preference file is missing or damaged, it will simply use `[NSColor whiteColor]` for the `backgroundColor` value.

You changed the `SlideImageView` to draw a solid background color only if one was supplied to its `setBackgroundColor:` method. Although the `SlideImageView` class could talk to `NSUserDefaults` directly to get the background color, it's better to make this class as reusable as possible. A view object such as `SlideImageView` shouldn't know anything about controller-level functionality such as user defaults. Also, when someone calls `SlideImageView`'s `setBackgroundColor:` method, the image view will redraw itself using the `setNeedsDisplay` method.

The `SlideShowWindowController` enables the new `backgroundColor` feature in `SlideImageView`. When a window is first opened, it sets the image view's background color to the current default value. It reapplies the background color value when it notices the value has changed.

> **NOTE** *Remember that color values can't be stored in* NSUserDefaults *directly as* NSColor *objects; instead Cocoa Bindings is embedding the* NSColor *object in an* NSData *object using* NSKeyedArchiver. *When you manually read color values from* NSUserDefaults *you must decode the resulting* NSData *with* NSKeyedUnarchiver. *Similarly, when manually setting color values, you must first encode them with* NSKeyedArchiver.

SlideShowWindowController uses Cocoa Bindings' Key Value Observing protocol to note when the preferences have been updated. You listen for changes using NSObject's addObserver:forKeyPath: options:context: method. You send this message to the object you want to watch, in this case the shared NSUserDefaults object. The first argument represents the object listening for changes; in this case, the SlideShowWindowController object. The second object defines the key the observer is listening for: backgroundColor. The third argument is an options field; two common option values are NSKeyValueObservingOptionNew and NSKeyValueObservingOptionOld. These values indicate if the observing object is interested in learning about the new value, the old value, or both values.

All observer objects must implement a observeValueForPathKey:ofObject:change:context: method, which is also part of the NSKeyValueObserving protocol. This method returns information about the observed value, including its parent object and its key path, and information about the change itself. SlideShowWindowController asks the change dictionary for the new value using NSKeyValueChangeNewKey. This value is available to SlideShowWindowController because it passed NSKeyValueObservingOptionNew in as the option to addObserver:forKeyPath:options: context:. After SlideShowWindowController has the new color value, it resets the image view's background color.

You must unregister an observer object before it is destroyed; otherwise you run the risk of sending a message to a freed object, which will result in your application crashing. SlideShowWindowController registers the observer in its initWithWindowNibName: function and unregisters itself in its dealloc function.

SUMMARY

Core Data helps embody the spirit of Cocoa by freeing you from the little details of managing a file format and handling undo. Although you get a lot of functionality "for free," you are still in charge. You decide what kind of data you want to store, how that data gets stored, and how it all relates to each other.

While learning about Core Data, you also got more practice working with Cocoa Bindings. You already learned how Cocoa Bindings and properties help you avoid writing controller code — code that shuttles data from one place to another. When used with Core Data, you hooked Slide Master's document files directly to their interface without writing any busywork code.

Neither Core Data nor Cocoa Bindings prevent you from writing your own custom code if you need it. You manually inserted objects into the slideshow document, you pushed automatically generated values into Core Data entities, and you even added a replacement `setBackgroundColor:` accessor for `SlideImageView` that requests redraw when the color changes.

There is a lot more to say about Core Data, especially as you try to model more and more complex relationships. Now you know the basics of using Core Data in a Cocoa document-based application. You can build on this experience to learn more on your own.

In this chapter you learned

➤   How to design a document data model in an object graph

➤   How to observe, change, and sort Core Data objects using Cocoa Bindings

➤   How to create your own Core Data objects and insert them into a managed object context

➤   How to manually set and get values from Core Data objects

➤   How Core Data and Cocoa Bindings interact with other Cocoa archiving technologies such as `NSKeyedArchiver`, property lists, and user defaults

In the next chapter, you learn about various scripting languages available in Mac OS X. Before proceeding, however, try the exercises that follow to test your understanding of the material covered in this chapter. You can find the solutions to these exercises in Appendix A.

EXERCISES

1.   Slide Master can display images as individual documents, as well as in a collection of slides in a slideshow. Extend Slide Master to open an image in its own document when you double-click an entry in the slideshow document's table view. Try to use `NSDocumentController` to open the requested file.

2.   Change the slideshow document to print the name of the current slide in the main slideshow window. Implement the feature by printing the name directly in the `SlideImageView`. No nib file changes should be necessary. AppKit provides some additions to Foundation's `NSString` class for drawing strings directly in a view; you may find these methods helpful.

3.   Currently Slide Master stores images by URL, which saves on disk space. If files are moved or renamed, Slide Master won't be able to find the images. You can use `NSURL`s to create bookmark data objects — `NSData` objects that hold Finder Alias information. Change Slide Master to save files as URL bookmarks.

▶ **WHAT YOU LEARNED IN THIS CHAPTER**

Entity	a class of objects known to Core Data, conceptually similar to an Objective-C class
Attributes	properties of an Entity that store discrete pieces of data
Relationships	entity properties that refer to other Entities
Managed Object	an object managed by Core Data, a subclass of `NSManagedObject`
Managed Object Context	an object that holds managed objects such as those in a document, represented by `NSManagedObjectContext`
Root Object	an object in an object graph to which all other objects are directly or indirectly related. It is used to find other objects
Fetch Request	a mechanism for looking up managed objects from a managed object context, represented by `NSFetchRequest`
Sort Descriptor	a mechanism for sorting objects in an array controller, represented by `NSSortDescriptor`
Transient Attributes	core Data attributes that are stored in Entities, but not archived in a data store

PART III
Script Programming

11

Overview of Scripting Languages

WHAT YOU WILL LEARN IN THIS CHAPTER:

➤ What a scripting language is, and how it differs from languages such as Java and Objective-C

➤ The strengths and weaknesses of the following scripting languages: Bash, AppleScript, Python, Ruby, and JavaScript

➤ The basic properties of each of the scripting languages, and how each language looks

➤ Where you can learn more about the various scripting languages

With its Unix heritage, Mac OS X comes laden with little surprises that are not traditionally of the Mac but now have a home on the platform. Scripting languages are a good example. Before Mac OS X the support for scripting was limited, aside from Apple's own solution — AppleScript. Now you can run any of the scripting languages found commonly on other Unix platforms and Linux directly from your Mac and not have to sacrifice anything. There are even some advantages to using Mac OS X with these languages, such as the Scripting Bridge, which allows you to write great-looking Cocoa apps in most of the popular scripting languages.

This chapter provides an introduction to scripting in general and an overview of the most important scripting languages on Mac OS X — from the Bash Shell to Python and Ruby. Because it would be impossible to cover all scripting languages in one short chapter, a selection of the most important scripting languages has been made. Each of the languages ships with the Mac OS X system, so you can start using them straight out of the box.

WHAT IS A SCRIPT?

In Chapters 6 and 7 you learned about the C and Objective-C programming languages, which form the basis of much of the development taking place on Mac OS X today. These languages are *compiled languages*, which means they have to be converted from source code into object code, which the CPU understands, by a program called a *compiler*. When you write in compiled languages, you have to build your program before you can run it.

A *script* is a program written in an interpreted language. An *interpreted language* is one that does not get compiled before it is executed. Instead, the source code of the program is read directly, one line at a time, by a program called an *interpreter*. An interpreter is similar to a compiler, in the sense that its job is to convert source code into instructions that the computer can execute. However, there is an important difference: a compiler performs the entire conversion before the program is run, generating an executable in a form that can be directly understood by the CPU. An interpreter performs the conversion on-the-fly, reading a line of code at a time, interpreting it, and carrying out the corresponding operations before reading the next line.

Another way of looking at it is that a compiled program runs directly on the CPU, whereas a script runs inside an interpreter, which runs on the CPU. This level of indirection means that scripts generally run quite a bit slower than compiled languages, but when this performance penalty is not a concern, they can make your life a lot easier. The flexibility afforded by an interpreter can provide considerable advantages. For example, it is possible for a script to generate and execute new source code while it is running. This is not possible with a compiled program, which must be fully compiled from source code before it is run.

WHAT IS A SCRIPTING LANGUAGE?

If a script is a program run by an interpreter, it won't come as much of a surprise that a *scripting language* is the programming language that a script is written in. Scripting languages tend to be high-level languages, operating closer to the human programmer than the computer CPU. For example, where C allows you to access addresses in memory via pointer variables (see Chapter 6), scripting languages do not generally provide such low-level operations. Instead, they include extensive libraries of functions for dealing with everything from text manipulation to file handling, and even access to databases. Scripting languages are very powerful, allowing you to get the most done with as little code as possible.

Each scripting language tends to specialize in a particular application domain:

➤ AppleScript is great for scripting applications with a graphical user interface (GUI).

➤ Perl has excellent text-manipulation facilities.

➤ Python and Ruby include powerful object-oriented (OO) features to aid in structuring large programs.

➤ Bash makes it easy to leverage other commands and programs.

➤ PHP is designed for building web sites, with features for accessing databases and producing HTML.

➤ JavaScript is designed to work in web browsers and can be used to create Dashboard widgets.

Scripting languages are often referred to as *glue languages*, because they are generally used to glue together other applications and programs. For example, the Bash Shell has a relatively small built-in set of functions; its usefulness stems from an ability to easily execute all the commands that ship with a Unix system. Languages such as Perl, Ruby, and Python are often used to make different programs work together. The output of one program may be reformatted by the scripting language in such a way that it can be used as the input to another program. AppleScript is typically used to glue together programs with GUIs, perhaps taking an image file from iPhoto, applying some filters to it in Photoshop, and inserting the finished product in a Microsoft Word file.

In the rest of this chapter, you are introduced in more detail to some of these scripting languages and their application domains. You learn how they can make your life a lot easier as a programmer. Even though you won't become proficient in any of the languages by the end of the chapter, you will have a good idea of what each is about, and where you can learn more if your interest is piqued. Three of the languages — Bash, AppleScript, and JavaScript — are so important to Mac OS X that they are given special attention in Chapters 12 through 14.

BASH

Bash is the default shell that ships on Mac OS X. A *shell* is basically an interpreter that offers the user the possibility of direct interaction, in addition to being able to run scripts. If you open the Terminal application, you are presented with a command-line prompt. This prompt is generated by the Bash Shell, and any command you enter is executed by the Bash Shell.

Bash is descended from the original Unix shell: Bourne Shell. The Bourne Shell is a subset of Bash, so you can do everything in Bash that you can do in the Bourne Shell. In fact, on Mac OS X, whenever you request a Bourne Shell, you get Bash.

It cannot be stressed enough how important shell programming, and Bash in particular, is to Mac OS X. Even if you never see a command-line prompt, or run a shell script yourself, you are indirectly making use of Bash every time you start your computer. For example, the configuration process that Mac OS X follows when it is booted is completely controlled by Bash Shell scripts. If you are not convinced, take a look in the `/etc/periodic/daily` directory. Open any of the files there in a text editor such as TextEdit. You are now looking at a Bash Shell script.

Why Bash?

Unix shells are not the most glamorous of languages. They tend to be syntactically eccentric, which can throw up some challenges when you are learning to use them. They do have considerable advantages though, which make it worth your while. Shells are particularly adept at running command-line programs, and combining them in ways you would never have thought possible.

Bash provides the usual programming constructions — variables, conditional branching, loops, and functions — but one of its greatest strengths lies in allowing you to easily redirect program input and output. With very few keystrokes, you can retrieve program input data from a file or channel it from the output of another program. The latter is known as a *pipe*, because it is similar to running the data down a pipe from one program to the next. A good shell scripter can do some amazing things, such as piping the output of one Unix command to the input of a second, and the output of the second command to the input of a third, and so forth.

Shells such as Bash are also the primary means of interacting with the Unix core of Mac OS X. If you need to install a new Unix command, move some files around in the heart of the operating system, or edit the Apache Web Server configuration files — you can best do so with Bash. Finder, quite rightly, puts up barriers for average users that try to enter places in the operating system traditionally reserved for Unix power users, but Bash invites you to come in. All you need to do to get an invitation is open the Terminal application in `/Applications/Utilities` and you are presented with a Bash Shell eagerly awaiting your instructions.

> **NOTE** *Other alternatives to Bash are available on Mac OS X. In fact, originally the default shell was TCSH, but was later changed. Bash is the default shell on the popular Linux operating system, which may have been the reason it was chosen, quite apart from being a very powerful shell. Apple probably wanted to make migrating from Linux to Mac OS X as painless as possible.*

A strength of shells is that they exist on all Unix-based operating systems. They are truly platform agnostic, so if you write a shell script on Mac OS X, it should run fine on a Linux system. The only thing to be aware of is that although the shell itself may not vary much from one system to the next, the commands it is using may. For example, the Linux version of a particular command may use different options from the Mac OS X variant.

Shell languages tend not to be very advanced, in comparison to other programming languages. Variables are limited to strings, numbers, and arrays. You can't easily create data structures such as C's `struct` (see Chapter 6), and object-oriented programming (OOP) (see Chapter 7) is a very foreign concept in the world of Bash. Given these restrictions, you shouldn't try to write your next monster-sized application in Bash. Shells are great for small scripts, up to a few hundred lines, but if you need to write a more extensive program, you are better off going for a more powerful scripting language such as Python or Ruby.

TRY IT OUT A Bash Example

Chapter 12 is dedicated to Bash scripting, so only a simple example is provided here to give you a feel for what Bash, and other shells, are about. The following script creates a disk image containing a file or directory of the user's choice:

```
#!/bin/sh

# Set variables with input arguments
VOLUME_NAME=$1
DISK_IMAGE_NAME=$1
DMG_SIZE=$2
DIR_PATH=$3

# Functions
```

```
CreateImage() {
  echo Creating a volume
  /usr/bin/hdiutil create -quiet "$DISK_IMAGE_NAME.dmg" -fs HFS+ \
      -volname "$VOLUME_NAME" -megabytes $DMG_SIZE
}

AttachVolume() {
  echo Attaching volume
  local TMPFILE=`mktemp -t "hdiutil_output"`
  /usr/bin/hdiutil attach "$DISK_IMAGE_NAME.dmg" > "$TMPFILE"
  DEV_FILE=`cat "$TMPFILE" | grep 'Apple_partition_scheme' | \
    awk -F' ' '{ print $1 }'`
}

DetachVolume() {
  echo Detaching volume
  hdiutil detach -quiet "$1"
}

# Main part of script
CreateImage
AttachVolume
cp -r "$DIR_PATH" "/Volumes/$VOLUME_NAME"
DetachVolume $DEV_FILE

echo Finished
```

code snippet MacOSXProg ch11/creatediskimage.sh

How It Works

The script begins by assigning a number of variables to arguments passed on the command line when the script was started.

```
VOLUME_NAME=$1
DISK_IMAGE_NAME=$1
DMG_SIZE=$2
DIR_PATH=$3
```

The name of the volume, and the name of the disk image itself, which are stored in the variables VOLUME_NAME and DISK_IMAGE_NAME, respectively, are both set to the first argument passed to the script. Arguments are stored in the variables $1, $2, and so forth, in the order passed to the script. The size of the disk image is passed as the second argument and is assigned to the variable DMG_SIZE. The DIR_PATH variable is assigned to the path of the directory or file that will be stored in the disk image.

A number of functions are defined next, beginning with a function that creates a new, empty disk image:

```
CreateImage() {
  echo Creating a volume
  /usr/bin/hdiutil create -quiet "$DISK_IMAGE_NAME.dmg" -fs HFS+ \
      -volname "$VOLUME_NAME" -megabytes $DMG_SIZE
}
```

This function first prints a message using the echo command to indicate that the image is being created. The hdiutil command is then used to create the disk image. It is passed a number of options, including

-fs HFS+, which instructs the command to create an HFS+ file system in the disk image. The -megabytes $DMG_SIZE option gives the size of the disk image. The variable DMG_SIZE is used for this purpose.

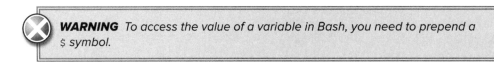

> **WARNING** *To access the value of a variable in Bash, you need to prepend a $ symbol.*

The name of the disk image is given as $DISK_IMAGE_NAME.dmg. DISK_IMAGE_NAME is a variable, and its value, $DISK_IMAGE_NAME, is a string. In Bash you can combine variable values and literal strings, such as .dmg, by simply using them together. The script replaces $DISK_IMAGE_NAME with its string value before invoking the hdiutil command. The hdiutil command gets passed a filename comprising the value of DISK_IMAGE_NAME, and the extension .dmg. hdiutil never sees the DISK_IMAGE_NAME variable itself.

After the image has been created, it needs to be attached as a volume, so that files can be transferred to it. The function AttachVolume achieves this:

```
AttachVolume() {
   echo Attaching volume
   local TMPFILE=`mktemp -t "hdiutil_output"`
   /usr/bin/hdiutil attach "$DISK_IMAGE_NAME.dmg" > "$TMPFILE"
   DEV_FILE=`cat "$TMPFILE" | grep 'Apple_partition_scheme' | \
     awk -F' ' '{ print $1 }'`
}
```

Again, a message is echoed to the script output indicating what is about to take place, purely for the benefit of the user. A local variable, TMPFILE, is declared next; a local variable is not visible outside the function in which it is declared. The TMPFILE variable is assigned to the output of the command on the right side, which is contained between backticks. When a command is contained between backticks, Bash evaluates it and replaces the whole command with its output. In this case, the command mktemp creates a temporary file, printing the path to the new file as output. This path replaces the contents of the backticks, and TMPFILE is assigned to the path.

The hdiutil command is again invoked, this time to attach the existing disk image, with the name $DISK_IMAGE_NAME.dmg. The output of the hdiutil command is piped to the file at the path stored in the TMPFILE variable. The > is used to redirect the output of a command to a file. The content of the file is replaced by the output of the command; if the file does not exist, a new file is created to contain the data.

The last line of the function defines a new variable called DEV_FILE, which is the device file associated with the attached volume. This file is needed later in the script to detach the volume again. To get the path of the device, the output of the hdiutil command is processed. To understand how this works, you really need to see the output of hdiutil. Here is how it looks:

```
Initializing...
Attaching...
Finishing...
Finishing...
/dev/disk2              Apple_partition_scheme
/dev/disk2s1            Apple_partition_map
/dev/disk2s2            Apple_HFS                   /Volumes/
   SomeVolumeName
```

The path of the device that is needed is the first one that appears, /dev/disk2, in the line with Apple_partition_scheme.

To extract this path, a number of different commands are chained together. The command used to get the path is enclosed between backticks and amounts to the following:

```
cat "$TMPFILE" | grep 'Apple_partition_scheme' | awk -F' '
    { print $1 }'
```

It begins with the cat command, which simply reads the contents of the temporary file and writes it to output. The output of cat is piped to another command: grep. The symbol | is used when you want to pipe the output of one command to another, just as > pipes output to a file. The grep command receives the output of cat as input and extracts all lines that contain the string Apple_partition_scheme. These lines are written to the output of grep, which is piped to the command awk. awk prints the first thing on the line, the /dev/disk2 path. This path is the output of the whole command, and is assigned to the DEV_FILE variable.

The DetachVolume function is considerably simpler, using the hdiutil command to detach the volume stored in the path passed to it as an argument:

```
DetachVolume() {
  echo Detaching volume
  hdiutil detach -quiet "$1"
}
```

Arguments are treated in functions the same as for a whole script. The first argument is stored in the variable $1 inside the script; the second in $2; and so forth.

The end of the script calls the functions in the appropriate order and copies the file or directory to the volume while it is attached:

```
CreateImage
AttachVolume
cp -r "$DIR_PATH" "/Volumes/$VOLUME_NAME"
DetachVolume $DEV_FILE
echo Finished
```

To pass the argument to the function DetachVolume, it is simply listed after the function name. Function arguments are separated by whitespace. The script ends by printing the string Finished.

This example demonstrates many aspects of Bash Shell programming. You have seen that:

➤ Bash includes the usual suspects, such as functions and variables.

➤ Shells make it particularly easy to redirect data streams between different commands with pipes.

➤ The power of a shell derives from the Unix commands it invokes. The shell itself is quite primitive in programming terms.

More Information

Chapter 12 covers Bash in detail, so if you are interested in learning to use it, that is the best place to start.

Aside from Chapter 12, the man page for Bash is a good resource for documentation. Open the Terminal utility and enter this command:

```
man bash
```

Use the spacebar to move down the page, and press **q** to quit the man program.

Countless sites on the Internet cover Bash in intimate detail. A quick Google search will generate the hits you need to begin exploring Bash. Here are two sites to get you started:

➤   *The Ooblick Guide to Bourne Shell Programming* is an easy-to-read quick introduction to shells (http://www.ooblick.com/text/sh/).

➤   The Free Software Foundation, which is responsible for developing Bash in the first place, includes the Bash Reference Manual on its web site (http://www.gnu.org/software/bash/manual/bashref.html).

APPLESCRIPT

Many different scripting solutions are presented in this chapter, but only one has been designed specifically to script applications with graphical interfaces: AppleScript. AppleScript was created by Apple in the old days of Mac OS, but is now well supported on Mac OS X, and has even been extended to allow fully functional applications to be developed via a software bridge.

Why AppleScript?

AppleScript is not only different to other scripting languages because its main purpose is scripting applications with a graphical interface, but it also looks a lot different because it is targeted not at programmers, but ordinary Mac users. The language reads to a large extent like English. This is a boon for the non-programmer, but some experienced programmers may be put off by the verbosity of the language, and the degree of redundancy; you can often choose between several different constructions to perform a single task in AppleScript.

In Mac OS X v10.6, AppleScript can also be used to develop complete applications in Xcode via a software bridge (see Chapter 13). Using the bridge, you can add a Cocoa user interface to your scripts. It makes it easy for non-programmers to develop Mac OS X applications that are indistinguishable from those written natively in Objective-C.

 NOTE *Originally, AppleScript was the only language on the Mac that could be used to script applications with a graphical interface. In Mac OS X 10.5, a new technology — the Scripting Bridge — was introduced, giving the same access to other scripting languages. In Mac OS X v10.6, you can script applications using any popular scripting language, not just AppleScript.*

If you want to script your Mac OS X applications, AppleScript is well suited, but for other tasks it may not be the best choice. To begin with, AppleScript is not a cross-platform solution; it runs only on Mac OS X, so don't expect your AppleScripts to run on your Linux or Windows computer. AppleScript is also not a very good solution for scripting command-line tools, and text processing is better handled with languages such as Python and Ruby. This doesn't mean AppleScript has no part to play when you are faced with such tasks, because the best solution may involve some combination of AppleScript for handling applications and another scripting language for processing text and data.

TRY IT OUT An AppleScript Example

AppleScript and its Cocoa bridge are covered in more detail in Chapter 13, so this section is kept quite brief. To give you an idea of how AppleScript looks, here is a simple script that creates and sends e-mails. The e-mails are personalized with the name of the person to whom they are sent. The user enters e-mail addresses and names via dialog boxes:

Available for
download on
Wrox.com

```applescript
set email_text to "Hello <name>. How are you?"
repeat
    (* Get name and address from user *)
    activate
    display dialog "Enter an email address:" & return ¬
        default answer "" as string buttons {"Cancel", "Continue"} ¬
        default button 2
    copy the result as list to {email_address, button_pressed}

    (* If user wants to proceed, get the name of the person in the email *)
    if the button_pressed is "Continue" then
        display dialog "Enter name:" & return ¬
            default answer "" as string buttons {"Continue"} default button 1
        copy the result as list to {persons_name, button_pressed}
        (* Create personalized email text *)
        set name_offset to offset of "<name>" in email_text
        set end_offset to name_offset + (length of "<name>")
        set text_length to length of email_text
        set email_beginning to get text 1 thru (name_offset - 1) of email_text
        set email_end to get text end_offset thru text_length of email_text
        set personalized_text to email_beginning & persons_name & email_end

        (* Compose and send email *)
        tell application "Mail"
            set new_message to make new outgoing message ¬
                at end of outgoing messages
            tell new_message
                set subject to "Hi!"
                set content to personalized_text as string
                set visible to false
                make new recipient at end of to recipients ¬
                    with properties {name:persons_name, address:email_address}
            end tell
            send new_message
        end tell
    else
        (* If user pressed Cancel button, exit *)
        exit repeat
    end if

end repeat
```

code snippet MacOSXProg ch11/sendemail.scpt

How It Works

This script begins by setting a variable called `email_text` to a string that contains the content of all the e-mails to be sent:

```
set email_text to "Hello <name>. How are you?"
```

The string contains a message, with a placeholder used to represent the name of the recipient. There is nothing special about the placeholder; in this case the text `<name>` has been used, but any unique string is fine. Later in the script, the `<name>` placeholder is sought in the e-mail text and gets replaced by the actual name of a recipient.

Most of the script is embedded in a loop, which begins with the keyword `repeat`, and ends with `end repeat`. This loop is similar to a `while` loop in C; it continues forever, unless an `exit repeat` statement is encountered.

The first block of code inside the `repeat` prompts the user to enter an e-mail address by displaying a dialog box:

```
(* Get name and address from user *)
activate
display dialog "Enter an email address:" & return ¬
    default answer "" as string buttons {"Cancel", "Continue"} ¬
    default button 2
copy the result as list to {email_address, button_pressed}
```

A comment appears first, which is ignored by the AppleScript interpreter, followed by the statement `activate`. This makes the script the foremost application. After `activate`, the `display dialog` command is used to display a dialog with the text `Enter an email address:`. The `default answer` `""` as `string` ensures that a text field will be included in the dialog for the user to enter the address. The text field is initialized with an empty string. The rest of the `display dialog` command gives a list of buttons that should appear and indicates which button should be the default.

The following line gets the result of the dialog, which is a list containing the e-mail address entered and the name of the button pressed. A *list* is a built-in type, similar to an array in other languages, which contains an ordered set of entries. The entries are assigned in this case to the variables `email_address` and `button_pressed`.

The next part of the script checks whether the user pressed the Continue button, and, if so, proceeds to request that the name of the e-mail recipient be entered:

```
(* If user wants to proceed, get the name of the person in the email *)
if the button_pressed is "Continue" then
    display dialog "Enter name:" & return ¬
        default answer "" as string buttons {"Continue"} default button 1
    copy the result as list to {persons_name, button_pressed}
```

If the user pressed Cancel in the e-mail address dialog, the `else` branch further down is executed, and the command `exit repeat` causes the `repeat` loop, and thereby the script, to terminate.

With the name and e-mail address in hand, the script proceeds to create the text that will become the content of the e-mail. The placeholder `<name>` must be replaced with the actual name obtained from the script user:

```
(* Create personalized email text *)
set name_offset to offset of "<name>" in email_text
set end_offset to name_offset + (length of "<name>")
set text_length to length of email_text
set email_beginning to get text 1 thru (name_offset - 1) of email_text
set email_end to get text end_offset thru text_length of email_text
set personalized_text to email_beginning & persons_name & email_end
```

The first non-comment line locates the <name> substring, using the command offset, which returns the index of the first character of the placeholder in the email_text string. The index of the last character of <name> is then determined by adding the length property of the placeholder string to the variable name_offset. The following lines split the email_text variable into two variables: the first, email_beginning, is the text preceding the placeholder and the second, email_end, is the text that follows the placeholder. Last, a new variable, personalized_text, is created for the e-mail content, which comprises the concatenation of email_beginning, persons_name and email_end. The & operator concatenates (joins) strings together.

With the content prepared, all that is left is to send the e-mail. The application Mail is used for this:

```
(* Compose and send email *)
tell application "Mail"
    set new_message to make new outgoing message ¬
        at end of outgoing messages
    tell new_message
        set subject to "Hi!"
        set content to personalized_text as string
        set visible to false
        make new recipient at end of to recipients ¬
            with properties {name:persons_name, address:email_address}
    end tell
    send new_message
end tell
```

A tell/end tell block allows you to direct a series of commands to a particular variable, in this case the application Mail. The first line in the tell block creates a variable called new_message, and sets it to a new outgoing message supplied by the Mail application. make new outgoing message instructs Mail to create a new message, and at end of outgoing messages instructs it to append the message to the list of all outgoing messages.

Another tell block is then formed to set properties of the new_message variable. The properties include the subject and content of the e-mail. The last command in the block creates a new recipient, appending it to the list of all recipients of the message, and sets the recipient properties with the name and e-mail address obtained from the script user.

NOTE *Setting the properties of the recipient has been achieved using the* with properties *command, rather than the* tell *block used to set properties of the* new_message *variable. Either approach is legitimate in AppleScript.*

After the `new_message` variable has been configured, the e-mail is sent using the `send` command of the `Mail` application. If all goes well, an e-mail should be sent to the e-mail address entered by the user, with the recipient's name replacing the placeholder in the e-mail content.

What you have seen in this example is that AppleScript:

➤   Is a verbose English-like language

➤   Makes it easy to carry out commands with applications such as Mail

➤   Allows you to interact with the user via a graphical interface

➤   Is not that adept at string manipulation

➤   Usually includes several ways to achieve any one task

More Information

Chapter 13 covers AppleScript in more detail and deals with building applications with the Cocoa bridge. This chapter is a good place to start if you are interested in learning more about AppleScript.

Your hard disk also includes a lot of reference material on AppleScript, including the documentation pages in Xcode and example scripts in the folder `/Library/Scripts`.

PYTHON

Python is an object-oriented scripting language designed by the Dutchman Guido van Rossum in the early 1990s. It competes to some extent with Ruby, which is covered in the next major section of the chapter. Python and Ruby are both powerful languages, used in a wide variety of situations, from simple text processing to web programming, from GUI development to bioinformatics.

Python is one of the most elegant and simple languages there is, without sacrificing anything in the way of power. The best way to convey the Python ethos is to reproduce some parts of *The Zen of Python*, which is a series of statements about Python written by Tim Peters:

➤   Beautiful is better than ugly.

➤   Explicit is better than implicit.

➤   Simple is better than complex.

➤   Readability counts.

➤   There should be one — and preferably only one — obvious way to do it.

You can read the full list at the Python web site (`http://www.python.org/doc/humor/#the-zen-of-python`) or by entering the following commands in a terminal window:

```
sample$ python
Python 2.6.1 (r261:67515, Jul  7 2009, 23:51:51)
[GCC 4.2.1 (Apple Inc. build 5646)] on darwin
Type "help", "copyright", "credits" or "license" for more information.
 >>> import this
```

To summarize The Zen of Python, Python aims to make things as simple as possible, yet still provide all the power you need.

Why Python?

Python provides very powerful programming constructs, such as object-orientation (OO), in a very simple syntax. OO features become particularly important as your programs grow in size and need to be structured. If you are writing a 100-line script, Bash may be fine, but if you want to write a web content management system, Python fits the bill. It competes with compiled languages such as C++ and Java in fields not generally associated with scripting, and more than holds its own.

> **NOTE** One of the most well-known companies for its use of Python is Google. Google uses Python for much of its internal scripting, and also as the basis for services such as Google App Engine. Google even employs the creator of Python, Guido van Rossum.

If you have read Chapter 7 on Objective-C, you understand some of the advantages of object-oriented programming (OOP). Python provides all those advantages in a scripting language. You can order your programs into classes, which contain data and methods, and one class can derive from another, inheriting all its data and methods.

As with Objective-C, Python is a *dynamically typed* language, which means you do not need to explicitly state the class of the objects in your scripts. However, Python is *strongly typed*, which means that you cannot do something with an object that is not allowed by its class. If you try to do something illegal with an object, an exception will be raised, and your script will exit (unless you catch the exception). With Python you get the ease of programming without explicitly declaring object classes, and the assurance that if you use an object incorrectly, you will find out as soon as your script is run.

Python provides powerful built-in types, such as dynamic arrays and dictionaries, much as those provided by the Cocoa Foundation framework for Objective-C. Python also includes an extensive library, with support for strings, regular expressions, mathematics, interacting with the operating system, running subprocesses, threading, networking, and much more. If it isn't in the Python Library, it is probably available as an extension; anyone can write modules that extend the functionality of Python.

One problem often associated with scripting languages is performance. For many applications, this is not a great concern, but in certain performance-critical cases, it is. Python alleviates this problem to a large extent because modules can be written in C. In fact, Python is even used in scientific applications, which traditionally have high performance demands. This is possible because those (usually small) parts of a program that consume most of the CPU time can be rewritten in C, or re-implemented to make use of existing modules written in C.

Python ships with every copy of Mac OS X and can be found in the framework `/System/Library/Frameworks/Python.framework`. It also runs on platforms such as Windows and Linux, and if you are careful, your scripts can be made to run on any platform without modification.

Mac OS X ships with a few Python packages that are not available on any other platform. First, there are a set of bindings for the CoreGraphics framework. These bindings allow you to access the Quartz graphics layer in your Python scripts. For example, you could use a Python script to generate PDF files or convert images from JPEG format to PNG. Basically, anything you can do with CoreGraphics, you can do with the Python bindings.

Another framework for Python developers on the Mac is PyObjC, which allows you to use Python to program with the Cocoa frameworks. You can write fully functional Cocoa programs in Python, which are indistinguishable from those written in Objective-C. In some ways, it is even easier to program Cocoa in Python than it is in Objective-C. For example, Python has powerful data containers built into the language, which can make scripts more concise. This, and other differences, can make Python scripts considerably shorter than the equivalent Objective-C program.

TRY IT OUT   **A Python Example**

Two of Python's strengths are its OO features and text handling. The following script demonstrates these aspects by moving through all the files and directories descended from a given root directory and counting the words in those files that have a particular extension. It not only counts all whitespace-separated words, but also produces a second count with XML tags removed. You could thus use this script to scan your web site directories, producing a word count with HTML tags removed.

> **NOTE** *XML, the eXtensible Markup Language, is a general language for defining how data is structured. It looks similar to HTML, but is more general; in fact, there is a variant of HTML called XHTML that is defined in XML.*

Available for
download on
Wrox.com

```python
#!/usr/bin/env python

#-----------------------------------------
# Counts words after removing HTML/XML tags
#-----------------------------------------
import re, string, sys, os

#---------------
# Classes
#---------------
class WordCounter:

    """
    Counts all whitespace separated words in a string.
    """

    def _reduceString(self, str):
        "Removes anything that should not be counted. Here it does
        nothing."
        return str

    def countWords(self, str):
        "Counts all words in a string"
        str = self._reduceString(str)
        return len( string.split(str) )
```

```python
class TagRemovingWordCounter (WordCounter):

    """
    Counts all whitespace separated words, after removing XML
    tags.
    """

    def __init__(self):
        self.tagRegEx = re.compile(r'\<\/?.+?\>')

    def _reduceString(self, str):
        # substitute space for XML tag
        str = self.tagRegEx.sub( ' ', str )
        return str

#----------------
# Functions
#----------------
def CountWords( wordCounter, fileExt, rootDir ):

    """
    Count words with the WordCounter passed in, for a given root directory
    and file extension. All files with the extension passed, that reside
    in the root directory, or any subdirectory, are scanned.
    """

    fileNameRegEx = re.compile( r'.*\.' + fileExt )
    wordCount = 0
    for currentDir, subDirs, files in os.walk(rootDir):
        for fname in files:
            if not fileNameRegEx.match(fname): continue
            filePath = os.path.join(currentDir, fname)
            f = file(filePath)
            fileContentsString = f.read()
            f.close()
            wordCount = wordCount + \

            wordCounter.countWords
            (fileContentsString)
    return wordCount

def Usage():

    "Return a string with the usage of the script"

    return "Usage: wc.py file_extension root_directory"

#----------------
# Main program
#----------------
def Main():

    """
    The script takes two arguments: a file extension, and a
```

```
        root directory path. All files with the extension in the root
        directory and subdirectories, are processed. The number of
        words in all the processed files are summed and printed. The
        number of words excluding XML-like tags are also printed.
    """

    # Check that two arguments have been passed to the script
    if len( sys.argv ) != 3:
        print Usage()
        sys.exit()

    # Calculate the word count with tags
    wordCounter = WordCounter()
    numWords = CountWords( wordCounter, sys.argv[1], sys.argv[2] )
    print "%-60s %6d" % ("total word count", numWords)

    # Calculate the word count without tags
    wordCounter = TagRemovingWordCounter()
    numWords = CountWords( wordCounter, sys.argv[1], sys.argv[2] )
    print "%-60s %6d" % ("word count without tags", numWords)

if ( __name__ == "__main__" ): Main()
```

code snippet MacOSXProg ch11/wc.py

How It Works

The script begins with a shebang, just like a Bash script:

```
#!/usr/bin/env python
```

A shebang is a line that tells the shell charged with launching a script which program should be used to run it. In this case, the shebang indicates that the script should be run by the `python` interpreter. A full path to the interpreter has not been provided, although that is also possible; instead, the `/usr/bin/env` command has been used, which searches for the `python` program and returns its path for you to the shell. This makes your script more portable because you don't have to keep changing the shebang every time the `python` interpreter is relocated.

A comment follows, describing briefly what the script is for.

```
#----------------------------------------
# Counts words after removing HTML/XML tags
#----------------------------------------
```

Comments in Python are indicated by a # symbol; anything on the line following the # is ignored by the interpreter.

Next, some modules are imported:

```
import re, string, sys, os
```

Python has many different modules in its library, and many more are available from third parties. To use the functions and classes in a module, you first must import it so that the interpreter knows that it must be loaded. In this case, the modules imported are `re`, for regular expressions; `string`, for string handling; `sys`, for aspects related to the environment the script is running in; and `os`, for interacting with the operating system in a platform-independent manner.

The script continues by defining a number of classes, the first of which looks like this:

```
class WordCounter:

    """
    Counts all whitespace separated words in a string.
    """

    def _reduceString(self, str):
        "Removes anything that should not be counted. Here it does
            nothing."
        return str

    def countWords(self, str):
        "Counts all words in a string"
        str = self._reduceString(str)
        return len( string.split(str) )
```

Classes appear in all OO languages, including Objective-C (see Chapter 7). The name of the class is given after the keyword `class`; in this case, the class is called `WordCounter`.

Just under the class name is an optional comment, which is used only for documentation purposes. In this case, a multiline comment has been used; Python uses `"""` to delineate the beginning and end of multiline comments. Documentation comments can be used with any class or function and can be extracted with the program `pydoc` to generate HTML documentation. If you run the command

```
pydoc -w ./script_file
```

in the Terminal utility, an HTML file will be generated that you can open in any web browser.

After the comment, the class includes two methods: `_reduceString`, and `countWords`. A *method*, in OO terminology, is a function that belongs to a class. The keyword `def` is used in Python to delineate the beginning of a function or method. It is followed by the name, and a comma-separated list of arguments in parentheses. A colon is used to close off the line.

Unusually for OO languages, the instance to which a method belongs is passed explicitly as the first argument in the argument list. By convention, this argument is called `self`, as in Objective-C (see Chapter 7).

To invoke a method, a Java/C++-like dot syntax is used. This is demonstrated in the `countWords` method:

```
str = self._reduceString(str)
```

The `_reduceString` method is invoked for the `self` object. The variable `str` is passed to the method and then assigned to the value returned by the method.

By now you may have noticed that there are no `end class` or `end def` keywords to indicate where a class or method finishes. How does the Python interpreter know when one method finishes and the next begins? The answer has to do with whitespace. Whitespace, or to be more specific, indentation, is part of the Python language. In most other languages you indent to make code more readable, but the compiler or interpreter ignores the indentation. In Python, indentation is used to delineate the nesting of blocks of code.

Take this simple example:

```
def hello():
    print "hello"
    print "nice day isn't it"
```

This is not the same as the following:

```
def hello():
    print "hello"
print "nice day isn't it"
```

In the second example, the second `print` statement does not belong to the function `hello`, but to the enclosing code block. In C, the first example would be:

```
void hello() {
    printf("hello");
    printf("nice day isn't it");
}
```

and the second would be:

```
void hello() {
    printf("hello");
}
printf("nice day isn't it");
```

Syntax aside, the `_reduceString` method of `WordCounter` takes an argument for the parameter `str`, and returns it again. This seems pointless, but has a good reason, as will become evident as you continue reading.

 WARNING *The prepended underscore in the name `_reduceString` has no special meaning to the Python interpreter, but there is a convention among Python programmers that this means a method is protected — it should be accessed only from inside the defining class and its descendents. The reason this convention has evolved is that the Python language itself does not provide any constructions for controlling access to data or methods. All instance variables and methods of a class can be accessed wherever the class itself is accessible.*

The `countWords` method accepts a string argument. It first calls `_reduceString` with the string, before splitting the string into a list of words with the `string.split` function, and returning the length of the list:

```
return len( string.split(str) )
```

The `split` function is from the module `string`, which is prepended to the function name. The `split` function returns a list of the words that are separated by whitespace in the string passed to the function.

A list is an array-like built-in type for storing objects in order; it is like `NSMutableArray` from the Cocoa frameworks (see Chapter 7). You can get the number of elements in a list, or its length, with the `len` function. This line thus counts the number of words in the string, and returns it.

The second class, `TagRemovingWordCounter`, is used to count words after XML tags have been removed:

```
class TagRemovingWordCounter (WordCounter):

    """
    Counts all whitespace separated words, after removing XML
    tags.
    """

    def __init__(self):
        self.tagRegEx = re.compile(r'\<\/?.+?\>')

    def _reduceString(self, str):
        # substitute space for XML tag
        str = self.tagRegEx.sub( ' ', str )
        return str
```

It is a subclass of `WordCounter`; super classes are given in a comma-separated list in parentheses after the class name. After a documentation comment, the method __init__ is defined. __init__ is the initializer method, which is called when a new object is created. There can only be one initializer per class in Python.

In the example, the __init__ method sets an instance variable called `tagRegEx`. To make a new variable in Python, it is not necessary to declare it; you simply use it on the left side of an expression. The type of the variable becomes the type of the object to which it is assigned. Everything in Python is an object, and every variable has the type of the object it is assigned to. If you reassign a variable to a different object, its type will effectively change to the type of the new object.

`tagRegEx` is assigned to an object representing a regular expression. A regular expression is like a formula that can be used to match patterns in strings. You can use them to test if a string matches a particular pattern, or search a string for matching substrings. Regular expressions are not restricted to Python, but are also integral to Perl and Ruby, and are even used in shell programming via commands such as `egrep`, `sed`, and `awk`. Regular expressions are very powerful, and are covered in Chapter 12, which deals with shell programming.

The function `compile`, from the module `re`, is used to create the regular expression object in this case. The regular expression itself, which matches any XML tag, is given between single quotes. The `r` that precedes the first quote indicates that the string is a *raw string*, which means that the Python interpreter will pass it to the `compile` function exactly as it is written in the program. If a string is not a raw string, `python` will substitute characters that have special meaning.

The `_reduceString` method of `TagRemovingWordCounter` uses the regular expression object initialized in `__init__` to replace all XML tags with whitespace. Because `TagRemovingWordCounter` is a subclass of `WordCounter`, this implementation of `_reduceString` overrides the implementation in `WordCounter`. When the `countWords` method is invoked on a `TagRemovingWordCounter` object, the `countWords` implementation in `WordCounter` is executed because it is inherited by the `TagRemovingWordCounter` class. `countWords` first calls `_reduceString`, replacing all tags with whitespace, before using the `split` function to split the string into words. Effectively, only words outside of tags are counted.

The function `CountWords`, which follows the classes, traverses the directory structure, visiting each file, and scanning the ones that have the correct file extension:

```
def CountWords( wordCounter, fileExt, rootDir ):

    """
    Count words with the WordCounter passed in, for a given
        root directory and file extension. All files with the
        extension passed, that reside in the root directory, or
        any subdirectory, are scanned.
    """

    fileNameRegEx = re.compile( r'.*\.' + fileExt )
    wordCount = 0
    for currentDir, subDirs, files in os.walk(rootDir):
        for fname in files:
            if not fileNameRegEx.match(fname): continue
            filePath = os.path.join(currentDir, fname)
            f = file(filePath)
            fileContentsString = f.read()
            f.close()
            wordCount = wordCount + \

            wordCounter.countWords
            (fileContentsString)
    return wordCount
```

A `for` loop is used to iterate over all the directories descended from the root directory. The `walk` function, from the `os` module, takes a single argument, which is the path to the root directory to be traversed. It returns an iterator object, which can be used in a `for` loop.

For each directory, the iterator returns three objects: the directory path, a list of subdirectories in the directory, and a list of files in the directory. Python allows you to return as many values from a function as you see fit, unlike most other languages where only one return value is allowed.

A second loop is nested in the first, to iterate over the list of files in each directory. A regular expression, `fileNameRegEx`, is first used in an `if` statement to test if the filename has the correct file extension. If it doesn't, the `continue` statement is executed, causing the `for` loop to begin its next iteration, skipping the code between the `continue` and the end of the `for` loop.

If the filename matches the regular expression, indicating that it has the right extension, the name is combined with the directory path using the function `os.path.join`, to give the path to the file. The built-in `file` function opens the file and returns an object giving access to its contents. The contents are read with the `read` method before the file is closed with the `close` method.

The `WordCounter` object passed to the function is used to count the words in the string read in, and the variable `wordCount`, which was initialized to the integer `0` at the beginning of the method, is increased by the word count for the file. When all files have been scanned, `wordCount` is returned.

The main program in the example script can be found in the `Main` function. `Main` is not a special function in Python; you can put your main program in any function you like, or keep it at global scope. `Main` is responsible in this case for creating `WordCounter` objects and printing results for the user:

```python
# Check that two arguments have been passed to the script
if len( sys.argv ) != 3:
    print Usage()
    sys.exit()

# Calculate the word count with tags
wordCounter = WordCounter()
numWords = CountWords( wordCounter, sys.argv[1], sys.argv[2] )
print "%-60s %6d" % ("total word count", numWords)

# Calculate the word count without tags
wordCounter = TagRemovingWordCounter()
numWords = CountWords( wordCounter, sys.argv[1], sys.argv[2] )
print "%-60s %6d" % ("word count without tags", numWords)
```

It first checks that the script was passed two arguments, namely, the file extension and the path. Arguments are passed via the list variable `sys.argv`. This contains the name of the script, followed by each argument, so its length should be one more than the expected number of arguments.

The next block of code initializes a `WordCounter` object. This demonstrates how you actually create instances in Python. You give the class name, followed by the arguments to the `__init__` initializer in parentheses, much as a function call. When you create a new object, memory is allocated for the new object, and then the `__init__` method is called with the arguments passed.

The `CountWords` function is passed the `wordCounter` object, along with the first two arguments of the script. Lists such as `sys.argv` provide access to their elements via indexes. Indexes begin at 0 and are given in square braces after the list variable. The integer returned by `CountWords` is printed on the next line using the built-in `print` function.

The last block of code is very similar, but uses a `TagRemovingWordCounter` object. This demonstrates nicely the strength of OO polymorphism (see Chapter 7) and Python dynamicism. Exactly the same function, `CountWords`, works equally well with a `WordCounter` object as a `TagRemovingWordCounter` object. Both classes include the method `countWords` needed by the `CountWords` implementation. Any other class defining a `countWords` method could also be used in the `CountWords` function.

The `Main` function is not called until the last line of the script:

```python
if ( __name__ == "__main__" ): Main()
```

This rather strange-looking `if` statement is common to many Python scripts. Often you will write Python scripts that could be run as standalone scripts or imported and used in another script. For example, you may want to use the `WordCounter` class in an entirely different setting. You want to import the classes and functions in the example script, but do not want the main program of the word counting script to be executed.

The `if` statement makes this possible, by comparing the built-in __name__ variable with the string "__main__". If the script is run as the main program, __name__ will be equal to __main__; if it is imported by another script, it will not be. `Main` will thus be executed only when the script is the main program.

This has been a lightning-fast introduction to Python, and it has barely scratched the surface. Hopefully you have been able to recognize that Python:

➤   Has a simple syntax, in which indentation is significant.

➤   Includes powerful OO features.

➤   Is dynamically and strongly typed. Variables take the type of the objects they are assigned to and can even change type when reassigned.

➤   Includes a broad library of modules, with regular expressions, string handling, and file system operations.

More Information

Your first stop for more information about Python is the main Python web site (http://www.python.org). This site includes the latest Python releases, documentation, tutorials, articles, and links to other Python web sites. It also includes a wiki for Python on the Mac platform (http://wiki.python.org/moin/MacPython).

You can find documentation and examples of Python in use in Mac OS X via the Xcode Documentation browser, including information for using the Python Quartz Bindings and PyObjC. You can also learn more about the latter at the PyObjC web site (http://pyobjc.sourceforge.net/).

RUBY

Ruby is a powerful scripting language introduced by Yukihiro "Matz" Matsumoto in the mid-1990s. It is a bit younger than Python, but has a similar syntax, powerful OO features, text manipulation capabilities, and an extensive library of modules. Ruby is generally considered a modernized version of the Perl scripting language, and — as with Perl — has text handling (for example, regular expressions) integrated directly into the language itself.

Ruby was popularized by the web application development framework Ruby on Rails (Rails for short). Ruby on Rails has seen a meteoric rise in the past few years, and is now the poster child of the Web 2.0 development community. It allows web developers to build database-backed applications much faster and simpler than older technologies such as Java. Ruby on Rails is included as standard in Mac OS X v10.6.

Why Ruby?

Ruby inherits a lot from the granddaddy of scripting languages, Perl. As Perl matures, it gains more and more functionality, but it began as basically the scripting equivalent of C. It did not have any OO features, but did provide functions, and more powerful data containers such as arrays and hashes (dictionaries). String manipulations were central, with regular expressions built into the language directly, rather than accessible via a library.

Ruby improved on Perl by adding modern features such as OOP, and a cleaner Python-like syntax. As with Perl, Ruby has very powerful string handling, and extensions such as Ruby on Rails, which make it a popular choice for server-side web development.

One of the central premises of Perl is that there should be several ways to achieve a single task. This flexibility gives the scripter a lot of leeway. If you use Perl regularly, you will likely be able to write scripts much more compactly than you can in other languages, which makes it good for writing small helper scripts. For major projects, a more structured style of programming is required to produce maintainable code; Perl can also be used for this, but it takes discipline on the part of the scripter not to lapse into the indecipherable code that Perl allows.

Ruby is much better suited to large projects than Perl. Although it is closer to the many ways approach from Perl than Python's one way approach, features such as classes make it a good choice for structuring large projects. Ruby also includes advanced language features such as blocks, which can simplify some aspects of your scripts.

On Mac OS X, Ruby can be used with the Cocoa frameworks via the RubyCocoa bridge. RubyCocoa is included in the operating system.

A more ambitious project — which does not yet form part of the operating system — is MacRuby (`http://www.macruby.org`). The goal of MacRuby is to build a port of Ruby directly on top of Mac OS X technologies such as the Objective-C runtime and Core Foundation framework. This will allow applications written with MacRuby to run at near native speeds.

Whether or not you decide to script in Ruby or Python is largely a question of what other technologies you will need. The languages themselves are both elegant and powerful, so available frameworks will generally be the determining factor for which of the two you adopt. If you need to use Rails, then it has to be Ruby. Want to use Google App Engine? Python is the language for that.

TRY IT OUT A Ruby Example

Because Ruby overlaps Python in many application domains, the example provided in this section has the same basic functionality as the Python example given earlier. This will allow you to compare the two languages more directly, to decide what appeals to you the most. The script itself traverses a directory tree, counting the number of words in files with a given extension. The total number of words is counted, along with the number of words with XML-style tags removed:

```
#!/usr/bin/env ruby

#----------------------------------------
# Counts words after removing HTML/XML tags
#----------------------------------------
require 'find'
```

```ruby
#----------------
# Classes
#----------------
class WordCounter

  # Counts all whitespace separated words in a string.

  def reduceString(str)
    # Removes anything that should not be counted. Here it does nothing.
    str
  end

  def countWords(str)
    # Counts all words in a string
    reduceString(str).split.length
  end

end

class TagRemovingWordCounter < WordCounter

  # Counts all whitespace separated words, after removing XML tags.

  def initialize
    @tagRegEx = /\<\/?.+?\>/
  end

  def reduceString(str)
    str.gsub(@tagRegEx, ' ')
  end

end

#----------------
# Functions
#----------------
def CountWords( wordCounter, fileExt, rootDir )

  # Count words with the WordCounter passed in, for a given root directory
  # and file extension. All files with the extension passed, that reside
  # in the root directory, or any subdirectory, are scanned.

  wordCount = 0
  Find.find(rootDir) do |path|
    if File.file?(path)
      next unless path =~ /.*\.#{fileExt}/
      f = File.open(path)
      fileContentsString = f.read
      f.close
      wordCount = wordCount + wordCounter.countWords(fileContentsString)
    end
  end

  return wordCount

end
```

```
def Usage
  # Return a string with the usage of the script
  "Usage: wc.rb file_extension root_directory"
end

#----------------
# Main program
#----------------
def Main

  # The script takes two arguments: a file extension, and a root directory path.
  # All files with the extension in the root directory and subdirectories, are
  # processed. The number of words in all the processed files are summed and
  # printed. The number of words excluding XML-like tags are also printed.

  # Check that two arguments have been passed to the script
  if ARGV.length != 2
    puts Usage()
    Process.exit
  end

  # Calculate the word count with tags
  wordCounter = WordCounter.new
  numWords = CountWords( wordCounter, ARGV[0], ARGV[1] )
  printf("%-60s %6d\n", "total word count", numWords)

  # Calculate the word count without tags
  wordCounter = TagRemovingWordCounter.new
  numWords = CountWords( wordCounter, ARGV[0], ARGV[1] )
  printf("%-60s %6d\n", "word count without tags", numWords)

end

if $0 == __FILE__
  Main()
end
```

code snippet MacOSXProg ch11/wc.rb

How It Works

When you see this script, you could easily mistake it for the Python example. Ruby and Python share many syntactic features.

The script begins with a shebang, just as the Python script does, but this script uses the ruby command instead of python:

```
#!/usr/bin/env ruby
```

A module is then imported: find. The Ruby require keyword is equivalent to Python's import. Just as in the Python script, two classes are defined. The first is WordCounter:

```
class WordCounter

  # Counts all whitespace separated words in a string.
```

```
def reduceString(str)
  # Removes anything that should not be counted. Here it does nothing.
  str
end

def countWords(str)
  # Counts all words in a string
  reduceString(str).split.length
end

end
```

A Ruby class begins with the `class` keyword followed by the class name, and ends with an `end` statement. Ruby uses `end` to close off code blocks, unlike Python, which uses indentation to delimit blocks.

Just as in Python, methods begin with the keyword `def`, but do not include the colon at the end of the line. The `self` variable is passed implicitly by Ruby, which can make the argument list a bit more compact.

The previous methods feature another aspect of Ruby methods and functions, namely that the `return` statement is optional. If no `return` statement is provided, Ruby will return the last value evaluated. In the example, neither method has an explicit `return`; both return the value from the last action in the method.

 NOTE *This is one aspect of the language that has been adopted from Perl, and it highlights a significant difference in philosophy with Python. Ruby and Perl tend to offer many ways to carry out a given task, and many syntactic shortcuts, whereas Python usually only offers one clear, explicit path. Python programmers will argue that the Ruby way makes code more confusing to read, and Ruby programmers will argue that Python is not flexible enough, and overly verbose. Which you prefer is largely a question of taste.*

The second class is a good example of the integration of regular expressions into the Ruby language:

```
class TagRemovingWordCounter < WordCounter

  # Counts all whitespace separated words, after removing XML tags.

  def initialize
    @tagRegEx = /\<\/?.+?\>/
  end

  def reduceString(str)
    str.gsub(@tagRegEx, ' ')
  end

end
```

The `TagRemovingWordCounter` class inherits from `WordCounter`, which is indicated using a < symbol in the first line. The initializer is called `initialize`, rather than __init__, as it is in Python.

In the Python script, a string was used to store a regular expression, and stored in an instance variable. In Ruby, a regular expression object is created directly in code and stored in the instance variable `tagRegEx`. In Ruby, the @ symbol is prepended to delineate an instance variable, rather than using the self variable.

You can create regular expressions in Ruby, just as in Perl, using a pair of forward slashes. The regular expression itself is everything that falls between the slashes:

```
/\<\/?.+?\>/
```

The `reduceString` method uses the regular expression object to replace all XML tags with a space. The `gsub` string method is for this purpose.

The `CountWords` function demonstrates another important aspect of Ruby, blocks:

```
def CountWords( wordCounter, fileExt, rootDir )

  # Count words with the WordCounter passed in, for a given root directory
      and file extension. All files with the extension passed, that reside
      in the root directory, or any subdirectory, are scanned.

  wordCount = 0
  Find.find(rootDir) do |path|
    if File.file?(path)
      next unless path =~ /.*\.#{fileExt}/
      f = File.open(path)
      fileContentsString = f.read
      f.close
      wordCount = wordCount + wordCounter.countWords
        (fileContentsString)
    end
  end

  return wordCount

end
```

A block is a piece of code that can effectively be passed between different program units, and yet still maintains access to the variables from its enclosing scope. This is the same as blocks in the C language, which were discussed in Chapter 6.

The block in the previous code is the following:

```
Find.find(rootDir) do |path|
  ...
end
```

It begins at the `do` keyword, and ends with `end`. This enclosed block of code actually gets passed to the `Find.find` method, which executes it for each file found, setting the path variable to a different value for each iteration.

When the block is executed, it has access to the variables from its enclosing scope. For example, `fileExt` is used inside the block, and it is an argument of the `CountWords` function.

In this particular example, a block is being called repeatedly much as if it were code in a for loop. In fact, a for loop was the solution used in the Python script. Ruby uses blocks in contexts where more traditional language constructs would be used in Python. Again, the approach you prefer is a matter of personal taste.

The `Main` function looks like this:

```
def Main

    # The script takes two arguments: a file extension, and a root
        directory path.
    # All files with the extension in the root directory and
        subdirectories, are
    # processed. The number of words in all the processed files are
        summed and
    # printed. The number of words excluding XML-like tags are also
        printed.

    # Check that two arguments have been passed to the script
    if ARGV.length != 2
      puts Usage()
      Process.exit
    end

    # Calculate the word count with tags
    wordCounter = WordCounter.new
    numWords = CountWords( wordCounter, ARGV[0], ARGV[1] )
    printf("%-60s %6d\n", "total word count", numWords)

    # Calculate the word count without tags
    wordCounter = TagRemovingWordCounter.new
    numWords = CountWords( wordCounter, ARGV[0], ARGV[1] )
    printf("%-60s %6d\n", "word count without tags", numWords)

end
```

The differences between this code and the Python code are largely superficial. It is worth noting that in Ruby you can use the `puts` function to print a string, and that you create a new object in Ruby by calling the `new` method of the class, rather than appending a list of arguments directly to the class name, as you do in Python.

Ruby is an advanced language and not easy to convey in such a short passage. Many subtleties exist, and they have been glossed over here to some extent. Nonetheless, from this example you should have been able to gather that Ruby:

➤ Is syntactically similar to Python, though somewhat more complex

➤ Adopts the Perl philosophy of providing many different ways to address a given problem, and offers many syntactic shortcuts

➤ Includes powerful OO features

➤ Has built-in regular expressions, similar to Perl

➤ Includes a broad library of modules similar to those available in Python

More Information

The Ruby language web site is a good place to begin your exploration of Ruby (`http://www.ruby-lang.org`). It includes links to many other Ruby resources.

If you want to start developing a web application with Ruby on Rails, visit the Rails web site first (`http://rubyonrails.org`).

You can find Ruby modules and libraries at RubyForge (`http://rubyforge.org`) and The Ruby Application Archive (`http://raa.ruby-lang.org`). Ruby also has a good built-in package management system called RubyGems, which you can access using the `gem` command.

To write Cocoa applications with Ruby, you can use RubyCocoa (`http://rubycocoa.sourceforge.net`), which ships with Mac OS X.

JAVASCRIPT

Netscape originally created JavaScript as a scripting language to make dynamic content for the Web. JavaScript code is usually found embedded in HTML and gets run in a web browser. By giving you access to all the elements of an HTML page via the so-called *Document Object Model (DOM)*, JavaScript allows you to take static HTML web content and change it as time passes.

JavaScript looks quite a bit like the Java programming language, but that is where the comparison ends. JavaScript is not Java, nor is it a subset of Java. JavaScript is a simple interpreted language that runs in web browsers, and Java is an extensive compiled language that can be used for a wide variety of different purposes — from developing web sites to creating desktop applications.

 NOTE *Java is a compiled language, but it is a compiled language with a difference. The Java compiler converts Java source code into something called byte code, rather than the machine code that runs on the CPU. The byte code is platform independent; when you run a Java application, a program called the Java Virtual Machine (JVM) reads the byte code and generates machine executable code, which is what is sent to the CPU. In short, the JVM is a bit like an interpreter. As you can see, the distinction between a compiled language and an interpreted language is not that clear when it comes to Java.*

Why JavaScript?

The importance of JavaScript has grown over time to the point where it is now perhaps the most widely used language on Earth. It began as a little scripting language to make web sites flashier, but it now underpins nearly all web development, including Web 2.0 technologies such as Asynchronous JavaScript and XML (Ajax) which are heavily used by companies such as Google.

The reason JavaScript has risen together with the Web is that it is so closely coupled to its other technologies: HTML and CSS. JavaScript gives you direct access to elements of a HTML document, including its CSS stylesheets. You can change these elements and effectively modify the page in time. JavaScript can also perform requests to a server. These two aspects — updating elements of a page and requesting data from a server — are what make JavaScript so suitable for modern client-side web development.

Quite aside from its importance in web development, JavaScript has an added attraction for Mac developers. When Apple introduced Dashboard in Mac OS X v10.4 (Tiger), JavaScript stepped outside the browser. As you undoubtedly know, Dashboard is a technology that allows you to develop and use *widgets*, which are little utilities that you can display with the press of a key or move of the mouse. What you may not know is that Dashboard is based on web technologies such as HTML, CSS, and JavaScript. Put simply, a Dashboard widget is not much more or less than a web page.

TRY IT OUT **A JavaScript Example**

Chapter 14 is largely dedicated to JavaScript scripting, so only a simple example is provided here to give you a feel for what JavaScript is about. The following is a HTML page with embedded CSS and JavaScript. It displays an image inside a box in your web browser (see Figure 11-1). When you click the image, a dialog is displayed, and when you dismiss it, the image moves to a new random position inside the box.

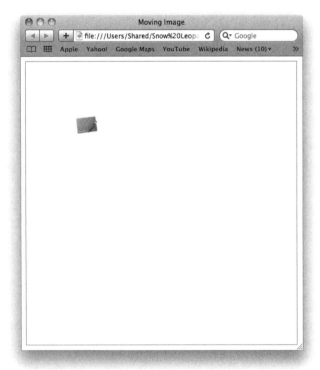

FIGURE 11-1

```
<?xml version="1.0" encoding="UTF-8"?>
<!DOCTYPE html PUBLIC "-//W3C//DTD XHTML 1.1//EN"
    "http://www.w3.org/TR/xhtml11/DTD/xhtml11.dtd">

<html xmlns="http://www.w3.org/1999/xhtml" xml:lang="en">
<head>
    <title>Moving Image</title>

    <style type="text/css">
    body {
        width:500px;
        height:500px;
        border:solid gray 1px;
    }

    img#movingimage {
        position:absolute;
        top:100px;
        left:100px;
    }
    </style>

    <script type="text/javascript">
function moveimage(image) {
    alert('About to move image');
    var top = Math.floor(Math.random() * document.body.offsetHeight);
    var left = Math.floor(Math.random() * document.body.offsetWidth);
    image.style.top = top + 'px';
    image.style.left = left + 'px';
}
    </script>

</head>

<body>
    <img id="movingimage" onclick="moveimage(this);"
        src="http://groups.google.com/group/coreplot-discuss/icon?v=1&hl=en" />
</body>
</html>
```

code snippet MacOSXProg ch11/movingimage.html

How It Works

When writing a full web site, HTML, CSS, and JavaScript would usually be separated into different files, but for the sake of simplicity, everything has been put into a single HTML document in this example.

After the usual HTML document declarations, some CSS appears in the head section:

```
<style type="text/css">
body {
    width:500px;
```

```
    height:500px;
    border:solid gray 1px;
}

img#movingimage {
    position:absolute;
    top:100px;
    left:100px;
}
</style>
```

The body is sized and given a border; it forms the gray box that the image moves inside. A second declaration sets the attributes and initial position of the image itself.

The JavaScript also appears in the head section of the document:

```
    <script type="text/javascript">
function moveimage(image) {
    alert('About to move image');
    var top = Math.floor(Math.random() * document.body.offsetHeight);
    var left = Math.floor(Math.random() * document.body.offsetWidth);
    image.style.top = String(top) + 'px';
    image.style.left = String(left) + 'px';
}
    </script>
```

You use `script` tags to delineate a block of JavaScript or import a JavaScript file. In this example, a single function has been declared: `moveimage`. It takes the image object as an argument, so it can be used with any image, not just the one displayed.

The `moveimage` function begins by displaying a dialog to the user, informing him or her that the image is about to move:

```
    alert('About to move image');
```

Although a fairly pointless action, this demonstrates that it is quite easy to use JavaScript to communicate with the user.

The function continues by evaluating two random numbers, and using those to set the location of the image:

```
    var top = Math.floor(Math.random() * document.body.offsetHeight);
    var left = Math.floor(Math.random() * document.body.offsetWidth);
    image.style.top = top + 'px';
    image.style.left = left + 'px';
```

The coordinates of the image are calculated by multiplying a random floating-point number between 0 and 1, which is returned by the `Math.random` function, by the dimensions of the body element. To get the dimensions of the body, the so-called DOM tree is queried: `document.body.offsetHeight` gives the height of the body, and `document.body.offsetWidth` gives the width.

The DOM is also used to set the position of the image. The `style` attribute of any element contains its CSS style information; in this example, the `top` and `left` attributes of the style are set, which effectively moves the image on the screen. Note that styles are always strings, so the coordinate numbers must first be converted to a string before the values are set in the DOM. In this case, the text *px* is appended to each value, which simultaneously converts it to a string and sets the appropriate units (that is, pixels).

The main body of the HTML document is very simple. It just contains an `img` tag for the image:

```
<body>
    <img id="movingimage" onclick="moveimage(this);"
        src="http://groups.google.com/group/coreplot-discuss/icon?v=1&hl=en" />
</body>
```

You may have been wondering how and when the JavaScript `moveimage` function gets called. The `img` tag contains the answer: the `onclick` attribute is set to a small piece of JavaScript — a single function call — that will get executed when someone clicks the image. The argument passed in the call is the variable `this`, which represents the current element in the DOM tree — in this case the `img`.

Hopefully, this example has shown you that:

➤   JavaScript is a language with Java-like syntax.

➤   JavaScript is closely coupled to HTML and CSS via the DOM.

➤   JavaScript is very important in the development of dynamic web sites.

More Information

One of the best places to learn about web technologies such as HTML, CSS, and JavaScript is the W3Schools web site (`http://w3schools.com`). It includes reference material on each technology, as well as tutorials and full coverage of the DOM.

Chapter 14 covers web technologies such as JavaScript in more detail, and shows how you can develop web apps and Dashboard widgets with the Dashcode application.

OTHER SCRIPTING LANGUAGES

Unfortunately, there isn't enough room in this book to cover all the scripting languages shipped with Mac OS X. Five of the more important languages have been addressed, but many other good languages have had to be omitted. The following list gives you a very brief overview of some of these remaining scripting languages:

➤   **Perl:** The ancestor of all modern scripting languages, Perl has impressive text manipulation facilities, and is often used in CGI programming for the Web (`http://www.perl.org`). Although the language continues to improve, and is still very popular with system administrators, Perl is slowly losing ground to more modern languages such as Python and Ruby.

➤ **PHP:** A language used mostly to build web sites. It can be mixed with HTML to produce web pages that get dynamically built by the web server whenever requested by a client web browser. PHP allows you to easily integrate a database with your web site, upload files via a web page, send e-mails from web forms, and much more. For general information on PHP, there is the PHP web site (`http://www.php.net/`), and for an introduction to PHP on Mac OS X, you need look no further than the Apple Developer Connection (`http://developer.apple.com/mac/articles/internet/phpeasyway.html`).

➤ **Tcl:** An easy-to-use scripting language tightly integrated with the Tk GUI toolkit. This combination allows you to write cross-platform GUI applications, though you shouldn't expect the polish of a Cocoa application. The Tcl/Tk frameworks provided with Mac OS X simulate the look of the Mac OS X controls, but it isn't really going to fool anyone — the interface is obviously not Mac native. Tcl is used as the base language of the MacPorts project (`http://www.macports.org/`), which aims to make Unix tools easy to install on Mac OS X. A good place to begin learning about Tcl/Tk is the Tcl Developer Xchange (`www.tcl.tk/`).

SUMMARY

A scripting language is a high-level language that is interpreted, rather than being compiled into object code by a compiler. Mac OS X ships with a many different scripting languages, each with its own application domain, strengths, and weaknesses. This chapter has introduced you to some of the more important of these languages.

In this chapter, you learned that:

➤ The Bash Shell can be used interactively, or to run shell scripts. It is a simple language, used extensively in the Mac OS X system, and is particularly good at gluing other commands and programs together.

➤ AppleScript is the best scripting language for scripting applications with a GUI on Mac OS X. It has a verbose, English-like syntax and is targeted at non-programmers.

➤ Python is a powerful object-oriented scripting language, with a simple syntax and extensive library. As with most modern scripting languages, it is very capable when it comes to text manipulation.

➤ Ruby is similar in appearance to Python, but has a philosophy closer to its immediate ancestor, Perl. It provides many different ways of achieving a single task. This is either a strength or weakness, depending on your perspective. It is a powerful object-oriented language, and has been made popular by the web application framework Ruby on Rails.

➤ JavaScript is a Java-like scripting language that can be used to make dynamic web content, but it is of particular interest to Mac developers because it underpins Dashboard.

➤ Other scripting languages on Mac OS X include Perl, PHP, and Tcl.

In the next chapter, you learn more about the Bash Shell. Before proceeding, however, try the exercises that follow to test your understanding of the material covered in this chapter. You can find the solutions to these exercises in Appendix A.

EXERCISES

1. A friend says to you that she is interested in scripting a weekly backup of her user directory. She asks you what you think the best scripting language to use would be. What would you advise, based on what you have learned in this chapter?

2. Another friend wants to build a complex web content management system. He asks your advice about scripting languages that he could use for the project. What do you suggest?

3. If you want to extract photos from your iPhoto library, and automatically send them to friends in your Address Book, what would be the best scripting language for the job?

▶ WHAT YOU LEARNED IN THIS CHAPTER

Script	a program that is interpreted line-by-line rather than being compiled into machine code
Scripting Language	a high-level language used to write scripts
Interpreter	a program that reads and interprets a script, or accepts commands interactively from a user
Shell	an interpreter that works with a shell scripting language, and can be used to run UNIX commands
Bash	the default Mac OS X UNIX shell
Python	a simple, yet powerful object-oriented scripting language
Ruby	a modern object-oriented scripting language based on Perl, and made popular by the Ruby on Rails web application framework
JavaScript	a scripting language that runs in web browsers and can be used to build dynamic web pages
DOM	the Document-Object Model, a hierarchical data structure used in JavaScript to manipulate a web page
AppleScript	an English-like scripting language used by Mac power users to script applications with a graphical interface
Perl	the granddaddy of modern scripting languages, with powerful text manipulation and web development features
PHP	a scripting language used for server-side web development

12

The Bash Shell

WHAT YOU WILL LEARN IN THIS CHAPTER:

➤ How to configure and use Bash interactively and for running scripts

➤ How to use the Terminal application for accessing the command line

➤ The most important Unix commands and where to find information about commands

➤ Some of the commands that are available only on Mac OS X

➤ Basic shell programming

At the heart of every Mac OS X system is a Unix core. If you don't look for it, you won't see it, but it's there. As with all Unix systems, Mac OS X relies heavily on shell scripts. When you log into your account at startup — whatever you happen to be doing on Mac OS X — chances are good that a shell script is involved in some way.

After reading Chapter 11, you know that scripts are simple programs that string together Unix commands to perform a task. Scripts are run by a program called a *shell*, which interprets one line of code at a time. On Mac OS X, the default shell is called Bash, which is a powerful shell that can be used interactively or to run scripts. Upon completing this chapter, you should have a good basis for working with the Bash shell.

GETTING STARTED

Before you can start interacting with the operating system via the Terminal application or writing your own shell scripts, some preliminaries need to be taken care of. First, you need to know what a *command-line interface (CLI)* is and the different ways in which it can be used. You need to have an application that can access the CLI and a way to edit scripts and other text files. Finally, you need to configure your Bash shell before you start using it. This section covers these aspects and prepares you for using the Bash shell (which you'll start doing in the next section).

The Command-Line Interface

The Mac has always had an excellent graphical user interface (GUI) — it's what made the Mac famous to begin with. With Mac OS X, Apple continues to lead the way when it comes to GUI design.

The original Mac OS may have had a great GUI, but it lacked a command-line interface (CLI). Where Windows users could start up MS-DOS and enter commands to copy files or execute programs, Mac OS users didn't have this option — in all honesty, most didn't want it.

A CLI is a means of interacting with the operating system via textual commands entered on the keyboard rather than by pointing and clicking the mouse. A CLI usually requires the user to enter commands at a simple prompt rather than interacting via controls and menus.

Mac OS X has a rich GUI, but it also offers a CLI as a bonus for the power user. The CLI of Mac OS X can be accessed with applications such as Terminal and X11 (with `xterm`).
The CLI in Mac OS X is actually the Bash shell, which listens for the commands you enter at the prompt, and takes action accordingly.

 NOTE *X11 is the GUI used on most other Unix systems, and is equivalent to Aqua on Mac OS X. You can run X11 alongside Aqua by installing the X11 application, which is an optional install with the Mac OS X system. To install it on your Mac, use a Mac OS X install disk.*

A CLI is not for everyone. Most will want to stick with what is offered in the GUI; but for others, the CLI offers an extra dimension. It is very powerful, usually offering more options to the user than can be accessed via a GUI. Some things are also much easier to do with the CLI than with a GUI. For example, Mac OS X includes Unix commands that enable you to manipulate files and text in many more ways than are possible using Finder and TextEdit.

Interactive versus Script

You can use the Bash shell in two different ways: interactively or for running scripts. When you type commands at a prompt, you are using the shell interactively. One command is performed at a time, as you enter it and press Return. But you can also put a series of commands in a file to form a *script*. You can use the same commands in a script as you enter at the prompt, but the script allows you to perform many commands together and execute that series of commands as many times as you please without having to retype them each time.

Working interactively does not preclude you running scripts. The two can, and usually are, interleaved. You can run any script you like from the shell prompt. A *subprocess* is usually started to run the script, such as an extra Bash shell. The shell initiating the script can either wait for the subprocess to exit, or it can continue without waiting.

The Terminal Application

The easiest way to access Bash on Mac OS X is to use the Terminal application, which you can find in the /Applications/Utilities folder. Terminal can be used to open windows, each of which contains a prompt that you can use to enter commands. Each Terminal window is running a different copy of the Bash shell, so the commands you enter in one window do not influence the Bash shell in another window.

When you open Terminal for the first time, you may want to change some configurations. One thing you may want to change is the default behavior of windows when the shell it is running exits. When you first use Terminal, windows remain open after a shell exits; you have to close them manually, even though they aren't useful anymore. If you want to change this behavior so that the window closes when the shell exits, choose Terminal ⇨ Preferences and then the Settings tab. Click Shell and then the When the Shell Exits pop-up button. You can choose either Close The Window or Close If The Shell Exited Cleanly.

 NOTE *The Close If The Shell Exited Cleanly option refers to the fact that each shell has an exit status when it terminates. The exit status is a simple integer number. If it is 0, the shell exited without any problem; a non-zero value indicates an error occurred. With this option, the window closes only if no errors arise.*

Apart from Terminal, you can also use the X11 application to access the command line. X11 is an optional install with Mac OS X; if you have installed it, it appears in /Applications/Utilities. When you start up X11, an xterm Terminal appears by default. xterm is a Unix command for starting a new Terminal window in the X Windows System, which is the windowing system started by the X11 application. You can create a new Terminal window in X11 either by choosing Applications ⇨ Terminal or by entering the following at the prompt of an existing Terminal:

```
xterm &
```

Editors

Many ways exist to edit text files on Mac OS X, including TextEdit and Xcode. Opening files in these applications from a Terminal is quite easy. You can simply issue this command:

```
open filename
```

This opens the file in the application assigned to the file type. You can choose the application for any given file type in the file's Info panel in the Finder (select the file and then choose File⇨ Get Info).

Using external editors with Terminal is certainly possible, but this may not be the most convenient solution. You may prefer to remain inside the Terminal window to edit files. Unix has a vast assortment of command-line, text-editing programs — the most widely used are vi and emacs. Both are powerful editors, but they have steep learning curves and are beyond the scope of this book.

NOTE *If you talk to Unix users about their preference for emacs or vi, you may hit a nerve. The competition between these two editors is something akin to a religious war and can prompt very lively discussions.*

Instead of discussing vi or emacs, this chapter introduces a very simple command-line editor that ships with Mac OS X: Nano. Nano is not as advanced as emacs or vi, but it is quite adequate for basic file editing and is intuitive to use. You can edit a file with Nano simply by entering the nano command followed by the filename, like this:

```
nano filename
```

If the file already exists, it will be opened; if it does not exist, it will be created. Figure 12-1 shows a sample editing session with Nano.

FIGURE 12-1

Using Nano is relatively self-explanatory. You enter text via the keyboard and navigate with the arrow keys. Also, many commands can be issued by holding down Control and pressing another key. Some of these commands appear at the bottom of the Nano editing window.

The following table provides a summary of some of Nano's more important commands. More commands are described in Help, which you can access by pressing Control-G.

COMMAND	DESCRIPTION
Control-X	Exits Nano. If you have unsaved changes, Nano prompts you for whether you would like to save them.
Control-K	Cuts the selected text, or a single line if there is no selection. You can't make a selection with the mouse; instead, you set the start position of the selection with Control-^ and move the cursor to the end position with the arrow keys.
Control-U	Pastes the text that was cut with Control-K at the position of the cursor.
Control-^	Sets the starting position of a selection. After issuing this command, use the arrow keys to move the cursor to the end position of the selection.
Control-V	Moves down one full page.
Control-Y	Moves up one full page.
Control-G	Opens the help pages.

Configuring Bash

When a Bash shell starts up, it can read a number of configuration files. You can customize your Bash shells by entering commands in one or more of these files. It is common, for instance, to set the PATH *environment variable* in these files. An environment variable is a variable stored by a shell and generally influences the behavior of the shell and any programs that it executes. The PATH variable is a list of paths that are searched-for commands and other executable programs.

When you open a Terminal window, an *interactive login shell* greets you. It is interactive because you can interact with it in real-time, and it is a login shell because it was not started by another shell. When Bash starts a login shell, it executes the commands in the file /etc/profile. Here is the /etc/profile provided with Mac OS X:

```
# System-wide .profile for sh(1)

if [ -x /usr/libexec/path_helper ]; then
        eval `/usr/libexec/path_helper -s`
fi

if [ "${BASH-no}" != "no" ]; then
        [ -r /etc/bashrc ] && . /etc/bashrc
fi
```

The first line is a comment. On the next three non-blank lines, the PATH variable is set using a command called path_helper. The last three lines of the file check whether a file exists at /etc/bashrc; if one does, the commands in the file are executed.

> **NOTE** *In this chapter, the word* directory *is used interchangeably with* folder. *These words are testimony to the heritage of Mac OS X, arising out of a marriage between Unix and Mac OS. The word* directory *is used in the Unix world, and* folder *was the equivalent term in the original Mac OS. On Mac OS X, either is appropriate.*

The `/etc/profile` file is read whenever a login shell is started for any user. It should be used for system-wide configuration and not for the configuration options of a particular user. Usually, you do not need to edit `/etc/profile` at all; you can simply customize the shell from user configuration files.

After `/etc/profile`, the login shell checks whether a file called `.profile` exists in the user's home directory. If it does, the commands it includes are executed. You can put into the `.profile` file any commands you would like to run when a login shell is initiated. You could, for example, add directories to the default PATH variable as follows:

```
PATH=$PATH:~/bin
export PATH
```

This adds the directory `bin` in your home directory to the existing PATH variable. The value of the PATH variable is retrieved by prepending a `$` symbol, as seen on the right side of the first expression. The `export` command updates the environment variable PATH; without this, the variable would only be changed locally and not outside the `.profile` file.

> **NOTE** *Bash allows you to represent a user's home directory by a tilde (˜) symbol. So a user's* `.profile` *file is located at the path* `~/.profile`.

Not all shells are login shells. You may start one shell from within another, for example, by simply entering the command `bash` at the prompt and then pressing Return. If you try this, you may not notice any change, but you are actually working inside a new shell. This type of shell is simply called an interactive shell; it is not a login shell.

When a new non-login interactive shell starts, the Bash shell checks for the existence of a file called `.bashrc` in the user's home directory. If this file exists, it is executed. The `.profile` file is not executed when a non-login shell starts up. You can use the `.bashrc` file to customize your shell configuration for non-login shells. Most users don't need to have different configurations for login and non-login shells, so the `.bashrc` file can be left empty or removed altogether.

In the following Try It Out, you use the Terminal application with the Nano editor to create the Bash configuration file `~/.profile` and add a few commands to customize your Bash shell.

TRY IT OUT   Configuring Your Bash Shell

1.   Start the Terminal application in `/Applications/Utilities`.

2.   Create the file `.profile` in your home directory using the Nano editor. To do this, simply issue the following command at the prompt:

```
nano .profile
```

3.   Type the following text into the Nano editor. You can use the arrow keys to move around. When you are finished, press Control-X, and answer with a **Y** when prompted whether you would like to save your changes.

```
export PATH=.:$PATH:~/bin
export PS1="\h:\u:\w$ "
alias h history
```

4.   When you are satisfied and want to terminate your Terminal session, enter the following command at the prompt:

```
exit
```

How It Works

This introductory example should help you get familiar with Terminal, Nano, and the Bash configuration files. When you start the Terminal application, a Bash shell starts, and you receive a prompt. The Bash shell always has a current working directory, and it begins in your home directory. When you create the `.profile` file with Nano, it is created in your home directory because that is the current working directory.

The commands added to the `.profile` file are intended to serve as examples and are not by any means compulsory. You can add whatever you like to `.profile`.

The first command extends the PATH variable.

```
export PATH=.:$PATH:~/bin
```

The PATH environment variable is initialized in `/etc/profile` before the `~/.profile` is read. The existing value is not discarded but is extended by the command. The new value of PATH is set to be the old value, as given by `$PATH`, with two directories added: `.` and `~/bin`. The directory represented by the period (`.`) is always the current working directory of the shell, and `~/bin` is the directory `bin` in your home directory. The directory `~/bin` does not have to exist; if it doesn't, Bash simply ignores it when searching for a command. If you create the `~/bin` directory, you could add your own scripts and other executables to it, and Bash would find and execute them no matter which directory you happen to be working in.

 NOTE *Any file that can be executed by the shell, whether it is a compiled program or script, is often referred to as an executable.*

Many users like to add the current working directory, as given by `.`, to their `PATH` variable. Adding `.` to the `PATH` means that the shell will look for executable programs in the current working directory, as well as at other paths. It is quite common to want to execute a program in your current directory, especially if you are writing your own scripts. If you don't include `.` in your path, you need to enter a path to run a script in your current working directory, as follows:

```
./script_name
```

The order of the paths in the `PATH` variable is significant. The shell searches the paths in the order they appear, for the first matching executable. When an executable is found, the rest of the paths are ignored. In the example, the shell searches in the current directory (.) first, followed by the directories originally in the `PATH` variable, and lastly in `~/bin`. If you want the executables in a particular directory to have priority, include that directory early in your `PATH` variable.

The second line of the `.profile` file sets an environment variable.

```
export PS1="\h:\u:\w$ "
```

The `PS1` environment variable is used to formulate the prompt string that you see when the Bash shell is waiting for you to enter a command. You can use any string you like for the prompt, as well as characters with special meanings that are substituted with another string before being displayed. In the example, the hostname (`\h`) is shown, followed by a colon and the username (`\u`). The current working directory (`\w`) is given last, followed by a `$` symbol and a space. The following table gives some of the more interesting special characters that you can use in your prompt.

SPECIAL CHARACTER	DESCRIPTION
\d	The date (as in "Wed Nov 20th")
\h	The first section of the hostname
\H	The full hostname
\t	The time in 24-hour format
\T	The time in 12-hour format
\A	The time in 24-hour format, excluding seconds
\w	The path of the current working directory
\W	The last directory in the current working directory path
\!	The number of the command in the history list

The `.profile` file finishes by defining an *alias*. An alias in Bash is an alternative name for a command; when you type the alias, the original command to which it corresponds is executed. In this case, the `history` command, which gives a list of the commands previously given to the shell, is assigned the alias `h`. With this alias in place, instead of having to type `history` when you want to list the history of commands, you can simply type `h`.

The `exit` command allows you to terminate a shell. You can also supply a number to the `exit` command, which is returned to the parent process as the exit code. This is usually used to indicate if an error occurred and what the error was.

UNIX BASICS

The Unix philosophy, which Mac OS X shares at its lower levels, can be summarized by the old adage that many hands make light work. Unix systems are full of *commands* — small programs that are highly specialized. Each command does one thing, and does it well. Even though the foundations are simple, you can achieve powerful tasks by combining Unix commands. This section covers basic aspects of Unix, some of the most important Unix commands, and how you can combine them to achieve your objectives.

Paths

Much of the time spent interacting with an operating system involves working with files and directories (that is, folders). You have to be able to locate files, view or edit them, move them, remove them, and so forth. But all these actions require that you be able to stipulate to the operating system a particular file or directory. In the Finder, you can select a file and drag it to the Trash if you want to remove it. On the command line, there are no file icons; so you need to give a path to any file or directory that you want to use in a command.

Unix paths can take one of two forms: *absolute paths* and *relative paths*. Absolute paths are spelled out in full with respect to the root directory. An absolute path begins with a forward slash, as in the following:

```
cd /Users/terry/Desktop
```

This line uses the `cd` command, which changes the current working directory of the shell. The current directory is set to the `Desktop` folder of user `terry`. The path begins with a forward slash and is thus an absolute path, taken with respect to the root directory of the file system.

Relative paths do not begin with a forward slash and are taken with respect to the current working directory of the shell. If the current working directory in the preceding example is user `terry`'s home directory, the `cd` command could be issued as follows:

```
cd Desktop
```

Because the current working directory is `/Users/terry`, which is the home directory of user `terry`, entering a relative path of `Desktop` results in the absolute path `/Users/terry/Desktop`.

When you're working with relative paths, there are a few special symbols that can help you navigate. If you want to refer to the current directory, you can use a single period. The following command, for example, lists the contents of the current working directory of the shell:

```
ls .
```

The period can also be used in paths; the presence of a period effectively leaves the path unchanged. For example, the following command lists the contents of the Desktop folder if issued from inside the user's home directory:

```
ls ./Desktop
```

This is completely equivalent to

```
ls Desktop
```

Given that the single period has no effect on paths, you may be wondering why you would even need it. Sometimes it is important to simply indicate that something is a path, and a period can achieve that. For example, when issuing commands, the shell searches the paths in your PATH environment variable, but the current working directory is not included unless you have added it yourself. If you have an executable in your current working directory, and you want to run it, you need to give an explicit path; otherwise, the shell won't find it. Here's how you provide the path:

```
./some_executable
```

Simply issuing the command without the period will result in an error message.

Another special symbol for use in paths is the double period. This moves up to the parent directory of a directory. For example, to list the contents of the /Users directory, you could enter the following from your home directory:

```
ls ..
```

Of course, the double period symbol (. .) can also be used in paths. Here is how you could list the contents of the /Applications directory from your home directory, using a relative path:

```
ls ../../Applications
```

Wherever the double period occurs in the path, it moves up to the parent directory. Two double periods, as in the preceding example, effectively shift you up two levels of directories: the first one moves you to the /Users directory, and the second one to the root directory /. When in the root directory, Applications selects the /Applications directory.

Locating and Learning Commands

Unix commands on Mac OS X tend to be stored in a number of standard directories. The most important commands appear in the /bin directory. bin stands for binary, and most commands are compiled programs, which means they are in a non-readable binary format rather than a text format.

NOTE *If you look for* /bin *in the Finder, you may be surprised to see that it's missing. It isn't actually missing, it's just hidden. Apple prefers that everyday users not be bothered by low-level details such as* /bin, *and hides them in Finder. You can still navigate to the* /bin *directory in Finder by choosing Go ⇨ Go to Folder and entering* **/bin.**

You can list the contents of the /bin command by using the ls command. Here is the output for the command on one particular system:

```
Macintosh:~ sample$ ls /bin
[              df            launchctl      pwd           tcsh
bash           domainname    link           rcp           test
cat            echo          ln             rm            unlink
chmod          ed            ls             rmdir         wait4path
cp             expr          mkdir          sh            zsh
csh            hostname      mv             sleep
date           kill          pax            stty
dd             ksh           ps             sync
```

The /bin directory includes the various shells, including bash, as well as fundamental commands for interacting with the file system, such as cp, chmod, mv, and rm. (Details of these commands are provided throughout this section.) Even the command used to list the directory contents, ls, resides in /bin.

Mac OS X systems include a second directory intended for binaries typically used by system administrators: /sbin. This directory includes commands for shutting down the system and mounting volumes via a network. The commands in /sbin do not belong to the core of Unix commands, and many are found only on Mac OS X.

Most commands are found in the directory /usr/bin. This directory is intended for less fundamental commands than the ones belonging in /bin. Apple adds commands to /usr/bin over time, but the contents of /bin are usually left intact. /usr/bin includes all sorts of commands, from file compression programs to compilers. Any command that is not in /bin, and not intended for system administrative purposes, tends to end up in /usr/bin. The /usr/sbin directory is the analog of /usr/bin for system administrative commands.

You can use the which command to get the path of a command, or to learn which particular path is used if there are multiple copies of a command. You simply enter which followed by the command name, and it prints out the path that is used if you issue the command in the shell. Here is an example of using which with the emacs command:

```
Macintosh:~ sample$ which emacs
/usr/bin/emacs
```

which works only with commands in the paths defined by your PATH environment variable. If you seek a command outside your path, you will need to use a more general file-searching command such as find or locate, which are described later in this chapter.

If you want to know how to use a command, or the options that it includes, you can use the man command. Typing in man, followed by a command name, opens documentation in a simple file viewer called less. You can navigate through the documentation by pressing the spacebar, and you quit less by pressing **q**. Figure 12-2 shows the Terminal window after the command man ls has been issued at the prompt.

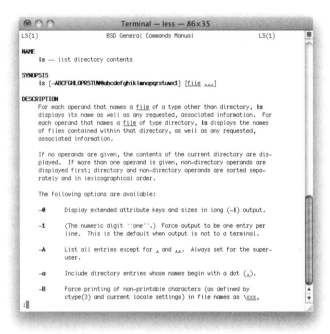

FIGURE 12-2

Running Commands and Other Executables

By now it should be quite clear that running an executable in a shell is simply a matter of typing its name and supplying any options required. If the command is not in one of the paths in your PATH environment variable, you can run the command by giving an explicit path. You can also use an explicit path if you want to override the search order used by the shell to locate a command. For example, perhaps you have two different versions of a particular command, and you want to specify explicitly which should be run. Using an explicit path to the command achieves this.

When a command or other executable is run, the shell can either wait for it to exit or continue processing other commands. When the shell blocks and waits, the command is said to be running in the *foreground*; if the shell continues without waiting, the command is running in the *background*. By default, a command runs in the foreground. If you want to run a command in the background, you need to append an & symbol to the end of the line, such as in this example:

```
find . -name "*.txt" &
```

This command searches for text files in the current directory and any of its subdirectories. Because this may take a while, it makes sense to run the command in the background so that you can continue issuing commands while the search proceeds. The & at the end of the line indicates to the shell that it should return from the find command immediately, rather than waiting for it to complete. You get a new prompt, and can continue to issue commands to the shell.

When you run a command or other executable, you are actually starting a new *process*. A process is simply a running program. Commands started from inside a shell are *subprocesses* or *child processes* of the shell and inherit the environment variables of the shell as a result. If the shell exits for some reason while the subprocess is running, the subprocess is terminated by the operating system.

You can pass arguments to a subprocess when it starts simply by including the arguments after the executable name. For example, the following find command is passed three arguments:

```
find / -name "*.doc"
```

The arguments are passed to find as the strings /, -name, and *.doc. The find command interprets the arguments and carries out the request. The shell itself has no understanding of what the arguments represent or which arguments the find command expects to receive; it simply breaks the line into separate strings and passes them to find.

When a command exits, it returns an exit value. This is an integer value, which is usually used to indicate when an error has occurred. A value of 0 means that everything went fine; a non-zero value usually indicates that an error occurred. Often the non-zero value returned is an error code, which can be used to find out exactly what type of error occurred.

To access the error code of a command in Bash, you use the special variable $?, which is the error code of the last command run by the shell. You can test the value of $? after a command has run to determine if anything went wrong; comparing it to zero, for example. You learn how to perform such tests later in this chapter in the "Shell Programming" section.

If you want to exit a shell, you can use the exit command. With no argument, the exit command sets the exit code to 0. If an error occurs, you will want to set the error code to a non-zero value. To do this, simply supply the error code as an argument to exit, as in the following example:

```
exit 127
```

Here, the exit code has been set to 127.

Bash provides a few other ways to run commands and scripts. For instance, the eval command can be used to run commands. The commands are executed in the existing shell; no subprocess is initiated. For example, the following lists the contents of the directory /usr/bin:

```
eval ls /usr/bin
```

This really becomes useful only when you can evaluate arbitrary strings of commands that are read from a file or entered by the user. Strings are covered in greater depth in the "Shell Programming" section later in this chapter.

The source command is similar to eval, but it executes commands from a file. The commands are again executed in the existing shell, with no subprocess initiated.

With the exec command, you can replace the shell with another running script or program. The initiating script is terminated, and the newly started executable replaces it. This newly started executable takes its environment, and the *process identity* — the number used to represent the process by the system. If you run

```
exec ls
```

the command ls replaces the Bash shell used to initiate it. When ls is finished listing the current working directory, it also exits. Because the shell has terminated, your prompt does not return. Depending on your preferences, your Terminal window may close.

If you issue

```
exec bash
```

it may seem as though the command changed nothing, but a new Bash shell has started, replacing the old one. If you decide you want to use a shell other than bash during a Terminal session, you can do it like this:

```
exec tcsh
```

This replaces the existing Bash shell with a new TCSH shell.

Redirecting Input and Output

The real strength of shells is their ability to easily combine relatively simple commands to perform complex tasks. To achieve this, it is important to be able to take the data output by one command and use it as input to another command, or to write data to a file and read it back in later for further processing. The Bash shell provides powerful, easy-to-use features for channeling data between commands and files.

Data is channeled from one command to another, or to and from a file, via *pipes*. Pipes are analogous to the plumbing in your bathroom, except that they transmit data instead of water. To pipe data from the output of one command to the input of another, you use the pipe (|) operator. Here is an example of taking the output of an ls command and piping it to a command called grep:

```
ls -1 /usr/bin | grep cc
```

Better ways exist to achieve the same effect as this command, but this example demonstrates the workings of a pipe. The command ls -1 /usr/bin produces a lot of output, which can be summarized as follows:

```
Macintosh:~ sample$ ls -1 /usr/bin
2to3
2to32.6
BuildStrings
CpMac
DeRez
```

```
GetFileInfo
...
zip
zipcloak
zipgrep
zipinfo
zipnote
zipsplit
zless
zmore
znew
zprint
```

Results differ depending on the commands you have installed in the /usr/bin directory. The output gets piped to the input of the command grep cc, which extracts any line containing the text cc. The original output of the ls command is reduced to only those commands containing the text cc, as shown here:

```
Macintosh:~ sample$ ls -1 /usr/bin | grep cc
cc
ccmake
distcc
distccd
distccmon-text
gcc
gcc-4.0
gcc-4.2
i686-apple-darwin10-gcc-4.0.1
i686-apple-darwin10-gcc-4.2.1
mpicc
perlcc
perlcc5.8.9
powerpc-apple-darwin10-gcc-4.0.1
powerpc-apple-darwin10-gcc-4.2.1
rpcclient
runocc.d
yacc
```

You are not limited to piping data between two commands; you can pipe together as many commands as you like. By way of example, imagine that you are only interested in commands in /usr/bin that contain cc and a digit in their names. Here is one way to list those commands:

```
ls -1 /usr/bin | grep cc | grep -e '[0-9]'
```

The output of this command is

```
Macintosh:~ sample$ ls -1 /usr/bin | grep cc | grep -e '[0-9]'
gcc-4.0
gcc-4.2
i686-apple-darwin10-gcc-4.0.1
i686-apple-darwin10-gcc-4.2.1
perlcc5.8.9
powerpc-apple-darwin10-gcc-4.0.1
powerpc-apple-darwin10-gcc-4.2.1
```

A second pipe has been added, taking the output of the `grep cc` command and piping it into the input of a second `grep`. The second `grep` prints only the lines that contain at least one digit.

You can also pipe data to and from files. To do this, you use the *redirection operators* < and >. The < operator redirects the standard input of a command causing it to be read from a file, like this:

```
grep -i TABLE < index.html
```

Here, the command `grep TABLE`, which prints any line of text containing TABLE, is applied to the contents of the file `index.html`. The shell reads `index.html`, channeling the data into the `grep` command, which prints those lines with TABLE in them.

Piping the output of a command to a file is similar, as shown here:

```
grep -i TABLE < index.html > table_results.txt
```

This command has been extended, with the output of the `grep` command now being piped to the file `table_results.txt`, rather than being displayed by the shell. After this command has executed, you should be able to open the file `table_results.txt` in an editor such as Nano or TextEdit and find the `grep` output there.

Notice that using > overwrites any existing file. If you want to append the data, rather than replacing the contents of the output file, you can use the >> operator like this:

```
grep -i TABLE < index.html >> table_results.txt
```

If `table_results.txt` doesn't exist before this command is issued, it is created, and the command's output is inserted. If the file does exist, the output is appended to the end of the existing data in `table_results.txt`.

Apart from standard output, every command also has a stream of data called *standard error,* which is intended for error messages. You can pipe the standard error to a file using the 2> operator, as in this example:

```
grep -sdf 2> grep_error.txt
```

The `grep` option given here is invalid, so it prints an error message to the standard error and exits. The file `grep_error.txt` ends up containing the following text:

```
grep: unknown directories method
```

The form of redirection operator used here is applicable not only to the standard error, but to any *file descriptor.* The standard error has the file descriptor 2, so the operator 2> pipes the standard error to a file. The standard output has the file descriptor 1, so 1> pipes data to standard output. (The standalone > operator is shorthand for 1>.) Standard input has the file descriptor 0; you can read from standard input with the operator 0<, as well as with the shorthand notation <.

In the next Try It Out, you learn how to redirect data by performing a series of commands interactively in the Bash shell. The objective is to determine the total amount of RAM available on your Mac by using the command-line tool `system_profiler`.

TRY IT OUT Determining Your Memory by Redirecting Data

1. Open a Terminal window in the Terminal application.

2. Enter the following command:

```
man system_profiler
```

3. Skim the information provided until you think you understand what the `system_profiler` command does. You can use the spacebar to move down and press **b** to move back up a page. Press **q** when you are ready to quit the `less` viewer.

4. Back at the Bash prompt, enter the following command:

```
system_profiler SPMemoryDataType
```

The output should look something like this:

```
Macintosh:~ sample$ system_profiler SPMemoryDataType
Memory:

    Memory Slots:

      ECC: Disabled

        BANK 0/DIMM0:

          Size: 2 GB
          Type: DDR3
          Speed: 1067 MHz
          Status: OK
          Manufacturer: 0x80CE
          Part Number: 0x4D4337314235363733344448312D4346382020
          Serial Number: 0x4765641B

        BANK 0/DIMM1:

          Size: 2 GB
          Type: DDR3
          Speed: 1067 MHz
          Status: OK
          Manufacturer: 0x80CE
          Part Number: 0x4D4337314235363733344448312D4346382020
          Serial Number: 0x476564F5
```

5. Now re-enter the command, but pipe the output to a temporary file, similar to this:

```
system_profiler SPMemoryDataType > sysoutput.tmp
```

6. Open the file `sysoutput.tmp` with Nano to make sure it contains this output:

```
nano sysoutput.tmp
```

7. Exit Nano again by pressing Control-X.

8. Use the `grep` command to read the `sysoutput.tmp` file, and extract the sizes of the RAM modules, like this:

```
grep -e 'Size: [0-9]' < sysoutput.tmp
```

You should see something similar to the following:

```
Macintosh:~ sample$ grep -e 'Size: [0-9]' < sysoutput.tmp
          Size: 2 GB
          Size: 2 GB
```

9. Repeat the command in step 8, but redirect standard output to a new file as follows:

```
grep -e 'Size: [0-9]' < sysoutput.tmp > grepoutput.tmp
```

10. Enter the following command to extract the numbers in `grepoutput.tmp`:

```
awk '{print $2}' < grepoutput.tmp
```

You should see output that resembles this:

```
Macintosh:~ sample$ awk '{print $2}' < grepoutput.tmp
2
2
```

11. Repeat the command in step 10, but pipe the output to a new temporary file:

```
awk '{print $2}' < grepoutput.tmp > awkoutput.tmp
```

12. Process the `awkoutput.tmp` file with the following command as follows:

```
perl -e '$sum=0; while(<>) { $sum+=$_; } print "$sum\n";' < awkoutput.tmp
```

The output displays the total RAM in your computer, similar to this:

```
Macintosh:~ sample$ perl -e '$sum=0; while(<>) { $sum+=$_; } print "$sum\n";'
  <  awkoutput.tmp
4
```

Notice that the command is one long line that has been wrapped by the Bash shell onto the next line. Do not insert a return in the command.

13. Repeat the first few commands of this chain, but instead of generating a temporary file to transfer data, just use a direct pipe from one command to the next, such as this:

```
system_profiler SPMemoryDataType | grep -e 'Size: [0-9]'
```

14. Enter the following long command to duplicate the result of steps 1 through 12 while avoiding temporary files:

```
system_profiler SPMemoryDataType |  grep -e 'Size: [0-9]' | awk '{print $2}' |
perl -e '$sum=0; while(<>) { $sum+=$_; } print "$sum\n";'
```

> Again, allow the command to be wrapped by Bash; do not type a return until you have entered the entire command.

15. Remove the temporary files by entering the following three commands at the prompt:

```
rm sysoutput.tmp
rm grepoutput.tmp
rm awkoutput.tmp
```

How It Works

This example is designed to give you lots of practice piping data to and from files and between commands. The commands used throughout the example are covered later in this chapter; for now, concentrate on how data is shifted between the commands, rather than on how the commands themselves actually work.

The `system_profiler` command is used to write information about the memory in your Mac to a temporary file, using the standard output redirection operator >. The data in the temporary file is then read back into the `grep` command using the standard input redirection operator <. This pattern is followed for the rest of the example, writing data to a file and reading it back in, with each command reducing the data a bit more until the final result is produced.

Rather than introducing temporary files that must be cleaned up later, it is often easier to pipe data directly between commands. This is the approach introduced in the last few steps of the example. Instead of writing the output of each command to a file and reading it back into the next command, a pipe is used to channel output data from one command to the next. With this approach, the entire sequence of commands can be reduced to a single line, and no temporary files are produced.

At the end of the example, the temporary files are deleted with the command `rm`. This command is covered in detail later in the section "Working with Files and Directories."

Navigating the File System

Navigating the file system is somewhat different with Bash than it is with Finder. The shell maintains an environment variable, `PWD`, containing the path to the current working directory. Any relative paths you enter into your commands are interpreted with respect to this path.

Just as you can open different folders in the Finder, you can also change the current working directory of a shell. The command `cd` is used for this purpose. To use `cd`, you simply pass the path to a new directory as an argument. The path can be either an absolute path or a relative path. Here is an example of using an absolute path to change to the `/Library/Frameworks` directory:

```
cd /Library/Frameworks
```

To affirm that the current directory did change, you can check the value of the PWD environment variable or use the pwd command, which prints the path of the current working directory as shown here:

```
Macintosh:/Library/Frameworks sample$ echo $PWD
/Library/Frameworks
Macintosh:/Library/Frameworks sample$ pwd
/Library/Frameworks
```

The echo command simply prints a string to standard output after values have been substituted for any variables by the shell.

You can also use relative paths with cd, in which case the path is taken relative to the current working directory. So, if the current working directory is your home directory, entering the following command will take you into your Desktop folder:

```
cd Desktop
```

A few special directories in your file system can be reached via shortcuts. Entering cd without any path will take you to your home directory. Your home directory is stored in the environment variable HOME and can also be represented by the tilde (~) symbol. Each of the following commands changes the current working directory to your home directory:

```
cd
cd $HOME
cd ~
```

To change to your Desktop directory, you could use this:

```
cd ~/Desktop
```

You can also access the home directory of another user by appending the username to the ~. For example, to change to the Desktop folder of the user terry, you could enter this:

```
cd ~terry/Desktop
```

 NOTE *By default, you do not have permission to change to the* Desktop *directory of another user on Mac OS X. To be allowed to do this, the other user would have to change the permissions of the directory to give you access. The "File Permissions" section discusses this in more detail.*

Another important directory is the root directory of the file system. This is given by a single forward slash. To change to the root directory, you can issue this command:

```
cd /
```

Navigating a file system is also about knowing what you can navigate to. In Finder, you are automatically presented with a list of available files and folders whenever you open a folder. In Bash, this is not the case; you have to enter a command to list the contents of a directory. The command in question is ls.

If you issue the ls command without any arguments, it lists the contents of the current directory. In the following example, the current working directory is /bin:

```
Macintosh:/bin sample$ ls
[               df              launchctl       pwd             tcsh
bash            domainname      link            rcp             test
cat             echo            ln              rm              unlink
chmod           ed              ls              rmdir           wait4path
cp              expr            mkdir           sh              zsh
csh             hostname        mv              sleep
date            kill            pax             stty
dd              ksh             ps              sync
```

If you supply a path to ls, absolute or relative, it lists the contents of that directory, no matter what the current working directory happens to be. For example:

```
Macintosh:/bin sample$ cd
Macintosh:~ sample$ ls /var/log/apache2/
access_log      error_log
```

The cd command changes the current working directory to the user's home directory. The ls command lists the contents of a different directory, namely the /var/log/apache2 directory used to store log files of the Apache web server.

> **NOTE** The /var/log/apache2/ *directory may be empty if you have never used your Apache web server before, in which case the* ls *command given will not print any filenames.*

The ls command has a number of useful options. The -l option allows you to get detailed information about files and directories, including their size, when they were last modified, and who owns them. Consider the following:

```
Macintosh:~ sample$ ls -l /var/log/apache2
total 24
-rw-r--r--  1 root  wheel  3346 Sep  8 19:00 access_log
-rw-r--r--  1 root  wheel  4347 Sep  8 19:00 error_log
```

In this example, the contents of /var/log/apache2 have been listed again, but this time by using the -l option. The first part of the line indicates the *file mode*, which gives the *permissions* of each file. These determine who is allowed to read, write, or execute a given file. The meanings of the various permissions are discussed later in this chapter.

The preceding example also lists other useful information, such as the file owner, which is `root` for both files in this case; the group of the file, which is `wheel` for both files; the size of the file in bytes, which is 3,346 bytes for `access_log` and 4,347 for `error_log`; and the date and time they were last modified.

The `-R` option is also quite useful, because it recursively lists subdirectories. For example:

```
Macintosh:~ sample$ ls -R ~demo/Sites
images          index.html

/Users/demo/Sites/images:
apache_pb.gif  gradient.jpg  macosxlogo.png  web_share.gif
```

This command lists the contents of the `Sites` directory of the user `demo`, as well as all the subdirectories of `Sites`.

Working with Files and Directories

Knowing how to navigate the file system is one thing, but being able to modify it is just as important. The coming sections cover how you can alter the file system by copying or moving files and directories, creating them, removing them, searching for them, and even compressing and archiving them.

To move a file or directory from one path to another, you use the `mv` (move) command. But this command does more than just move a file or directory from one place to another. It can also be used to change the name of a file or directory or replace one file with another. `mv` simply changes one path, the *source path*, to another path, the *destination path*; if that involves changing the name of the file or directory, that is what happens.

To begin with, consider simply moving a file from one directory to another as follows:

```
mv somefile somedir
```

In this simple example, the file called `somefile` in the current working directory is moved into the directory called `somedir`, which is also located in the current working directory. Of course, `mv` also works with any form of the relative or absolute path as in this example:

```
mv ~/Desktop/somefile .
```

In this case, `mv` moves the `somefile` file in the `Desktop` folder into the current working directory.

If a file already exists at the destination path, *it will get overwritten by the file you are moving.* You need to be careful not to accidentally overwrite files you want to keep.

Changing the name of a file is no more involved. You simply ensure that the destination path either doesn't exist or is a file that you want to overwrite. In either case, `mv` moves the file to the destination path, changing its name appropriately. For example, to change the name of a file called `autumn.txt` to `spring.txt`, with both files in the current working directory, you can do this:

```
mv autumn.txt spring.txt
```

After this operation, `autumn.txt` no longer exists, and the file that used to be called `autumn.txt` is now called `spring.txt`.

Other forms of paths are also possible, of course. Here is an example where a file is moved from the user's Desktop folder into the Documents folder and renamed at the same time:

```
mv ~/Desktop/project.doc ~/Documents/lastproject.doc
```

The file originally called project.doc is not only moved to another directory, but its name also gets changed to lastproject.doc. If there is already a file called lastproject.doc in the Documents folder, it will be overwritten and lost.

If you want to avoid accidentally overwriting files when you use mv, you can use the -i option. This will cause mv to prompt you before it overwrites any file. You can even add an alias to the .profile file to be certain you don't accidentally overwrite a file, similar to this:

```
alias mv="mv -i"
```

Now, whenever you enter mv, it will be executed with the -i option, which is included automatically.

Moving directories is similar to moving files, but there are some differences. To change the name of a directory, you simply use a destination path that does not already exist. For example, if there is a directory called projects in the current working directory, and you want to rename it lastyearsprojects, you could do this:

```
mv projects lastyearsprojects
```

Note that if there is already a directory called lastyearsprojects, the projects directory will not replace it as would happen in the case of files. Instead, the projects directory becomes a subdirectory of lastyearsprojects. If you want to replace one directory with another, you first have to either move or remove it. (Removing directories is covered shortly.)

Copying files and directories is similar to moving them. The cp command is used to copy files from one path to another as follows:

```
cp sourcefile destinationfile
```

Unlike mv, the sourcefile continues to exist after the cp operation; destinationfile is a duplicate of sourcefile. Just as with mv, all manner of paths can be used to stipulate the source and destination files, and if the destination file already exists, it is overwritten.

 WARNING *The cp command on Mac OS X not only copies the file itself, but also the resource fork of a file. The resource fork is metadata describing the file. Mac OS X uses a combination of file extensions and metadata to identify file types and other properties.*

To copy a directory, you have to use the -r option with cp, like this:

```
cp -r ~/Desktop/sourcedir ~/Documents
```

This copies the directory sourcedir in the Desktop folder, plus all its contents, into a new directory called sourcedir in the Documents folder. If you want to rename the copied directory, you can simply do this:

```
cp -r ~/Desktop/sourcedir ~/Documents/destdir
```

The copy is now called destdir, although it is still located in the Documents folder. If the destination directory already exists, cp will not replace it but will make the new copy a subdirectory of the destination directory.

Both mv and cp can be used with multiple sources, as long as the destination is a directory. For example, the command

```
mv file1 file2 file3 destdir
```

moves the files file1, file2, and file3, which are in the current working directory, to the destdir directory, which is also in the current working directory. As always, any form of path can be used for the files and directories in the command.

Removing files is fairly straightforward; you simply use the rm command and give the path to the file like this:

```
rm somefile
```

This removes the file somefile in the current working directory. You can also remove multiple files simply by including their paths as arguments to rm, as shown here:

```
rm ~/Desktop/temp.txt ~/rubbish.doc ~/Documents/project.txt
```

This command removes three different files, which are located in three different directories.

To remove a directory, you either have to supply the -r option to rm or use the rmdir command. Here is an example of each approach:

```
rm -r ~/Desktop/somedir
rmdir ~/Desktop/somedir
```

Making a new directory is achieved using the mkdir command. You give the path to the new directory as an argument like this:

```
mkdir /Users/demo/Desktop/newdir
```

This creates a directory called newdir in the Desktop folder of the user demo.

In the following example, an error will result if you try to issue the command before first creating the newdir directory:

```
mkdir /Users/demo/Desktop/newdir/otherdir
```

`mkdir` only makes a new subdirectory of an existing directory unless you supply the `-p` option, in which case it also generates any non-existing intermediate directories. So the preceding command could be made to succeed by changing it to this:

```
mkdir -p /Users/demo/Desktop/newdir/otherdir
```

File Permissions

All the commands discussed so far will succeed only if you have permission to perform the requested operation. Every file and directory in the file system has a set of permissions; in the Finder, you have limited access to these permissions when you select a file, choose File ⇨ Get Info, and open the Sharing & Permissions section of the Get Info window. This tells you who owns the file and the operations you are allowed to perform. If you are the owner, you can also change the permissions of the file or folder.

 WARNING *This section discusses traditional Unix file permissions. Mac OS X includes a second means of setting permissions for a file: Access Control Lists (ACLs). ACLs are considerably more flexible than traditional Unix permissions, but they are also more involved. If you want to learn about ACLs, you can start by reading the man page for the* `chmod` *command. This command can be used to interact with ACL attributes.*

The Bash shell gives you even more control over permissions and ownership. You can find out the permissions of a file or directory using the `ls -1` command, as explained earlier. For example, to learn the permissions of the commands in /bin, you could enter the following:

```
ls -l /bin
```

The output of this command lists one line for each file. Each line looks similar to this:

```
-r-xr-xr-x  1 root  wheel  44272 May 18 21:35 cat
```

The owner or user of the file is the third entry on the line — in this case `root`. The permissions of three different types of users are given in the string at the start of the line. The first character in the string indicates the file type, with a hyphen for a file and `d` for a directory. The rest of the string can be broken into three blocks of three characters, giving the permissions of the owner, group, and other users, respectively. Figure 12-3 shows the string in detail.

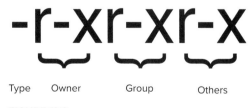

FIGURE 12-3

The permissions applying to the owner of the file are in places 2–4, which are r-x in this example. The first of these three characters indicates whether the owner has read permission, allowing the contents of the file to be examined or copied, for example. A letter r indicates that read permission is granted; a hyphen indicates that reading is not allowed.

The second character indicates if the owner is allowed to write to the file by replacing it with another file or changing its contents. A w means writing is allowed; in this example, the owner is not allowed to change the file, so a hyphen appears as the second character.

The last of the three characters pertains to whether the owner can execute the file. If a file is executable, it can be run as a program or script. An x here indicates that the file can be executed by the owner, and a hyphen indicates that this is not allowed. This permission is somewhat different for directories, because they cannot be executed. For a directory, an x indicates that the owner can examine the directory's contents; for example, by listing them with the ls command.

The remaining six characters in the string are divided between permissions for the file's group and permissions for all other users. Each file has a group, as well as an owner. The group that a file belongs to is given as the fourth entry on the line printed by ls -l; in this example, it is wheel. Each user belongs to one or more groups, and if a given user is in the group that a file belongs to, that user has the group permissions.

If a user is not the owner of the file and is not in the group that the file belongs to, the permissions given by the last set of three characters applies.

If you are the owner of a file, you can change its permissions. The command chmod is used for this purpose. chmod allows you to add or remove permissions for the owner, group, or other users. For example, to make a file executable by the file owner, you could do this:

```
chmod u+x ~/Desktop/somefile
```

The argument u+x indicates that the owner of the file, as indicated by the u, should be granted execute permissions for the file at the path ~/Desktop/somefile. The plus symbol (+) indicates that permissions should be granted, whereas a minus symbol or hyphen (-) indicates that permissions should be withdrawn.

Just as you can change the permissions for the file's owner by using a u in the argument string, you can also change permissions for the group by using g and other users by using o. You can even simultaneously update permissions for more than one type of user and/or multiple permission types. Take the following example:

```
chmod ug+rw somefile
```

This command grants read and write permission to the file owner and group users. To remove these permissions again, you can use this command:

```
chmod ug-rw somefile
```

The root user can change a file's owner or group. The chown command is used for this purpose, as in this example:

```
chown terry somefile.txt
```

This changes the owner of the file given as the second argument to user `terry`. The group of the file is left unchanged.

> **NOTE** `root` *is known as the superuser and can do anything, regardless of permissions. If you are an administrator on your Mac, you can carry out commands as if you are the superuser using the* `sudo` *command, which is discussed shortly. You need to be careful when you are carrying out commands as the root user, because the results of a mistake could be drastic. A mistyped command could easily delete all the files on your file system, so be careful.*

To change the group of a file, the root user can issue a `chown` command like this:

```
chown :admin somefile.txt
```

The `root` user can also change the group and owner of a file, or multiple files, simultaneously with `chown`. Here is such an example:

```
chown terry:admin file1 file2 ~/Desktop/file3
```

The new owner is listed before the colon, and the group after it. The rest of the line contains the paths to the files for which ownership is to be modified.

If you are an administrator of your Mac and need to perform an operation for which you do not have permission, you can use the `sudo` command. `sudo` performs an operation as the user `root`.

By way of example, suppose you want to move a new executable to the `/usr/bin` folder. `/usr/bin` is writable only by the `root` user, so trying to move a file into it causes an error, as shown here:

```
Macintosh:~ sample$ mv exefile /usr/bin
mv: rename Desktop/temp.py to /usr/bin/temp.py: Permission denied
```

To overcome this restriction, you can use `sudo` as follows:

```
sudo mv exefile /usr/bin
```

You will be prompted to enter your password; if you enter it, the `mv` command will succeed. You can use `sudo` in this way to perform any command for which you don't have permission, including `chown`.

> **WARNING** *The* `sudo` *command expects you to enter your own password when prompted, not the password of the superuser* `root`*.*

Globbing

If you want to perform a command for several files, it can become tedious typing full names and paths. The Bash shell allows you to take some shortcuts, using pattern matching within filenames and paths. This is known in the world of shell scripting as *globbing*.

To use globbing, you insert pattern-matching characters into strings to match certain filenames or paths. The pattern-matching characters match zero or more characters in the name or path. Probably the most widely used pattern-matching character is the wildcard *. This special character will match any zero or more characters. For example, used on its own, it matches all files and directories:

```
Macintosh:/bin sample$ cd /bin
Macintosh:/bin sample$ echo *
[ bash cat chmod cp csh date dd df domainname echo ed expr hostname kill ksh
    launchctl link ln ls mkdir mv pax ps pwd rcp rm rmdir sh sleep stty sync
    tcsh test unlink wait4path zsh
```

This example uses the echo command to print out all the names that * matches, in the directory /bin. Because * matches any number of characters, all the files in /bin are echoed. The Bash shell replaces the wildcard with the names that it matches before passing the resulting filenames as arguments to the echo command. The echo command itself is not passed the wildcard — the shell interprets any globbing characters before it runs the echo command.

The * character is also useful in combination with non-special characters. For example, suppose you want to list all the text files in your Desktop folder. Here is how you could do it:

```
ls ~/Desktop/*.txt
```

The path ~/Desktop/*.txt matches any file or directory located in the Desktop folder with the extension .txt. The * matches any string, of any length, and .txt only matches names that end in exactly those characters. Together, *.txt matches any name ending in .txt.

The * character is also useful in the middle of a path. Suppose you want to find all .txt files in a subdirectory of the Desktop folder. Here is how to do that:

```
ls ~/Desktop/*/*.txt
```

Notice that you can use more than one pattern-matching character in each path. The first asterisk matches any directory in the Desktop folder, and the second one, together with .txt, matches any file or directory name ending with the extension txt.

If you want a wildcard that matches any single character, rather than zero or more characters that are matched with the * character, you can use ?. The ? wildcard matches only one character. The following lists files that have exactly five characters in their names, with blah as the first four:

```
ls blah?
```

A file called blah will not match, but blah0 or blaht will. blah00 will not match, because ? matches exactly one character.

If you want to limit the number of possible characters matched, you can enter the allowed characters in square braces, like this:

```
ls blah[01]
```

This would match `blah0` or `blah1`, but not `blah2`, for example. You can add as many characters between the braces as you like — any of them can match.

You can use various characters to modify the behavior of the pattern-matching braces. If you insert a ^ character directly after the first brace, only characters not included between the braces will match. For example,

```
ls blah[^01]
```

will match `blah2`, but not `blah0` or `blah1`.

There are also some sets of characters that you can specify within the braces. For example, `:alpha:` represents alphabetic characters and `:upper:` represents uppercase characters. So

```
ls blah[:alpha:]
```

matches `blaht`, but not `blah0`. For a complete list of character sets, see the Bash man page.

> **WARNING** *Some of the need for pattern matching is removed by Bash's autocompletion feature. If you enter the beginning of a file or directory name at the Bash prompt, you can press the Tab key to see if Bash can complete it for you by considering the possibilities in the given context.*
>
> *If Bash can find a unique possibility, it inserts it for you, saving you some typing. If it can't, it does nothing. But if you press the Tab key a second time, it shows you all the possible matches. You can then add a few more characters to ensure a unique match and use autocompletion again to finish entering the name.*
>
> *Autocompletion also works with commands. Try entering* `system_` *and pressing the Tab key. Bash should find the* `system_profiler` *command in your path and fill in the rest of the command for you.*

In the next Try It Out, you put theory into practice by interacting with your Mac's file system via the Bash shell. In doing so, you use fundamental commands such as `ls`, `cd`, `mv`, `mkdir`, `chmod`, `chown`, `sudo`, and `rm`.

TRY IT OUT   Interacting with the File System

1.   Open the Terminal window in the Terminal application.

2.   Change to the /usr/bin directory and list all commands that contain gnu.

```
Macintosh:~ sample$ cd /usr/bin
Macintosh:/usr/bin sample$ ls *gnu*
gnuattach       gnudoit         gnuserv
gnuclient       gnumake         gnutar
```

3.   Copy the commands containing gnu to your Desktop folder and then change to the Desktop folder. After typing Desktop in the cd command, try pressing the Tab key to use Bash's autocompletion feature to finish off the path.

```
Macintosh:/usr/bin sample$ cp *gnu* ~/Desktop/
Macintosh:/usr/bin sample$ cd ~/Desktop
```

4.   Make a subdirectory of the Desktop folder called **somecommands** and move the commands that you just copied into that subdirectory.

```
Macintosh:~/Desktop sample$ mkdir somecommands
Macintosh:~/Desktop sample$ mv *gnu* somecommands
```

5.   Change to the somecommands directory and list its contents.

```
Macintosh:~/Desktop sample$ cd somecommands/
/Users/terry/Desktop/somecommands
Macintosh:~/Desktop/somecommands sample$ ls
gnuattach       gnudoit         gnuserv
gnuclient       gnumake         gnutar
```

6.   List full details of the gnutar command, using ls -l.

```
Macintosh:~/Desktop/somecommands sample$ ls -l gnutar
-rwxr-xr-x  1 sample sample 991552 Sep 10 14:29 gnutar
```

7.   Change the permissions of gnutar, removing read and execute permissions for all users that are neither the file's owner nor in the file's group.

```
Macintosh:~/Desktop/somecommands sample$ chmod o-rx gnutar
```

8.   Change the owner and group of the gnutar file to some other user on your system. In the example given here, the new user and group are demo. You should use a user that exists on your system in place of demo. First try to use chown without the sudo command. An error should arise. When it does, use the sudo command to force the change of ownership. You will be prompted for your password.

```
Macintosh:~/Desktop/somecommands sample$ chown demo:demo gnutar
chown: gnutar: Operation not permitted
Macintosh:~/Desktop/somecommands sample$ sudo chown demo:demo gnutar
Password: *********
```

9. List full details of the `gnutar` command again. Notice how the permissions, owner, and group have changed.

```
Macintosh:~/Desktop/somecommands sample$ ls -l gnutar
-rwxr-xr-x  1 demo  demo  991552 Sep 10 14:29 gnutar
```

10. Move down one directory to the `Desktop` directory and remove the `somecommands` directory. Answer **y** when prompted as to whether you would like to override the permissions of the `gnutar` command.

```
Macintosh:~/Desktop/somecommands sample$ cd ..
Macintosh:~/Desktop sample$ rm -r somecommands
override rwxr-x---  demo/demo for somecommands/gnutar? y
```

How It Works

Most of this example involves fairly straightforward changes of the directory, and the copying and moving of files. These are very common actions when working in a shell, and you should learn them well.

To list the files containing `gnu` in the `/usr/bin` directory, two special globbing characters were used.

```
Macintosh:/usr/bin sample$ ls *gnu*
```

Because the `*` character matches zero or more characters, `*gnu*` matches any file or directory name containing `gnu`, including cases where `gnu` is at the beginning or end of the name.

After copying the files containing `gnu` to the `Desktop` folder, a new directory is created with `mkdir`, and the commands are moved into it with `mv`. The `gnutar` command is then used to practice the modification of ownership and permissions. First, the rights of other users to read or execute the file are removed, using `chmod` with the argument `o-rx`. `o` refers to users that are neither the owner nor in the file's group. The hyphen means that rights are being revoked, and the `rx` indicates that the rights being revoked are for reading and executing. (Other users did not have write permissions to begin with, so they do not need to be revoked.)

Next, an attempt is made to change the owner and group of the `gnutar` file. This does not succeed at first, because normal users are not allowed to change ownership of a file; only `root` can change ownership. To overcome this impedance, the `sudo` command is used to run the `chown` command.

To finish the example, the `somecommands` directory is deleted. Because you do not own the `gnutar` file, you are prompted about whether the permissions should be overridden. If you answer in the affirmative, the `gnutar` file and the rest of the `somecommands` directory are deleted.

Searching for Files

With the integration of Spotlight search technology, you have some pretty powerful tools for finding files and directories available to you on Mac OS X. In addition to the GUI, Apple has provided tools for searching with Spotlight from the command line. You can use Spotlight to search for files by name, but it also searches file content and metadata.

Metadata is data about data. It includes information such as a file's name, the date it was created, the type of data it contains, and much more. If you want to know what metadata is associated with a particular file, you can use the `mdls` command to find out, as shown in this example:

```
Macintosh:~ sample$ mdls Sites/index.html
kMDItemContentCreationDate     = 2007-11-22 20:48:36 +0100
kMDItemContentModificationDate = 2007-11-22 20:48:36 +0100
kMDItemContentType             = "dyn.age80u7drru"
kMDItemDisplayName             = "index.html"
kMDItemFSContentChangeDate     = 2007-11-22 20:48:36 +0100
kMDItemFSCreationDate          = 2007-11-22 20:48:36 +0100
kMDItemFSCreatorCode           = ""
kMDItemFSFinderFlags           = 0
kMDItemFSHasCustomIcon         = 0
kMDItemFSInvisible             = 0
kMDItemFSIsExtensionHidden     = 0
kMDItemFSIsStationery          = 0
kMDItemFSLabel                 = 0
kMDItemFSName                  = "index.html"
kMDItemFSNodeCount             = 0
kMDItemFSOwnerGroupID          = 504
kMDItemFSOwnerUserID           = 504
kMDItemFSSize                  = 5
kMDItemFSTypeCode              = ""
kMDItemKind                    = "HTML document"
kMDItemLastUsedDate            = 2007-11-22 20:48:36 +0100
kMDItemUsedDates               = (
  "2007-11-22 09:00:00 +0100"
)
```

Spotlight command-line tools are located in the `/usr/bin` directory and begin with the letters `md`, which stand for *metadata*. As you can see from the output of the `mdls` command, even a simple HTML file has a lot of metadata associated with it. Each *metadata attribute* is associated with a key; the keys can be seen in the left column of the output of `mdls`, with the data value itself given in the right column.

To search the metadata and content of files, you can use the `mdfind` command. For example, to find all files that include the text `Personal Web Sharing` in the metadata or content, you could issue the following command at the prompt:

```
mdfind "Personal Web Sharing"
```

You can restrict your search to particular metadata attributes by using a simple query string. For example, to search only the metadata attribute `kMDItemFSName` of each file, which contains the filename, you could issue the following command:

```
mdfind "kMDItemFSName == 'Personal Web Sharing'"
```

The string passed to `mdfind` is a query string. In this case, the path to any file whose `kMDItemFSName` attribute includes `Personal Web Sharing` will be written out.

There are also some traditional Unix tools that can help you locate files and directories by name. One of the easiest ways to find paths containing a given string is to use the `locate` command. For example, to find all paths containing the string `NSApplication.h`, you could issue the following command:

```
Macintosh:~ sample$ locate NSApplication.h
/Developer/SDKs/MacOSX10.4u.sdk/System/Library/Frameworks/AppKit.framework/
    Versions/C/Headers/NSApplication.h
/Developer/SDKs/MacOSX10.5.sdk/System/Library/Frameworks/AppKit.framework/
    Versions/C/Headers/NSApplication.h
/Developer/SDKs/MacOSX10.6.sdk/System/Library/Frameworks/AppKit.framework/Versions/
    C/Headers/NSApplication.h
/System/Library/Frameworks/AppKit.framework/Versions/C/Headers/NSApplication.h
```

As you can see, even a reasonably unique string such as this can generate several results. Bear in mind that the string can match anywhere in the path. If it matches a directory name, for example, the whole contents of the directory, and all its subdirectories, will be printed. Try to be specific about what you are searching for when using `locate`.

The `locate` command works with a database of all the files on your file system, which gets updated weekly by Mac OS X. This means that new files are unlikely to be found by the `locate` command. `locate` is useful for finding files that do not change often, such as commands, libraries, and header files. It will not be very effective for finding regularly changing files and directories, such as those in your own projects.

 WARNING *The* `locate` *database gets updated once a week on Mac OS X, but only after it has been created. You usually have to create the initial database yourself. To do this, issue the command* `sudo /usr/libexec/locate.updatedb` *in Terminal.*

A command you can use to search the file system in its current state is `find`. Of course, `find` doesn't have the benefit of a database, so it is slower than `locate`. It has to go through the file system one file or directory at a time, checking the filename and reporting results. But `find` has many more options than `locate`, and it's a powerful command to learn.

The most common way of using `find` is like this:

```
find /System/Library/Frameworks -name NSApplication.h
```

This command searches in the directory `/System/Library/Frameworks`, and all subdirectories, for any file or directory with the name `NSApplication.h`.

You can also use globbing characters in the name you pass to `find`. To search for any file with a name containing `darwin` in the current working directory or any subdirectory, you could enter this:

```
find . -name "*darwin*"
```

The `*` characters match zero or more characters in the name, so the path of any file whose name contains `darwin`, including those that begin or end with `darwin`, will be printed.

You can also carry out commands on the files you locate with `find`. For this, you use the `-exec` option, which runs a command that you provide, like this:

```
find . -name rubbish -exec rm {} \;
```

This command finds files called `rubbish` in the current working directory or any of its subdirectories. When a file called `rubbish` is found, the command given after `-exec` is performed. The command in this case is `rm`, to remove the file. The path of the located file can be accessed using the special character `{}`, so `rm {}` is the same as typing `rm` followed by the path to the file. Commands following the `-exec` option need to be terminated by a semicolon, but because the semicolon has a special meaning to the Bash shell, it is escaped with a backslash.

The `find` command is very powerful, with many options. For example, you can list or carry out commands on files that were last modified before a given date. Perhaps you want to remove them after a while. In fact, your Mac OS X system uses the `find` command every day to clean up old files. Take a look in the file `/etc/periodic/daily/110.clean-tmps`, which is a Bash script run by Mac OS X every day. You should be able to find a section similar to this:

```
rc=$(for dir in $daily_clean_tmps_dirs
    do
        [ ."${dir#/}" != ."$dir" -a -d $dir ] && cd $dir && {
            find -dx . -fstype local -type f $args -delete $print
            find -dx . -fstype local ! -name . -type d $dargs -delete $print
            } | sed "s,^\\., $dir,"
    done | tee /dev/stderr | wc -l)
```

In short, this complicated set of commands uses `find` to remove files and directories located in `/tmp` and other directories used for temporary file storage, after they have not been accessed for a number of days. For more information on the options used in these commands, and `find` in general, read the `find` man page.

Working with Text

An important part of using a shell is being able to manipulate text, whether the text is the contents of a file or the output of a command that needs to be piped into a second command. Unix systems have a number of powerful tools for working with text, including `grep`, `sed`, and `awk`. This section covers the most important commands for handling text on Mac OS X.

A simple but commonly used command is `echo`, which simply prints out whatever follows it on the line, after the shell has substituted any variable values or special characters. For example, to print a greeting to standard output, you could do this:

```
Macintosh:~ sample$ echo Hello Cupertino !
Hello Cupertino !
```

But you can make your message a bit more flexible by including variables and other special Bash characters. Consider the following example:

```
Macintosh:~/Desktop sample$ touch Cupertino
Macintosh:~/Desktop sample$ GREETING=Hello
Macintosh:~/Desktop sample$ echo $GREETING Cuper* !
Hello Cupertino !
```

The `touch` command simply updates the timestamp of the file given as an argument; or, if the file doesn't exist, it creates a new empty file with that name. In this case, an empty file called `Cupertino` is created.

A variable called `GREETING` is then initialized to `Hello`, and the `echo` statement combines the value of the variable, as given by `$GREETING`, with the names of all files and directories in the current directory beginning with `Cuper`. `Cuper*` is interpreted by the shell as a glob and expanded before the string is passed to `echo`. The net result is precisely the same as the first example, which employed the `echo` command.

The `cat` command can be used to concatenate (join) a number of files, printing the result to standard output. If used with a single file, it simply writes the contents of the file to standard output. To join two files, creating a third, you could do this:

```
cat file1 file2 > file3
```

After this command, `file3` will first contain the contents of `file1`, followed by the contents of `file2`. `file1` and `file2` themselves will be unaltered. If `file3` exists prior to the operation, it will be overwritten.

`cat` is often used to initiate a chain of operations on the contents of a file rather than using the `<` redirection operator. For example, you could extract all lines of a file containing the word `Cupertino` by issuing the following command:

```
cat somefile | grep Cupertino
```

The `cat` command writes the contents of `somefile` to standard output. The standard output is piped into a `grep` command, which prints any line containing the text `Cupertino`.

`grep` is a very useful command that can be used to extract lines of text matching some pattern. In the simplest case, it just searches for a literal match to a string as in the following example:

```
Macintosh:~/Desktop sample$ grep '<TABLE' index.html
<TABLE WIDTH="85%" BORDER="0" CELLSPACING="15" CELLPADDING="0">
```

The `grep` command searches the file `index.html` for any lines that include `'<TABLE'`, which is an opening tag for a HTML table. Notice the use of single quotes; this is necessary because the `<` character has a special meaning to the shell (it is the input redirection operator). If you enclose a string in single quotes, the shell will ignore any special meanings and pass the string unaltered to `grep`.

`grep` can also be used with special pattern-matching strings called *regular expressions*. You can think of regular expressions as being similar to globbing, but do not confuse the two: although the characters used for pattern-matching in globs and regular expressions are often the same, their meanings can be quite different.

Here is a simple example of using a regular expression with `grep`:

```
Macintosh:~/Desktop sample$ grep 'BORDER.*CELLSPACING' index.html
<TABLE WIDTH="85%" BORDER="0" CELLSPACING="15" CELLPADDING="0">
```

The pattern to be matched is `'BORDER.*CELLSPACING'`. This regular expression matches any line that includes the text BORDER, followed by zero or more arbitrary characters, and then the text CELLSPACING. The period (.) character is special in regular expressions; it matches exactly one character, similar to the ? in Bash globbing. The * character has a very different implication in regular expressions. It means that the preceding character can occur zero or more times. In this case, the period is the preceding character, so it can be used to match zero or more arbitrary characters. The complete pattern thus matches any string beginning with CELLSPACING and ending with BORDER, with any characters in between.

Two types of regular expression that you can use with `grep` are *basic* and *extended*. There is not enough room to cover all the intricacies of regular expressions in this chapter, but they are powerful and well worth learning. To get you started, the following table describes the most important extended regular expression patterns and what they match. To use extended regular expressions, insert the `-E` option in front of the regular expression. Basic regular expressions are similar to extended regular expressions, but more restrictive. See the man page of `grep` for more details.

PATTERN	DESCRIPTION	EXAMPLE	DOES MATCH	DOESN'T MATCH
.	Matches any single character.	char.t	char0t chartt	chart
*	Modifies the meaning of the previous character. A match can occur with zero or more of the previous character in the regular expression.	char*t	chat chart charrt	
+	Similar to *, but requires at least one match. Zero occurrences does not match.	char+t charrt	chart charrrt	chat
{n}	Matches exactly *n* occurrences of the previous character.	char{3}blah	charrrblah	chablah charblah charrblah
[...]	Matches any character given in the square braces.	char[xYz]t	charxt charYt charzt	chart charyt charwt

PATTERN	DESCRIPTION	EXAMPLE	DOES MATCH	DOESN'T MATCH
(...)	Used to group characters together.	char(xyz)*blah	charblah charxyzblah charxyzxyzblah	charxblah charxyblah
|	Allows two different expressions to match.	char(x|yz)+blah	charxblah charyzblah charxxblah charxyzblah charyzxblah charyzyzblah	charblah charzyxblah charyyzzblah

grep is a good command for extracting lines of text, but it can't help you much if you want to modify text. For that, you need a more powerful tool, such as sed or awk.

awk is named after its creators — Aho, Weinberger, and Kernighan — and is actually a whole language unto itself. Unfortunately, there isn't the space here to do it justice. It can be used for complex text manipulation, but you can also use it for simple tasks such as extracting a word based on its position in a line. For example, suppose you wanted to use the wc command to count the number of words in a file. You could do something like this:

```
Macintosh:~/Desktop sample$ wc index.html
     125     799    5754 index.html
```

wc provides the number of lines, words, and characters in the given file. But in this example, you are interested only in the number of words. You can extract this number with the following command involving awk:

```
Macintosh:~/Desktop sample$ wc index.html | awk '{ print $2; }'
799
```

In this case, the output of wc has been piped to awk. An awk program is given in-between single quotes. awk programs process one line of text at a time, in a repetitive manner. This very simple awk program prints the second whitespace-separated entry on each line that it reads. Because only one line is output by the wc command, awk prints only the string 799, which appears second on the line.

> **NOTE** The number of words in a file can be obtained more easily by simply supplying the -l option to wc. However, this would not have demonstrated the usefulness of awk, which was the purpose of the preceding example.

The sed command is not a complete programming language as is awk, but it is a very powerful editor. A common use for sed is to replace one regular expression with another. For example, the following command replaces any occurrences of the text Apple with Apple Inc:

```
sed -e 's/Apple/Apple Inc/g' somefile.txt
```

The resulting text is written to standard output. The first argument to `sed`, which is enclosed in single quotations, is an editing command; it tells `sed` what text substitution to make. A substitution command takes the form `s/.../.../g`, with the regular expression between the first and second forward slashes replaced by the text between the second and third slashes.

Here is a more advanced example, leveraging the possibilities of regular expressions:

```
sed 's/< *[Tt][Aa][Bb][Ll][Ee].*>/<table class="tableclass">/g' index.html
```

This example scans the file `index.html` for any HTML opening tags for tables. These tags take the basic form `<TABLE ...>` and can include attributes after the `TABLE` label. The `sed` command searches for these tags and replaces them with `<table class="tableclass">` when found.

The regular expression used to find the `TABLE` tags is quite involved. It looks like this:

```
< *[Tt][Aa][Bb][Ll][Ee].*>
```

It begins with the `<` character, which is followed by a space and a `*` character. The `*` indicates that a match can include zero or more of the previous character, which in this case is a space. A series of five square braces follow, each containing an upper- and lowercase letter. Together, these braces account for the case-insensitivity of HTML, allowing for every legal form of the string `table`, including `TABLE`, `table`, `TaBlE`, and `tabLE`. The regular expression handles the possibility of attributes by including the characters `.*`, which match zero or more arbitrary characters after the `table` label. The `>` terminates the tag.

In the following Try It Out, you use some of the commands you have learned for manipulating text to change the table cell widths in an HTML file.

TRY IT OUT   **Editing an HTML File with sed**

1.   Open a window in the Terminal application.

2.   At the prompt, change to your `Desktop` directory using the `cd` command as follows:

```
Macintosh:~ sample$ cd ~/Desktop
/Users/sample/Desktop
```

3.   Copy the default `index.html` file from your `Sites` folder to the current working directory.

```
Macintosh:~/Desktop sample$ cp ~/Sites/index.html.
```

4.   Use `cat` to pipe the contents of the `index.html` file into the input of `grep`, extracting any lines that include style declarations of the form `font-family: "Lucida Grande"`.

```
Macintosh:~/Desktop sample$ cat index.html | grep -i 'font-family: "Lucida Grande"'
            p { color: #666; font-size: 16px; font-family: "Lucida Grande", Arial,
              sans-serif; font-weight: normal; margin-top: 0; }
            h1 { color: #778fbd; font-size: 20px; font-family: "Lucida Grande",
              Arial, sans-serif; font-weight: 500; line-height: 32px; margin-top:
              4px; }
```

```
                   h2 { color: #778fbd; font-size: 18px; font-family: "Lucida Grande",
                     Arial, sans-serif; font-weight: normal; margin: 0.83em 0 0; }
                   h3 { color: #666; font-size: 60px; font-family: "Lucida Grande", Arial,
                     sans-serif; font-weight: bold; text-align: center; letter-spacing:
                     -1px; width: auto; }
```

5. Using `sed`, replace all these tags with the style declaration `font-family: Helvetica`, and put the resulting HTML in a file called `new.html`.

```
Macintosh:~/Desktop sample$ sed 's/font-family: "Lucida Grande"/font-family:
    Helvetica/g' index.html > new.html
```

6. Confirm that the tags have been substituted by using `grep` on the file `new.html`.

```
Macintosh:~/Desktop sample$ grep font-family new.html
                   p { color: #666; font-size: 16px; font-family: Helvetica, Arial,
                     sans-serif; font-weight: normal; margin-top: 0; }
                   h1 { color: #778fbd; font-size: 20px; font-family: Helvetica, Arial,
                     sans-serif; font-weight: 500; line-height: 32px; margin-top: 4px; }
                   h2 { color: #778fbd; font-size: 18px; font-family: Helvetica, Arial,
                     sans-serif; font-weight: normal; margin: 0.83em 0 0; }
                   h3 { color: #666; font-size: 60px; font-family: Helvetica, Arial,
                     sans-serif; font-weight: bold; text-align: center; letter-spacing:
                     -1px; width: auto; }
```

How It Works

If you haven't modified your `Sites` directory since installing Mac OS X, it should still include a default `index.html` file, which is used in this example. If you don't have this file anymore, you can use any HTML file you like. Just pick out a string in the file, and try to replace it.

In step 4, `grep` is used to extract any line containing a particular declaration for the font Lucida Grande. The `-i` option stands for *case-insensitive*, so `grep` ignores case.

The `sed` command substitutes the font declaration for a different declaration with the font Helvetica. Results are redirected with the > shell operator to the file `new.html`.

The last `grep` command confirms that the styles have been updated as expected. You can also examine the `new.html` file for yourself with Nano if you want to be sure everything went as planned.

Process Control

Running short subprocesses in the foreground is fairly straightforward, but if you have something more time-consuming, you will want to run it in the background. You need to be able to monitor the progress of your background process, to find out its status and whether it has exited. Even if you don't initiate background processes very often yourself, many are run by the `root` user to handle all sorts of administrative activities.

> **WARNING** *Many background processes are daemons. Daemons run continuously, and are often started when the system boots up. They typically listen for requests on a network port and act on them when they are received, perhaps starting up other programs.*
>
> *If you want to see what sort of daemons are running on your system, open the Activity Monitor utility. In an Activity Monitor window, select System Processes from the Show pop-up button in the toolbar.*

The ps command is used to check the status of processes running on your system. If you use it without any arguments, it prints the processes associated with the shell you are using. For example:

```
Macintosh:~ sample$ ps
  PID  TT  STAT     TIME COMMAND
 1112 std  S      0:00.14 -bash
```

Only one process is shown in this case: the Bash shell itself. Other information given includes the PID, or process identifier; STAT, the status of the process; and TIME, the CPU time consumed. The PID is needed to identify the process in any commands that you issue. The possible status values are given in the following table.

STATUS VALUE	DESCRIPTION
D	The process is in disk, and cannot be interrupted.
I	The process is idle. It has been sleeping for longer than 20 seconds.
R	The process is running.
S	The process has just been put to sleep. It has been sleeping for less than 20 seconds.
T	The process is stopped.
U	The process is waiting in an uninterruptible state.
Z	The process is a zombie. It is dead.

When you start a process in the background, it appears in the list produced by ps. For example, the following runs the sleep command in the background:

```
Macintosh:~ sample$ sleep 10 &
[1] 18700
Macintosh:~ sample$ ps
PID TTY          TIME CMD
17963 ttys000   0:00.06 -bash
18700 ttys000   0:00.00 sleep 10
```

The `sleep` command simply pauses for the time you give as an argument, which in this case is 10 seconds. The `&` has been used to put the command into the background. When you do this, the `PID` of the subprocess is printed, which is `18700` in this example. When the `ps` command is issued, the `sleep` process shows up with the expected `PID` of `18700`.

Without options, `ps` only supplies information about the processes that you own and that were started from the shell. You can get information about other processes that you own using the `-x` option. The output of `ps -x` includes any applications that are running, whether you started them yourself or not. For example, apart from the applications you initiated yourself, there are processes for the Finder, Dock, and iCal, which you may not have realized existed.

`ps` can also be used to get information about other processes running on the system. Many options are available, and you should take a look at the `ps` man page to decide which ones you would like to include. Using `-xj` with the command provides enough information for most purposes, as you can see here:

```
Macintosh:~ sample$ ps -xj
USER      PID  PPID  PGID  SESS JOBC STAT   TT       TIME COMMAND
sample    146    1   146  7da8000   0 Ss     ??    0:10.58 /sbin/launchd
sample  25427   146 25427 7da8000   1 S      ??    1:32.79 /System/Library/
   CoreServices/Dock.app/Contents/MacOS/Dock
sample  25428   146 25428 7da8000   1 S      ??    2:26.54 /System/Library/
   CoreServices/SystemUIServer.app/Contents/MacOS/SystemUIServer
sample  25429   146 25429 7da8000   1 S      ??    0:36.11 /System/Library/
   CoreServices/Finder.app/Contents/MacOS/Finder
sample  25431   146 25431 7da8000   1 S      ??    0:00.01 /usr/sbin/pboard
sample  25442   146 25442 7da8000   1 S      ??    0:03.80 /System/Library/
   Frameworks/ApplicationServices.framework/Frameworks/ATS.framework/Support/fontd
sample  25451   146 25451 7da8000   1 S      ??    0:00.79 /usr/libexec/
   UserEventAgent -l Aqua
sample  25458   146 25458 7da8000   1 S      ??    0:00.29 /Users/sample/Library/
   Application Support/Textcast/httpd/textcast_httpd
sample  25464   146 25464 7da8000   1 S      ??    0:00.39 /Applications/
   iTunes.app/Contents/Resources/iTunesHelper.app/Contents/MacOS/iTunesHelper
   -psn_0_6018493
sample  25465   146 25465 7da8000   1 S      ??    0:03.27 /Applications/
   Yojimbo.app/Contents/MacOS/Yojimbo -psn_0_6022590
...
```

The output has been truncated, but you can see that this set of options gives you information about all processes, and for all users.

One time you will need `ps` is when something goes wrong, and you want to terminate a process. If you can find out the process identifier using `ps`, you can issue a `kill` command to stop it. To demonstrate, the `sleep` command is utilized again in the following example:

```
Macintosh:~ sample$ sleep 3600 &
[1] 18707
Macintosh:~ sample$ ps
PID TTY           TIME CMD
17963 ttys000    0:00.06 -bash
18707 ttys000    0:00.00 sleep 3600
Macintosh:~ sample$ kill -9 18707
```

```
Macintosh:~ sample$ ps
PID TTY           TIME CMD
17963 ttys000    0:00.06 -bash
```

The `sleep` process is set to sleep for 3,600 seconds, or one hour. Instead of waiting for it to exit by itself, the `kill` command is used with the option `-9` and the `PID` to terminate the process. The last `ps` command confirms that the `sleep` process has exited.

> **WARNING** *You can use* `kill` *to terminate a process in the background, but what about when the process is in the foreground? Simply press Control-C, and the foreground process will be killed.*

You can also stipulate processes to kill by name, rather than process identifier. The `killall` command is for this purpose, as shown in the following example:

```
Macintosh:~ sample$ sleep 3600 &
[1] 1183
Macintosh:~ sample$ killall sleep
[1]+  Terminated              sleep 3600
```

`killall` kills any process belonging to you that matches the name you pass. Processes of other users, including `root`, are unaffected.

If you do need to kill a process belonging to the root user, or some other user, you can use the `sudo` command along with either `kill` or `killall`. `sudo` performs the command as `root`, and can thus terminate any process. Be careful not to terminate vital processes on your system, or you could crash your Mac.

One drawback of `ps` is that it is static. It prints information about processes running at the time you issue the command, but it never updates. The `top` command gives similar information to `ps`, but it continuously updates. Simply issue

```
top
```

and press **q** when you are ready to exit. `top` gives all sorts of information, too much to cover here. It is particularly useful though for monitoring the percentage of CPU time that each process is using. Perhaps your system is responding slowly, and you want to know if there is a process hogging the CPU. `top` can tell you. If you use the `-u` option, it even orders the processes based on the percentage of CPU time they are using so that you can quickly find the culprit at the head of the list.

Mac OS X Exclusive Commands

If you have experience with other Unix systems, most of the commands discussed in this chapter will be familiar to you. But Mac OS X has a number of commands that are non-standard, but very useful. There are too many to cover in detail, but the following table should give you an idea of what's available. By referencing the man pages, you should be able to figure out how to use each one. If a man page is not available, most commands provide help when you supply the `-h` option.

COMMAND	PURPOSE
diskutil	Command-line equivalent of the Disk Utility application; can be used to check and repair disks and permissions, and erase and partition disks.
hdiutil	Creates, mounts, and manipulates disk images.
installer	The command-line interface to the Installer application; used to install applications that come in packages.
launchd	Starts and stops background processes when certain events occur, such as network traffic or user login. You do not generally interact directly with launchd, but use launchctl instead.
launchctl	Configures the processes run by the launchd daemon. You can have processes start on login, at a certain time, or even periodically. For example, this command runs regular cleanup scripts. launchd is a very flexible tool.
mount_afp	Mounts an AppleShare file system. This is akin to choosing Go ⇨ Connect to Server in Finder.
open	Opens any document or application, just as you would by double-clicking an icon in the Finder.
pmset	Used to control power management. This is of interest to laptop users, because pmset offers more control than is available through the System Preferences application.
system_profiler	Provides the same information found in the System Profiler utility.

Overview of Other Commands

It is impossible to cover all Unix commands in a single chapter, so a selection of the most important has been presented here. But there are many other commands that you may have use for. The following table gives some of the standard Unix commands that have not been discussed in detail so that you can decide for yourself which are useful. Use the man pages to learn more.

COMMAND	PURPOSE
curl	Command-line tool for downloading and uploading files; supports FTP and HTTP protocols.
dig	Tool for interacting with domain name servers (DNS); can be used to determine the IP address of a host, for example.
ftp	Used for transferring files to and from servers using the FTP protocol.
gzip/gunzip	Compresses/decompresses files with the GZIP format.

continues

(continued)

COMMAND	PURPOSE
`netstat`	Used to get detailed information about the network that the computer is attached to.
`nice/renice`	Used to set or change the priority of a running process so that the kernel allots more or less CPU time to it.
`sftp`	Secure version of `ftp`, based on the SSH protocol. Use this to securely transfer files to or from a server.
`ssh`	Secure shell for remotely accessing a system. It can be used to login to a remote system, giving access to a command-line interface. It can also be used to run commands on a remote system, and even allows you to encrypt network traffic between two computers using a technique known as *tunneling*. Tunneling can also be used to avoid limitations imposed by a firewall.
`tar`	Creates and extracts archives of files and directories. An archive is a single file that can contain the data of many files and/or directories.
`zip/unzip`	Compresses/decompresses ZIP archives.

SHELL PROGRAMMING

You can do a lot with Unix commands, but if you have to issue the same commands over and over, it can become pretty tedious. Luckily, it's possible to combine a sequence of commands into a script, which can be run as often as you like. This section shows you how to write and run scripts.

Bash also offers a number of rudimentary programming constructions, such as conditional branching and loops, which may be familiar to you from other programming languages. Although these aspects of Bash can be used when working you're interactively, they are most useful when you're writing shell scripts. The programming aspects of Bash are also covered in this section.

Scripts

Bash scripts are made up of nothing more or less than the commands you enter at the prompt when working interactively. If you enter these commands in a text file, one per line, in the order they are issued, and you change the permissions of the file so that it can be executed, you have a Bash shell script.

Consider this interactive session:

```
Macintosh:~ sample$ cd ~/Desktop/
/Users/sample/Desktop
Macintosh:~/Desktop sample$ touch blah
Macintosh:~/Desktop sample$ mkdir blahdir
Macintosh:~/Desktop sample$ mv blah blahdir/
```

If you find yourself repeating these commands often, you might consider inserting them into a script. The script would look like this:

```
#!/bin/bash
cd ~/Desktop/
touch blah
mkdir blahdir
mv blah blahdir
```

The script simply contains the same commands that were entered at the interactive prompt. The only difference is the first line, which is called a *shebang*. A shebang begins with the characters #!, and ends with a path. It tells the shell that is running the script which program to use to interpret it. In this case, another Bash shell is being used, so the path to the bash command is given. If this were a Perl script, for example, the path to the perl command would be given in the shebang.

When you have added this script to a file, you can run it in two ways. The first is to explicitly use the bash command with the file as an argument, like this:

```
bash scriptfile.sh
```

The bash command is used to run the script in scriptfile.sh. If you take this approach, you do not need to have execute permissions for the file scriptfile.sh. Also, the shebang will be ignored, because you are explicitly passing the script as an argument to bash rather than letting the shell decide what to run the script with.

The second and more common way to run a script is to give the script file execute permissions, in this way:

```
chmod u+x scriptfile.sh
```

With the script now executable, you can run it like this:

```
./scriptfile.sh
```

You need to include an explicit path to the file, unless you have the current working directory in your PATH environment variable.

When you issue this command, the shell you are using examines the shebang and starts a new Bash shell that interprets the script.

Variables

You are already acquainted with environment variables in Bash, but not all variables are environment variables. A variable becomes an environment variable when the export command is used. If a variable is not exported, it is visible within the script in which it is defined, but not, for example, in any subprocesses.

Variables are defined by simply assigning them. They do not have to be declared beforehand, as in some other languages. Here is a simple example of defining and using a variable:

```
ADDRESS='1 Shell Street'
echo $ADDRESS

ADDRESS='2 Shell Street'
echo $ADDRESS
```

Running this script results in the following output:

```
1 Shell Street
2 Shell Street
```

The ADDRESS variable is initially assigned to the string '1 Shell Street'. The quotation marks are important; without them, the ADDRESS variable would be assigned only to 1, and the shell would not know how to interpret the rest of the string, resulting in an error. Later in the script, the ADDRESS variable is reassigned to '2 Shell Street'.

To access the value of a variable, you prepend a $ symbol. To summarize, when assigning a value to a variable, you use the variable name without a $, and when you want to substitute the value of a variable, you do use the $. In cases where the shell cannot determine the variable name, you can use curly braces to clarify matters. Consider this script, for example:

```
SUBJECT=care
echo $SUBJECTless
```

This results in an error, because the shell looks for a variable called SUBJECTless, which doesn't exist. Curly braces are used to fix the problem, as shown here:

```
SUBJECT=care
echo ${SUBJECT}less
```

The script will now print the text careless.

You will have noticed by now that variable names are usually written in capital letters. This is purely a convention; it is not compulsory. You can use lowercase letters or mix upper- and lowercase; however, if you want your scripts to be easily read by others, consider sticking to the convention.

In each of the preceding examples, the shell substitutes the value of any variables *before* the echo commands are called. This applies to all commands, not only echo. Unless you take certain steps to explicitly prevent variable substitution (discussed in the next section, "Quoting"), the shell substitutes any variables before running the command.

The Bash shell also provides array type variables. Arrays allow you to include multiple values in a single variable. You access the stored values using an index. Here is an example of defining and using an array:

```
ADDRESS[0]=Hello
ADDRESS[1]=there
ADDRESS[10]=Bob!
echo ${ADDRESS[0]} ${ADDRESS[1]} ${ADDRESS[2]} ${ADDRESS[10]}
```

This script prints the following output:

```
Hello there Bob!
```

You index an array using an integer in square braces, with indexes beginning at 0. As you can see, it is not necessary to assign a value for all indexes. In this example, values have been assigned only for indexes 0, 1, and 10. In the echo statement, the value for index 2 is requested. No value has been assigned for index 2, but it does not result in an error; instead, the value is simply an empty string. Only the values of the other three array entries actually appear in the printed output.

When you access the value of an array element, you have to use the curly braces, as shown in the example. If instead you write something like:

```
echo $ADDRESS[1]
```

the shell first tries to retrieve the value of $ADDRESS. In Bash, this evaluates to the first element in the array, ${ADDRESS[0]}. This value will be substituted and combined with [1], resulting in the output Hello[1], which is not what was intended.

Variables in Bash are global; that is, they are visible throughout the whole script after they have been defined. If you want to limit the visibility of a variable, you can use the local keyword. The following example shows a function that defines two variables, one global and one local:

```
VarFunc() {
  VAR1=value1
  local VAR2=value2
}
VarFunc
echo VAR1 is $VAR1
echo VAR2 is $VAR2
```

Here is the output of this script:

```
VAR1 is value1
VAR2 is
```

Without going into the semantics of functions, which are discussed a little later in this chapter, it should be clear that VAR1 is visible outside the function VarFunc, and VAR2 is not, as witnessed by the fact that an empty string is printed in the second line of the output, rather than the text value2.

You can perform arithmetic with integer variables using the let command. You simply write the expression you want to evaluate on the line after let, as follows:

```
Macintosh:~ sample$ ONE=1
Macintosh:~ sample$ let THREE=$ONE+2
Macintosh:~ sample$ echo $THREE
3
```

 NOTE *You cannot perform arithmetic with decimal (floating-point) numbers directly in Bash. If you want to do this, you need to use the command bc or a more powerful language such as Ruby or Python (see Chapter 11).*

Apart from the variables that you define yourself, the Bash shell defines a number of useful variables. For example, the process identifier of the shell running the script is given by $$. You can use this when naming files to avoid overwriting output from other runs, as in the following example:

```
echo It\'s a good day, la la la la la > goodday_output_$$.txt
```

This one-line script writes a string to a file. The filename includes the process identifier (for example, `goodday_output_5006.txt`) to avoid overwriting output produced by the same script in a different run. Other important shell variables are *positional parameters*, which correspond to the arguments passed when the script is run. The path of the script is passed in the variable $0, and the arguments are passed in the positional parameters $1, $2, $3, and so forth. The variable $# gives the number of positional parameters. To illustrate, suppose that the following script is inserted into the file `argscript.sh`:

```
#!/bin/bash
echo The script is called $0
echo There are $# positional parameters
echo First argument is $1
echo Second argument is $2
echo Third argument is $3
```

If you run this script as

```
./argscript.sh arg1 arg2 arg3
```

the following output is produced:

```
The script is called ./argscript.sh
There are 3 positional parameters
First argument is arg1
Second argument is arg2
Third argument is arg3
```

All arguments can also be found in the variable $@. Inserting the following line in the preceding script:

```
echo The arguments are $@
```

results in this additional line of output:

```
The arguments are arg1 arg2 arg3
```

Another commonly used shell variable is $?. This gives the exit status of the last command executed in the foreground. Usually, a value of 0 indicates that the command succeeded, and a non-zero value indicates failure. Here is an example:

```
smkdir tempdir$$
echo Exit code of mkdir was $?
mkdir tempdir$$
echo Exit code of mkdir was $?
```

The second `mkdir` command causes an error, because the directory already exists. The exit code of the successful command is `0`, and that of the unsuccessful operation is `1`, as you can see from the following script output:

```
Exit code of mkdir was 0
mkdir: tempdir5224: File exists
Exit code of mkdir was 1
```

Quoting

Several different types of quotation marks are used in shell programming, and it is important to know the implications of each. For example, double quotation marks do not have the same meaning as single quotation marks, and the two are often *not* interchangeable.

Double quotation marks are used to form strings, as you might expect. The shell will perform variable substitution within double quotations, as you can see in the following interactive session:

```
Macintosh:~/Desktop sample$ NAME=David
Macintosh:~/Desktop sample$ TIME="6 o'clock"
Macintosh:~/Desktop sample$ MESSAGE="Meet $NAME at $TIME"
Macintosh:~/Desktop sample$ echo $MESSAGE
Meet David at 6 o'clock
```

The definition of the `TIME` variable shows that single quotes have no special meaning in a double-quoted string. When defining the `MESSAGE` variable, the values of the `NAME` and `TIME` variables are substituted before the string is assigned to the `MESSAGE` variable.

If you want to avoid the special meaning of `$NAME` and `$TIME` in the shell, you can use single quotation marks as shown here:

```
Macintosh:~/Desktop sample$ NAME=David
Macintosh:~/Desktop sample$ TIME="6 o'clock"
Macintosh:~/Desktop sample$ MESSAGE='Meet "$NAME" at $TIME'
Macintosh:~/Desktop sample$ echo $MESSAGE
Meet "$NAME" at $TIME
```

Just as you can use single quotes in a double-quoted string, you can also use double quotes in a single-quoted string. The variable substitutions made in the preceding double-quoted string are not made when single quotes are used.

If you want to use double quotation marks, but force the shell to treat certain characters literally, even when they have a special meaning, you can use the backslash, like this:

```
Macintosh:~/Desktop sample$ NAME=David
Macintosh:~/Desktop sample$ TIME="6 o'clock"
Macintosh:~/Desktop sample$ MESSAGE="Meet \$NAME at $TIME"
Macintosh:~/Desktop sample$ echo $MESSAGE
Meet $NAME at 6 o'clock
```

A backslash preceding a character escapes any special meaning that that character has. It applies not only to variables, as demonstrated here, but to any characters that have special meaning to the shell.

Another type of quotation mark that is used often in shell programming is the *backtick*. When a command is enclosed in backticks, the command is executed, with the output replacing the command itself. Here is how you could use this approach to rewrite the previous example:

```
Macintosh:~/Desktop sample$ NAME=David
Macintosh:~/Desktop sample$ TIME="6 o'clock"
Macintosh:~/Desktop sample$ MESSAGE="Meet `echo $NAME` at `echo $TIME`"
Macintosh:~/Desktop sample$ echo $MESSAGE
Meet David at 6 o'clock
```

In this case, the echo commands given in the definition of MESSAGE are carried out by the shell and substituted before the string is assigned to MESSAGE. Backticks can be very useful when you want to store the results of a command for further processing. For example, you could list the contents of a directory, storing the resulting string in a variable, as demonstrated by this command:

```
DESKTOP_CONTENTS=`ls ~/Desktop`
```

The ls command lists the contents of the user's Desktop folder and assigns the resulting output to the DESKTOP_CONTENTS variable.

Conditional Branching

Most programming languages provide a mechanism for branching based on a condition or the outcome of a test. This is called *conditional branching*, and Bash also supports it with the if command.

The most difficult aspect of learning to use if in Bash is constructing conditions. Here is how you could use if to test whether an error occurred during the execution of a mkdir command:

```
if mkdir hellodir
then
    echo Making hellodir succeeded
else
    echo Making hellodir failed
fi
```

The if statement tests if the command given as the condition has an exit value of 0, which indicates success. If so, the commands after the then command are executed. If the exit value of the command is non-zero, the commands after the else command are executed. The fi keyword is used to close the if statement.

NOTE In Bash, the closing keyword of a command is often just the command written back-to-front. For example, the closing keyword for if is fi, and the closing keyword for case is esac.

This `if` command may seem confusing at first, because languages such as C and Java behave in an opposite manner: the `if` block is executed when the condition is non-zero or `true`, and the `else` block is executed when the condition is `0` or `false`. This difference comes about because Bash treats an exit value of `0` as success, and all other values as errors.

There is an operator in Bash that allows you to get behavior more similar to what you find in other languages: the `((...))` operator. The preceding example can be rewritten like this:

```
mkdir hellodir

if (( $? ))
then
    echo Making hellodir failed
else
    echo Making hellodir succeeded
fi
```

In this example, the exit value of the `mkdir` command, which is given by the shell variable `$?`, is tested with the `((...))` operator. The `((...))` is an arithmetic evaluation operator, which is actually equivalent to the `let` command. It evaluates the expression, returning `0` if the expression evaluates to a non-zero value, or `1` if the expression is `0`.

If rather than performing arithmetic operations, you want to compare strings, you can use the `[[...]]` operator. Here is an example in which the values of three variables are compared using various operators:

```
VAR1="some string"
VAR2="$VAR1"
VAR3="other string"

if [[ $VAR1 == $VAR2 ]]; then
    echo VAR1 and VAR2 are the same
else
    echo VAR1 and VAR2 are different
fi

if [[ $VAR1 != $VAR3 ]]; then
    echo VAR1 and VAR3 are different
else
    echo VAR1 and VAR3 are the same
fi
```

Here is the output of this script:

```
VAR1 and VAR2 are the same
VAR1 and VAR3 are different
```

First, notice that the `then` command, which was previously included on the line following the `if`, is on the same line in this example. This is made possible by the addition of a semicolon behind the `if` command. Separate shell commands can either be written on separate lines or appear on the same line separated by semicolons. Using the semicolon with an `if` command makes the code a bit more compact.

The assignment of the variables to various strings at the beginning is fairly straightforward, except for VAR2. You may be wondering why double quotation marks have been used around the value $VAR1 on the right side of the assignment. If you don't do this, the shell will expand $VAR1 as the two words some and string. The quotation marks used to assign VAR1 are *not* part of the variable; they are simply there to group the separate words into a single string. If you don't use quotation marks when assigning VAR2, it gets assigned to the first word, some, and the shell won't know how to treat the extra word string. It's a good idea to get into the habit of using double quotes when accessing the value of any string variable, including paths, which often contain spaces.

The conditional expressions themselves are comparisons between strings. The [[...]] operator returns 0 if the expression is true, and 1 otherwise. The operators == and != can be used in the string comparisons and test for equality and inequality of the strings, respectively. You can also use logical operators, as demonstrated by the following example, which extends the preceding script:

```
if [[ $VAR1 == $VAR2 && $VAR2 == $VAR3 ]]; then
    echo VAR1, VAR2, and VAR3 are all equal
elif [[ $VAR1 == $VAR2 && !($VAR2 == $VAR3) ]]; then
    echo VAR1 and VAR2 are equal, but VAR2 and VAR3 are not
elif [[ $VAR1 != $VAR2 && $VAR2 == $VAR3 ]]; then
    echo VAR1 and VAR2 are not equal, but VAR2 and VAR3 are
else
    echo VAR1 and VAR2 are not equal, and neither are VAR2 and VAR3
fi
```

Here is the output for this section of the script:

```
VAR1 and VAR2 are equal, but VAR2 and VAR3 are not
```

This example introduces the elif command, which stands for *else if*. If the condition of an if command is not met, control moves to the first elif. If the condition of the elif is met, such that the expression evaluates to 0, the commands after the next then command are evaluated, and then control jumps down to fi. If the elif condition is not met, control moves to the next elif, and so on. If none of the elif conditions are met, the commands after else are executed.

The conditional expressions in this example make use of many of the available operators. && is the logical AND, which evaluates to true if the expressions on either side of it are true. ||, which is not used here, is logical OR, which is true if either expression is true. Parentheses, such as those used in the first elif expression, can be used to group terms. The unary ! operator is the NOT operator and negates the value of the expression, changing true to false, and vice versa.

The final way of writing test conditions is with the test command, which is equivalent to the [...] operator. test can be used for arithmetic comparisons, but it is most useful for testing file attributes. Here is an example that tests whether a particular file exists:

```
if test -e ~/Desktop/tempfile
then
    echo tempfile exists
fi
```

This can also be written as follows:

```
if [ -e ~/Desktop/tempfile ]
then
    echo tempfile exists
fi
```

The test command takes an option used to determine the type of test to be performed for the file given. In this case, the -e indicates that the existence of the file is being tested. If the file exists, the test command evaluates to 0 and the if block is performed.

You can perform many other tests with the test command by using various options. The following table shows some of the more useful ones.

OPTION	TEST DESCRIPTION
-a or -e	Tests if a file exists. A directory is also considered a file, for this purpose.
-d	Tests if a file exists and is a directory.
-f	Tests if a file exists and is a regular file, not a directory.
-r	Tests if a file exists and is readable.
-w	Tests if a file exists and is writable.
-x	Tests if a file exists and is executable.
-O	Tests if a file exists and is owned by the user.
-G	Tests if a file exists and is owned by a group of the user.
-nt	Binary operator used to determine if one file is newer than another. The comparison is based on the last modification dates of the two files. The test is true if the file to the left of the operator is newer than the file to the right.
-ot	Similar to -nt, but tests if one file is older than another.

The Bash shell includes a second conditional branching command that will not be demonstrated here: case. A case command can be used to test an expression for equality with a number of possible values. For more information on the case command, see the bash man page.

Looping

Loops allow you to perform a series of commands repetitively, without having to duplicate them. The `while` loop continues until the exit status of a command is no longer 0. For example, here is a `while` loop that has a fixed number of iterations:

```
let i=0
while (( $i < 5 ))
do
    echo $i
    let i=$i+1
done
```

Here is the output of this script:

```
0
1
2
3
4
```

The command given after the `while` keyword is executed, and its exit value is checked. If it is 0, indicating success, the commands between `do` and `done` are executed. This repeats until a non-zero exit value is encountered.

In the example, the command utilizes arithmetic evaluation to determine whether the variable `i` is less than 5. If so, the loop continues; if not, it exits. The commands inside the `while` block echo the variable and then increment it by 1, using the `let` command.

 NOTE *The Bash shell also includes an* `until` *loop, which has the same structure as the* `while` *loop. The difference between the two is that the* `until` *loop continues as long as the conditional command returns a non-zero exit status and stops when an exit status of zero is encountered.*

`while` loops are often used to iterate over command-line arguments, using the `shift` command. Assume the following script is in a file called `script.sh`:

```
#!/bin/bash
while (( $# ))
do
    echo $1
    shift
done
```

When run with the command

```
./script.sh 1 2 3 4
```

the output is as follows:

```
1
2
3
4
```

In this example, the `while` tests how many input arguments are left, which is given by the shell variable $#. When there are none, the `while` loop exits. On each iteration, the command `shift` removes one input parameter — the one in the $1 variable — and moves all the others to a lower index. $2 becomes $1, $3 becomes $2, and so forth.

The `for` loop is capable of performing the same operations as the example shown at the beginning of this section, with somewhat less code.

```
for (( i=0 ; i<5 ; i++ ))
do
     echo $i
done
```

This is very similar to the `for` loop in the C language, which is described in Chapter 6. Three arithmetic expressions are given inside the arithmetic evaluation parentheses ((...)). The first is evaluated just once, at the beginning. This is usually used for initializing a counting variable, such as `i`. The next is evaluated every iteration, including the first. If it is true, the loop continues; if not true, the loop exits with control transferred immediately to the `done` statement. If the second statement is true, the third statement is evaluated and usually increments the counter variable; the `++` operator increases a variable by 1. On each iteration, the commands between `do` and `done` are executed.

Another form of the `for` loop can be used to iterate over a list of words. In the example that follows, it is used to echo a number of names from a string variable:

```
NAMES="Bill Bob Barry Bernice Beatrix"
for name in $NAMES
do
     echo $name
done
```

This is the output:

```
Bill
Bob
Barry
Bernice
Beatrix
```

The `for` ... `in` ... form of the `for` loop sets the variable given after the `for` keyword to each of the whitespace-separated words in the string given after `in`.

A useful variation on this loop involves leaving out the `in` part of the loop. When you do this, the `for` loop iterates over the input arguments, as demonstrated by this script:

```
#!/bin/bash
for name
do
        echo $name
done
```

Inserting this in a file called `script.sh`, and running it as

```
./script.sh Bill Bob Barry Bernice Beatrix
```

leads to this output:

```
Bill
Bob
Barry
Bernice
Beatrix
```

Functions

If your scripts start to become large, or you find yourself duplicating a lot of code, you may consider using *functions*. Functions allow you to group commands together, so that they can be executed from anywhere in a script with a *function call*.

You write a function like this:

```
function ChangeToDesktopAndList() {
        cd ~/Desktop
        ls
}
```

This function is called `ChangeToDesktopAndList`. The `function` keyword is optional, but the parentheses following the function name, and the braces, are required. To call this function, you simply enter the function name like this:

```
ChangeToDesktopAndList
```

The function definition must precede the function call in the script so the shell knows about the function's existence. Wherever you call the `ChangeToDesktopAndList` function, the commands in the function are executed.

As with scripts, functions can also take arguments. And arguments in functions are also accessed using the shell variables $1, $2, $3, and so forth. Here is a more general function than ChangeToDesktopAndList:

```
function ChangeToDirAndList() {
    cd "$1"
    ls $2
}

ChangeToDirAndList ~/Desktop -l
```

This function changes to a directory passed as the first argument, and lists the contents, with the options of the ls command passed as the second argument. The function call simply lists the arguments separated by whitespace, just as if it were a script. In the example, the Desktop folder is the first argument, and the -l option is the second.

Note that if your arguments include spaces, you need to use quotation marks to group them. Quotation marks have also been used in the function around the $1 argument, just in case the path passed includes spaces. Here is a function call in which the arguments include spaces:

```
ChangeToDirAndList "$HOME/Desktop/some dir" "-l -a"
```

The only complication is that the environment variable HOME has to be used in place of the ~, because the shell does not substitute for the ~ in a quoted string.

If you need to explicitly return from a function to the calling code, you can use the return command. For example, in

```
function ReturningFunc() {
    ls ~/Desktop
    return
    ls ~
}
```

the last ls command is never performed, because the function jumps from the return command back to the calling code.

In the next Try It Out, you use various shell programming constructions to develop a script that will find and compress any large files in a given directory and any of its subdirectories.

TRY IT OUT   **Writing a Shell Script to Compress Large Files**

1.   Open a Terminal window in the Terminal application.

2.   Change to the Desktop directory by issuing the following command:

```
cd Desktop
```

3.   Create a new file with Nano called `compress.sh` as follows:

```
nano compress.sh
```

4.   Enter the following script with Nano in the `compress.sh` file:

```bash
#!/bin/bash

# Check exit status in $?.
# If non-zero, print it, along with the message in $1.
# If $? is non-zero, exit script if $2 is equal to "YES".
function CheckExitStatus() {
    local EXIT_STATUS=$?
    if (( $EXIT_STATUS )); then
        echo An error occurred, with status $?
        echo Message: $1
        if [[ $2 == "YES" ]]; then
            exit $EXIT_STATUS
        fi
    fi
}

# Function that finds any files larger than 5Mb, and compresses them.
# The directory path $1, and subdirectories, are searched for large files.
function CompressFilesInDirTree() {
    find "$1" -size +5000000c -type f -exec gzip "{}" \;
    CheckExitStatus "Find command failed" YES
}

# Main program. Loop over directories passed via command line arguments.
# Compress any large files in each directory tree.
for dirPath
do
    CompressFilesInDirTree "$dirPath"
done
```

code snippet MacOSXProg ch12/compress.sh

5.   Change the permissions of the `compress.sh` file so that it is executable.

```
chmod u+x compress.sh
```

6.   Locate a directory tree with a variety of files smaller and larger than 5MB. Copy the whole directory to a temporary directory in the `Desktop` folder like this:

```
cp -r source_directory ~/Desktop/temp_dir
```

   `source_directory` should be the path to the directory you want to copy.

7.   Run the `compress.sh` script to compress the large files in `temp_dir`.

```
./compress.sh temp_dir
```

8. Check that the files larger than 5MB that reside in `temp_dir` and its subdirectories have been compressed by the `gzip` command and have the `.gz` extension.

9. Remove the `temp_dir` directory when you are ready.

```
rm -r temp_dir
```

How It Works

The `compress.sh` script begins with a function that checks the exit status of the last command executed and acts based on whether an error occurred.

```
# Check exit status in $?.
# If non-zero, print it, along with the message in $1.
# If $? is non-zero, exit script if $2 is equal to "YES".
function CheckExitStatus() {
    local EXIT_STATUS=$?
    if (( $EXIT_STATUS )); then
        echo An error occurred, with status $?
        echo Message: $1
        if [[ $2 == "YES" ]]; then
            exit $EXIT_STATUS
        fi
    fi
}
```

Before the function definition, there is a comment. A comment can be created by simply using the # symbol; anything after the # on the line is ignored by the shell.

The function name is `CheckExitStatus`, and the first executable line defines a variable called `EXIT_STATUS`, which is visible only inside the function because of the presence of the `local` keyword. `EXIT_STATUS` is assigned to the last exit status, which is given by `$?`. Because `$?` will be reset every time a command is issued, its value is saved in the `EXIT_STATUS` variable.

The `if` block checks whether the exit status is non-zero, in which case, a couple of messages are echoed. The first argument to the function is a message to the user that is printed if a command failed. The second argument is used in the nested `if` command; if the argument is equal to the string `YES`, the script exits.

The second function does the bulk of the work, searching for files in a particular directory tree and compressing the large ones.

```
# Function that finds any files larger than 5Mb, and compresses them.
# The directory path $1, and subdirectories, are searched for large files.
function CompressFilesInDirTree() {
    find "$1" -size +5000000c -type f -exec gzip "{}" \;
    CheckExitStatus "Find command failed" YES
}
```

The `find` command performs the search. It has a number of options passed to it. The first argument to the function is also used as the first argument to the `find` command. This argument is the root directory of the search. (Note that double quotes have been used to ensure that any spaces in the directory path are not misinterpreted.)

The first option passed to find is –size +5000000c. This means that find should ignore any file smaller than 5,000,000 bytes, or around 5MB. The –type f option is included so that find searches only for regular files and not directories or other file types. The -exec option executes the command given for any file found that matches all criteria. In this case, files are compressed with the gzip command.

The CheckExitStatus function is called after the find and is passed two strings: one is printed if the command has failed, and the other is a string that indicates whether a failure should cause the script to exit. If YES is passed as the second argument, a failure will cause the script to terminate.

The end of the script, which could be considered the main program, uses a for loop to iterate over any directory paths passed as command-line arguments.

```
# Main program. Loop over directories passed via command line arguments.
# Compress any large files in each directory tree.
for dirPath
do
    CompressFilesInDirTree "$dirPath"
done
```

For each iteration, the CompressFilesInDirTree function is called, passing the directory path as the only argument. The argument is given in quotation marks in case the path includes any spaces, which would cause it to be passed as multiple arguments.

SUMMARY

The Bash shell plays a vital part in Mac OS X operations; it's used at system startup and for system maintenance. You can use Bash to access a wealth of different Unix commands and combine them to undertake complex operations. These operations would be much more difficult to do with the Finder.

In this chapter you learned

➤   How to use Bash interactively and write scripts with the Terminal application and the Nano editor

➤   The most important Bash commands for performing fundamental operations on files and text

➤   About other less fundamental commands, some of which are found only on Mac OS X

➤   How you write shell scripts with the programming constructs available in Bash, including conditional branching, looping, and functions

In the next chapter, you learn how to work with AppleScript and the AppleScriptObjC bridge. AppleScript is quite different from Bash in that it is generally used for scripting applications with a GUI rather than Unix commands. Before proceeding, however, try the exercises that follow to test your understanding of the material covered in this chapter. You can find the solutions to these exercises in Appendix A.

EXERCISES

1. With the Terminal application, use Bash interactively to create a compressed archive of all the files of a particular type (that is, with a particular extension) located in your home directory or subdirectories.

First locate the files with the `find` command and copy them to a temporary directory. Use the `cp` command to make the temporary copy, the `ditto` command to compress the archive, and `mv` to move it to a backup directory.

Refer to the man pages of the various commands to learn how they are used.

2. Convert the interactive commands you used to complete Exercise 1 into a backup script. You can use the `history` command to see what commands you typed. For more information, see the `history` man page.

Restructure the commands to make the script more readable and robust if necessary, and don't be afraid to introduce shell programming constructs such as conditional branches and functions. Have the script check for errors and send you an e-mail you if one occurs. (Hint: See the man page of the `mail` command.)

▶ **WHAT YOU LEARNED IN THIS CHAPTER**

Command-Line Interface (CLI)	an interface based on textual commands rather than on-screen graphics
Shell	a program that interprets textual commands and can launch programs and execute scripts
Bash	the default shell on Mac OS X
Shell Script	a textual program run in a shell, and interpreted one line at a time
Process	a program running in the operating system
Subprocess	a process that was started by another process
Terminal	an application used to access the CLI on Mac OS X
Environment Variable	a global variable accessible from within a process which relates to the environment in which it is running
Resource File	a file containing commands that configure a shell when it launches
Path	a list of directories searched when locating a command or program to run
Pipe	a construct to carry data from one process to another, or in and out of files
Command	a program with a text-based interface that gets run from a shell
Globbing	a scheme for pattern matching filenames in a shell
File Permissions	a system for controlling access of users to resources in the file system
Variable	a labeled piece of data in a shell script
Conditional Branching	following a different path through a script based on whether certain conditions are met
Looping	repetitive execution of a block of statements in a script
Function	a block of code that can be invoked via calls made at different locations in a script

13

AppleScript and AppleScriptObjC

WHAT YOU WILL LEARN IN THIS CHAPTER:

➤ The different ways you can use AppleScript scripts, and the tools you can use to create them

➤ The basics of the AppleScript language

➤ How to script applications such as Finder, iPhoto, and QuickTime

➤ How to develop complete applications with the AppleScriptObjC bridge

AppleScript is a scripting language developed by Apple primarily for scripting applications that have a graphical user interface (GUI). It reads like English and is targeted more at the general Mac user than the programming professional. Nonetheless, even the serious programmer has something to gain from AppleScript. AppleScript allows you to take full advantage of the functionality offered by applications ranging from iPhoto to QuickTime, Mail to Microsoft Word. AppleScript is to GUI applications what the Bash Shell is to Unix commands — the glue that binds them together. (If you don't know what this means, read Chapter 12 on the Bash Shell.)

In recent years, AppleScript has ventured beyond its traditional hunting grounds into application development. By integrating AppleScript with the Cocoa frameworks (see Chapter 8); Apple has made it possible to develop complete Mac OS X applications with AppleScript, using a *scripting bridge*. This makes it possible for non-programmers to easily write applications that look stunning and behave as any other Cocoa application.

 NOTE *Just as AppleScript has been moving into the realm of application development, the traditional stomping ground of AppleScript — scripting applications with a GUI — has been opened up to other scripting languages. You can now send commands between applications using languages such as Objective-C, Python, and Ruby, in addition to AppleScript.*

APPLESCRIPT

This section introduces you to the AppleScript language and the many ways it can be utilized. AppleScript scripts have access to the internals of running applications and can issue commands or request data. By extracting data from one application and feeding it into another, you can create complex workflows with AppleScript. This can save you a lot of repetition in your daily activities, freeing you up for the activities that demand more creativity.

Creating an AppleScript

The tool used to write a basic AppleScript script is the purpose-built AppleScript Editor application, which you can find in the `/Applications/Utilities` folder. AppleScript Editor is a basic editor, but it is designed for AppleScript and has some useful features, such as syntax checking and reformatting, which can make scripts easier to read.

Each window of AppleScript Editor (see Figure 13-1) is for a separate script. In the toolbar are buttons for recording a script, stopping the operation in progress, running a script, and compiling a script. (The latter checks syntax and reformats.)

The AppleScript Editor also gives you a means to browse the *dictionary* of any application. The dictionary includes the various properties and commands that can be accessed by AppleScript. You can open an application's dictionary by choosing File ➪ Open Dictionary and then choosing an application.

In this first Try It Out, you write a very simple script with AppleScript Editor, and then compile and run it. You also open a dictionary to better understand the script.

FIGURE 13-1

TRY IT OUT   **Using AppleScript Editor**

1.   Open the AppleScript Editor application.

2.   In the editor window, enter the following script:

```
tell application "Finder"
    activate
    set someFolder to path to applications folder
    open someFolder
end tell
```

code snippet MacOSXProg ch13/Open Applications Folder.scpt

3. Click the Compile toolbar button and note the changes in the script.

4. Click the Run toolbar button. A Finder window should appear, displaying the `Applications` folder.

5. Choose File ➪ Open Dictionary. In the panel that appears, select StandardAdditions.osax in the table and then click the Choose button.

6. In the browser view at the top, click File Commands and then select the first of the two Path To commands in the second column. Try to understand the information displayed in the text view at the bottom in relation to the script you entered in step 2.

7. Save the script by choosing File ➪ Save and typing the name `Open Applications Folder`. Make sure the File Format pop-up button is set to Script. Close the script window in AppleScript Editor, and then reopen it by double-clicking the `Open Applications Folder` script file in Finder.

8. Now save the script again using the File ➪ Save As... menu item, this time selecting Application from the File Format pop-up button. Locate the saved file in the Finder, and double-click it. What happens, and how does it vary from what happened in step 7?

How It Works

The script in this example is very simple. It sends several commands to the Finder application. The `tell` block indicates that commands should go to the application called `Finder`. The first command is `activate`, which tells Finder to become the frontmost application.

The next line sets a variable called `someFolder` to the path to the `Applications` folder. Note how similar that last sentence is to the line in the script. AppleScript often reads as English.

The last command to Finder is `open`, with the path `someFolder` passed as an argument. This causes Finder to open a new window with the `Applications` folder selected.

When you click the Compile button, the AppleScript interpreter checks the syntax of the script for correctness, adds some highlighting and coloring, and sometimes reformats. Reformatting can involve changing indentation, for example, to make the script easier to read. To actually run the script, you need to click the Run button.

The dictionary of Standard Additions documents various standard commands and classes that can be used in your AppleScripts. In this case, the command `Path To` was used to get the path to the `Applications` directory. The dictionary tells you what arguments can be used with the `path to` command, and other assorted information.

When you save a script, you can choose various formats. If you choose the Script format, the file opens in AppleScript Editor when you double-click it in Finder. If you want to run the script, you need to use the Run button in AppleScript Editor.

If you save a script as an application, it is given a different extension (`.app`), which identifies it as an application to the Mac OS X system. When you double-click the application, it does not open in AppleScript Editor but runs immediately, as any other application. In this example, it opens the `Applications` folder in Finder, and exits.

NOTE *AppleScript applications can also be referred to as applets.*

Scriptable and Recordable Applications

Not all applications are *scriptable*. A scriptable application is one that can be accessed from an AppleScript. Many applications are not scriptable because the developers did not take the necessary steps to make them so. Making an application scriptable is not difficult, but it also does not happen automatically.

In addition to being scriptable, an application can also be *recordable*. Even fewer applications are recordable than are scriptable. Scripts can be developed for recordable applications simply by opening AppleScript Editor, clicking the Record toolbar button, and carrying out the tasks you want to include in the script. When you are finished, click the Stop button in the AppleScript Editor toolbar, and you have your AppleScript.

Using this approach is easy because you don't need to write the code yourself, but it has some drawbacks. The first is simply that many applications are not recordable, so you still have to write scripts by hand for those that aren't. The second drawback is that the code produced by AppleScript Editor is very verbose and difficult to follow. It also doesn't include any flow-control constructs such as loops or branches; it is simply a list of all the commands you carried out while Record was pressed.

Recording can be useful for simple repetitive tasks and for laying the foundation of a script. You can record a number of actions and then edit the script, introducing more powerful flow-control statements and generally cleaning up the code to form a well-rounded script.

Apple Events

AppleScript scripts communicate with one another and with running applications by using *Apple Events*. Apple Events are a means of performing *interapplication communication* and can be used to send messages between scripts and applications running on a single machine or across a network. Each Apple Event can be seen as encapsulating a command sent by one script or application to another script or application, where it is interpreted and usually results in some action being undertaken.

For example, if you have written a line of AppleScript requesting the Finder to open a particular folder, an Apple Event is created to represent this request and is sent to the Finder application. Finder attempts to open the folder and sends a reply, in the form of a second Apple Event, back to your script to indicate whether or not the operation was successful.

Apple Events are represented and transmitted via a *messaging protocol* called Open Scripting Architecture (OSA), which was devised by Apple in the early 1990s. OSA is language-agnostic and can be supported by any scripting language. In Mac OS X, it is now possible to send Apple Events from an Objective-C Cocoa application, and even use scripting languages such as Python and Ruby.

WARNING *The ideas behind OSA are shared by other more recently developed messaging protocols such as SOAP and XML-RPC. The latter are built on top of the eXtensible Markup Language (XML) and are used primarily for Web Services. Web Services allow communication between computers via the HTTP protocol, which is the protocol upon which the Web is based.*

 WARNING *Another form of interapplication messaging on Mac OS X is provided by the Cocoa frameworks. It is called* Distributed Objects *(DO) and allows you to send messages to an object that exists in a different application or even on a different computer, as if it existed locally.*

Variables and Data Types

As with most languages, AppleScript uses *variables* to store data. Variables are named vessels for data stored in memory; they can store anything from a simple number, to a string, or even a whole script. AppleScript provides the usual simple data types such as `real` (decimal) and `integer` numbers, and `boolean`, which represents truth values. But there are also more advanced data structures such as `string`, which contains text; `list`, which is an ordered collection of data; and `record`, which stores data in key-value pairs. AppleScript even supports object-oriented programming (OOP), which is covered later in the "Scripts and Objects" section.

Variable names are case-insensitive in AppleScript and have the usual restrictions: they can contain only alphanumeric characters and the underscore character and cannot begin with a digit. You do not need to declare a variable's type before you use it; to create a variable, you simply assign it a value, as follows:

```
set _some_variable to 12.0
```

The `set ... to ...` command is the usual means of setting a variable. In this example, `_some_variable` gets the real number value `12.0`. You can also force a variable to take a particular type by using the `as` keyword:

```
set _some_variable to 12.0 as string
```

In this case, the real number `12.0` is first coerced to the string value `"12.0"` before being assigned to `_some_variable`. *Coercion* in AppleScript is similar to what is known as *casting* in other languages, such as C (see Chapter 6). In each case, some data is simply converted from one type to another type.

 NOTE *The limitations placed on variable names can be overridden by enclosing the variable name within | symbols. For example,* |5 `times as many $'s`| *is a legal AppleScript variable name.*

When you use `set`, you are actually creating a shallow copy of some data, meaning that the variable you assign shares the data with any other variable assigned to the same data. If you want to make a deep copy, in which the data is actually duplicated before being assigned to the variable, you use the `copy` command:

```
copy 12.0 to _some_variable
```

or

```
copy 12.0 as string to _some_variable
```

In most cases, including this example, there is little difference between using `set` and `copy`. But with the more advanced data types, it can be important which you choose, as discussed in the following paragraphs.

As already stated, variables don't have a *static type*; they are *dynamically typed*, taking on the type of whatever data they are assigned to. This also means they can change type. Here is an example of a variable first assigned to a real number and then to a string:

```
set x to 5.0 + 5 as number
set x to 5.0 + 5 as string
```

In the first line, x takes the real number value `10.0`. In the second line, x is reassigned and has the string value `"10.0"`. You may have thought x would be equal to the string `"5.0 + 5"`, but this is not so. The latter would require the following assignment:

```
set x to "5.0 + 5" as string
```

A string literal is enclosed in double quotation marks.

 NOTE *The value* `5.0` *in the preceding examples was coerced to a type called* `number`. `number` *is a type that can be used for both real and integer numbers.*

Another simple data type, *boolean,* can take the values `true` and `false`. You can use the usual comparison operators to create expressions with `boolean` values. Here are a couple of examples of setting `boolean` variables:

```
set someBool to true
set anotherBool to 4 < 5
```

In the second example, the variable `anotherBool` is assigned to the value of the expression `4 < 5`, which is `true`.

String variables are important in any language. In AppleScript, strings are *immutable,* meaning they cannot be changed after they are created. If you need to edit a string, you simply create a new string based on the original one.

AppleScript's string manipulations are relatively primitive when compared to a language such as Python, but you can perform basic operations. You join strings in AppleScript using the concatenation operator &:

```
set address to "18 Hills Hoist Lane, " & "Berryhappy"
```

The variable address is assigned the string value "18 Hills Hoist Lane, Berryhappy".

If a line in your script gets too long, you can press Option-Return to insert the line continuation character (¬) to continue to the next line. In the preceding example, it would look like this:

```
set address to "18 Hills Hoist Lane, " & ¬
    "Berryhappy"
```

The ¬ is the continuation character. Unlike Objective-C or Java, AppleScript does not have a line termination character. A logical line of code is equivalent to a line in the script, unless a line continuation character is inserted.

AppleScript also includes two important compound data types, which can be used to store collections of data. The first is list, which stores ordered collections of data entries, with each entry associated with an index.

 NOTE *A list is similar to an* NSMutableArray *in Cocoa (see Chapter 8); it is a dynamic array that can grow to accommodate new data.*

List literals are defined by enclosing comma-separated entries in curly braces as in:

```
set someList to {1,2,3}
```

The variable someList is associated with the list containing the integer numbers 1, 2, and 3. It is not necessary for the entries to all be the same type. The following is also legal:

```
set someList to {1,"2",3}
```

Now the second entry is the string "2", rather than an integer.

To access the entries in a list, you can do this:

```
set someEntry to item 2 of someList
```

Here the variable someEntry is set to the second entry in the list someList. In the previous example, this was the string "2". List indexes begin at one in AppleScript, not zero as in C and many other languages.

Data types can have various attributes, and AppleScript has a very specific naming scheme for these. An attribute can be either an *element* or a *property*. In the preceding example, item is an element of the list type. An element is an attribute that can have any number of different values. You use the item element of list to access the entries in the list. A property is an attribute that has exactly one value. Recognizing the differences between properties and elements is important because you need to use them in distinctive ways with AppleScript.

Setting entries of a list after it has been created is also possible:

```
set someList to {"one", "two", "three"}
set item 2 of someList to "2"
```

After the second line has been executed, someList will be equal to the list {"one", "2", "three"}.

To extend a list by appending a new value, you can do this:

```
set end of someList to "four"
```

And to insert a value at the beginning you can do this:

```
set beginning of someList to "zero"
```

Finally, the number of entries in a list is accessible via the length property:

```
set list_length is length of {1,2,3,4}
```

The variable list_length is assigned the value 4, which is the number of elements in the list literal. A nice feature of lists is that you can use them to assign multiple variables at once, as in this example:

```
set {x, y, z} to {1, 2, 3}
```

This assigns the entries in the first list to those in the second. x is assigned to 1; y to 2; and z to 3.

The second compound data type available in AppleScript is record. A record stores unordered key-value pairs. In other languages, a record is called a *dictionary, hash table,* or *map.* A record literal in AppleScript is created with curly braces, just as is a list, but keys are also supplied:

```
set friends_ages to {bob:42, joe:36}
```

The keys are given to the left of each colon, and the values to the right.

To access the values in the friends_ages record, you supply a key as so:

```
set friends_ages to {bob:42, joe:36}
set bobs_age to bob of friends_ages
set joe of friends_ages to 38
```

In the second line, a value is retrieved from the record using the keyword of. In the third line, an entry in the record is modified, changing the value corresponding to the key joe to 38 from 36.

Extending a record involves the concatenation operator &:

```
set friends_ages to friends_ages & {jack:36, jill:37}
```

This actually creates a new `record` by combining the old `friends_ages` record with the literal `record` containing ages for `jack` and `jill`. The newly formed `record` is then assigned to `friends_age`.

Unlike the `list` type, a `record` doesn't have an element called `items` because the entries in a `record` are unordered. It does have the property `length`, which is the number of entries it contains. In addition, every key used in a `record` is automatically made a property. That is why they work with the `of` keyword, which is usually used to access properties.

It is important to realize that when you assign to a `list` or `record`, you are not actually copying its contents; rather, you are simply creating a reference to the existing data container. A reference is a type similar to a pointer in the C language (see Chapter 6); it basically just stores a memory address. If you actually want to copy the contents, you need to use the `copy` command, rather than `set`:

```
set birthdays to {¬
    terry:date "December 2, 1972", ¬
    ellen:date "May 28, 1968" }
 —  Create one reference, and one copy
set ref_to_birthdays to birthdays
copy birthdays to copy_of_birthdays
 —  Change terry's birth year to 1974
set terry of birthdays to date "December 2, 1974"
 —  Check values
terry of ref_to_birthdays      —  Should give year as 1974
terry of copy_of_birthdays     —  Should give year as 1972
```

This example contains a few new aspects of AppleScript. The first is the `date` type. As you can see, you can create a `date` by using an appropriately formatted string, along with the keyword `date`. The format of the date is quite flexible, but it must be consistent with the settings in the International pane of your System Preferences.

This example also uses comments for the first time. Single-line comments are signified using two hyphens (`--`); anything following the hyphens on the line is ignored. Multiline comments are delineated by an opening symbol (`(*`), and a closing symbol (`*)`).

The main point of this example is to demonstrate that if you use `set`, you get a reference to the `record`. If you change the original record, which is `birthdays`, the `set`-assigned `record` also gets updated. On the next to last line, the `terry` entry in `ref_to_birthdays` is retrieved; this entry should be the same as in `birthdays` and show the new year of `1974`. The copy will *not* show the new year because it is a completely different record and is not altered by the change to `birthdays`.

On the last two lines of the script, the `terry` entries in the two derived `records` are retrieved. You can use this type of statement to test values in AppleScript Editor. If you open the Result tab in an AppleScript Editor window, you can see the value of the last command run. This can be used to check the values of variables. In this example, you could enter the next to last line if you wanted to see the value of the `terry` entry in `ref_to_birthdays` and enter the very last line for the value of `terry` in `copy_of_birthdays`.

AppleScript has many other data types, but none are as important as the ones covered in this section. You will encounter some of the others as you work through the rest of this chapter.

In the following Try It Out, you build up experience with the data types discussed in this section by storing information about a fictional group of friends.

TRY IT OUT | **Working with Data**

1. Open AppleScript Editor and enter the following in a script window:

```
set joe to { ¬
    full_name:"Joe Blockhead", ¬
    birthday:date "12 February, 1969", ¬
    favorite_colors:{"green", "purple"}, ¬
    favorite_meal:"Spaghetti"}

set belinda to { ¬
    full_name:"Belinda Blockhead", ¬
    birthday:date "13 February, 1971", ¬
    favorite_colors:{"lilac", "indigo"}, ¬
    favorite_meal:"Beans"}

set peter to { ¬
    full_name:"Peter Whoknows", ¬
    birthday:date "26 June, 1952", ¬
    favorite_colors:{"red", "blue", "pink"}, ¬
    favorite_meal:"Turkey"}
```

Available for download on Wrox.com

code snippet MacOSXProg ch13/Addresses.scpt

2. Click the Compile button to check the script.

3. Add a new line to the end of the script to access the value of Belinda Blockhead's birthday:

```
birthday of belinda
```

4. Run the script by clicking the Run button. Open the Result tab at the bottom of the window and confirm that the birthday shown is correct.

5. Replace the new line added in step 3 with a line to extract the first favorite color of Peter Whoknows:

```
item 1 of favorite_colors of peter
```

6. Rerun the script, again checking the output in the Result tab.

7. Replace the last line of the script again, this time to retrieve the second favorite color of Peter:

```
peter's (item 2 of favorite_colors)
```

8. Rerun the script and check the results.

How It Works

The script defines records for three different individuals. A record can contain any data types; in this case, each record contains a variety: a date, two strings, and a list. It is also perfectly acceptable to embed one record within another.

The rest of the exercise centers on accessing the stored data. Retrieving the birthday of Belinda Blockhead is straightforward, but the favorite colors of Peter Whoknows present more of a problem. How do you access data contained in a compound type that is an entry in another compound type?

You can use one of two approaches. The first involves what is sometimes called an *inside-out reference*. In step 5, you used an inside-out reference:

```
item 1 of favorite_colors of peter
```

The of keyword is used in a chain beginning with the most deeply nested property (the list favorite_colors) and ending with the container at the highest level (the record peter).

The second approach utilizes a *possessive reference*, which is used in C-like languages, including C++ and Java. Step 7 uses this approach:

```
peter's (item 2 of favorite_colors)
```

An apostrophe followed by s is used to denote possession. (You were warned that AppleScript is very much like English.) The parentheses are necessary to make clear precisely what is possessed — namely, the second entry of the list favorite_colors.

To compare the AppleScript way with another common form of describing containment relationships, here is how you might write step 7 in Java:

```
peter.favorite_colors.getItem(2)
```

As you can see, the order is exactly opposite to the inside-out approach and is similar to the AppleScript possessive reference form.

In general, the inside-out reference is easier to understand in AppleScript and is the form most commonly used.

Handlers

Handlers are AppleScript subroutines, similar to functions in the C language (see Chapter 6). A handler includes a block of code that is executed whenever the handler is *called* from somewhere in your script. It has zero or more parameters, which are variables used to pass arguments in, and an optional return value for passing a result back to the *caller*. Unlike C and some other languages, a handler does not need to have been declared or defined before it is used in a script; it can be defined after a call.

Here is a simple handler that adds two numbers together and returns the result. A call is made to the handler to add one and one:

```
on addTwoNums(firstNum, secondNum)
  return firstNum + secondNum
end addTwoNums

addTwoNums(1, 1)  -  return value is 2
```

The `on` keyword precedes the handler's name, followed by a comma-separated list of parameters in parentheses. If there are no parameters, empty parentheses must be used. The handler is terminated by the keyword `end`, followed by the handler's name. The body can contain any number of statements, and control can be passed back to the caller using the `return` statement, which may also pass a *return value*.

 NOTE *If you don't enter the name of the handler after the* end *statement, AppleScript Editor does it for you.*

The `return` statement can be used to pass a result back to the caller, but it isn't necessary to include a value or have a `return` statement at all. If there is no `return` statement, the value of the last command executed in the handler implicitly becomes the return value. If no value should be returned, a `return` statement can be used without an argument.

The parameters defined in the preceding example are known as *positional parameters* because they are assigned to the arguments passed to the handler based purely on their position in the parameter list. It is also possible to have *labeled parameters*, in which each parameter is preceded by a preposition, making calls to the handler read more as English. For example, the preceding handler could be rewritten as follows:

```
on summing for firstNum against secondNum
  return firstNum + secondNum
end summing

summing for 1 against 1 -- result is 2
```

One advantage of labeled parameters is that the order of the arguments can be varied in the calling code. For example, the following is also a legal call to the `summing` handler, although it doesn't make much sense:

```
summing against 1 for 1
```

A limited number of prepositions are allowed when using labeled parameters, which can sometimes make coming up with appropriate labels a creative challenge. The prepositions available are listed in the following table.

above	below	from	out of
against	beneath	instead of	over
apart from	beside	into	thru
around	between	of	under
aside from	by	on	
at	for	onto	

The of preposition is the odd one out; it can be used only for the first label in a handler parameter list. Other than that, there are no restrictions on order.

Labeled parameters are quite restrictive, but luckily AppleScript provides something more flexible: *named parameters*. With named parameters you can call a parameter just about anything you like. Here is an example:

```
on sum given firstNumber:x, secondNumber:y
   return x + y
end sum

sum given firstNumber:5.0, secondNumber:2.0  -- Result is 7.0
```

The keyword given must precede the named parameters. The parameters themselves are comma-separated, and each includes a colon, with the parameter name on the left and the variable or value on the right. As with labeled parameters, any order of arguments can be used for named parameters in the calling code.

 NOTE *Named parameters in AppleScript closely resemble the segmented names used in Objective-C (see Chapter 7).*

It is also possible to include both labeled parameters and named parameters in one handler. The labeled parameters must come first, and the named parameters last:

```
on append onto firstString given other:secondString
   return firstString & secondString
end appendstring

-- Result of this call is "hello there"
append onto "hello " given other:"there"
```

To understand the mechanics behind argument passing with handlers, it is best to imagine that the parameters in a handler are variables that have been assigned to the arguments passed using the set command. If you think like this, you will be able to predict what will happen when you pass a particular type of value.

For example, arguments with simple types such as `real`, `integer`, and `string` are effectively *passed-by-value*. If you change the value of a parameter corresponding to a simple-typed argument, the original argument remains unaffected. If you think about it, this is exactly what would happen if you assigned one variable, say x, to another simple-valued variable, y. If you later change x, y will not be affected. This is what you observe passing simple types to handlers.

The same is not true of compound data types, such as `list`, `record`, `date`, and `script` objects (which you learn about later in the section "Scripts and Objects"). Compound data types are effectively *passed-by-reference*. When you alter the value of a parameter with a compound type, the argument is also changed. This makes sense because if you use `set` to assign a variable x to a compound data value y, and then perform an operation on x, such as appending a new entry to a `list`, y will also be modified.

Here is an example to demonstrate the semantics of argument passing in AppleScript:

```
on changes(numVar, listVar, recordVar)
   set giraffe of recordVar to "A tall animal"
   set end of listVar to 4
   set numVar to 4.0
end changes

set n to 3.0
set l to {1, 2, 3}
set r to {giraffe:"A long animal"}

changes(n, l, r)

n -- value is 3.0
l -- value is {1,2,3,4}
r -- value is {giraffe:"A tall animal"}
```

The argument n is not affected by the reassignment of the parameter `numVar` because it is a simple type. The `list` and `record` variables l and r each reflect the operations performed in the `changes` handler after the call is made.

To finish off this section on handlers, we should point out that not all handlers need to be called from within your scripts. Handlers can also be written to intercept Apple Events sent from outside your code. There is a special `run` handler, for example, that is called to run the main code of a script. If you don't define it explicitly, the statements found in your script at the highest level are executed; but if a `run` handler is found, it is called instead. Here is an example:

```
on run
   say ("hello")
end run

on say (w)
   display dialog w
end say
```

The `run` handler is called when the script is started; it, in turn, calls the `say` handler, which displays a dialog box with the text `hello`. Note that the `run` handler does not need a parameter list because it is special; usually, if you write a handler that has no parameters, you need to include empty parentheses in the definition of the handler.

Control Statements

Control statements relate to the flow of execution of a script and include conditional branching and looping, among other things. AppleScript provides the usual constructions for flow control but adds one or two that you probably won't recognize from any other programming language.

Conditional Branching

AppleScript includes the `if` construct for conditional branching purposes. It tests a boolean condition and executes a block of code only if that condition evaluates to `true`. Here is a simple example:

```
if true then
   display dialog "Must have been telling the truth"
end if
```

This is not a particularly interesting example because the condition, which appears after `if`, is always `true`, so the dialog will always be displayed. The `if` statement includes the keyword `then` after the condition, and the block is closed with `end if`. If the condition is `true`, the code between `if` and `end if` is executed; otherwise, it is skipped.

The `if` statement becomes more useful when you actually perform a test:

```
set x to 5.0
set y to 3.0
if x < y then
  display dialog "x was less than y"
else
  display dialog "x was not less than y"
end if
```

The expression `x < y` has been used as the condition in this example. In addition, an `else` block has been included. The code after the `else` is only evaluated if the condition is `false`. In this example, because x is not less than y, the `else` block will be evaluated, and a dialog displayed with the text "x was not less than y".

The `if` statement can include multiple conditions, using the `else if` keyword. Here is an example:

```
set x to 5.0
set y to 3.0
set z to 1.0
if (x ≤ y and y ≤ z) or (z ≤ y and y ≤ x) then
  display dialog "y is between x and z"
else if (y ≤ x and x ≤ z) or (z ≤ x and x ≤ y) then
  display dialog "x is between y and z"
else if (x ≤ z and z ≤ y) or (y ≤ z and z ≤ x) then
  display dialog "z is between x and y"
else
  display dialog "An error occurred"
end if
```

Each condition is tested in order, beginning with the condition after `if`, and proceeding to each `else if` condition. The block of code following the first condition that evaluates `true` is executed, and all others are skipped. If no condition is `true`, the `else` block is executed.

In this example, three different tests compare the three variables x, y, and z. The operator ≤ is generated automatically by AppleScript Editor when you enter `<=` and compile or run the script. The conditions also include the logical operators `and` and `or`, and parentheses are used to group terms. When you run the script, a dialog appears displaying the text "y is between x and z."

There is one more form of the `if` statement: the single-line form. If an `if` statement has no `else` block and only a single executable command, it can all be written on a single line, such as this:

```
set friends_name to "Bob"
if friends_name is equal to "Bob" then display dialog "Hi Bob!"
```

In addition to demonstrating the use of the single-line form of `if`, this example includes the operator `is equal to`, which has been used to compare whether two strings are the same.

Looping

AppleScript includes several different constructions for looping. Loops always begin with the keyword `repeat` and end with the keyword `end repeat`; however, there are many different variations on the `repeat` loop. The most basic form loops forever, or until an `exit repeat` statement is encountered:

```
set x to 0

repeat
  set x to x + 1
  if x = 100 then exit repeat
end repeat

display dialog x as string
```

This example displays a dialog containing the number 100. The code inside the `repeat ... end repeat` block is executed until x is equal to 100, at which point the `exit repeat` command causes the loop to terminate.

> **NOTE** *The operator* = *is used in the example above to compare the variable* x *to the number* 100. *In AppleScript, you can use* = *interchangeably with the text* `is equal to`. *Which you choose is merely a question of preference.*

The loop exit condition in this example can be included in the `repeat` statement itself using the `while` or `until` keywords, as so:

```
set x to 0

repeat while x < 100
  set x to x + 1
end repeat

display dialog x as string
```

or this:

```
set x to 0

repeat until x = 100
  set x to x + 1
end repeat

display dialog x as string
```

In each of these examples, the condition supplied after the while/until keyword is tested *before* each iteration of the loop. The repeat while loop continues as long as the condition is true, and the repeat until continues as long as the condition is false. This explains why the conditions are different in each case. The end result of each example is the same: a dialog is displayed with the number 100.

Often you need to loop over a sequence of regularly spaced integer numbers. There is a repeat loop to handle this too; it is called the repeat with loop. The preceding examples can be rewritten to use this form of repeat:

```
repeat with x from 0 to 100 by 1
end repeat

display dialog x as string
```

As you can see, this is actually the most compact form in this particular instance. The loop variable x is first initialized in the loop to the integer given after from, which is 0. The number given after by is added to x *after* each iteration of the loop, until x is equal to the number after the to keyword, at which point execution jumps to the end repeat and continues from there.

The by keyword is optional in repeat with loops. If you exclude it, the loop variable is incremented by 1 after each iteration. Thus, in this example, it could have been left out. If you need to use numbers other than 1, you need to include by. The numbers supplied must be integers but do not have to be positive. For example, you can have x count backward to -100 using an increment of -1 and an end value of -100 after the to keyword.

 NOTE *The* repeat with *loop is similar to the* for *loop in the C programming language (see Chapter 6).*

The final form of `repeat` allows you to iterate through the items in a `list`. For example, the following loop sums items:

```
set sum to 0

repeat with x in {10, 9, 8, 7}
  set sum to sum + x
end repeat

display dialog "The sum is " & sum as string
```

This example displays a dialog with value 34, which is the sum of 10, 9, 8, and 7. The variable after `with`, `x`, is repeatedly assigned to values in the `list` supplied after the `in` keyword. The `list` values are assigned in the order in which they appear in the `list`.

`tell` Command

The control statements covered so far are all fairly standard; you could find similar constructions in just about any language. But AppleScript has a few control statements that are peculiar, and very important. The most widely used of these is the `tell` statement, which is used to send commands to applications, among other things.

`tell` can appear in block form or on a single line. The one-line form looks like this:

```
tell application "Finder" to activate
```

This issues a command to Finder to activate, which means to become the frontmost application. The `tell` statement consists of the keywords `tell` and `to`. A `tell` statement includes a command, which is `activate` in this case, and a target to which the command is to be sent, which is Finder. If you run the example script, the Finder application should become active.

> **NOTE** *Each scriptable application defines a set of commands that can be used in* `tell` *statements. To see which commands a particular application defines, you can examine its dictionary by choosing File* ➪ *Open Dictionary in AppleScript Editor.*

The block form of `tell` looks like this:

```
tell application "Finder"
    activate
    open desktop
end tell
```

A `tell` block can contain zero or more commands. In this example, two commands are issued, one to activate and the other to open the `Desktop` folder. If you run the script, the Finder should become the frontmost application, and a window with the `Desktop` folder should appear.

`tell` blocks can also be nested, with each block targeting a different property. For example, imagine that you wanted to get the path to the first photo in your iPhoto library. Here is how you could do it:

```
tell application "iPhoto"
    tell photo library album
        set first_photo to item 1 in photos
        display dialog image path of first_photo as string
    end tell
end tell
```

The outer `tell` block selects the iPhoto application to receive commands. The nested `tell` block targets an object of the class album. This is accessed via a property of the iPhoto application called `photo library album`.

 NOTE *You learn about classes in the "Classes" section later in this chapter. For now, it is enough to know that they can be treated as applications when it comes to issuing commands and accessing properties.*

Inside the nested `tell` block, a variable is set to the first photo in the element photos, which belongs to the `album` class. Because any commands issued in a `tell` block are directed at its target, you do not need to use the `of` keyword to stipulate the album. The next line displays a dialog containing the path to the photo represented by `first_photo`, which is retrieved from the property `image path`.

Punctuation

Two unusual control statements in AppleScript are `ignoring` and `considering`. These are most commonly used to explicitly inform AppleScript to ignore or consider some aspect of text, such as whitespace or punctuation. For example, to compare two strings while ignoring any punctuation, you could do this:

```
ignoring punctuation
    if "Hello, Tom!" = "Hello Tom" then
        display dialog "Strings are equal"
    end if
end ignoring
```

This script displays the dialog indicating that the strings are equal, even though they clearly aren't. The `ignoring` block means that any punctuation in the strings is not considered in the comparison; because all the other characters are the same, the strings are equivalent.

You could rewrite the example to use a `considering` block, like this:

```
considering punctuation
    if "Hello, Tom!" = "Hello Tom" then
        display dialog "Strings are equal"
    else
        display dialog "Strings are not equal"
    end if
end considering
```

In this case, punctuation is taken into account, and the strings are not equal. If you run the script, a dialog will be displayed to that effect.

Exception Handling

Most modern languages provide some form of *exception handling*. Exception handling gives you a mechanism for treating exceptional circumstances and errors. AppleScript includes the `try` block for exception handling. In the following example, an attempt is made to open a file in the `Desktop` folder:

```
set somePath to (path to desktop folder as string) & "temp file"

try
    set fileNum to open for access file somePath with write permission
on error
    close access file somePath
    return
end try

write "Hello Bob!" to fileNum
close access file somePath
```

The `try` block begins with `try`, includes `on error`, and ends with `end try`. The commands given between `try` and `on error` are evaluated, and if an error arises, control is transferred immediately to the `on error` block, and the commands between `on error` and `end try` are executed. These commands are executed only if an error arises; if everything proceeds normally, they are skipped.

This example begins by defining a path. The path to the `Desktop` folder is retrieved first, using the `path to` command from the Standard Additions dictionary. The `path to` command is included in the File Commands group. Paths returned by the `path to` command are colon-delimited. To create a path for a temporary file, the string `"temp file"` is appended to the `Desktop` folder path.

> **NOTE** *Standard Additions are a set of helpful commands and classes included with AppleScript. You can read more about them by choosing File ⇨ Open Dictionary in AppleScript Editor and then selecting the StandardAdditions.osax item in the table.*

An attempt is then made in the `try` block to open the file with `open for access`. This command is also from Standard Additions, in the File Read/Write group. If an error arises during the attempt to open the temporary file, the `close access` command from Standard Additions is used to close the file, and the script returns. If no error results, execution continues after the `try` block and the text `"Hello Bob!"` is written before the file is closed.

When exceptional circumstances arise, you can *throw* an error, which can optionally include a message string, and/or error number:

```
error "Could not open file." number -52
```

When you do this, control jumps to the `on error` command of the enclosing `try`, even if that `try` block is at a higher level of the script. For example, if an error is thrown from inside a handler, control can jump out of the handler if that is where the enclosing `try` block is located. The `try` block is said to *catch* the error. If there is no enclosing `try` block, the script stops with an error dialog box displayed.

The `try` blocks in the preceding example did not access the message or error number, but you can do that by extending the `on error` command, as in the following example:

```
try
    error "Hi Mum, I failed!" number 2
on error msg number n
    display dialog msg & return & "Error num: " & n as string
end try
```

Parameters in the `on error` block are retrieved just as they are supplied to the `error` command. In this case, the error message is assigned to the `msg` variable, and the error number to the variable n. A dialog is then displayed with this information. The `return` keyword is a global property in this case, *not* the `return` command; it represents the line break character.

There are a couple of other things that you should know about the `on error` block. First, it is optional; if you leave it out, exceptions are caught by the `end try` statement and ignored. Second, you can throw errors from inside the `on error` block. In this way, you can catch an error and throw a different one, perhaps with extra information supplied.

In the following Try It Out, you take the skills you have learned so far, from writing handlers to catching exceptions, and use them to create a stock quote repository. An AppleScript is used to download stock quotes from a Web Service and store them in files.

TRY IT OUT Downloading and Saving Stock Quotes

1. Open a new script window in AppleScript Editor.

2. Enter the following script in the window:

Available for download on Wrox.com

```
-- Initialize the stock repository, if necessary. It is simply a folder
-- on the Desktop.
on setup_stock_repository()
    set desktop_path to path to desktop folder as string
    tell application "Finder"
        set the repository_folder to desktop_path & "Stock Repository"
        if not (folder repository_folder exists) then
            make new folder at desktop with properties ¬
                {name:"Stock Repository"}
        end if
    end tell
end setup_stock_repository

-- Uses HTTP GET to download a delayed stock quote
on download_quote(stock_symbol)
    try
        set download_url to ¬
```

```applescript
            ("http://www.webservicex.net/stockquote.asmx/GetQuote?symbol=" & ¬
                stock_symbol)

        -- Download XML with embedded quote
        tell application "URL Access Scripting"
            set temp_file to "/var/tmp/stockdownload.xml"
            download download_url to temp_file replacing yes
        end tell

        -- Read in downloaded XML
        open for access temp_file
        set download_string to (read temp_file)
        close access temp_file

        -- Search for last quote, which is between "Last&gt;" and "&lt;/Last"
        set open_tag_offset to (offset of "Last&gt;" in download_string)
        set quote_offset to open_tag_offset + 8
        set close_tag_offset to (offset of "&lt;/Last" in download_string)
        set quote to (text quote_offset thru (close_tag_offset - 1) of ¬
            download_string)

        return quote
    on error msg
        display dialog "Download failed: " & msg
        return ""
    end try
end download_quote

-- Save a price in the repository for the stock symbol given
on save_latest_price given stock:stock_symbol, price:price
    set desktop_path to path to desktop folder as string
    set the repository_folder to desktop_path & "Stock Repository"
    set stock_file_path to repository_folder & ":" & stock_symbol
    try
        set file_number to open for access file stock_file_path ¬
            with write permission
    on error
        close access file stock_file_path
        return
    end try
    set end_of_file to get eof of file_number
    write (price as string) & return to file_number starting at end_of_file + 1
    close access file stock_file_path
end save_latest_price

-- Download and save the price
on archive_stock_price(stock_symbol)
    set price to download_quote(stock_symbol)
    save_latest_price given stock:stock_symbol, price:price
end archive_stock_price

-- Main script
setup_stock_repository()
archive_stock_price("AAPL")
```

```
archive_stock_price("IBM")
archive_stock_price("MSFT")
```

Code Snippet MacOSXProg ch13/Stocks.scpt

3. Compile the script by clicking the Compile button to make sure it was entered correctly.

4. Run the script by clicking the Run button. You need to be connected to the Internet for the script to work.

5. In Finder, open your `Desktop` folder and look for a folder called Stock Repository. If you find the folder, open it, and examine the contents of the files contained there. Run the script again, and note how the file contents change.

How It Works

This example brings together many of the aspects of AppleScript that you have learned up to this point in this chapter and a few tricks you haven't seen yet. It defines these handlers:

➤ `setup_stock_repository`: For setting up a repository to store stock quotes, which is nothing more than a folder containing text files.

➤ `download_quote`: For downloading a stock quote for a given symbol.

➤ `save_latest_price`: For saving a quote for a given symbol to the repository.

➤ `archive_stock_price`: For carrying out the full cycle of downloading and saving a stock quote in the repository.

The `setup_stock_repository` handler creates a folder for the repository, using the Finder:

```
on setup_stock_repository()
    set desktop_path to path to desktop folder as string
    tell application "Finder"
        set the repository_folder to desktop_path & "Stock Repository"
        if not (folder repository_folder exists) then
            make new folder at desktop with properties ¬
                {name:"Stock Repository"}
        end if
    end tell
end setup_stock_repository
```

It uses the Standard Additions command `to path` to retrieve the path to the `Desktop` folder. In the `tell` block, it appends the string `"Stock Repository"` to this path to create the path to the repository folder, and then checks whether the folder already exists. The `exists` command is defined in the Standard Suite of every application dictionary, including Finder. If the folder does not exist, a new one is created, using another command from the Standard Suite: `make`.

The `download_quote` handler uses an HTTP GET to access a Web Service. With Web Services, you can request a server located somewhere on the Internet to return some data or perform a calculation. In this case, a Web Service is requested to return a time-delayed stock quote for a given symbol:

```
on download_quote(stock_symbol)
    try
```

```
            set download_url to ¬
                ("http://www.webservicex.net/stockquote.asmx/GetQuote?symbol=" & ¬
                    stock_symbol)

            -- Download XML with embedded quote
            tell application "URL Access Scripting"
                set temp_file to "/var/tmp/stockdownload.xml"
                download download_url to temp_file replacing yes
            end tell

            -- Read in downloaded XML
            open for access temp_file
            set download_string to (read temp_file)
            close access temp_file

            -- Search for last quote, which is between "Last&gt;" and "&lt;/Last"
            set open_tag_offset to (offset of "Last&gt;" in download_string)
            set quote_offset to open_tag_offset + 8
            set close_tag_offset to (offset of "&lt;/Last" in download_string)
            set quote to (text quote_offset thru (close_tag_offset - 1) of ¬
                download_string)

            return quote
        on error msg
            display dialog "Download failed: " & msg
            return ""
        end try
    end download_quote
```

The URL of the Web Service is stored in the `download_url` variable. This is passed to the `download` command in the URL Access Scripting suite, which downloads the data to a temporary file, replacing it if it already exists. The file contents are read in, and a search for the stock quote is performed using the `offset` command from the String Commands Suite.

To save a stock quote in the repository, the `save_latest_price` handler uses file-writing capabilities provided by the Standard Additions dictionary:

```
    on save_latest_price given stock:stock_symbol, price:price
        set desktop_path to path to desktop folder as string
        set the repository_folder to desktop_path & "Stock Repository"
        set stock_file_path to repository_folder & ":" & stock_symbol
        try
            set file_number to open for access file stock_file_path ¬
                with write permission
        on error
            close access file stock_file_path
            return
        end try
        set end_of_file to get eof of file_number
        write (price as string) & return to file_number starting at end_of_file + 1
        close access file stock_file_path
    end save_latest_price
```

First, a path to a file is built up. The file is in the repository folder and has the same name as the stock symbol. In the `try` block, the `open for access` command is used to open the file for writing. It returns a file reference number, which is used to refer to the file in other commands.

If opening the file fails, the `try` block catches the error, closes the file, and returns. If the file opens successfully, the `write` command is used to append the price to the end of the file. The `get eof` command gives the number of bytes in the file, which is equivalent to the index of the last character. To append, the new data is written to an index one greater than the index given by `get eof`. The handler finishes off by closing access to the file.

The `archive_stock_price` handler does nothing more than call the `download_quote` handler and pass the quote returned to the `save_latest_price` handler:

```
on archive_stock_price(stock_symbol)
    set price to download_quote(stock_symbol)
    save_latest_price given stock:stock_symbol, price:price
end archive_stock_price
```

The main part of the script sets up the repository and then archives quotes for a few big players in the computer industry:

```
setup_stock_repository()
archive_stock_price("AAPL")
archive_stock_price("IBM")
archive_stock_price("MSFT")
```

This is a bit simplistic. A more advanced implementation might prompt you for a stock symbol via a dialog box, or perhaps repeatedly download a particular set of stock quotes at a regular time interval.

Operators

AppleScript includes the usual set of operators found in programming languages, which are used for constructing arithmetic expressions, comparing values, and evaluating logic. The following table describes the operators available and gives simple examples of their use.

OPERATOR	DESCRIPTION	EXAMPLE	RESULT
+	Addition operator. Adds numbers together.	1 + 1	2
–	Subtraction operator. Subtracts the second number from the first.	2 - 1	1
*	Multiplication operator. Multiplies one number by another.	2 * 2	4
/	Division operator. Divides the first number by the second number.	4.0 / 2	2.0

continues

(continued)

OPERATOR	DESCRIPTION	EXAMPLE	RESULT
`()`	Parentheses. Overrides operator precedence, forcing a different evaluation order.	`(1 + 1) * 2`	4
`=, is, is equal to`	Equality comparison operator. `true` if the left and right numbers are equal.	`2 = 2`	
`≠, /=, is not is not equal to`	Inequality comparison operator. `true` if the left and right numbers are not equal.	`1 ≠ 2`	
`<, is less than`	Less-than operator. `true` if the left number is less than the right one.	`2.0 < 5.0`	true
`>, is greater than`	Greater-than operator. `true` if the left number is greater than the right one.	`2.0 > 5.0`	
`≤, <=, is less than or equal to`	Less than or equal operator. `true` if the left number is less than or equal to the right one.	`2.0 <= 2.0`	true
`≥, >=, is greater than or equal to`	Greater than or equal operator. `true` if the left number is greater than or equal to the right one.	`3.0 ≥ 3.1`	false
`div`	Integer division operator. Returns the whole number of times that the right number goes into the left one. This is similar to the `/` operator, except that the decimal part of the result is effectively discarded. Even though this is the integer division operator, it works with `real` number operands; the result, however, is always an `integer`.	`-6.0 div 5`	-1
`mod`	Modulus operator. Returns the remainder of a division of the left number by the right number. This is equivalent to what is left after using the `div` operator. The result is a `real` number if one or both operands are `real`; otherwise it is an `integer`.	`-6.0 div 5`	-1.0
`^`	Power or exponentiation operator. Raises the first number to the second number.	`2 ^ 3`	8
`and`	Logical AND operator. `true` if the left and right boolean expressions are both `true`, and `false` otherwise.	`1 < 2 and 2 > 1`	true

OPERATOR	DESCRIPTION	EXAMPLE	RESULT
or	Logical OR operator. `true` if either the left or the right boolean expression is `true` `false` only if both expressions are `false`.	`1 > 2 or 1 > 0`	`true`
not	Logical NOT operator. Has the value `false` if the expression is `true` and `true` if the expression is `false`.	`not 1 > 0`	`false`

Equality and Inequality Operators

The equality and inequality operators require more attention than the others. First, those coming from languages such as C may be surprised to find that these operators are not == and !=. The reason = can be used for equality is that it is not used for assignment in AppleScript: the `set` keyword is used for assignment. In languages such as C, = is the assignment operator, so a different operator is needed for testing equality.

Another aspect of the equality and inequality operators is that they can be used not only to compare numbers but also to compound types such as lists and records. Here is an example of comparisons between some of these data types:

```
{1, 2} = {1, 2} -- true
{2, 1} = {1, 2} -- false
{1, 2, 3} = {1, 2} -- false
{1, 2, 3} ≠ {1, 2} -- true
{Harry:"gray", Bob:"green"} = {Harry:"gray", Bob:"green"} -- true
{Harry:"gray", Bob:"green"} = {Bob:"green", Harry:"gray"} -- true
{Harry:"gray", Bob:"green"} is {Tom:"gray", Bob:"green"} -- false
{Harry:"gray", Bob:"green"} is equal to {Harry:"gray", Bob:"purple"} -- false
```

As you can see, the entries in the `list` or `record` must all be equal for the data containers to be considered equal. Also, the same number of entries must exist in each container. In the case of a `list`, the entries must be in the same order; and in the case of a `record`, both the keys and values must match (the order is not important).

The Concatenation Operator

AppleScript includes a number of other operators, not related to arithmetic or logic. Some you have already seen, such as the concatenation operator &. This is used to join `strings` and other types, such as `records` and `lists`. Here are some examples of using the concatenation operator:

```
"Hello " & "there."              -- "Hello there."
{Bob:"gray"} & {Chris:"orange"} -- {Bob:"gray", Chris:"orange"}
{1, 2, 3} & {4, 5, 6}            -- {1,2,3,4,5,6}
```

You can also concatenate types that are not the same. In this case, *implicit coercion* is used to convert the types of the operands such that they can be joined. For example, here are some cases where implicit coercion is needed:

```
1 & 2 & 3                                -- {1,2,3}
{1, 2} & 3                               -- {1,2,3}
{1, 2} & "three"                         -- {1,2,"three"}
"three" & {1, 2}                         -- "three12"
{1, 2} & {Bob:"gray", Chris:"blue"}      -- {1,2,"gray","blue"}
{Bob:"gray", Chris:"blue"} & {1, 2}      -- Error. Can't coerce list to record.
```

Concatenating two or more `numbers` results in a `list`. You can append simple types such as `numbers` and `strings` to the end of a `list` using the concatenation operator, and you can even add the values of a `record` to a `list` using concatenation. You can't add the values of a `list` to a `record` because there is no way for AppleScript to assign a key to each value in the list.

The order of operands is important when concatenating. The AppleScript interpreter tries to coerce the operand on the right to a type that can be concatenated to the operand on the left. That is why concatenating a `string` to a `list` is different from concatenating a `list` to a `string`. In the former case, the `string` is implicitly coerced to a `list` and the concatenation operator ends up joining together two `lists`. In the latter case, the `list` is coerced to a string by combining its entries, and the concatenation operator ends up combining two `strings`.

The Contains Operator

AppleScript includes a number of operators that can be used to determine whether or not a `string`, `list`, or `record` contains a given entry or entries. The `contains` operator is one such operator:

```
"Happy Birthday" contains "Birthday"                     -- true
{1, 2} contains {1}                                      -- true
{1, 2} contains 1                                        -- true
{1, 2} contains 3                                        -- false
{1, 2, 3} contains {1, 2}                                -- true
{1, 2, 3} contains {1, 3}                                -- false
{Bob:34, Tom:36, Penny:43} contains {Penny:43, Tom:36}   -- true
{Bob:"gray", Tom:"green"} contains "green"               -- Error
```

The `contains` operator works with operands of the same type, such as two `lists` or two `records`, but it also works with mixed types if implicit coercion can be used to create compatible types. With `strings`, `contains` evaluates to `true` if the `string` given on the right is a sub-`string` of the one on the left.

When used with `lists`, `contains` determines whether the `list` on the right is a sub-`list` of the one on the left. A sub-`list` must completely match some contiguous segment of the full `list`. It is not enough simply to include entries from the full `list` in the sub-`list`; the entries must also be in order and contiguous.

The example above demonstrates how coercion can be used to check for entries in a `list`. Whenever `contains` is used with a `number`, the `number` is first coerced to a `list`, and then the `contains` operator checks if the newly formed `list` is a sub-`list` of the other operand.

The rules for `records` are similar. `contains` can compare only two `records`; because no other type can be coerced to a `record`, you can use the operator only with explicitly created `records`. Note that when testing for containment of one `record` in another, it is sufficient that all key-value pairs are found — the order is not important.

Aside from `contains`, there are a number of other similar operators. The following table provides descriptions and simple examples of these operators.

OPERATOR	DESCRIPTION	EXAMPLE	RESULT
contains	true if the first argument contains the second argument.	{1,2} contains {1}	true
does not contain	true if the first argument does not contain the second one.	{1,2} does not contain {1}	false
is in	true if the second argument contains the first argument.	{1} is in {1,2}	true
is not in	true if the second argument is not contained in the first one.	{1} is not in {1,2}	false
begins with	true if the first argument begins with the first one.	{1,2,3} begins with {1,2}	true
ends with	true if the first argument ends with the second one.	{1,2,3} ends with {2,3}	true

Specifying Elements

As you learned earlier in the chapter, elements are attributes of a data type that can hold any number of different values. One question that this raises is how you specify a particular element. AppleScript gives you lots of different *element specifiers*, each with its own little piece of English grammar — it can all become quite confusing. This section covers these grammatical nuggets and hopefully flattens the learning curve somewhat.

Often you specify an element by name, such as in the following example where an `account` element is requested from the Mail application:

```
tell application "Mail" to get account "tom@completely-fictional.com"
```

The `get` keyword is used, followed by the element and the name as a `string`.

It is also quite common for elements to include an `id`, which is unique. Whereas a name may be able to change, an `id` is immutable and does not change. You can use an `id` to retrieve an element, as in this example:

```
tell application "Address Book"
    set friendsId to get id of person "Erik the Viking"
    set middle name of (get person id friendsId) to "Boris"
end tell
```

This example first stores the id of a person from the Address Book application called "Erik the Viking". It then sets the middle name for Erik, using the id to access the person. The expression in parentheses retrieves the person corresponding to Erik. The result is that "Erik the Viking" is renamed to "Erik Boris the Viking".

Another common way to access elements is by index. You have already seen this put to use many times with the list type. The item element gives access to the list's entries:

```
get item 2 of {"one", "two", "three"} -- Result is "two"
```

Or, equivalently, to:

```
tell {"one", "two", "three"} to get item 2
```

You can also use negative indexes; these count back from the last element:

```
get item -1 of {"one", "two", "three"} -- Result is "three"
```

Last, you can use a variety of English expressions to refer to specific indexed elements. For example, you can write get first item, get second item, and so forth. You can also use get last item or get back item to refer to the last entry in the list.

> **NOTE** *None of these element specifiers are restricted solely to the item element of the* list *type — they work with ordered elements of any type.*

You may also want to specify a range of indexes of elements. This is quite easily achieved in AppleScript:

```
get items 2 thru 4 of {1,2,3,4,5} -- Result is {2,3,4}
```

Notice that the plural form of the element label has been used, followed by a beginning index, the keyword thru, and an end index. The result is a list containing the requested elements. The word through can be exchanged with thru, and you can optionally designate the beginning index of the list with the keyword beginning and the end by end.

If the elements you want to extract are not stored contiguously, you can use a logical condition to specify them. The where keyword is used for this purpose:

```
tell application "iTunes"
    set play_list to first library playlist of first source
    set track_list to tracks of play_list where artist begins with "Bruce"
    play first item of track_list
end tell
```

If all goes well, this script should play a song by an artist going by "Bruce," assuming there is one in your iTunes library. The logical condition is provided in this line:

```
set track_list to tracks of play_list where artist begins with "Bruce"
```

The where keyword causes each track element in the play_list variable to be tested. Whenever the artist property of the track begins with the text Bruce, the track is added to a list, which is returned after all tracks have been considered.

You can use whose in place of where, and also optionally include the words it or its to make expressions read more naturally. For example, you could write the statement from the preceding example thus:

```
set track_list to tracks of play_list where its artist begins with "Bruce"
```

or

```
set track_list to tracks of play_list whose artist begins with "Bruce"
```

You may end up with a grammatical horror story, but AppleScript doesn't care.

So far, you have seen how you can refer to ordered elements in absolute terms by using indexes, but it is also possible to refer to them in terms of their positions relative to other elements. The keywords before/in front of and after/behind can be used to do this. If you run the following script, with a single document containing the text Once upon a time... open in TextEdit, the expressions should evaluate to the values indicated by the comments in the script:

```
tell application "TextEdit"
    tell text of document 1
        get word after word 1          -- "upon"
        get word behind word 1         -- "upon"
        get word in front of word 2    -- "Once"
        get word before word 3         -- "upon"
    end tell
end tell
```

after and behind are equivalent, as are in front of and before.

Sometimes you don't want to refer to a specific element, but to all elements or any element. The every keyword can be used to return a list of all elements, as follows:

```
tell application "Finder" to get every folder of home
```

This line returns all the folders in the user's home directory in a list.

The some keyword allows you to randomly select an element:

```
get some item of {1, 2, 3, 4, 5} -- Random results.
```

This line randomly selects an entry in the list each time it is run.

Scripts and Objects

You have seen properties and elements used throughout this chapter, but you haven't yet seen how they are created. A property can be created in a script, as in:

```
property greeting:"Good Morning"
display dialog greeting    -- Displays "Good Morning"
set greeting to "Goedemorgen"
display dialog greeting    -- Displays "Goedemorgen"
```

The property is just a global variable as any other, with an initial value assigned to it — in this case the string `"Good Morning"`. Its value can change just as any other variable, as demonstrated on the third and fourth lines.

As you well know by now, you can access properties using the `of` keyword. To demonstrate this, the following script explicitly creates a *script object*:

```
script Greeter
    property greeting : "Good Morning"
    display dialog greeting
    set greeting to "Goedemorgen"
    display dialog greeting
end script

set greeting of Greeter to "Bonjour"
run Greeter
```

A script object is virtually the same as a top-level script, which is what you create whenever you type something into AppleScript Editor. A script object can have properties, handlers, and other executable statements. The commands in a script object are not executed when they are first read, but when the script is run, using the `run` command.

As you can see from this example, the properties of a script can be accessed from outside the script itself using the `of` keyword. In this case, two dialogs appear: one with the text "Bonjour", and the other with "Goedemorgen". The initial value of the property, "Good Morning", is not displayed because the `greeting` property gets changed before the script is run.

Surprisingly, you can't create elements for script objects. Elements are provided only by scriptable applications and built-in AppleScript types.

Script objects allow you to use object-oriented programming (OOP) in AppleScript. Because they can contain data, in the form of properties and other variables, as well as handlers, they have all the ingredients for OOP. (To learn more about OOP, see Chapter 7, which deals with Objective-C.)

The following simple example shows how you can use script objects for OOP. This example involves script objects representing operating systems; the first script is called `OperatingSystem`:

```
-- Script object representing general operating systems
script OperatingSystem
    property version : "Unknown"

    on displayDetails()
```

```
        display dialog "Version: " & my version
    end displayDetails

    on run
        my displayDetails()
    end run
end script
```

This script object has a single property, `version`, and two handlers, `displayDetails` and `run`. `run` was discussed earlier; it is a special handler that all scripts have. When a script is run with the `run` command, this handler gets called. The `run` handler here simply invokes the `displayDetails` handler.

`displayDetails` itself just displays a dialog containing the text "Version:," along with the version number stored in the `version` property. The use of the keyword `my` is optional in this case; `my` refers to the enclosing script object and can be used to distinguish a variable or handler belonging to the script from one at a higher level. If there were a global handler called `displayDetails`, for example, using `my` would make explicit that the version of `displayDetails` in the `OperatingSystem` script should be used.

Things start to get interesting only when you have multiple script objects relating to one another in various ways. Here is the next script object in the example, which is a child of `OperatingSystem`:

```
-- Script object representing the Snow Leopard OS, which is special
script SnowLeopard
    property parent : OperatingSystem
    property version : "10.6"

    on displayDetails()
        display dialog "Snow Leopard Baby!"
        continue displayDetails()
    end displayDetails
end script
```

The `SnowLeopard` script object has its parent property initialized to `OperatingSystem`. You do this in AppleScript to define an *inheritance relationship*. `SnowLeopard` inherits all the properties and handlers of `OperatingSystem` without having to include them explicitly. So even without adding anything more to the `SnowLeopard` script object, it already has a property called `version` and handlers called `displayDetails` and `run`. (All script objects have `run`, of course.)

The rest of the `SnowLeopard` script modifies some of the aspects it inherits. This is called *overriding* in object-oriented (OO) terminology. For example, rather than initializing `version` to `"Unknown"`, it is initialized to `"10.6"`. Without this line of code, `SnowLeopard` would inherit the version `"Unknown"`. The `displayDetails` handler is also overridden; the implementation in `SnowLeopard` displays the message `"Snow Leopard Baby!"`, before calling the `displayDetails` method in `OperatingSystem`. The `continue` keyword is used to stipulate that a handler should be sought in the parent script.

You can pass script objects to handlers just as you can pass other data types to handlers. Script objects, such as `lists` and `records`, are passed-by-reference. Their contents are not copied, so any changes made to the object inside the handler still apply after the handler has returned. Here is the next part of the example, which is a handler that displays details of an OperatingSystem script object:

```
-- Handler to display an OperatingSystem
on displayOperatingSystem(os)
    os's displayDetails()
end displayOperatingSystem
```

This demonstrates an aspect of OOP known as *polymorphism*. The handler displayOperatingSystem simply calls the displayDetails handler of the OperatingSystem script object passed to it. But the displayOperatingSystem handler also works for any script object that has the handler displayDetails, including the child script SnowLeopard. Even though the handler only mentions the OperatingSystem class, any script object descending from OperatingSystem can also be passed to this handler. (For more details on polymorphism, see Chapter 7.)

The last part of the example script uses the script objects and handler defined earlier:

```
-- Create a OperatingSystem object for Leopard
copy OperatingSystem to leopardObject
set version of leopardObject to "10.5"
displayOperatingSystem(leopardObject)

-- Create a SnowLeopard object for the Snow Leopard OS, and run it
copy SnowLeopard to snowLeopardObject
run snowLeopardObject
```

To create a new object, you use the copy command. You copy the script object to a variable that you then use to represent the object. You can't use the set command for this, because set does not copy the data contained in the script — it only stores a reference to the script. If you used set instead of copy, whenever you tried to change the data in one variable, all others would also change because they would all refer to the same object.

You can access the properties of a script object in the usual ways, stipulating that the property belongs to the script using the of keyword or the possessive form. In this example, an OperatingSystem object is created and has its version set to "10.5". It is then passed to the displayOperatingSystem handler, which displays a dialog box.

Finally, a SnowLeopard object is created, and the run command is used to run it. Note that the SnowLeopard class does not explicitly define a run handler; the run handler used is inherited from OperatingSystem and calls the displayDetails handler. The particular displayDetails handler executed is the one in the SnowLeopard script, not the one in the OperatingSystem script. This is yet another example of polymorphism, in which the handler that ends up being executed depends on the type of the object that is the subject of the call.

NOTE *Handlers belonging to script objects are called "methods" in the OO parlance, and calling such a handler is known as messaging because it is similar to sending a message to the object. (See Chapter 7 for more information.)*

Classes

This discussion of different types of objects leads nicely into a discussion of *classes*. A class is a type in AppleScript. Earlier in the chapter, the term *data type* was frequently used, but the more correct terminology is class. You can use the `class` property of an object to determine its class:

```
script Classy
end script
class of 15                 -  integer
class of "82"               -  string
class of {1,2}              -  list
class of Classy             -  script
class of class of Classy    -  class
```

Classes are themselves types, as you can see from the last line. They can be compared just as other types; so you can easily test, for example, whether an argument passed to a handler is a `list` or a `record`.

Working with Scripts

You can run AppleScripts from within other AppleScripts, and even from within other programming languages. You use the `run script` command to run a script from within another AppleScript:

```
run script file "DiskName:Users:username:Desktop:somescript.scpt"
```

`run script` is defined in the StandardAdditions.osax dictionary and takes a `file` as an argument. In this case, a `file` object has been created from a path to a script, given in colon-delimited form.

You can also store and load scripts from inside an AppleScript. This is a way to create libraries of commonly used script objects and handlers. Loading is different from running because the `run` handler is not called; the entities in the script are read in but not executed. Here is an example of loading an existing script that was created with AppleScript Editor:

```
set someScript to load script file "DiskName:Users:username:somescript.scpt"
```

The `load script` command is also from the StandardAdditions.osax suite.

To use anything from the loaded script, you have to ensure that you indicate the containment relationship explicitly. For example, if this script has a handler called `doSomething`, you could call it in any of the following ways:

```
tell someScript to doSomething()
someScript's doSomething()
doSomething() of someScript
```

You can also store a script using the `store script` command from the StandardAdditions.osax suite. This is less common than loading and is not demonstrated here.

AppleScript scripts can also be run from shells such as Bash (see Chapter 12). The `osascript` command, which can be found in the `/usr/bin` directory, allows you to do this. You can run a script or execute a single command. To run a script file, you needn't do more than enter the `osascript` command in a Terminal window, followed by a path to the script file:

```
/usr/bin/osascript script_name.scpt
```

To execute a single command, use the `-e` option:

```
/usr/bin/osascript -e 'tell application "Finder" to activate'
```

To learn more about `osascript`, open the man page in Terminal by entering:

```
man osascript
```

You can also run shell scripts from inside AppleScript. To do this, use the `do shell script` command from StandardAdditions.osax. Here is an example of using the Unix `grep` command to retrieve all lines in a file containing the word "giraffe":

```
do shell script "grep giraffe ~/Desktop/file_name.txt"
```

To learn more about `grep` and other Unix commands, read Chapter 12.

The next two Try It Outs let you consolidate all the elements of AppleScript you have learned about in this chapter. You write a script that extracts photos randomly from an album in your iPhoto library and combines them into a QuickTime slideshow. In the first Try It Out, you develop the simple interface that prompts the user for information used to create the slideshow. In the second Try It Out, you add the AppleScript to create the slideshow with the information entered.

TRY IT OUT   Creating the User Interface for Slideshow Maker

1.   Open AppleScript Editor and in a new document, enter the following script:

Available for download on Wrox.com

```
on run
    try
        set num_photos to prompt_for_number_of_photos_in_show()
        set the_album to prompt_for_album_choice()
    on error msg
        display_error_message(msg)
    end try
end run

on display_error_message(message)
    display dialog message buttons {"OK"} default button 1
end display_error_message

on prompt_for_number_of_photos_in_show()
    set number_of_photos to 0
    repeat while number_of_photos is 0
        try
            display dialog ¬
```

```
                "How many photos do you want to include in the slideshow?" ¬
                buttons {"OK"} default answer 10 default button 1
            set dialog_result to result
            set number_of_photos to (text returned of dialog_result) as integer
            if number_of_photos ≤ 0 then error "Enter a non-zero positive number"
        on error msg
            display_error_message(msg)
            set number_of_photos to 0
        end try
    end repeat
    return number_of_photos
end prompt_for_number_of_photos_in_show

on prompt_for_album_choice()
    tell application "iPhoto" to set album_names to name of albums

    set selected_albums to false
    repeat while selected_albums is false
        choose from list album_names with prompt "Choose an album" ¬
            without multiple selections allowed and empty selection allowed
        set selected_albums to result
        if selected_albums is false then ¬
            display_error_message("Please make a selection")
    end repeat

    set album_name to first item of selected_albums
    tell application "iPhoto" to set the_album to get album album_name
    return the_album
end prompt_for_album_choice
```

code snippet MacOSXProg ch13/Slideshow Maker Part 1.scpt

2. Click the Compile button to check that everything has been entered correctly.

3. Click the Run button and respond to the requests provided by the dialog boxes that appear.

4. Rerun the script and try to cause it to crash by entering invalid values for the number of photos to include in the slideshow. Note how the script responds to your attempts to confuse it.

How It Works

This version of the Slideshow Maker script begins by prompting the user to enter a value for the number of photos in the slideshow, and concludes by asking the user to choose an iPhoto album. The main part of the script comes first and has been included in the run handler. You could just as easily write the contents of the handler at the top level of the script, and nothing would change; if the run handler is not included explicitly, it is generated implicitly.

The run handler looks like this:

```
on run
    try
        set num_photos to prompt_for_number_of_photos_in_show()
        set the_album to prompt_for_album_choice()
    on error msg
```

```
            display_error_message(msg)
        end try
    end run
```

Two different handlers are called to request information from the user. The `prompt_for_number_of_photos _in_show` handler requests that the user enter a positive integer representing the number of photos that should be extracted from the iPhoto album and used in the slideshow. The `prompt_for_album _choice` shows the user a list of iPhoto albums and asks that a selection be made. The return value of the handler is an object of the `album` class from the iPhoto application.

The commands issued in the `run` handler are all embedded in a `try` block. If any error arises, it is caught at `on error`, and the handler `display_error_message` is called to inform the user of the problem. This handler, which appears directly after the `run` handler, does little more than display a dialog box:

```
on display_error_message(message)
    display dialog message buttons {"OK"} default button 1
end display_error_message
```

The `buttons` option for the `display dialog` command from the StandardAdditions.osax dictionary allows you to supply a `list` of button titles. In this case, only the OK button is needed. Using the `default button` option, you can give the index of the selected button. By providing a default, you allow the user to dismiss the dialog by simply pressing Return, rather than having to use the mouse to click the button.

The first handler used to interact with the user asks for the number of photos to use in the slideshow:

```
on prompt_for_number_of_photos_in_show()
    set number_of_photos to 0
    repeat while number_of_photos is 0
        try
            display dialog ¬
                "How many photos do you want to include in the slideshow?" ¬
                buttons {"OK"} default answer 10 default button 1
            set dialog_result to result
            set number_of_photos to (text returned of dialog_result) as integer
            if number_of_photos ≤ 0 then error "Enter a non-zero positive number"
        on error msg
            display_error_message(msg)
            set number_of_photos to 0
        end try
    end repeat
    return number_of_photos
end prompt_for_number_of_photos_in_show
```

The dialog box displayed includes a text field for entering the requested value. The `default answer` option indicates to the `display dialog` command that a field should be included, with the initially displayed value set to `10` in this case. You can include as many text fields as you like in a dialog simply by including multiple `default answer` options.

The value entered by the user is retrieved using the `result` keyword, which always holds the value of the last command executed. `result` has been used in this example to make the code slightly more legible, but it would also be completely acceptable to combine the `display dialog` and `set` commands into a single line, beginning with `set dialog_result to display dialog ...`.

The result of the `display dialog` command is a `record`. To get the text entered by the user, you access the value corresponding to the `text returned` key. In the example, this is coerced to an `integer` and then compared with `0` to make sure it is a positive number. Any error that occurs is caught by the `try` block, and a `repeat while` loop continues to prompt the user for the number of photos until a valid value is entered. This type of construction, with a loop and error handling code, is a common way of ensuring that your scripts robustly handle user interaction.

The second handler requests that the user choose one of the albums in iPhoto:

```
on prompt_for_album_choice()
    tell application "iPhoto" to set album_names to name of albums

    set selected_albums to false
    repeat while selected_albums is false
        choose from list album_names with prompt "Choose an album" ¬
            without multiple selections allowed and empty selection allowed
        set selected_albums to result
        if selected_albums is false then ¬
            display_error_message("Please make a selection")
    end repeat

    set album_name to first item of selected_albums
    tell application "iPhoto" to set the_album to get album album_name
    return the_album
end prompt_for_album_choice
```

The first line retrieves the names of the albums from iPhoto. The iPhoto application includes an element called `album`; by using the `of` operator to access the name property, with the plural form `albums`, an implicit loop is formed. Effectively, the script loops over `albums`, with the `name` retrieved from each one, and then added to a `list`. The resulting `list` is what gets assigned to `album_names`. You could achieve the same end result with an explicit `repeat` loop, but the implicit loop is often more elegant.

The `choose from list` command from the Standard Additions dictionary is used to present the albums to the user in a dialog, and accept the user's choice. Two labeled parameters are provided to the command, using the `without` keyword: multiple selections and empty selections are both disallowed. The return value of the `choose from list` command is a `list` of the selected values when a selection was made by the user, and the boolean value `false` when the Cancel button was clicked. The result is retrieved with the `result` keyword, and stored in the `selected_albums` variable.

Because only one `album` gets used by the script, the `album_name` variable is set to the first `item` of the `selected_albums` `list`. iPhoto is then told to set the variable `the_album` to the `album` with the `name` `album_name`; `the_album` is returned from the handler.

In the next Try It Out, you make the Slideshow Maker script fully functional, such that it takes photos from the iPhoto album selected by the user and converts them into a QuickTime slideshow.

Finishing Off Slideshow Maker

1.   Open the Slideshow Maker script in AppleScript Editor and modify the `run` handler as follows:

```
on run
    try
        copy Photo_Archive to photo_arch
        set photo_arch's archive_folder_name to "Test Photo Archive"
        tell photo_arch to setup_archive_folder()
        set num_photos to prompt_for_number_of_photos_in_show()
        set the_album to prompt_for_album_choice()
        add_photos_from_album given Photo_Archive:photo_arch, ¬
            album:the_album, number_of_photos:num_photos
        create_image_sequence_from_folder(photo_arch's archive_folder, 2)
        tell photo_arch to delete_archive()
    on error msg
        display_error_message(msg)
    end try
end run
```

code snippet MacOSXProg ch13/Slideshow Maker Part 2.scpt

2.   Add the following to the end of the Slideshow Maker script:

```
script Photo_Archive
    property original_photo_paths : {}
    property archive_folder_name : "Photo Archive Folder"
    property archive_folder : false

    on setup_archive_folder()
        tell application "Finder"
            set desktop_path to path to desktop folder as string
            set archive_folder_path to desktop_path & archive_folder_name
            if not (folder archive_folder_path exists) then
                set archive_folder to make new folder at desktop ¬
                    with properties {name:archive_folder_name}
            else
                error "Folder called " & archive_folder_name & ¬
                    " already exists on Desktop." number 1
            end if
        end tell
    end setup_archive_folder

    on add_photo_to_archive(the_photo)
        tell application "iPhoto" to set photo_path to image path of the_photo
        if photo_path is not in original_photo_paths then
            set photo_file to POSIX file photo_path as alias
            tell application "Finder" to duplicate photo_file to archive_folder
            set end of original_photo_paths to photo_path
            return true
        else
            return false
        end if
```

```
        end add_photo_to_archive

        on delete_archive()
            if archive_folder is not false then delete archive_folder
        end delete_archive

    end script

    on add_photos_from_album given Photo_Archive:the_archive, ¬
        album:the_album, number_of_photos:number_of_photos
        tell application "iPhoto"
            set num_photos_in_album to count of photos of the_album
            if number_of_photos is greater than num_photos_in_album then
                set number_of_photos to num_photos_in_album
            end if
            set i to 0
            repeat until i is number_of_photos
                the_archive's add_photo_to_archive(some photo of the_album)
                if result is true then set i to i + 1
            end repeat
        end tell
    end add_photos_from_album

    on create_image_sequence_from_folder(the_folder, seconds_per_photo)
        tell application "QuickTime Player 7"
            launch
            activate
            set first_image to first file of the_folder as alias
            open image sequence first_image seconds per frame seconds_per_photo
        end tell
    end create_image_sequence_from_folder
```

code snippet MacOSXProg ch13/Slideshow Maker Part 2.scpt

3. Click the Compile button to check that everything has been entered correctly.

> **NOTE** *You need QuickTime Player 7 to run this script. QuickTime Player 7 may have been moved to the* `/Applications/Utilities` *folder when you upgraded to Snow Leopard. If not, you can download it at* `http://www.apple.com/quicktime`*. At the time of this writing, the new QuickTime Player (version 10) does not support creating movies from image sequences.*

4. Click the Run button and respond to the dialog boxes. You should end up with a QuickTime slideshow made up of photos from the album that you selected.

> **NOTE** *If you don't use iPhoto for digital photos, you can download a few images from the Web and import them into your iPhoto library.*

How It Works

This script is by the far the most involved you have seen up to this point in the chapter. You may want to read through it several times to better understand how it works. After the user has been prompted for the number of photos in the slideshow and an iPhoto album, Finder, iPhoto, and QuickTime Player 7 are used to create and display the slideshow. It is a good example of how AppleScript can *glue* Mac OS X applications together to achieve a task in a way not possible in other languages.

The `run` handler now maps out all the stages required to create the slideshow:

```
on run
    try
        copy Photo_Archive to photo_arch
        set photo_arch's archive_folder_name to "Test Photo
          Archive"
        tell photo_arch to setup_archive_folder()
        set num_photos to prompt_for_number_of_photos_in_show()
        set the_album to prompt_for_album_choice()
        add_photos_from_album given Photo_Archive:photo_arch, ¬
            album:the_album, number_of_photos:num_photos
        create_image_sequence_from_folder(photo_arch's
          archive_folder, 2)
        tell photo_arch to delete_archive()
    on error msg
        display_error_message(msg)
    end try
end run
```

First, a new instance of a script object called `Photo_Archive` is created using the `copy` command. A `Photo_Archive` simply represents a folder containing photo files. The name of the archive folder is set to `"Test Photo Archive"`, and the handler `setup_archive_folder` is called to create the folder so that photos can be added to it.

The two handlers written in the previous Try It Out are called next, and then the handler `add_photos_from_album` is used to add the requested number of photos from the iPhoto album to the `Photo_Archive`. In practice, this involves locating the photos in the file system and copying them to the archive folder using Finder.

With the `Photo_Archive` populated with photos, `create_image_sequence_from_folder` uses QuickTime Player 7 to load them as an image sequence. The `archive_folder` property of `Photo_Archive` is a folder class from the Finder application; it is retrieved from `photo_arch` and passed to the `create_image_sequence_from_folder` handler. The second argument to the handler is the number of seconds each photo is displayed in the slideshow.

The last action taken is to delete the folder controlled by the `Photo_Archive` script object, using the handler `delete_archive`.

The `Photo_Archive` script object begins by defining some properties:

```
script Photo_Archive
    property original_photo_paths : {}
    property archive_folder_name : "Photo Archive Folder"
    property archive_folder : false
```

The `original_photo_paths` property is a `list` used to store the paths of the photos in the archive before they were copied. This is used to avoid copying the same photo more than once into the archive. The `archive_folder_name` was set in the `run` handler and is simply a name for the folder used to store the photos. In this example, the folder is always located in the user's `Desktop` folder. `archive_folder` is used to store a Finder `folder` class object representing the archive folder. It is initialized to `false` but later set to the `folder` object.

The `setup_archive_folder` was called in the `run` handler to create the folder used to store the copied photos. It does this using the Finder application:

```
on setup_archive_folder()
    tell application "Finder"
        set desktop_path to path to desktop folder as string
        set archive_folder_path to desktop_path &
            archive_folder_name
        if not (folder archive_folder_path exists) then
            set archive_folder to make new folder at desktop ¬
                with properties {name:archive_folder_name}
        else
            error "Folder called " & archive_folder_name & ¬
                " already exists on Desktop." number 1
        end if
    end tell
end setup_archive_folder
```

It creates a path to the archive folder by concatenating the path to the `Desktop` folder and the name of the archive folder. Using the `exists` command, a check is made to ensure that the folder doesn't already exist. The `exists` command is in the Standard Suite of every application's dictionary.

The remainder of the `Photo_Archive` script object provides handlers for adding photos to the archive and deleting the archive:

```
on add_photo_to_archive(the_photo)
    tell application "iPhoto" to set photo_path to image path
        of the_photo
    if photo_path is not in original_photo_paths then
        set photo_file to POSIX file photo_path as alias
        tell application "Finder" to duplicate photo_file to
            archive_folder
        set end of original_photo_paths to photo_path
        return true
    else
        return false
    end if
end add_photo_to_archive

on delete_archive()
    if archive_folder is not false then delete archive_folder
end delete_archive

end script
```

The `add_photo_to_archive` handler has one parameter, which is an object of the class `photo` from the application iPhoto. The first line of `add_photo_to_archive` requests iPhoto to get the path to the `photo`. An `if` block checks if this photo path has already been encountered by using the `is not in` operator with the property `original_photo_paths`. If the photo has previously been added to the archive, `false` is returned, indicating that the photo was not added in the current call.

If the photo has not been added to the archive previously, an `alias` object is created to represent it. To do this, a `POSIX file` is created and coerced to an `alias`. A `POSIX file` is used when the path is given as a POSIX path, with forward slashes separating directories; this is the type of path used on Unix systems. The `file` class expects a colon-separated path, which was used on versions of Mac OS before Mac OS X. The `image path` property of `the_photo` retrieved from iPhoto is a POSIX path, explaining why a `POSIX file` must be created first.

The next line of `add_photo_to_archive` tells Finder to make a copy of the `photo`'s file in the archive folder. The `duplicate` command, which is used to make the copy, is in the Standard Suite of every application.

The last action taken is to add the `photo`'s path to the `list original_photo_paths` so that it will not be added a second time by a later call. The return value is `true`, indicating the `photo` was added to the archive.

The `delete_archive` handler is very simple. It checks to make sure the `archive_folder` property has been set to something other than the initial value `false`, and if so, uses the `delete` command from the Standard Suite to remove it. The folder is not actually deleted but moved to the Trash. If you want to delete it permanently, you have to empty the Trash.

After the `Photo_Archive` has been set up and the iPhoto `album` is known, `photos` can be randomly selected from the `album`, and added to the archive; this is the role of the `add_photos_from_album` handler:

```
on add_photos_from_album given Photo_Archive:the_archive, ¬
    album:the_album, number_of_photos:number_of_photos
    tell application "iPhoto"
        set num_photos_in_album to count of photos of the_album
        if number_of_photos is greater than num_photos_in_album
          then
            set number_of_photos to num_photos_in_album
        end if
        set i to 0
        repeat until i is number_of_photos
            the_archive's add_photo_to_archive(some photo of
              the_album)
            if result is true then set i to i + 1
        end repeat
    end tell
end add_photos_from_album
```

This handler uses a `tell` block to communicate with iPhoto. The first part of the handler compares the `number_of_photos` parameter with the number of photos in the `the_album` parameter. If there are too few `photos` in the `album`, the `number_of_photos` variable is set to the number of `photos` in the `album`.

The last half of the handler includes a loop that adds one randomly selected `photo` at a time from the `album` to the archive. A counter variable, `i`, is used to keep track of how many `photos` have been added to the archive. The result of the `add_photo_to_archive` handler is checked after each call; if it is `true`, indicating the `photo` was successfully added to the archive, the counter is incremented.

The last handler in the script uses QuickTime Player 7 to open the photos in the archive folder as an image sequence:

```
on create_image_sequence_from_folder(the_folder,
    seconds_per_photo)
    tell application "QuickTime Player 7"
        launch
        activate
        set first_image to first file of the_folder as alias
        open image sequence first_image seconds per frame
          seconds_per_photo
    end tell
end create_image_sequence_from_folder
```

QuickTime Player 7 is told to `launch`, which causes it to start up without displaying any dialog and then `activate`, which makes it the foremost application. The first `file` in the `folder` parameter is retrieved, coerced to the class `alias`, and assigned to the variable `first_image`.

It is important not to confuse the general `file` class with the `file` class from the `application` Finder. In this case, the class of the first `file` in the `folder` is Finder's `file` class. This can be coerced to the `alias` type, which is very similar to a `file`, with a few subtle differences that are not discussed here. The handler concludes with the QuickTime Player 7 command `open image sequence`; the `alias` is passed as an argument, along with the time (in seconds) to use for each photo.

This example not only utilizes many aspects of AppleScript that you have been exposed to earlier in this chapter, but it also includes more user interaction than previous scripts. In the next section, you learn to go beyond the simple user interfaces you've seen so far and develop complete applications with AppleScript and the Cocoa frameworks.

APPLESCRIPT APPLICATIONS

In Snow Leopard, Apple introduced a new means for you to leverage the power of Mac OS X's frameworks from AppleScript: the AppleScript/Objective-C bridge (or AppleScriptObjC for short). AppleScript scripters are now full-fledged members of the Apple software development universe, and can develop their applications with exactly the same frameworks that Objective-C programmers use. And just as Objective-C programmers develop their software with tools such as Xcode and Interface Builder, AppleScript scripters can do the same.

The *software bridge* between AppleScript and Objective-C not only allows AppleScript to invoke methods belonging to Objective-C objects, and vice versa, it also allows the two languages to be mixed together in a single class. An AppleScript script can inherit from an Objective-C class, effectively sharing its methods and properties. This level of integration was not available before Snow Leopard.

In the next section, you learn about the facilities in Xcode and Interface Builder for writing AppleScript applications, as well as how to use the AppleScriptObjC bridge. Several Try It Out examples demonstrate how to write complete applications with AppleScript and take advantage of its greatest strength — scripting other applications.

The AppleScriptObjC Bridge

The AppleScriptObjC bridge allows you to develop complete Cocoa applications in AppleScript, without having to write any Objective-C code (see Chapter 7). To achieve this, the bridge effectively mirrors Objective-C objects in AppleScript, and AppleScript scripts in Objective-C. It then maps AppleScript commands to Objective-C methods and vice versa. You can issue a command to a particular object in AppleScript, and have the command sent across the bridge to the corresponding Objective-C object where it results in a method being invoked. The Objective-C object behaves exactly the same as if the method invocation had come from an Objective-C program. If the method has a return value, it is sent back over the bridge and converted into an AppleScript object in the process. The reverse is also true: Objective-C code can call into AppleScript and retrieve returned data.

Although you don't need to write any Objective-C in an AppleScript application — unless you want to — it is necessary to understand the syntax of Objective-C methods and how they are invoked. The names of the handlers used in AppleScript to reference Objective-C methods are based on the Objective-C method names, so you need to at least be able to understand the signature of an Objective-C method. (Objective-C is covered in detail in Chapter 7.) Objective-C uses an unusual segmented approach to name its methods. It might seem strange at first, but let it grow on you. Take this method, for example:

```
-(void)performOperation:(NSString *)op withPriority:(NSInteger)priority;
```

This method is called `performOperation:withPriority:`. It has two segments in its name, and each segment corresponds to a different argument.

To invoke this method from AppleScript, you replace the colons in the name with underscores, and put the arguments in parentheses:

```
my_object's performOperation_withPriority_("operation string", 5)
```

Exposing an AppleScript handler to Objective-C follows the same rules. If you create a script and want to make a method called `convert:` visible from the Objective-C side of the bridge, you would define a handler as so:

```
script Converter
    on convert_(sender)
        ...
    end convert_
end script
```

Objective-C classes are directly accessible in AppleScript and have the same name when used in AppleScript as they do in Objective-C. An AppleScript script can even inherit from an Objective-C class:

```
script Converter
    property parent : class "NSObject"
    ...
end script
```

In this example, by setting the `parent` property of the `Converter` script, it has been made a subclass of the Objective-C class `NSObject`.

When native AppleScript data types such as `string`, `list`, and `record` cross the bridge, they are automatically converted to fundamental Objective-C classes like `NSString`, `NSArray`, and `NSDictionary`. The bridge even converts an AppleScript `list` or `record` into an Objective-C struct such as `NSPoint` or `NSRect`.

Contrary to what you might expect, when Objective-C objects belonging to fundamental classes such as `NSString` are passed back to AppleScript, they are not automatically converted to native AppleScript types. This is to allow you access to the Objective-C methods of these objects from AppleScript. If you need a native AppleScript object, you can simply coerce the data to the type you need. For example, if you retrieve an `NSString`, you can coerce it to the type `text`:

```
set control_string to control's stringValue()
display dialog(control_string as text)
```

The `control_string` variable is of the `NSString` class, which means you can invoke any of the `NSString` methods. However, the `display dialog` command expects to be passed an AppleScript `text` object, not an `NSString`. A simple coercion of the `NSString` to `text` resolves the issue.

Using Xcode

When you develop an application with AppleScriptObjC, you use the same development environment as you would if you were programming in Objective-C, and that's Xcode. Xcode includes provisions for managing and editing source code, and building and browsing documentation. Learning to use these facilities is an important part of learning to develop with AppleScriptObjC, and with a good basis in Xcode, you are 90 percent of the way there.

 NOTE *Xcode is covered in detail in Chapter 3. If you need help with the basics, we recommend turning to Chapter 3 before proceeding further.*

To create a new AppleScriptObjC project, choose File ➪ New Project in Xcode, and then select Application under Mac OS X in the source list on the left. Finally, select Cocoa-AppleScript Application from the pane on the right.

You can choose to build one of two different types of AppleScript projects: a standard application or a document-based application. You should check the Create document-based application check box if you want an application that works with multiple documents.

If you choose to create a standard application, and follow the instructions, you end up with an AppleScriptObjC project. This project initially includes a number of files that form the basis of any AppleScriptObjC application. Some of these files are summarized in the following table.

FILE OR BUNDLE	DESCRIPTION
`AppKit.framework`	The Application Kit framework, which contains the elements of Cocoa used for user interfaces.
`Foundation.framework`	The Foundation framework, which contains the non-graphical elements of Cocoa.
`Cocoa.framework`	An umbrella framework that contains both `AppKit.framework` and `Foundation.framework`.
`CoreData.framework`	A framework that can be used for storing data on disk (see Chapter 10).
`AppleScriptObjC.framework`	The framework that contains the code that bridges AppleScript and Objective-C.
`<Project Name> AppDelegate.applescript`	File containing an AppleScript script that acts as the application delegate. The application delegate usually takes responsibility for tasks that need doing when the application launches or is about to terminate.
`<Project Name>-Info.plist`	A property list file found in all Mac OS X applications. It defines metadata for an application, for example giving its version number.
`main.m`	The `main` function, which is written in Objective-C. This is called when the application first launches. The `main` function provided includes code to load the AppleScript scripts and pass control to the `NSApplication` object.
`MainMenu.xib`	The primary Interface Builder file, which contains the main menu and can be used to set up the application's graphical interface.

AppleScript files are given the extension `.applescript`. To create a new AppleScript file, you simply choose File ➪ New File and select Cocoa Class in the source list under Mac OS X, and then AppleScript Class from the pane on the right. You can use the Subclass Of pop-up button to choose a superclass for the new class.

After you have entered your source code and defined a user interface by editing the `MainMenu.xib` file in Interface Builder, you will want to build your application. Building an AppleScript application is no different from building any other type of application in Xcode. It simply involves selecting the Build ➪ Build menu item or clicking the Build toolbar button. If all goes well, you should end up with a self-contained application bundle in your build directory that can be run either from inside Xcode, or by double-clicking it in the Finder.

Unfortunately, when you are working on an AppleScript file in Xcode and do a complete build, the error messages you get are not very useful. One way to get better errors is to run the Compile command just on the file you are editing. You can find the Compile command in the Build menu, or press Command-K. If there is a problem, you will see a dialog appear with information describing the error.

Errors that are caught during the build phase are generally syntactical in nature, but many other errors can arise at runtime. To see what errors occur when you run your application, you should open the console by choosing Run ➪ Console.

One of the limitations of AppleScriptObjC at this point is that the Xcode debugger will not work in AppleScript code. For example, you cannot set a breakpoint and have execution pause in a piece of AppleScript. This means you have to be a bit creative when debugging. One very useful command is log; it can be used to dump objects to the console. By inserting log statements in your code, you can usually figure out where things are going astray:

```
set str to "What is this?"
log str

set i to {1,2}
log {str, i}
```

If you want to dump more than one object in a single statement, just enclose them in a list.

One of the major tasks you are confronted with when learning to use AppleScriptObjC is simply learning what classes and commands are available to you. Cocoa is large, and it is all exposed in AppleScript, making for a relatively steep learning curve. You will probably want to make regular use of Xcode's documentation browser to find Cocoa classes and commands. In addition to Cocoa documentation, Xcode also allows you to browse AppleScript documentation. You can open the documentation window by choosing Help ➪ Developer Documentation. To access AppleScript content, simply search for AppleScript with the search field on the right.

Using Interface Builder

Another important developer application is Interface Builder. Without it, it would be much more difficult for you to create user interfaces for your applications. Interface Builder allows you to lay out the elements of your user interface and connect them to your AppleScript scripts. You can also indicate which handlers should be called when the user performs an action, such as clicking a button.

 NOTE *For a detailed introduction to Interface Builder, read Chapter 4.*

With AppleScriptObjC, you set up your interface in exactly the same way an Objective-C programmer does, connecting outlets and selecting actions for targets in Interface Builder. The same skills you learned in Chapter 4 for Objective-C can be used when building AppleScript applications.

An *action* is a method that gets called when an event is triggered by the user. It takes a single argument, which is the interface element sending the message (for example, a button). To write an action in AppleScript, you add a handler that takes the sender as an argument:

```
script Controller
    property parent : class "NSObject"

    -- Action method updateView:
    on updateView_(sender)
        ...
    end updateView_
end script
```

Because the action is called from Objective-C, it needs to conform to the standard naming convention, with one underscore per argument.

An *outlet* is a reference to an object that can be assigned in Interface Builder. In AppleScript, it is just a standard property:

```
script Controller
    property parent : class "NSObject"

    -- Outletsproperty button : missing valueproperty textView : missing value

    -- Action method updateView:
    on updateView_(sender)
        ...
    end updateView_
end script
```

Outlets should be set to `missing value` initially. This is equivalent to the Objective-C value `nil`, which basically means *no object*. When a property is initialized to `missing value`, it will show up in Interface Builder as an outlet, and you can connect it to an element in your interface.

In the next couple of Try It Out examples, you use AppleScriptObjC to develop an application called Piles of Pictures. This application uses AppleScript to retrieve photos from one or more albums in iPhoto, and draws them at random positions to form a poster. The drawing is achieved with the aid of Cocoa classes.

The user interface of Piles of Pictures is shown in Figure 13-2. In this first example, you create the user interface in Interface Builder; in the next Try It Out example, you add script code to make the application functional.

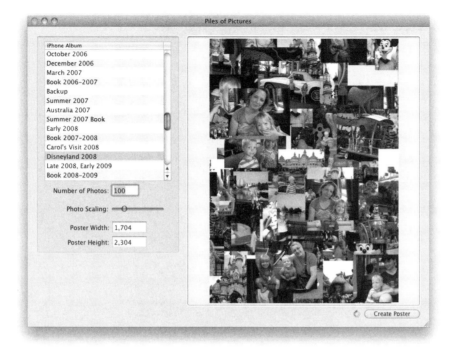

FIGURE 13-2

TRY IT OUT   Creating the Piles of Pictures User Interface

1. Start up Xcode and choose File ➪ New Project. When presented with the New Project panel, select Application from the Mac OS X section in the source list on the left, then select Cocoa-AppleScript Application from the top pane on the right. Make sure the "Create document-based application" checkbox is unchecked, and then click the Choose . . . button. Fill in Piles of Pictures for the Project Name and select the directory you would like the project to reside in. Click the Save button to create the new project.

2. In the Groups & Files pane on the left, open the Resources group, which is in the Piles of Pictures group, and double-click MainMenu.xib. The file should open in Interface Builder.

3. Begin laying out the main window, as shown in Figure 13-3. Bring up the Library window by choosing Tools ➪ Library. Select the Objects tab at the top, and then select Cocoa from the list in the Library group.

4. Start by dragging an NSImageView from the Library to the main window of the application. (Use the filter field at the bottom of the Library window to locate the NSImageView.) Position the image view on the right as shown. Add an NSButton underneath, and open the Inspector window for the button by choosing Tools ➪ Inspector. Select the first tab in the Inspector window and enter the title Create Poster. Drag the round NSProgressIndicator from the Library window and position it next to the button.

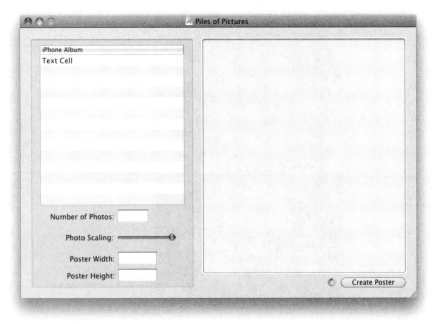

FIGURE 13-3

5. Drag an NSBox to the left of the window and resize it to fit. Set the Title Pos. option of the box in the Inspector to None, so that the title is not displayed. Drag an NSTableView, and position it as shown inside the box. Select the NSTableView and enter 1 in the Columns field in the first tab of the Inspector window. Also make sure the Empty check box is deselected in the Selection section of the Inspector, and the Multiple Selection check box is checked. You can also check the Alternating Rows check box if you wish.

6. Select the NSTableColumn by double-clicking the header cell of the NSTableView. Enter iPhoto Album as the Header title.

7. Drag an NSForm from the Cocoa palette in the Library window into the box. Position it under the NSTableView. Reduce the number of fields in the form to 1 by holding down the Option key while you drag the center-bottom handle upward. Double-click the form cell's label to edit it, and enter Number of Photos. Drag an NSNumberFormatter from the Cocoa palette in the Library onto the editable field of the NSFormCell. Click the Number of Photos label twice, and when the formatter button appears — it is a $ sign — click it to edit the formatter in the Inspector. Select Decimal from the Style pop-up button, and enter 1 in the Constraints Minimum field.

8. Repeat step 7 to create the NSForm shown at the bottom of the box in Figure 13-3. This form has two NSFormCells, with the labels Poster Width and Poster Height. Add an NSNumberFormatter to each, selecting the same format as in step 7, but setting the Minimum value to 0 in each case.

9. Add an NSSlider to the box, as shown in Figure 13-3, by dragging it from the Library window. In the Inspector window, select the Size tab, which is third from the left, and choose Small from the Size pop-up button. In the Attributes tab, which is on the far left, enter 0.0 and 1.0 for the Minimum and Maximum values, respectively. Drag a Label from the Cocoa palette in the Library into the box next to the slider and edit it to read Photo Scaling:.

10. Prepare to adjust the Window settings by selecting it in the MainMenu.xib document window. Deselect the Close and Resize check boxes, and enter Piles of Pictures for the Window Title.

11. Edit the File menu in the MainMenu instance. Click the File menu and delete all the menu items it contains except Save. To delete a menu item, select it and press Backspace. Rename the Save menu item to Save Poster by clicking its title and entering the new name.

12. Go to Xcode and edit the file Piles_of_PicturesAppDelegate.applescript so that it contains this source code:

```
script Piles_of_PicturesAppDelegate
    -- Outlets
    property albumTableView : missing value
    property posterImageView : missing value
    property progressIndicator : missing value
    property numberOfPhotosFormCell : missing value
    property scalingSlider : missing value
    property widthFormCell : missing value
    property heightFormCell : missing value
    property createPosterButton : missing value

    -- Actions
    on createPoster_(sender)
    end createPoster_

    on savePoster_(sender)
    end savePoster_
end script
```

code snippet MacOSXProg ch13/Piles of Pictures 1/Piles_of_PicturesAppDelegate.applescript

13. Return to Interface Builder and connect the outlets that you just declared. For each outlet, hold down Control, and click and drag from the Piles of Pictures Application Delegate icon (which is a blue box) to each of the elements in the main window of the application. Select the appropriate outlet each time.

14. Connect the actions defined in the application delegate by Control-dragging separately from the Create Poster button and the Save Poster menu item to the Piles of Pictures Application Delegate icon, and selecting the appropriate action for each.

15. Connect the dataSource outlet of the Album table view to the application delegate by Control-dragging from the table view to the delegate and selecting the dataSource outlet. Make sure you select the table view before starting the drag. The first click on the table view will select the scroll view containing the table view, not the table view itself. Click a second time to select the table view.

16. Save the changes you have made to the MainMenu.xib file.

How It Works

Most of this assignment simply involves laying out a user interface with Interface Builder and should not be particularly new to you. If you have read Chapter 4, which covers Interface Builder in detail, you should not find any of this too challenging.

What you probably haven't had to do before is declare outlets and actions in an AppleScript script, and then connect them in Interface Builder. This process is very similar to the way it is done in an Objective-C program. After you have declared an action or outlet in the script, it automatically becomes visible in Interface Builder and can be connected to the appropriate target object.

Two actions were declared in this example: savePoster: and createPoster:. When the user clicks the Create Poster button, the createPoster_ handler is called and a poster created with the settings retrieved from the various outlets. When the poster is ready, it can be saved. If the user chooses File ⇨ Save Poster, the savePoster_ handler will save the image data to file.

In the following Try It Out, you write the Piles_of _PicturesAppDelegate.applescript script to form a working AppleScript application. This script responds to the action messages sent by the interface components that you set up in this Try It Out, and will refer to the interface components using the outlets previously defined.

TRY IT OUT   Writing the Piles of Pictures Application Delegate Script

1. Open the Piles of Pictures project in Xcode and click the Piles_of_PicturesAppDelegate. applescript file in the Classes group of the Groups & Files pane on the left. The script should appear in the main editor.

2. Update the script as follows:

Available for
download on
Wrox.com

```
property NSSavePanel : class "NSSavePanel"
property NSImage : class "NSImage"
property NSFileHandlingPanelOKButton : 1
property NSCompositeSourceOver : 2

script Piles_of_PicturesAppDelegate
    property parent : class "NSObject"

    -- Outlets
    property albumTableView : missing value
    property posterImageView : missing value
    property progressIndicator : missing value
    property numberOfPhotosFormCell : missing value
    property scalingSlider : missing value
    property widthFormCell : missing value
    property heightFormCell : missing value
    property createPosterButton : missing value

    -- Model data
    property albumNames : {}
```

```
        property posterImage : missing value

        -- Launching
        on applicationDidFinishLaunching_(notification)
            my setControlDefaults()
            my setupTable()
        end applicationDidFinishLaunching_

        on setControlDefaults()
            widthFormCell's setIntegerValue_(1704)
            heightFormCell's setIntegerValue_(2304)
            numberOfPhotosFormCell's setIntegerValue_(50)
        end setControlDefaults

        on setupTable()
            tell application "iPhoto" to set my albumNames to name of albums
            tell albumTableView to reloadData()
        end setupTable

        -- Actions
        on createPoster_(sender)
            -- Create image for poster
            set posterWidth to widthFormCell's integerValue() as number
            set posterHeight to heightFormCell's integerValue() as number
            set posterImage to initWithSize_({|width|:posterWidth, ¬
                height:posterHeight}) of NSImage's alloc()

            -- Start progress indicator spinning
            -- and disable button
            progressIndicator's startAnimation_(me)
            set createPosterButton's enabled to false

            -- Add images to poster
            -- Allow button to conclude push by delaying to next
            -- run loop iteration
            my performSelector_withObject_afterDelay_("addImagesToPoster", ¬
                missing value, 0.1)
        end createPoster_

        on savePoster_(sender)
            set |panel| to NSSavePanel's savePanel()
            |panel|'s setAllowedFileTypes_({"tiff"})
            |panel|'s runModal()
            if result is not equal to NSFileHandlingPanelOKButton then return
            set |url| to |panel|'s |URL|()
            set |image| to posterImageView's |image|
            set imageData to |image|'s TIFFRepresentation()
            imageData's writeToURL_atomically_(|url|, false)
        end savePoster_

    -- Retrieving selected albums
        on getSelectedAlbums()
            set theAlbums to {}
            set numberOfAlbums to length of my albumNames
```

```
        repeat with row from 0 to numberOfAlbums - 1
            if albumTableView's isRowSelected_(row) then
                set selectedAlbumName to item (row + 1) in albumNames
                tell application "iPhoto" to get album selectedAlbumName
                set the end of theAlbums to result
            end if
        end repeat
        return theAlbums
    end getSelectedAlbums

    -- Retrieving Photos from iPhoto
    on getPathsToRandomPhotos(theAlbums, numberOfPhotos)
        tell application "iPhoto"
            set photoPaths to {}
            repeat numberOfPhotos times
                set end of photoPaths to image path of some photo ¬
                    of some item of theAlbums
            end repeat
        end tell
        return photoPaths
    end getPathsToRandomPhotos

    -- Adding images to Poster
    on addImagesToPoster()
        -- Draw images
        set numberOfPhotos to numberOfPhotosFormCell's integerValue()
        set theAlbums to my getSelectedAlbums()
        set imagePaths to my getPathsToRandomPhotos(theAlbums, numberOfPhotos)
        set scaleFactor to scalingSlider's floatValue()
        set i to 0
        repeat with imagePath in imagePaths
            set img to initWithContentsOfFile_(imagePath) of NSImage's alloc()
            addImageToPoster(img, scaleFactor)
            set i to i + 1
        end repeat

        -- Update image in interface
        posterImageView's setImage_(posterImage)

        -- Stop progress indicator
        -- and reenable button
        progressIndicator's stopAnimation_(me)
        set createPosterButton's enabled to true
    end addImagesToPoster

    on addImageToPoster(img, scaleFactor)
        -- Determine size and position
        set imgSize to img's |size|()
        set posterSize to posterImage's |size|()
        set scaledWidth to scaleFactor * (|width| of imgSize as number)
        set scaledHeight to scaleFactor * (height of imgSize as number)
        set originX to (random number from -scaledWidth to ¬
            (|width| of posterSize as number))
        set originY to (random number from -scaledHeight to ¬
            (height of posterSize as number))
```

```
        -- Destination rect in poster image
        set s to {|width|:scaledWidth, height:scaledHeight}
        set o to {x:originX, y:originY}
        set destRect to {|size|:s, origin:o}

        -- Source rect of current image
        set srcRect to {|size|:{|width| of imgSize as number, ¬
            height of imgSize as number}, origin:{0, 0}}

        -- Draw into poster image
        posterImage's lockFocus()
        img's drawInRect_fromRect_operation_fraction_(destRect, ¬
            srcRect, NSCompositeSourceOver, 1.0)
        posterImage's unlockFocus()
    end addImageToPoster

    -- Table View data source methods
    on numberOfRowsInTableView_(tableView)
        return length of albumNames
    end numberOfRowsInTableView_

    on tableView_objectValueForTableColumn_row_(tableView, tableColumn, row)
        return item (row + 1) of albumNames
    end tableView_objectValueForTableColumn_row_

end script
```

code snippet MacOSXProg ch13/Piles of Pictures 2/Piles_of_PicturesAppDelegate.applescript

3. Build and run the application by clicking the Build and Go toolbar button. If you encounter an error, try debugging it using the Compile command from the Build menu, and the `log` statement.

4. Assuming that you have an iPhoto library, select one or more albums in the iPhoto Album table view. Set the number of photos you want to include in the poster and adjust the scaling of the photos. If you want, you can also change the width and height of the poster. Lastly, click Create Poster and wait for the poster to be generated. This can take a minute or two, depending on your settings and computer.

> **NOTE** Remember, if you don't use iPhoto for your digital photos, it doesn't mean you can't use it for this example. You can simply open your iPhoto library and import a few images from your hard disk or the Web.

5. Save the poster by choosing File ➪ Save Poster. Open the saved poster by double-clicking it in Finder, or use QuickLook to examine your handiwork.

How It Works

Hopefully the `Pile of Pictures.applescript` script has demonstrated how easy it is to create a useful application with AppleScriptObjC, one that is practically indistinguishable from an Objective-C–Cocoa application. With around 150 lines of AppleScript, you can extract photos from iPhoto, draw them on a new image taking full advantage of Cocoa and Quartz, and export the resulting image to a file.

The script begins by declaring some properties:

```
property NSSavePanel : class "NSSavePanel"
property NSImage : class "NSImage"
property NSFileHandlingPanelOKButton : 1
property NSCompositeSourceOver : 2
```

Cocoa classes and constants belong to the `current application` object in AppleScript; rather than having to continuously write expressions such as `current application's class "NSSavePanel"`, it is convenient to declare properties at the top of the script for use throughout. You can then simply refer to `NSSavePanel`, rather than the previous mouthful.

Cocoa constants are supposed to be visible via the AppleScriptObjC bridge, but this is not always the case. The `NSFileHandlingPanelOKButton` and `NSCompositeSourceOver` constants are examples of this. Because they are not available via the bridge, their values have been set to match their Cocoa numerical values.

The application delegate script appears here:

```
script Piles_of_PicturesAppDelegate
    property parent : class "NSObject"

    -- Outlets
    property albumTableView : missing value
    property posterImageView : missing value
    property progressIndicator : missing value
    property numberOfPhotosFormCell : missing value
    property scalingSlider : missing value
    property widthFormCell : missing value
    property heightFormCell : missing value
    property createPosterButton : missing value

    -- Model data
    property albumNames : {}
    property posterImage : missing value
```

It begins by setting the `parent` property so that it inherits from the Cocoa class `NSObject`. The outlets defined earlier appear next, followed by two new properties for storing the list of photo album names, and then the image of the poster being created.

The first methods do some setup when the application launches:

```
    -- Launching
    on applicationDidFinishLaunching_(notification)
        my setControlDefaults()
        my setupTable()
    end applicationDidFinishLaunching_

    on setControlDefaults()
        widthFormCell's setIntegerValue_(1704)
```

```
            heightFormCell's setIntegerValue_(2304)
            numberOfPhotosFormCell's setIntegerValue_(50)
        end setControlDefaults             .

        on setupTable()
            tell application "iPhoto" to set my albumNames to name of
              albums
            tell albumTableView to reloadData()
        end setupTable
```

The `applicationDidFinishLaunching_` handler is a delegate method of the `NSApplication` class, and gets called after the application has concluded launching. In this example, it is used to initialize the input fields in `setControlDefaults`, and to retrieve the photo album names from iPhoto to store in the `albumNames` property. After the names are stored, the table view is told to reload its data using the `reloadData` method.

The table view uses its `dataSource` outlet — which was set inside Interface Builder earlier — to retrieve the data it displays. The application delegate script defines methods that tell the table view what it needs to know:

```
        -- Table View data source methods
        on numberOfRowsInTableView_(tableView)
            return length of albumNames
        end numberOfRowsInTableView_

        on tableView_objectValueForTableColumn_row_(tableView,
          tableColumn, row)
            return item (row + 1) of albumNames
        end tableView_objectValueForTableColumn_row_
```

The `numberOfRowsInTableView_` handler returns the total number of rows, which is the length of the `albumNames` list. The `tableView_objectValueForTableColumn_row_` handler returns the title of an album corresponding to a particular row of the table.

 NOTE *You need to be careful when working with indexes, because AppleScript begins at 1, and Objective-C begins at 0. This means you often have to add or subtract 1 when working with the AppleScriptObjC bridge.*

The code to save the poster image to file is in the `savePoster_` action handler:

```
        on savePoster_(sender)
            set |panel| to NSSavePanel's savePanel()
            |panel|'s setAllowedFileTypes_({"tiff"})
            |panel|'s runModal()
            if result is not equal to NSFileHandlingPanelOKButton
              then return
            set |url| to |panel|'s |URL|()
            set |image| to posterImageView's |image|
            set imageData to |image|'s TIFFRepresentation()
```

```
        imageData's writeToURL_atomically_(|url|, false)
    end savePoster_
```

This handler gets a save panel by calling the NSSavePanel class method savePanel, and sets it up to create TIFF files. The runModal method puts the panel on-screen. After the user enters a file and location, the return value of the runModal method is checked to see whether the OK button was pressed. If not, the handler returns; if so, the URL of the user's selection is retrieved, and the poster image is converted to data in the TIFF format using the TIFFRepresentation method. Lastly, the NSData method writeToURL:atomically: is invoked to dump the data to disk.

One aspect of this code that may be confusing at first is the use of vertical bars around variable and handler identifiers. AppleScript has many built-in keywords, and it is very easy to have a variable or handler name conflict with an existing keyword. You can avoid this by putting vertical bars on either side of the identifier. If you are unsure whether a particular identifier is reserved for use by AppleScript, you should probably just insert the bars anyway, because they can't do any harm.

When the user clicks the Create Poster button, the createPoster_ handler is called. It initiates the chain of events that retrieves photos and draws the poster:

```
on createPoster_(sender)
    -- Create image for poster
    set posterWidth to widthFormCell's integerValue() as number
    set posterHeight to heightFormCell's integerValue() as number
    set posterImage to initWithSize_({|width|:posterWidth,height: posterHeight}) ¬
        of NSImage's alloc()

    -- Start progress indicator spinning
    -- and disable button
    progressIndicator's startAnimation_(me)
    set createPosterButton's enabled to false

    -- Add images to poster
    -- Allow button to conclude push by delaying to next run loop
        iteration
    my performSelector_withObject_afterDelay_("addImagesToPoster", ¬
        missing value, 0.1)
end createPoster_
```

It begins by retrieving the values of the controls in the user interface. These are coerced to AppleScript numbers and stored in variables. A new poster image is also created using the NSImage methods alloc and initWithSize_. This shows the standard way you can create a new Objective-C object in AppleScript, a two-step process in which memory is first set aside (alloc) and then initialized (initWithSize_).

The initWithSize: method takes an NSSize struct as argument. As you learned earlier, you can pass a list or record whenever a standard struct such as NSSize is expected; in this case, a record with keys width and height has been used.

After initializing the poster image, the createPoster_ action handler starts the progress indicator spinning, disables the button so that the user can't press it twice, and then does a delayed call to the handler addImagesToPoster. To delay the call, the NSObject method performSelector:withObject: afterDelay: is used. This method is asynchronous, which means it returns before the call has been made, allowing the main thread to continue executing. After the delay has past, the method passed in via the selector argument is invoked. If the second argument is non-nil, it is passed to the method.

The performSelector:withObject:afterDelay: method is very common in Objective-C programs. It allows tasks to be postponed for a period of time. In this case, it is used to allow the Create Poster button to complete its animation and pop back up again. If a direct call to addImagesToPoster is made, the button has to wait until the poster is fully drawn before completing its animation.

The addImagesToPoster method oversees the drawing of the poster:

```
on addImagesToPoster()
    -- Draw images
    set numberOfPhotos to numberOfPhotosFormCell's
      integerValue()
    set theAlbums to my getSelectedAlbums()
    set imagePaths to my getPathsToRandomPhotos(theAlbums,
      numberOfPhotos)
    set scaleFactor to scalingSlider's floatValue()
    set i to 0
    repeat with imagePath in imagePaths
        set img to initWithContentsOfFile_(imagePath) of
          NSImage's alloc()
        addImageToPoster(img, scaleFactor)
        set i to i + 1
    end repeat

    -- Update image in interface
    posterImageView's setImage_(posterImage)

    -- Stop progress indicator
    -- and reenable button
    progressIndicator's stopAnimation_(me)
    set createPosterButton's enabled to true
end addImagesToPoster
```

It uses the getSelectedAlbums handler to retrieve the photo albums from iPhoto that correspond to the user's selection in the table view, and then gets paths to random photos from these albums. The NSImage initializer initWithContentsOfFile_ is used to read in each of the photos from disk, at which point they are passed off to the addImageToPoster handler, which does the actual drawing. The method concludes by setting the newly formed poster in the NSImageView in the main window, so the user can see the result.

The addImageToPoster is responsible for drawing a single image into the poster:

```
on addImageToPoster(img, scaleFactor)
    -- Determine size and position
    set imgSize to img's |size|()
    set posterSize to posterImage's |size|()
    set scaledWidth to scaleFactor * (|width| of imgSize as
      number)
    set scaledHeight to scaleFactor * (height of imgSize as
      number)
```

```
        set originX to (random number from -scaledWidth to ¬
            (|width| of posterSize as number))
        set originY to (random number from -scaledHeight to ¬
            (height of posterSize as number))

        -- Destination rect in poster image
        set s to {|width|:scaledWidth, height:scaledHeight}
        set o to {x:originX, y:originY}
        set destRect to {|size|:s, origin:o}

        -- Source rect of current image
        set srcRect to {|size|:{|width| of imgSize as number, ¬
            height of imgSize as number}, origin:{0, 0}}

        -- Draw into poster image
        posterImage's lockFocus()
        img's drawInRect_fromRect_operation_fraction_(destRect, ¬
            srcRect, NSCompositeSourceOver, 1.0)
        posterImage's unlockFocus()
    end addImageToPoster
```

To draw into an NSImage in Cocoa — in this case the one referenced by the posterImage variable — you first call the method lockFocus, and, after drawing is complete, the method unlockFocus. Doing this creates an offscreen buffer where the drawing can take place. The drawing itself is achieved using the drawInRect_fromRect_operation_fraction_ method of the image object that is being drawn into the poster. All this code can be found in the last few lines of the addImageToPoster method.

The majority of the addImageToPoster handler is concerned with the arithmetic of determining the rectangle that the photo will be drawn into on the poster. Rectangles are represented by the NSRect struct in Objective-C; in AppleScript, this is equivalent to a record with the keys size and origin. The value corresponding to the size key is another record representing an NSSize. It has keys width and height, and the origin key corresponds to a value for an NSPoint, which is a record with keys x and y.

The code involves randomly selecting a position for the photo on the poster, and scaling the image dimensions based on the scaleFactor variable. Random values are chosen for the origin of the photo, which is in the bottom-left corner. These values get combined to define the rectangle in which the photo image will be drawn in the coordinates of the poster image.

The getSelectedAlbums handler retrieves the rows of the albums selected by the user in the table view, and then requests the album objects corresponding to these rows from iPhoto:

```
    on getSelectedAlbums()
        set theAlbums to {}
        set numberOfAlbums to length of my albumNames
        repeat with row from 0 to numberOfAlbums - 1
            if albumTableView's isRowSelected_(row) then
                set selectedAlbumName to item (row + 1) in
                    albumNames
                tell application "iPhoto" to get album
                    selectedAlbumName
                set the end of theAlbums to result
```

```
            end if
        end repeat
        return theAlbums
    end getSelectedAlbums
```

A `repeat` loop iterates over the rows in the table, and a call to the table view's `isRowSelected_` method is used to determine whether the corresponding album should be included. If an album name has been selected, it is used to get the `album` object from iPhoto, which is added to a `list` that is eventually returned from the handler.

The last handler in the script is `getPathsToRandomPhotos`:

```
on getPathsToRandomPhotos(theAlbums, numberOfPhotos)
    tell application "iPhoto"
        set photoPaths to {}
        repeat numberOfPhotos times
            set end of photoPaths to image path of some
                photo ¬
                    of some item of theAlbums
        end repeat
    end tell
    return photoPaths
end getPathsToRandomPhotos
```

This code is very similar to code used earlier in the chapter to randomly access photos in the iPhoto library. It retrieves the number of photos requested at random from the `list` of `album` objects passed to it. Notice that there is no attempt made to prevent a photo from being selected more than once, so a poster may contain the same photo two or more times.

SUMMARY

AppleScript is in a category by itself because it is the only scripting language designed to interact with Mac OS X applications while they are running. For this reason, it fills an important role in Mac OS X programming. Even if your applications are written in languages other than AppleScript, there will often be tasks better left to an AppleScript script. It also helps users if they can write scripts that work with your applications — your software becomes a first-class citizen on the Mac platform. Some knowledge of the language is thus a decided advantage for any Mac OS X developer.

In the next chapter, you learn how to develop widgets and web applications with JavaScript and Dashcode. Before proceeding, however, try the exercises that follow to test your understanding of the material covered in this chapter. You can find the solutions to these exercises in Appendix A.

1. Modify the script you completed in the fifth Try It Out example, "Finishing Off Slideshow Maker," so that the user is prompted for the duration of each slide. Make sure you handle invalid user input appropriately.

2. The Piles of Pictures application works fine if the user does not try to do anything unusual, but it doesn't do a good job of taking into account exceptional circumstances. In particular, it doesn't consider the possibility that the user's iPhoto album contains no albums, or that the albums selected by the user are all empty.

Modify the Piles of Pictures script so that it checks that the user selected at least one album, and that the selected albums are not all empty. If either of these circumstances arises, throw an error, and catch it again in the `addImagesToPoster` handler. Display an alert panel if an error occurs. (Hint: Read about the `NSAlert` class in the Developer Documentation accessed through the Xcode Help menu.)

3. Piles of Pictures allows you to vary the scaling of the photos drawn in the poster, but the same scaling factor applies to all photos. The purpose of this exercise is to allow the user to randomly vary the scaling from one photo to the next, so that the poster ends up with a distribution of different sizes.

Add a second slider to the Piles of Pictures user interface to allow the user to choose a variation factor from 0.0 to 1.0. Choose a random value for each photo from the range stipulated by the variation factor, and add it to the original scaling factor such that each photo has a different scaling.

The variation factor should range over positive and negative values, corresponding to larger and smaller sizes, respectively. You need to ensure that the overall scaling factor of a photo — after applying the variation factor — is between 0.0 and 1.0.

▶ **WHAT YOU LEARNED IN THIS CHAPTER**

AppleScript	AppleScript is an English-like language that appeals to non-programmers and is designed for scripting graphical Mac OS X applications.
AppleScript Editor	AppleScript Editor is a tool located in `/Applications/Utilities` that can be used to edit and run AppleScript scripts. You can use it to open application dictionaries to learn what commands are available.
Language Basics	How to define variables and store data, as well as how collection types such as `list` and `record` are used in scripts.
Flow Control and Organization	How to use branching constructs such as the `if` statement, as well as several varieties of the `repeat` loop. How you use handlers and scripts for the high-level organization of code.
Properties and Elements	The differences between properties and elements, and the various ways you can access each.
Applications	How to script applications such as iTunes, iPhoto, Finder, and QuickTime.
AppleScriptObjC	How you can use the AppleScriptObjC scripting bridge to leverage Cocoa frameworks from AppleScript scripts, calling from AppleScript to Objective-C and vice versa.
Development Tools	The provisions in Xcode and Interface Builder for developing fully functional Cocoa applications with AppleScriptObjC.

14

JavaScript, Dashboard, and Dashcode

WHAT YOU WILL LEARN IN THIS CHAPTER:

➤ The basics of the JavaScript scripting language

➤ How to write Dashboard widgets with JavaScript, Cascading Style Sheets (CSS), and HTML

➤ How to use WebKit CSS Animations to make visually stunning web pages and widgets

➤ How to develop a web client application in Dashcode

JavaScript is one of the most widely used scripting languages around, and is essential for the operation of the Web. When it was initially introduced, its primary purpose was to add dynamic behavior to static web sites — graphical tricks such as making buttons change appearance when pressed, or animating a sequence of images.

Nobody at that point in time could have predicted that JavaScript would one day evolve into the language that underpins nearly all client-side web development. JavaScript is now much more than just flashy graphics — though it is that too — it also plays a big role in Web 2.0 technologies such as Ajax. (The 'j' stands for "JavaScript.") In contrast to the hack-ish use of JavaScript in the early days, now there are large, well-engineered frameworks developed entirely in JavaScript. In short, Web 2.0 would probably not have happened without JavaScript.

 NOTE *Some of the most well-known JavaScript frameworks include Prototype, Scriptaculous, jQuery, Dojo, SproutCore, and Cappuccino. Many of these frameworks actually extend the JavaScript language, making up for its limitations.*

The last few years, Apple has also started to embrace JavaScript. The WebKit framework, which is the basis of the Safari web browser, but also Dashboard and the iTunes Music Store are leading the way in terms of JavaScript runtime performance.

Apple has also introduced Dashcode, a tool that is primarily designed for developing Dashboard widgets and client-side web applications in JavaScript. Dashcode is a powerful tool, comparable in many ways to Xcode. Dashcode makes JavaScript a first-class citizen on the platform.

JAVASCRIPT

Netscape originally created JavaScript as a scripting language to make dynamic content for the Web. JavaScript code is usually found embedded in HTML and gets run in a web browser. By giving you access to all the elements of an HTML page via the so-called *document object model* (DOM), JavaScript allows you to take static HTML web content and change it as time passes.

JavaScript looks quite a bit like the Java programming language, but that is where the comparison ends. JavaScript is not Java, nor is it a subset of Java. JavaScript is a simple, interpreted language that runs in web browsers. Java is an extensive compiled language that can be used for a wide variety of purposes — from server-side web development to desktop application development.

 NOTE *Java is a compiled language, but it is a compiled language with a difference. The Java compiler converts Java source code into something called byte code, rather than the machine code that runs on the CPU. The byte code is platform independent; when you run a Java application, a program called the Java Virtual Machine (JVM) reads the byte code and generates machine executable code, which is what is sent to the CPU. In short, the JVM is a bit like an interpreter. As you can see, the distinction between a compiled language and an interpreted language is not that clear when it comes to Java.*

JavaScript is a relatively simple language to learn. It sticks to many of the conventions of C, with curly braces used to delineate blocks of code, and semi-colons used to terminate lines. You will learn more about JavaScript as you go through the examples in this chapter. To get you started, what follows is a short introduction to the basics of JavaScript.

JavaScript can be embedded directly into HTML files or included from separate script files. You can import a JavaScript file using the `script` tag:

```
<html>
    <head>
        <script type='text/javascript' src='CoolEffects.js' charset='utf-8'/>
    </head>
    ...
</html>
```

This imports the file `CoolEffects.js` and executes the JavaScript in it. The `script` tag usually appears in the `head` section of an HTML file, but this is not a requirement.

The `script` tag is also used if you want to embed a short JavaScript script directly into an HTML file:

```
<html>

<head>
...
</head>

<body>
...

<script type="text/javascript">
var pageTracker = _trackingObject.getTracker("HDFS-98");
pageTracker._trackPage();
</script>

</body>

</html>
```

This code, which could come from a web site statistics package, is embedded directly into the HTML at the end of the `body` section.

As with all programming languages, JavaScript allows you to define variables. It uses the `var` keyword for this purpose:

```
var age = 10;
var name = "Bob";
var _name2 = "Gray";
```

Variables take on the type of whatever they are assigned to, so you don't have to explicitly declare the variable type. All the usual data types are allowed, including numbers and strings. Variable names follow the standard C naming rules, with alphanumeric characters and underscores allowed, but with digits forbidden from occupying the first position.

In addition to simple numerical and character types, JavaScript also has built-in collections. The first is an `Array` type, which can hold multiple objects that can be referenced by an index:

```
var array = new Array();
array[0] = 'hi';
array[1] = 'there';
array[2] = 2.0;
```

This example shows that you create an array object using `new Array()`, and then add values to it. As with C, JavaScript uses square brackets to specify array indexes, and indexes begin at zero.

Another very common collection is one that stores key-value pairs. In Objective-C this is called a dictionary, and in AppleScript it is a record. Whatever the term, most languages have such a collection type, but not JavaScript . . . at least not an obvious one.

JavaScript doesn't have a dedicated key-value container, but standard JavaScript objects can be used in much the same way, so it is not really needed:

```
var keysAndValues = new Object();
keysAndValues.color = 'red';
keysAndValues['type'] = 'fast';
alert("This thing is " + keysAndValues.type)
```

This script displays an alert dialog with the text `This thing is fast`. As you can see, you can use either the dot notation to access values, or you can use the square bracket notation that is used for the array type.

JavaScript has the same basic set of arithmetic operators as C and other similar languages. These include ++ and -- for incrementing and decrementing an integer, respectively, and += for adding the right side of an expression to the variable on the left side.

The + operator can be used not only with numbers, but also for concatenating strings. It can even convert a number to a string:

```
var string1 = 'This is it.';
var string2 = "This time I know it's number " + 9 + '.';
alert(string1 + ' ' + string2);
```

This example shows that you can use single or double quotes to define string literals, and the + operator to concatenate them. The alert that appears contains this text:

```
This is it. This time I know it's number 9.
```

Note that the number 9 was implicitly converted to a string and concatenated. This can be used to change a numerical value into a string, as in the following example.

```
var num = 9;
var numAsString = num + '';
```

By adding an empty string to a number, you convert it into a string representation of the numerical value.

Of course, JavaScript also has the standard allotment of looping and branching constructs. To loop over elements in an array, you can do this:

```
var a = new Array();

var i = 0;
for ( i = 0; i < 3; i++ ) a[i] = i;

for ( i in a ) {
   alert('' + i);
}
```

This example shows two different types of `for` loops: the traditional C variety that ranges over integers, and a second type that ranges over the contents of an array. The first loop fills the array with integer values, and the second one displays alerts with the value of each element in the array.

The `if` statement can be used for conditional branching, just as in C:

```
var i = 5;
if ( i == 5 ) {
    alert('Good!');
}
else {
    alert('Nope');
}
```

You can also add `else if` to create further branches.

JavaScript has functions to help you order your code. A great aspect of JavaScript functions is that they are *closures*: they can be used inline and passed around as objects. They can also access variables that are defined in the function's parent scope:

```
function showAlert( arg ) {
    alert(arg);
}

showAlert("Alert!");
```

This simple example takes a single argument, assumes it is a string, and displays it in an alert dialog. But take this more complex case:

```
function showFuncResult( func ) {
    alert( func() );
}

function main() {
    var isFullyFunctional = false;
    showFuncResult(
        function() {
            if ( isFullyFunctional )
                return "Fully Functional!";
            else
                return "Not Functional";
        } );
}
```

What is interesting in this example is that the argument to `showFuncResult` is a function. When `showFuncResult` is called, it is passed as an anonymous, inline function. When the anonymous function gets called inside `showFuncResult`, it accesses the value of the variable `isFullyFunctional`, even though that variable is not visible inside `showFuncResult`.

A JavaScript function is thus a closure — an object that can be passed around, and that carries with it any variables that existed in the scope in which it got defined. You can assign functions to variables, or pass them to other functions, as was the case in the above example.

NOTE *JavaScript's functions are actually very similar to blocks in the C language, which you can read about in Chapter 6.*

That pretty much covers the basics of the JavaScript language. It is small, yet flexible. But that is not the whole story, because one of the great strengths of JavaScript is that it works seamlessly with the DOM, a tree-like internal representation of all the elements that make up an HTML page. By manipulating the DOM with JavaScript, you can make a page update on-the-fly, effectively introducing dynamic behavior.

Each element in a web site becomes an object in the JavaScript DOM. Consider this example:

```
<html>
<body>

<head>

<script type="text/javascript">
function updateText( obj ) {
    obj.innerHTML = "Yes, this is text. I concur.";
}
</script>

</head>

<span id="firstpara" onclick="updateText(this);">This is some text.</span>

</body>
</html>
```

This HTML page only has one visible element, namely a span containing some text. By setting the onclick handler to a short piece of JavaScript, a function call can take place whenever the user clicks the text. The JavaScript calls the function updateText, and passes the argument this. The variable this represents the object that is executing the code, in this case the span element.

Inside the updateText function, the innerHTML attribute of the object passed in gets set to a new string. The net effect is that if you click the text in the browser, it changes. By modifying the DOM, JavaScript is effectively modifying the web page displayed in the browser.

You can use this to easily access the current DOM element, but often you need to access other parts of the DOM tree. You could traverse the whole tree in search of the element you seek, or you could use the very handy method getElementById. Using getElementById, you could rewrite the previous example as follows:

```
<html>
<body>

<head>

<script type="text/javascript">
```

```
function updateText( obj ) {
    obj.innerHTML = "Yes, this is text. I concur.";
}
</script>

</head>
<span id="firstpara">This is some text.</span> <br />
<span style="color:white; background-color:gray;"
    onclick="updateText( document.getElementById('firstpara') );">Click Here</span>
</body>
</html>
```

A second span has been added and styled with CSS to look like a gray button (see Figure 14-1). The `onclick` handler of this button makes the call to `updateText`. The `this` object is of no use here, because the text needs to be updated elsewhere in the document — namely, in the first `span`. So the `getElementById` method of the document is used to retrieve the element corresponding to the first `span`, which is then passed to the `updateText` function.

FIGURE 14-1

The DOM gives you access to all aspects of an HTML document, but also the CSS styles. You can also modify these on-the-fly, which is very important for changing the physical appearance of a web page.

Imagine that you want to have the button in the previous example change color when pressed. You do that by altering the `style` attribute of the button `span`:

```
<span style="color:white; background-color:gray;"
    onclick="this.style.color='red'; this.style.backgroundColor='black';">
    Click Here</span>
```

When the user clicks the button, the `onclick` handler is called. It accesses the `style` attribute of `this`, setting `color` and `backgroundColor` to different string values. This is equivalent to changing the CSS style of the element, and causes the button's text and background to change color.

Before finishing this short section on JavaScript, it is worth mentioning a very powerful tool for working with the language: Safari. Apple's browser has hidden features targeted at web site and widget developers. To turn on these features, open the Safari preference pane, and under the Advanced tab, check the Show Develop menu in the menu bar check box (see Figure 14-2).

You should now see a new Develop menu appear. You can use this to view error messages, browse CSS styles for a page, or even bring up a JavaScript debugger. It is a very useful feature and should be your first port of call when things go wrong.

FIGURE 14-2

 NOTE *If you use the Firefox browser, you needn't fret, because it also has powerful features for debugging web pages.*

Dashboard

Quite apart from its important place in web development, JavaScript has an added attraction for Mac developers — on Mac OS X, JavaScript has stepped outside the browser. As you are undoubtedly aware, Dashboard is a technology that allows you to develop and use *widgets*, which are little utilities that you can display with the press of a key or move of the mouse. What you may not know is that Dashboard is based on web technologies such as HTML, CSS, and JavaScript. Put simply, a Dashboard widget is not much more or less than a web page.

If you have experienced Dashboard as a user, you are aware that widgets can come in a variety of forms. Some are like small standalone applications, such as a calculator or notepad. Others, such as the Weather and Flight Tracker widgets provided by Apple, give you an easy way to access web content. And a third category provides simplified interfaces to existing programs such as iTunes.

Dashboard widgets are *bundles*, which are simply folders with a special extension. All applications on Mac OS X are also bundles — folders with the extension `.app`, which the Finder treats as a single file for most purposes. Widgets also come in bundles, but the extension you give them is `.wdgt`.

A widget bundle must include a number of different files, including the following:

➤ A main HTML file

➤ A PNG file for the widget bar icon

➤ A PNG file for the default image of the widget, which is displayed during loading

➤ An Info.plist property list file that includes metadata that describes various aspects of the widget, such as its size on-screen

A widget bundle can also include any other files needed for it to function properly, such as images or JavaScript source code.

Dashboard widgets can leverage any technology included with Mac OS X, from AppleScript to OpenGL, but most are built using just three technologies:

➤ **HTML**: Defines the structure of a widget

➤ **Cascading Style Sheets (CSS)**: Defines the look of a widget

➤ **JavaScript**: Defines the behavior of a widget

In the next two Try It Outs you test your JavaScript, HTML, and CSS by creating a Dashboard widget. The widget in question, called DashBall, is a standalone utility variety. DashBall, shown in Figure 14-3, is a simple game in which the user hits a tennis ball against the walls of a brick box.

You will create this widget manually, with simple tools such as Finder, Safari, and a text editor. This allows you to better understand how a widget is constructed. The Dashcode tool, which is covered later in this chapter, can also be used to develop Dashboard widgets.

In this first Try It Out, you set up the widget so that it can be displayed but doesn't do anything. In the second Try It Out, you finish the widget, adding ball movement and responding to whenever the ball gets hit by the user's cursor.

FIGURE 14-3

TRY IT OUT **Beginning the DashBall Dashboard Widget**

1. Create a new folder called DashBall in the Finder. Create a new text file in the folder called DashBall.js using any editor (for example, Xcode or TextEdit), and enter the following source code:

Available for
download on
Wrox.com

```
// Wall Coordinates
var wallCoords = {left:40, right:225, bottom:175, top:15};

// Ball Properties
var ball = {
    x:(wallCoords.right + wallCoords.left ) * 0.5,
    y:(wallCoords.top + wallCoords.bottom) * 0.5,
    velocityX:200.0,
    velocityY:200.0 }
```

```
if (window.widget)
{
    widget.onshow = onshow;
    widget.onhide = onhide;
}

// Called when widget is loaded
function setup()
{
    setBallPosition();
}

// Called when dashboard is shown
function onshow()
{
}

// Called when dashboard is hidden
function onhide()
{
}

function setBallPosition()
{
    var ballImage = document.getElementById("ball");
    ballImage.style.top = ball.y;
    ballImage.style.left = ball.x;
}
```

code snippet MacOSXProg ch14/DashBall 1/DashBall.js

2.   Add another text file called DashBall.css, and enter the following text:

Available for download on Wrox.com

```
body {
    margin: 0;
}

img#ball {
    position: absolute;
}
```

code snippet MacOSXProg ch14/DashBall 1/DashBall.css

3.   Add a file called DashBall.html to the DashBall folder, and enter the following contents:

Available for download on Wrox.com

```
<html>

<head>

<style type="text/css">
    @import "DashBall.css";
</style>
```

```
<script type='text/javascript' src='DashBall.js' charset='utf-8'></script>

</head>

<body onload='setup();'>
    <img src='Default.png' />
    <img id='ball' src='TennisBall.png' />
</body>

</html>
```

code snippet MacOSXProg ch14/DashBall 1/DashBall.html

4. Now add a text file called `Info.plist` to the `DashBall` folder, and insert the following property list code:

```
<?xml version="1.0" encoding="UTF-8"?>
<!DOCTYPE plist PUBLIC "-//Apple Computer//DTD PLIST 1.0//EN"
    "http://www.apple.com/DTDs/PropertyList-1.0.dtd">
<plist version="1.0">
<dict>
    <key>AllowMultipleInstances</key>
    <true/>
    <key>CFBundleIdentifier</key>
    <string>com.beginningmacosxprogramming.widget.dashball</string>
    <key>CFBundleName</key>
    <string>DashBall</string>
    <key>CFBundleShortVersionString</key>
    <string>1.0</string>
    <key>CFBundleVersion</key>
    <string>1.0</string>
    <key>DefaultImage</key>
    <string>Default</string>
    <key>MainHTML</key>
    <string>DashBall.html</string>
    <key>Height</key>
    <integer>225</integer>
    <key>Width</key>
    <integer>300</integer>
</dict>
</plist>
```

code snippet MacOSXProg ch14/DashBall 1/Info.plist

5. Use a drawing or painting program to create the graphics files for DashBall, and save them in the `DashBall` folder. All files should be in PNG format. Use Figure 14-1 as a reference for how the graphics should look. The following table gives details of each of the graphics you need to create.

FILENAME	DESCRIPTION OF IMAGE	WIDTH	HEIGHT
Default.png	A rectangular border made of bricks, with a black background.	300 pixels	225 pixels
Icon.png	A square region of brick wall with rounded corners, and a tennis ball in the center.	82 pixels	82 pixels
TennisBall.png	A tennis ball.	36 pixels	36 pixels

If you do not have the talent or desire to create these images, you can use the ones supplied in the sample code for this chapter, which you can download from www.wrox.com.

6. Use the Finder to make a copy of the `DashBall` folder, and rename the copy `DashBall.wdgt`. The icon of the folder should change to indicate that `DashBall.wdgt` is a Dashboard widget.

7. Double-click `DashBall.wdgt` to install it in Dashboard. The Finder will display a dialog asking whether you wish to install the widget. Agree to the request. When in Dashboard, drag the widget around on-screen and then close it again.

How It Works

The `Info.plist` file that you supply in a widget's bundle gives Dashboard important information about the widget, such as its size on-screen and the name of the main HTML file. The `Info.plist` file is in Apple's XML property list format, which allows you to include basic types such as integers and strings, and to structure data into arrays and dictionaries.

 NOTE *You do not have to edit property lists manually in a text editor if you don't want to. Instead, you can use the Property List Editor application, which is located in the* `/Developer/Applications/Utilities` *directory, after you install the Xcode developer tools.*

Here is a table describing the entries in the `Info.plist` file of DashBall:

DICTIONARY KEY	TYPE	DESCRIPTION
AllowMultipleInstances	Boolean	Whether or not a user is allowed to create more than one instance of the widget on-screen. For DashBall, this is allowed.
CFBundleIdentifier	String	A unique identifier for the widget. This is used, for example, to store preferences.
CFBundleName	String	The name of the widget in Dashboard.
CFBundleShortVersionString	String	The version number of the widget, as a short string.
CFBundleVersion	String	The full version number of the widget.
DefaultImage	String	The name of the PNG file that is displayed while the widget is loading. The extension should not be included in the name.
MainHTML	String	The name of the main HTML file of the widget. The extension should be included.
Height	Integer	The height of the widget in pixels.
Width	Integer	The width of the widget in pixels.

The only optional key in the table is `AllowMultipleInstances`; the others have to be supplied in every widget you write.

The `Info.plist` file supplies Dashboard with metadata for your widget, but the structure of the widget itself is defined in the main HTML file. For DashBall, this file is called `DashBall.html`, as stated in the `Info.plist` file for the key `MainHTML`. If you have any experience with HTML, the `DashBall.html` file should not pose any challenges. It begins by importing the CSS file `DashBall.css`, which is used to define some aspects of the appearance of the widget:

```
<style type="text/css">
    @import "DashBall.css";
</style>
```

The CSS file is very simple in this case:

```
body {
    margin: 0;
}

img#ball {
    position: absolute;
}
```

The first block indicates that the body of the widget's HTML page should have a margin with a width of 0. The second block refers to the image representing the tennis ball. The `position` property is set to `absolute`, which means the ball's position can be set to any position on the page.

After importing `DashBall.css`, the `DashBall.html` file includes the JavaScript file `DashBall.js`:

```
<script type='text/javascript' src='DashBall.js' charset='utf-8'>
   </script>
```

`DashBall.js` determines the behavior of the widget, such as how it reacts to events, user generated or otherwise.

The body of the HTML file includes two image files — one of the brick wall box, `Default.png`, and the other of the tennis ball, `TennisBall.png`:

```
<body onload='setup();'>
    <img src='Default.png' />
    <img id='ball' src='TennisBall.png' />
</body>
```

The `body` tag also includes the `onload` attribute, which is assigned to a piece of JavaScript code that gets executed when the HTML is first loaded. In this case, the JavaScript function `setup`, which is defined in `DashBall.js`, is called. The `setup` function initializes various aspects of the widget.

The JavaScript file `DashBall.js` begins by defining some variables for the positions of the four walls and the position and velocity of the tennis ball:

```
// Wall Coordinates
var wallCoords = {left:40, right:225, bottom:175, top:15};

// Ball Properties
var ball = {
    x:(wallCoords.right + wallCoords.left ) * 0.5,
    y:(wallCoords.top + wallCoords.bottom) * 0.5,
    velocityX:200.0,
    velocityY:200.0 }
```

You define variables in JavaScript using the `var` keyword. The `wallCoords` variable is assigned to an object that has the attributes `left`, `right`, `bottom`, and `top`. These attributes are initialized to 40, 225, 175, and 15, respectively. Together they define the region that the tennis ball is allowed to explore. The values themselves are taken relative to an origin at the top-left of the page. They were determined by trial and error to make the ball appear to bounce off the brick walls.

The ball's attributes are its position, given by x and y relative to the top-left corner, and its velocity, given by `velocityX` and `velocityY`. The attributes x and y are initialized such that the ball is located in the center of the box defined by `wallCoords`. The velocity attributes have been chosen arbitrarily; they could just as easily be set to other values to give the ball a different initial speed and/or direction of travel. The next lines of the `DashBall.js` script set the `onshow` and `onhide` attributes of a JavaScript object called `widget`:

```
if (window.widget)
{
    widget.onshow = onshow;
```

```
        widget.onhide = onhide;
    }
```

`widget` is created by Dashboard and can be used to interact with Dashboard and the rest of the operating system. For example, you can use `widget`'s `system` method to run shell commands and other programs.

The preceding code uses an `if` statement to check whether the `widget` object exists. You need to do this if you want to be able to test your widgets in a web browser such as Safari because the `widget` object exists only when running in Dashboard, not in a browser.

If the `widget` object does exist, two of its attributes, `onshow` and `onhide`, are set to functions defined later in the script:

```
// Called when dashboard is shown
function onshow()
{
}

// Called when dashboard is hidden
function onhide()
{
}
```

In this case, the functions have also been given the names `onshow` and `onhide`, but this is not a requirement. Neither function takes any action at this point; functionality is introduced in the next Try It Out. The function `onshow` is called when Dashboard gets displayed on-screen, and `onhide` is called when Dashboard gets hidden. These attributes of `widget` are quite important because they allow you to halt any expensive calculations that your widget might perform while Dashboard is not in view.

The `setup` function is called when the HTML body is loaded, as you saw in the preceding HTML file. It calls a second function, `setBallPosition`, which positions the ball's image according to the initial coordinates of the ball:

```
// Called when widget is loaded
function setup()
{
    setBallPosition();
}
```

`setBallPosition` moves the ball's image to whatever point in the page corresponds to its x and y coordinates at that point in time:

```
function setBallPosition()
{
    var ballImage = document.getElementById("ball");
    ballImage.style.top = ball.y;
    ballImage.style.left = ball.x;
}
```

This function demonstrates how you can retrieve objects representing elements of a web page using JavaScript. The `getElementById` method of the `document` object, which is the root object for the web page, is passed a string identifier for the object sought. The identifier itself is set in the HTML file using the `id` property; in DashBall, the `id` property of the `img` tag corresponding to the ball's image was set to `ball`.

The object returned by `getElementById` corresponds to the `img` element of the ball's image. You can use JavaScript to set attributes of this tag, and thereby affect the relationship of the ball's image to the page. In this case, the `style` attribute of the `img` element is modified. The `style` attribute represents the element's CSS style, and modifying it effectively changes the CSS style of the image. The `setBallPosition` function sets the `left` and `top` attributes of the `img` element's `style` attribute to the `x` and `y` attributes of the ball, respectively. This results in the ball's image moving on the page to the coordinates given.

The DashBall widget is not yet complete. You can view it in Dashboard and move it around, but it doesn't do anything. In the following Try It Out, you finish the widget, making the ball move in time and allowing the user to hit it.

TRY IT OUT   Finishing the DashBall Dashboard Widget

1. Use a text editor to open the `DashBall.js` file in the `DashBall.wdgt` bundle. To open the `DashBall.wdgt` bundle in Finder, you need to Control-click it and select the Show Package Contents item from the contextual menu. Edit the top of the file as highlighted here:

```
// Ball Properties
var ball = {
    x:(wallCoords.right + wallCoords.left ) * 0.5,
    y:(wallCoords.top + wallCoords.bottom) * 0.5,
    velocityX:200.0,
    velocityY:200.0 }

// Physics
var frictionFactor = 0.9;
var elasticityFactor = 0.95;

// Timersvar theTimer = {step:100};
var powTimerId = 0;

// Variables for hitting
var hitting = false;
var hitCoords = new Object();
var ballCoordsAtHit = new Object();
```

code snippet MacOSXProg ch14/DashBall 2/DashBall.js

---

2. Edit the `setup`, `onshow`, and `onhide` functions in `DashBall.js` as indicated here:

```
// Called when widget is loaded
function setup()
{
    setBallPosition();
```

```
    theTimer.id = setInterval("updateBall()", theTimer.step);
}

// Called when dashboard is shown
function onshow()
{
    if ( !theTimer.id ) theTimer.id = setInterval("updateBall()", theTimer.step);
}

// Called when dashboard is hidden
function onhide()
{
    clearInterval(theTimer.id);
    theTimer.id = 0;
}
```

code snippet MacOSXProg ch14/DashBall 2/DashBall.js

3. To finish DashBall.js, add the following code to the end of the file and save your changes:

```
function updateBall()
{
    // Apply gravity
    ball.velocityY += 50.0 * ( theTimer.step / 1000.0 );

    // Update position
    ball.x += ball.velocityX * ( theTimer.step / 1000.0 );
    ball.y += ball.velocityY * ( theTimer.step / 1000.0 );

    // Handle bounces. Include a little friction, and inelasticity.
    if ( ball.x > wallCoords.right || ball.x < wallCoords.left )
    {
        ball.velocityX *= -elasticityFactor;
        ball.velocityY *= frictionFactor;
    }
    if ( ball.y < wallCoords.top || ball.y > wallCoords.bottom )
    {
        ball.velocityY *= -elasticityFactor;
        ball.velocityX *= frictionFactor;
    }

    // Make sure ball is in court
    ball.y = Math.max(ball.y, wallCoords.top);
    ball.y = Math.min(ball.y, wallCoords.bottom);
    ball.x = Math.max(ball.x, wallCoords.left);
    ball.x = Math.min(ball.x, wallCoords.right);

    setBallPosition();
}

function startHit() {
    hitting = true;
    hitCoords.x = event.x;
    hitCoords.y = event.y;
```

```
        ballCoordsAtHit.x = ball.x;
        ballCoordsAtHit.y = ball.y;
    }

    function finishHit() {
        if ( hitting ) {
            ball.velocityX += 2 * (event.x - hitCoords.x -
                (ball.x - ballCoordsAtHit.x));
            ball.velocityY += 2 * (event.y - hitCoords.y -
                (ball.y - ballCoordsAtHit.y));
        }
        var pow = document.getElementById("pow");
        pow.style.top = ball.y;
        pow.style.left = ball.x;
        pow.style.opacity = '1.0';
        pow.style.webkitAnimationName = 'spinin';
        if ( powTimerId ) clearTimeout(powTimerId);
        powTimerId = setTimeout('hidePow();', 2000);
        hitting = false;
    }

    function hidePow() {
        var pow = document.getElementById("pow")
        pow.style.webkitAnimationName = 'fadeout';
        pow.style.opacity = '0.0';
        powTimerId = 0;
    }
```

code snippet MacOSXProg ch14/DashBall 2/DashBall.js

4. Open the `DashBall.css` file in the `DashBall.wdgt` bundle. Add the following to the end and save the changes:

```
@-webkit-keyframes spinin {
    0% {
        opacity: 0.2;
        -webkit-transform: scale(0.5) rotate(0deg);
    }
    80% {
        opacity: 0.4;
        -webkit-transform: scale(2) rotate(540deg);
    }
    100% {
        opacity: 1;
        -webkit-transform: scale(1) rotate(720deg);
    }
}

@-webkit-keyframes fadeout {
    0% {
        opacity: 1;
        -webkit-transform: scale(1);
    }
    100% {
```

```
        opacity: 0;
        -webkit-transform: scale(2);
    }
}

.powtext {
    font: 26px "Lucida Grande";
    font-weight: bold;
    color: white;
    position: absolute;
    opacity:0;
    -webkit-animation-duration: 0.5s;
    -webkit-animation-timing-function: ease-in;
}
```

code snippet MacOSXProg ch14/DashBall 2/DashBall.css

5. Open the `DashBall.html` file in the `DashBall.wdgt` bundle and make the highlighted changes:

Available for
download on
Wrox.com

```
<body onload='setup();'>
    <img src='Default.png' />
    <span id='pow' class='powtext'>Pow!</span>
    <img id='ball' src='TennisBall.png'
        onmouseover='startHit();'
        onmouseout='finishHit();' />
</body>
```

code snippet MacOSXProg ch14/DashBall 2/DashBall.html

6. After you have saved all your changes, copy the bundle, append .wdgt to the folder name, and double-click the new copy in Finder to install DashBall in Dashboard. The ball should now move. Try hitting the ball with your cursor to see what happens.

7. Open Dashboard and locate the DashBall icon on the widgets bar at the bottom of the screen. Drag out a new instance of the widget and confirm that it works as expected. Hide Dashboard and then show it again. Confirm that the ball begins moving again from the position it had when hidden.

How It Works

Some small changes are made to the elements in the `DashBall.html` file. In particular, a span element is added that includes the text `Pow!`:

```
<span id='pow' class='powtext'>Pow!</span>
```

This text gets displayed for a couple of seconds whenever the user successfully hits the ball. It pops onto the screen spinning like a record, and then jumps out of the screen as it disappears.

The `id` of the element, `pow`, is used to refer to the text in `DashBall.js`. The `class` of the span element, `powtext`, is defined in `DashBall.css`:

```
.powtext {
    font: 26px "Lucida Grande";
    font-weight: bold;
    color: white;
    position: absolute;
    opacity:0;
    -webkit-animation-duration: 0.5s;
    -webkit-animation-timing-function: ease-in;
}
```

This CSS code sets a number of attributes of the text, including its font and color. The position of the text on-screen also needs to be changed based on where the ball is hit. So the `position` attribute is set to `absolute`, just as it was for the ball's image. The position of the text can then be given relative to the coordinate system of the page. The attribute `opacity` determines whether or not the text is visible. Here it is initialized to `0`, which means the text is completely transparent and thus invisible.

WebKit CSS Animations are used to animate the text onto and off of the screen. When the ball is hit, the WebKit Animation `spinin` is activated:

```
@-webkit-keyframes spinin {
    0% {
        opacity: 0.2;
        -webkit-transform: scale(0.5) rotate(0deg);
    }
    80% {
        opacity: 0.4;
        -webkit-transform: scale(2) rotate(540deg);
    }
    100% {
        opacity: 1;
        -webkit-transform: scale(1) rotate(720deg);
    }
}
```

The animation has been labeled 'spinin', but any valid identifier could have been used. This block of code defines the key frames of an animation, which are values taken by attributes at different points in time. In this particular animation, the opacity begins at 0.2, which is quite transparent. The WebKit Transform property is set to have a scale of 0.5 and a rotation of 0. This causes the text to start out at half its normal size.

After 80 percent of the animation is complete, the opacity has been increased to 0.4, the scale corresponds to double natural size (2), and the text has been rotated 540 degrees. Finally, at the completion of the animation, the scale is returned to natural size, the text is fully opaque, and it has rotated twice around. The net effect of all these changes is that the text spins out of the screen and then settles to its natural size and position.

The `fadeout` transition is a bit simpler, with no rotation:

```
@-webkit-keyframes fadeout {
    0% {
        opacity: 1;
        -webkit-transform: scale(1);
    }
```

```
    100% {
        opacity: 0;
        -webkit-transform: scale(2);
    }
}
```

To trigger the animations and react to the user hitting the ball, two attributes were added to the existing `img` element used to represent the ball's image in the `DashBall.html` file:

```
<img id='ball' src='TennisBall.png'
        onmouseover='startHit();'
        onmouseout='finishHit();'>
```

The `onmouseover` attribute defines a piece of JavaScript that is executed whenever the user moves the cursor into the region covered by the image. The code executed in this case calls the function `startHit`, which is defined in `DashBall.js`. The `onmouseout` attribute is similar, but it is used when the mouse leaves the area covered by the image. When this event occurs, the `finishHit` function is called.

The `startHit` function sets a number of global variables that are declared at the top of `DashBall.js`:

```
function startHit() {
    hitting = true;
    hitCoords.x = event.x;
    hitCoords.y = event.y;
    ballCoordsAtHit.x = ball.x;
    ballCoordsAtHit.y = ball.y;
}
```

The `hitting` global variable is used to keep track of whether the user is in the process of hitting the ball. It is `true` when the cursor has entered the region of the ball, and `false` at all other times.

The `hitCoords` global variable is used to store the coordinates of the cursor when the ball is hit. It is declared and initialized at the top of `DashBall.js`:

```
var hitCoords = new Object();
```

The `new` keyword creates a new object. `hitCoords` is initialized to a new object of the class `Object`, which you can simply view as an empty container. To put data in the container, you assign values to attributes as demonstrated in `startHit`; you do not need to declare the attributes before assigning them.

The `event` object in `startHit` contains information about the event that triggered the function call. The attributes `x` and `y` indicate where the event occurred, and these are stored in the `hitCoords` object for later reference. The coordinates of the ball are also stored when it is hit, in the `ballCoordsAtHit` variable.

All the variables set in `startHit` are used in the `finishHit` function to determine the change in the velocity of the ball resulting from the hit:

```
function finishHit() {
    if ( hitting ) {
        ball.velocityX += 2 * (event.x - hitCoords.x -
            (ball.x - ballCoordsAtHit.x));
        ball.velocityY += 2 * (event.y - hitCoords.y -
```

```
                (ball.y - ballCoordsAtHit.y));
    }
    var pow = document.getElementById("pow");
    pow.style.top = ball.y;
    pow.style.left = ball.x;
    pow.style.opacity = '1.0';
    pow.style.webkitAnimationName = 'spinin';
    if ( powTimerId ) clearTimeout(powTimerId);
    powTimerId = setTimeout('hidePow();', 2000);
    hitting = false;
}
```

This function first makes sure that the `hitting` variable is `true`; if it is, it adjusts the `velocityX` and `velocityY` attributes of the `ball` object. The change in velocity is determined by subtracting the coordinates at which the ball was hit, which are stored in `hitCoords`, from the coordinates of the event leading to the `finishHit` call, which are in the `event` object. The movement of the ball is then subtracted, to give the direction of the hit. The change in velocity is set to two times this direction; this scaling was determined simply by trial and error, to give the right "feel" when the ball is hit. You can adjust it to your own liking.

 NOTE *The algorithm used to change the velocity of the ball when it is hit is quite primitive. For example, it does not account for the speed of the cursor when the ball is hit. If you like, you can improve the widget by coming up with a more advanced algorithm for hitting the ball.*

The rest of the `finishHit` function displays the `Pow!` text. It first gets an object representing the text using the `getElementById` function; then it sets the `style` attribute of the element to position the text at the same point as the ball. The `style.opacity` attribute is also set to `"1.0"` so that the text appears on-screen.

To trigger the WebKit Animations, the `webkitAnimationName` style attribute is set to the string `"spinin"`. This starts the `spinin` animation defined earlier in the `DashBall.css` file. The `hidePow` function, which is called to hide the text, triggers the `fadeout` animation by setting the `webkitAnimationName` style attribute to the string `'fadeout'`:

```
function hidePow() {
    var pow = document.getElementById("pow")
    pow.style.webkitAnimationName = 'fadeout';
    pow.style.opacity = '0.0';
    powTimerId = 0;
}
```

The call to `hidePow` is made with the help of a timer, which delays for two seconds to allow the text to remain on-screen temporarily. The `setTimeout` function is used in JavaScript to create a timer that fires only once. The first argument is the JavaScript that is executed when the timer fires. In this case, the `hidePow` function is called. The second argument is the time interval before the timer fires, in milliseconds.

The return value of the function is an identifier for the timer. It gets stored in the powTimerId variable. The identifier can be passed to the clearTimeout function to cancel the timer; an example of this can also be found in finishHit, where any previously created timer that has yet to fire is cancelled before a new timer is created with setTimeout.

Another timer is used to animate the ball; the timer in question, however, fires repeatedly at regular intervals, rather than just once. The animation timer gets created in the onshow function that is called whenever Dashboard appears on-screen; it gets cancelled in onhide whenever Dashboard disappears from the screen:

```
// Called when dashboard is shown
function onshow()
{
    if ( !theTimer.id ) theTimer.id = setInterval("updateBall()",
        theTimer.step);
}

// Called when dashboard is hidden
function onhide()
{
    clearInterval(theTimer.id);
    theTimer.id = 0;
}
```

As you can see, the setInterval function is used to create a repeating timer, rather than setTimeout.

> **WARNING** *By starting and stopping the animation in this way, the DashBall widget does not take up precious CPU cycles when Dashboard is not on-screen. You should take a similar approach to every widget you write. Be sure that your widgets do not keep running while Dashboard is off-screen.*

The animation timer makes repeated calls to the updateBall function. This function updates the ball's coordinates and velocity, and finishes off by moving the ball's image on-screen using a call to setBallPosition. The updateBall function is simple enough from a programming point of view, but it's a bit involved in terms of the physics it uses to modify the state of the ball. For example, it adjusts the velocity for gravity and accounts for collisions with the walls, including the effects of friction and inelasticity. The details are left for you to consider; if they are too complicated for your liking, you can either ignore them or change the algorithm to something simpler.

This DashBall example has only scratched the surface of what is possible with Dashboard widgets. For example, no use was made of preferences for storing data persistently. You could use preferences to allow the user to set the initial velocity of the ball or the strength of gravity acting on the ball, to name but two possibilities.

No direct use of Quartz drawing was made in DashBall either. Dashboard offers an extension to HTML, the canvas tag, and a matching JavaScript class, Canvas, which allows you to use Quartz to draw on your widget. You could, for example, rewrite DashBall such that the space inside the brick box corresponded to a canvas, and the ball was drawn using the methods of the JavaScript Canvas class, which in turn invokes Quartz drawing functions.

Hopefully, the DashBall example has shown you that:

➤   JavaScript is a language with a Java-like syntax.

➤   JavaScript is closely coupled to HTML and CSS via the document object model (DOM).

➤   Dashboard widgets are not much more than dynamic web pages.

➤   Dashboard widgets are generally constructed out of HTML, for structure; CSS, for appearance; and JavaScript, for behavior.

➤   WebKit CSS Animations are quite easy to use and add an extra dimension to a web page or widget.

DASHCODE

Dashcode is to web technologies what Xcode is to Objective-C: an integrated development environment (see Figure 14-4). With Dashcode, which you can find in /Developer/Applications, you can create widgets for Dashboard, iPhone web applications, and even web applications for the desktop. In this section, you see how to create a complete client-side web application with Dashcode and just a few lines of JavaScript.

Dashcode has all the features you would expect in an integrated development environment. It has tools to help you organize your code, lay out your user interface, and make connections between the two. It also has a very good editor, with syntax highlighting for HTML, CSS, and JavaScript, as well as code completion. It even has a first-class JavaScript debugger. Set a breakpoint in your JavaScript code, and you'll be able to inspect the values of any variables or view the complete call tree.

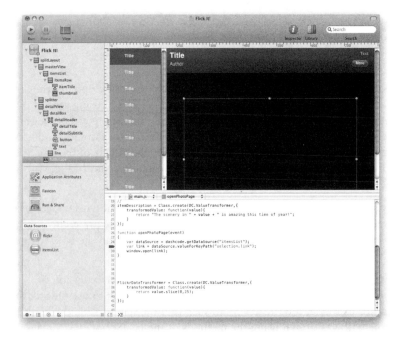

FIGURE 14-4

Dashcode is actually a bit more than just a development environment, because it includes an entire JavaScript framework that adds standard widgets such as buttons and list views to your toolkit. The Dashcode JavaScript framework is built in an object-oriented manner, much as the Cocoa frameworks (see Chapter 8), and can be extended in your own code.

Dashcode also includes templates that act as the starting point of a project. You can even create a complete RSS reader application for your web site just by entering the feed URL. There are templates for different types of Dashboard widgets, iPhone web applications, and desktop web applications.

The building, testing, and deploying of applications is also handled by Dashcode. When you build a project, Dashcode opens a simulator for testing so that you don't have to upload to a web server. When you are ready to go live with your app, Dashcode will bundle everything and deploy it for you.

You will be introduced to Dashcode by way of example. In the next two Try It Outs, you will develop a desktop web application for the popular Flickr (`http://www.flickr.com`) photo-sharing web site (see Figure 14-5). In the first, you lay out the interface in Dashcode, and in the second you implement data download and populate the interface elements.

FIGURE 14-5

TRY IT OUT Laying Out the Flick It! Interface

1. Launch Dashcode from the `/Developer/Applications` folder. In the project template sheet that appears, select Safari on the left, and the Browser application type on the right. Look for the label Develop for and uncheck the Mobile Safari option. Click the Choose button.

2. You should be presented with a project window that looks similar to Figure 14-6. Choose Save from the File menu, and save the project under the name Flick It! somewhere on your hard drive.

FIGURE 14-6

3. Take a look at the Workflow Steps in the bottom-left corner of the screen. These can help guide you as you work through the project. The first step is to lay out the interface. Click the Library button to bring up the Library panel. Now click the Inspector button to bring that up.

4. Select the view in the left column of the canvas on the right. Make sure you select the whole column, not one of the sub-views. The selection in the source list on the left should be `masterView`. (You can also click `masterView` to make the selection.)

5. In the Inspector window, click the second tab to edit the visual properties of the object (Figure 14-7). Open the color panel by clicking the swatch next to Background Color. In the color panel, choose a dark gray color.

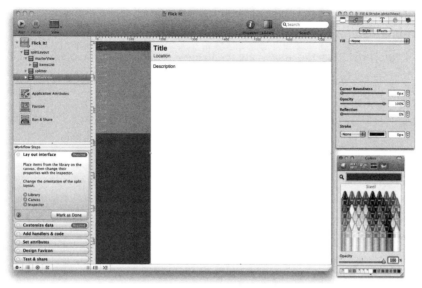

FIGURE 14-7

6. Select the first row of the list on the left. To do this, you have to click it somewhere outside the Title field. In the Inspector, choose the Metrics tab (third) and set the Height to 60px.

7. Now select the Title text field in the first row of the list on the left of the canvas. In the Inspector, open the fourth tab, and choose White from the Color pop-up button. Set the Shadow pop-up button to None (Figure 14-8).

8. Go to the Metrics tab (third tab), and in the Autoresize section, click the strut (line) that extends outward from the top of the box. It should transform into a spring (Figure 14-9).

FIGURE 14-8

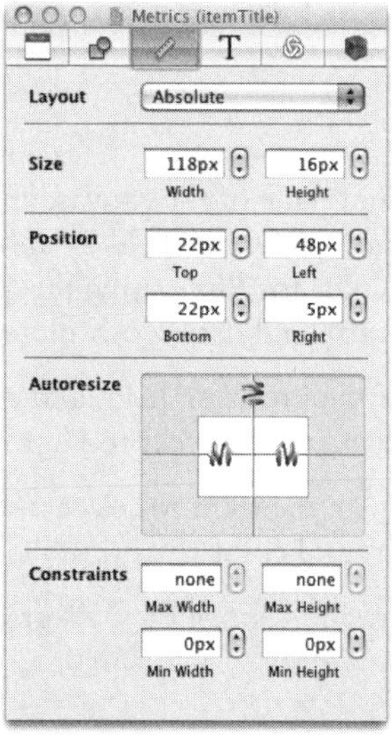

FIGURE 14-9

9. Return to the canvas and resize the first Title text field by dragging the resizing handle on the left in the middle toward the right. Also drag the field downward so that it is centered.

10. In the Library panel, select the Parts tab and locate the Image part. (You can use the filter field at the bottom to find it quicker.) Drag the Image part into the first row of the list just to the left of the Title field. Resize it so that it completely fits inside the row (Figure 14-10).

FIGURE 14-10

11. Select the Description field in the right pane of the canvas, and delete it by pressing backspace. Select the Title field on the right, and shorten the field by about half, dragging the right-middle handle to the left. Change the text color to White using the Text tab in the Inspector. Open the Metrics tab of the Inspector (third tab), and choose Absolute from the Layout pop-up button.

12. Repeat step 11 to reduce the size of the Location field, and change its text color to White. Also double-click the field to edit it, and change the text to Photographer.

13. Click the background of the header on the right to select it. Use the Fill & Stroke tab (second tab) to set a dark gradient as the background color (Figure 14-11).

14. Select the bottom pane on the right, and change the background color to solid black.

15. Drag an Image part from the Parts section of the Library panel into the bottom pane on the right of the canvas. Open the Metrics tab in the Inspector, and choose Absolute from the Layout pop-up button. Set the struts and springs in the Autoresize section as shown in Figure 14-12. This allows the image to resize laterally, but pins it to the top of the parent view. Drag the image to position it just above the center of the pane. Finally, in the Fill & Stroke Inspector tab (second), set the reflection slider to 50 percent.

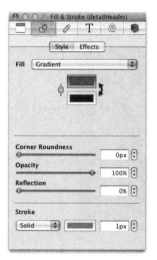

FIGURE 14-11

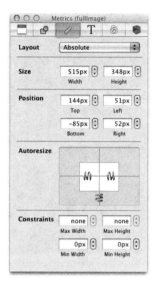

FIGURE 14-12

16. Drag a Text part from the Library into the header view on the right of the canvas. In the Metrics Inspector pane, change the Layout to Absolute. Now position the field to the top right, approximately in line with the Title field. In the Inspector's text pane (fourth tab), change the font size to 11px, the color to a very light gray, and the alignment to right. In the Metrics tab of the Inspector, set the spring on the left of the Autoresizing box, and set all other connections to struts (straight lines).

17. Locate the Lozenge button in the Library Parts tab. Drag one into the header section on the right of the canvas. In the Metrics pane of the Inspector, choose Absolute for the Layout, and set a spring on the left of the Autoresizing box so that the button is pinned to the right of the view. Drag the button under the text on the right of the canvas. Resize the button to make it smaller. Set the text color to White, and set the button color to gray, using the Fill & Stroke pane of the Inspector (second tab). Click the button's title and change it to More.

18. Make sure your project window looks similar to Figure 14-13, and save the project.

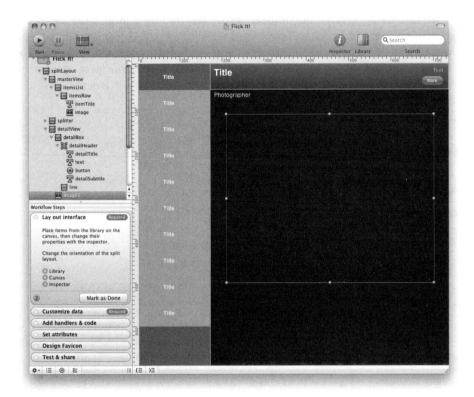

FIGURE 14-13

How It Works

This Try It Out has been largely an exercise in laying out a user interface. If you have any experience with Interface Builder, it will probably seem very familiar. It is quite repetitive when you understand how the interface tools work.

The Browser template was used for this project. This template allows you to build an application that has different levels of detail. In this case there are just two levels: the master list on the left, and the detail view on the right.

The project could also have been based on the RSS template. In fact, this would have made things even easier, only requiring that the URL of the RSS feed be entered. Or you could start the project with the Custom template and lay out the whole interface yourself. The Browser template seems like a good compromise between no work at all, and doing it all from scratch.

The list on the left will eventually contain the latest photos from the public RSS stream on Flickr. There will be a thumbnail and the title of the image, which is often no more than a device-generated identifier. The pane on the right houses the detail view. This shows the photo in full, as well as giving the title, author, and date it was uploaded on the right.

When clicked, the More button is intended to take you to the `flickr.com` page that corresponds to the photo shown.

Most of the attributes you changed should be self-explanatory. Size of text, alignment, and color need no explanation. But the Metrics tab of the Inspector may need some clarification, particularly if you have never used Interface Builder before.

In Dashcode, objects on-screen can be positioned and resized in one of two modes: Absolute and Document Flow. If they are in Absolute mode, they can be positioned anywhere inside their parent view, and will be repositioned and resized according to the Autoresize settings. If you choose Document Flow as the mode, the object is automatically positioned to fit after other Document Flow objects.

The Autoresize control is based on Interface Builder. You can set various aspects of an object to either be flexible — in which case you use a spring — or fixed, which requires a strut. You can have settings which allow an object to grow in size with its parent view — such as the main image in this example — which can broaden to fit. Or you can set the size of the object to be fixed, and just have it pinned to one or the other side of the parent view. This approach has been used for the text labels and More button.

In the next Try It Out, you set up Flick It! to download data from `flickr.com` and populate the user interface that you previously created. You will also see how to add your own JavaScript source code, and interact with the Dashcode framework from JavaScript.

TRY IT OUT   Handling Data in the Flick It! Web Application

1.   In the Workflow steps, click the Mark as Done button, and close the Lay out interface pane by clicking its title bar. Open the Customize data pane by clicking it. Press the Data Sources button to bring up the list of data source objects.

2.   Change the title of the first data source to `flickrPublicStream`. Select the data source and enter the following URL in the field on the right, before pressing return: `http://api.flickr.com/services/feeds/photos_public.gne?format=rss_200_enc`.

3.   You should see an outline of the feed appear in the bottom-right pane. Use the disclosure triangle to open the row entitled `item` in the `channel` section. Mouse over the `title` row, and click the circle that appears to the right. Still holding the mouse button down, drag to the Title field of the first row in the left canvas list (Figure 14-14). Let go when the Title field is selected, and then select `text` from the contextual menu that appears.

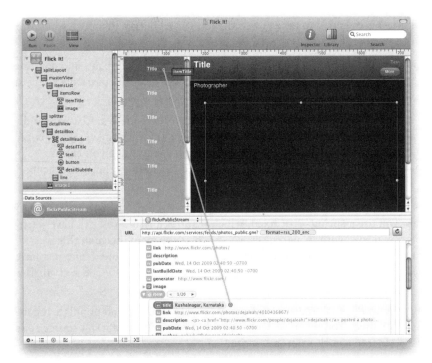

FIGURE 14-14

4. Locate the `media:thumbnail` section of the data source outline and open it. Using the same technique as in step 3, drag from the `url` to the thumbnail image to the left of the `Title` field in the first row of the list. Choose `src` from the menu that appears.

5. To test what you already have, click the Run button in the toolbar. You will get a warning that you are only allowed to retrieve data from the same domain as the feed. Click the Simulate button. You should get a window similar to that in Figure 14-15.

6. Close the simulator to return to Dashcode's project window. You will notice that a new data source, called `itemsList`, has appeared in the Data Sources list. Select it. In the outline, drag from the `title` attribute in the `selection` section to the `Title` field in the header of the detail pane on the right. Choose `text` from the menu.

7. Drag from the `media:credit` attribute to the `Photographer` field, and choose `text` from the menu. Also drag from the `url` attribute inside the `media:content` section to the main image on the right of the canvas, and choose `src` from the menu.

FIGURE 14-15

8. Scroll to the bottom of the data source outline. Drag from hasSelection to the main image, and choose visible from the menu. Repeat this for the Photographer text field. Finally, drag again, this time from hasSelection to the More button, but choose enabled rather than visible from the menu.

9. Drag from the pubDate attribute to the text field in the header on the right, and choose text. With the text field selected, open the Bindings tab in the Inspector (fifth). Click the disclosure triangle to open the text pane, and enter FlickrDateTransformer in the Value Transformer field.

10. You should see the main.js file open automatically in an editor in the project window. Edit the code beginning with FlickrDateTransformer as follows:

```
FlickrDateTransformer = Class.create(DC.ValueTransformer,{
    transformedValue: function(value){
        return value.slice(0,25);
    }
});
```

11. Select the More button, and choose the Behaviors tab in the Inspector (last). For the onclick handler, enter openPhotoPage in the right column. The editor should again open automatically with source code for the openPhotoPage function. Replace it with the following:

```
function openPhotoPage(event)
{
    var dataSource = dashcode.getDataSource("itemsList");
    var link = dataSource.valueForKeyPath("selection.link");
    window.open(link);
}
```

12. Save the project and click the Run toolbar item to test it. Notice how the elements in the detail pane behave when there is no selection. Now click a thumbnail and watch how the detail views update. Resize the window and notice how the different views reposition or resize. Finally, click the More button to test the effect.

How It Works

This Try It Out has been concerned with retrieving the Flickr public photo RSS stream, and connecting the elements of the data stream to the interface.

Dashcode can work with data in XML or JSON formats. It represents each stream by a data source object. When you set the URL of a data source, it downloads the latest document and represents it in a structured outline view in the editor. You can then connect elements of the data source to elements of the interface, a process known as *binding*.

Each type of interface control has a number of different bindings that can be connected to a data source. For example, many have a text binding, which simply represents the text displayed in the interface. You can see which bindings are available for a particular control by selecting it and opening the Bindings tab of the Inspector (fifth tab).

 NOTE *Dashcode bindings are very similar to Cocoa bindings, which were introduced in Chapter 8.*

Dashcode allows you to easily bind controls to elements of the data source by dragging from one to the other. This is just a convenience, because ultimately all bindings end up being stored as a target data source, and a key path to the required element in the document. You can see this in the Bindings pane of the Inspector. In fact, you could set up all your bindings in the Inspector, without using the dragging technique at all.

In the Bindings pane, you can also control other aspects of a binding, such as what text should be displayed if there is no selection, or more than one selection. You can use bindings to display a text value, but you can also set bindings for whether or not a control should be visible on-screen, or whether it should be enabled, and so forth.

The main XML data stream represents the primary data source in this example, but when you bind items in the stream to the list in the interface, an interesting phenomenon occurs: the list itself becomes a data source. The reason for this is that otherwise it would be very difficult to bind the detail view or a sub-list.

With the `itemsList` data source selected, it is possible to bind data from the current selection of the list to controls in the detail view of the interface. There is even a `hasSelection` node that is very useful for hiding or disabling controls when there is no selection. The `visible` and `enabled` bindings are available for this purpose.

Sometimes the data you are binding to is not quite in the right form. A good example of this would be a control that should be displayed when there is no selection. You can't just bind to the hasSelection node, because that will cause the control to be visible when there *is* a selection.

Dashcode offers value transformers to help with this. Value transformers can be connected to any binding, and can transform the data from the data source before passing it to the interface. Some value transformers can also perform the reverse transformation.

There are a number of built-in value transformers, which you can find by clicking the Value Transformer combo box in the Bindings pane of the Inspector. The DC.transformer.Not value transformer, for example, applies the logical NOT operator to the data before passing it to the interface. This allows you to solve the problem posed earlier where the control should be displayed when there is no selection in the list: just bind to the hasSelection node and set the value transformer to DC.transformer.Not.

Although Dashcode has a number of useful prebuilt value transformers, much of the time you need to write your own. As soon as you enter the name of a value transformer that does not exist, Dashcode generates stub code for it in main.js.

In Flick It!, the date in the XML data is very long, so a value transformer was used to abbreviate it:

```
FlickrDateTransformer = Class.create(DC.ValueTransformer, {
    transformedValue: function(value){
        return value.slice(0,25);
    }
});
```

A value transformer must be a subclass of the DC.ValueTransformer class, which is part of the Dashcode framework. This small snippet of code shows how you define a class in Dashcode. The FlickrDateTransformer is a subclass of DC.ValueTransformer and contains a single method called transformValue, which takes a single argument — the value to be transformed.

 NOTE *Although JavaScript itself is not an object-oriented programming language, it is flexible enough to behave as one. Most JavaScript frameworks introduce a system for defining classes and subclasses, and Dashcode is no exception.*

In this extremely simple example, the transformValue method shortens the string to 25 characters, and returns it. You could easily conceive of more advanced algorithms that show the time that has passed since the photo was uploaded (for example, 53 minutes), or use a localized representation of the date.

Not all interface behavior can or should be handled by bindings. For example, when a button is pressed, it is more natural to have it call a handler to take some action. The Behaviors pane of the Inspector can be used to associate events with particular handlers. If you enter a handler that does not yet exist, Dashcode will again generate stub code in main.js.

In the current application, the openPhotoPage handler was associated with the onclick event of the More button:

```
function openPhotoPage(event)
{
```

```
    var dataSource = dashcode.getDataSource("itemsList");
    var link = dataSource.valueForKeyPath("selection.link");
    window.open(link);
}
```

This code shows you how you can access a data source object from JavaScript. The `getDataSource` method of the global `dashcode` object is used to retrieve the data source object. The method `valueForKeyPath` can then be used to retrieve a value from the data source. Alternatively, `setValueForKeyPath` can be used to change the value inside a data source.

You might be wondering how the interface knows to update when a data source changes its data. For example, if the selection of the photo list changes, how do the detail views in the interface know to refresh?

The technology behind this is called *key-value observation* (KVO), and it is based largely on the Cocoa technology of the same name. In short, an object can subscribe for change notifications from another object for a given key. When that key changes, they get informed of the change and can refresh.

One subject that wasn't covered in this Try It Out was actually deploying the web application on a server. Dashcode makes this reasonably easy: click the Run & Share icon in the project source list (see Figure 14-16). You can deploy your application via Mobile Me, or have Dashcode upload it automatically with FTP or WebDAV.

FIGURE 14-16

One thing that is easy to forget when creating Dashcode applications is that they can only work with data from your own web domain. In that sense, the previous Flickr example is just a nice exercise — only Flickr could actually deploy the app on the Web, because only Flickr has access to the `flickr.com` domain. You can only run the app in simulation mode.

What this means is that Dashcode only gives you half the solution. You still need to code the server-side of your application; the side that actually generates the XML that the Dashcode app ingests. For this you can use languages such as PHP, Java, Ruby, and Python (see Chapter 11).

SUMMARY

Over the years, JavaScript has grown from a quick and dirty way to add some eye candy to your web site to the foundation of nearly all client-side web application software development. With the advent of Web 2.0 technologies such as Ajax, JavaScript has started to be taken seriously, and there are now powerful frameworks built on top of it that make developing web applications that much easier.

One of those technologies is Dashcode, Apple's integrated development environment (IDE) for web technologies. Dashcode can be used to develop Dashboard widgets, iPhone web applications, and even full desktop web applications. Using the Dashcode JavaScript frameworks, you can put together web applications that look great in just an hour or two.

In this chapter, you have seen how you can develop a basic photo browser with Dashcode. You've also seen how Dashboard widgets are pieced together, and how you can use web technologies such as HTML, CSS, and JavaScript to build them. You made acquaintance with WebKit CSS Animations too, which make it relatively simple to declaratively animate web pages and widgets. With all these tools at your disposal, you have no excuse for not creating inspired web applications on your Mac.

EXERCISES

1. Modify the DashBall widget so that it has two balls inside the box. Allow the user to hit either of the balls, and adapt the physics so that balls bounce off each other when they collide. Add a new piece of text that appears on-screen when two balls collide. Use WebKit CSS Animations to animate the appearance and disappearance of the text.

2. Beginning with the Browser Dashcode project template, develop a basic reader app for the JavaScript RSS stream of the Stack Overflow web site (http:// stackoverflow.com). The app should have a list of the latest posts on the left, and a detail view on the right. These details should include the author's handle, the title of the post, and the HTML content of the post. Include a button that takes you to the selected post on the Stack Overflow web site. You can use this URL for the data source: http://stackoverflow.com/feeds/tag/javascript.

▶ **WHAT YOU LEARNED IN THIS CHAPTER**

HTML	Hypertext markup language, a format used to structure web pages
JavaScript	A scripting language designed to run in a web browser, which can be used to make web pages dynamic
CSS	Cascading style sheets, a standard for assigning visual styles to the elements of a web page
Dashboard	A desktop environment on Mac OS X where you can run widgets
Dashcode	An integrated development environment and framework for building Dashboard widgets and web pages
Widget	A small application written with web technologies that runs in Dashboard
WebKit CSS Animations	Extensions to the CSS standard that allow a developer to declaratively animate a web page via CSS styles
Data Source	A controller object in a Dashcode application that makes data available to interface elements via bindings
Bindings	A means of using key paths to stipulate connections between interface controls and nodes in data source

Answers to Exercises

CHAPTER 1

Exercise 1 Solution

The first two apropos commands return far too much information to be useful. The third command, apropos "copy file" returns a reasonable amount of information.

```
Macintosh:~ sample$ apropos "copy file"
CpMac(1), /usr/bin/CpMac(1) - copy files preserving metadata and forks
File::Copy(3pm)         - Copy files or filehandles
cp(1)                   - copy files
cpio(1)                 - copy files to and from archives
```

From this result, you might surmise that CpMac, cp, or cpio would be an appropriate tool for copying files. Of course, the manual entry for each command provides more helpful information.

Exercise 2 Solution

The command man -k "copy file" is equivalent to apropos "copy file" and yields the same results as Exercise 1.

CHAPTER 2

Exercise 1 Solution

Use the following steps to collect the sample:

1. Launch /Developer/Applications/Instruments. The program starts and displays a list of available templates.

2. Choose the Time Profiler template. Instruments configures your document with the Time Profiler instrument.

3. Click the Record button in the toolbar. This brings up an open panel where you can specify which program you want to start along with other options.

4. Select /Applications/Stickies in the Open panel and click the Choose button. The Stickies application appears in the Dock, and the Dock's windows appear behind the Instruments application.

5. Switch to Stickies and use the application. Type some notes, change the color a few times, and do the usual things you do with Stickies. Then quit Stickies and return to Instruments. The Instruments window will resemble Figure A-1.

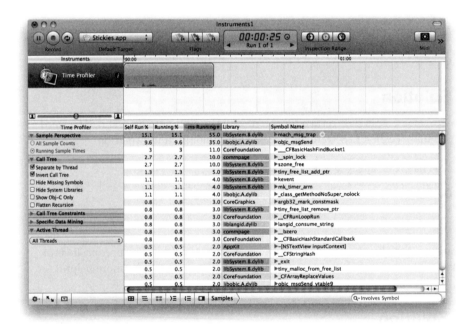

FIGURE A-1

The table area shows a tree containing all the frames recorded by Instruments. The Symbol Name column displays a most commonly occurring frame where your program spent its time. You can reveal other frames in the backtrace by opening the symbol name's disclosure triangle. If you let Stickies run for a few seconds without using it, the first item in this table should be a function called mach_msg_trap, as shown in the figure.

This means Stickies was just waiting for user input from the window server. Because programs waiting for user input (or sitting in mach_msg_trap in general) use no CPU time, this is normally a good thing.

Exercise 2 Solution

You can use `man -a intro` to list all the `intro` man pages. To get a complete list of all the sections, you could simply make note of the sections yourself as they appear in the pages.

You could also use `man -k intro` to list all the man pages that match the `intro` keyword, as shown in the following code. Although this returns the section information you're interested in, it also returns information for a bunch of other man pages as well.

```
Macintosh:~ sample $ man -k intro
...
glut(3)                  - an introduction to the OpenGL Utility Toolkit
intro(1)                 - introduction to general commands (tools and utilities)
intro(2)                 - introduction to system calls and error numbers
intro(3)                 - introduction to the C libraries
intro(5)                 - introduction to file formats
intro(9)                 - introduction to system kernel interfaces
kerberos(1)              - introduction to the Kerberos system
math(3)                  - introduction to mathematical library functions
networking(4)            - introduction to networking facilities
...
Macintosh:~ sample $
```

If you want an exact list, you can ask for a list of all the pages named `intro` using `man -a -w intro` as shown in the following code. `-a` displays all files with the specified name, and the `-w` flag tells `man` to print the pages' paths rather than their content. You can then deduce the manual section from the file's directory and file extension.

```
Macintosh:~ sample $ man -a -w intro
/usr/share/man/man1/intro.1.gz
/usr/share/man/man8/intro.8.gz
/usr/share/man/man2/intro.2.gz
/usr/share/man/man3/intro.3.gz
/usr/share/man/man5/intro.5.gz
/usr/share/man/man7/intro.7.gz
/usr/share/man/man9/intro.9.gz
Macintosh:~ sample $
```

CHAPTER 3

Exercise 1 Solution

Use the proper man page requests that appear in the following table. Note that `printf` overlaps with a command-line function, so you must specifically request the section for C functions. The section is optional for other man pages.

FUNCTION	MAN PAGE
printf	"3 printf"
scanf	"scanf" or "3 scanf"
pow	"pow" or "3 pow"

Exercise 2 Solution

1. Change the instances of int in Calculate.h to double. This includes

```
double calculate(const double a, const double b, const char op);
```

2. Change the instances of int in Calculate.c to double. This includes

```
double calculate(const double a, const double b, const char op)
{
    double result;
```

3. Replace the main function in main.c with the following code:

```
int main (int argc, const char * argv[])
{
    int count;
    double a, b, answer;
    char op;

    // print the prompt
    printf("Enter an expression: ");

    // get the expression
    count = scanf("%lg %c %lg", &a, &op, &b);
    if (count != 3) {
        printf("bad expression\n");
        exit(1);
    }

    // perform the computation
    answer = calculate(a, b, op);

    // print the answer
    printf("%lg %c %lg = %lg\n", a, op, b, answer);

    return 0;
}
```

Exercise 3 Solution

1. Add the following include after the other includes in Calculate.c:

```
#include <math.h>
```

2. Add the following `case` entries to the `switch` statement. Here is the final `switch` statement:

```
case '/':
    result = a / b;
    break;
case '\\':
    result = (int)a / (int)b;
    break;
case '%':
    result = (int)a % (int)b;
    break;
case '^':
    result = pow(a, b);
    break;
```

Your `Calculate.c` file should look like the following:

```
#include "Calculate.h"

#include <stdio.h>
#include <stdlib.h>
#include <math.h>

double calculate(const double a, const double b, const char op)
{
    double result;

    switch (op) {
        case '+':
            result = a + b;
            break;
        case '-':
            result = a - b;
            break;
        case '*':
            result = a * b;
            break;
        case '/':
            result = a / b;
            break;
        case '\\':
            result = (int)a / (int)b;
            break;
        case '%':
            result = (int)a % (int)b;
            break;
        case '^':
            result = pow(a, b);
            break;
        default:
            printf("unknown operator: %c\n", op);
            exit(1);
    }

    return result;
}
```

CHAPTER 4

Exercise 1 Solution

1. Change all the labels so that they are pinned to the upper-left corner. The Autosizing control should look similar to the one shown in Figure A-2.

2. Change all the text fields so that they are pinned to the upper edge of the window, and so that they are flexible in the horizontal direction. The Autosizing control should look similar to the one shown in Figure A-3.

3. Change the OK and Cancel buttons so that they are pinned to the lower-right corner. The Autosizing control should look similar to the one shown in Figure A-4.

4. Enable the window's close, minimize, and resize controls by checking them in the window Inspector's Attributes view.

5. Set the window's minimum size to the window's current size by checking Minimum Size and clicking the Use Current button in the Inspector's Size view.

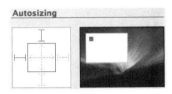

FIGURE A-2

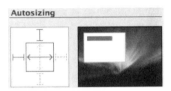

FIGURE A-3

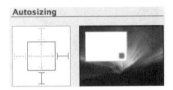

FIGURE A-4

Exercise 2 Solution

1. Create a new Cocoa ⇨ Window project. Your nib window appears, containing a window instance.

2. Drag a Tab view from the Library to your window.

3. Use the guides to align the Tab view near the upper-left corner and resize the Tab view to fill the window. Hold down the Option key and move the mouse over the window to verify the Tab view's position. Its edges should be 20 pixels from the window's edges, except for the top one, which should be 12 pixels.

4. Double-click the View tab and name it **Advanced**.

5. Double-click the Tab tab and name it **Game**.

6. Drag a Label from the Library into the Tab view. A selection box should appear within the Tab view, as shown in Figure A-5. This indicates that you're dragging the control into the Tab view itself, not simply into the window.

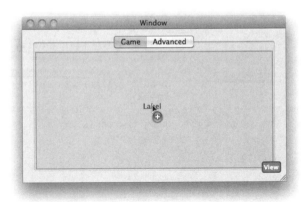

FIGURE A-5

7. Use the guides to position the label a comfortable distance from the upper-left edge of the Tab view. Hold down the Option key and move the mouse over the Tab view to verify the label's position. The top and left edges should be 20 pixels from the left edge of the Tab view, and 30 pixels from the top edge of the Tab view.

8. Change the label to read `Player Name`: . Make sure the label fits this new text exactly.

9. Right-align the text using the Attribute Inspector.

10. Drag a Text Field from the Library into the Tab view. Position it directly to the right of the label. Use the Size Inspector to make the text field 200 pixels wide.

11. Duplicate the label and text field, and move the new objects directly below the old ones. They should line up horizontally. Verify that the text fields are 8 pixels apart by first selecting one text field and then pointing at the other field while holding down the Option key.

12. Change the second label to read `Team Name`: .

13. Click the Advanced tab to select it. The controls in the Game tab will disappear.

14. Drag a Check Box from the Library into the Advanced Tab view. Position it in the upper-left corner of the window: 20 pixels from the left and 30 pixels from the top.

15. Change the text box to read `Log in automatically`.

16. Create two more check boxes, `Respawn Immediately` and `Unlimited Ammunition`, and position them immediately below the first checkbox. All three checkboxes should be 20 pixels from the left edge and 6 pixels from each other.

17. Switch back to the Game tab. Note that the contents of this tab are wider than the contents of the Advanced tab, but the contents of the Advanced tab are taller.

18. Resize the Tab view horizontally to fit the Game tab's contents. There should be 20 pixels between the text fields' right edges and the Tab view. You may have trouble finding the Tab view's resize controls if you're editing its contents; in this case, the Tab view will use a special bounding box without resize controls. If so, try clicking the window's content view and then clicking back on the Tab view to select it.

19. Switch to the Advanced tab and resize the Tab view vertically until its bottom edge is 20 pixels away from the third checkbox.

20. Select all three checkboxes, hold the Option key, and move the mouse over the tab control. The checkboxes will be 20 pixels away from the left and bottom edges, and 30 pixels away from the top edge. If you have trouble selecting the checkboxes, try clicking one of the boxes and using Command-A to select all.

21. While holding down the Option key, use the arrow keys to center the checkboxes in the Tab view. You can nudge 10 pixels at a time by also holding down the Shift key when pressing an arrow key.

22. Switch back to the Game tab.

23. Select all the controls, hold down the Option key, and center the controls in the Tab view.

24. Resize the window horizontally so there are only 20 pixels between the Tab view and the window edge. Leave plenty of space below the Tab view to add buttons.

25. Drag a Push button from the Library to your window and use the guides to position it below and to the right of the Tab view. It will be 10 pixels from the lower edge of the Tab view and 20 pixels from the window's edge.

26. Rename this button **OK**.

27. Drag a second Push button from the Library and use the guides to position it about 12 pixels to the left of the OK button.

28. Rename this button Cancel.

29. Resize the window vertically so there are only 20 pixels between the OK and Cancel buttons and the window's edge.

30. Test your handiwork by choosing File ⇨ Test Interface.

CHAPTER 5

Exercise 1 Solution

a. TextEdit's `Info.plist` file describes the following 12 document types:

➤ Rich Text Format documents (called `NSRTFPboardType`)

➤ Rich Text Format with attachments (called `NSRTFDPboardType`)

➤ HTML documents

➤ Apple web archives

➤ Open Document Text documents

➤ OpenOffice documents

➤ Microsoft Word 2007 documents

➤ Microsoft Word 2003 XML documents

➤ Microsoft Word 97 documents

➤ Plain Text documents (called `NSStringPboardType`)

➤ Apple SimpleText documents

➤ Unknown documents—used to view any arbitrary file, regardless of type

b. Preview's bundle signature is `prvw`.

c. Terminal's bundle identifier is `com.apple.Terminal`.

d. The exact contents of an `xcodeproj` file bundle will depend on your username, the usernames of those working with you, and what Xcode features you use. Files commonly found in Xcode project files include the following:

> ➤ the `project.pbxproj`

> ➤ `<username>.`

> ➤ `<username>.mode1v3`

e. The current bundle version of the AppKit framework has been C throughout the Mac OS X releases to date. Note that the version is a single English letter.

Exercise 2 Solution

a. `defaults domains`

b. `defaults -currentHost domains`

c. `defaults read com.apple.Terminal`

Recall that preferences are stored using an application's `CFBundleIdentifier`. You learned Terminal's bundle identifier in the preceding exercise (1c).

d. `defaults write MyExamplePref Autosave 1`

Unlike other `defaults` commands, the `defaults write` command creates a preference file if one doesn't already exist.

e. `defaults write MyExamplePref colors -array red orange yellow`

The `-array` flag tells `defaults` that the following values are actually members of an array. Other flags exist as detailed in the `defaults` man page.

f. `defaults delete MyExamplePref Autosave`

CHAPTER 6

Exercise 1 Solution

1. Open the Grepper project in Xcode, and make the highlighted changes in the following code to the `main.c` file:

```
#include <stdio.h>
#include <string.h>

// Global constants
const int MAX_STRING_LENGTH = 256;

// Main function
int main (int argc, const char * argv[]) {
    // Get string to search for, which is the last argument
    const char *searchString = argv[argc-1];

    // Loop over files
    unsigned int fileIndex;
    for ( fileIndex = 1; fileIndex < argc-1; ++fileIndex ) {
        // Get input file path from standard input
```

```
        const char *inpPath = argv[fileIndex];

        // Open file
        FILE *inpFile;
        inpFile = fopen(inpPath, "r");

        // Loop over lines in the input file, until there
        // are none left
        char line[MAX_STRING_LENGTH];
        int lineCount = 0;
        while ( fgets(line, MAX_STRING_LENGTH-1, inpFile) ) {
            ++lineCount;
            if ( strstr(line, searchString) ) {
                printf("In file %s, line %d:\t%s", inpPath, lineCount, line);
            }
        }

        // Close files
        fclose(inpFile);

    } // End loop over files
    return 0;
}
```

2.   Select the Grepper executable in the Executables group of the Groups & Files panel on the left of the project window. Choose Get Info from the File menu and select the Arguments tab in the Info window that appears. Using the + button, add arguments to the Arguments table at the top. Add the paths of two or more text files first, and a string to search for as the last argument.

3.   Compile and run the program by clicking the Build and Run toolbar item in the main project window.

4.   Choose Console from the Run menu and verify that all the files entered have been searched; also note that line numbers now appear for each line printed.

Exercise 2 Solution

1.   Open the MyAddressBook project in Xcode and select the AddressBook.h file in the Source group of the Groups & Files panel. In the editor, add the following function signature:

```
int RemovePerson( AddressBook *addressBook, char *name );
```

2.   Open the AddressBook.c file in the editor and add the following function:

```
int RemovePerson( AddressBook *addressBook, char *name ) {
    int n = addressBook->numPersons;

    // Search for person with the name passed
    int i;
    for ( i = 0; i < n; ++i ) {
        Person *person = addressBook->persons[i];
```

```
            if ( strcmp( person->name, name ) == 0 ) {
                // Found Person, so delete
                DeallocPerson(person);

                // Reduce number of persons in address book.
                // Also move the last person to the fill the hole formed
                // in the persons array by the removal.
                addressBook->numPersons = n - 1;
                addressBook->persons[i] = addressBook->persons[n-1];

                return 1; // succeeded
            }
        }

        return 0; // failed
    }
```

3. In the `Controller.h` file, add the following function signature:

```
void ProcessDeletePersonRequest(Controller *controller);
```

4. In the `Controller.c` file, add the following function definition:

```
void ProcessDeletePersonRequest(Controller *controller) {
    char name[256];
    printf("You chose to delete an address.\n");
    printf("Please enter the name of the person to delete: ");
    gets(name);

    int personWasRemoved = RemovePerson( controller->addressBook, name );
    if ( personWasRemoved )
       printf("%s was deleted from the address book.\n", name);
    else
       printf("The address of %s could not be found.\n", name);
}
```

5. Modify the `ProcessUserChoice` function in `Controller.c` as indicated by the highlights in the following code:

```
int ProcessUserChoice(Controller *controller, char choice) {
    int shouldStop = 0;
    switch (choice) {
        case 'a':
            ProcessNewPersonRequest(controller);
            break;
        case 'f':
            ProcessFindPersonRequest(controller);
            break;
    case 'd'
        :ProcessDeletePersonRequest(controller);
         break;
        case 's':
```

```
                    ProcessSaveRequest(controller);
                    break;
                case 'q':
                    ProcessSaveRequest(controller);
                    shouldStop = 1;
                    break;
                default:
                    printf("You entered an invalid choice. Try again.\n");
            }
            return shouldStop;
        }
```

6.   Modify the `PrintUserOptions` function similarly, according to the highlights in this code:

```
void PrintUserOptions(Controller *controller) {
    printf("\nYou can either\n"
            "a) Add an address\n"
            "f) Find an address\n"
        "d) Delete an address, or\n"
            "s) Save your addresses\n"
            "q) Save and Quit\n");
    printf("Please enter your choice (a, f, s, d, or q): ");
}
```

7.   Compile and run the program by clicking Build and Run in the toolbar of the main project window. Open the console and try adding a number of addresses, and then delete some. Make sure you can still find addresses that haven't been deleted in the address book afterward.

Something to note about this solution is that there are several places in the existing code that need to be updated. The changes made were not localized to a small part of the code, but were spread throughout. Having to update many different parts of a program when you need to make changes can introduce bugs and make a program difficult to learn for someone not familiar with it. Object-oriented programming (OOP), which you learn about in Chapter 7, localizes changes, reducing the impact of changes to existing code.

CHAPTER 7

Exercise 1 Solution

After you have created the Discus project, replace the contents of the `Discus.m` file with the following code:

```
#import <Foundation/Foundation.h>
int main (int argc, const char * argv[]) {
    NSAutoreleasePool * pool = [[NSAutoreleasePool alloc] init];

    // Store data in an array of dictionaries
    NSArray *discs =
        [NSArray arrayWithObjects:
```

```
        [NSDictionary dictionaryWithObjectsAndKeys:
            @"CD",                      @"Type",
            [NSNumber numberWithInt:3], @"LengthInMinutes",
            @"Lounge Room",             @"Location",
            @"BB Bonkas",               @"Artist",
            nil],
        [NSDictionary dictionaryWithObjectsAndKeys:
            @"CD",                      @"Type",
            [NSNumber numberWithInt:4], @"LengthInMinutes",
            @"Attic",                   @"Location",
            @"CC Charmers",             @"Artist",
            nil],
        [NSDictionary dictionaryWithObjectsAndKeys:
            @"DVD",                        @"Type",
            [NSNumber numberWithInt:121],  @"LengthInMinutes",
            @"Attic",                      @"Location",
            @"TJ Slickflick",              @"Lead Actor",
            @"LJ Slickflick",              @"Director",
            nil],
        nil];

    // Extract a few entries, and print them in the console
    NSLog(@"The third entry in the library is a %@",
        [[discs objectAtIndex:2] objectForKey:@"Type"]);
    NSLog(@"The director is %@",
        [[discs objectAtIndex:2] objectForKey:@"Director"]);

    // Write the array to file
    NSString *path =
        [NSHomeDirectory() stringByAppendingPathComponent:@"Desktop/discus.plist"];
    [discs writeToFile:path atomically:YES];

    // Read the array back from the file, and write it to the console
    NSArray *newDiscs =
        [[[NSArray alloc] initWithContentsOfFile:path] autorelease];
    NSLog(@"The database contents are:\n%@", newDiscs);

    [pool release];
    return 0;
}
```

The dictionaries and arrays have been populated directly using the methods
dictionaryWithObjectsAndKeys: and arrayWithObjects:. Each of these methods takes a
comma-delimited list and must be terminated with nil.

The objectAtIndex: method extracts an entry from an NSArray, and objectForKey: is used to
get a particular value out of an NSDictionary after it has been retrieved from the array. Values are
written to the console with NSLog. The %@ formatting character can be used to format any object,
including the NSStrings and NSNumbers in this example.

The NSString class has a number of methods for working with paths;
stringByAppendingPathComponent: has been used in this example. The NSHomeDirectory
function returns the path to the home directory, and the rest of the path is supplied to the method as
the string @"Desktop/discus.plist".

The `writeToFile:atomically:` method can be used to write Foundation classes such as `NSArray`, `NSDictionary`, and `NSString` to a file in property list format. The property list format is a structured XML format, as you would see if you opened the file in a text editor. Using this method, along with `initWithContentsOfFile:`, makes reading and writing structured data a breeze with Cocoa.

Exercise 2 Solution

1. Open the MyAddressBook Objective C project in Xcode, and select the `AddressBook.h` file in the Source group of the Groups & Files panel. In the editor, add the following method declaration to the class interface block:

```
-(Person *)removePersonForName:(NSString *)name;
```

2. In the file `AddressBook.m`, add the following method definition to the implementation block of `AddressBook`:

```
-(Person *)removePersonForName:(NSString *)name {
    id person = [[personForNameDict objectForKey:name] retain];
    [personForNameDict removeObjectForKey:name];
    return [person autorelease];
}
```

3. In the `Commands.h` file, add the following interface block:

```
@interface RemovePersonCommand : Command
{
}
@end
```

4. Open the `Commands.m` file in the editor and add the implementation of the `RemovePersonCommand` class, as follows:

```
@implementation RemovePersonCommand

+(NSString *)commandIdentifier {
    return @"d";
}

+(NSString *)commandDescription {
    return @"Delete an address";
}

+(NSArray *)requiredInfoIdentifiers {
    return [NSArray arrayWithObject:@"Name of person"];
}

-(NSString *)executeWithInfoDictionary:(NSDictionary *)infoDict {
    NSString *name = [infoDict objectForKey:@"Name of person"];
    Person *p = [[self addressBook] removePersonForName:name];
    return ( p == nil ? @"Address not found" :
```

```
        [NSString stringWithFormat:@"Address for %@ was removed", name]);
    }

    @end
```

5.   While in the `Commands.m` file, modify the `initialize` method of the `Command` class as highlighted here:

```
+(void)initialize {
    commandClasses =
        [[NSArray arrayWithObjects:
            [NewPersonCommand class],
            [FindPersonCommand class],
            [RemovePersonCommand class],
            [SaveAddressBookCommand class],
            [QuitCommand class],
            nil] retain];
}
```

6.   Compile and run the program by clicking the Build and Run toolbar item. Enter a number of addresses, and then try removing some. Also try to remove someone not in the address book. Test the program to ensure that entries that should remain in the address book are still there after you have removed other addresses.

What should strike you about the changes required in the Objective-C version of MyAddressBook is that they are reasonably isolated from existing code in the sense that very few methods need to be edited. The only existing method that needs changing is the `initialize` method of the `Command` class, and the change is very minor. Most of the changes to the program that were made involved extending it with new methods and classes, rather than modifying what already existed. This reduces the risk of introducing bugs when changing a program, and usually makes it easier to understand.

The `AddressBook` class was modified in much the same way that the `AddressBook` ADT was modified in the C program of Exercise 2 from Chapter 6. A new method was introduced to remove an entry, in this case by removing it from the `NSMutableDictionary` `personForNameDict` instance variable that is used to store instances of `Person` in the `AddressBook`. Note that this method is quite a bit simpler than the corresponding C version. That is because the Objective-C version leverages powerful Foundation classes of Cocoa, such as `NSMutableDictionary`.

CHAPTER 8

Exercise 1 Solution

1.   In Xcode, create a new Cocoa Application project named `Color Calculator`.

2.   Open `MainMenu.xib` in Interface Builder.

3. Build the interface shown in Figure A-6. You can find the Color Well control in Interface Builder's Library.

4. In Xcode, create files for an Objective-C class named **Color**.

5. In Interface Builder, drag an Object item from the Library to your nib's instances window, and change the Object's Class to **Color**.

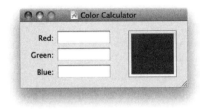

FIGURE A-6

6. Drag an Object Controller from the Library to your nib file, and connect its `content` outlet to your Color object. Also change the object controller's Class Name to **Color** using the Attributes Inspector.

7. Bind the Red text field to your Object Controller's `red` Model Key Path.

8. Bind the Green text field to your Object Controller's `green` Model Key Path.

9. Bind the Blue text field to your Object Controller's `blue` Model Key Path.

10. Bind the Color Well to your Object Controller's `color` Model Key Path.

11. Save your nib file.

12. In Xcode, add the following code to `Color.h`:

```
#import <Cocoa/Cocoa.h>

@interface Color : NSObject
{
    NSNumber *red;
    NSNumber *green;
    NSNumber *blue;
}

@property (nonatomic, retain) NSNumber *red;
@property (nonatomic, retain) NSNumber *green;
@property (nonatomic, retain) NSNumber *blue;
@property (nonatomic, readonly) NSColor *color;

@end
```

13. Change the contents of `Color.m` to match the following:

```
#import "Color.h"

@implementation Color

+ (NSSet *)keyPathsForValuesAffectingValueForKey:(NSString *)key
{
    NSSet *keyPaths = [super keyPathsForValuesAffectingValueForKey:key];

    if ([key isEqualToString:@"color"]) {
        NSSet *dependentKeys = [NSSet setWithObjects:@"red",
                                @"green",
```

```
                                      @"blue",
                                      nil];

            keyPaths = [keyPaths setByAddingObjectsFromSet:dependentKeys];
        }

        return keyPaths;
    }

    @synthesize red;
    @synthesize green;
    @synthesize blue;

    - (NSColor *)color
    {
        return [NSColor colorWithCalibratedRed:self.red.floatValue
                                    green:self.green.floatValue
                                     blue:self.blue.floatValue
                                    alpha:1.0f];
    }

    @end
```

14. Save your files and build and run the Color Calculator. When you change the text fields, the Color Well updates.

Exercise 2 Solution

1. In Xcode, open `Color.h` and make the color property read-write with `assign` semantics. Because your class doesn't synthesize the `color` property, the `assign` keyword is simply advisory.

```
@property (nonatomic, assign) NSColor *color;
```

2. Switch to `Color.m` and add the following method to the `Color` class:

```
- (void)setColor:(NSColor*)color
{
    color = [color colorUsingColorSpace:[NSColorSpace genericRGBColorSpace]];

    self.red = [NSNumber numberWithFloat:color.redComponent];
    self.green = [NSNumber numberWithFloat:color.greenComponent];
    self.blue = [NSNumber numberWithFloat:color.blueComponent];
}
```

CHAPTER 9

Exercise 1 Solution

1. In Xcode, create a new Cocoa document-based Application project named Text Editor.

2. Open `MyDocument.xib` in Interface Builder.

3. Replace the "Your document contents here" label with a text view from the Library.

4. Resize the text view to fill the window, and make the view resizable using the Size Inspector.

5. Click near the top of the scroll view area to select the text view.

6. In the Text View Attributes Inspector, turn off Rich Text.

7. In the Bindings Inspector, bind Value to the File's Owner's `stringValue` Model Key Path.

8. Save your nib file.

9. In Xcode, open `MyDocument.h` and change the object definition so it matches the following code:

```
@interface MyDocument : NSDocument
{
    NSString *stringValue;
}

@property (nonatomic, retain) NSString *stringValue;

@end
```

10. Switch to `MyDocument.m` and replace its contents with the following code:

```
#import "MyDocument.h"

@implementation MyDocument

- (id)init
{
    self = [super init];
    if (self) {
        self.stringValue = @"";
    }
    return self;
}

- (NSString *)windowNibName
{
    return @"MyDocument";
}

- (void)windowControllerDidLoadNib:(NSWindowController *) aController
{
    [super windowControllerDidLoadNib:aController];
}

@synthesize stringValue;

- (NSData *)dataOfType:(NSString *)typeName error:(NSError **)outError
{
    NSData *data = [self.stringValue dataUsingEncoding:
NSMacOSRomanStringEncoding];

    return data;
```

```
}

- (BOOL)readFromData:(NSData *)data ofType:(NSString *)typeName error:(NSError
**)
   outError
{
   NSString *string = [[NSString alloc] initWithData:data encoding:
     NSMacOSRomanStringEncoding];
   self.stringValue = string;
   [string release];

   return YES;
}

@end
```

11. Double-click Xcode's Text Editor target and switch to the Properties tab.

12. Change the document type's Name from **DocumentType** to **Text File** and change the Extensions from **????** to **txt**.

13. Add a new document type, name it **Unknown File**, change the Extensions to *****, and change the Class to **MyDocument**.

14. Save, compile, and run your program. When you save your document, Text Editor suggests a .txt extension. Text Editor also accepts any file type in the Open panel when you're dragging files onto its Dock icon.

Exercise 2 Solution

1. In Xcode, open MyDocument.m and replace the dataOfType:error: and readFromData: ofType:error: methods with the following code:

```
- (NSData *)dataOfType:(NSString *)typeName error:(NSError **)outError
{
    NSData *data = [self.stringValue dataUsingEncoding:
NSMacOSRomanStringEncoding];

   return data;
}

- (BOOL)readFromData:(NSData *)data ofType:(NSString *)typeName error:(NSError
**)
   outError
{
   NSString *string = [[NSString alloc] initWithData:data encoding:
     NSMacOSRomanStringEncoding];
   self.stringValue = string;
   [string release];

   return YES;
}
```

2. Save, compile, and run Text Editor.

CHAPTER 10

Exercise 1 Solution

1. In Xcode, add the following instance variable to `SlideShowWindowController.h`:

```
IBOutlet NSTableView        *mTableView;
```

2. Switch to `SlideShowWindowController.m` and add a `tableDoubleClick:` method declaration to `SlideShowWindowController`'s class extension. Also, import the `Slide.h` header file as follows:

```
#import "Slide.h"


@interface SlideShowWindowController ()
- (void)openPanelDidEnd:(NSOpenPanel *)openPanel returnCode:(int)returnCode
    contextInfo:(void *)contextInfo;
- (void)tableDoubleClick:(id)sender;
@end
```

3. Set the table view's double-click action using the following line of code. You need to add this line to `SlideShowWindowController`'s `windowDidLoad` method:

```
[mTableView setDoubleAction:@selector(tableDoubleClick:)];
```

Normally, double-clicking a row in a table view begins an editing session; this is a common way of changing contents in a table view. If the rows in a table view aren't editable, the table view sends a double-click action along the responder chain. `NSTableView` doesn't have a double-click action by default, so you must supply one if you are interested in handling double-clicks. The double-click action otherwise behaves as an `NSControl` instance's action.

4. Define the following `tableDoubleClick:` method in `SlideShowWindowController`'s implementation section:

```
#pragma mark Table Support

- (void)tableDoubleClick:(id)sender
{
    NSDocumentController* docController = [NSDocumentController
        sharedDocumentController];

    for (Slide *slide in mSlidesController.selectedObjects) {
        NSURL* url = slide.imageURL;
        [docController openDocumentWithContentsOfURL:url display:YES error:
nil];
    }
}
```

The `NSDocumentController` singleton class is responsible for keeping track of the kinds of documents your application is capable of opening, among other things. You can ask the NSDocumentController to open a file at a specific path or URL. If the application is capable of displaying the file, NSDocumentController creates a document for that file and, if necessary, displays its window on-screen.

5. Save your changes to SlideShowWindowController.m.

6. Open SlideShowDocument.xib in Interface Builder.

7. Connect the File's Owner's mTableView outlet to the table view in the document window.

8. Build and run Slide Master. When you double-click a row in the table view, the image file opens in its own image document.

Exercise 2 Solution

One way to detect selection changes is to observe the array controller's selectedObjects property. That's essentially what the binding used by the main image view is doing. You can also implement table delegate methods that fire when the selection changes. For this example, watching the array controller is more direct.

SlideImageView must track a file's name to display it with the image data. That's a simple matter of creating accessors for an mFileName instance variable. SlideShowWindowController sets this information when the table view's selection changes.

1. In Xcode, add an mFileName instance variable and property to SlideImageView.h, as shown here:

```
@interface SlideImageView : NSImageView
{
    NSString    *mURLKeyPath;
    NSColor     *mBackgroundColor;
    NSString    *mFileName;
}

@property (nonatomic, retain) NSString *URLKeyPath;
@property (nonatomic, retain) NSColor *backgroundColor;
@property (nonatomic, retain) NSString *fileName;

@end
```

2. Switch to SlideImageView.m and release the mFileName variable in the SlideImageView's dealloc method as follows:

```
- (void)dealloc
{
    [mURLKeyPath release];
    [mBackgroundColor release];
    [mFileName release];

    [super dealloc];
}
```

3.   Synthesize the fileName accessor like this:

```
@synthesize URLKeyPath = mURLKeyPath;
@synthesize fileName = mFileName;
```

4.   Add code in `drawRect:` to draw the filename in the lower-right corner of the screen, as shown in the following:

```
- (void)drawRect:(NSRect)rect
{
    if (mBackgroundColor) {
        [mBackgroundColor set];
        NSRectFill(rect);
    }

    [super drawRect:rect];

    if (mFileName) {
        NSRect bounds = [self bounds];
        NSRect stringRect = NSZeroRect;

        stringRect.size = [mFileName sizeWithAttributes:nil];
        stringRect.origin.x = bounds.size.width - stringRect.size.width;

        [mFileName drawInRect:stringRect withAttributes:nil];
    }
}
```

AppKit provides additional methods on the `NSString` class to draw strings directly into views, and `SlideImageView` uses these methods to draw its filename. First, it calls `sizeWithAttributes:` to measure the visual size of the filename. When it knows the area required to draw the string, `SlideImageView` builds a rectangle describing exactly where the string should be drawn. `SlideImageView` then draws the string to the screen using `drawInRect:withAttributes:`. `SlideImageView` passes in `nil` to use the default drawing attributes for its string.

5.   Open `SlideShowWindowController.m` and start observing the `mSlidesController` array controller's `selectedObjects` property from within `windowDidLoad`.

```
// watch for selection changes
[mSlidesController addObserver:self
                    forKeyPath:@"selectedObjects"
                       options:NSKeyValueObservingOptionInitial
                       context:NULL];
```

6.   Stop observing `mSlidesController` from within `dealloc`. The entire `dealloc` method is shown here:

```
- (void)dealloc
{
    NSUserDefaults *userDefaults = [NSUserDefaults standardUserDefaults];
```

```
        // remove backgroundColor observer
        [userDefaults removeObserver:self forKeyPath:@"backgroundColor"];
        [mSlidesController removeObserver:self forKeyPath:@"selectedObjects"];

        [super dealloc];
    }
```

7. Change `observeValueForKeyPath:ofObject:change:context:` to handle selection changes as well as background color changes. This requires you to be more careful about checking the incoming key path.

```
- (void)observeValueForKeyPath:(NSString *)keyPath ofObject:(id)object change:
    (NSDictionary *)change context:(void *)context
{
    if ([keyPath isEqualToString:@"backgroundColor"]) {
        NSData *data = [change objectForKey:NSKeyValueChangeNewKey];
        NSColor *color = [NSKeyedUnarchiver unarchiveObjectWithData:data];

        [mSlideImageView setBackgroundColor:color];
    }
    else if ([keyPath isEqualToString:@"selectedObjects"]) {
        NSArray *selectedObjects = mSlidesController.selectedObjects;
        if (selectedObjects.count > 0) {
            Slide *slide = [selectedObjects objectAtIndex:0];
            if (slide) {
                NSURL *url = slide.imageURL;
                [mSlideImageView setFileName:url.lastPathComponent];
            }
        }
    }
}
```

If the array controller has only one selected object, get it and retrieve its URL. This is easy, because the `mSlidesController` manages `Slide` objects.

8. Save your changes, and then build and run Slide Master. When you view an image in the slideshow window, its name appears in the lower-right corner. The name is drawn in black, using a default font value. Note that this filename does not appear when you view images in their own document.

Exercise 3 Solution

NSURL objects can be converted to NSData objects containing Finder Alias information. The NSURL API calls these data objects *bookmarks*. One solution to this problem is to change the Slide object to record these bookmarks into the data store, while continuing to use NSURLs as computed transient values.

1. In Xcode, open the `SlideShowDocument.xcdatamodel` file.

2. Add a new `imageBookmark` attribute to the Slide entity and set its Type to Binary data.

3. Change the `imageURL` attribute to Transient.

4. Open `Slide.h` and add an `imageBookmark` property beside the `imageURL` property as follows:

```
@property (nonatomic, retain) id imageURL;
@property (nonatomic, retain) id imageBookmark;
```

5. Switch to `Slide.m` and change the `Slide` implementation to the following code:

```
@implementation Slide

@dynamic image;
@dynamic imageURL;
@dynamic imageBookmark;
@dynamic creationDate;
@dynamic slideShow;

- (void)awakeFromInsert
{
    [super awakeFromInsert];

    self.creationDate = [NSDate date];
}

- (void)awakeFromFetch
{
    [super awakeFromFetch];

    BOOL isStale;
    NSURL *url = [NSURL URLByResolvingBookmarkData:self.imageBookmark
                                    options:0
                                relativeToURL:nil
                            bookmarkDataIsStale:&isStale
                                    error:nil];
    if (url) {
        [self setPrimitiveValue:url forKey:@"imageURL"];

        NSImage *image = [[[NSImage alloc] initWithContentsOfURL:self.imageURL]
            autorelease];
        [self setPrimitiveValue:image forKey:@"image"];
    }
}

- (void)setImageURL:(NSURL*)url
{
    NSData *bookmarkData = [url bookmarkDataWithOptions:0
                        includingResourceValuesForKeys:nil
                                    relativeToURL:nil
                                        error:nil];
    if (bookmarkData) {
        [self setPrimitiveValue:bookmarkData forKey:@"imageBookmark"];
    }

    [self setPrimitiveValue:url forKey:@"imageURL"];
}

@end
```

6.   Save your changes and then build and run Slide Master. You can still create and save documents just as before. Now if you move or rename your source images, Slide Master keeps track of them.

CHAPTER 11

Exercise 1 Solution

Backing up files and directories is easily achieved using a standard shell such as Bash. Bash can find and copy files using commands such as `find` and `ditto`. You could use other languages, but Bash is the simplest and most universal solution.

Exercise 2 Solution

A web content management system is a complex piece of software, and demands a powerful scripting language. Python or Ruby would be most appropriate for this purpose. The object-oriented features of these languages make them particularly attractive for building such an advanced system, and the availability of web application development frameworks like Django for Python (http://www.djangoproject.com) and Ruby on Rails for Ruby (http://rubyonrails.org) make them even better suited to developing a web content management system.

Exercise 3 Solution

AppleScript is probably the best choice here, though other languages like Python and Ruby could be used in combination with the Scripting Bridge. AppleScript allows you to directly access data in applications like iPhoto, Address Book, and Mail, and is thus a good choice.

CHAPTER 12

Exercise 1 Solution

1.   Open a Terminal window in the Terminal application.

2.   Change to the `Desktop` folder using the `cd` command.

```
cd ~/Desktop
```

3.   Make a directory to temporarily store copied files in. You should choose a directory name that is appropriate for the type of files you are copying. In this case, the directory name is `TextFilesBackup`.

```
mkdir TextFilesBackup
```

4. Issue the following `find` command to locate files with the extension `txt` that reside in your home directory or a subdirectory thereof. The command copies each file found to the backup directory.

```
find ~ -name *.txt -exec cp {} ~/Desktop/TextFilesBackup \;
```

The globbing wildcard character * matches zero or more characters, so *.txt matches any text file. Each file found is copied by the `cp` command passed with the -exec option.

5. Use the following command to compress the backup folder with ZIP compression:

```
ditto -c -k ~/Desktop/TextFilesBackup ~/Desktop/TextFilesBackup.zip
```

The -k option forces `ditto` to use the universal ZIP format, which can be read on most operating systems. The name of the directory to be compressed is specified after the options, followed by the archive file path.

6. Issue the following three commands to remove the `TextFilesBackup` directory, create a directory for storing backups, and move the ZIP file to it:

```
rm -r ~/Desktop/TextFilesBackup
mkdir ~/Backups
mv ~/Desktop/TextFilesBackup.zip ~/Backups/
```

Exercise 2 Solution

1. Open a Terminal window in the Terminal application and change to your Desktop directory.

```
cd ~/Desktop
```

2. Using the Nano editor, create a file called **backup.sh** and enter the following script. Then replace the e-mail address fred@blah.com with your own e-mail address. Save the file and exit Nano.

```
#!/bin/bash

# Set email address for error messages
ERROR_EMAIL=fred@blah.com

# Functions
StopWithError() {
    local MSG="An error caused backup script to terminate: $1"
    echo $MSG | mail $ERROR_EMAIL
    exit 1
}

CheckExitStatus() {
    if (( $? )); then
        StopWithError "$1"
    fi
}
```

```
# Configuration variables
FILE_EXT=txt
BACKUP_DIR=~/Backups

# Create backup directory if necessary
if [ -e "$BACKUP_DIR" ]; then
    # Make sure the backup directory is actually a directory
    if [ ! -d "$BACKUP_DIR" ]; then
        StopWithError "The backup path is not a directory"
    fi
else
    # If the backup directory doesn't exist, create it
    mkdir -p "$BACKUP_DIR"
    CheckExitStatus "mkdir failed to create backup directory"
fi

# Variables for temporary files and directories
ARCHIVE_DIR_PATH=`mktemp -d /var/tmp/backupdir_XXXX`
BACKUP_FILE_NAME=TextFilesBackup_`date +%F_%H-%M`.zip
BACKUP_FILE_PATH="$BACKUP_DIR/$BACKUP_FILE_NAME"

# Locate files with extension given, and copy to archive directory
find ~ -name "*.$FILE_EXT" -type f -exec cp "{}" "$ARCHIVE_DIR_PATH" \;
CheckExitStatus "Find command failed"

# Compress the archive directory
ditto -c -k "$ARCHIVE_DIR_PATH" "$BACKUP_FILE_PATH"
CheckExitStatus "ditto command failed to compress archive"

# Remove the archive directory
rm -r "$ARCHIVE_DIR_PATH"
CheckExitStatus "Could not remove archive directory"
```

The mktemp command is used to create a temporary directory to copy the files to. The output of this command is the path to the new directory. The -d option indicates that a directory should be created, rather than a regular file. The path of the temporary directory is given last. The XXXX part of the directory name gets replaced by the mktemp command with a unique number.

3. Change the mode of the backup.sh file so that it is executable.

```
chmod u+x backup.sh
```

4. Run the script.

```
./backup.sh
```

5. When the script completes, use Finder to check the contents of the directory ~/Backups for a ZIP archive. Double-click the archive to expand it, and see if it contains text files from your home directory.

6. Try to force an error by removing the backup directory and replacing it with a regular file. See if you receive an e-mail about the error when you rerun the script.

WARNING *This script takes no account of multiple files with the same name. If more than one file shares a name, only one of the files will appear in the archive; the others will be overwritten. You need to improve the script if you want to archive multiple files with the same name.*

CHAPTER 13

Exercise 1 Solution

Insert the following handler code into the slideshow script:

```
on prompt_for_slide_duration()
    set slide_duration to 0
    repeat while slide_duration is 0
        try
            display dialog ¬
                "How many seconds should each slide in the " & ¬
                "slideshow be displayed?" ¬
                buttons {"OK"} default answer 2 default button 1
            set dialog_result to result
            set slide_duration to (text returned of dialog_result) as real
            if slide_duration ≤ 0 then error "Enter a positive number"
        on error msg
            display_error_message(msg)
            set slide_duration to 0
        end try
    end repeat
    return slide_duration
end prompt_for_slide_duration
```

This handler is very similar to other handlers in the script that prompt the user for input. A dialog is displayed, asking the user to enter the number of seconds per slide in the show. The value entered must be a number greater than zero; otherwise an error will arise, and the user will be prompted again.

To complete the exercise, modify the run handler to call the `prompt_for_slide_duration` handler, and pass the result to the `create_image_sequence_from_folder` handler.

```
on run
    try
        copy Photo_Archive to photo_arch
        set photo_arch's archive_folder_name to "Test Photo Archive"
        tell photo_arch to setup_archive_folder()
        set num_photos to prompt_for_number_of_photos_in_show()
        set slide_duration to prompt_for_slide_duration()
        set the_album to prompt_for_album_choice()
        add_photos_from_album given Photo_Archive:photo_arch, ¬
            album:the_album, number_of_photos:num_photos
```

```
                create_image_sequence_from_folder(photo_arch's archive_folder, ¬
                        slide_duration)
                tell photo_arch to delete_archive()
            on error msg
                display_error_message(msg)
            end try
        end run
```

Exercise 2 Solution

Begin by adding a `try` block to the `addImagesToPoster` handler to catch any `errors` that get thrown.

```
    on addImagesToPoster()
        try
            -- Draw images
            set numberOfPhotos to numberOfPhotosFormCell's integerValue()
            set theAlbums to my getSelectedAlbums()
            set imagePaths to my getPathsToRandomPhotos(theAlbums,
    numberOfPhotos)
            set scaleFactor to scalingSlider's floatValue()
            set i to 0
            repeat with imagePath in imagePaths
                set img to initWithContentsOfFile_(imagePath) of NSImage's
    alloc()
                addImageToPoster(img, scaleFactor)
                set i to i + 1
            end repeat

            -- Update image in interface
            posterImageView's setImage_(posterImage)
        on error errorMsg
            set anAlert to init() of NSAlert's alloc()
            tell anAlert to addButtonWithTitle_("OK")
            tell anAlert to setMessageText_(errorMsg)
            tell anAlert to setAlertStyle_(NSWarningAlertStyle)
            tell anAlert to runModal()
        end try

        -- Stop progress indicator
        -- and reenable button
        progressIndicator's stopAnimation_(me)
        set createPosterButton's enabled to true
    end addImagesToPoster
```

The `NSAlert` class is used to display alert panels in Cocoa, which in this case is a warning. The message passed via the `error` is displayed in the panel. After the `NSAlert` has been configured, it is displayed by invoking the `runModal` method.

Add two lines at the top of the script to define a property for the `NSAlert` class, and a constraint. The constant is used to configure the alert in the preceding code.

```
    property NSSavePanel : class "NSSavePanel"
    property NSImage : class "NSImage"
    property NSAlert : class "NSAlert"
```

```
property NSFileHandlingPanelOKButton : 1
property NSCompositeSourceOver : 2
property NSWarningAlertStyle : 0
```

In the `getSelectedAlbums` handler, add a check to ensure that at least one album has been selected.

```
on getSelectedAlbums()
    set theAlbums to {}
    set numberOfAlbums to length of my albumNames

    if numberOfAlbums is 0 then
        error "There were no albums selected. " & ¬
            "Select one or more albums, and try again.
"end if

    repeat with row from 0 to numberOfAlbums - 1
        if albumTableView's isRowSelected_(row) then
            set selectedAlbumName to item (row + 1) in albumNames
            tell application "iPhoto" to get album selectedAlbumName
            set the end of theAlbums to result
        end if
    end repeat
    return theAlbums
end getSelectedAlbums
```

If the number of selected rows is zero, an `error` is thrown, which gets caught in the `addImagesToPoster` handler.

Finally, modify the `getPathsToRandomPhotos` handler so that it checks the number of photos available in the selected albums.

```
oon getPathsToRandomPhotos(theAlbums, numberOfPhotos)
    tell application "iPhoto"
        -- Check that there is at least one photo in the albums
        set atLeastOnePhoto to false
        repeat with theAlbum in theAlbums
            if (count of photos in theAlbum) ∠ 0 then
                set atLeastOnePhoto to true
                exit repeat
            end if
        end repeat
        if not atLeastOnePhoto then
            error "There were no photos in the selected albums. " & ¬
                "Add some photos to the albums, and try again."
        end if

        -- Choose random paths
        set photoPaths to {}
        repeat numberOfPhotos times
            set end of photoPaths to image path of some photo ¬
                of some item of theAlbums
        end repeat
    end tell
    return photoPaths
end getPathsToRandomPhotos
```

The new code uses a `repeat` loop to iterate over the `albums` passed in. The number of `photos` in each `album` is retrieved using the `count` command, and if it is non-zero, the `atLeastOnePhoto` variable is set to `true` and the loop exits. If the `atLeastOnePhoto` variable is still `false` after the loop has completed, an `error` is thrown.

Exercise 3 Solution

To update the user interface, follow these steps:

1. In the `Piles_of_PicturesAppDelegate.applescript` file, add a new outlet property called `variationSlider`.

   ```
   property albumTableView : missing value
   property posterImageView : missing value
   property progressIndicator : missing value
   property numberOfPhotosFormCell : missing value
   property scalingSlider : missing value
   property variationSlider : missing value
   property widthFormCell : missing value
   property heightFormCell : missing value
   property createPosterButton : missing value
   ```

2. Open the `MainMenu.xib` file in Interface Builder by double-clicking its icon in the Groups & Files pane of the Piles of Pictures Xcode project window.

3. Select the Photo Scaling slider and the Photo Scaling text field by holding down the Shift key and clicking each in turn. Duplicate these two views by choosing the Edit ⇨ Duplicate menu item. Double-click the new text field and enter **Scaling Variation:**.

4. Position the new controls to make the interface more aesthetically pleasing. You may need to resize the window and other views to achieve this.

5. Control-click the application delegate object in the `MainMenu.xib` document window, and drag to the new slider. Select `variationSlider` from the pop-up window that appears when you release the mouse button.

6. Save your changes to `MainMenu.xib` and return to the Xcode project.

Now add the following new handler to the `Piles of PicturesAppDelegate.applescript` script:

```
on varyScalingFactor(scalingFactor, variance)
    set randomVariance to (random number from -variance to variance)
    set scalingFactor to scalingFactor + randomVariance
    if scalingFactor < 0.0 then set scalingFactor to 0.0
    if scalingFactor > 1.0 then set scalingFactor to 1.0
    return scalingFactor
end varyScalingFactor
```

This handler takes the scaling factor and the variation factor. It forms a new scaling factor by adding a random value to the original scaling factor, in the range stipulated by the variation factor. The random number is chosen in the range from -`variance` to `variance`. Negative values result in a smaller scaling factor, and positive values give a larger scaling factor.

The random number is added to the `scalingFactor` variable. Because this could potentially result in a scaling factor greater than 1 or less than 0, two `if` statements check the value of `scalingFactor` and adjust it if necessary, so that it ends up in the range 0.0 to 1.0.

To finish, it is only necessary to call this new handler at the appropriate point in the script. In the `addImagesToPoster` handler, you need to make the following modifications:

```
on addImagesToPoster()
    try
        -- Draw images
        set numberOfPhotos to numberOfPhotosFormCell's integerValue()
        set theAlbums to my getSelectedAlbums()
        set imagePaths to my getPathsToRandomPhotos(theAlbums, numberOfPhotos)
        set scaleFactor to scalingSlider's floatValue()
        set scaleVariation to variationSlider's floatValue()
        set i to 0
        repeat with imagePath in imagePaths
            set img to initWithContentsOfFile_(imagePath) of NSImage's alloc()
            set photoScaleFactor to varyScalingFactor(scaleFactor, scaleVariation)
            addImageToPoster(img, photoScaleFactor)
            set i to i + 1
        end repeat

        -- Update image in interface
        posterImageView's setImage_(posterImage)
    on error errorMsg
        set anAlert to init() of NSAlert's alloc()
        tell anAlert to addButtonWithTitle_("OK")
        tell anAlert to setMessageText_(errorMsg)
        tell anAlert to setAlertStyle_(NSWarningAlertStyle)
        tell anAlert to runModal()
    end try

    -- Stop progress indicator
    -- and reenable button
    progressIndicator's stopAnimation_(me)
    set createPosterButton's enabled to true
end addImagesToPoster
```

Rather than passing the `scaleFactor` retrieved from the user interface directly to the `addImageToPoster` handler, it is first adjusted using `varyScalingFactor`, with the result stored in the variable `photoScaleFactor`. This adjusted scaling factor is what is passed to `addImageToPoster`. Because the factor is different for each photo, each photo will be scaled differently in the resulting poster.

CHAPTER 14

Exercise 1 Solution

1. Open the `DashBall.css` file in a text editor and make the following change:

```
    body {
          margin: 0;
    }

 img.ball {
        position: absolute;
 }
```

2. In the DashBall.html file, make these changes:

```html
<html>

<head>

<style type="text/css">
    @import "DashBall.css";
</style>

<script type='text/javascript' src='DashBall.js' charset='utf-8'></script>

</head>

<body onload='setup();'>
    <img src='Default.png' />
    <span id='pow' class='powtext'>Pow!</span>
    <span id='splat' class='powtext'>Splat!</span>
    <img class='ball' id='ball0' src='TennisBall.png'
        onmouseover='startHit(0);'
        onmouseout='finishHit(0);' />
    <img class='ball' id='ball1' src='TennisBall.png'
        onmouseover='startHit(1);'
        onmouseout='finishHit(1);' />
</body>

</html>
```

3. Lastly, update the DashBall.js file as follows:

```javascript
// Wall Coordinates
var wallCoords = {left:40, right:225, bottom:175, top:15};

// Ball Properties
var balls = new Array()
balls[0] = {
    x:(wallCoords.right + wallCoords.left ) * 0.5,
    y:(wallCoords.top + wallCoords.bottom) * 0.5,
    velocityX:200.0,
    velocityY:200.0,
    radius:13.0,
    imageId:"ball0" };
balls[1] = {
    x:(wallCoords.right + wallCoords.left ) * 0.25,
    y:(wallCoords.top + wallCoords.bottom) * 0.25,
    velocityX:-200.0,
    velocityY:200.0,
```

```
        radius:13.0,
        imageId:"ball1" };

// Physics
var frictionFactor = 0.9;
var elasticityFactor = 0.95;

// Timers
var theTimer = {step:100};
var powTimerId = 0;
  var splatTimerId = 0;

  // Variables for hitting
  var hitting = false;
  var hitCoords = new Object();
  var ballCoordsAtHit = new Object();

  if (window.widget)
  {
      widget.onshow = onshow;
      widget.onhide = onhide;
  }

  // Called when widget is loaded
  function setup()
  {
      var i;
      for ( i = 0; i < balls.length; i++ ) {
          setBallPosition(balls[i]);
      }
      theTimer.id = setInterval("updateBalls()", theTimer.step);
  }

  // Called when dashboard is shown
  function onshow()
  {
      if ( !theTimer.id ) theTimer.id =
          setInterval("updateBalls()", theTimer.step);
  }

  // Called when dashboard is hidden
  function onhide()
  {
     clearInterval(theTimer.id);
     theTimer.id = 0;
  }

  // Handy Math functions
  function distanceBetweenPoints(point1, point2)
  {
      return Math.sqrt( Math.pow(point2.x-point1.x, 2) +
        Math.pow(point2.y- point1.y, 2) )
  }
```

```
function dot(vector1, vector2)
{
    return vector1.x*vector2.x + vector1.y*vector2.y;
}

function unitVector(vector)
{
    var length = distanceBetweenPoints({x:0,y:0}, vector);
    return {x:vector.x/length, y:vector.y/length};
}

// Ball functions
function setBallPosition(ball)
{
    var ballImage = document.getElementById(ball.imageId);
    ballImage.style.top = ball.y;
    ballImage.style.left = ball.x;
}

function updateBalls()
{
    // Update each ball separately
    var i;
    for ( i = 0; i < balls.length; i++ ) {
        updateBall(balls[i]);
    }

    // Now handle interaction of balls with each other
    var i, j;
    for ( i = 1; i < balls.length; i++ ) {
        for ( j = 0; j < i; j++ ) {
            var separation = distanceBetweenPoints(balls[i], balls[j]);
            if ( separation < balls[i].radius + balls[j].radius ) {
                // Colliding
                var interCenterVec = {x:balls[j].x-balls[i].x,
                                      y:balls[j].y-balls[i].y};
                var unitVec = unitVector(interCenterVec);

                // Determine collision speed
                var ballVelocity = {x:balls[i].velocityX, y:balls[i].
                velocityY};
                var interCenterSpeed_i = dot(ballVelocity, unitVec);
                ballVelocity = {x:balls[j].velocityX, y:balls[j].velocityY};
                var interCenterSpeed_j = dot(ballVelocity, unitVec);
                var collisionSpeed = interCenterSpeed_i - interCenterSpeed_j;

                // Adjust balls by the collision speed,
                // such that they elastically
                // bounce in the opposite direction.
                var adjustment = {x:collisionSpeed*unitVec.x,
                                  y:collisionSpeed*unitVec.y};
                balls[i].velocityX -= adjustment.x;
                balls[i].velocityY -= adjustment.y;
                balls[j].velocityX += adjustment.x;
```

```
                    balls[j].velocityY += adjustment.y;

                    // Move balls apart so that they are not overlapping
                    var overlap = balls[i].radius + balls[j].radius - separation;
                    balls[i].x -= 0.5 * unitVec.x * overlap;
                    balls[i].y -= 0.5 * unitVec.y * overlap;
                    balls[j].x += 0.5 * unitVec.x * overlap;
                    balls[j].y += 0.5 * unitVec.y * overlap;

                    // Display Splat sign
                    point = {x:0.5*(balls[i].x+balls[j].x),
                             y:0.5*(balls[i].y+balls[j].y)};
                    showSplat(point);
                }
            }
        }
}

function updateBall(ball)
{
  // Apply gravity
  ball.velocityY += 50.0 * ( theTimer.step / 1000.0 );

  // Update position
  ball.x += ball.velocityX * ( theTimer.step / 1000.0 );
  ball.y += ball.velocityY * ( theTimer.step / 1000.0 );

  // Handle bounces. Include a little friction, and inelasticity.
  if ( ball.x > wallCoords.right || ball.x < wallCoords.left )
  {
      ball.velocityX *= -elasticityFactor;
      ball.velocityY *= frictionFactor;
  }
  if ( ball.y < wallCoords.top || ball.y > wallCoords.bottom )
  {
      ball.velocityY *= -elasticityFactor;
      ball.velocityX *= frictionFactor;
  }

  // Make sure ball is in court
  ball.y = Math.max(ball.y, wallCoords.top);
  ball.y = Math.min(ball.y, wallCoords.bottom);
  ball.x = Math.max(ball.x, wallCoords.left);
  ball.x = Math.min(ball.x, wallCoords.right);

    setBallPosition(ball);
}

function startHit(ballIndex) {
  hitting = true;
  hitCoords.x = event.x;
  hitCoords.y = event.y;
    ballCoordsAtHit.x = balls[ballIndex].x;
    ballCoordsAtHit.y = balls[ballIndex].y;
}
```

```
    function finishHit(ballIndex) {
        var ball = balls[ballIndex];
    if ( hitting ) {
        ball.velocityX += 2 * (event.x - hitCoords.x - (ball.x -
                            ballCoordsAtHit.x));
        ball.velocityY += 2 * (event.y - hitCoords.y - (ball.y -
                            ballCoordsAtHit.y));
    }
    var pow = document.getElementById("pow");
    pow.style.top = ball.y;
    pow.style.left = ball.x;
    pow.style.opacity = '1.0';
    pow.style.webkitAnimationName = 'spinin';
    if ( powTimerId ) clearTimeout(powTimerId);
    powTimerId = setTimeout('hidePow();', 2000);
    hitting = false;
}

function hidePow() {
    var pow = document.getElementById("pow")
    pow.style.webkitAnimationName = 'fadeout';
    pow.style.opacity = '0.0';
    powTimerId = 0;
}

    function showSplat(point) {
        var splat = document.getElementById("splat");
        splat.style.top = point.y;
        splat.style.left = point.x;
        splat.style.opacity = '1.0';
        splat.style.webkitAnimationName = 'spinin';
        if ( splatTimerId ) clearTimeout(splatTimerId);
        splatTimerId = setTimeout('hideSplat();', 2000);
    }

    function hideSplat() {
        var splat = document.getElementById("splat")
        splat.style.webkitAnimationName = 'fadeout';
        splat.style.opacity = '0.0';
        splatTimerId = 0;
    }
```

There are quite a lot of changes to the JavaScript file, but by far the most significant is that the global variable `ball` has been replaced by an array called `balls`. Functions that previously acted on the global variable are instead passed a `ball` object as argument, or an index for the ball to use.

The `updateBalls` method, which continually updates the dynamic state of each ball, is quite involved, in particular the section that accounts for collisions between balls. The physics behind this code is somewhat complex, but the code itself is not. Feel free to glaze over it if you are not interested in the mathematics.

The `Splat!` text is handled much the same as the `Pow!` text. It appears when two balls collide, and a global timer is used to remove the text from the screen after it has been there for two seconds. Web Kit CSS animations are used for both showing and hiding the text.

Exercise 2 Solution

1. Launch Dashcode. In the project template sheet, select Safari on the left and the Browser application type on the right. Uncheck the Mobile Safari option next to the Develop For label. Click the Choose button.

2. Choose Save from the File menu, and save the project under the name **StackOverflow**.

3. Click the Library and Inspector buttons in the Lay Out Interface section of the Workflow Steps pane at the bottom left.

4. Select the Location field on the right of the canvas, and delete it by pressing the Backspace key.

5. Locate the Lozenge button in the Parts tab of the Library panel, and drag it just under the Title field on the canvas. Use the Inspector to change the title of the button to View (first tab). Make the button smaller by dragging the handles on the sides, and use the Inspector to make the button light gray in color (second tab). When you are finished, it should look similar to Figure A-7.

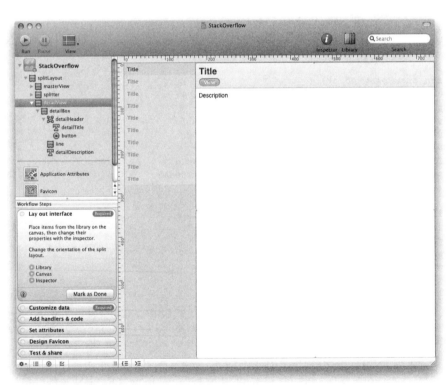

FIGURE A-7

6. Open the Customize data section of the Workflow Steps pane, and click the Data Sources button. Select `dataSource` in the Data Sources list that appears.

7. Enter the URL http://stackoverflow.com/feeds/tag/javascript in the URL field at the bottom on the right, and press Return.

 NOTE *If you would rather follow a Dashcode feed instead of JavaScript, you can enter* `http://stackoverflow.com/feeds/tag/dashcode` *for the URL.*

8. In the outline that appears at the bottom-right, locate the section called `entry`. Mouse over the `title` property in that section, and click-and-drag from the circle on the right to the `Title` field in the first cell in the list on the left of the canvas. Choose `text` from the pop-up menu options that appear when you release the mouse button.

9. Select the `itemsList` data source, and drag from the `title` attribute in the `selection` section to the `Title` field in the header of the detail pane on the right. Choose `text` from the menu.

10. Drag from the `summary` property in the selection to the `Description` field on the canvas, and choose `html` from the menu.

11. Select the View button in the canvas, and open the Behaviors tab of the Inspector (last tab). Enter `openPage` in the Handlers column for the `onclick` row. In the JavaScript editor that appears at the bottom, edit the boilerplate text for the `openPage` function.

```
function openPage(event)
{
    var dataSource = dashcode.getDataSource("itemsList");
    var link = dataSource.valueForKeyPath("selection.link.$href");
    window.open(link);
}
```

12. Save the project, and click the Run button to test it. Select `posts` from the list on the left, and notice how the detail views change. Click the View button to open the corresponding page on stackoverflow.com.

Developer Resources

A number of useful developer resources are available to Mac OS X programmers. These include web sites, mailing lists, and other resources. This appendix provides information about these resources.

WEB SITES

Apple Developer Connection (http://developer.apple.com/)

You can find a wealth of Mac OS X programming information at Apple Developer Connection (ADC), including online documentation, sample code, and software downloads. Most of the ADC content is free or available through a free membership, although some of its services are available only to paid ADC subscribers.

CocoaDev (http://www.cocoadev.com/)

CocoaDev is a Wiki web site dedicated to Cocoa programming on Mac OS X. Wiki web sites encourage public participation by allowing anyone to post and edit content directly on the site. Not only can you browse CocoaDev for answers to your questions, but you can also post your own questions in a discussion area. Later on, you can even post answers to other people's questions.

Cocoa Dev Central (http://www.cocoadevcentral.com/)

Cocoa Dev Central is a Cocoa programming web site featuring articles and tutorials. Although less collaborative than the CocoaDev web site, the content on Cocoa Dev Central is presented as full-length magazine articles. Also, Cocoa Dev Central links to other Cocoa programming resources on the Internet, so you can find even more information about Cocoa programming.

MacScripter.net (http://macscripter.net/)

MacScripter.net is a collection of web forums dedicated to AppleScript programming. You can find additional information about writing AppleScripts on Mac OS X there, as well as resources for AppleScript Studio and the Automator tool found in Mac OS X 10.4 "Tiger." MacScripter.net also includes a large section of sample scripts and a section where you can share code with other people.

MacTech (http://www.mactech.com/)

MacTech provides a ton of information aimed at the Mac OS X programmer, including Macintosh news, development articles and tutorials, and sample code. You will find a wide variety of programming content on MacTech, including information for both Carbon and Cocoa programmers.

The Omni Group Developer (http://www.omnigroup.com/developer/)

The Omni Group is a Mac OS X software company best known for the OmniWeb web browser, but it also has a large Cocoa developer web site. For example, the web site offers information about writing and porting games on Mac OS X. You can even download some of Omni's source code for use in your own projects.

Stack Overflow (http://stackoverflow.com/)

Stack Overflow is a collaborative programming Q&A web site that covers virtually any programming topic. The questions and answers come from web site readers. Questions are tagged by programming language, company, topic, and so on. Readers rank answers by quality and relevance, so good answers bubble up to the top.

MAILING LISTS

Apple Mailing Lists (http://lists.apple.com/mailman/listinfo/)

Apple runs mailing lists for a variety of programming topics, including Carbon, Cocoa, AppleScript, and other technologies. Apple engineers frequently contribute to these lists, so they are a good place to get detailed answers to your questions. You can find mailing list archives online at http://lists.apple.com/archives/.

Omni Mailing Lists (http://www.omnigroup.com/mailman/listinfo/)

The Omni Group sponsors a few mailing lists for Mac OS X, including development lists for Cocoa and WebObjects, and a mailing list for Mac OS X administration. Archives are also available online.

OTHER RESOURCES

CocoaDev Chat Rooms

A number of contributors to the CocoaDev web site are available in the CocoaDev chat room on the AOL Instant Messenger network. For example, you can connect to CocoaDev from iChat by choosing File ➪ Go to Chat and entering CocoaDev as the chat name. IRC channels are also available. You can find out more on CocoaDev's web site: http://www.cocoadev.com/index.pl?ChatRoom.

MacTech Magazine

MacTech Magazine has been providing monthly articles on Macintosh programming for more than 20 years. Current issues feature information about application development in Carbon, Cocoa, and AppleScript. You can also find articles on other technologies such as OpenGL, QuickTime, and various scripting languages. MacTech articles are usually written for a beginning or intermediate programming audience, so there's something there for everyone. You can find out more at MacTech's web site: http://www.mactech.com/.

INDEX